MEDIEVAL ARABIC PRAISE POETRY

This book gives an insight into panegyrics (*madīḥ*), a genre central to understanding medieval Near Eastern society. Poets in this arabophone multiethnic society would address the majority of their verse to rulers, generals, officials, and the urban upper classes, its tone ranging from celebration to reprimand and even to threat.

Beatrice Gruendler discusses this panegyric genre as represented by Ibn al-Rūmī, who dedicated many of his poems to the last Ṭāhirid governor of Baghdad. Ibn al-Rūmī's work is ideally suited to this study, as it addresses the issue of literary patronage and provides a self-portrait of the artist and his social position.

This book will be of interest to scholars of comparative literature, anthropology, linguistics, medieval studies and Near Eastern studies.

Beatrice Gruendler is Professor of Arabic Language and Literature at Yale University. She has published widely on Arabic poetry and paleography, including *The Development of the Arabic Scripts: From the Nabatean Era to the First Islamic Century* (Atlanta, Georgia: Scholars Press, 1993) and, with Verena Klemm, *Understanding Near Eastern Literatures: A Spectrum of Interdisciplinary Approaches* (Wiesbaden: Reichert, 2000).

ROUTLEDGECURZON STUDIES IN ARABIC AND MIDDLE-EASTERN LITERATURES

Edited by James E. Montgomery, *University of Cambridge*, Roger Allen, *University of Pennsylvania*, and Philip F. Kennedy, *New York University*

RoutledgeCurzon Studies in Arabic and Middle-Eastern Literatures is a monograph series devoted to aspects of the literatures of the Near and Middle East and North Africa both modern and pre-modern. It is hoped that the provision of such a forum will lead to a greater emphasis on the comparative study of the literatures of this area, although studies devoted to one literary or linguistic region are warmly encouraged. It is the editors' objective to foster the comparative and multi-disciplinary investigation of the written and oral literary products of this area.

SHEHERAZADE THROUGH THE LOOKING GLASS
Eva Sallis

THE PALESTINIAN NOVEL
Ibrahim Taha

OF DISHES AND DISCOURSE
Geert Jan van Gelder

MEDIEVAL ARABIC PRAISE POETRY
Beatrice Gruendler

MEDIEVAL ARABIC PRAISE POETRY

IBN AL-RŪMĪ AND THE PATRON'S REDEMPTION

Beatrice Gruendler

Routledge
Taylor & Francis Group
LONDON AND NEW YORK

First published in 2003
by Routledge
2 Park Square, Milton Park, Abingdon, Oxon, OX14 4RN

Simultaneously published in the USA and Canada
by Routledge
270 Madison Ave, New York NY 10016

Routledge is an imprint of the Taylor & Francis Group

Transferred to Digital Printing 2010

Typeset in Times New Roman by LaserScript Ltd, Mitcham, Surrey

British Library Cataloguing in Publication Data
A catalogue record of this book is available from the British Library

Library of Congress Cataloging in Publication Data
A catalog record for this book has been requested

ISBN10: 0–7007–1490–1 (hbk)
ISBN10: 0–415–59579–7 (pbk)

ISBN13: 978–0–7007–1490–2 (hbk)
ISBN13: 978–0–415–59579–7 (pbk)

Publisher's Note

The publisher has gone to great lengths to ensure the quality of this reprint but points out that some imperfections in the original may be apparent.

'Isn't there for every writer a particular thing of that sort, the thing that most makes him apply himself, the thing without the effort to achieve which he wouldn't write at all, the very passion of his passion, the part of the business in which, for him, the flame of art burns most intensely? Well, it's *that!*'

... It was something, I guessed, in the primal plan; something like a complex figure in a Persian carpet. He highly approved of this image when I used it, and he used another himself. 'It's the very string', he said, 'that my pearls are strung on!'

(Henry James 1958, 141–2, 149)

Es ist anzunehmen, daß vor allem die Erfindungsgabe der Autoren den wissenschaftlichen Dialog zum literarischen Dialog nie abreißen lassen wird.

(Anne Betten 1994, 538)

CONTENTS

Preface ix
Acknowledgments xi
Abbreviations xii
Note on quotes and translations xiii
Note on transliteration and dating xiv
Glossary xv

PART I
Setting the stage **1**

1 The background: Poetry and poets in early Abbasid society 3

2 The form: The Abbasid praise *qaṣīda* 13

3 The approach: *Madīḥ* and pragmatics 26

4 The protagonists: Ibn al-Rūmī and his patron ʿUbaydallāh b. ʿAbdallāh 42

5 The *madīḥ* exchanged between Ibn al-Rūmī and ʿUbaydallāh 48

PART II
Speech and characterization **77**

6 Speech as action 79

7 The dramatis personae 94

PART III
The dramaturgy **123**

8 The scene 125

9 The episode and its witnesses 145

10 'The passion of him whose parting has grayed is affectation' (L191) 156

11 'They aimed at my heart from the gaps of veils' (L1042) 182

PART IV
Verbal ornament **197**

12 Supporting figures of speech 199

13 Phantasmagoria 219

PART V
Ibn al-Rūmī's ethics of patronage **227**

14 In the mirror of *madīḥ* 229

15 Mutual duties and rights of benefactor and protégé 233

16 Acts and words between panegyrist and model 247

Conclusion: Dramaturgy as a rhetoric of ethics 263

Appendices
A. Themes of the *qaṣā'id* 269
B. Speech acts in the *qaṣā'id* 271
C. Witnesses in the episodes 272
D. Poetry dedicated to ʿUbaydallāh b. ʿAbdallāh 273
E. Concordance with Boustany 276
Notes 278
Bibliography 316
Index of verses 327
General index 331

PREFACE

Why study medieval Arabic praise poetry? To give a straightforward response, this genre is pivotal for anyone interested in the 'Golden Age' of the medieval Near East – a time when Baghdad and Samarra were capitals of a cosmopolitan, if turbulent, civilization, and every person of merit, from lute-player to lexicographer, sought entry to the Abbasid court. This significance of praise poetry, or *madīḥ*, may come as a surprise. More likely the reader has encountered the loose wine song (*khamriyya*) from the taverns of Baghdad and nearby cloisters or the flirtatious love lyric (*ghazal*) from the Baghdadian and Samarran courtly circles. Both were restricted to intimate settings, as they flouted, or at least sidestepped, the official Islamic doctrine. *Madīḥ* in contrast was performed in the caliph's public audiences, as praise poetry enshrined the Abbasid ruler ideology and its Islamic world-view. Historiography attests to victories or enthronements of caliphs by the panegyrics composed for them, as it conversely documents times of strife through poets' satires and lamentations. The lighter *adab* literature preserves innumerable accounts (*akhbār*) of *madīḥ* performances, and in poets' collected works (*dīwāns*), *madīḥ* almost always occupies the prominent position. For these (and other) reasons, *madīḥ* is omnipresent as well as replete with the doctrinal, ideological, and ethical values of Abbasid urban society, and its study affords important insights about Medieval Arabic-Islamic civilization.

The high visibility of *madīḥ* can be explained by the literary prestige it conferred upon a ruling dynasty – a validation no other cultural practice could confer. As a continuous literary tradition since the time before Islam, *madīḥ* linked the Abbasid caliphate with the heroic Arab past (*Jāhiliyya*) as well as comparing it to the ancient civilizations of Byzantium and Persia. This required that poets possess an in-depth knowledge of their poetic heritage and the ability to recall any part of it on a given occasion, which led some to compile systematic anthologies of quotable verse. More important, they were called upon to ply this heritage to a new literary aesthetic, while heeding prevailing political agendas. A poet who mastered these challenges gave leadership figures a verbal aura they highly prized.

Recent scholarship has begun to remedy the long-standing neglect of *madīḥ*, owing to its textual difficulty as much as to its suspect quality of merchandise.

Regarding the first point, the study of Arabic *madīḥ* is still a sum of single efforts, lacking a systematic survey of the genre and its themes, motifs, and styles. Regarding the second point, there is no better time than the twenty-first century to concede the fact that art and commerce might form a complex, if ambivalent, symbiosis. In medieval Arabic praise, trade appears as a frequent image and it lacks intrinsic negative connotations as well as the (modern) distinction between moral and material exchange. The 'usefulness' of *madīḥ* was not only unobjectionable, it constituted part of this poetry's very value. The key to a fair evaluation of *madīḥ* lies then in choosing an adequate framework of enquiry; to do justice to this poetic quest requires taking into account its status and function within the contemporary Abbasid society. What role did *madīḥ* play between author and recipient? How did it shape, and how was it shaped by, the process of exchange? Which higher authorities did it invoke? And which gains and losses were at stake on either side?

These and related questions are posed here in a representative case, the long-standing relationship between the versatile Ibn al-Rūmī and his first patron, the governor of Baghdad, ʿUbaydallāh b. ʿAbdallāh b. Ṭāhir, scion of a highly cultured Khurāsānian dynasty. Their exchanges of over two decades (253–76/867–90) inspired a rich and varied body of *madīḥ*, which constitutes the subject of this book. Ibn al-Rūmī's poems range from the celebratory encomium (*qaṣīda*) and felicitation (*tahni'a*) to the admonition (*ʿitāb*), marking high and low points of the patronage.

Salient features of the poetry itself and the type of questions asked suggest a synchronic, pragmatic approach. This resulted, through a dialogical process between source and method, in a compound model of dramatic discourse and speech act theory. Thus adapted, the model sheds light on the poems' dramatic profile without glossing over their subtleties and variations. Should it be applied to other genres and authors, this model will doubtlessly need modification. At this stage, it offers a new perspective on two major issues: Ibn al-Rūmī's transformation of ancient and novel poetic elements into a cohesive dramaturgy, inscribed with his self-portrait as a panegyrist, and his instatement through this dramaturgy of an ethics of literary patronage.

ACKNOWLEDGMENTS

It is a pleasure to acknowledge my indebtedness to my advisor Wolfhart Heinrichs for his confidence, inspiration, and constructive criticism since the earliest stages of this book as a dissertation. My further thanks are owed to my readers, Sandra Naddaff, Wheeler Thackston, and Ahmad Mahdavi-Damghani.

In the various stages of this work, I benefitted from the comments and criticism of J. Christoph Bürgel, William Granara, Dimitri Gutas, Roy Mottahedeh, Gregory Nagy, Michael Sells, Oktor Skjaervo, and Manfred Ullmann, though any remaining errors and inconsistencies are entirely mine. To Anthony Brandt, Andi Brittan, Thomas Stewart, and particularly the Wolfsdorf family I am grateful for more than intellectual support, to Tara Zend for her improvements to my style, and to Mary E. Butler for assistance in library matters.

The completion of this work, as a Ph.D. thesis at Harvard University, was made possible through grants from the Studienstiftung des deutschen Volkes, the Harvard Graduate School, the Harvard Graduate Society, and the Committee on General Scholarships under the aegis of Margot Gill. Its publication was supported by the Whitney Humanities Center, Yale University. I also thank the *Harvard Review of Arabic and Islamic Studies* for their permission to reprint my article from volume 3 (1996), pp. 104–60 on Ibn al-Rūmī's ethics of patronage.

I am thankful to James E. Montgomery for accepting this book in the RoutledgeCurzon Studies in Arabic and Middle-Eastern Literatures and to Jonathan Price, Rachel Saunders, Moira Eminton, and David McCarthy for their pleasant co-operation on all publishing matters.

The most cherished place belongs to my family for whom this book is but a small excuse for my absence, and to my husband Steve to whom I owe infinite gratitude for bearing with me through its circuitous history.

B. G.

ABBREVIATIONS

A	Admonition (*ʿitāb*)*
AEL	Lane, *Arabic-English Lexicon*
GAS ii	Sezgin, *Geschichte des arabischen Schrifttums, vol. 2: Poesie bis ca. 430 H.*
GAP ii	Gätje (ed.), *Grundriß der arabischen Philologie, vol. 2: Literaturwissenschaft*
E	Epigram*
EAL	Meisami and Starkey (eds), *Encyclopedia of Arabic Literature*, 2 vols
EI²	*Encyclopaedia of Islam*, second edition, 11 vols to date
F	Felicitation (*tahniʾa*)*
H	Satire (*hijāʾ*)*
JAL	*Journal of Arabic Literature*
L	Long encomium (praise *qaṣīda*)*
Lis	Ibn Manẓūr, *Lisān al-ʿarab*
S	Short encomium*
WKAS	Ullmann, *Wörterbuch der klassischen arabischen Sprache*, 2 vols
ZDMG	*Zeitschrift der Deutschen Morgenländischen Gesellschaft*

*These sigla precede a poem's number (following the edition of Ibn al-Rūmī's *Dīwān* by Naṣṣār *et al.*) and indicate its form, e.g. 'E462' stands for 'epigram no. 462'. For full references, see Appendix D.

NOTE ON QUOTES AND TRANSLATIONS

Some poem numbers appear twice in the *Dīwān*; vol. vi reaches no. 1657 and then starts anew from no. 1178' through to no. 1562'. An apostrophe designates the second appearance of a respective number, distinguishing, e.g. L1250' (*Dīwān*, vi: 2366–77), a *madīḥ* of ʿUbaydallāh, from the earlier no. 1250 (*Dīwān*, iv: 1624), a *mujūn* poem. Nos. 673, 674 and 1359 also appear twice, due to overlaps between volumes.

As all poetry quoted or cited is listed in the Index of Verses, discussions of identical passages under different aspects are not usually cross-referenced.

Except for the Koran, cited after Arberry (1955), all translations are the author's.

NOTE ON TRANSLITERATION AND DATING

This book follows the Library of Congress transliteration system but without indicating the final *tāʾ marbūṭa* or the graphic form of *alif*. In connected discourse, the *hamzat al-waṣl* is dropped. Diacritics are omitted in common place names and Anglicized words (e.g. Baghdad, Koran) and English derivatives of Arabic terms (e.g. Abbasids). Dates are given according to both the Hijrī and the Common Era, with 1/622 indicating the first year of the Islamic calendar.

GLOSSARY

adab (pl. *ādāb*): (a) good breeding, social grace; (b) professional (scribal, judicial) knowledge; (c) general culture; initially restricted to Arabic letters, expanded during the third/ninth and fourth/tenth centuries to encompass translated foreign letters and sciences, and finally reaching encyclopedic scope (cf. *muruwwa*, *ẓarf*).

adīb (pl. *udabāʾ* f. *adība* pl. *adībāt*): a person possessing *adab* (q.v.) (cf. also *ẓarīf*).

akhdh: see *sariqa*.

ʿarabiyya: the Arabic prestige language, used in writing and formal speech, codified in the Abbasid period based on pre-Islamic literature and the Koran.

aṭlāl: literally 'traces'; one of the motifs of the *nasīb* (q.v.), containing the evocation of abandoned campsite traces; often leading to the remembrance and description of a former beloved (*ḥabīb*), who once dwelt there.

badīʿ: literally 'novel, new style'; (a) poetic mannerism that arose during the Abbasid era (cf. *muḥdath*); (b) the tropes and rhetorical figures characterizing this style; (c) attribute of good verse in this style.

bayān: literally 'clarity, clear expression'; (a) in philosophy, verbal and non-verbal communication; (b) in later poetics, *ʿilm al-bayān* denotes the branch treating imagery; (c) a figure of speech.

dīwān (pl. *dawāwīn*): (a) army payroll, register; (b) branch of the government (revenue, taxation); (c) the collected poetic works of an individual or a tribe.

duʿāʾ: literally 'prayer'; the invocation of blessing for the patron in a poem.

fakhr or *mufākhara*: boast on a variety of poetic themes.

gharaḍ (pl. *aghrāḍ*): literally 'goal'; (a) the purpose pursued with a poem (e.g. satire); (b) the thematic intention of a verse (e.g. description).

gharīb: rare, obscure, and difficult vocabulary.

ghazal: a poem celebrating present (tragic, erotic, or courtly) love, as different from the *nasīb* (q.v.), remembering a lost or former love.

ḥabīb: the (male or female) beloved; protagonist of *nasīb* and *ghazal* (q.v.).

hijāʾ (pl. *ahājī*): a poem of satire or invective.

ḥikma (pl. *ḥikam*): (a) a wise saying, adage in poetry or prose; (b) sayings of wisdom as the introductory part of a *qaṣīda* (q.v.).

iltifāt: a rhetorical figure consisting of a change of grammatical person, or theme, within a single verse.
ism (pl. *asmāʾ*): given name, personal name (e.g. Aḥmad).
istiʿāra: literally, 'borrowing'; (a) a metaphor; (b) a metaphor generated on the basis of an analogy.
istidlāl: deduction, inferential thinking.
ʿitāb: a poem of admonition.
Jāhiliyya: the 'Period of Ignorance' before Islam; from it derives the bulk of the poetic canon, which became constitutive for the *ʿarabiyya* (q.v.).
jalīs (pl. *julasāʾ*): familiar, courtier (cf. *nadīm*).
jinn (s. *jinnī*): invisible, supernatural beings endowed with Muslim faith; together with humans (*ins*), they constitute the living universe and the totality of believers.
kalām: speech.
kātib (pl. *kuttāb*): scribe or government functionary of any rank (up to that of vizier); member of a largely non-Arab professional class, instrumental in the shaping of *adab* (q.v.).
khaṭṭ: script.
khayāl: the (dream) apparition of the beloved, or *ḥabīb*, in *nasīb* and *ghazal* (q.v.).
kināya: (a) allusion, circumlocution, euphemism; (b) metonymy.
kitāb (pl. *kutub*): (a) a piece of writing, letter; (b) book.
kunya (pl. *kunā*): agnomen, a parent's naming after his or her son (e.g. Abū Bakr).
lafẓ (pl. *alfāẓ*): utterance; in poetic criticism, the verbal form, one of the two components of poetry, the other being *maʿnā*, or meaning (q.v.).
madīḥ (pl. *madāʾiḥ*): (a) the entire genre of praise poetry; (b) the part of a poem concerned with praise.
majlis (pl. *majālis*): literally 'place of sitting'; by extension a group of people sitting together in regular meetings, or sessions, whether for the purpose of learning or (literary, musical, convivial, or licentious) entertainment.
mamdūḥ: 'the praised one'; the addressee, or dedicatee, of a praise poem.
maʿnā (pl. *maʿānī*): literally 'meaning, content'; (a) in poetry, the general theme or subject of a poem; (b) poetic motif; (c) the generating idea underlying a complex motif, *concetto* (also *maʿnā al-maʿnā*).
marthiya (pl. *marāthī*): personal or official lament, dirge.
mufākhara: see *fakhr*.
muḥdath: literally 'modern'; (a) a poetic style flourishing in the Abbasid era, as opposed to 'ancient' poetry from the pre-Islamic through Umayyad periods (cf. *badīʿ*); (b) epithet of a poet using this style (pl. *muḥdathūn*).
mujūn: licentious, ribald poetry.
muruwwa: comparable to Latin *virtus*; catalogue of individual virtues in Bedouin, or later, urban culture (cf. *adab*, *ẓarf*).

muṭābaqa: see *ṭibāq*.
nadīm (pl. *nudamāʾ*): boon companion, courtier (cf. *jalīs*).
nasab: (a) a person's lineage, or genealogical chain, beginning with his or her patronymic, a main topic of *madīḥ* (as opposed to individual achievements, or *ḥasab*); (b) the discipline of genealogy.
nasīb (pl. *manāsib*): one of the introductory themes of the *qaṣīda*, containing usually one of three framing motifs: *aṭlāl* (q.v.), morning of separation from the beloved (*ḥabīb*), or (dream) apparition of the beloved (*khayāl*).
qaṣīda (pl. *qaṣāʾid*): (a) a ceremonial ode, comprising different themes (variously arranged and connected) and serving many purposes (praise, boast, message, advice, and devotion); formed in early sixth-century Arabia, it developed Persian and Hebrew branches in the fourth/tenth and fifth/eleventh centuries and survives today in many Asian and African languages; (b) in this book, mostly used in the narrow sense of the Abbasid panegyric ode.
raḥīl: camel description or camel journey, part of the *qaṣīda* (q.v.).
rithāʾ: see *marthiya*.
ṣanʿa: in poetry: (a) its craft or artistry; (b) the pursuit of poetry as a self-conscious, intellectual endeavor, or *shiʿr maṣnūʿ*, as opposed to *shiʿr maṭbūʿ*, the poetry flowing from natural talent (*ṭabʿ*).
sariqa (pl. *sariqāt*): also *akhdh*, a poetic plagiarism or borrowing, considered praiseworthy, blameworthy, or neutral, depending on the (more or less) creative treatment of its model, which may already be a *sariqa*.
shabāb: see *al-shayb wa-l-shabāb*.
shāʿir (pl. *shuʿarāʾ*): literally 'knower'; one who composes poetry in long verse, or *shiʿr*, a poet, as opposed to the *rājiz* who composes poetry in half-verse, or *rajaz*, using only the *rajaz* meter.
al-shayb wa-l-shabāb: literally 'white hair and youth'; one of the introductory themes of the *qaṣīda*, containing a lament of old age and nostalgia for, or boast of, former youth.
shiʿr: see *shāʿir*.
ṣināʿa: the trade or craft, e.g. of poetry or prose (cf. *ṣanʿa*).
tahniʾa (pl. *tahānī*): felicitation, a poem of congratulation on a specific occasion.
tajnīs: paronomasia.
takassub: gain through one's labor; in poetry, gain through eulogy, panegyrics.
takhalluṣ: transition from the (Arabic) *qaṣīda*'s introduction to its main theme.
takhyīl: literally 'make-believe'; (a) in poetic imagery, most often an illusory interpretation of a state of affairs (e.g., mock etiology, mock analogy); (b) in philosophical poetics, the evocation through figurative language of an image to a listener's mind, prompting his or her visceral response or persuasion; (c) in Koranic exegesis, the visualization of an abstract notion, such as God's omnipotence as a holistic, indivisible picture; (d) term for various figures of speech.

tamthīl: literally 'the adducing of a likeness'; (a) in grammar, the citation or definition by example; (b) in rhetoric, either the producing of a *mathal* (meaning either proverb, parable, or fable) or a figure of speech (simile, metaphor) that is based on an analogy, i.e. in which a set of elements at the level of the topic is matched with another set of elements at the level of the image.

tashbīh: simile, comparison.

ṭibāq and *muṭābaqa*: antithesis, antithetical parallelism.

waṣf (pl. *awṣāf*): descriptive poetry, or ecphrasis, either as an independent poem or as part of a *qaṣīda*.

ẓarf: elegance, sophisticated deportment in moral matters and material culture, a social ideal of the third/ninth century urban elite (cf. *adab*, *muruwwa*).

ẓarīf (pl. *ẓurafā'*): a person possessing *ẓarf* (cf. *adīb*).

Part I

SETTING THE STAGE

1

THE BACKGROUND

Poetry and poets in early Abbasid society

Before presenting the two protagonists of this book, the stage for Abbasid court society must be set, and the practices surrounding panegyrics briefly surveyed. The genre's most salient literary form, the panegyric *qaṣīda*, has become the goal of several scholarly approaches, including the present one, which will be discussed shortly. The remainder of the first part introduces the poet Ibn al-Rūmī and his brilliant patron, the Ṭāhirid governor ʿUbaydallāh b. ʿAbdallāh (d. 300/913), including an overview of the poetry their relationship inspired. The English renditions of the Arabic term *madīḥ*, 'panegyrics' or 'praise poetry,' may mislead one into believing that the poetry so designated limited itself to flattery. Indeed, *madīḥ* was much broader than that and included, next to praise, other tones of address ranging from advice and exhortation to criticism, direct accusation, and warning. In the following poem, quoted in part, Ibn al-Rūmī admonishes Muḥammad (d. 253/867), the brother and predecessor of the above-mentioned ʿUbaydallāh or, according to one manuscript, ʿUbaydallāh himself:[1]

أَلا لَيْتَ شِعْرِى لِمْ مطلْتَ مَثوبتِى   ولَمْ تُؤْتَ مِن بُخْلٍ ولَمْ تُؤْتَ مِن عُسْرِ؟
إخالُكَ إذْ جوَّدْتُ فيكَ مدائِحِى   منعْتَ ثوَابِى حاسِدًا لِى على شِعْرِى
أَتَحْسُدُنِى تجْويدَ رَيْطٍ نَسَجْتُهُ   لِتَلبَسَه؟ يا لِلْعجيب مِن الأَمرِ
تَذَكَّرْ – هَداك اللّهُ – أنِّىَ مادِحٌ   وأَنَّكَ ممدوحٌ ولا تَعْدُ بِى قَدْرِى
يُنافِسُ فى الشِّعْرِ النَّظيرُ نَظيرَهُ   وجلَّ ملوكُ النّاسِ عنْ ذلك النَّجْرِ
وما يَتجارَى الشاعِرانِ لغايةٍ   وراءَ اعْتِفاءِ الفَضْلِ مِنْ سَيِّدٍ غَمْرِ
وأَنتَ الَّذِى تعْفو العُفاةُ فُضولَه   ويُجرِى إلى معروفِه الشِّعْرَ مَنْ يُجرى ...
عَلَيْكَ بأَفعالِ الملوكِ وخَلِّنِى   وتقْريظَ ما تَأْتِى مِنَ العُرْفِ والنُّكْرِ

Oh, if only I knew, why you have postponed my reward
– you are stricken neither with parsimony nor with poverty.

I imagine, since I have bestowed my good praises on you,
you withheld my reward, envying me for my poetry.

Do you envy me for bestowing a fine mantle, which I have woven
for you to wear? Oh, help me with a strange matter!

Remember – God be your guide – that I am praising
and that you are praised! Do not wrong me in my rank![2]

In [all] poetry, one challenges one's equal,
and the sovereigns of people are above that endeavor.[3]

Two poets do not race with each other for any goal
but to request the grace of a magnificent leader.

And you are the one to whose graces supplicants come
and towards whose kindness a sender of poetry dispatches it ...

Busy yourself with the acts of kings and leave to me
the praising of your kindness [to your subjects]
and your cunning [against your enemies]!

(A694: 2–8, 12)

The poet voices two concerns with remarkable directness: he complains about a withheld reward for his poetry (2–3) and accuses his patron of trying to compete with him in poetry (5–12). The poet takes his dissatisfaction as an occasion to raise the question of poetic patronage and the function of reward. Ibn al-Rūmī also sets clear boundaries between the tasks of sovereign and praise poet and proceeds to lecture his patron about the dos and don'ts of a sovereign. He distinctly reminds Muḥammad (or ʿUbaydallāh) of his *passive* role in poetry, that of being a model for depiction (5, 12), as opposed to his *active* role in imparting mercy and generosity (7–8, 12). The poem is qualified in the *Dīwān* as an admonition (*ʿitāb*), which belongs to the genre of panegyrics (*madīḥ*), and not to satire (*hijāʾ*). Arabic poetry is in general characterized by having a purpose, such as to boast, praise, satirize, or describe, and the concept of poetry as 'pure art' and social grace only emerged in the Abbasid period among the dilettante poets from the ruling elite. If this admonitory poem forms part of Abbasid panegyrics, then the understanding of this genre must be revisited. What background and which assumptions could have guided the concerned parties to interpret such explicit admonishing and warning in a positive way?

Madīḥ adopted different literary forms. They included the long encomium (panegyric *qaṣīda*), the felicitation (*tahniʾa*), shorter poems (*qiṭʿa*) and epigrams. The long encomium characteristically combined praise with at least one other theme, such as nostalgia for a former love (*nasīb*) or lost youth (*al-shayb wa-l-shabāb*), a description of spring (*waṣf al-rabīʿ*), a boast (*fakhr*), or a wine-song (*khamriyya*). Although all forms belonged to the genre of praise[4] (*madīḥ*) some – as demonstrated – presented requests, excuses (*iʿtidhār*) or admonishments (*ʿitāb*). Allusions to satire (*hijāʾ*), the other side of *madīḥ*, sometimes played an indirect role. Open satire, however, stigmatized the recipient beyond repair and signalled the poet's desire to terminate his relationship with his patron.

Based on the current state of research, only a sketchy overview of Abbasid *madīḥ* practices can be given.[5] It owes much to Jamal Eddine Bencheikh,[6] whose excellent work is limited unfortunately to the first half of the third/ninth century, from the end of the Civil War and the ascent of caliph al-Maʾmūn (r. 198–218/813–33), to the assassination of caliph al-Mutawakkil (d. 247/861). This covers only half the career of Ibn al-Rūmī (221/836–283/896) and leaves out a major change that affected Ibn al-Rūmī's later career, namely the return of the caliphate to his hometown, Baghdad. Caliph al-Muʿtaṣim had moved the court to the newly-built Samarra (221/836), where a wealth of opportunity attracted young aspiring poets, and Baghdad, the cosmopolitan metropolis and center of patronage was relegated to the cultural backwaters. In this era, the capitals drew their most famous poets from elsewhere: Abū Tammām and al-Buḥturī came from Syria, Diʿbil and Abū l-ʿAtāhiya from Kufa, Abū Nuwās, Bakr b. al-Naṭṭāḥ, and al-Ḥusayn b. al-Ḍaḥḥāk from Basra, and only ʿAlī b. al-Jahm and Ibn al-Rūmī were native Baghdadians.[7] More than most poets, Ibn al-Rūmī kept faith with his city and saw it restored to the rank of residence by caliph al-Muʿtamid (278/892) a few years before his death (283/896).

The audience

By the Abbasid era, poetry fell into lighter and ceremonial genres. Light poetry included epigrams, wine, love, licentious and descriptive poetry; ceremonial poetry, praise, boast, lament, and satire. The ceremonial genres, longer and more complex, were the domain of professional poets. Literary circles (*majālis* s. *majlis al-uns*) became the audience for the performance of both kinds, though ceremonial poetry may have been presented in larger official settings as well. The circles brought together members of the highest social class, which included the caliphal family, ministers, scribes, religious dignitaries, military leaders, and governors, with the refined Baghdadian middle class, consisting of wealthy merchants, lower scribes, landowners and lower ranking military leaders, provided they could appear as *ẓurafāʾ* (s. *ẓarīf*) 'refined ones.'[8] A third class was represented by their affiliated clients, protégés, and educated slaves, as in the case of most of the female musicians and singers. If the caliph himself hosted the circle, participants included on the one hand, his retinue and high state officials, as well as selected scholars and judges; and on the other, individuals whose profession it was to entertain, such as poets, musicians, singers, and jesters. Of course, caliphs differed in the way they shaped their circles and conducted themselves as patrons. Caliph al-Maʾmūn, for instance, divided scholars and poets into separate sessions and banned musicians for a long time from the poets' circle. He neglected wine and love poetry and patronized ceremonial poetry, his preferred style being the archaic Bedouin verse of ʿUmāra b. ʿAqīl.[9] The audience of these *majālis* was well-versed in the finer points of language, literature, music, and social manners (*adab*) and possessed sophisticated tastes (*ẓarf*).[10] Besides poetry, they appreciated wine and song to such a degree that not even a caliph could restrain them. The ban on wine by al-Muhtadī (r. 255–6/869–70) only aroused the people against him, and his ban on song ended with his reign.[11] Among this audience, the chancellery scribes,[12] many of whom were non-Arabs who had risen through merit to high administrative positions, hastened to acquire *adab* and *ẓarf*. This was facilitated by a number of handbooks written by and for scribes. In imitation of the caliph, members of the higher classes, ministers, governors, scribes, and even one famous female poet formed their own circles. Members of the caliphal circle were esteemed guests at these lower circles, and their assistance was sought to gain introduction to the *majālis* of the caliph. An individual could then simultaneously assume different functions, such as being a member of the audience in one setting and a patron in another. ʿUbaydallāh b. ʿAbdallāh b. Ṭāhir, himself a celebrated patron, offered in turn a series of poems of gratitude to the powerful scribe al-ʿAlāʾ b. Ṣāʿid b. Makhlad.[13] The audience also derived from diverse ethnic backgrounds: Arabic, Aramean, Byzantine, Persian, and Turkish, including even the caliphs, some of whom were born to non-Arab mothers. Yet all of them shared one courtly culture that was based on the classical *ʿarabiyya*.[14]

As the audience included specialists from different disciplines – poets, scribes, philologists, and theologians – it not only savored every detail of the poetic performance, but also showed a readiness to criticize. A poet anticipated close scrutiny of his work and took care to ensure its linguistic and poetic soundness and ethical propriety. But he also relied on his audience to gauge his technical bravado.[15] In particular he assumed their knowledge of themes and motifs, enabling them to identify how much of a line or hemistich came from an existing verse and how he enhanced it by giving it a new form and meaning. The *sariqa* 'theft' or *akhdh* 'taking over', as well as *talmīḥ* 'allusion' and *taḍmīn* 'quotation' by which modern poets referred to each other and the ancients formed an integral part of Abbasid poetry, designed for an audience steeped in the classical tradition. Borrowing was then not frowned upon in general, but depended in each case on how elegantly a poet appropriated and recast a *sariqa* in his own verse. The double resonance of a borrowed phrase or motif in a verse rather enhanced it for an educated listener. In this sense, Wolfhart Heinrichs defines the common denominator of a good *sariqa* as follows. 'It endows one's poem with a quality of intertextuality, which for the connoisseur enriches it beyond what its mere words say.'[16] This strong reliance on pre-existing poetry rather than reality is the main argument for Heinrichs in describing Abbasid poetry as mannerist.[17]

Well-represented in those *majālis* were the chancellery scribes (*kuttāb*) who combined a high level of education with a relatively stable financial situation. The scribes themselves composed poetry for their own pleasure and hence became a threat to the professional poets. The scribes could even afford to hold their own literary circles and garner compliments for their verses from attending professional poets, whose praise need not have been candid. A conflict of interest arose for the poet if his patron was more ambitious in mastering poetry than in receiving it. Ibn al-Rūmī complains about the unfairness of this situation:

قَدْ بُلِينا فى دهْرِنا بمُلوكٍ   أُدباءٍ – عِلمتُهمْ – شُعراءِ
إنْ أَجَدْنا فى مَدْحِهِمْ حَسَدونا   فحُرِمْنا منهمْ ثَوابَ الثَّناءِ
أَوْ أَسَأْنا فى مدْحِهم أَنَّبونا   وهَجَوْا شِعْرَنا أَشَدَّ هِجاءِ
قَدْ أَقاموا نُفوسَهمْ لِذوِى المَدْ   حِ مُقامَ الأَنْدادِ والنُّظَراءِ

We are tried in our era by sovereigns I have known,
who are literati and poets.

If we say their praises well, they envy us,
and we are denied the reward of the eulogy.

Or, [if] we say their praises badly, they blame us
and vociferously satirize our poetry.

They have put themselves in the place
of competitors and equals to the panegyrists.

(E19)[18]

Usually, the dilettante poet-scribes limited themselves to the lighter genres which sufficed for elegant conversation and were easily set to music, a frequent ingredient of the circles. At the same time, Bencheikh notes a decline in the level of discourse from erudite discussion to shallow *divertissement*:

> Poetry becomes for most of them [sc. the scribes] an exercise in style, an agreeable occupation that lends itself to the most diverse occasions. It is the mode of communication *par excellence*, the mainstay of a culture; it reveals all of the attitudes these men take towards existence. But, what it gains in terms of sociocultural expression, it loses in terms of artistic exploration. Practiced too frequently as a habit and in the most banal circumstances, it dilutes itself in [its] daily [use] and is saved only by taking on the forms of mannerism.[19]

The scribes' success derived from their administrative skills, and their primary domain was prose. When indulging in versifying, they occasionally encroached on the genre of *madīḥ*, the domain of professional poets.[20] Even if such praises remained short and mediocre, they exposed the scribes to the poets' criticism, such as Diʿbil al-Khuzāʿī who disapproved of a *madīḥ* by Khālid b. Yazīd for al-Muʿtaṣim.[21] The Tunisian poetic critic Ibn Rashīq (d. 463/1070) took a different position and protected such attempts by distinguishing between scribes and professional poets:

> The secretary (*kātib*) is not obliged to compete with the poet (*shāʿir*) in mastering the craft (*ṣanʿa*) of poetry, because of the scribes' desire for the sweetness and lightness of words, artlessness, and the presentation of something that comes easily. Moreover, most of their poetry comes merely as an elegant exercise, neither out of desire nor fear; they are free and relaxed in their pleasures, indulged in their styles, since they only produce poetry out of choice and as an elegant pursuit, as the secretary Kushājim says:
>
> وَلَئِنْ شَعُرْتُ فما تَعَمَّدْتُ الهِجاءَ ولا المَديحَهْ
> لكِنْ رَأَيْتُ الشِّعْرَ لِلآدابِ تَرجَمَةً فصيحَهْ
>
> > If I compose poetry, I intend neither satire nor praise,
> >
> > But I have found poetry to be an eloquent translation of the refined ways of life (*ādāb*).
>
> The same rule [of not being beholden to the strictures of the poetic craft] applies to the poetry of caliphs, princes, and the wealthy people of rank. They are not held answerable like the illustrious poet, whose trade (*ṣināʿa*) is poetry, and whose merchandise panegyrics (*madīḥ*).[22]

While a scribe's mediocre poetry could not be faulted, his beautiful verse was all the more appreciated. The scribes could turn their lack of technique into an advantage by striving for elegance and simplicity. In addition they prided themselves on not subjecting poetry to a specific purpose – praise or blame – but practicing it as pure art. Their rank rested on their administrative skills and their epistolary style; poetry only added a, however valued, social grace. With this advantage, the scribes were both in a safer and more honorable position than the vocational poets, who depended solely on poetry for their income and had to humor their patrons' caprices. A similar tension existed among musicians; for instance, between the professional composer Isḥāq al-Mawṣilī and the composing son of a caliph, Ibrāhīm b. al-Mahdī. The famous singer ʿAmr b. Bāna (d. 278/891) left his teacher Isḥāq for the princely amateur, because he preferred art for pleasure (*taṭarrub*) to art for gain (*takassub*).[23]

Another group partaking in the literary circles and significant for the poets, were the singers and musicians. Song did not compete with but complemented poetry, for a singer could make the fame of a poem by setting it beautifully to music, or introduce a new poet at court, by intoning some of his verses.[24] However, the singers usually preferred the light genres, which lent themselves to musical performance,[25] and in which they drew from both professional and dilettante poets and composers. Moreover, song was associated with wine-drinking and licentious behavior, and a singer could only appear at a caliph's familiar sessions devoted to light *divertissement*, whereas a poet might offer praises both at public ceremonies and familiar sessions. Therefore singers could not easily serve as go-betweens for panegyrists and patrons. If a panegyrist needed to contact a new patron or patch up a *faux pas* with a current sponsor, he approached an honorable individual who had access to the patron's circle and was in his confidence, thus being better equipped to intervene on the poet's behalf. These intercessors gave rise to a new sub-genre of praise poetry, the poem of intercession, which praised the intercessor and the one who responded to intercession alike. The act of (asked and granted) intercession itself became doubled generosity. Ibn al-Rūmī once asked his friend, the courtier and polymath ʿAlī b. Yaḥyā b. al-Munajjim to intercede on his behalf with the minister Ismāʿīl b. Bulbul (d. 278/891).[26] On another occasion he implored his former teacher, the grammarian al-Mubarrad (d. 286/900), for a similar favor with al-ʿAlāʾ (272/886), the son and secretary of the minister Ṣāʿid b. Makhlad.[27]

The patrons

The patrons were derived from the upper and middle classes of the audience described above; prominent among them were the scribes (*kuttāb*), many of whom had risen in the ranks of the Abbasid administration. From the beginning of the Abbasid age, scribes took an active role as functionaries up to the highest levels. Although the majority of them doubtlessly had little influence, some ascended to the head of government offices and the vizierate. During the second half of the third/ninth century, the vizierate was occupied by a few families of Aramean and Persian background all of whom heavily patronized the arts as well as the foreign sciences and the translation movement.[28] The Abbasid patron did not choose a poet for his political or religious leaning, which the poet usually concealed when disadvantageous. Although it was not a prerequisite, an ethnic or religious affiliation between a poet and his patron could enhance their relationship. Ultimately, however, the poet owed his patron loyalty against his own personal preferences.[29] His benefit rather derived from an exchange of his literary services for protection and compensation from the patron. The poet invested his talent and renown to justify his patron's claims to rank and merit and to portray him favorably, and the patron accepted and rewarded this portrayal of himself.

With the proliferation of dilettante poetry in this period, a new type of patron emerged that caused the boundaries between poet and patron to blur. Scribes as patrons no longer received praises passively (in response to generous gifts) but rather recited to the members of their literary circles the prose and poetry they themselves had composed.[30] With his stronger position as a patron and the double standards between dilettante and professional poetry in his favor, the host of a literary circle could count upon the polite applause of his protégés at the least.[31] Abū Tammām and al-Buḥturī understood the importance of creating a space for their patrons' literary skills and they included praises of these skills in their encomia.[32] A patron also indirectly influenced his poets' compositions by challenging them with poetic acrobatics or giving them a verse or a theme on which to improvise. He might even ask his poets to write poetry, which he would then promulgate as his own. In sum, the Abbasid patron was no longer only an *object* of poetry but an *active* partner and participant. This role of the patron placed him under new obligations. He had to comment as a connoisseur on the poetry he received, acknowledging the technical challenges the poet had braved.[33] A patron's ignorance in poetic matters was inexcusable and exposed him to embarrassment and ridicule, such as the vizier Ismāʿīl b. Bulbul, mistaking a very daring hyperbole in Ibn al-Rūmī's *madīḥ* of him for *hijāʾ* (satire).[34] A patron also took part more consciously in the patronage system; in other words, to be a perfect patron became an art in itself. While the patron of earlier times indiscriminately lavished favors on poets and thereby motivated them to praise him, the Abbasid patron-*adīb* became a connoisseur, suggesting themes, criticizing poems he received, or entrusting them to a consulting third party. The position of the expert patron *vis-à-vis* his poet became increasingly complex. In material matters he kept his superiority; in poetic matters he claimed to stand on equal basis with his poet. Al-Buḥturī and Abū Tammām played along with this, ostensibly acknowledging their patrons' literary talents. Ibn al-Rūmī went a step further and exploited the situation by taking it literally; to concede the excellence of a patron's poetry entailed for the poet the renouncing of the same claim for his own work, on which his very rank rested. Ibn al-Rūmī once dramatized the dilemma of the versifying patron in a felicitation.[35] In it he asked the question whether, if the poem's addressee commanded unequalled excellence in *all* achievements including poetry, how could one dare to offer him verses that were by definition second-rate? In putting the question to his patron, Ibn al-Rūmī kept the balance between respecting him in the role of a poet and reminding him gently of his other duties.

The poets

In the third/ninth century two trends came to the fore that affected both the poets' status and their craft. The roots of the former trend reached back into the period before Islam. Then, the poets had shared and defended the collective political stance of their audiences. They were the spokesmen of their tribes and occupied within them a certain rank by birth and conformity with the honor code (*muruwwa*). Poetry was the vehicle to enact this honor code and was counted as one of the virtues constituting it. The poet celebrating *muruwwa* did not restrict himself to setting in verse what he had personally experienced; rather he portrayed a shared heroic ideal. The Umayyad period with its vast socio-political changes brought forth little *madīḥ*, which was to resurface in force only in the Abbasid period. At that stage, the collective identification between poet and audience was no longer a given. The poets no longer spoke as members of a tribal community but as city-dwelling professionals who sought the protection of individual patrons without necessarily sharing their political and religious views. After having served in pre-Islamic and early Islamic times as a medium of political propaganda, poetry lost ground against the emerging prose in the

Abbasid age. Doctrinal propaganda for the Abbasid revolution was carried out predominantly by missionaries (*duʿāh*)[36] and only a few poets.[37] Instead, between the caliphates of al-Ma'mūn and al-Mutawakkil, the dissemination of governmental decisions was entrusted to a writer of prose, the famous essayist al-Jāḥiẓ (d. 255/868–9).[38] In addition, the 'Bureau of Poetry' (*dīwān al-shiʿr*), which had dispensed allocations to the best panegyrists, ceased to exist.[39] Al-Jāḥiẓ epitomizes these changes in his comparison between poet and orator: the poet has not only lost the role of defending the Abbasid dynasty and doctrine to the fields of historiography, dogmatic theology, and the doctrinal epistle, but has also forfeited his rank as the speaker of his tribe.[40] But while one role was lost, another one emerged with the consolidation of the Abbasid dynasty. From its very beginning, the Abbasid rule was exposed to Sasanian advice literature translated from Pahlavi, as well as mirrors of princes (*Fürstenspiegel*) either translated or composed by scribes of Iranian background, notably Ibn al-Muqaffaʿ.[41] The new caliphs saw themselves more as the successors of the Sasanians and adopted their court ceremonial which included the role of the accomplished and educated courtier.[42] The panegyrists filled that role and became the caliph's familiars (*julasāʾ* s. *jalīs*) and boon companions (*nudamāʾ* s. *nadīm*).[43] But the protection of a praise poet by a particular ruler entailed for him the loss of an independent status. The courtier-poet had little leverage against his princely patron, as exemplified in al-Mutawakkil's circle. This caliph reduced his poets literally to buffoons, pitting them against each other and instigating animosities between them for his own entertainment.[44] This treatment was extreme yet symptomatic of the lack of clout of the panegyric profession. In addition, with the increasing poetic activity of the patrons, the poets lost their exclusive right to a field of expertise on which they had based their claims. The poetic carpet had been literally pulled out from under their feet. They praised their patron's compositions as matchless, declaring their own verse second to them. In the dedication of the encomium, the poet could freely boast of his own work, but only in its function as a tribute for the excellence of his patron. This first trend then stripped the poets of a larger, abstract authority – the pre-Islamic tribal *muruwwa* – and curtailed their authority in poetic matters, leaving them to their own devices in seeking patronage and protection or a position as a courtier.

The second trend affecting poets in the third/ninth century was of a literary order. Half-a-century earlier, Bashshār b. Burd (d. 167/783)[45] and Muslim b. al-Walīd (d. 208/823)[46] had inaugurated the *muḥdath* 'modern' style or *badīʿ* 'new style'. This style was characterized by an increased use of rhetorical figures and fantastic imagery as well as its indebtedness to existing, especially classical, poetry. The *muḥdath* poet gleaned the themes, motifs (*maʿānī*), and the rare vocabulary (*gharīb*) from his pre-Islamic and Umayyad predecessors as well as his contemporaries and arranged it in ways as to create additional effects, be they rhetorical figures, or *metaphorae continuatae* with multiple terms drawn from one semantic field, or descriptions of one theme with the vocabulary of another. As a result, *muḥdath* poetry was double-layered, presenting the familiar in a stylish new setting. This building on pre-existing poetry combined with its distance (or estrangement) from the depicted reality has earned *muḥdath* poetry the label of mannerism.[47] A fervent battle ensued around this style, with the adherents of Abū Tammām (d. 231/845)[48] marking the extreme position, and those of his disciple al-Buḥturī (d. 284/897)[49] the more moderate. The debate between these two trends of *badīʿ* overshadowed styles of other poets, who differed more significantly from both than the two did from one another, namely Diʿbil al-Khuzāʿī (d. 244/859 or 246/860),[50] ʿAlī b. al-Jahm (d. 249/863),[51] and Ibn al-Rūmī who developed forms of dialogue.[52]

The flourishing of the *badīʿ*-style concurred with the emergence of the scribes and their dilettante poetry. The scribes followed this literary vogue as well, but in using *badīʿ*, stuck to lighter and shorter genres. The professional poets in turn were able to flaunt their knowledge of the vast ancient repertory.[53] If anything, the *muḥdath* style contributed to widening the gap between professionals and dilettantes, as it rendered the composition of the ceremonial genres, which strongly relied on classical precedent, very difficult. Coryphées such as Abū Tammām, al-Buḥturī, and Ibn al-Rūmī, who only served caliphs and the high elite, thrived on this challenge and elevated the craft (*ṣanʿa*) of poetry to new heights. Their mannerist techniques as well as the sheer length of some of their pieces[54] lay far beyond the aspirations of the most excellent amateur. It may not be far-fetched to imagine the professional poets grasping the opportunity to demonstrate the great difference between themselves and the dilettantes, thus safeguarding their beleaguered profession at least on the technical level. Whether they did so consciously or as an intuitive protective reaction may only be speculated upon. In any case, the poets prided themselves on their technical mastery; Abū Tammām revelled in his audience's struggle with his thorny vocabulary, while Ibn al-Rūmī intimidated (or annoyed) his addressees with poems of daunting length and difficult rhyme letters,[55] though he occasionally felt compelled to accompany a poem with glosses for less erudite listeners.[56]

As a result of the two trends, the change in the poets' status and the rise of the 'new style', the poets' basis of authority shifted from a collective identity to individual skill. Meanwhile the latter expanded to include the composition of modern carefully-crafted poetry (*ṣanʿa*) and the social skills (*adab*, *ẓarf*) of court conduct and entertainment. Naturally these changes articulated themselves within the poetry, such as in the formation of new themes[57] and a reconfigured persona of the poet, reflecting his new rights and duties.[58]

2

THE FORM

The Abbasid praise *qaṣīda*

Of all verse dedicated to Abbasid caliphs, governors, generals and scribes, only a part represented the ceremonial genres of *madīḥ* (panegyric) and *rithā'* (lament); the remainder included the informal genres of *ghazal* (love poetry), *khamriyya* (wine poetry) and *waṣf* (descriptive poetry). Ceremonial genres could be recited at both official (*majlis 'āmm*) and semi-private audiences (*majlis al-uns*); informal only at the latter. Only *madīḥ* (and *rithā'*) could render the public portrayal of a patron, and its most traditional, prestigious and therefore poetically most challenging form was the *qaṣīda*. For much the same reasons, i.e. difficult language, style, and imagery as well as a limited catalogue of themes, the panegyric *qaṣīda* has only recently received due scholarly attention. With the concern for representative results, however, many interpretative approaches address the *qaṣīda* sequence of *nasīb*, *raḥīl*, and *madīḥ*, as described by Ibn Qutayba in the preface of his handbook on poetry and identified by Renate Jacobi as a popular Umayyad form.[1] While the insights gained about this 'typical' *qaṣīda* are inestimable, it is equally vital to realize that poets took great freedom in the thematic composition of their *qaṣā'id* (pl. of *qaṣīda*). The second half of this chapter, a comparison between two contrasting pieces by al-Buḥturī and 'Alī b. al-Jahm, will dispel any impression of uniformity in *qaṣīda* composition.

History of research

Modern scholarship has recognized the Abbasid *qaṣīda* as a complex layered composition. Medieval Arabic poetic critics lacked a terminology for larger forms of composition and instead classified poetry by content, based on the states of mind of the poet as well as on the themes or intentions (*aghrāḍ*) of the poetry.[2] But some specimens of poetry clearly display a larger composition, for example a poem of Ibn al-Rūmī with repetitions, a consistent structure, and a transition from *nasīb* to *madīḥ*.[3] Some medieval critics, however, discussed the composition of certain sections and implicitly acknowledged the *qaṣīda* as a whole in their treatment of headings, such as the beginning of poems (*ibtidā'*) and the transition from *nasīb* to *madīḥ* (*takhalluṣ*).[4] There is further internal and external evidence for readers' reception of larger forms. The anthologist al-

Marzūqī (d. 421/1030) and the Koranic exegetes al-Rāzī (d. 606/1209) and al-Iskāfī (d. 1026), for instance, recognized and appreciated large and non-contiguous forms.[5]

Much of the research on the Abbasid praise *qaṣīda*, a genre of extreme longevity, emerges from the issues raised by the pre-Islamic and Umayyad *qaṣīda*. Therefore, the following paragraphs summarizing previous work on the Abbasid *qaṣīda* touch on earlier forms as well. It should be noted, however, that the *qaṣīda* was only one of many poetic forms. What is more, the famous *qaṣā'id* mostly discussed in secondary literature may present a more homogenous order of themes than warranted by the historical reality, as they may have been rearranged by transmitters (*ruwāh* s. *rāwī*) as well as edited by the Abbasid collectors who elevated them to classics.[6] No account is taken here of the subsequent development of the *qaṣīda* in Arabic or other languages, notably Hebrew and Persian.[7]

Recent study on the *qaṣīda* can be said to respond to the triple accusation of pre-Islamic Arabic poetry by early orientalists: they perceived it to be molecular in structure, stereotyped in its imagery, and lacking introspection and individual emotion.[8] These earlier perceptions have been countered by recent interpretations, which can be divided into three axes of approach: textual, intertextual, and contextual. (The terms should be understood as keywords, rather than all-inclusive descriptions.) In general, the methodological scope of modern scholars includes literary theory, which opens new ways of appreciating classical Arabic poetry.

The textual approach

This responds to the judgment of molecularity. This approach is concerned with establishing the coherence of a *qaṣīda*, analyzing its structure, its order of themes, and its unity. In his discussion of the genesis of the *qaṣīda*, Alfred Bloch attributes its tripartite structure – the succession of *nasīb*, camel description, and the final part (message, praise or elegy) – to its use as a travel song. The *nasīb* and *raḥīl* entertained the messenger on his journey, and only the final part was intended for the addressee.[9] Bloch stresses the importance of the message formulae in *qaṣā'id* and uni-thematic poems (*qiṭa'* s. *qiṭ'a*). He even notes a continuity of argument in some *qaṣā'id*, where the morning-of-separation motif of the opening part, containing the poet's argument with a female speaker, is echoed in the final part, containing an aggressive message to the addressee of the poem.[10] Renate Jacobi proposes that first two, then three *qiṭa'* were combined to *qaṣā'id* in an interactive process with the audience during the first part of the sixth century.[11] Her analysis of a large pre-Islamic corpus[12] empirically demonstrates the great variety in the thematic order of pre-Islamic *qaṣā'id*, which she classes into three types: memorial *qaṣīda*, message *qaṣīda*, and praise *qaṣīda*.[13] She notes further the poets' emerging tendency to connect the *qaṣīda*'s parts with motifs of transition.[14] Moreover, multiple correspondences within and across the *qaṣīda*'s parts have been identified by Jaroslav Stetkevych and Michael Sells on the level of etymon, symbol, and semantic field.[15]

For the Umayyad *qaṣīda*, Jacobi shows the continuation of the trend toward molding the *qaṣīda* into a narrative continuity (*nasīb*, *raḥīl* to patron + *madīḥ*) as well as a gradual reduction from three *qaṣīda* types to one: the praise *qaṣīda*. Within the *qaṣīda*, the former three parts have shrunk to two, since the *raḥīl*, previously a camel description, has been reinterpreted as a camel ride to the patron, and subsumed under the *madīḥ*.[16]

The Abbasid *qaṣīda* further reduces or wholly eliminates the *raḥīl* and remains essentially bipartite.[17] Here the search for unity has thus focussed on the relationship between its two parts. Of special importance to the present study is the identification of extended binary rhetorical figures, such as parallelism and antithesis, that serve as structuring devices for the overall composition of the *qaṣīda*.

In the poetry by al-Muʿtamid b. ʿAbbād (d. 487/1095), parallelism is extended to a structuring device on the level of the section.[18] In a *qaṣīda* of Bashshār b. Burd (d. 167/783), the correlation of *nasīb* and *madīḥ* forms one pervasive parallelism. Both the *ḥabīb* (the beloved), the protagonist of the *nasīb*, and the *mamdūḥ* (the praised one), the protagonist of the *madīḥ*, are depicted as the goal of the poet's love and ambition. The similarity in the poet's attitude to both creates a parallelism, which places them in analogous positions. Having so established *ḥabīb* and *mamdūḥ* as equivalents, the poet states explicitly about the *ḥabīb*, in the *nasīb*, what courtly etiquette prevents him from pronouncing about the patron, in the *madīḥ*. The parallelism between the two makes the criticism of the *ḥabīb* applicable to the patron as well. In this way, parallelism becomes a means of indirection; the hearer detects from the similar description of *mamdūḥ* and *ḥabīb* that both are interchangeable and deduces from the description of the *ḥabīb* as aloof and stingy that the same is true of the patron, without the poet ever saying so directly.[19]

Antithesis has also been used as a larger form, either of thematic or rhetorical order. Like parallelism it serves as a structural element of sections[20] or of entire poems, as shown in a panegyric *qaṣīda* by Abū Tammām.[21] Panegyric *qaṣāʾid* for caliphs tend to be antithetical in structure, and Stefan Sperl reflects this with a new terminology, designating as *strophe* the first part, containing *nasīb*, *al-shayb wa-l-shabāb*, etc., and as antistrophe the second part, containing the *madīḥ* proper. The *ḥabīb*, protagonist of the *nasīb* (strophe), and the ruler, protagonist of the *madīḥ* (antistrophe), as well as their respective powers (fate and rulership) and their realms (*aṭlāl* and state), constitute binary oppositions. As a whole, the *qaṣīda* moves from affliction to redemption or from the sensual to the spiritual realm.[22] Both binary structures reveal an inherent logic in the *qaṣīda*'s separate themes, by ascribing the first part (Sperl's strophe) a functional role as a foil for or a contrast to the second part, concerned with the ruler (Sperl's antistrophe).

For smaller sections, Andras Hamori and Raymond Scheindlin have found further structural devices. Sections are opened by vocatives, parallel syntax, past tense verbs and switches of the grammatical person.[23] Devices of closure are *ḥikam*, aphorisms, rhetorical questions, apostrophes, balanced hemistiches, and slowing patterns.[24] Further structural devices govern, for instance, the internal order of sections, such as the progression from summary to detail (*mujmal–mufaṣṣal*) or the narrative.[25] Others again bind elements scattered throughout the poem such as partial repetition or explanation (*bayān*) of a verse several lines later.[26] Beyond these syntactical and rhetorical figures, other interrelations operate at the level of motif and imagery. Together, the textual approaches show the nearly unlimited number of features that can be adduced in favor of the *qaṣīda*'s cohesiveness, internal logic and functional unity.

The intertextual approach

This addresses the judgment concerning stereotyped themes and imagery. While acknowledging the indebtedness of each poem to pre-existing poetry in its fidelity to received themes, comparisons, and metaphors, this approach acknowledges the author's agency in selecting, arranging, and transforming these elements. Precisely because the poet used familiar topoi and filled his mouth with the metaphors of others, was the audience able to detect and appreciate his elaboration and improvement of them. Every motif or metaphor did not merely please because of its given articulation, but because of its resuscitation of previous versions in the hearers' minds. The glamour of a new line of poetry thus resulted from its simultaneous distance from, and closeness to, earlier renditions.[27]

In the Abbasid period, intertextuality did not exhaust itself in varying earlier motifs, but also combined them, and dislocated them from their original themes. The poet constructed *concetti*[28] with comparisons, tropes, and rhetorical figures. This technique allowed the poet to intertwine the levels of topic and image or to construct duplicitous verse, with a coherent meaning both at the topical and the figurative level. The resultant complexity of poetic expression and the focus on its rhetorical arrangement led to a rift between poetry and reality. Poetry became an aim in itself and grew increasingly distanced from the depicted object; in other words, it became manneristic.[29] Without taking intertextuality into account, the modern reader misses the nature of Abbasid verse.

The contextual approach

Both the first (textual) and second (intertextual) approach treat the *qaṣīda* as a phenomenon of language and style. A tribal or courtly surrounding is assumed but only touched in passing.[30] This is the domain of contextual approaches, which respond to the view that the *qaṣīda* is 'objective' and lacking individual emotion and introspection. Instead of searching for individual expression, these approaches explore the *qaṣīda* as embedded in a tribal or urban elite society. Its specific character is attributed to the role it plays therein, as an embodiment of collective concepts and ideals. These may be of ritual, religious, social or political order. Despite their methodological diversity, drawing on anthropology, sociology and history, all approaches share the treatment of the *qaṣīda* as an intrinsic part of a situational whole.

For the pre-Islamic *qaṣīda*, scholars focus on its collective and mythical or ritual functions.[31] But whereas Jacobi describes the diversity of the *qaṣā'id* in their own terms, based on ample material, other interpretations presuppose an ideal tripartite *qaṣīda* scheme and decipher selected specimens along the lines of structuralist and anthropological theories. James Montgomery's approach occupies a middle ground. He identifies a central concept of Arab society, the Bedouin honor code of *muruwwa*, as a unifying principle of poetic themes. The balance between *muruwwa* and pessimism provides the underlying tension in many *qaṣā'id*.[32] This notwithstanding, pre-Islamic poets could express individual emotion or gratify a more expert audience with unusual compositions if they so chose.[33]

As to the Abbasid praise *qaṣīda*, two approaches explain its interactional role. First, its ideological message has received emphasis. As an amalgamation of *Jāhiliyya* and Islamic history, the *qaṣīda* served both to celebrate an ideal ruler's image and to legitimize a specific ruler.[34] Second, it performed a ceremonial function as a type of court literature. Its language, the elevated poetic *ʿarabiyya*, distinguished an educated class.[35] In particular, the *badīʿ*-style of the *qaṣīda* suited courtly life because it mirrored its duplicity; it provided the courtier with a medium for indirect didactic and ethical injunctions to his superiors.[36] Studies of ideological or ceremonial aspects take the single *qaṣīda* as a point of juncture in the interaction of a poet with a ruler or a courtly audience. Treating the *qaṣīda* as a stable literary form, they create at times an impression of uniformity – an impression which is heightened by the few number of poets studied, for knowledge about the Abbasid praise *qaṣīda* derives almost exclusively from the panegyrists of (multiple) rulers, such as Abū Tammām, al-Buḥturī and al-Mutanabbī (d. 354/965).[37] One can diversify this uniform picture by adding the role of lesser patrons, particularly important in the light of patronage being practiced by many members of the educated class other than rulers, and providing a livelihood for any number of professional poets. Another aspect are the long-term relationships between particular poets and their patrons. It was the patron who offered a poet protection and supplied his income, and the patron's taste was the one the poet first obeyed. This book contributes to the last aspect by examining the *interactive* potential of the praise *qaṣīda* within the long-standing and successful patronage relationship in early Abbasid Baghdad between Ibn al-Rūmī and ʿUbaydallāh b. ʿAbdallāh.

Constraint and variety

Before presenting the selected approach, the complementariness of the above-described three types must be stressed. In particular, intertextual and contextual approaches look at similar phenomena from different angles. The choice of the one or the other often depends on cues given by the medieval poet, privileging in a given *qaṣīda* either the (vertical) textual tradition or the (horizontal) historical situation as the dominant frame of reference.

An intertextual analysis of a number of contemporary texts can provide a framework for identifying a poet's agency within the inherited conventions. Bencheikh distinguishes, for instance, between shared themes and their linguistic articulation in a specific poem. In his view, the themes of a *qaṣīda* only steer a poet's creative effort, but do not contain it:

> Mais la convention, si elle oriente la création, ne la contient pas .... Or ce n'est pas parce que le poète entreprend de construire une *qaṣīda* selon les lois établies qu'il fait oeuvre de poète; c'est parce que son écriture, sur un schéma fixé, crée la *qaṣīda* que celle-ci devient une oeuvre poétique .... En déployant sa série thématique, le créateur détermine en fait le lieu de son language.[38]

The poetic achievement lies in the linguistic rendition:

> Aux séquences [thématiques] mises en evidences par la critique, se substitue une articulation de *languages* qui constituent la substance du poème et révèlent sa véritable structure.[39]

Thus, the Abbasid poet oriented himself toward the textual tradition, consisting of the sum of existing *qaṣā'id*. But the poet could choose to give more room to the historical situation and subject the thematic sequence to a particular topic, develop new structural devices, or even introduce new themes.[40] An intertextual approach can reveal and describe such innovations with precision. But to understand the underlying motivation for them, a mere textual comparison does not suffice; instead one needs to establish links with the poet's surrounding reality. This is accomplished by the contextual approaches described above, which look beyond the *qaṣīda* as a convention to detect its function. For the poet had two larger frames of reference at his disposal: the poetic tradition consisting of pre-existing *madīḥ*, and the historical background including his courtly audience, his individual benefactor, and the occasion at hand. The poet, however, had the choice to privilege the historical situation over the textual tradition or vice versa, and he signalled it to this audience by direct (or indirect) cues.[41] The following two cases illustrate the different weight that might be given to context and convention.

When ʿUbaydallāh b. ʿAbdallāh b. Ṭāhir, the subsequent governor of Baghdad, came to the city in 253/867, al-Buḥturī sent him an encomium celebrating his arrival.[42] In it he follows the conventional bipartite structure of *nasīb* (1–9) and *madīḥ* (10–31) with dedication (32–9). The *nasīb* unites a plethora of ancient motifs: the morning of separation, halting at the abandoned campsite traces (*aṭlāl*), the address of two companions, regret of youth, and consolation. The old motifs are brought into parallelisms (5, 9) or antithetical parallelisms (3, 4, 6), and then create a coherent action at the metaphorical level (3, 4, 8). The description of the poet's feelings does not form a continuous development. Rather, the concept of unfulfilled love is split into separate facets. Neither the poet nor his beloved become palpable figures.

The *madīḥ* exhibits the same absence of a palpable poet figure and supplies a very vague description of the addressee, except for his name (11, 32) and a brief ancestral affiliation (14). The poet limits his praise to all-encompassing hyperbolae for the patron (Spring, 11–12; Kaaba, 28–9) and the ascription of the common virtues of generosity, gentility, and courage:

وبانَتْ به حتّى تفرَّدَ بالعُلا　　غرائبُ أفعالٍ قليلٍ شُكولُها ...
مَوازينُ حِلْمٍ ما يُوازَنُ قَدْرُها　　وساعاتُ جودٍ ما يُطاعُ عَذولُها
وقدْ تُسْعَرُ الهَيْجاءُ مِنْهُ بمِرْجَمٍ　　تُوَفّى به أوْتارُها وذُحولُها

With him appeared amazing acts, the likes of which are few,
so that he singled himself out by [his] high rank . . .[43]

Measures of gentility – their size cannot be weighed,[44]
moments of generosity whose constant blamer is spited.

Sometimes war is kindled by him, a fierce warrior, by whom
[the thirst of war for] retaliation and blood-revenge is fulfilled.
(no. 679: 16, 24–5)

If one compares praise poems to fitted garments,[45] this one is a wide tent. No specific attribute or achievement distinguishes the patron. The poet appears only once in the first person, expressing tempered joy: 'It pleased me that the noble deeds began to lay down their loads on the earth of Iraq' (10). Then he disappears from the *madīḥ* only to reappear in the dedication in an equally vague stance:

أبا أحْمدٍ والحَمْدُ رَهْنُ مآثِرٍ　　تُؤَثِّلُها أوْ عارفاتٍ تُنيلُها
وَصَلْتُ بكَ الحاجاتِ جَمْعًا وإنّما　　بطَوْلِ جليلِ القومِ يُقْضَى جليلُها ...
وأرْسَلْتُ أفوافَ القوافي شَوافعًا　　إليْكَ وقدْ يُجْدي لدَيْكَ رَسولُها
بَوادٍ بإحسانِ الثَّناءِ وخَلْفَها　　عوائدُ لمْ تُطْلَقْ إليكَ كُبولُها
زواهرُ نَوْرٍ ما يَجِفُّ جَنيُّها　　وأنْجُمُ لَيْلٍ ما يُخافُ أُفولُها
وما بصوابٍ أنْ يُؤَخَّرَ حَظُّها　　وقدْ سَبَقَتْ أوْضاحُها وحُجولُها
إذا ما البُزاةُ البيضُ لمْ تُسْقَ رِيَّها　　على ساعةِ الإحسانِ خيفَ نُكولُها

> Abū Aḥmad,[46] praise is a pledge of glorious deeds you firmly [re]establish or [a pledge] of benefits you accord.
>
> With you, I have met all my needs, since a great need can only be granted by a great man . . .[47]
>
> I have sent to you as intercessors white striped coats of rhymes – perhaps the messenger in them[48] is of use to you:
>
> First ones, performing excellent praise, after them, others again, whose tethers have not [yet] been loosened [to go] to you.
>
> Blooming white blossoms, [although] a plucked one of them does not wither, stars of the night, [although] one need not fear their setting.
>
> It is not right that their share be postponed, after the ones with white blazes and fetlocks have been the first.[49]
>
> When the white buzzards are not given to drink to satiation at the moment of [their] excellent performance, one fears their cowardice [in the future].
>
> (no. 679: 32–3, 35–9)

In the dedication the poet sets poetry and gifts in relation, but without clarifying his own standpoint towards the patron. On the one hand, the poet states 'With you, I have met all my needs' (33). On the other, the poet makes his verses intercede for him and offer their services (35). He announces more verses to come (36) and mentions that the reward for the present ones should not be deferred (38). The poet vaunts them as striped coats (35), ever-blooming white blossoms, fixed stars (37), and winning steeds (38). His demand for reward remains comparatively subtle (38): reward is merely motivated in general statements at the beginning and end of the dedication. In the opening sententia, verses are declared pledges for glory and benefits (32), i.e. they precede them. The closure reiterates this with an analogy between verses and buzzards who continue to hunt only if rewarded immediately after killing their prey (39). Directly speaking, initial praises anticipate reward, but further praises depend on reward of the present ones. The poet attempts to entice the patron to earn these further praises by gifts (32, 36, 39) and does not insist on reward as a right owed to him (38). While the poet's persona remains aloof from the discussion, he lets his verses address the patron, for instance, in the metaphor of the birds of prey ʿUbaydallāh has to train. It depends on him whether they will benefit him or not. If the patron's duties are formulated indirectly, the description of his actual achievements is kept even more vague. He distinguishes himself with 'amazing acts' (16) and by his beneficence 'great needs are granted (33)', but whether he has indeed proven that with al-Buḥturī is left open to question. The poet's vagueness reflected the specific situation; he contacted a potentially generous patron for the first time, giving him the benefit of the doubt and leaving it to him to prove his generosity.[50] At the same time, the poem's ornate combinations of metaphors and rhetorical figures in the *muḥdath* style made it a worthy introductory present.

When al-Mutawakkil came to power in 232/847 he banned the Ḥanafī/Muʿtazilī doctrine of the created Koran, officially instated by al-Maʾmūn.[51] ʿAlī b. al-Jahm[52] celebrated al-Mutawakkil as restorer of the *Sunna* and dedicated this first *qaṣīda* to him.[53] In it, he refers to al-Mutawakkil's abolishment of the process of *miḥna* ('testing') to which all judges and, in one instance, prisoners of war[54] were subjected. The caliph began the process with a formal edict in 234/848–9, then gradually replaced all the important judges supporting the doctrine and ended with releasing all those imprisoned on its account in 237/851–2. The *qaṣīda* lacks a *nasīb* and is structured entirely as a dialogue. The poet's persona faces a bystander (*qāʾil*) in five turns of question and answer.[55]

وقائِلٍ أيُّهما أنْوَرُ   الشَّمْسُ أَمْ سَيِّدُنا جعْفَرُ؟
قُلتُ لقدْ أَكبَرْتَ شَمْسَ الضُّحَى   جَهْلاً وما أَنْصَفْتَ مَن تَذْكُرُ
هَلْ بَقِيَتْ فيكَ مَجوسِيَّةٌ   فالشَّمْسُ فى مِلَّتِها تُكْبَرُ
أَمْ أَنْتَ مِن أبنائِها عالِمٌ   وزَلَّةُ العالمِ لا تُغْفَرُ
فقُلْ مَعاذَ اللَّهِ مِن هَفْوَةٍ   قال فَهَلْ يَغْلَطُ مُستَخْبِرُ
الشَّمْسُ يَوْمَ الدَّجْنِ مَحْجوبَةٌ   واللَّيلُ يُخْفيها فلا تَظْهَرُ
فَهْيَ على الحالَيْنِ مَملوكةٌ   لا تَدْفَعُ الرِّقَّ ولا تُنْكِرُ
فكيْفَ قايَسْتَ بها غُرَّةً   غَرّاءَ لا تَخْفَى ولا تُسْتَرُ؟
فِى كُلِّ وقْتٍ نورُها ساطِعٌ   وكُلُّ وَصْفٍ دونَها يَقْصُرُ

[When] someone said: 'Which of both shines brighter, the sun or our lord Jaʿfar?'

I said [to him]: 'You have glorified ignorantly the morning sun and done injustice to the one you mention.

Does Zoroastrianism[56] survive in you?
For their sect glorifies the sun.

Or are you a scholar of their lineage?
For, a scholar's error is inexcusable.

Say: "[I take] refuge to God from [committing] a sin!"'
He said: 'But is someone who asks [liable to] be wrong [or right]?'

[I said:] 'The sun is veiled on a cloudy day, and the night [also] hides it, so that it does not appear.

It (sc. the sun) is enslaved in these two cases, neither repelling nor rejecting slavery.

How do you compare it to a shining face (sc. of the caliph), neither hidden nor covered?

Its light shines at every moment,
and every description falls short of it.'

(no. 23: 1–9)

In the first two turns, the poet argues as a poetic expert. He finds fault with 'brightness' as a term of comparison between his caliph and the sun (2). Based on the bystander's unjustified flattery to the sun (to be compared to the caliph), the poet suspects him of Zoroastrianism (3–4). The accusation already foreshadows the poem's central theme: the triumph of orthodoxy (*Sunna*) over a heretic doctrine. Then the poet's persona draws out in detail why the comparison between sun and caliph is improper: the sunshine is interrupted by clouds and night, whereas the caliph's splendor perdures. The inverted hyperbole of the ruler as more brilliant than the sun is commonplace. ʿAlī b. al-Jahm, however, dramatizes it as a dialogue. In addition, he presents himself as a supporter of the caliph, accusing the bystander of heresy. In the fifth and last turn, the bystander inquires about the caliph's courage in war. The poet reacts, as if the interlocutor should have known the answer: 'The great news has reached you: He arose, and the people of the earth were trembling, when he struck the advancing and retreating [enemy].' Following the defeat of the heretics, the poet delivers his final *plaidoyer* in which he gives the word to both the caliph, speaking for the *Sunna*, and Satan, speaking for the heretics. Al-Mutawakkil attributes his victory humbly to God:

وقالَ والألْسُنُ مَقْبوضةٌ   لِيُبْلِغِ الغائِبَ مَن يَحْضُرُ
أَنِّى تَوَكَّلْتُ على اللهِ لا   أُشْرِكُ باللَّهِ ولا أَكْفُرُ
لا أَدَّعِى القُدْرَةَ مِن دونِهِ   باللَّه حَوْلى وبه أَقْدِرُ
أَشْكُرُهُ إنْ كنْتُ فى نِعْمةٍ   منهُ وإنْ أَذْنَبْتُ أَسْتَغْفِرُ

He (sc. al-Mutawakkil) said while [people's] tongues
were tied: 'The present shall tell it to the absent,

That I have relied (*tawakkaltu*) on God,
not taking associates to God, nor being an unbeliever.

I do not claim power other than by him,
my might is by God, I exert power by him.

I thank him, if I enjoy his grace,
and if I sin I ask [his] forgiveness.'

(no. 23: 27–30)

Satan laments that the family of the prophet – which includes the Abbasids – did not give him enough of a respite to corrupt the people:

وصاحَ إبليسُ بأَصْحابهِ   حَلَّ بِنا ما لَمْ نَزَلْ نَحْذَرُ
ما لِى ولِلْغُرِّ بنِى هاشِمٍ   فِى كُلِّ دَهْرٍ منهُمْ مُنْذِرُ
أَكُلّما قلْتُ خَبَا كوكْبٌ   منهُمْ بدا لِى كوكْبٌ يَزْهَرُ

Satan and his companions screamed:
'That which we constantly guarded against has befallen us!

What is wrong with me and the noble leaders, the Banū Hāshim?
In every era there is a warning one from among them.

Does every time I say, "A star of them is extinguished",
[another] shining star appear to me?'

(no. 23: 36–8)

The ruler as vanquisher of fate, Satan, unbelievers, and all other evil forces is a common theme in *madīḥ*. ʿAlī b. al-Jahm, however, has fitted it to the concrete occasion and dramatized it as a dialogue containing three intercalated frames of speech. The first frame consists of an encounter of the poet with a bystander in five turns of question and answer. The second frame, contained in the poet's long last answer (18b–45), opposes the caliph (27–33) and Satan (36–45), and the third frame, through the speech of Satan, reiterates his earlier words (38). The poet begins his last answer with a lecture to the bystander, boasting of the caliph's restoration in a tone that would not befit the pious caliph himself. The praise introduces the quoted speeches of the caliph and Satan, the caliph as a victorious fighter for God,[57] Satan as a frustrated defender of heresy. The caliph's humble God-fearing words stand out against Satan's saucy complaint. The poet's idea of quoting Satan shocked the attending judge Ibn Abī Du'ād who had never heard anything of the kind before.[58] By dramatizing the *qaṣīda* as a dialogue, the poet gave a distinctive portrayal of the caliph as a restorer of the *Sunna* (46–50), and of himself, as his loyal supporter and defender. The poem's dedication continues the theme of religious orthodoxy:

فَاسلَمْ لنا يا خَيْرَ مُسْتَخْلَفٍ   مِن مَعْشَرٍ ما مِثْلُهُ مَعشَرُ
واسمَعْ إلى غَرّاءَ سُنِّيَّةٍ   يَسطَعُ مِنها المِسْكُ والعَنَبَرُ
مَوْقِعُها مِن كُلِّ ذِى بِدعَةٍ   مَوْقِعُ وَسْمِ النَّارِ أَو أَكثَرُ

Be safe for us, you best descendant[59] of a group
(sc. the Banū Hāshim) that has no equal!

> And listen to a noble orthodox [*qaṣīda*]
> exuding musk and amber.
>
> Her effect on every heretic reformer
> is like the effect of branding fire or more powerful.
>
> (no. 23: 49–51)

The poet presents his *qaṣīda* as noble and orthodox and compares its impact to branding the heretics. In its description he reuses images and words previously applied to the caliph. He has a noble shining face (*ghurratun gharrāʾu*, 8) that casts light (*nūruhā sāṭiʿun*, 9);[60] the *qaṣīda* is noble (*gharrāʾu*, 50) and exudes (*yasṭaʿu minhā*) amber and musk. Like the caliph it is orthodox (*sunniyya*, 50) and inflicts harm on heretics (51). Nowhere in the *qaṣīda* did the poet mention his needs or the caliph's duties towards him. In this first address to the caliph, he sought to ingratiate himself by subordinating his poem wholly to the caliph's religious stance.

Al-Buḥturī privileged the poetic tradition as a frame of reference, whereas ʿAlī b. al-Jahm depicted one particular patron, al-Mutawakkil, within a specific situation: the abolishment of the official doctrine of the created Koran. Al-Buḥturī left his piece vague in view of the uncertain circumstances of its composition. His avoidance of historical reference does not imply unawareness, rather he chose not to commit his poem too much, being as yet unsure of the addressee. If the poem failed with the first patron, it would still be reusable for another. Instead of gambling on a single occasion, al-Buḥturī availed himself of the textual tradition. Moreover, the many detachable, quotable verses could easily be transmitted to subsequent audiences and by greater currency raise the value of poet and poem.[61]

ʿAlī b. al-Jahm invested his poem wholly in one patron and one historical circumstance. Stylistically, he molded the entire *qaṣīda* as a dramatic dialogue, designed to persuade patron and audience and endowed with a distinct self-portrayal. The historical occasion left the strongest imprint on this poem. But its originality as well as the compelling structure and dramatic argument were lost in the quotation of single verses. To compose such a *qaṣīda* posed a certain risk because the poem's power spent itself in a single performance.

But no poet can predict his reception, and ʿAlī b. al-Jahm secured seven years of patronage with al-Mutawakkil before he became a victim of intrigues. The circumspect Buḥturī had not found favor with ʿUbaydallāh b. ʿAbdallāh. On the contrary, the erudite governor attacked the famous poet later for cleaving slavishly and against all logic to the poetic tradition.[62] In that sense ʿAlī's gamble had proved more successful.

The foregoing shows the great difference in the ways a poet could orient his *qaṣīda*. Naturally the two examples do not exhaust the range of possible variations, although they show that contextual approaches to the Abbasid praise *qaṣīda* – the present one included – cannot expect to reveal uniformity among different poets. Changing scenarios must be anticipated even within the same patronage relationship. This book makes a beginning in this direction by examining how Ibn al-Rūmī, in his *madīḥ, depicted and directed* the patronage of ʿUbaydallāh b. ʿAbdallāh in a distinct, imposing way.

3

THE APPROACH

Madīḥ and pragmatics

That a poet could choose in principle between targeting one audience and winning currency among many is easily evident. To truly understand the play on tradition, in the second case, requires an in-depth intertextual approach for which the wealth of medieval Arabic poetry and poetic criticism can be tapped.[1] This book, however, studies the first case, the strategies a poet devised in reaching one contemporary audience. In this pragmatic approach, the contextualized meaning, that is, the speaker's meaning, is considered the essential meaning.[2] This makes the praise *qaṣīda* part of an interaction larger than the text, while taking full account of the *qaṣīda*'s specific speech character. Textual and contextual aspects can then be linked within the limits of Ibn al-Rūmī's subjectivity.[3]

The praise *qaṣīda* had existed since pre-Islamic days and gained currency in Abbasid society because time-honored features could be rallied to new purposes and social needs. At court the *qaṣīda* became a meaningful part of the ceremonial celebrating the caliph; in literary circles it offered a medium of patronage for members of the elite who sought to distinguish themselves. In addition to a poet's choice of focus between present and future audiences (shown in the second chapter), he variously engaged with the different constituents of his momentary audience. First a praise *qaṣīda* was received by the audience at large whom a poet involved, for example, with indirect language or patterns of anticipation and resolution.[4] Second a praise poet entertained, before the audience, a personal relationship or friendship with an individual addressee. Every performance or recitation of a praise poem thus addressed itself to a bipartite public: the court or literary circle and the patron, the expectations of each being not only directed toward the poet, but also toward each other. The patron expected the audience's applause and the subsequent dissemination of his panegyric; the audience expected the poetically proper celebration and portrayal of their host. The poet was only acquitted of his duty by the simultaneous, complementary (collective and individual) reception of his poem: the audience's witnessing of the patron's eulogy. Their expectations for the patron gave the poet leverage, since the patron applauded, rewarded or criticized the literary offering for the sake of the audience as much as for that of the poet.

The disentangling of the *qaṣīda*'s interactive role between poet, audience and patron requires a synchronic perspective.[5] If *madīḥ* is the vehicle of this sort of interaction, there must be traces of performance in its text that reflect its function[6] to varying degrees. It may lie, for instance, in the ways in which a poet anticipated his two audiences, since on their reaction his reputation and livelihood depended. What did he take for granted? What did he deem to be in need of justification? And where did he deploy his strongest rhetoric? These questions can best be tackled with an eclectic pragmatic approach, suited to analyze the spectrum of interaction bundled within the prism of the *qaṣīda*. It entails a macro-level of dramatic discourse for intercalated communicative settings, and a micro-level of speech act theory for specific intersections between text and historical situation.[7] Readers familiar with these theoretical tools are invited to proceed to the fourth chapter.

Literary speech situation (context) and genre

The pragmatic approach understands Abbasid panegyrics as communication and therefore includes in its meaning the context that surrounds it. The poems of Ibn al-Rūmī to ʿUbaydallāh are not considered for their textual properties in isolation, but for their potential to persuade and affect audiences. The poems further represented items of exchange between the poet and his addressee, endowed with a material and ethical value that was matched with the counter-values of reward and protection, outside of the text.

The pragmatic approach neglects later performances or quotes of a praise poem, as they disrupt the entirety of a poem and select verses that match the receiving text or occasion of performance. When for instance, the historian Ibn al-Jawzī cited one of Ibn al-Rūmī's admonitions to Muḥammad b. ʿAbdallāh, he omitted verses specific to that patronage relationship and so divested the poem of the marks of its original delivery.[8] It is this original context, surrounding a poem's first dedication, that the pragmatic approach considers. It allows one to incorporate the conditions of the context into the textual analysis, and it provides the means to identifying and systematically describing those parts of a linguistic utterance that inform about, and react to, the situation that generated it.

In everyday language, the context-dependent meaning of an utterance or text is what it conveys within the particular circumstances (utterance meaning), as opposed to what it says literally (sentence meaning). A simple situation may illustrate this: the statement 'You are standing on my foot', uttered to someone who stepped on the speaker's foot, conveys the indirect request 'Please get off my foot'.[9] The appropriate reaction would be to step away; to respond to the literal meaning 'Yes, I am standing on your foot' would be construed as a joke or a provocation. Context should, however, not be taken as a monolithic whole. In any interpretation, the 'context' is necessarily a result of limitation and selection of significant and available data of the immediate image, topic, theme, or genre at large.[10]

How is context understood in a literary text? If a statement is part of a literary text, it is therefore not devoid of a context, rather, context is conceived of in a different way. In a literary text, the conventions of literary production constitute the context, while the conditions that define which utterances are appropriate represent the literary genre.[11]

Mary Louise Pratt and Ernest W. B. Hess-Lüttich regard the dialogue of an author with a reader in literature as not generically different from everyday speech. The rules and expectations of conversation are not suspended, but altered.[12]

> In sum, speech act theory provides a way of talking about utterances not only in terms of their surface grammatical properties but also in terms of the context in which they are made, the intentions, attitudes, and expectations of the participants, the relationships existing between participants, and generally, the unspoken rules and conventions that are understood to be in play when an utterance is made and received.... The real lesson speech act theory has to offer is *that literature is a context* too, not the absence of one.[13]

According to Pratt and Hess-Lüttich, the literary speech situation distinguishes itself from the everyday speech situation by the two characteristics of unidirectionality and preparation. Unidirectionality implies that only the author speaks, using a stable medium.[14] The hearers relinquish their turn in the conversation and voluntarily commit to being an audience. The yielding of their turn reflects the hearers' expectation, which the speaker will have to fulfill in order to prove that their engagement was worthwhile.[15] Preparation signifies that a lapse of time separates composition from presentation – that process of preparation and selection a work of literature passes through, until it is published or performed.[16] The awareness of this preparation influences the reader to assume deviations as largely intentional and to construct the author's meaning.

> The literary pre-paration and pre-selection processes are designed to eliminate failures which result from carelessness and lack of skill. The more selection and revision processes we know a work has gone through, the less likely we will be to attribute apparent inconsistencies and inappropriatenesses to random and unintentional error.[17]

Pratt adds two further characteristics, tellability and implicature. Tellability is a consequence of the above-mentioned unidirectionality. The speech presented to the audience must be relevant to the situation it is brought to, or 'tellable'. It is prone to share a problematic state of affairs, invite the audience to evaluate and contemplate, and call for their affective and imaginary involvement. Such tellable phrases or 'display-texts' are commonly detachable from a conversational situation and more elaborate.[18] The second characteristic, implicature, has been coined by Paul Grice to 'refer to the various kinds of calculations by which we make sense of what we hear'.[19] In literature, implicature expresses the fact that the literary speaker is still bound by the rules of conversation which Grice formulated as the 'co-operative principle':

> Make your conversational contribution such as is required, at the stage at which it occurs, by the accepted purpose or direction of the talk exchange in which you are engaged. One might label this the CO-OPERATIVE PRINCIPLE.[20]

But, as in regular conversation, the literary speaker can intentionally and blatantly violate and exploit a maxim of the co-operative principle in order to point to an indirect meaning.[21] Drawing on an example of irony in *Pride and Prejudice*, Pratt demonstrates how the reader resolves Jane Austen's violation of clarity by understanding that she is implying indirect criticism. Pratt emphasizes that it is the literary speech situation that invites the reader to a greater tolerance for such violations.

> I suggested that exploitation is virtually the only kind of intentional nonfulfillment of maxims that the literary speech situation allows, that intentional failure to fulfill a maxim in literature always counts as flouting and is thus always intended to be resolved by implicature.... Again, it is our tacit knowledge of the literary speech situation that enables us to make the flouting interpretation, not the intrinsic features of the utterances themselves. The literary speech situation is such that it is virtually impossible for an author to be guilty of any of the other kinds of intentional nonfulfillment [of the conversational maxims] Grice mentions.[22]

In everyday conversation the so-called 'conditions of appropriateness' of speech acts[23] help to determine when implication is called for. In literary speech the genre fulfills this function, for the conventions of a genre determine the set of experiences and expectations a reader or hearer brings to a text. We would construct the same statement read in a novel differently from the way we would construct it in a satire.

> Given his knowledge of how literary works come into being, the reader is entitled to assume ... that the writer was aware of the appropriateness conditions for the literary speech act situation and for the genre he has selected; that he believes this version of the text successfully accomplishes his purpose, and is 'worth it' to us.[24]

The literary speech situation (or context) of Abbasid poetry required the audience to understand poetry as a courtly practice, within the grammatical rules and the literary conventions of the *ʿarabiyya*. The audience could assume a poet's authorial intention and endeavor for excellence down to every detail and expect to recognize familiar themes and motives in new arrangements and formulations. As a genre, *madīḥ* differed, for instance, from the musical performance or the recitation of wine and love poetry, which obeyed other rules. The panegyric presupposed a patron deserving and affording praise, a poet who composed it in a complex poetic idiom as a *tahniʾa*, *qaṣīda* or other form and offered it to a patron before an audience. The following examples illustrate the role of *madīḥ* as a genre for understanding particular verses and correctly decoding their meaning. As a work and effort (*ʿamal, jahd*) of high skill, *madīḥ* was understood to deserve remuneration. But what if the poet ostensibly denied that fact, as Ibn al-Rūmī did in his praise for ʿAlī b Yaḥyā b. al-Munajjim al-Nadīm?[25]

وتَعلّمْ أنّى وإن أنا أُذلِلْـ ـتُ بما قلتُ فيكَ مِن أقوالِ
عارِفُ النَّفسِ أنّنِى لَمْ أُجاوِزْ فيك قولَ العِدا بجَهدِ احْتِفالِ
مِثلَ ما لا يُجاوِزون الَّذِى قُلْـ ـتُ إلى غيرِه بوَجْهِ احتيالِ
ليسَ يَسطيعُ أَنْ يقولَ المُعادِى فيك إلّا الَّذِى يقولُ المُوالِى

Learn, that, even if I were humiliated
for the things I said about you,

My soul knows, that I did not, in your case,
transgress the speech of enemies, by eager exaggeration.

In the same way they do not transgress
what I said about you, by falsification.

An enemy cannot but say
the same about you as a friend.

(L1600: 248–51)

The poet literally denies his share in enhancing the patron's record. The denial of merit concludes the praise section, taking the place of a request usually made at this point. In a *qaṣīda* of 337 verses in *khafīf* meter, an enormous length even for *madīḥ*,[26] the poet ostensibly disowns his merit because there cannot be the least doubt about it. The conventions of *madīḥ* make the poet's denying of the undeniable read as modesty. Inversely, the conditions of *madīḥ* let a literal protestation of truthfulness (249) be understood as a causal hyperbole. The fact that both literal utterances require interpretation is given by the literary speech situation; how exactly they are to be deciphered is indicated by the genre of *madīḥ*.

This literary speech situation and the genre must be kept apart from the specific historical background, the relationship of the actual Ibn al-Rūmī, ʿUbaydallāh b. ʿAbdallāh, and the members of his circle, including third parties, such as a famous *adīb* attending a panegyric performance.[27] Although the historical patronage is amply evidenced by the sum of datable poems, particular encounters of Ibn al-Rūmī and ʿUbaydallāh are scarcely attested. Al-Marzubānī (d. 384/994)[28] reports, however, an anecdote of Ibn al-Rūmī with another patron. It is adduced here to illustrate the fact that the correct deciphering of poetry according to generic conventions required familiarity with these – in a similar way the correct reading of the vowelless Arabic script required familiarity with the rules of the classical *ʿarabiyya*. In praising the vizier Abū l-Ṣaqr Ismāʿīl b. Bulbul[29] for his ancestry Ibn al-Rūmī used a bold inverted hyperbole:

قالوا أَبو الصَّقْرِ مِن شَيْبانَ قلتُ لَهُمْ   كلّا لَعمرِى ولَكِنْ مِنهُ شَيْبانُ

They said 'Abū l-Ṣaqr derives from Shaybān.' 'No, by my life,'
I said, 'it is rather the Shaybān who derive from him!'
(L1302': 86)

The patron understood this as lampooning, since it literally negated his noble Arab lineage, which happened to be fake. The patron's failure to decode the implied meaning was due to his ignorance of poetic genres. Al-Marzubānī, however, interpreted the verse by the rules of the *madīḥ*. Quoting the next following verse he proved that the affiliation of Abū al-Ṣaqr with the Shaybān was not at all put into question, but its direction was hyperbolically reversed to elevate Abū al-Ṣaqr above them: the glorious descendant decorates his ancestors in a fantastic reversal of the course of history. Al-Marzubānī cited the poet's own words in support of the non-literal reading. It is an analogy with the prophet Muḥammad and the Northern Arabs, represented by their eponymous ancestor ʿAdnān:

وكمْ أَبٍ قد علا بِابْنٍ ذُرَى شَرَفٍ   كما علا بِرَسولِ اللَّهِ عَدْنانُ

How many a father rose through his son to peaks of honor,
like the [descendants of] ʿAdnān rose through the prophet of God.
(L1302: 87)

Al-Marzubānī sees the meaning of the verse as determined by its genre and theme – ancestral praise – and attributes Abū l-Ṣaqr's inability to decode the hyperbole to his confusion between lampoon and encomium, two diametrically opposite poetic genres.[30] Al-Marzubānī also thought it unjust that the secretary withheld the reward. The historical background may explain Abū l-Ṣaqr's over-sensitivity, for the Persian secretary had purchased a forged Arab genealogy. To such a vain, self-conscious *mamdūḥ*, the literal wording of the hyperbole posed the hazard of ridicule. Therefore the purpose of praise failed and the poet remained unrewarded. As a scholar and transmitter, al-Marzubānī saw no ambiguity in the *madīḥ* verse, whereas the patron, ignoring the *madīḥ* genre, isolated it and read into it inappropriate allusions to his non-Arab background.

In another respect, the anecdote shows a patron's anticipation of an attack in public, as well as a poet's power to embarrass him. The success of the panegyrist then lay in pressuring a patron indirectly into proving his reputation (with a show of generosity) without the poet's letting the patron lose face.

In sum, both anecdotes exemplify a poet's reliance on the literary speech situation and the genre of *madīḥ* to indicate how his words were to be interpreted by audience and patron. But an uneducated hearer could misconstrue implied meanings because of wrong assumptions or mistake them as literal. The audience's knowledge of genres also included their familiarity with famous pre-Islamic and Islamic classics, which were constantly referred to, or transfigured, by the Abbasid poets.[31] Previous poetry as reflected in the hearers' knowledge set a standard, and a poem was deemed worthy of presentation depending on how it deviated from that accepted standard – and it had to deviate to a certain extent. In sum, as a ceremonial genre, *madīḥ* presupposed a particularly educated and critical audience. In view of this audience and subsequent transmission, poets themselves critically reviewed and pruned their texts, a process I have accounted for above with the concept of tellability.[32] The fulfillment of this condition is indeed often mentioned explicitly in a praise poem, in the self-descriptive passage accompanying the dedication.[33]

Thus far only the interaction via poetry between the historical poet on one side and his patron and the larger audience on the other has been visualized. But one also finds in Ibn al-Rūmī's panegyrics (as well as some of his other genres) a second level of spoken interaction *within* his poetry, which is ingeniously related to the surrounding situation.

The criteria and types of poetic dialogue

One of the striking features in Ibn al-Rūmī's *madīḥ* and a major means of style are his dramatic scenes.[34] There fictional or historical personae encounter and address each other or soliloquize. At times, these scenes are clustered together to establish larger plots that display some dramatis personae from different sides. These personae vary substantially in their range of speech and action. Fictional ones, such as the accuser, personified old age (*shayb*, literally 'white hair'), and youth (*shabāb*), adhere to one grammatical person, and their appearance is limited to the length of one scene, so that their entering and exiting define that scene. The historical personae of poet and patron reappear in subsequent scenes, throughout which they switch grammatical persons, entering and exiting the prevailing dialogue situation.[35] Several consecutive scenes with the same persona render it three-dimensional. For instance, in some series of scenes, alternating fictional personae cast the poet from one argument into another. In these instances, the fictional personae serve as auxiliaries for the dialectic development of the poet's persona. But how do these verbal interactions look? What are their ingredients? And how can dramatic encounters be distinguished from each other and from non-dramatic passages?

A vital clue lies in the change of the grammatical person of the speaker in poetry. A recent study devoted to this feature traces its expansion from a simple rhetorical figure to a dramatic device in longer passages.[36] In the first part of his analysis, Geert Jan van Gelder reviews the medieval criticism concerning the change of person, as represented by the discussions of al-Sakkākī (d. 626/1229) in his *Miftāḥ al-ʿulūm* on *iltifāt* 'turning aside' and Ḍiyā' al-Dīn Ibn al-Athīr (d. 637/1239) in his *Mathal al-sā'ir* on *tajrīd* 'abstraction'.[37] The feature is treated as a rhetoric figure, remaining within the scope of a single line of poetry. Both critics understand the poet's address of himself as 'you', as a way for him to distance himself from his emotions, and for the audience, to empathize with him. This self-addressed 'you' becomes an impersonal common ground and therefore a meeting place for the poet and his audience.[38] Ibn al-Athīr appreciates, in particular, ambiguous cases where a second person might refer either to poet or audience. In the second part of his analysis dealing with the change of person as used in poetry, Gelder finds that the 'you' of pre-Islamic poetry has a generalizing effect. It appears in formulae, *loci* of passion and disillusionment, and exhortations. He finds little of it among the neo-classical poets al-Buḥturī and al-Mutanabbī, but he does not consider poets such as ʿAlī b. al-Jahm, Diʿbil, and Ibn al-Rūmī who use a more discursive style. However, in a poem of al-Muʿtamid b. ʿAbbād, he observes a correlation between the shifts of the *mamdūḥ* from third to second person and of the poet's persona from second to first[39] – a feature well present and developed further in Ibn al-Rūmī's *madīḥ*.[40] The dearth of single-line *iltifāt* in Abbasid poetry, van Gelder justifiably claims, may have resulted from the general trend of extending rhetorical figures into larger forms, as has been documented in the case of parallelism and antithesis.[41] In Ibn al-Rūmī's encomia, the switch of grammatical person becomes a device of the largest scope; it constitutes an integral part of his dramaturgy:[42] a switch of person opens and closes a single dramatic scene, and during an ongoing scene, the first and second person indicate the dramatis personae present in a dialogue, as opposed to the third person who, representing an absent figure, is spoken about, conjured up, criticized, or vainly implored. We will see below how consistently the direct address distinguishes the personae of the present (accuser and *shayb*) from those of the past (*shabāb*).

The specific power of such drama flows from the simultaneousness of the outer communication between the historical poet and his patron and audience, and the interior dialogue between the poet's persona and other dramatis personae at the moment of initial performance. My discussion of those interior dialogues relies on dramatic discourse, specifically, the notion of *reciprocal* communication between speakers as proposed by Hess-Lüttich in modification of Roman Jakobson's unidirectional model.[43] Within this *reciprocal* relationship speakers differ further as initiators or acceptants and according to their asymmetrical scopes of action. The dramatic discourse model of Hess-Lüttich is based on German drama and needs to be adjusted to Abbasid panegyrics. Hess-Lüttich distinguishes for instance between the personal dialogue and mass media.[44] Abbasid panegyrics, however are at the same time dedicated to an individual *and* addressed to a public. What is more, both levels of dialogue are designed to interface with each other, and the dialogue reveals a number of strategies, playing out the two audiences against each other.[45] I have therefore expanded Hess-Lüttich's paradigm of dramatic dialogue to include this simultaneous double audience.[46] Finally, the encomia contain not only scenes involving a dramatized interlocutor, but also episodes addressed directly to the anonymous hearer without intermediary, thus requiring a different paradigm.

The first paradigm (fig. 1) constitutes a dramatic scene involving the (fictional or historical) personae 'A' and 'B'. Three concentric frames define as many levels of communication, to be described from the outside to the inside. The outer frame stands for the historical relationship between the panegyrist who communicates simultaneously with the anonymous hearer and the individually addressed patron. Their circumstances cannot be retrieved from a single poem. The second frame limits the relationship as it manifests itself in the text, to wit, between the implied author (the trace in the text of its creator) and the implied recipient (as anticipated by the author). The group of encomia as a whole shows the set of expectations the implied author entertains with regard to the addressee. These constitute the poet's ethics of patronage, discussed in Part 5. The inner frame delimits the dialogue between the (fictional or historical) personae 'A' and 'B', for instance, the dramatized personae of poet and patron. This last level represents the literary dialogue in the narrow sense, which will be detailed below in this chapter. To illustrate the distinction between the implied author[47] and the poet's persona: the poet's persona may deny the work done for a praise poem, whereas the implied author's work is evident in the form of the poem. Or, the poet's persona may pretend to despair of the patron's persona, suppress the dedication, and ostensibly turn his back on him, whereas the implied author still addresses the whole poem to the implied patron, disguised as an indirect plea.[48] Conversely, the poet's persona may declare his trust in future reward, while the implied author omits the praise of generosity from the standard catalogue of *madīḥ*, indirectly admitting that he lacks evidence of it.[49]

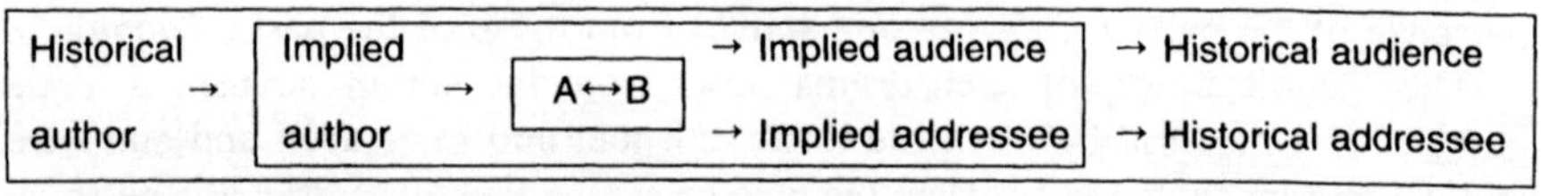

'A↔B' stands for 'A is communicating with B, and B is communicating with A' as a reciprocal, simultaneous event. The double arrrow graphically translates the reciprocity of Hess-Lüttich's (synonymous) simple arrow

Figure 1 Model of communication for the scene

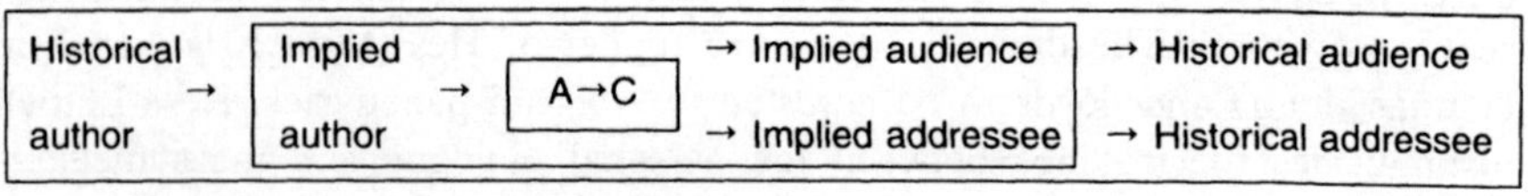

Figure 2 Model of communication for the episode

Dramatic scenes, however, do not cover all of the encomium. In the descriptive type of passage, or narrative episode (fig. 2), the poet's persona 'A' sporadically addresses an anonymous hearer 'C'. The paradigm again reflects the simultaneous anonymous audience and individual addressee.

Besides a different structure of their interior dialogue, the scene and episode can be distinguished by further criteria – leaving aside for the moment the implied and historical participants of the outer frames. Dramatic discourse provides a set of criteria which are very inclusive, accommodating both everyday and fictional dialogue. In keeping with Hess-Lüttich, I have selected those criteria (fig. 3) that are suited to grasp Ibn al-Rūmī's sketchy poetic rendering of dialogue.[50] My selection of criteria also suits dialogues of 'Alī b. al-Jahm[51] and Diʿbil al-Khuzāʿī,[52] but may have to be modified for other Abbasid praise poets. The two communicative paradigms (hereafter 'scene' and 'episode') can then be described by the criteria of the participants' 'constellation', their mutual 'relationship', their social 'position', the 'scheme of action' of the passage and the respective speaker's 'orientation' towards the addressee. All these criteria help to extract the dialogue typology of Ibn al-Rūmī's praises.[53] In the scene, the constellation of speakers is dyadic, i.e. between two parties, even in monologues, which are really interior dialogues. Composite scenes involve more than two speakers in succession, but each scene is still dyadic, with the previous or next interlocutor presumed absent. As to the relationship of the speakers, scenes do not take place with equal representation of both parties before the public eye, because the hearers are not faced with a literal transcript, but a poetic rendering of dialogue. The poet's persona, or direct speaker 'A', controls entirely how, how much, and where his interlocutor 'B' participates in the discussion. Half of the dialogue is conveyed indirectly from the standpoint of the poet's persona. He speaks directly, while his interlocutor is quoted or paraphrased. The scope of action of the poet's persona is therefore incomparably larger than that of his

Criteria	*Scene*	*Episode*
Constellation of participants	Strictly dyadic	One (marginal, implicit, or impersonal) speaker and/or one group
Relationship of participants	Participants differ in range of verbal action	Participants have a similar, limited range of verbal action
Position of participants	*Active role*: fictional or historical personae with moral standpoints	*Passive, reactive role*: perceiving, attesting personae
Scheme of action	Argumentative or informative (the dialogue *is* the action)	Rhetorical, phatic (the dialogue *relays* another action or circumstance)
Orientation to hearer	Persuasive or demonstrative	Demonstrative, directive, informative

Figure 3 Dramaturgic criteria for the distinction of scene and episode

interlocutor, and their dialogical relationship asymmetrical. The social position of the fictional characters is defined in relation to the poet's persona, that of the historical personae, in relation to the patron's persona. Both fictional and historical personae assume moral standpoints; the set of relationships between the poet's and the patron's personae grows quite complex, warranting a treatment of its own in Part 5.

The action of a scene may unfold in two ways. When its scheme is argumentative, the partners' viewpoints differ and the poet's persona assumes a persuasive orientation towards the other persona. In contrast, when the scheme of action is phatic–rhetorical (univocal), the speakers hold similar views, and the poet's persona shows this in a demonstrative, affirmative orientation towards the interlocutor.[54]

In the episode,[55] the constellation of the participants varies between two people and a small group. The speaker and addressee form a very loose relationship, which is articulated merely in the pronouns 'I ' (or 'we') and 'you'; in some cases they disappear altogether. The 'we' and 'you' in particular include the anonymous audience. Here, the function of speaker and addressee lies in experiencing or acknowledging the events described. Their testimony validates the action without taking a direct part in it. The action of the episode obeys a phatic–rhetorical scheme in which the viewpoints of the speaker and addressee converge. The speaker's orientation is directed towards conveying a state of affairs and gaining the hearers' acquiescence, a role in which the poet's persona remains very restricted. Essentially, the episode stands for the dialogue of the poet's persona with the audience without any interposed fictional interlocutor. However, the dialogue form is loose and pronouns for the speaker and hearers only sporadic. The episode's true focus lies in the events related about a third, absent party. The criteria mentioned here serve broadly to define scene and episode; and further criteria will be adduced in Part 3 to draw finer distinctions among their subtypes.

Excursus into the theory of speech acts

Returning to the outer frames of the dialogue paradigm, Ibn al-Rūmī reveals an intriguing strategy. He lets the interior dialogue parallel the exterior circumstances of a panegyric poem. This occurs in such scenes where the dramatic personae stand for the historical figures between whom the poem is transferred, so their spoken words intrude upon the historical surrounding and involve it directly. The grammatical first person, taken by the poet's persona, addresses the second person filled by the patron's persona. Such direct speech affects the very moment of its delivery, but it also transcends it, recalling and commenting on the situation's prehistory, and predicting and reflecting on its future. This nature of speech as part of human interaction with all of a speaker's expectations, intentions and commitments is brought forth in the theory of speech acts. This initially philosophical–linguistic theory has been applied to

French and English literature with moderate success, but it is far better suited to analyze Abbasid *madīḥ* with its vital components of ethics and accountability.[56] In the following, I present a short excursus on speech act theory before detailing its areas of relevance to Ibn al-Rūmī's *madīḥ*.

The speech act essentially suspends the notion that talking and acting are opposites. It places speech alongside other symbolic human acts by which we affect the people around us, although the complex conventions and regulations of speech distinguish it from other non-verbal symbolic acts. As acts of speech involve intention and benefit on the part of the speaker, as well as responsibility, they represent an 'interested transaction'.[57] Stanley Fish renders the gist of speech act theory succinctly in his analysis of Shakespeare's *Coriolanus*:

> It is *about* what the theory is 'about', the conditions for the successful performance of certain conventional acts and the commitments one enters into or avoids by performing or refusing to perform those acts ... The questions it [sc. speech act theory] is able to ask and answer – what is involved in a request? what is one doing when one greets? what enables one to banish? – are the questions about which the action [of *Coriolanus*] revolves.... It [sc. *Coriolanus*] is also about what the theory is about, language and its power: the power to make the world rather than mirror it, to bring about states of affairs rather than report them, to constitute institutions rather than (or as well as) serve them.[58]

The methodology of speech act theory varies among different philosophical, linguistic or anthropological proponents,[59] as well as in the scope of its application between the macro and micro-level. The former is addressed more often in linguistic anthropology, the latter in linguistics and philosophy. While interaction is certainly not restricted exclusively to the syntax of single sentences, there are certain direct utterances in Ibn al-Rūmī's poems that can be elucidated with the help of speech act theory. This is why Stanley Fish's more restrictive application drawing on John Searle offers itself as a model for analysis. But approaches differ even for the generic performative speech act. John L. Austin defined as performatives such speech acts that simultaneously combine action and utterance. This concept of performative was refined by Émile Benveniste, who restricted it to explicit cases and excluded from it clichés, infelicitous acts, and such acts that are not sanctioned by the force of authority or social convention. To this effect, he added to Austin's concept the condition that the person performing the act must have the legitimacy to do so. Benveniste further pointed out that the performative is self-referential, denoting the performer and the situation of its occurrence, and that every incident of a performative is unique; when repeated, it becomes *another* act.[60] Developing Austin's ideas, Searle divided an utterance F(p) into the two aspects of illocutionary[61] force F and propositional content p. He subdivided Austin's performative into different types of speech acts,[62] such as request, assertion, question, thanks, advice, warning, greeting, and congratulation. These he arranged into a taxonomy of illocutionary acts, comprising five subtypes:[63] the *assertive*, committing the speaker to the truth of a proposition, e.g. 'state' and 'hypothesize'; the *directive*, getting the hearer to do something (the propositional content), e.g. 'beg', and 'defy', as well as questions; the *commissive*, committing the speaker to something, e.g. 'promise' and 'pledge'; the *expressive*, expressing a state of sincerity about a propositional content, e.g. 'congratulate', 'praise', and 'thank'; and the *declarative*, an act of speech whose successful performance brings about a correlation between propositional content and reality, e.g. 'Hereby I baptize you', 'I pronounce you guilty', 'You are fired', and 'I resign'. This last type is identical with Benveniste's performative. The first four types can coincide with the fifth, as, for example, 'to boast' and 'to deduce' are actions that simultaneously declare something and assert it; a pledge is both a commitment and a declaration of that commitment.

A speech act cannot be true or false; rather it succeeds, falls short of its goal, or fails. To find out how a speech act succeeds or fails, Searle dissected it into constituent parts, which he called 'rules' and which govern the form and background of the speech act and the sincerity of its participants, as far as declared. For example, the act of congratulation is based on some event related to the hearer, called the propositional content. The congratulation then requires, as a preparatory condition, that this event is in the hearer's interest and that the speaker believes so, and, as a sincerity condition, that the speaker is equally pleased at the event. As an essential condition, the congratulation counts as an expression of pleasure at the event, so that in this act of speech, sincerity condition and essential condition coincide. Finally a congratulation also says what it does, namely to congratulate, which makes it also a declaration.[64] In his analysis of Shakespeare's *Coriolanus*, Stanley Fish defines the act of praise in accordance.[65] Praise is based on some event (act, property, quality, etc.) related to the hearer. As a preparatory condition, the event reflects creditably on the hearer and the speaker believes that it does. As a sincerity condition, the speaker values this event positively, and as an essential condition, the act counts as a positive valuation of the event. Similar to the congratulation, the act of praise has a double nature, asserting an event and expressing appreciation for it. Searle's rules do not merely regulate the act, rather they constitute it, and the lack of one or more of them makes it ineffective.

In the light of these rules, we can consider certain phrases that recur in Ibn al-Rūmī's praise poems as direct speech acts, most importantly the concluding phrase of dedication at the end of each poem, *manaḥtukahā* 'I have [herewith] dedicated it (sc. the poem) to you'. This phrase formally transfers the prestigious piece to its dedicatee. Other performative phrases include the declaration of the intention to praise, felicitations, and messages, all of which are studied in detail in chapter 5.

But action through speech is not limited to these few performative phrases – even if they show its most immediate and powerful form. In a drama, all speech is action, or more precisely, all action is channelled through the vehicle of speech, and in a similar way all (quoted or paraphrased) direct speech in Ibn al-Rūmī's scenes, whether performative or not, is part of their dramaturgy; personae may be characterized by their utterances, and their verbalized antagonistic attitudes towards each other create the dynamic tension of their encounters. The entire poetically-scripted interaction between the personae of poet and patron – beyond the mere performative acts – comments upon the historical situation with a counter image of literary patronage, be it a positive, accurate parallel, an enticing higher ideal, or a threatening vision of what should be avoided.

Characterization, dramaturgy, poetic argument, and ethics

The foregoing has sketched the different levels of dramatic discourse and the intersections between text and historical situation as grasped by speech act theory. Combined, these tools offer four areas of analysis and interpretation. First, dramatis personae may be characterized by the speech acts they use.[66] Coriolanus in Shakespeare's drama of the same title[67] is characterized by his predilection for commitment and rejection, acts that are self-reliant, and his avoidance of thanks, request, and greeting, acts that would acknowledge his indebtedness to others. His preferred speech acts characterize him as an individual who despises society and accepts only his own measure of himself. Shoshana Felman[68] characterizes the Don Juan of Molière's comedy by the act of promise. His infinite repetition of failed promises (of marriage) shows his world-view as oriented between felicity and infelicity, while the other personae are concerned with truth or falsehood. The difference between the performative, which succeeds or fails, and the statement, which is true or false, sets Don Juan apart from all other characters.

Ibn al-Rūmī's encomia yield ample material for a similar characterization of their personae. Apart from the already mentioned historical personae of poet and patron, fictional personae abound, among them the conventional figures of the poet as hero, the female accuser, the observer, and the neighbor; the jealous one, the competitor, and the bystander; as well as the personifications of fate, white hair and youth. Only the historical personae can adopt several roles. Their personal pronouns ('I' and 'you' for the poet and 'you' or 'he' for the patron) alternate between these roles and facilitate the staging of controversial arguments and inner tensions. The characterization of figures through their speech forms the gist of Part 2.

The personae's encounters or soliloquies constitute the larger dramaturgy. They order, defy, greet, and wish, or argue, conveying with their utterances attitudes and feelings. The poet's persona of the aging theme (*al-shayb wa-l-shabāb*), for instance, expresses his grief by invoking rain upon youth, and characterizes his former youth as not knowing this nostalgic wish. Quotes of past speech inserted into monologues add the depth of time. Even personified objects and abstract concepts are endowed with direct speech or symbolic action and partake in the drama. The coming of old age, for instance, is represented as white hair, arriving to warn the poet of his death. As in a play, speech is the 'vehicle of the action'.[69] Part 3 of the book classifies the different dramatic encounters, and shows their composition into long passages.

The language of most praise poems for ʿUbaydallāh b. ʿAbdallāh is not overly rich in tropes and rhetorical figures and sometimes borders on the plain. Imagery, however, heightens the tension of encounters and supports the speaker's argument. In passages where the personae are marginalized (i.e. the episodes) artful imagery and description of themes of *madīḥ* and *fakhr* (boasting) supply the veritable 'action'. Here syntactical figures that order the description and dense clusters of abstract, fantastic tropes (phantasmagoria), infused with a human dimension, abound. These figures of speech that support the poetic argument, are represented in Part 4.

It is above all the ethical component of panegyrics that speech act theory is suited to analyze. On the level of direct interaction, the dedication and other discrete acts of speech perform *and* describe the panegyric relationship in which they are embedded. They administer exact stipulations and explicitly connect the rights and benefits of one partner with the duties and benefits of the other through reciprocity or cooperation. These discrete phrases are firmly integrated into scenes that portray the patronage relationship as a whole. Thus the panegyric art of Ibn al-Rūmī consists of choosing an iconology and imposing it – by means of poetic speech – onto the historical patron whose name it immortalizes.

In one important point, Ibn al-Rūmī even goes beyond the model of Searle: he includes within the dedication of *madīḥ* the acts and attitudes of the dedicatee.[70] This relationship is briefly indicated in two encomia, but developed at length in poems of felicitation and admonition.[71] In this point, Ibn al-Rūmī may be said to extend the impact of the speech act beyond what Austin, Searle, or Benveniste conceived. Richard Ohmann, who defined the speech act more broadly, requires, like Ibn al-Rūmī, the appropriate *ulterior* behavior of the participants as evidence for the 'felicity' of a speech act: 'Both parties must behave appropriately afterward'.[72] According to him, a promise is infelicitous, if the person giving it does not fulfill it, or an order is not executed by the hearer. Fish strongly criticized this perspective and clarified that felicity concerns only the speaker's proper execution of the speech act, not the hearer's favorable reaction.[73] Ibn al-Rūmī's use of the performative is perhaps even subtler than that by Ohmann, for the poet succeeds in enlisting the hearer's complicity not only as a response to a speech act, but as an intrinsic part of that act. His dedication presupposes that the addressee has already fulfilled certain conditions imposed on him. This is achieved by the implication of the addressee in the sincerity condition, as will be explained in detail in the last chapter. To a single speech act, the dramatic frame adds the background, showing the poet's vacillation between trust and faith in the patron, and his doubt in him. Only full trust allows the poet to put his sincerity and integrity at risk in offering a praise poem. As a result, the addressee is morally obliged to justify the pledged trust of the poet and assure the truth of the poem, by ratifying its portrayal of him as generous. Grander and more unique than the greatest array of a patron's perishable material gifts is the generosity given in the form of a poet's trust, which is unique and irreplaceable if once forsaken. In this way, Ibn al-Rūmī attaches his unilateral dedication of the poem to a dramatized relationship between himself and his patron, in consonance with an idealist ethics of patronage. His well-built poetic dramaturgy casts an inescapable net of words over the addressee, as is demonstrated in Part 5.

4

THE PROTAGONISTS

Ibn al-Rūmī and his patron ʿUbaydallāh b. ʿAbdallāh

Who was this poet who made the case for his profession and enlightened patronage? His life remains frustratingly elusive, for his transmitted biography revolves around topoi of superstition, pessimism, and failure brought upon himself – topoi which grew increasingly elaborate over time and typecast Ibn al-Rūmī as a cantankerous satirist and misanthrope. By 424/1033 al-Maʿarrī (d. 449/1058) had already called superstition 'the way of Ibn al-Rūmī' (*madhhab Ibn al-Rūmī*),[1] and the label stuck. This medieval characterization – which survives in modern school books – is contradicted by the support Ibn al-Rūmī received from numerous and long-standing patrons, as documented in his voluminous *Dīwān*. The so-attested relationships, three of which are discussed below, add detail to the poet's professional life.

ʿAlī b. al-ʿAbbās b. Jurayj, called Ibn al-Rūmī, 'son of the Byzantine', was born in Baghdad 221/836 to a half-Greek father and a Persian mother. Before the age of thirty he lost both parents as well as a maternal aunt and uncle. Late in life he married and founded a family only to lose within a short period his wife, his sons Muḥammad, Hibatallāh, and two other children. Their names are not recorded, but their existence is confirmed by two laments with which their father mourned them. Illness, or according to some biographies, poison or suicide, put an end to the poet's life in 283/896 at the age of 59.[2] Ibn al-Rūmī had received a solid philological education. As a young boy he attended the local *kuttāb* (Koran school). He pursued further education with the philologist, historian and genealogist Muḥammad b. Ḥabīb (d. 245/859), and the famous Basran grammarian al-Mubarrad (d. 286/900), who had moved to Baghdad in the year of al-Mutawakkil's assassination, 247/861. The sessions of Thaʿlab, a famous rival grammarian of the Kufan school, and of the above-mentioned essayist al-Jāḥiẓ may have easily attracted the young poet, for both taught in Baghdad at that time.[3] In terms of his creed, Ibn al-Rūmī was a Shiite with Muʿtazilite inclinations, but he usually reserved the expression of his religious feelings for patrons of similar persuasion – with one notable exception.[4] After the Abbasid caliph had the Alid rebel Yaḥyā b. ʿUmar executed, Ibn al-Rūmī lamented him as a martyr and accused the entire Abbasid family of injustice against the offspring of ʿAlī b. Abī Ṭālib. If they based their legitimacy as caliphs on their descendance from the prophet through his paternal uncle ʿAbbās, how could they fail to protect the descendants of the prophet through his paternal cousin ʿAlī? The lament branded the Abbasids as betraying their sacred duties and marked them for divine punishment.[5]

By the age of twenty Ibn al-Rūmī earned his living by writing poetry, the main source of his income being *madīḥ*, which fills 90 per cent of his *Dīwān*.[6] He dedicated poetry to one governor, several viziers and many functionaries of the second rank, a sizeable yet less glamorous clientèle than that of al-Buḥturī, who eulogized seven caliphs and the leading dignitaries.[7] In addition to the sheer amount of Ibn al-Rūmī's panegyrics, his originality and variety of styles impress;[8] this sets him apart from the better-known caliphal panegyrists, Abū Tammām and al-Buḥturī, around whom the medieval critical debate of the 'new style' (*badīʿ*) revolved, and who have dominated modern scholarship on Abbasid poetry.[9]

Among the many patrons recorded in Ibn al-Rūmī's *Dīwān*, the Ṭāhirid ʿUbaydallāh b. ʿAbdallāh (d. 300/913) was the first major figure as well as his closest and poetically most stimulating partner.[10] This last ruler of the Arabized Iranian dynasty of the Ṭāhirids was reduced to commanding the police governorship (*shurṭa*) of Baghdad and Samarra after his ancestors had once governed Khurāsān and lead caliphal armies.[11] ʿUbaydallāh assumed the governorship in 253/867 as his brother Muḥammad's designated successor, only to lose and regain it at least twice. First another brother, Sulaymān, ousted him in 255/869. Siding with ʿUbaydallāh, Ibn al-Rūmī criticized Sulaymān's appointment to the governorship as undeserved. When the brothers reconciled, he composed a *tahniʾa* in which he declared the rulership as something innate to ʿUbaydallāh and independent of any official post.[12] ʿUbaydallāh was restored as governor in 266/880 shortly after his brother's death (265/879). Then the Ṣaffārid *condottiere* ʿAmr b. Layth replaced him, but reappointed ʿUbaydallāh as his deputy in 276/890. At ʿAmr's subsequent removal from power by the caliph, ʿUbaydallāh was reconfirmed as governor.[13] Despite his discontinuous political career, ʿUbaydallāh lived the life of a well-rounded *adīb*. Besides his interest in philosophy, he was a brilliant composer of music, a prose-stylist, and a talented poet. His poetry in the lighter genres is amply quoted in the *adab* literature.[14] Al-ʿAskarī (d. *c*. 400/1010) singles out a verse by him as the best poetry ever composed.[15] ʿUbaydallāh exchanged light poetry and epistles with other *udabāʾ*, for example, his brother Muḥammad, the princely poet Ibn al-Muʿtazz, the scribe al-ʿAlāʾ b. Ṣāʿid[16] and the Banū Wahb, a family of courtiers and viziers. His illustrious literary circle included, next to Ibn al-Rūmī and his friend Dimashqī, an official panegyrist called Ibrāhīm al-Bayhaqī, his friend and singer Muḥammad b. ʿAlī al-Bayn and the poets al-Buḥturī, Aḥmad b. Abī Ṭāhir Ṭayfūr (d. 280/893) and Abū ʿAlī Muḥammad [b. Muḥammad] b. ʿArūs al-Shīrāzī (d. before 290/903).[17]

Ibn al-Rūmī's relationship with ʿUbaydallāh lasted at least twenty-three years, from 253/867 to 276/890.[18] The earliest encomium (L994), datable to 253/867, congratulates the young governor on his appointment. Several felicitations celebrate a renewal of this appointment (F1124, F1122, and F1174), but only one (L1611) that mentions ʿAmr b. Layth clearly refers to the second reappointment in 276/890, which makes it the latest datable piece. A further felicitation (F1557) can be dated to 268/882, for it mentions the coincidence of four religious festivals within one week during that year. The image used in this *tahniʾa*, of the four festivals – the Breaking of the Fast, *Nawrūz*, Passover, and Easter – mounted on four steeds symbolizing the different religions and racing against each other for the patron's grace, recalls the cloverleaf racecourse in Samarra, where the caliph would sit at the center and watch all competitors simultaneously.[19] With sixty-four poems (in 2373 verses) dedicated to him, ʿUbaydallāh ranked third with Ibn al-Rūmī in terms of the number of poems to his name. This excludes twelve further pieces he dedicated to the Banū Ṭāhir collectively.[20] ʿUbaydallāh received praise *qaṣāʾid*, short praises, felicitations (*tahānī*), admonitions (*ʿitāb*), and a mere six verses of mild satire (*hijāʾ*). He also suggested topics and verses for the poet's improvisation.[21] Being himself a poet, ʿUbaydallāh proved to Ibn al-Rūmī both a challenge and an inspiration. He appreciated his protégé's choice of difficult rhyme letters and rare words and his stamina in long *qaṣāʾid*.[22] Ibn al-Rūmī also became involved in his patron's poetic dispute with al-Buḥturī. ʿUbaydallāh attacked a poem by al-Buḥturī with a versified critique, the gist of which is given by Wolfhart Heinrichs as 'the rational objection of someone trained in philosophy against the views prescribed in poetry by tradition'.[23] In his famous retort, al-Buḥturī rejected logic as out of place in poetry, with which Ibn al-Rūmī must have disagreed, given his predilection for logical argument. He directed an invective against al-Buḥturī which included praise of ʿUbaydallāh,[24] and he also composed, reusing the same prosody as the poems of the dispute, a praise *qaṣīda* for ʿUbaydallāh, which included a harsh sermon to an unidentified proud 'friend', most likely al-Buḥturī (L215: 39–65).[25] After 276/890, ʿUbaydallāh's relationship with Ibn al-Rūmī dwindled, perhaps because of the patron's falling into poverty[26] and Ibn al-Rūmī's courting of other patrons, but the end of the relationship was not marked by any satire of the poet.[27]

Ibn al-Rūmī also counted among his patrons the Persian Ismāʿīl b. Bulbul, (d. 278/891), minister of al-Muʿtamid since 265/878.[28] They first met in 251/865, and remained in contact for a minimum of twenty years. The vizier received with ninety-one pieces (in 1824 verses), the second highest number of poems in Ibn al-Rūmī's *Dīwān*.[29] An above-related dispute over an encomium (L1302) is dated by al-Ḥuṣrī (d. 413/1022) to the beginning of the relationship in 265/878, when Ismāʿīl became vizier;[30] the final break-up must have occurred much later, when the patron had become remiss in his rewards. This prompted Ibn al-Rūmī's first to send him poems of reproach (*ʿitāb*) and then to seek the intercession of ʿAlī b. Yaḥyā al-Munajjim (L1600) – to no avail. After that, he resorted to satire.[31] During the caliphate of al-Muʿtaḍid whom Ismāʿīl b. Bulbul had mistreated as a crown prince, he fell into disgrace. The caliph's resentments and suspicions against Ismāʿīl were heightened by the vizier's excessive gifts to the Banū Shaybān, with whom he claimed an affiliation, and his generosity to other allies. Moreover, his love for the Greek sciences had earned him the label of *zindīq*.[32] He was imprisoned, tortured, and finally executed. His successor to the vizierate, ʿUbaydallāh b. Sulaymān b. Wahb, patronized Ibn al-Rūmī in turn.

Among the Banū Makhlad, a family of scribes of Nestorian origin, Ibn al-Rūmī established the first contact with al-ʿAlāʾ b. Ṣāʿid in 261/875 through the intercession of his old teacher al-Mubarrad, whom he had asked for this service (L585). In 269/882 when al-ʿAlā's father Ṣāʿid b. Makhlad was appointed 'Holder of the Two Vizierates' (Dhū l-Wizāratayn) – for the caliph al-Muʿtamid and his brother al-Muwaffaq, the true regent[33] – Ibn al-Rūmī addressed him also with an encomium of ninety verses (L1091). If al-Buḥturī is to be believed, the recipient's son al-ʿAlāʾ consulted him for an appropriate reward, and al-Buḥturī recommended one *dīnār* per verse.[34] The reward, however, never reached Ibn al-Rūmī, who sent poems of reproach and then abandoned the fruitless endeavor. When the Banū Makhlad were disgraced and imprisoned in 272/885, he vented his frustration in gloating satire.[35]

A further family of patrons of Nestorian descent were the Banū Wahb from Najrān, who had also patronized al-Jāḥiẓ and Abū Tammām. The vizier Sulaymān b. Wahb (d. 272/886) had been ousted in 265/878 in favor of the above-mentioned Ismāʿīl b. Bulbul,[36] and during Sulaymān's disgrace, Ibn al-Rūmī established ties with his son ʿUbaydallāh (d. 288/901) and his grandson al-Qāsim (d. 291/904).[37] When the Wahb family was restored to the vizierate with ʿUbaydallāh in 278/891, the poet reaped the benefit of his earlier loyalty. Al-Qāsim, who served his father as an assistant and deputy, allotted the poet ample gifts and a monthly pension of 500 *dīnār*s, unusual for the time, and to him the poet dedicated the greatest number of poems in the *Dīwān* (120 pieces in 3436 verses).[38] Ibn al-Rūmī's position was so strong that he interceded with al-Qāsim on behalf of others, for instance his disgraced and banned architect.[39] Therefore, the poet was taken aback by the sudden withdrawal of al-Qāsim, and he sent the deputy vizier a series of apologetic poems (*iʿtidhār*), excusing himself for any unwittingly committed offenses. As the silence persisted, he satirized al-Qāsim's chamberlain (*ḥājib*), but he spared the person of his old patron. Some medieval sources claim that al-Qāsim forestalled the poet's vitriolic invective by enlisting the help of Ibn al-Rūmī's old acquaintance, Ibn Firās to poison him.[40]

Ibn al-Rūmī's stance towards the Abbasids was initially hostile due to their anti-Shiite policies, while they took no notice of him. The first Abbasid whose patronage he actively sought was the regent al-Muwaffaq, who instituted more tolerant policies towards the Shiites. No poetry was dedicated to him directly, but Ibn al-Rūmī often praised al-Muwaffaq in encomia addressed to his appointees, many of whom were Ibn al-Rūmī's patrons.[41] At an advanced age and after his rival al-Buḥturī had left Baghdad, Ibn al-Rūmī became a familiar of the regent's son Abū l-ʿAbbās, who ascended the throne in 279/892 as al-Muʿtaḍid. For seven years until his death, Ibn al-Rūmī enjoyed the honors of an official court poet, celebrating in his felicitations the yearly *Ḥajj*, *ʿĪd al-Fiṭr*, *Nawrūz*, and *Mihrajān* festivals.[42]

His three long-term patrons, the governor ʿUbaydallāh b. ʿAbdallāh b. Ṭāhir, the vizier Ismāʿīl b. Bulbul, and the deputy-vizier al-Qāsim b. ʿUbaydallāh b. Sulaymān b. Wahb received together a third of Ibn al-Rūmī's *madīḥ*, which indicates a balanced and moderately successful career – not to mention his numerous short-term patrons. This alone contradicts the description of him by al-Marzubānī (d. 384/994) almost a century later as a luckless panegyrist.

> I do not know anybody among rulers and subjects whom he praised without turning on him with satire, regardless of whether [the patron] had rewarded him well or badly. Therefore he benefitted little from saying poetry, the rulers avoided him, and it became a cause of his death.[43]

His invective, it seems, received more attention than warranted by its rather small proportion in his *Dīwān*. Al-Khaṭīb al-Baghdādī (d. 463/1071), for example, made no mention of it.[44] Ibn al-Rashīq finally put the poet's satire into perspective with his panegyrics.

> As to Ibn al-Rūmī, he was the one among people who most deserved the name of poet ... but satire was most frequent with him, until he became famous for it, and one said 'more satirical (*ahjā*) than Ibn al-Rūmī', for he who does something often is known by it. Ibn al-Rūmī's satire is neither better nor ampler than his praise, but a little bit of damage goes a long way.[45]

Ibn al-Rūmī was by no means unique in his satire, though the medieval reception has not treated him even-handedly in this respect; al-Buḥturī's similar behavior was tacitly accepted, as al-Marzubānī admits.

> Many of the *ahl al-adab* decry the foul tongue of ʿAlī b. al-ʿAbbās al-Rūmī and denounce him for his profuse satire to the point of singling him out in that; but they fail to associate al-Buḥturī with him and join them together ... for al-Buḥturī satirized nearly forty leaders he had praised, among them two caliphs, namely al-Muntaṣir and al-Mustaʿīn, and [he] treated in likewise fashion ministers, generals, and their companions in suffering among high functionaries, governors, honorable judges and great men, after he had praised them and accepted their presents. Herein his case demonstrates bad companionship and a foul behavior.[46]

In conjunction with Ibn al-Rūmī's praise poetry, his talent for satire served as a latent threat, which he kept alive with intermittent allusions. But with his long-term patrons, satire came only as a last resort, when a relationship had deteriorated beyond repair, such as with Ibn Bulbul. The poet first spent a long time waiting, gently reminding and admonishing a non-paying dedicatee, before he actually switched to lampooning him. But he did not always go that far, as his restraint with al-Qāsim shows. When it happened, his satire might even be justified from the poet's strict ethical perspective; his praise having been offered as an advance in good faith, failure to reward it made the praise lapse. In lampooning the dedicatee, the poet then tipped the balance back and stripped the *mamdūḥ* of the ascribed good repute that, for lack of reward, had not become a truth. A more subtle option consisted in the poet's ostensibly upholding his loyalty and revealing indirectly the patron's unworthiness to the audience:

إذا ما مدحْتُ المرْءَ يومًا ولمْ يُثِبْ   مديحِى وحقُّ الشّعْرِ فى الحُكْمِ واجِبُ
كفانِى هجائيهِ قِيامِى بمَدْحِهِ   خطيبًا وقوْلُ النّاسِ لِى أنْتَ كاذِبُ

When I have praised a man and he did not reward me
– the due of praise being by legal determination obligatory –

Then, it suffices me as satire of him that I stand up declaiming
his praise, and the people say to me, 'You are a liar!'

(E110)[47]

5

THE *MADĪḤ* EXCHANGED BETWEEN IBN AL-RŪMĪ AND ʿUBAYDALLĀH

The relationship with ʿUbaydallāh b. ʿAbdallāh dominated Ibn al-Rūmī's formative years and furnishes an ideal opportunity for studying poetic patronage. Some general remarks about the practice of panegyrics at the time precede a survey of the *madīḥ* dedicated, its textual sources, and its inventory of forms – the longest and most elaborate among them being the *qaṣīda*.

The practice of praise

Scholars distinguish between formal ceremonies and familiar literary sessions (*majālis al-uns*), but consider praise to be part of both.[1] For a caliph, there were many official occasions for praise, including his enthronement, the designation of his heir apparent, the celebration of a victory, the birth of a child in his household, and the yearly festivals of *Ḥajj*, *ʿĪd al-Fiṭr*, *Mihrajān* and *Nawrūz*.[2] The poems were either offered to or commissioned by the caliph or a high official. Such occasional poems belong to the genre of the felicitation (*tahniʾa*), which lacks the *qaṣīda*'s thematic introduction (*nasīb*, *al-shayb wa-l-shabāb*, etc.) and opens instead with a congratulation to the addressee on the festive occasion. As *tahānī* for appointments to official positions and yearly festivals can often be dated, they allow one to establish the (minimal) duration of a patronage relationship.

As for the weekly sessions of the caliph with his familiars (*julasāʾ*) and boon companions (*nudamāʾ*), they followed their own protocol and etiquette.[3] Descriptions of *madīḥ* performances are rare, and the few recorded occasions seem outside the norm, such as Bashshār, described as spitting and gesticulating, Abū Tammām, prevented from reciting because of his rough (*ajashsh*) voice, and al-Buḥturī, as hysterically running about, vaunting his verse and attacking the audience for not applauding.[4] Praise poetry, however, was not a fixed ingredient in these *majālis*; it did play a part, for instance, in the inaugural session of the circle of caliph al-Rāḍī (r. 322–9/934–40). His familiar Abū Bakr al-Ṣūlī (d. 335/946) presented to him a previously-composed encomium and thereby set the theme for the conversation of the entire *majlis*. No praise occurred in another recorded session, held by the caliph al-Muʿtamid (r. 256–79/870–92), where he set the theme by asking a question about a musical instrument and received an array of elaborate responses in prose and verse.[5]

The Caliphal court was not alone in holding literary sessions; they were widespread among the elites of Samarra and Baghdad, as shown by those of the viziers ʿAlī b. al-Furāt (d. 312/924) and al-Ṣāḥib Ibn ʿAbbād (d. 385/995) in the fourth/tenth century.[6] Another forum for the public recitation of poetry was the *majlis al-shuʿarāʾ*, a weekly meeting of poets every Friday in the 'Dome of the Poets' (*qubbat al-shuʿarāʾ*) in the Manṣūr Mosque in Baghdad. There they recited to each other their newly-composed pieces, and newcomers presented themselves to the poets' community.[7]

When and how did a poet receive his reward? In accounts of official ceremonies, it immediately followed the poem, as a public demonstration. Sometimes, coins were showered like rain over the reciting poet, or his mouth filled with jewels.[8] The amounts for single poems recorded in the sources vary from 10,000 to 120,000 *dirham*s or 500 to 10,000 *dīnār*s.[9] Poets' life-income was similarly disparate: the 100,000 *dirham*s earned by al-Mukhayyim al-Rāsibī (fl. 170–93/786–809) are dwarfed by fifty times this amount, or 200,000 *dīnār*s, gained by Marwān b. Abī l-Janūb (d. after 240/854).[10] In relation to this, al-Buḥturī's suggested ninety *dīnār*s for one of Ibn al-Rūmī's *qaṣāʾid* seems paltry, and al-Buḥturī himself rejected a reward of ten *dīnār*s as an insult.[11] However, this falls within the range of a scribe's average monthly income of 300 *dirham*s or twenty-five *dīnār*s.[12] The higher amounts were most likely given on exceptional occasions and as a demonstration of their givers' munificence within the context of the *akhbār* in which they occur, such as a Barmakid lavishing the astronomical sum of 100,000 *dirham*s on an anonymous man for a single verse of praise.[13] Other kinds of rewards included settling a poet's debts, awarding him a fief or a lucrative position, such as postmaster or tax-collector, or bestowing robes of honor, mounts, and expensive educated slaves.

Some patrons paid the members of their literary sessions regular stipends, such as the vizier Alī b. al-Furāt, who set aside 20,000 *dirham*s a year for pensions at the turn of the fourth/tenth century, one his beneficiaries being al-Ṣūlī. Others rewarded each poem individually, such as the Būyid vizier al-Ṣāḥib Ibn ʿAbbād, who dispensed smaller occasional gifts of 50–100 *dirham*s half-a-century later.[14] To assess a poem's worth before compensating the author, a patron might solicit an *adīb*'s estimate.

How did a poem reach its addressee? With the onset of the manufacture of paper in Baghdad, people had at their disposal a writing material that was cheaper than the expensive papyrus, produced under government monopoly.[15] But how acceptable was it to send a poem to its addressee instead of personally delivering it? And once a poem had been recited and requited, how did it reach subsequent audiences, for its value was supposed to grow with its currency? Did any obligations arise from a rejected praise poem? With a broad investigation of official ceremonies and *majālis* still lacking, these questions cannot yet be answered. Neither can the admittedly copious accounts in the biographical and *adab* literature touching on these issues simply be foraged for data. Their various genres – whether anecdote, *faraj ba'da l-shidda* narrative, *adab* story about a type of behavior, or literary and historical *khabar* – all obey their own specific plot structures and require a separate study. At this stage, I rely on Ibn al-Rūmī's poetry for a case illustration of patronage. His panegyrics, for instance, impart information about their occasion, delivery and reception.

The relationship with a patron and access to his literary session could be won through the intercession of a third party. Once a relationship had been established, the initiation of a poem could come from the poet's side, and he might either send it or recite it himself. After the dedication, the poet accepted an immediate reward, a promise of later reward, but never a refusal of payment, which was interpreted as dishonorable. Returning a poem to its sender was considered unjust on the part of the patron, since it wasted the poet's effort. A returned poem could not serve any claim for reward, nor be 'recycled' for another patron. In the following retort Ibn al-Rūmī rejected a proposal in this vein made by Ibrāhīm b. al-Mudabbir (d. 279/892–3) as outrageous and offensive.

You have returned to me my praise after long waiting,
you have soiled its fresh attire.

'Praise with it whom you please except me', you said,
but who is willing to accept rejected praise?

Especially since you earned for yourself
shame that will not fade.[16]

Can a living person don the shrouds
of a corpse, soaking with pus?

(A446)[17]

For Ibn al-Rūmī, a poem was a personal gift and neither reusable nor transferable. Al-Buḥturī had different standards: he was known for frequently recycling his old praise poems, as in the example given above.[18] In numerous shorter pieces, Ibn al-Rūmī reminds his patrons of their promises and excuses himself for potential offenses (that may have justified a delay of reward). In others, he acknowledges received favors or asks for more.

A patron could also initiate an exchange with a sumptuous gift, to which the poet responded with a poem of gratitude (L1250', A464). The exchange could stop at that, if either side was dissatisfied, or develop into a long patronage.

One poem often referred to a previous one, explaining it (E1398), re-sending it (F1578), or recalling that it had been underpaid (A1204) or not paid at all (A1171, A1241, A1368, A1510). Inversely, a poem could announce a future one (F1124). Beyond that, each poem symbolized a continuation of the patronage, which signified much more than the sum of poem-for-favor exchanges.

In all this, the public was always summoned to witness both the acts of praise and reward. A lack of public acknowledgment voided the exchange (A1160: 1–7, L1250': 180–4), but in some, its place is taken by an individual *adīb* or poet; al-ʿAlāʾ b. Ṣāʿid asked Ibn al-Rūmī, for instance, to judge the *Risālat al-Shukr* addressed to the scribe by ʿUbaydallāh b. ʿAbdallāh.[19] The poems themselves also contained passages that predicted their future transmission and quotation, advertising their value for the patron.

Finally, the poems give indication of their author's idealized patronage. Especially in the third part of the long encomia (praise *qaṣāʾid*), as well as in smaller poems of reminder or admonition mixed with praise (*ʿitāb*), Ibn al-Rūmī formulates and advocates an idealized ethic of patronage. All in all, the wealth of information contained in Ibn al-Rūmī's *madīḥ* offsets to some degree the dearth of accurate information on panegyric practice.

A note on the textual sources

Ibn al-Rūmī's poetry is cited according to the only complete critical edition by Ḥusayn Naṣṣār *et al.* with variant readings taken from the incomplete edition by Sharīf Salīm (covering rhyme letters أ–ب). Three recent complete editions by ʿAbd al-Amīr Muhannā, Aḥmad Ḥasan Basaj, and Majīd Ṭarrād *et al.* reproduce Naṣṣār's text without the critical apparatus. Naṣṣār *et al.* followed the anonymous MS Cairo, Dār al-Kutub 139 (abbreviated as د) dated 884 AH (rhyme letters أ–ه), which Sezgin ascribes to al-Ṣūlī after the poet's friend and *rāwī* Ibn al-Musayyab (or al-Musayyabī) al-Kātib. The editors annotated variations and additions from another medieval *Dīwān* recension by Aḥmad b. Muḥammad b. Ṭāhir al-ʿUqaylī al-Shāʿir after Ibn al-Rūmī's servant and *rāwī* Mithqāl (abbreviated as ع), contained in the MSS Istanbul, Topkapı, Revan Köşkü 701 (rhyme letters أ–د), Nuruosmaniye 3859 (د–ض) and 3860 (ض–ك), and Escurial 277 (ل–ي) all dated 651–2 AH, as well as from other partial copies of the same redactor, Istanbul, Topkapı, Ahmet III 2558 (abbreviated as ق) and several more recent mostly partial manuscripts as well as a selection of Ibn al-Rūmī's poems by Ibn Nubāta (d. 768/1366), contained in MS Istanbul, Aya Sofya 4261.[20] Al-ʿUqaylī is singular because of his ordering of the poems by addressee: within each rhyme letter, he lists first, separately for each addressee, the long praises, short praises (*madāʾiḥ*), admonitions (*ʿitāb*), laments (*marāthī*), long invectives, and short invectives (*hijāʾ*); then all love poetry (*ghazal*), descriptive poetry (*awṣāf*), and licentious poetry (*mujūn*); and finally any single verses. This is a logical classificatory choice in a mainly panegyric oeuvre, but it is also tempting to see the arrangement as underscoring the role of the addressee for understanding a poem's meaning.[21] A third medieval *dīwān* recension by Ibn al-Ḥājib, a poet and servant of Ibn al-Rūmī, mentioned in the *Fihrist* (166/241–2) seems lost. The MS Princeton, Garret 19 is a late copy of Dār al-Kutub 139 (د). The letters indicating poem types are explained in the Abbreviations.

Themes of the *Qaṣā'id*

Among the *madīḥ* dedicated to ʿUbaydallāh and varying in length, structure, thematic complexity and style, one can recognize four forms, each with its characteristic themes and personae: the long encomium (praise *qaṣīda*), the felicitation (*tahni'a*), the short encomium and the admonition (*ʿitāb*). Excluded are epigrams, improvisations and linguistic acrobatics such as *taṣḥīf*, performed by request of ʿUbaydallāh. The same holds for the alphabetical series of poems addressed to ʿUbaydallāh in answer to his *Risālat al-Shukr*, dedicated to al-ʿAlāʾ b. Ṣāʿid, since it was al-ʿAlāʾ who commissioned the composition from Ibn al-Rūmī.[22]

The long encomia stand out with their structural versatility and thematic wealth that builds upon pre-Islamic and Umayyad models. Stefan Sperl has identified in some Abbasid *qaṣā'id* a bipartite and antithetical 'strophe-antistrophe' structure.[23] From this Ibn al-Rūmī deviates, with a tripartite structure and the lack of larger antithetical relations, except in one case.[24] However, I retain Sperl's strophe as a designation for the *qaṣīda*'s first thematic block, containing *al-shayb wa-l-shabāb*, *nasīb* etc., and Sperl's antistrophe for the *madīḥ* up to the dedication. The *qaṣīda*'s end with the dedication and related issues, such as the description of the poem, the attitudes implied by the poet, and the acknowledgment of the patron's contribution, has undergone such development as to require a separate section. It is here referred to as 'metastrophe', using the Greek prefix *meta-* in its double meaning of 'after' and 'about', because the section follows logically after the conclusion of the praise whose goals and conditions it discusses, in the same way meta-communication discusses the goals and conditions of communication. As will be seen in the individual encomia, the poet debates in the last section his professional relationship with the patron. In the preceding antistrophe, the poet has praised him, pledged his word for the patron's (generous) qualities, and placed his own credibility at stake. In the metastrophe, this completed performance of *madīḥ* becomes the basis for the poet's credits and claims *vis-à-vis* his patron. A metastrophe bears not only on the poem to which it belongs; in it the *qaṣīda* reflects on its status and the ethics of the exchange of which it forms a part, namely the long-term commitments of the patronage relationship. The antistrophe and metastrophe also differ in the way the patron is addressed; in the antistrophe, he is predominantly referred to in the third person, in the metastrophe he is addressed in the second person. If not filled by the patron, the second person in the antistrophe may address bystanders, enemies, supplicants, or other personae called upon to witness and experience the patron's described acts and attributes. The transition from antistrophe to metastrophe occurs in steps, with demands of the poet dovetailed with hyperbolic *madīḥ* of the patron.[25]

In terms of length, Ibn al-Rūmī's encomia of 100–300 verses dwarf those of Abū Tammām, al-Buḥturī and other early Abbasid poets, which rarely exceed eighty verses. Ibn al-Rūmī's L1611 to ʿUbaydallāh represents with its 303 verses the second longest piece in his *dīwān*.[26] The longest, L1600, dedicated to ʿAlī b. Yaḥyā b. Abī l-Manṣūr al-Munajjim, contains 337 verses. Altogether, Ibn al-Rūmī dedicated nine long encomia to ʿUbaydallāh (see Appendix A).[27] Their respective parts – strophe, antistrophe, and metastrophe – are articulated with various recurring groups of themes.

The strophe

This initial part consists most often of several themes that show no explicit connection with the occasion of the poem, contrary to the congratulations at the beginnings of *tahānī*.[28] Seven out of the nine encomia open with the theme of *al-shayb wa-l-shabāb*, about old age, symbolized by hoariness (*shayb*), which marks the loss of youth (*shabāb*). Ibn al-Rūmī modulates subthemes and moods with an extraordinary finesse. The theme of aging begins always in a melancholic mood but develops in a variety of ways. In L1611, the regret at old age and complaint about the injustice (*ẓulm*) of time and women motivate a long sequence, beginning in verse 5, of *fakhr* themes: women's love (as oryx[29] hunt), *khamriyya* (including a description of wine and a female cupbearer and musician), onager hunt, battle, desert journey by night and midday heat. In L1250', *shayb* plays the part of justice, of a divine symbol (*āya*) at which the poet's persona repents his frivolous past. After that, he mourns his lost youth and depicts his present failure in love and drinking. Only then, in verse 39, does the *fakhr* sequence commence, rephrasing the lost capacity to love and drink in a boastful remembrance of former occasions. The poet follows with a long *raḥīl* in the guise of an independent description of an oryx bull. In both poems, L1611 and L1250', the defeat and intimidation of the poet's persona by *shayb* yields to a sequence of *fakhr* episodes, marked by *wa-rubba*. The apparent weakness of old age simply motivates a show of former virility as the mood changes from subdued to triumphant. Poetically, the elapsed era of youthful exploits is reclaimed as an asset, and the poet's viewpoint shifts from the present to a past that becomes timeless. The language of the *fakhr* episodes in both strophes abounds in ornate rhetorical figures and imagery.[30]

Elsewhere, the mood of *al-shayb wa-l-shabāb* remains subdued and wistful. In L215, the regret of lost youth leads the poet to renounce love (*aṭlāl* motif) and reflect on the unsteadiness and deceptiveness of time. This is followed by moral admonitions and a sermon on panegyric ethics in which the initially sad mood turns sober and defensive. Other, shorter strophes sustain a single mood. In L1307, the poet's persona merely defends the dignity of his grief and feebly protests the injustice of fate. In L434, a detached and almost serene poet drily describes his loss of faculties; love plays only a minor part. In L1306, the poet's persona invokes rain over his distant youth and bids it farewell in a tone of acceptance.

The most torn and melancholic mood appears in L191; gray hair arrives as an announcer of death and murderer of youth.[31] Fear and grief are depicted, then scenes of youth pass in revue, introduced by anaphora (*yudhakkirunī l-shabāba* ... 'What reminds me of youth is ...'). The scenes move from pain over unrequited love to descriptions of nature: gardens, streams, and the East wind. Then, the poet bids the threadbare coat of youth farewell. The viewpoint of the poet's persona never departs from the present state of *shayb*. His memory remains something forsaken, not a repository of triumphant escapades. Every image of nature recalls his present grief and permanent separation from happier times.

Two encomia contain a *nasīb*, a reminiscence of women's love. In L994 departing women give way to a description of spring flowers, before the women defeat the flowers in a *mubārāh*.[32] The women are then described in floral imagery, as if dressed in the spoils of their defeated competitor. In L1042, aloof urban beauties eye the poet through gaps in their veils; the description vaunts their nobility but also shows them as hostile and disdainful towards the poet. Both *nasīb*s display the sumptuous descriptive style already noted in the *fakhr* episodes of other strophes (L1611 and 1250').

The strophes run to impressive lengths, in series of *fakhr* episodes (L1611, L1250') or dramatic scenes (L191, L215). Ibn al-Rūmī is clearly fascinated with the dilemma of the aging man, as he shows in his dramatization of *al-shayb wa-shabāb*. For this single theme, the poet creates an astounding spectrum of nuances, either remaining within the melancholy of *shayb*, old age, or transcending it to the boastful account of his memories of *shabāb*, youth. In L1306: 9, the ensuing *madīḥ* (antistrophe) causes the poet's recovery from grief, somewhat in keeping with Sperl's antithetical structure.[33] In the other poems, however, the poet's recovery already begins within the strophe and the positive mood only continues in the antistrophe. Less often, Ibn al-Rūmī uses themes of the conventional *nasīb*. He adds modern motifs such as the descriptions of flowers, a woman in floral imagery (L994), and urbane noblewomen (L1042).

The antistrophe

This section's main building block is a standard catalogue of praiseworthy individual acts and qualities, including generosity, honorable ancestors, powerful rulership in peace and war, and – only in L1611 – reliable and fruitful patronage. Hyperbolic praise appears throughout and especially at the closure of the antistrophe and transition to the metastrophe. The patron's attributes are often cast in oppositional pairs, e.g. protection and destruction, self-control and fury, bravery and cunning. The contrasting individual virtues engender a wider paradox between the patron's unity in his striving and his diversity in excellent attributes. Dualism and paradox leave the character of the *mamdūḥ* ambivalent, abstract and beyond the scope of definition and predictability – despite the generally familiar topoi of excellence. Every antistrophe adds and emphasizes certain aspects or conspicuously *leaves out* others of the standard catalogue. The use of mythical, pre-Islamic, Islamic and Iranian imagery offers further shading.

One group of antistrophes (L215, L434, L994, L1611, L1250') contains the standard catalogue of virtues – individual praiseworthy acts, ancestry, and rulership – with only minor variations. The longest and most detailed antistrophe appears in L1611; the individual section emphasizes the respectability, generosity, and universal perfection of the *mamdūḥ* in view of his youth, in successive abstract images, framed by anaphora (*fatan* ... 'a youth ...'). The ancestral praise is centered around the *mamdūḥ* as his father's favorite son, and as someone who increased his inherited honor. As a ruler, his reliability, but also his ferocity, courage, cunning, and unpredictability are emphasized. His courtliness, his legitimacy as governor, and an invocation conclude the rulership section. The following section on the virtues of patronage is unique to this poem. It portrays the ideal *mamdūḥ*: a man easy to praise, benevolent to his supplicants, indulgent towards the faults of his poets, appreciative of and erudite in poetry. L434 contains a terser version of the catalogue: ancestral, individual, and rulership praise, the latter including support of the caliphate. L1250' lacks ancestral praise; the praise of the *mamdūḥ* as fate-defying ruler is based on divine investiture and guidance in two anaphorae (*fa-hwa* ... *wa-hwa* ... and *ṣāḥibu*...). His generosity is celebrated in Islamic imagery. The praise concludes with *hieros gamos* and apotheosis.[34] In L215, acts of succor and protection dominate the individual praise; the ancestral section represents the *mamdūḥ* as renewing the family honor. Throughout both sections, the patron appears as an easy subject to praise. There follow two long sections on generosity and rulership, divided among military and administrative skills. Hyperbolic praise closes the antistrophe. In L994, the ancestral praise introduces the patron's individual praise, emphasizing reliability, which is continued in the section on generosity. Again, courtliness and knowledge of poetry appear as items of praise. Finally, the patron is congratulated on his new position as governor. In L1611, L215, and L994, aspects of individual praise such as generosity, reliability and sincerity, and aspects of good rulership such as courtliness, benevolence and erudition, mold the image of an 'ideal patron' as a poet would wish him; this is distinct from the 'ideal ruler' depicted in L434, L1250' and (also) L1611. But only L1611 gathers the qualities of an ideal patron into a separate section of praise; elsewhere (L215, L994, L1306 and L1307) they appear scattered among the standard sections on individual and rulership praise. Notable in the ancestral praise is the emphasis on the descendant's active role in confirming and increasing inherited glory.

In a second group of antistrophes (L191, L1306, L1307, L1042), the praise deviates significantly from the standard catalogue. In the fragment L1307, the praise limits itself to generosity and specific qualities: the patron's praise is said to have spread itself, without the words of people. Sincerity pervades his word and deed. He is a renewer of royalty, solves intricate problems, and protects the people.[35] L1306, however, omits generosity from the discussion of individual praise and only describes the *mamdūḥ*'s invincible power and reliability in promises. L191 similarly reduces the antistrophe to individual praise without generosity, only featuring protection and formidable power, described with an imagery that hardly inspires confidence. All of L1306, L1307 and L191 highlight qualities of the long-term patron: reliability, sincerity, and protective power, while they say little or nothing about generosity. Their praises appear more as pleas of the speaker to be proven true than statements of accomplished facts. The poet's monologues in the metastrophe of L191, in which he tries to convince himself of the patron's worthiness, make this clear. L1307 and L191 are silent about generosity, as an indirect message that the poet, not having witnessed it, could not truthfully extol it and refuses to lie.[36] At the same time, his knowledge of the patron's reliability leads him to expect it in the future. L1042 keeps praise for the individual patron extremely short and lavishes the greater part on his Ṭāhirid forefathers instead. The ancestors shall serve to incite the patron to emulate them. The *qaṣāʾid* of this second group with a modified catalogue of virtues admonish more than they praise. But they do so by stressing the patron's potential for generosity. In L1307, the desired behavior of the ideal patron is explicitly prescribed and encouraged. In the other cases, the same argument is made *e silentio*: the meager praise of individual virtues (L1042) and the lacking praise of generosity (L191 and L1306) indicate softly but clearly the patron's failure of having shown these qualities *de facto*.

The metastrophe

This final part of the *qaṣīda* represents Ibn al-Rūmī's most important contribution to the Abbasid *qaṣīda*, which does not imply a total lack of precedent. From the earliest pre-Islamic times onwards, poets used *qiṭʿa* and *qaṣīda* to convey messages, warnings and threats.[37] From these Ibn al-Rūmī borrows the old message formula with which he demarcates the end of the *qaṣīda* as a discrete entity.[38] The theme of the metastrophe is the patronage relationship; its tone oscillates between respectful gratitude and glaring exhortation. The core of the metastrophe is the dedication, surrounded by assertions bearing upon the state of satisfaction of the poet's persona – or lack thereof.

In shorter metastrophes (L215, L434, L1306, L1307, L1250'), the poet accompanies the dedication either with assurances of his exclusive loyalty and gratitude to ʿUbaydallāh and this patron's uniqueness and irreplaceability for him; or it is accompanied with an argument in support of a request, excuse or complaint. To the first kind belong L434 with a pledge of undivided loyalty and a rejection of another suitor for praise; L215 with a dedication, interlocked hyperbolic praises of patron and poem, and an invocation of blessings;[39] and L1307 with a protestation of loyalty, acknowledgment of received protection, and an invocation to the patron to enjoy his renewed governorship. In L1306, the dedication takes a hyperbolic form: all extant praise of ancients and moderns is said to be 'returned rightfully' to the patron, who alone can 'wear' it. L1250' presents a rather indirect, respectful variant. The poet declares his pure love for the patron and expresses his gratitude by invoking for him long life on earth and eternal afterlife. An explicit dedication is avoided as a token of self-effacement and gratitude: the poet refrained from mentioning his 'modest' composition to emphasize the matchlessness of the patron's kindness to him.

In a second, longer type of metastrophe (L994, L191, L1042, L1611) the poet places himself and his work in the proper light by describing his professional sacrifices and merits. In L994, this simply amounts to a praise of his composition preceding the dedication and several invocations. However, in a hyperbolic praise, the poet also gives the patron credit for helping him to compose the praise by contributing his name and attributes.

In the other three long metastrophes (L191, L1042, L1611), the poet not only points to his rights, but *explicitly* inquires about his reward, argues his case, and reprimands ʿUbaydallāh face to face. A metastrophe can run to considerable length, reaching thirty-one and eighty-three verses in L1611 and L191 respectively. In L1042, the poet proposes his departure, accusing ʿUbaydallāh of starving him, whereas his own services have been duly performed. He blames his emaciated state first on ʿUbaydallāh, then on his own anxiousness for his patron's sake; because a starved panegyrist is his patron's ridicule and stuff of satire. Thereupon he recalls his patron's former support and challenges him to show justice again. But the poet remains unconvinced about the outcome of his poem. He calls out his wish not to fall prey to delusion and phrases his pledge of loyalty as a rhetorical question. In L191, the poet asks a series of questions, showing surprise at the patron's generosity to others, while he himself is overlooked. The poet recalls his former trust in the patron's character and wonders in anaphoric rhetorical questions (*a-lasta l-marʾa* ... 'Are you not the man who ...') whether the patron is still the noble man he knew him to be. Ambiguous hyperbolic praise and an invocation interrupt the poet's doubts.[40] In the following *fakhr*, the poet insists on his sincerity, accuses his patron of turning his praise into lies, and boasts his need for a patron who matches his own noble rank. He visualizes his fictive departure from ʿUbaydallāh and, upon that, his return to him as his sole refuge, the poet's loyalty having finally triumphed over his reservations. A statement about the eternity of his praises concludes the *qaṣīda*. A more formal admonition appears in L1611. The antistrophe prepares the ground with a long praise of the patron as an ideal subject of *madīḥ*, protector, and urbane benevolent patron.[41] In the subsequent metastrophe, the poet highlights his own penury. He openly asks why the patron abandoned him after a life of service. His own absence from the patron's sessions is motivated by an elegant excuse: the patron's generosity not being limited in quantity and time, slothfulness proves the poet's faith in its permanence, whereas hurrying towards generosity would insult it as finite. This combines hyperbolic praise with a declaration of trust. After that, the poet proceeds to justify his need for reimbursement of expenses incurred for the many dependants his high rank entails. Finally, he dedicates the poem, vaunting it as a year's work of weaving, and invokes ʿUbaydallāh both as a ruler and rightly praised patron. In all three metastrophes, L191, L1042, and L1611, the poet argues that there is a rift between the patron's present acts and the poet's knowledge of his past ideal acts; and he spends his rhetoric on harmonizing the disparity between experience and expectation. For his own part, the poet demonstrates his own fulfillment of his panegyric role as well as his full trust and loyalty offered to his patron. The acts of patron and poet merge in the concepts of the praise's truth (or the poet's sincerity), which, in Ibn al-Rūmī's definition, lie beyond his sole control and within the combined responsibilities of poet and patron. In the whole corpus, very few verses openly reprimand the patron, but the antistrophe's standard catalogue of praise and the metastrophe's dramatization of the poet's doubts and struggles, place a moral burden upon the patron.

The nine encomia show an immense compositional richness. The development of their themes and the changing proportions of their parts cannot be explained by any of the binary structures previously proposed, but need to be acknowledged as continuous developments.[42] Strophe and metastrophe, for instance, often outweigh the antistrophe and the poem's official core in length and verbal artistry. When beholding the poems' very different parts – the ornate strophe varying between description and drama, the more predictable, list-like antistrophe, and the dramatic metastrophe – one might wonder what holds them together. First of all, the musical coherence of meter and rhyme and the conventions of *qaṣīda* poetry held great sway over an educated audience. Still, I argue for an additional *functional* coherence, which finds support in certain pronouncements made by the persona of the poet himself.

The strophe is characterized by the abundance of sumptuous *fakhr* episodes and dramatic scenes. The long sequences of *fakhr* episodes in the strophes of L1250 and L1611 support the idea of a *functional* connection between the strophe and the antistrophe, as formulated by Jamel Eddine Bencheikh:

> Plus celles-ci [sc. developments of conventional themes] seront habiles, plus sera vibrant l'enthousiasme suscité par le *nasīb* ... et plus l'éloge en sera rehaussé. Car c'est d'une véritable démonstration préalable qu'il s'agit: sa réussite donne sa dimension vraie au dithyrambe, il le légitime par avance.[43]

Thomas Bauer states the same for the pre-Islamic and Umayyad *qaṣīda*:

> Ein inhaltlicher Zusammenhang [of the onager episode] zum Rest der Qaṣīde ist nicht erkennbar. Trotzdem hat sie eine klar erkennbare Funktion: Erst duch sie (und den Nasīb) wird das Gedicht zu einer längeren Qaṣīde and damit zu einem Kunstwerk.[44]

First, the poet displays his skill in conventional themes, where his audience can follow and evaluate him best; then he fulfills the *qaṣīda*'s purpose, namely, the praise (or admonition) and request. The innovative dramatic scenes of the strophe, although very different from the *fakhr* episodes, must have served the same function. Their reception at the time has not been recorded, but later medieval critics praise Ibn al-Rūmī for inventing motifs that capture true or imagined human behavior.

The antistrophe includes one new theme of praise: patronage. Still developing, this theme is usually scattered and appears only once consolidated in a thematic block (L1611). It differs from the praise of the patron as author, invented by Abū Tammām, for it not only praises the patron's literary abilities, but also his appreciation and knowledge of poetry and his gracious treatment of poets – the whole range of human interaction in literary patronage.[45] The antistrophe hardly contains dramatic scenes, ornate descriptions and adventurous imagery, instead it shines with hyperbolic exaggeration of virtues that are familiar. The thematic goal (*gharaḍ*) of this section that involved the patron directly, ran the greatest risk of misinterpretation by him or less astute audiences, and it is plausible to assume that linear enumeration, syntactical figures, straightforward description, and exaggeration of the familiar virtues proved the safest course for a poet.

The metastrophe again contains dramatic scenes. Here, the poet casts himself as a character in the theme of patronage. Ibn al-Rūmī again goes further than Abū Tammām in not merely vaunting his panegyrics but redefining them as a form of human interaction with wide implications.[46] As such, the metastrophe complements and interprets the antistrophe: the latter fulfills the immediate goal of the *qaṣīda*, to praise; the former safeguards the ulterior purpose of patronage, the fulfillment of the poet's rights, needs, and claims.

The speech acts of praise

In the previous section, the complementary functions of a *qaṣīda*'s different parts give it coherence: the strophe conveys the literary rank of a *qaṣīda*, the antistrophe performs the praise proper, and the metastrophe safeguards the interests of the author. But beyond the functions of its parts, the *qaṣīda* as a whole has a communicative function. This finds its most direct expression in the voice of the poet as panegyrist, when he explicitly informs the hearers about the motive of a poem and the (ongoing) procedure of praise. Direct phrases to that effect intersperse the *madīḥ* proper and the patronage section and include: the naming of the patron, the intention to praise him, invocations and advice, messages, and the dedication. Among these, the intention to praise and the dedication hold between them the antistrophe and metastrophe, the two parts of the *qaṣīda* that directly bear upon patronage (see Appendix B). Both phrases are self-referential, i.e. the poet's persona uses them to explain what the poem 'does' for the patron and simultaneously carries this out. Their performative double nature makes the phrases operate both within the poem and engage, across it, with the surrounding historical situation. The dedication is further tied up with far-reaching stipulations of the panegyric act. All the phrases together lay down, step-by-step, a procedural framework for Ibn al-Rūmī's *madīḥ*.

The naming identifies the patron immediately at the onset of the antistrophe either by his proper name (*ism*) ʿUbaydallāh, his agnomen (*kunya*) Abū Aḥmad, or an ancestral name (*nasab*), for example, Ṭāhir, or a combination of these:[47]

أَضحَى أَبو أَحمدَ الأميرُ عُبيـ　　ـدُ اللَّهِ والحمدُ فِى الورَى عِيَبُهْ
وكيف لا يَنحَلونَ حمدَهُمْ　　أَبًا شديدًا علَيهِمُ حَدَبُهْ

As to Prince Abū Aḥmad ʿUbaydallāh,
by morning time [all] praise of humankind is [devoted to]
his [gift-filled] leather bags (sc. no praise is left for others).[48]
How can they not lend their praise
to a strong father whose care belongs to them?

(L215: 73–4)

The ancestors Banū Zurayq, Banū Muṣʿab, or Banū Ṭāhir, often accompany the addressee's name:

عبيدِ اللَّهِ قَرمِ بنى زُريقٍ　　وحسبُكَ باسمِهِ فَصلَ الخِطابِ

ʿUbaydallāh, Lord of the Banū Zurayq; his name
suffices as a decision [between truth and falsehood].[49]

(L191: 71)[50]

Sometimes the ancestors even precede by many lines the naming of the addressee:

بنى مُصعَبٍ فُزْتم بكلِّ فَضيلةٍ　　وآثرْتمُ حُسّادَكُمْ بالنَّقائص ...
ومنكمْ عبيدُ اللَّهِ فُتُّم بسَعْيِهِ　　ذَوِى السَّعْىِ فوتًا بائصًا أَىَّ بائصِ

Children of Muṣʿab, you have reached every virtue,
and treated those who wish you ill, to imperfections ...
From you is ʿUbaydallāh. With what forbidding distance
did you surpass – by his striving – all those who strive!

(L1042: 14, 41)[51]

The intention to praise accompanies the patron's name, but it is not always uttered as explicitly as here:

يا آلَ طاهِرٍ المطهَّرِ كاسْمِهِ　　إنَّ اللِّسانَ بمدْحِكُمْ لَطَليقُ
إن يُنْسِنِى عصرَ الشَّبابِ وعَهْدَهُ　　عَصْرٌ فعصرُكُمُ لذاكَ خَليقُ

> O tribe of Ṭāhir [lit.: 'pure'], pure as his name,
> the tongue is loose with your praise.
>
> If any time let me forget the time of youth
> and its closeness, your time would be capable of this.
>
> (L1306: 8–9)[52]

More often the intention is expressed indirectly, either by the poet exhorting himself or speaking about the patron in the third person. So firm is his design that he forgets youth and disregards bad omens – and he does not need to guard against false exaggeration with an outstanding patron like ʿUbaydallāh:

تَعَدَّ وأَسْرِفْ فِى مديحِ ابنِ طاهرٍ   فلَسْتَ على الإسرافِ فيه موبَّخا

> Transgress and exaggerate in praising Ibn Ṭāhir,
> for you cannot be blamed of exaggerating in it
> (sc. it is impossible to speak too well about him).
>
> (L434: 18)[53]

عِفْ حمدَ سُؤّالِه ولا يثْنِكَ الـ   أَخطَبُ عنْ قصدِهِ ولا خَطَبُهْ
ولا يعوقَنْكَ عنْ زيارتهِ الـ   أَعضَبُ مُستقبَلاً ولا عَضَبُهْ

> Spurn the [distant way of] praising of his supplicants!
> Neither the [ill-boding] ash-gray [raven] nor his gray [hue]
> shall deter you from going to him [yourself]!
>
> Nor shall the encounter of a[n ill-omened] broken-horned [beast],
> nor the break hinder you from visiting him!
>
> (L215: 106–7)

أَعُمُّهُمْ مدحًا وأَختصُّ منهُمْ   أَخاهُمْ عُبيدَ اللّهِ والحقُّ يُلزَمُ

> I enclose them all in my praise and single out
> their brother ʿUbaydallāh, for truth must be obeyed.
>
> (L1611: 104)

At times, the poet remains impersonal as in L215: 73–4, quoted in the previous paragraph.

Invocations (*duʿāʾ*) occur in various places at the end of the antistrophe and in the metastrophe. They use the imperative 'live' (*ʿish*), the optative, 'may you not cease to be ...' (*lā zilta*), or the jussive, 'let him boast' (*li-yafkhar*).[54] Some invocations are made solely on behalf of the patron; others, on behalf of his poet and supplicants; and many are mutual, invoking an act or virtue that benefits both sides, such as the poet's sincerity (L1611: 303). For the patron, long life, comfort, happiness, strong rule, glory, freedom from sinning, and a blessed afterlife are invoked by the poet:

فَعِشْ فى غِبطَةٍ ونعيمِ بالٍ ومُلْكٍ لا يَخافُ يَدَ اغتِصابِ

Live in joy, ease of mind, and a kingdom
that does not fear the hand of usurpation!
(L191: 150)

فَعِشْ سالِمًا لا زالَ مَجْدُكَ باقِياً وإنْ رَغِمَتْ مِن حاسِديكَ المعاطِسُ

Live safely, may your glory subsist,
even if those who envy you are spited!
(L994: 110)

وعِشْ عَيْشَ ثاوٍ خَيْرَ دارٍ فَما لَهُ على غَيْرِ زادٍ صالِحٍ مُتَلَوَّمُ ...
ولا زِلتَ ممدوحاً لمُطْرِيكَ مَصْدَقٌ إذا كان للمُطرينَ فِى النَّاسِ مَزْعَمُ

Live as the dweller in the best house and [as one]
in whom no bad provision [for the afterlife] can be blamed ...

May you never cease to be a patron who is an object
of sincerity for his praisers, when those who praise
have among [other] people [only] objects of pretense.
(1611: 301, 303)

The sincerity invoked in the last verse benefits both poet and patron. Abstract concepts wished for reach cosmic dimensions, and they are often personified. For instance, eternity grants the world, personified as ʿUbaydallāh's wife, the generous allotment of his millenary life span before she will be divorced from him.

فَجزاهُ الإلهُ عنّي خُلودًا ونَعيمًا فى ظِلِّ دارِ السَّلامِ
بَعْدما يُنْعِمَ البقاءُ به الدُّنـ ـيا صَحيحًا مُمَتَّعًا أَلفَ عامِ

May God reward him for my part with eternity
and ease of life in the shade of Eden![55]

After eternity will have favored[56] the world with him
for a thousand years, as a handsome compensation [of a divorcee].
(L1250': 189–90)

Other personifications invoked include the patron's glory as his child and his noble deeds as his wives:

أبا المجْدِ لا يَفقُدْكَ مُدّةَ عُمْرِهِ　　عزيزًا فإنّ المجْدَ بَعْدكَ يَيْتَمُ
ولا آمَتِ العَلْياءُ مِنكَ فإنَّها　　لِمِثْلِكَ قبلَ اليومِ كانَتْ تَأَيَّمُ

Father of glory, may it (sc. glory), dear [to you], not lose you
in its lifetime! Since glory will be an orphan after you.

Neither may the noble deeds be widowed from you!
Since they have remained [unmarried] widows
until today for one like you.

(L1611: 269–70)

For his own benefit, the poet invokes hope, desires, and wishes, personified as supplicants:

لِتَعُذْ بِسَيْبِكُمُ المطامِعُ والمُنَى　　فعلَيْكُمُ لِعِداتِها التّصْديقُ
ما زِلْتُمْ تَرقَوْنَ فى دَرَجِ العُلى　　حتَّى أَشارَ إليْكُمُ العَيّوقُ

May the desires and wishes take refuge with your downpour,
for you are obliged to prove their promises true.

You did not cease to ascend the stairs of high rank,
until Capella pointed at you!

(L1306: 14–15)[57]

In the preceding quote, the invocation of the poet's wishes is complemented by an assertion of the patron's accomplished glory.[58] Similarly invocation and advice can complement each other, as in the two following verses that both call for generous reward, but present it from the opposite perspectives of poet and patron:

فلا أكُنِ المُهريقَ فَضْلَةَ مائِهِ　　غُرورًا بِرقْراقٍ من الآلِ وابِصِ
ولا تبْخَسَنِّى حَقَّ مَدْحِى فإنّنِى　　أرى باخِسِى سِيّانِ عندِى وباخِصِى

Heaven forfend that I be one who pours away the rest of his water,
being deceived by the glittering pool of a mirage!

Do not undercut the right of my praise,
for I see as equal him who undercuts me
and him who gouges out my eye.

(L1042: 66–7)

The poet's wish not to be deceived and the advice to the patron not to underpay him have an identical goal: adequate reward. The next example adds the poet's rank to his claim:

فلا تَضعَنَّ رِفْدَكَ دونَ قَدْرِى   فليس يَفوتُ بَسْطَتَكَ انتِصابِى ...
ولا يَكنِ الَّذِى أَمَّلْتُ مِنه   كرقراقِ السَّرابِ على الحِدابِ
ولا كرمادٍ اشْتَدَّتْ رِياحٌ   بِهِ عُرْضَ الصَّحاصِحِ فَهْوَ هابِ

Do not stay with your gift below my rank,
since my height does not exceed your reach! . . .

That which I hoped for in him must not be
like a glistening mirage on elevated grounds,

Nor like ashes scattered by strong winds
across the plains, whirled up in the air.

(L191: 117, 121–2)

Here we find direct entreaties to respect the poet's rank coinciding with the demand for a respectable reward. Both invocation and advice show the tendency to match the rights and benefits of the poet with the duties and benefits of the patron. One encomium contains a felicitation identical to the openings of *tahānī*. They usually begin with an optative of *hana'a* 'to benefit' or *hanna'a* 'to congratulate', such as in the following incipit of a felicitation to the autumnal *Mihrajān* festival:[59]

لِيَهنِك لُبْسُ المِهْرجانِ وإنْ غدا   تُهنِّئُهُ الدُّنيا بإنَّكَ لابِسُه

May the garb of *Mihrajān* benefit you! Even if the world
congratulates it (sc. the garb) for your wearing it.

(F952: 1)

Within the *qaṣīda*, the poet who pronounces the felicitation may indirectly designate himself:

لِتَهْنِكَ يا ابنَ الأَكْرَمينَ إمارةٌ   بِطالِعِ سَعْدٍ جانَبَتْها المَناحِسُ
مقالةُ لا مُستَعْظِمٍ ما وَلِيتَهُ   ولو كان ما هبَّتْ عليْهِ الرَّوامِسُ

O son of the noblest, may a governorship with
auspicious ascendant, shunned by evil omens, benefit you!

[This is] said by him who does not deem too vast the rule
you have assumed, even though [what you are in charge of]
is equal to [the distance] far-travelling dust winds blow across.[60]

(L994: 84–5)

According to another invocation, ʿUbaydallāh's governorship of Baghdad shall perdure for his entire lifetime:

بِحَسْبِكَ هذِى ما حُيِيتَ إمارةً   تُجَلُّ بها حَقَّ الجلالِ وتُعظَمُ

> As long as you live,[61] you deserve this governorship,
> by which you are rightly honored and exalted.
>
> (L1611: 207)

Lengthy messages are dispatched in two encomia. They are introduced with the imperatives *qul/qulā li-* 'say (s./dl) to someone' or *aliknī ilā* 'convey [a message] from me to someone'.[62] These phrases addressing fictional messengers were already in use in pre-Islamic times, mainly in shorter poems containing missives to friend or foe.[63] In the first example, the poet sends two messengers to the patron himself:

فَقولا للأميرِ وإنْ رآنى   بمَزْجَرِ ما يُهانُ مِنَ الكِلابِ

> Say (dl) to the prince, even if he sees me
> in the position of scorned, chased dogs: ...
>
> (L191: 96)[64]

In the crucial part of the message, the poet recalls himself as the speaker, while admonishing the patron:

وآخِرُ خُطبَةٍ لِى فيكَ قَولى   ولَيْسَ عِتابُ مِثلِكَ بالغِلابِ

> My last speech about you are my words
> – and admonishing you is not trying to vanquish –
>
> (L191: 151)

The other message informs ʿAmr b. Layth, the new governor of Baghdad, of the merits of ʿUbaydallāh, which the poet vaunts to him:

أَلِكْنِى إلى عمرِو بنِ ليثٍ رِسالةً   لها حينَ يُدوَى الغَيْبُ غيْبٌ مُسَلَّمُ

> Deliver to ʿAmr b. Layth from me a message,
> which holds a future that is safe [from evil],
> when the future is consumed [by rancor].[65]
>
> (L1611: 146).

The dedication concludes the metastrophe and plays the double role of offering the *qaṣīda* and declaring so at the same time. Two types of phrases occur; in the first, *manaḥa* 'to dedicate', includes the speaker directly:

'[Herewith] I dedicate it to you' (*manaḥtukahā*). A single word reunites the three panegyric essentials supported by the perfective aspect of the verb, indicating completion:[66] the poet (*manaḥtu-*), the addressee (*-ka-*), and the encomium (*-hā*). In the second type of phrase, the imperative 'take it' (*khudhhā*, *dūnakahā*, *hākahā*), only the respective addressee (*-ka-*) and the poem (*-hā*) are explicitly named. The speaker remains implicit, although he may appear in the immediate context. Similar to the message, the dedication derives from pre-Islamic origins.[67] This phrase, formally completing the act of praise, is often accompanied by a *ḥāl* clause or *ḥāl* accusative, which describes the entire *qaṣīda* (or *tahni'a*). The description may be modest, with the poem failing to match the patron's uniqueness; or boastful, pleasing him like an ornament, entertainment, or a beautiful garden:

وكُلُّ أَشْباهِهِ الَّتى ذُكِرَتْ   دونَ الَّذِى بَلَّغَتْ بِهِ رُتَبُهْ
خُذْها أَميرِى قِلادَةً نُظِمَتْ   من لؤلؤٍ لا يَشينُها ثُقَبُهْ
وأَحْسَنُ الحلْىِ مَنطِقٌ حَسَنٌ   يَكْثُرُ محفوظُهُ ومُكتَتَبُهْ

All the similes that have been mentioned
are beneath what his ranks have achieved.

Take them, my prince, as a necklace
strung of pearls unspoilt by borings!

The best jewelry is beautiful speech
much memorized and asked to be dictated.

(L215: 150–52)[68]

فدونكَها يا ابنَ سَيْفِ المُلو   كِ لَهْوَ المجالِسِ زادَ الرُّفَقْ

Take it then, son of the sword of kings,
as an entertainment for [convivial] sessions,
as a provision for people travelling together.

(L1307: 47)

مِنَ اللآئِى لا يُخزِى الوجوهَ نَشيدُها   إذا مُنشِدٌ باهَى بها مَنْ يُجالسُ
تهُزُّ قناةَ الظَّهْرِ عن أَرْيَحِيَّةٍ   كما هزَّ رُمْحًا لِلطِّعانِ مُداعِسُ

Made of those [meanings] whose song does not abase the faces,
when he who sings them boasts with a companion in a *majlis*.

They make the spine shiver with pleasure
like a warrior makes a lance shiver by the thrust.

(L994: 103–4)

مَنَحْتُكَها كالرَّوضِ جادَتْهُ دِيمةٌ   بكَتْ فوقَه حتّى تَضاحكَ عابِسُهْ

I dedicate them to you, like a garden on which
long-lasting rain fell copiously, weeping above it
until what frowned in it laughed.

(F952: 74)

The long and sumptuous encomium L1611 is dedicated twice, first, as a woven garb, and then, personified as a bride:

مَنَحْتُكَها حَوْلِيَّةَ النَّسجِ لمْ تزَلْ   تُعانَى مَدَى حَوْلٍ دكيكٍ وتُخْدَمُ ...
فَدونكَها مَغْبوطَةً بكَ لو غَدا   سِواكَ لها مَوْلىً غَدَتْ وَهْىَ تُرْجَمُ

I dedicate it to you, as a year's work of weaving,
it was tended to ceaselessly and served for a full twelve months . . .[69]

Take her, as one who is envied for [belonging to] you,
if someone other than you becomes her master, she will be stoned.

(L1611: 297, 300)

The descriptions also highlight the power of the *qaṣīda*; it keeps the traveller alert by night and defies the passing of time.[70] Even the poet subordinates himself to his *qaṣīda*, posing as its 'son':

ومهما تبَّ مِن عَمَلٍ وقَوْلٍ   فما عَمَلُ ابنِ مَدْحِكَ لِلتَّبابِ

Whatever work and word perish, the work of
the 'son' of your praise is not destined for ruin.

(L191: 175)

We see Ibn al-Rūmī on one occasion extend the dedication to an entire passage in which he interprets his composition as a physical *and* mental journey to his patron:

إليكَ ذَعَرْتُ الوَحْشَ من كلِّ مأْمنٍ   لهُنَّ به عنْ سَخْلِهِنَّ مَلاحِسُ
إليكَ تَداعَتْنِى القَوافِى ولمْ أَقُلْ   إلَيْكَ تداعَتْنِى الفيافِى البَسابِسُ
أَتيْتُكَ مِنْ أَدْنَى مَزارِى يَخُبُّ بِى   إلَيْكَ رَجائِى لا القِلاصُ العَرامِسُ
أُجاوِزُ بيْتاً بَعْدَ بيْتٍ وأَمتَطِى   هواجسَ فِكْرٍ بعْدَهُنَّ هواجِسُ
دَعَوْتُ غَريبَ الشِّعْرِ باسمِكَ فارْعَوَى   إلىَّ مُجيباً وَهْوَ باسْمِكَ آنِسُ
فأَلَّفْتُ مِنه إذْ تجمَّعَ وَحْشُهُ   وهُنَّ رُتوعٌ بالفَلا وكوانسُ
فجاءتْ قوافيه تُبارِى صُدورَه   كما تَتبارَى القارِباتُ الخوامِسُ
مَنَحْتُكَها تَحْدو المَطِىَّ على الوَنَى   وتَنفِى الكَرَى عن ذِى السُّرَى وَهْوَ ناعِسُ

I chased towards you the wild oryx,
away from their calves from every covert where they lick them.

The rhymes called me to you, I did not say,
'The endless deserts called me to you'.

I came to you from my closest domicile,
my hope trotting with me to you, not robust camels.

I crossed house after house riding
idea upon idea of thought.

I called the rare poetry by your name,
and it turned around to answer me, tamed by your name.

I composed it, when its wild oryx had gathered,
grazing in the plain and hiding in the coverts.

Then its end rhymes came to race with its beginnings,
like approaching five-day-thirsty camels racing with each other.

I dedicate them to you: they spur on the mounts despite [their] fatigue
and chase slumber from the drowsy night traveller.

(L994: 95–102)[71]

The homonym *bayt* in verse 98, signifying 'house' and 'verse', epitomizes the passage's double meaning: the poet's physical journey, literally passing house after house in Baghdad on the way from his home to the patron – a gentle mockery of the conventional camel journey (*raḥīl*) – and his figurative journey, 'riding' his ideas through verse after verse in the process of composition. Both journeys have the patron as their physical or thematic goal (*gharaḍ*), and both entitle a poet to reward; the real exertion of desert travel belonging to the pre-Islamic poet, and the mental exertion of bending rare words to novel meaning in Ibn al-Rūmī's time.[72]

In connection with the *qaṣīda*'s merits and its benefits for the patron, the poet explains what it means to himself. Exaltation of a patron also entails his poet's high rank:

فليْسَ يَنالُنِى إلّا مُنيلٌ   يُطِلُّ علىَّ إطلالَ السَّحابِ

Only such a benefactor can reach me,
who looks down on me like the clouds.

(L191: 162)[73]

A true friendship is presupposed to exist between the patron and himself, and the poet owes his patron sincerity and steadfastness:[74]

ولكنّى – وما بِى مدْحُ نفسِى أرى عابَ التّكذُّبِ شرَّ عابِ

But I think – not praising myself –
that forged lies are the worst fault.

(L191: 154)

So precious are these virtues to Ibn al-Rūmī that he begs his patrons not to trifle with them, supported with a paraphrase of Sūrat al-Zumar 39/10:

بمهما شِئتَ دونَك فامْتَحِنّى فإنّكَ غايَتِى والصّبْرُ دابِى ...
سأَصبِرُ موقِنًا بوُفورِ حَظّى وأجرُ الصّابِرينَ بلا حِسابِ

Try me with anything you please, other than yourself,
for you are my goal, and patience is my habit ...

I will be persistent, sure of my ample share,
since the reward of the persistent is not calculated.

(L191: 152, 174)

Loyalty is the most cherished virtue Ibn al-Rūmī's panegyrist has to offer:

يابْنَ الأكارِمِ خُذْها مِدْحةً صَدَرَتْ عن مَورِدٍ لَكَ صافٍ غَيْرِ مَوْرودِ

Son of nobles, take it, as an encomium
from a source not visited by others, loyal to you.

(F458: 66)

Loyalty still persists when everything else induces doubt in the patronage-friendship. Loyalty holds the poet back when circumstances would otherwise require his departure. In the following example, which precedes the dedication, he adapts the Koranic term for the human-divine bond:[75]

ولى فيكَ آمالٌ وقدْ عَلِقَتْ يدِى بعُرْوَتِكَ الوُثْقَى فَهَلْ أنا مُسْلَمُ؟

I hold hopes in you and my hand is joined
to your indissoluble bond, am I abandoned?

(L1611: 273)

When strong doubts and admonitions preclude a dedication, protestations of loyalty take its place:

ولوْ أنّى قطعْتُ الأرْضَ طولاً لكان إليْكَ مِنْ بَعْدُ انقلابِى
إذا كنتَ المآبَ ولا مآبَ سِواكَ فأيْنَ عنْكَ بِذِى الإيابِ؟

If I were to cross the length of the whole earth,
I would thereupon turn back to you.

When you are the haven of return, and there is no haven
but you, to whom except you might one return?[76]

(L191: 172–3)

The most intriguing aspect of the dedication lies in the way it engages the patron as a third party with the poet and the poem. The double (literal and figurative) journey quoted above has shown what a dedication presupposes on behalf of the patron. He casts a spell on the rhymes to summon the poet (L994: 96), his name attracts rare words as if they were tamed oryx (95, 100) or thirsty camels (101).[77] Most importantly, ʿUbaydallāh, the model patron, contributes his acts and qualities as the substance of the poem:

إذا مادِحٌ أسْدَى وألْحَمَ باطلاً   فمَدْحُكَ مُسْدًى بالَّذِى فيكَ مُلْحَمُ

If some panegyrist weaves warp and woof in vain,
the warp and woof of your praise
is woven firmly with you [as material].

(L1611: 231)

وما زِلتَ لَبَّاسًا مديحًا تَحوكُه   مساعيكَ لمْ يَلبَسْه قبلَكَ لابِسُ
ولا مَدْحَ ما لمْ يمدَحِ المرْءُ نَفْسَهُ   بأفعالِ صِدْقٍ لمْ تشُبْها الخسائِسُ

You do not cease to wear praise that your acts
have woven, and nobody has yet worn.

It is not praise if a man does not extol himself
by true deeds unstained by meanness.

(L994: 105–6)[78]

ʿUbaydallāh's true excellence lets his acts and the words of poetry about them match so completely, that they allow a sincere poet to speak:

ألا رُبَّ قولٍ فيه أمكنَ قائلاً   ولوْ رامَهُ فِى غَيرِهِ ظَلَّ يَكعَمُ

Many a speech about him is possible for a speaker,
if he had wanted it for someone else,
he would have stayed muzzled.

(L1611: 252)[79]

The words cannot add anything to the deeds, so the poet dispenses with embellishment:

وما سَدَّ قَوْلٌ فِى فَعالِكَ خَلَّةً   ولا وَجَدَ المُدّاحُ نقْصًا فتَمَّموا

No speech closes gaps in your acts, nor do praisers
find an imperfection and complete it.

(L1611: 226)

In the invocations, we have already seen benefits and duties of the patron mesh with benefits and rights of the poet. The dedication ties a firm and far-reaching bond between the two. Unilaterally the poet's action is reinterpreted by him as part of a reciprocal or co-operative relationship between himself and the patron, which reaches beyond the text and the occasion of a single *qaṣīda*. The tendency to establish *reciprocal* moral relationships pervades the microcosm of the encomia. It recurs in the dramatic scenes and the imagery and provides the elements for an ethics of patronage.

In some cases, however, the direct dedication is replaced by an *implicit* one. The poet, for instance, refuses to dedicate praise to anybody else:

ومُستَمْنِحِى مدْحًا كمَدْحيهِ بعدما   تَمَكَّنَ إخلاصِى له فتَمَخَّخا
فَقُلْتُ له عنِّى إليكَ فلَنْ أَرَى   هواك لمِثْلِى فى رمادِكَ مَنْفَخا

To someone who asked me for praise, like my praise
of him (sc. ʿUbaydallāh), after my exclusive allegiance
to him had grown strong and deep,

I said, 'Be gone! I shall never see your yearning for the likes of me
[result in] a blowing on your ashes [to kindle the fire].'

(L434: 34–5)

The declaration of exclusive loyalty to ʿUbaydallāh and the categorical refusal to consider praising anybody else conveys indirectly that the poet devotes all his praise to him. In another poem, praise is not an offering but a right that the poet 'returns' to the Banū Ṭāhir:

مهما سَرَقْتُ عن الأَوائلِ فيكُمُ   فلِغَيْرِ باعٍ بالمديحِ يَضيقُ
لكنَّهُمْ نَحَلوا سِواكمْ مجْدَكُمْ   فرَدَدْتُ حَقَّكُمُ وذاكَ حَقيقُ
ما المدْحُ مسْروقٌ لكم مِن غيْرِكُمْ   بل منكُمُ فِى غيْرِكُمْ مَسْروقُ

Whatever I have borrowed from the ancient [poets
to say] about you (pl.), it was not because of an arm too weak for *madīḥ*,

Rather, they attributed your glory wrongfully to someone
other than you, so I returned your right to you – that is deserved.

Praise is not borrowed for you from others,
but it is borrowed for others from you.

(L1306: 16–18)[80]

Three encomia are left without a dedication for different reasons. In L1250' a pronouncement of the poet's gratitude and affection (176–83) in lieu of a dedication, mentioning his own labor, gives it the flair of a spontaneous response to kindness. In L191 and L1041 the poet calls in his dues and complains of neglect. The praises both encomia contain are mixed with unequivocal requests. To offer these poems formally would weaken their challenge; instead, the poet points to the fulfillment of his own duties in his earlier praises. In the more moderate request of the two, L191, this fulfillment includes the longevity of his past praise (175), his loyalty (129, 152–4, 172–4) and his continuing endorsement of his earlier praise:

وإنْ جاوَزْتُ مَدْحَكَ لمْ يَزَلْ بِى　　تَكَذُّبِىَ المدائحَ واجْتلابِى
مَتى أَجِدُ المدائحَ ليْت شِعرِى　　تُواتِى فِى سِواك دونَ كِذابِ

Even if I relinquish [my] praising you, the forging of false praises
and demanding [favors from other patrons] does not stop for me.

If I only knew when I will ever find [my] praises
fitting people other than you without lying?

(L191: 155–6)[81]

In the more forceful request L1042, friendship still urges the poet to warn his patron (66–7), but his trust is shaken:

أَيَظلِمُنِى مَن ليْسَ فى الأَرْضِ غيْرَه　　إذا نيصَ مِن ظُلْمٍ مَناصٌ لنائِصِ

Does he mistreat me, other than whom there is no refuge on this earth
for a refugee, when seeking refuge from injustice?[82]

(L1042: 68)

The group of phrases interspersing antistrophe and metastrophe points to the poem's historical context: through them the poet's persona *interacts* with the patron, that is, he performs acts and adopts attitudes that relate the patron's acts to his own in co-operation or as reciprocal obligation. Meanwhile, the phrases are not predictable formulae; rather, they respond to every poem's specific situation. The omission of the dedicatory phrase in the requests L191 and L1042 has the far-reaching implication of the praise remaining incomplete, which tarnishes the poems' celebratory force. In this way, the poet reprimands the patron indirectly for what he perceives as unjust neglect. Hence the phrases both reflect and affect their addressee and the surrounding conditions. Considering them in the light of speech act theory elucidates their specific *modus operandi*. Ibn al-Rūmī's five types of phrases fit the conditions of direct speech acts:[83]

The *naming* does not in itself constitute a direct act of speech, but it identifies the persona of the patron with the historical dedicatee who witnesses his *qaṣīda*'s première. He is further referred to as 'he' and 'you' in the antistrophe and metastrophe. The naming binds him to all the obligations, implied or explicitly pronounced, that the acceptance of Ibn al-Rūmī's praises entails.

The *intention to praise* is simultaneously a declarative and expressive speech act, for the poet announces his praise and his readiness to undertake it. The fact that this phrase is often replaced by indirect formulations, such as the poet's addressing himself or remaining impersonal, does not void the intention, which is implicit in a praise poem's very composition.

Invocations and *felicitations* are similarly expressive speech acts. They refer to and express the speaker's emotions towards the addressee. The sincerity of the poet's utterance is a condition of their validity.[84] *Advice* counts as a directive speech act, enjoining the addressee to do something. It also implies the speaker's intention. Advice, invocation, and felicitation all presuppose the belief of the speaker in the benefit of what they intend for the addressee.

The sending of a *message* appears as a directive speech act; however the messengers themselves never take shape or interact with the poet. Rather, the phrase introduces an issue of consequence for the addressee (L191) or specifies an addressee other than the primary recipient of a poem (L1611).

The dedication in the form of *manaḥtukahā* is a declarative speech act (or performative), for the poet refers to the act, and accomplishes it at the same time. It closely connects the speaker, the recipient and the poem offered in a single word.

Four of the phrases, in their explicit form, can then be identified with direct acts of speech and as such presuppose the speaker's authority as a praise poet. Within a poem, that authority is every time reasserted through the artful, difficult and often lengthy strophe. Among the phrases, the declaration of intention and dedication stand out because of their performative self-reflexive character. This signifies for the agents involved that the 'I', contained in the performative utterance, *identifies* the person who pronounces and executes it as the praising poet, and the 'you' as the historical addressee previously named. At the moment of recitation, the personal pronouns 'I' and 'you' provide an empty space for the historical poet (or his *rāwī*) and the patron to step into their literary portrayals and to act out the presentation and acceptance of the poem. This vital role of the first (and second) person pronoun has been demonstrated by Émile Benveniste. Seeing a fundamental difference between two kinds of pronouns in speech, he distinguishes between the first and second grammatical person as true 'persons' and the third as 'non-person', excluded from the intersubjectivity of language:

> *I swear* is a form with a singular value in that it places the reality of the oath onto him who utters *I*. This utterance is the *fulfillment* of an act [*accomplissement*, author's emphasis]: 'to swear' consists precisely of uttering *I swear*, by which the ego is bound. The utterance *I swear* is the very act engaging me, not the description of the act I accomplish.... The consequences (social, judicial, etc.) of my oath, or my promise, ensue from the moment of speech containing *I swear*, *I promise*.... This condition is not given in the meaning of the verb; rather the 'subjectivity' of speech makes it possible. One will see the difference by replacing *I swear* with *he swears*. Whereas *I swear* is a commitment, *he swears* is only a description on the same level as *he runs*, *he smokes* .... Many notions in linguistics, perhaps even in psychology, will appear in another light once one re-establishes them within the framework of speech, that is, language as assumed by a speaking human being, and in the condition of *intersubjectivity*, which alone makes linguistic communication possible.[85]

Interestingly enough Benveniste credits the medieval Arabic grammatical tradition with recognizing this difference.[86] The first and second pronouns of the performatives then emerge as those points at which the *qaṣīda* is grounded in the real world. Accordingly, the poet does not perform speech acts in the strophe, where he plays a fictional hero; performatives occur only in those strophes that are devoted to the two main actors in the exchange. The intention to praise opens the antistrophe containing the patron's catalogue of virtuous acts and attributes; the dedication dominates the metastrophe, which discusses and renews all reciprocal obligations between him and his poet. Both performatives restate succinctly what their surrounding strophes convey in longer illustrative or indirect ways. The dedication represents the more stable one of the two performatives, and it is tied with such dramatic ingenuity into the metastrophe, that it accomplishes more than most proponents of speech act theory would have it. To test its efficacy, one can, like Stanley Fish,[87] adapt John Searle's constituting rules. The dedication's propositional content is the offering of the *qaṣīda*. For a preparatory condition the *qaṣīda* should honor the addressee and be worthy of him. Here belong the vaunting descriptions of the poem accompanying the dedication. As a condition of sincerity, the poet should be truly convinced of the *qaṣīda*'s worthiness for the patron. The claim for sincerity and truth is indeed made in conjunction with the dedication. Essentially, the dedication counts as the poet's offering of the *qaṣīda* to the patron as something that honors and benefits him. So far, Searle's constituting rules are fulfilled in the dedication for those poems containing the full dedication phrase *manaḥtukahā*. The poem is the gift offered with the dedication and, as such, part of a reciprocal exchange. It may take the initiative as a first gift, expecting a counter-gift in the sense of *do ut des*, or respond to a previous favor.[88] As a result the *unilateral performative* of dedicating locks into a *chain of reciprocal acts*. However,

Searle's rules cannot cover all the aspects mentioned in the verses around the dedication, for instance, the poet's offered friendship, steadfastness, and loyalty have no place in his speech act model.

And what about the patron's worthiness and his contribution to the praise, mentioned in the dedications of L994 and L1611? Searle's model accounts even less for the behavior of the addressee as part of a speech act. All the same, Ibn al-Rūmī's encomia make the acts and attributes of the patron part of the act of dedication. The addressee gives the praise substance and makes it consistent with the truth.[89] That necessitates a sincerity condition different from Searle's, which is already fulfilled when only the *speaker's* word and act coincide. In some of Ibn al-Rūmī's dedications, however, sincerity is reached only when the speaking poet's word coincides with the act of the *addressed patron*. In one particular case, the poet proposes future acts which the patron must 'ratify'. As a consequence, the truth value of the praise depends on the patron, and by failing to conform to his portrayal, he belies it. The meaning of the praise is thus not stable and immutable, but preserves or loses its truth-value in accordance with the behavior of the addressee. Dedications of this kind do not fully transfer a panegyric to the patron, but propose it to him on conditional terms. The dedication presupposes, then, the patron's *co-operation* with the poet.

Ibn al-Rūmī's dedication has proved to be a two-faced coin, on the one hand, a gift and, on the other, an obligation with specific stipulations. It relates the poem it concludes, in some way or other, to the long-term relationship between the poet and his patron. This chapter has isolated such features as directly enter into the speech act of the dedication. But other strategies of poetic speech appear throughout the metastrophes of *qaṣāʾid* and poems of admonition, where the illocutionary force of single performatives is orchestrated with the dramaturgy of long passages. Both at the micro and macro levels, the poet tries to pre-empt the patron's reaction to his poem and to control its final interpretation with his means of poetic speech. In this, he explicitly formulates the procedure of praising and discusses the power of his word: he formally declares his own fulfillment of his role of enunciating praise and spells out how it should be received, accepted, rewarded, and remembered – leaving nothing to chance (or to the patron's imagination). In sum, the poet advocates a whole model of patronage down to every detail. As a result one can extract from Ibn al-Rūmī's poems his concept of poetic speech as action and persuasion and the underlying ethics of poetic patronage.

Recalling the double nature of the performative, Ibn al-Rūmī not only portrays and attests to the patronage, he also partakes of it and prescribes its future, all within the same event of speech. The fact that the poems try so explicitly to shape the reciprocal relationship (between panegyrist and patron) and stipulate its conditions, is remarkable and may betray a prudence arising from the historical situation. The result at any rate is a novel dramatis persona and altered reincarnation of the pre-Islamic poet as hero: the ideal (and idealizing) panegyrist of Abbasid society.[90]

Direct speech, however, is not restricted to the interaction between the personae of poet and patron, but pervades the entire encomium, characterizing speakers as personae, building dramatic tensions between them, and imbuing the imagery with a fantastic dimension. Moreover, speech is intimately intertwined with ethics at many levels. Part 2 is devoted to the different levels of speech and the dramatis personae, Part 3, to dramatic scenes and their combination, and Part 4, to poetic figures and imagery. The composition of all these elements into an ethics of patronage forms the subject of the book's last part.

Part II

SPEECH AND CHARACTERIZATION

6

SPEECH AS ACTION

The multifarious uses of speech pervading Ibn al-Rūmī's panegyrics strike the seasoned reader of *madīḥ* as unfamiliar. Ibn al-Rūmī deftly dramatizes himself and other personae. Similar to an action on stage, the direct speech of his and other dramatis personae creates scenes of dialogue whose key utterances are underscored by imagery. Scenes assemble in a larger dramaturgy, whose elements are conventional, yet novel in their composition. The speech of these dramatic scenes has two functions: first, it symbolizes feelings and actions to the point that monologue and dialogue no longer merely describe and accompany action, but rather they contain it. Second, utterances (and the acts they perform) characterize the dramatis personae. Such scenes of verbal action are counter-balanced by purely descriptive passages. But even there, speech may occur through the personification or fantastic reinterpretation of inanimate objects and abstract concepts. To the poet's mind, these things and ideas speak figuratively, on an abstract level of fantastic action. In this way, Ibn al-Rūmī creates drama even in mute static scenes. These functions of speech expand the limited realm of the performative as identified in the direct phrases of praise.

Three basic types of verbal action occur, which are briefly sketched before delving into detail. First, the poet's persona soliloquizes in self-contained passages, or encounters other personae with whom he converses. As in a drama, all action occurs through the exchange of words, speech being the sole vehicle of interaction. Simultaneously, the speech alludes to the larger course of action and sketches the characters of its speakers. For instance, the hero of the theme of aging (*al-shayb wa-l-shabāb*) begs women farewell with the following words:

هيْهاتَ أيَّتها الكواعبُ كالدُّمَى   ما لِى بكنَّ مع المَشيبِ صديقُ
منِّى عليكنَّ السَّلامُ تحيَّةً   إنَّ الشَّبابَ هراقَهُ مُهريقُ
لمْ تجمَعِ الأيّامُ شَمْلَ أَحِبَّةٍ   إلّا وشرْطُ صُروفِها التَّفْريقُ

How far [are you], O full-breasted ones like statuettes! With my hoariness I do not have a [single] friend among you.

Peace be upon you from me as a greeting!
For someone has poured away [my] youth.

The days have not reunited lovers, without separation
being the condition of their vicissitudes.

(L1306: 5–7)

The poet bids the women farewell, explaining his surrender with the certainty that fate puts an end to all love. The act of greeting performs the poet's mental reconciliation with old age, signalling his acceptance of it. But the greeting also traces the course of events of which this utterance forms the turning-point. The farewell follows upon the passage of youth (*shabāb*, 6) and lovers' encounter (*shamlu aḥibbatin*, 7), and it proudly forestalls the women's own scornful desertion of the poet, as seen for example in the quote after the next. Moreover, the speech characterizes the still-vigorous, lucid mind inhabiting the poet's decaying body.

Second, acts and circumstances can 'speak' for themselves in a figurative way. This occurs when speech is attributed to inanimate objects or abstract concepts by means of a trope, such as metaphor, metonymy, etiology or causal hyperbole, which usually entails the personification of the 'speaking' object or concept. For instance, when the hair on the poet's head begins to turn white (*shayb*), he addresses it as a bearer of good tidings:

أَلسْتَ مُبشِّرِى فى كلِّ يومٍ   بوَشْكِ تَرحُّلِى إثْرَ الشَّبابِ؟
لقدْ بَشَّرْتَنى بِلَحاقِ ماضٍ   أَحَبَّ إلىَّ مِن بَرْدِ الشَّرابِ

Do you not bring me daily the good tidings
of my swift departure in the wake of youth?

You brought me the news of my catching up
with a past dearer to me than the coolness of drink!

(L191: 10–11).

The poet sees in the appearance of hoariness an announcement of death. By his question he personifies the white hair (10) and puts its meaning – the advent of old age – into words. In the following line (11), he reverses that meaning from a death message to a joyful reunion with youth. The silent process of graying has become an audible debate between the aging man and (a part of) his body. Again, the larger course of action is traced: youth (*shabāb*) has been forced to depart, and death awaits the poet. His debate with white hair characterizes him as someone who grapples with approaching death and tries to outwit the course of time.

Third, verbal acts such as wishing and promising are themselves figuratively reinterpreted. For instance, a wish may be personified as a supplicant seeking refuge with the one to whom it was addressed. The granting of protection to the refugee being a moral obligation, a mock analogy with it makes the fulfillment of the wish equally imperative. Ibn al-Rūmī chooses this device frequently to reinterpret unilateral commitments as mutual obligations. These three types of verbal action will be illustrated in the remainder of this chapter, and the following chapter will show how they characterize fictive and historical personae.

Speech of humans

Human speakers appear either as quoted directly or paraphrased in the answer of the poet's persona.[1] A paraphrased statement is often condensed or even collapsed into a single apostrophe, such as, '[O] my accuser!' (*ʿādhilatī*). However brief, the direct phrase indicates a previous criticism by the addressed woman of the poet's behavior, yet the poet records only that part of the dialogue in which he responds to the charge. The conventions observed in the portrayal of most human figures populating the strophe allow such dramaturgic economy. In most examples, the women's quoted mocking of the poet as 'uncle' replaces their entire speech. The poet allots more space to his own scornful reaction:

جارتِى إنْ أَكُنْ كبِرتُ وأَوْدَى بعُرامِى اتِّقاءُ غِبِّ الأَثامِ
ودَعَتْنى النِّساءُ عماً وقدْ كنْـ ـتُ لديْهِنَّ من بنِى الأَعْمامِ
فلقدْ أَغْتدِى يُفيِّؤُ غُصْنِى خُيَلاءُ الشَّبابِ حىَّ العُرامِ

My neighbor (f.), if I have aged, and [if] fear
of final punishment has killed my verve,

And [if] the women have called me 'paternal uncle,' although I had been to them [one] of the paternal cousins,[2]

I did often go out early, with youthful vanity
shading my branch, as verve itself.

(L1250': 63–5)

In this very conventional theme of the poet and the female neighbor (*jāra*), the latter's blaming of the poet's immoral behavior is understood by convention and omitted. The encounter is represented only by the poet's response, which begins with a conditional clause. In the protasis (63–4), he admits his present fear of sin; in the apodosis, he boasts of his making light of sin when he was still young. The boasted youthful appearance takes the metaphor of a pliable verdant bough. The bough is then reified and extended to the shade protecting it, which corresponds on the level of reality to the vanity that accompanies youth.[3] The poet's encounter with the neighbor also recalls his earlier ones with women (*al-nisāʾ*). When he quotes their present mocking of him as 'paternal uncle'

(*ʿamm*) at the end of the protasis, he refers to a previous time when his position was rather that of a paternal cousin (*ibn al-ʿamm*), typically an ideal consort. The quote encapsulates the poet's past in its contrasting present. In responding to the neighbor, the poet also speaks to the women, justifying himself both to present and absent personae.

Here and in other examples, the speech of fictional personae produces the poet's reaction; less frequently, his speech prompts theirs.[4] Speech represents action: by insulting him, the women spurn the poet. Speech, condensed into the poet's response, furthermore epitomizes his physical encounter with his neighbor. The dimension of time and an (ever so sketchy) plot sequence is added by the poet's recalling in his retort the women's earlier rejection of him.

Most encounters are restricted to one persona's statement and the poet's response. A more complex encounter takes places between the poet's persona and 'a friend' in seven turns of moral argument. In each exchange of statement and response, the friend is paraphrased as slightly modifying his attitude to be contradicted every time anew by the poet's persona.[5]

In the above encounters, speech is the main vehicle of action. This can be supplemented or replaced by a persona's non-verbal gestures, such as a woman's laughing, averting her eyes, or observing the poet, which indicate attitudes and warrant responses.[6] Such is the case of the 'laughing one' (*ḍāḥik*):

وضاحكٍ ساءَنِى بضحْكتِهِ وقدْ عَلَتْنِى مِن البِلَى نُقَبُهْ

أبكانِىَ الشَّيبُ حين أَضْحَكَهُ حتَّى جرى الدَّمعُ واكِفًا سَرَبُهْ

لا بلْ أَسًى إذْ بدا ففجَّعَنِى بمَلَثَمٍ مِنه راقِنِى شَنَبُهْ

عَلَّلْتُ خدَّىَّ بالدُّموعِ له إذْ فاتَنِى أَن يَعَلَّنِى ثَغَبُهْ

[I recall] a laughing one, whose laughter hurt me,
after the scab of decay had covered me.

Hoariness made me weep, when it made him[7] laugh,
until tears came forth in steady flow.

No, rather [it was] sadness [that made me weep],
when he appeared and hurt me
with lips of his whose sparkling teeth I loved.[8]

I soaked my cheeks with tears for him,
since his clear puddle no longer quenched my thirst.

(L215: 9–12).

The poet's beloved here of the male gender, laughs about the poet's white hair, while the poet weeps about it; both reactions seem caused by white hair. But then, the poet connects the two acts: he ascribes his weeping directly to the beloved's cruel mockery (11) and his refusal to kiss him (12). It is because of this rejection, and not his graying hair, that the poet sheds tears. The sad turn in the once fulfilled relationship is sketched in the actions of the beloved's mouth, literally 'place of kissing', which used to be a satiating 'clear puddle' (i.e. its saliva), and whose formerly adored 'sparkling teeth' are bared now in cold laughter.

In encounters with humans, the poet follows conventional themes. By means of speech or non-verbal gestures, he establishes a plot between himself and another persona. In that, he takes a position either by resisting or submitting to the stance of his counterpart. Although only a single encounter is sketched, flashbacks to former ones establish a temporal sequence.

Speech figuratively attributed to inanimate objects and abstract concepts

Animals and inanimate objects may also convey meaning through various ways. Only in a few instances are they quoted verbatim, e.g. a camel and a spear.[9] More often, their speaking is a metaphor for acts or circumstances that are apparent in themselves. Such are the parcels carried by a group of supplicants who have just departed from the patron:

وينْصَرِفُ العافونَ تُثنِى عِيابُهم   عليْكَ ولمْ يَنبِسْ مِنَ القوْمِ نابِسُ

The supplicants depart with their bags praising you,
though none of the people has breathed a [single] word.

(L994: 109)

The bags filled with presents from the patron display his generosity. The supplicants need not be asked for the result of the patron's generous act; the filled bags give a more direct and truthful testimony than any human tongue. The bags' physically attesting to the patron's praiseworthy act is then cast into the metaphor of their 'praising' him. The patron's eloquent sayings similarly leave their own traces:

هو المُرْسِلُ الأمْثالَ فى كلِّ منْطِقٍ   يَظَلُّ بماءِ العَيْنِ فِى الخدِّ يُرْسَمُ

He is the one who coins proverbs in every utterance,
constantly painted on the cheek by the water of the eye.

(L1611: 197)

His utterances enrich the language with proverbs and move people to tears. The mere presence of the tears shows the hearers' delight, the metaphor of the tears' 'painting', however, makes them an immediate response to the patron's eloquence. Both the coined proverb and the visible tear thus attest directly to the patron's eloquence without the need for human speech. The patron's acts and words become evident in the effects they have upon inanimate objects.

In the second example, the power of the patron's eloquence has also been exaggerated, for *every* saying of his was described as proverbial. Another way of magnifying the effect of the patron's acts and sayings is the causal hyperbole, which consists of the transfer of a causal framework from image to topic.[10] In the following example, the pungency of musk is transferred to the mention of the patron among people and serves as a mock etiology, explaining why his mention cannot remain hidden:

إذا ما أَسرَّتْ أَنفُسُ القومِ ذِكرَهُ   تبيَّنتَهُ فيهِمْ ولمْ يَتكلَّمُوا
تطَيبُ به أَنفاسُهُ فتُذيعُه   وهلْ سِرُّ مِسْكٍ أُودِعَ الرّيحَ يُكْتَمُ؟

When people's souls (*anfus*) conceal his mention,
you detect it in them without their speaking:

Their breath (*anfāsuhū*) is sweet from it and spreads it.
Can the secret of musk be kept that is entrusted to the wind?[11]
(L1611: 127–8)

People could not conceal mention of the patron, even if they wanted to: their very breath exudes it. The breath's 'proclaiming' of the patron is a simile-based metaphor (*istiʿāra*) in the sense of ʿAbdalqāhir al-Jurjānī (d. 471/1078).[12] It derives from the underlying simile between the topic (the patron's mention) and the image (pungent musk) in their quality of spreading. The pungency of musk is then transferred to the mention of the patron and serves as a mock etiology for why its concealment is impossible.

The causal hyperbole also extends the patron's promise and threat to cosmic proportions.[13] The causal hyperbole belongs to the realm of poetic *takhyīl*, literally 'make-believe', a trend in Abbasid poetry of molding topic and image into diverse imaginary relationships.[14] In other examples, the mention of the patron appears as sweet tasting and sounding, his names and acts as tattooed on women's hands, his praise as branded without pain onto people's foreheads, and his nobility as a visible sign (*sīmā*) on his own forehead.[15] Even on the elapsing days do his acts leave their imprints.[16] In general, causal hyperbolae cast the patron's acts into images that endow the acts with the ability to indicate, spread, and preserve meaning.

What is more, the metaphors of bags that 'praise', tears that 'paint' and sweet breath that 'proclaims' the patron, make objects more powerful carriers of meaning than human dramatis personae. The figurative speech of things bypasses the mediation and interference of human speech, which allows for concealment, falsification, and embellishment. Things speak directly and truly through their mere physical presence. Their speech even overcomes human speech (or silence): if people wanted to conceal (*asarrat*) the patron's mention, their breath would divulge it; if they remained silent about (*lam yanbis… nābisū*) his generosity, their bags would proclaim it. By so attributing speech to objects, Ibn al-Rūmī produces seemingly 'objective' statements. The figurative language of things serves him as a device to let the patron's acts and words speak for themselves. This aspect will be shown below as a crucial ingredient of Ibn al-Rūmī's ethics of patronage.[17]

Though on the surface, the speech of objects may reveal itself as tropes (metaphor and causal hyperbole), it is worth devoting a brief excursus to some fundamental assumptions of medieval Arab scholars about verbal and non-verbal communication. This commonly falls under the heading of philosophical *bayān*, which, unlike poetry, targets the intellect, not the imagination (and which should not be confused with the later *ʿilm al-bayān*, the branch of poetics dealing with imagery). Ibn al-Rūmī's earlier contemporary al-Jāḥiẓ (d. 255/868) understood *bayān* as including the 'indication of meaning' (*dalāla*) by both humans and animals, with humans possessing alone also 'inferential thinking' (*istidlāl*). Human *dalāla* or *bayān* fell into five types: utterance (*lafẓ*), writing (*khaṭṭ*), counting on fingers (*ʿaqd*), gesture (*ishāra*), and posture or attitude (*niṣba*).[18] A century later, al-Rummānī (d. 384/994) subsumed the inanimate world among the producers of a *bayān* that is fourfold, encompassing speech (*kalām*), situation (*ḥāl*), gesture (*ishāra*) and sign (*ʿalāma*). His discussion, however, is limited to the first category.[19] The most in-depth and systematic treatment is the book-length study by Abū al-Ḥusayn Isḥāq b. Ibrāhīm b. Sulaymān b. Wahb al-Kātib (d. *c.* end third/ninth century) according to whom *bayān* occurs in four ways; through the contemplation of things intelligible by their essences (*iʿtibār*), through the persuasion by things coming into the heart when thought and intellect are applied (*iʿtiqād*), through utterance, i.e. the sound of the tongue (*ʿibāra*), and through writing for those distant or still unborn (*kitāb*).[20] Under the first heading falls the 'speaking' of the creation, which reveals itself not in words (*ḥiwāran*) but through the viewer's reflection on it (*iʿtibāran*). 'Even if things themselves are silent, they are speaking through their apparent circumstances.' Isḥāq was not primarily concerned with poetry, but he used the pre-Islamic *aṭlāl* motif (the poet's address of deserted habitations) as a convenient example. 'In this way the Arabs asked the [deserted] abode to speak, addressing the campsite traces and giving themselves the answer for them by way of figurative expression in speech.' After adducing a Koranic verse (Sūrat al-Rūm 30/9) about the earth as bearer of the traces of previous generations, Isḥāq quotes an example of the poetic motif:

يا رَبْعَ بِشرةَ بالجَناب تَكَلَّمِ   وأَبِنْ لنا خَبَرًا ولا تستعجِمِ

ما لِى رأَيتُكَ بعد أَهلِكَ موحِشًا   خَلَقًا كحوْضِ الباقِرِ المُتهدِّمِ؟

O abode of Bishra in Janāb, speak and express clearly
a message to us, and do not stay mute!

How come have I seen you deserted
after [the presence of] your inhabitants,
decayed like a broken watering trough of a cow herd?

The author comments, 'He asked a thing to speak that does not speak with a tongue (sc. the abode), because its situation expressed itself clearly.' A further poetic quote about a speaking mountain receives a similar explanation, 'He answered for a silent thing that does not answer (sc. a mountain) because its situation became obvious to the heart'. Isḥāq's discussion also makes clear that the so-called *bayān* of things in themselves really manifests itself within the consciousness of the receptive observer or investigator. He explicitly states, 'Only to him who considers them do these things express meaning and to him who seeks clarity do they impart it.'[21] In sum, Isḥāq's argument supplies the underlying reasoning of a poet who derives meaning from traces. But from the moment the poet verbalizes his silent perception, it becomes figurative poetic speech (*istiʿāra*).[22] As it is poetry I am concerned with here, I discuss the figurative speech of inanimate objects in poetic terminology. Still, the *bayān* theory helps one to understand how the figurative speech of objects in Ibn al-Rūmī's encomia can conflict with real human speech and rival it as the more direct and truthful way of stating meaning.

Sometimes the patron's acts and words even dispense with the silent testimony of things (bags, tears, human breath) and either 'speak' themselves or govern human (poetic) speech. Their own speaking is rare. It occurs only once in a verse about the governorship to which ʿUbaydallāh was reappointed as a deputy by ʿAmr b. Layth.[23] In the quoted verse, the governor's renewed bond with his subjects is personified and vows its own permanence to God:

وأثْبَتَ للأمْرِ الّذِى يستديمهُ أَواخِيَّ صِدْقٍ أقْسَمَتْ لا تَجَذَّمُ

For a matter he wanted to perdure he fixed sincere ties
that vowed they will not break.

(L1611: 153)

The figurative vowing of the rulership ties is a purely fictive action without counterpart on the topical level and belongs to the realm of poetic *takhyīl*. In the Būyid period, the public vow was a common way for a ruler to commit himself to a task. He pledged something to God with his subjects as a benefitting third party.[24] Here, the ruler's tie with his subjects borrows the legally-binding vow as a metaphor, based on reliability as the point of similarity. The vowing image then claims for ʿUbaydallāh's renewed governorship the validity of a solemn public commitment. Poetically speaking, it is a causal hyperbole for ʿUbaydallāh's reliability.

More often, qualities of the patron do not borrow but only govern human speech – again by causal hyperbole. His name passes decisions; his generosity causes the deaf to hear and the dumb to recite poetry; his glorious acts magically weave their own praise.[25] This glory can even reverse time and literary ownership. The Ṭāhirid glory, for instance, claims for itself praises dedicated by ancient poets to their bygone patrons, because those praises fit the Ṭāhirids better than their original addressees:

مهْما سَرَقْتُ عنِ الأَوائِلِ فيكُمُ   فَلِغيرِ باعٍ بالمديحِ يَضيقُ
لكنّهُمْ نحلوا سِواكُمْ مجْدَكُمْ   فرددْتُ حقّكُمُ وذاكَ حَقيقُ
ما المدْحُ مسروقٌ لكُمْ مِن غيْرِكُمْ   بل منْكُمُ فى غيْرِكُمْ مَسْروقُ

Whatever I have borrowed from the ancient [poets to say] about you (pl.), it was not because of an arm too weak for *madīḥ*,

Rather, they attributed your glory wrongfully to someone other than you, so I returned your right to you – that is deserved.

Praise is not borrowed for you from others, but it is borrowed for others from you.

(L1306: 16–18)

The supremacy of Ṭāhirid glory over all other glory is clothed in the image of the right to own all praise poetry. With a causal hyperbole, the concept of ownership (of praise poetry) is transferred onto the supremacy in praiseworthy glory. As a result, sublime glory becomes a legal title to all praise poetry, past and present. Such 'rightful' borrowing was more common among famous poets who took verses from their predecessors, claiming they were more deserving of them. This is formulated in the concept of *istiḥqāq*, according to which the best formulation (*lafẓ*) of a subject (*maʿnā*) conveys the ownership of it.[26] Ibn al-Rūmī's argument inverts the concept of *istiḥqāq*; it is the excellent subject who deserves the best verbal expression. In terms of *madīḥ*, the patrons themselves create with their glory the basis for their claim to praise, which the poet merely executes. This causal hyperbole reverses the course of history, portraying the ancient poets as thieves, whereas Ibn al-Rūmī's persona restores the stolen poetic good to its rightful owners. Moreover, this rhetorical figure ties acts and attributes of the patron directly to their traces in the world. Their causal relationship can be further heightened with an inverted hyperbole, i.e. one that exaggerates the importance of acts for speech through a feigned inversion of cause and effect. The personified speech now ostensibly selects the acts for itself, or alternatively, comes to the acts on its own accord. In addition to speech, personifications of poetry, its rhymes or motifs, accord the patron their exclusive allegiance.

أَلا رُبَّ قولٍ فيه أَمكنَ قائلاً   ولوْ رامَهُ فى غَيرِهِ ظَلَّ يكعَمُ
تَفورُ ينابيعُ القَريضِ بمدْحِهِ   إذا جَعَلَتْ فى آخرين تَسدَّمُ
أَطاعتْ معانِى الشّعرِ فيه وأَصْبَحَتْ   قوافيه حتَّى قيلَ لِى أَنْتَ مُلهَمُ

Many a speech about him empowered a speaker,
and if he had intended it about someone else,
he (sc. the speaker) would have stayed muzzled.

The springs of well-wrought poetry are brimming with his praise,
while they begin to dry up [if attributed] to others.

The motifs of poetry about him obey [me],
the rhymes become such that one says to me,
'You receive divine inspiration!'

(L1611: 252–4)

In parallel inverted hyperbolae, the personified poetry refuses itself to any subject but ʿUbaydallāh (252), and only about him, poetry gushes forth like a divine inspiration (254). In further images for poetry, springs flow for him (253), wild oryx are tamed by him, and thirsty camels race toward him. All of these express the poetry's dependence upon the patron and his sole worthiness of being its subject.[27] Elsewhere, the very rhymes summon the poet to dedicate them to the patron.[28] Poetry seems to be dictated by its subject and beyond its author's control.

In sum, the patron's acts (and sayings) figuratively 'speak' in two ways. First, they leave their imprint on inanimate objects that carry meaning, independent of human language or even counteracting human silence. Second, the acts have the power to summon human speech or poetry to express them. Here, acts and the words about them are connected by imported causal frameworks, for instance the concept of praise as an owned asset, or the personification of praise as loyal and obedient servant. In this, the praise poetry follows acts, is magically drawn and wholly devoted to them. With all its fantastically ascribed powers, poetry can only convey that which acts have supplied.

Both kinds of attributed speech relate to acts without any mediation of the poet's persona, but rather by the power of the acts themselves to leave physical traces or attract human speech. The close contact of acts and words operates in the patron's favor, in that he owes his praise poetry only to himself, and not the inventiveness of his panegyrist. But he is equally responsible in the reverse case: lack of praises and telling traces of generosity point to a lack of praiseworthy deeds. This applies, for example, to the omission of praise for generosity in some poems – its absence 'speaks' loudly about the missing generous acts. This interdependence of acts and the poetic speech about them is a cornerstone of Ibn al-Rūmī's ethics of patronage.

In the previously cited verses, all of which belonged to the antistrophe, objects and elements of speech are sporadically personified, yet they never grow into dramatized personae. In contributing to the patron's portrayal they do not choose their utterances, but simply submit to his greater power. They may convey nothing but the affirmation of his excellent acts and attributes, which constitute the predictable message of the antistrophe. Their only alternative option would be silence, refusing the patron their affirmation. In the strophe of the encomia, however, one inanimate object, namely white hair (*shayb*) becomes a full-fledged acting persona. I limit myself here to the speech of *shayb*, leaving the full discussion of its dramatized persona to the following chapter. White hair can impart four distinct messages: it prohibits the sinful acts of youth, it warns and guides the poet towards the straight path of sinlessness, it announces the poet's impending death, and it sarcastically brings the 'good news' of the poet's reunion with youth in his afterlife.[29] In all cases, white hair acts in lieu of old age and not by virtue of any properties of its own.

ولاحَ شيْبي فراعَ قاليَتي   بلْ خُلَّتي بلْ خليلتي شَهَبُهْ
بلْ راعَني أنَّه دَليلُ بِلىً   والعودُ يَذْوِي إذا ذوى هَدَبُهْ

My hoariness appeared and its whitish gray scared my enemy, no, rather my true love, no, my friend.[30]

No, rather its being a sign of decay scared me
– wood withers when its fronds have withered.

(L215: 2–3)

Not the graying of the hair itself but its implications scare the poet; as a metonymy, it foreshadows the decay of his whole body, which causes first the loss of women and passion, then the advent of death and final punishment.[31] In the same poem (10–11), the poet also blames white hair for making him weep, but then reveals the true cause of his tears to be the laughter of his former beloved.[32] The beloved's mockery is not just due to the poet's white hair, but his whole aging process.

One passage pits *shayb*, in the role of a warning sign, against the most formidable divine warning of the Koran.

وكِلا الشَّيْبِ والكتابِ جميعًا   واعِظٌ زاجِرٌ عنِ الآثامِ
غيْرَ أنَّ الكتابَ يُكتَبُ بالأقـ   ـلامِ والشَّيْبُ ليْس بالأقلامِ
بلْ بِرَدْعِ الحوادثِ المصمَئِلّا   تِ ومَرِّ الشُّهورِ والأعوامِ
لنْ ترى مثلَهُ كِتابًا مُبينًا   لا بِشَكْلٍ له ولا إعجامِ
خطَّ غُفْلَ الحروفِ يقرؤه الأُمْـ   ـمِيُّ كالصُّبحِ غيرَ ذي استعجامِ
فيه للقارئيهِ أيُّ نذيرٍ   بِبِلى جِدَّةٍ ووَشْكِ اخْترامِ

Both white hair and [Holy] Book
preach and restrain from sin.

Only the book is written with reed pens,
and the white hair, not with reed pens,

No, rather [the white hair is written] with the staining
of intertwined events and the elapsing of months and years.

You will not see a clear book like it, not even [one]
with vowel signs or diacritical marks.[33]

Written without subdivision, the illiterate reads it
like the [bright] morning without finding difficulty.[34]

What a warning it (sc. white hair) is for its readers
of the decay of youth and sudden death![35]

(L1250': 33–8)

An analogy (*tamthīl*) between white hair, preventing passion and preceding death, and the Koran, warning of sin and punishment after death, forms the basis for the causal hyperbole.[36] In it the Koran's attributes of 'being written' and 'legible' are transferred as metaphors to the hair on the poet's head. The instruments writing the metaphorical warning are not, however, reed pens but the events, and their 'script' is universally intelligible though 'unmarked' by helping vowels and diacritics. The writing material is the recalcitrant sinner himself, who cannot ignore a warning, written onto his very head, in the way he ignored the warning of the Koran. The hyperbole extols white hair as delivering a clearer and more powerful warning than the Koran.

Besides *shayb*, the abstract notions of youth and fate also adopt speech (or silence) in the strophe. Youth, although intensely imagined and implored by the speaking poet's persona, never responds to him.[37] The vicissitudes of fate, however, directly interfere with the poet. For instance, they forbid women to him. Their lasting effect is brought out by the metaphor of writing. They abrogate the poet's youth, and inscribe themselves onto the poet's head as an etiology for the process of graying.[38]

In sum, the capacity of objects and concepts to carry meaning, and the possibility of figuratively attributing speech to them are essential means of style in Ibn al-Rūmī's *madīḥ*. In the antistrophe, most of the objects and concepts are briefly personified without becoming fully *dramatized* personae. Their 'speaking' is a metaphorical or hyperbolic expression for the patron's all-pervasive excellence. Conversely the strophe contains personifications that become true dramatis personae, such as white hair, youth, and fate. White hair engages the poet in particularly dramatic debates. As its speech occurs by figurative attribution, its message is more flexible than the strongly conventional speech of the human personae.

Figurative reinterpretation of verbal acts

Certain verbal acts are extended beyond their literal meaning by reinterpretation. Such is the case of the patron's promise. Its binding force for the patron is, for instance, augmented by comparison with an official pact.[39] Often the meaning of the promise is enlarged to include its own fulfillment *in a single act*. To depict a promise by the patron simultaneously as his fulfillment of it may be counted as a hyperbolic expression of his reliability. Such 'guaranteed promises' are likened to unripe fruit already present in its calyx in hidden form.

وعطايا كَوامنٍ فى المواعيـ ـدِ كُمونَ الثِّمار فى الأكمامِ

[He does not cease with] presents hidden in the promises
like the hiding of fruit in calyxes.

(L1250': 153)

The collapsing of promise and fulfillment into one act changes the essence of the promise from an as yet unfulfilled, unilateral commitment to a completed performance (of a favor). Promise and gift become one. In the same way, a promise not yet executed is a bad gift.[40] But even then, non-fulfillment is not usually envisaged, only delay. The patron's excuse takes on the same metaphors of the pact and the anticipated fulfillment.[41] But verbal acts of one person can also be transferred figuratively to another; utterances of the poet's persona to the patron are reinterpreted as obligations incumbent on the latter. So the poet's request for favors and the patron's granting of them are similarly collapsed into a single act.

يُعَدُّ رجائِى فيكَ مالاً مُحَصَّلاً أُدنَّرُ فى قومِى به وأُدَرْهَمُ

My asking you is counted as riches [already] obtained,
with it I am called among my people
wealthy in both currencies [of gold and silver].

(L1611: 292)

To depict a request as its own granting highlights not only the patron's reliability, but his care for his protégé. The patron's care is still greater when he accords a wish or desire even before it has been formulated.

Both the poet's wish and the patron's promise are analogous in craving fulfillment, but the binding character of the promise is applied figuratively to the non-binding wish in a causal hyperbole:

لا كذِبُ المُنْيَةِ الّتى وَعَدَتْ معْروفَه يُشْتكَى ولا لَعِبُهْ

The wish that promises his favor
is not complained about as a lie or fake.

(L215: 115)[42]

As a result, the poet's secret wish elicits the same guarantee of fulfillment as the patron's formal promise. Elsewhere, two causal hyperbolae, the images of the promise and the search for protection, are combined into a conceit.[43] (Conceit is understood in the narrow sense of a two-step procedure, combining an existing trope with a rhetorical or paralogical figure and resulting in an original idea and a tension between topic and image.)[44] The wishes and desires not only promise their own fulfillment but are also personified as supplicants, seeking refuge with the personification of the patron's generosity.[45]

لِتَعُذْ بسَيْبِكُم المطامعُ والمُنَى   فعليْكُمُ لِعداتِها التَّصْديقُ

May the desires and wishes find refuge with your (pl.) downpour,
for you are obliged to prove their promises true.

(L1306: 14)

In the verse's second image, the wishes, posing as promises, impose fulfillment on the patron, as has already been seen. Their fulfillment by someone who honors his promises is (literally) taken for granted. The first image, however, adds a precondition; the personified wishes must first gain the protection of the patron's generosity. Logically, the first appeal must be granted before the second one can proceed; without this access no favorable reception can ensue. This prior appeal targets only one aspect of the patron, the personification of his generosity, whereas the subsequent, confident appeal evokes the patron's reliability. Here Ibn al-Rūmī's genius has parts of the patron intercede with his very self, and both aspects – generosity and reliability – belong to the iconology of the ideal patron.

In the discussed examples, single verbal acts are reinterpreted as mutual commitments between a benefactor and his protégé. Hopes, wishes, desires, and requests of the poet are depicted as promises, pacts, and protection granted by the patron. The unilateral acts become figurative mutual commitments. Particularly the patron's promise is extended in two directions. On the one hand, the promise hyperbolically includes its fulfillment; on the other, it comprises the poet's hopes and desires as of yet unpronounced. This extension of the promise is based on the image of the patron as a protector, deserving trust and honoring obligations.

Ibn al-Rūmī has been shown to use real and figuratively-attributed speech to build dramatic scenes and *madīḥ* episodes as well as to implement ethical principles. Such speech covers a broad spectrum: first, the real speech of humans, quoted or paraphrased; second, imaginary speech attributed to inanimate objects and abstract notions, by use of metaphor, metonymy, causal hyperbole, and personification; and finally, certain verbal acts, such as the wish and the promise, that are reinterpreted as part of a reciprocal relationship between the personae of poet and patron.

Dramatization is mostly restricted to human personae as well as white hair, fate and youth, all of which occur in the strophe. Their speech supplies the argument, and they become actors, with imagery playing a minor role.[46] Human speakers differ from the others in that the poet builds on pre-Islamic conventions. In inanimate objects and abstract notions, he can attribute dramatic speech more freely, as will be shown in more detail in the characterization of white hair in the following chapter.

The speaking objects and notions of the antistrophe are only fleeting personifications, tied to a metaphor or conceit within a single verse, such as the wishes in the guise of refugees. The speech of objects and notions occurs either by metaphor, such as the 'vowing' of the ties of rulership, by causal hyperbole, such as the 'proclaiming' of breath, or by mock etiology, such as the patron's glory 'weaving' its own praise. This speaking largely falls within the realm of fantastic imagery (*takhyīl*), a feature of the *muḥdath* style contemporary with Ibn al-Rūmī which offered him a wide range of metaphoric association. He skillfully uses *takhyīl* to establish two relationships: that between the patron and the poetry about him and that between the patron and himself. In the first, the patron is given an active part in the praise about him, through the direct connection of his acts to poetic speech. In the second, the poet connects his own demands to the duties of the patron, locking him into a mutual relationship with shared responsibilities.

7
THE DRAMATIS PERSONAE

Humans as well as inanimate objects and abstract notions gifted with some form of speech have been referred to in the preceding chapter as personifications. These do not, however, grow into dramatized characters. Rather, human action is ascribed to them only through figures of speech, which rarely exceed a single verse. But another group of speaking and acting characters, both human and non-human, populates the poetry. They distinguish themselves from the first kind by being true dramatis personae who confront the poet and involve him in debates.

The different personae are related to specific themes within the praise *qaṣīda* and vary in their development and the range of speech they command. Most human personae are fictional types, derived from ancient motifs, but some have historical counterparts, such as the addressee ʿUbaydallāh b. ʿAbdallāh b. Ṭāhir, his ancestors the Banū Ṭāhir or Banū Zurayq, and ʿUbaydallāh's temporary overlord the Ṣaffārid condottiere ʿAmr b. Layth. Ibn al-Rūmī identifies himself as 'I' in dedicatory statements and, in one admonition, names his Byzantine genealogy (*al-shāʿiru l-rūmiyyu*, A694: 15).

Fictional personae

In *al-shayb wa-l-shabāb*, the most common theme of the strophe, three personae recur – the female accuser, white hair, and youth – to whom the bulk of the discussion is devoted. In the strophe's *nasīb* and *fakhr* themes, personae scarcely appear and even less so in the antistrophe. Their few occurrences are listed at the end of this section.

The accuser

The persona of the accuser, or admonisher (*ʿādhila, ʿādhil*),[1] makes her entrance already in pre-Islamic poetry, and later in Umayyad and Abbasid love and wine poetry, where her objections are usually belittled and disregarded by the poet's persona.[2] In Ibn al-Rūmī's *madīḥ* for ʿUbaydallāh, the poet's persona addresses such a woman in three instances (*ʾa-ʿādhila*, L191: 2; *ʾa-ʿādhilatī*, L1307: 7; and

ʿādhilī L1250': 39[3]), describing her action as blaming and admonishing (*malām*, L1250': 2; *ʿadhl* L1250': 39). She behaves as a most intransigent opponent (*aladda l-khiṣāmi*, L1250': 1), alluding to the stubborn sinner in Sūrat al-Baqara 2/204. Her blame is delivered as a sermon (*khiṭāb*, L1250': 2) that lists the poet's faults (*al-mufannidī*, L1250': 3), namely his passion for women and wine and his intemperate grief for lost youth. Though her truthfulness is not attacked (*fī ṣawābi Ḥaẓāmi*, L1250': 39), the poet ignores her words. In one scene of excessive mourning for lost youth (L1307), he flatly refuses to heed the admonisher's criticism. Instead he vindicates his grief and his anger at fate without allowing her another word.

But the woman not only strives to subdue the poet with words; she wants to actively curb his passionate behavior (*iqtiḍāb*, L191: 2). In this she receives help from the larger forces of fate and time that cause the poet's aging. The poet, however, makes clear to her that she alone would not be his match (*wa-lawlā dhāka aʿyāki qtiḍābī*, ibid.) and that he has succumbed only to white hair (*rāḍanī laki l-shaybu*, ibid.; *aghnāki shaybī ʿan malāmī*, L191: 4). Old age alone compels him to abstain from sin and to repent. Having once adopted his new faultless attitude, the poet now turns around to blame the accuser for continuing her futile tirades. He orders her to stop (*fa-nziʿ ʿani l-ʿadhli*, L1250': 39; *daʿi l-lawma*, L1250': 43), to acknowledge his humiliation gracefully, (*fa-rḍa*, L1250': 40) and to 'wake up', for she embarrasses herself with reprimands without any substance (*fa-lūmī sāmiʿan laki aw afīqī faqad ḥāna ttiʾābuki wa-ttiʾābī*, L191: 3). In the sequence of the plot, the poet meets the accuser only after he has turned hoary and given up what she criticized.[4] Still, the woman persists in the act[5] and despite the poet's appeal never changes her attitude. Beyond evincing blame, she has no function: in order to broach other subjects, the poet turns, for instance, to a female neighbor.

White hair

As a motif white hair (*shayb*)[6] has already appeared within the pre-Islamic *nasīb* and has occasionally replaced it. In Islamic times it becomes one of the strophe's most popular themes. In Ibn al-Rūmī's *madīḥ*, the poet's hair turned white provides one of the two subjects of the *shayb wa-l-shabāb* theme and it often becomes a protagonist. As shown above, the speech of white hair represents by metonymy the effects of age on the poet and his surroundings.[7] The same applies to the actions of white hair; the conduct of certain personae toward the aging poet is metonymically represented as its effect. It follows that the dramatized action of white hair as a persona depends on the other actors involved.

As far as the women are concerned, old age repulses them. Their withholding of love, figuratively the failure of the poet's 'hunting' or 'quenching of his thirst', becomes the action of white hair. It stands for any impact of the poet's age on the women: it masks the poet (L1307: 1–2; L1250': 4), makes him a laughing stock (L215: 9, L1250': 64) or a scarecrow (L1307: 2, 5).[8] It further obstructs his friendship with women (L1306: 5; L1611: 4; L1250': 8) and causes his separation from his beloved (L215: 17). It literally forbids the poet to pursue passionate love at all, calls him back (191: 7), warns, and guides him.[9] To obey the summon of white hair is hard for the poet who has not lost his passion (L191: 1). The hair's white color itself, in the simile 'like white [stalks of the] *thaghām* plant' (*mithla l-thaghāmi, shabīhi l-thaghāmi*, L1250': 1, 26)[10] and the death message in the 'scab of death' (*mina l-bilā nuqabuh*, L215: 9) play minor roles here, since they do not affect the women. They do, however, appear as apparent causes of phenomena that are subsequently explained by the women's behavior.[11]

In conjunction with the accuser and the spy (*raqīb*, L215: 15–16), old age prevents sinful behavior. This reforming effect is metonymically attributed to white hair, which becomes the female accuser's ally (*ẓahīr*, L1250': 2) or, figuratively, a bridle (*lijām*, L1250': 3) or nose-rein (*khiṭām*, L1250': 46) for her to restrain the poet. To the spy, white hair brings restful sleep. The authority of white hair is greater than that of the human personae and spares them their efforts. But white hair does not act independently; it is a mere consequence of fate (*dahr*), time (*zamān*, L215: 15–16), elapsing nights (*al-layālī*, L1611: 4), or events (*ḥawādith*, L1250': 35). Whenever it appears side-by-side with other personae, white hair is one-dimensional, a metonymy of old age and its conditions.

As a sign of death, however, white hair encounters the poet alone and its actions become less predictable. In one monologue (L1250': 1–38), it appears and denies certain things to the poet (*ḥarumat bi-l-mashībi ashyāʾu*, 12–14), which were not allowed, but concerning which the poet boldly defied God and the scripture before (*waʿaẓa llāhu wa-l-kitābu fa-ṣammamtu wa-aqdamtu*, 16–17). His present repentance, his abstaining from sin, and his awe are due to white hair, not to God (*tanāhaytu muʿẓiman li-mashībī*, 19–21). Waking up to the misguided nature of his devotion to white hair (*ayyu ʿudhrin li-tāʾibin lā ilā llāhi*, 22–28) the poet fears he has committed an act of heresy. Gradually however, he recognizes white hair as a God-sent sign and not God's rival:

راعَنِى بالمشيبِ عَمَّا نَهَى عنْـ　　ـهُ بآىِ الكتابِ ذِى الإحْكامِ
كمْ بدا فِى الكِتابِ لِى مِنْ ضِياءٍ　　كان مِنْ قبْلُ دونهُ كالقَتامِ
هَتَكَ الشَّيْبُ ذلك السِّتْرَ لِى عنْـ　　ـهُ فزالَ العَمَى وراحَ التَّعامِى

He (sc. God) scared me by white hair from
what he had forbidden [before]
by the well-established signs of the Book.

How much light appeared to me in the Book,
which had before been like darkness without it.

The white hair tore away for me that curtain from it (sc. the Koran), so
that blindness ceased and feigned blindness subsided.

(L1250': 30–2)

In the subsequent passage, white hair and the holy book are compared in their manners of warning, and white hair emerges as the more powerful of the two. It scares the poet, uncovers his blindness and reaches even the illiterate (33–8).[12] The reforming role of white hair, already seen in conjunction with the women, the accuser, and the spy, is now elevated to a religious level. White hair acquires an ontological significance and stands on a par with the Koran as a bearer of a divine message. The initial misguided portrayal of white hair as a heathen idol underscores by contrast its true interpretation as a symbol of Islam.

White hair announcing death is reinterpreted most originally in *qaṣīda* L191. The poet speaks to it in a passage quoted in its entirety:

وقلْتُ مُسَلِّمًا للشَّيْبِ أَهلاً   بِهادِى المُخطِئينَ إلى الصَّوابِ
أَلستَ مبشِّرِى فِى كُلِّ يَوْمٍ   بوشْكِ تَرَحُّلِى إثْرَ الشَّبابِ؟
لقدْ بشَّرْتَنِى بلَحاقِ ماضٍ   أَحبَّ إلىَّ من بَرْدِ الشَّرابِ
فلستُ مُسَمِّيًا بُشراكَ نَعْيًا   وإنْ أَوْعَدْتَ نفسِى بالذَّهابِ
لكَ البُشرَى وما بُشراكَ عِندِى   سِوى ترقيعِ وهْيِكَ بالخِضابِ
وأَنتَ وإنْ فتكْتَ بِحِبِّ نفسِى   وصاحبِ لَذَّتِى دونَ الصِّحابِ
فقد أَعْتَبْتَنِى وأَمَتَّ حِقْدِى   بحَثِّك خَلْفَه عَجِلاً رِكابِى
إذا أَلحَقْتَنِى بشَقيقِ عَيْشِى   فقدْ وَفَّيْتَنِى فيه ثوابِى
وحَسْبِى مِن ثوابِى فيه أَنِّى   وإيّاه نَؤوبُ إلى مَآبِ
لعمْرُكَ ما الحياةُ لِكلِّ حَىٍّ   إذا فَقَدَ الشَّبابَ سِوى عَذابِ
فَقُلْ لبَناتِ دهْرِى فلْتُصِبْنِى   إذا ولَّى بأَسهُمِها الصِّيابِ

I said greeting hoariness, ‘Welcome,
you guide of the erring towards the truth!

Do you not bring me daily the good tidings
of my swift departure in the wake of youth?

You brought me the news of my catching up
with a past dearer to me than the coolness of drink.

I do not call your good tidings an announcement of death,
even if you are threatening my soul with departure.

Yours is the good tidings, on my part the good thing is this:
“I’ll mend your weakness with dye.”

Even if you have slain the beloved of my soul
and the matchless companion of my pleasure,

You have mended your way and stilled my rancor
by sending my mount quickly after him.

When you reunite me with the twin brother
of my [former] good life (sc. youth),
you grant me thereby my eternal reward.

It is sufficient reward for me regarding him,
that I and he return home.

By your life, for every living creature,
life, after losing its youth, is mere punishment.

Tell the calamities of my fate, that they must hit me
with their best arrows[13] when he (sc. youth) turns away.'

(L191: 9–19)

The poet first welcomes white hair as a guide towards the truth (9) and denies its harboring a message of death (12). Four times, he addresses it as a bearer of good news (10–13). Sarcastically, he offers to white hair in return his own 'good news', that he will simply ignore and dye it. After this first retort, the poet moves to a more detailed explanation of why 'his fast departure after youth' (10) is good tidings. Youth, personified as the poet's beloved had been slain by white hair, i.e. old age (14). The murderer, having brought rancor upon himself, redeems his crime by announcing to the bereaved the encounter with his lost lover (15), analogous to the paying of blood-money to redeem a murder. The posthumous reunion of the poet with his youth in death is then elevated to the hero's reward with his afterlife (16–17). In contrast to their eternal union, life at old age is pure punishment. The poet concludes the dialogue, expressing his eagerness to end this punishment and to be killed by fate's arrows (18–19). During the entire scene the poet argues against white hair as a messenger of death but welcomes it as an announcer of his reunion with youth. By presenting death as reward and life as punishment, the poet has turned the tables on this messenger of death. White hair, the rueful repenting murderer, arrives just in time to execute the poet's death wish. His sarcastic eager welcome and the remark about dying breathe contempt for death. He literally exhorts white hair not to let the fates of death miss him. This verbal duel between the poet and his harbingers of death reaches high dramatic tension.

White hair has emerged as a more versatile actor than the accuser. Its actions within each encounter depend on the involvement of other characters. Joined with human personae (women, accuser, and spy) it remains one-dimensional and all actions attributed to it are merely the effects of physical decay and the concomitant loss of women's passionate love. This role builds on pre-Islamic and Umayyad motifs. In conjunction with abstract notions (youth, death, and God), its range of action and development (i.e. its dramatized persona) expand considerably. In the two preceding passages, where white hair encounters the poet on its own, it undergoes a metamorphosis. Once it changes from a potential competitor of God to his messenger; another time it changes from the murderer of youth to the one who offers redemption and reunion with the deceased.

Youth

The other subject of *al-shayb wa-l-shabāb* is youth (*shabāb*). The poet's attitude towards it is governed by the chosen time frame of the scene. If set in the present (which is most common), the advent of white hair signals that youth is past and lost. When the poet mentally resurrects the past and relives the time of youth, then it is brought back to life.

Depending on the timeframe, youth either remains a purely abstract notion or becomes a protagonist. If set in the past, youth remains abstract. It stands for the resurrected ideal period in the poet's life, whose many facets – love, hunt, drink – fill episodes of *fakhr*. In L1611, the time of youth introduces a sequence of eight *fakhr* episodes, forming the bulk of the strophe.[14] In opposition to the period of old age, epitomized by white hair, youth is called metonymically 'the days of my pitch-black head' (*ayyāma raʾsiya asḥamū*, L1611: 6) or merely the 'blackness of the head' (*sawāda al-raʾsi*, 8). Its comparison with a nocturnal dream and fantasy (*ḥulm*, 8; *ʿahduhu l-mutawahhamū*, 9) is based on similes of hair and night as black, and youth and night-time as fleeting.[15] This youth is nothing but a brief span of enjoyment, and the common time frame of *fakhr* episodes.

In the present time frame of *shayb*, the abstract notion of youth appears in anaphoric expressions of grief (*lahfa nafsī ʿalā l-shabābi*, L1250: 48; *yudhakkirunī l-shabāba* ... L191: 31). Youth is the favorite era remembered (*qāʾilun qawla dhākirin khayra ʿaṣrayhi*, L1250: 47), while the anaphoric lamentations mark the hoary speaker's present.[16] In all the examples cited to this point, youth remains an abstract notion.

As an elapsed span of life, youth appears metaphorically as a failed hunt, a dry branch, and a lost beautiful garment (*burd*, *thawb*, *sirbālu l-naʿmāʾ*).[17] The bough and garment metaphors focus on the evanescence of youth, and only viewed from this perspective does youth materialize as a persona. The garment also allows the introduction of fate as the one bestowing youth upon people and later rescinding it.[18] Using this last metaphor of a threadbare mantle, the poet dramatizes the remnants of youth in a long passage:

أَيا بُرْدَ الشَّباب لَكنْتَ عندِى　　من الحَسَناتِ والقِسَمِ الرِّغابِ
بَليتَ على الزَّمان وكلُّ بُردٍ　　فبَيْنَ بِلىً وَبَيْنَ يدِ اسْتِلابِ
وعزَّ علىَّ أَنْ تَبلَى وأَبقَى　　ولكِنَّ الحوادِثَ لا تُحابِى

لبِسْتُكَ بُرْهةً لُبْسَ ابتِذالٍ　　　على عِلمِى بفضْلِكَ فِى الثِّيابِ
ولوْ مُلِّكْتُ صونَكَ فاعْلَمَنْهْ　　　لَصُنْتُكَ فِى الحَرِيزِ مِن العِيابِ
ولم أَلبَسْكَ إلّا يَوْمَ فخْرٍ　　　ويومَ زِيارةِ المَلِكِ اللُّبابِ

O mantle of youth, for me you were
a good deed and great luck.

You have been worn out with time,
since every mantle is between decay and robbery.

It hurts me that you wear out and I remain,
but [life's] events have no respect.

I wore you for a while not minding to wear [you] out,
though I knew your excellence among garments.

If it had been given me to preserve you,
be assured, I would have kept you in a safe bag.

I would have only worn you on a day of pride
and the day of visiting the true king.

(L191: 65–70)

The metaphor shows youth as a cherished and unwillingly surrendered material object distinct from the poet's persona: a precious garb one dons and wears out. But unlike the wearing of the real mantle, the wearing of this garb is not in the hands of man, for he cannot take it off and safely stash it away. Instead he is forced to abuse it in daily wear, painfully aware of its fading uniqueness (68). The dilemma of the garb of youth lies in the fact that enjoying it and destroying it are one and the same (67). The poet's apologetic address to the garb, defending himself with his inability to preserve it (69), lets the mantle come to life as someone who may understand and forgive. Both the metaphors of the bough and the garment share with youth their ephemerality. The bough's drying up and the mantle's wearing out are analogous to human aging. The worn out coat he addresses does not stand for youth in its radiance, but for the traces of its departure, inviting the association with the *locus classicus* for abandoned traces in Arabic poetry, the *aṭlāl* motif. In speaking to the mantle, the poet not only recalls his lost youth but describes his own aged body.

In L215, youth is personified as a deceased male beloved. The remembrance of lost youth in the poet's mind is analogous to the remnants of a beloved in a distant grave.[19] This image is developed further in the mourning poet's addresses to youth as a mourned friend, asking him not to be far, asking to be consoled for his loss, and sending rain to refresh the 'time of youth' in its metaphorical grave.[20] All of these are motifs of the lament; they personify lost youth in a way that places it beyond reach.[21] Lost youth takes a more dramatic role, when the poet accuses *shayb* of having murdered it: 'You killed the love of my soul and the companion of my pleasure' (*fatakta bi-ḥubbi nafsī wa-ṣāḥibi ladhdhatī*, L191: 16). The following quote dramatizes the murdered friend and the poet mourning for him. In it, the personified time of youth is associated with the *ḥabīb*, the former inhabitant of the *aṭlāl* remnants in the pre-Islamic *nasīb*.[22]

يا صاحبًا فاتَنِى المشيبُ به　　أَجْزَعَنِى يومَ بانَ مُنشَعَبُهْ
فارقَنِى مِنه يومَ فارقَنى　　تِلعابَةٌ لا يذُمُّه صُحُبُهْ
ما عيبُه غيرَ أَنَّ صاحِبَه　　يَطولُ عِند الفِراقِ مُنتَحَبُهْ
وقَلَّ مِن صاحِبٍ أُصيبَ بِهِ　　لمِثْلِهِ حزْنُه ومُكتَأَبُهْ
لَهْفِى لشَرْخِ الشَّباب أَنْ نَسَخَتْ　　مناسبَ اللَّهوِ بَعْدَه نُدُبُهْ
يا دارُ أَقوَتْ مِنَ الشَّبابِ أَلا　　حيَّاكِ غيثٌ فُروغُه جُوَبُهْ
دارَ شبابِى الجديدِ والعَيْشِ ذِى الـ　　ـحَبَرَة والصَّيْدِ يَرْتَمِى كُثَبُهْ
يَحسَبُه مَن بكاكِ ممتَثِلاً　　مُنسَكِبَ الدَّمعِ فيكِ مُنْسَكِبُهْ
أَصبَحْتِ خرساءَ بعد مِزهَرِكِ الـ　　ـناطِقِ يَحْدو بكأْسِهِمْ صَخَبُهْ
خلّاكِ ذَيْلُ الصِّبَى وساحِبُهُ　　يَعفوكِ ذيلُ الصَّبا ومُنسَحَبُهْ
وكنتِ للخُرَّدِ الحِسانِ فأَصْـ　　ـبَحْتِ لهَيْقٍ خلَيطُه شَبَبُهْ

O friend, whom hoariness took from me,
his separation made me despair on the day he departed.[23]

On the day he departed from me,
a playful youth, not blamed by his flocks of companions departed from me with him.

He has no fault, except that his friend
sobs long at his departure.

Rarely, in a friend afflicted with it (sc. loss),
is his sadness and dejection [felt] for one like him (sc. youth).[24]

Alas for the prime of youth, that laments [of him] have abrogated *nasībs* of pleasure [in his company]!

O abode, deserted by youth, may you be greeted by a shower, the [only] clearings between [whose clouds] are its pores![25]

Abode of new youth and of a life in bliss,
and of game, running along in small flocks.

He who weeps over you (f. sc. abode),
thinks that the downpour of it (sc. the shower)
imitates his [own] pouring of tears for you (f.).[26]

You (sc. abode) have turned dumb, after your talking lute, whose sound urged on their cups.

The skirts of youthful love and he who drags them
forsook you, the skirts of the East wind and their dragging are effacing you.

You belonged to the beautiful soft-spoken girls,
and you came to an ostrich with an oryx bull as companion.[27]

(L215: 17–27)

Youth is mourned in the first half (17–21) as a friend (*ṣāḥib*) and playful youth (*tilʿābatun*). Its qualities are described by negation in the way of laments (18–19).[28] He is 'not blamed by his friends', 'has no faults' except burdening his surviving friend with grief (19–20). In the final line of the evocation, the poet reveals the friend's name as 'prime of youth' (*sharkhi l-shabābi*, 21). This verse preempts the second passage: laments (*nudabuh*) will be composed for him instead of love poetry (*manāsibu l-lahwi*). The scholion explains *manāsib* (pl. of *nasīb*) as flirtatious love *mughāzalāt*, which describes love at the time of youth. But in the pre-Islamic *qaṣīda*, the *nasīb* is the nostalgic evocation of former love and connotes the irrevocability of its loss. It also contains the motif of weeping over the beloved's dilapidated abode (*aṭlāl*), the subject of the second passage (22–7) in which the poet turns his attention to the present time. He places the memory of youth and its reminders in analogy to the departed beloved and the remnants of her dwelling. These campsite traces become the metaphorical 'abode of youth' (*yā dāru; dāra l-shabābi*, 22–3) and are addressed with the traditional motifs of the *nasīb*: the greeting by rain (*ḥayyāki ghaythun*, 22) and its desolate state, inhabited by animals instead of humans (27). As in the pre-Islamic *nasīb*, the desolate abode shows the poet the irreversible force of time; the 'abode of youth' gives the same message to the Abbasid poet, yearning for his 'departed beloved youth'. The abode's silence affirms that youth has departed, and its dilapidated state mirrors the poet's own physique marked by age.

Youth moves between an abstract notion and a dramatized persona. If the time frame of a poem is set in the past, previous to *shayb*, youth remains a period of gregarious experiences, of loving, drinking, and hunting. If the time frame is set at the coming of *shayb*, youth is more defined and often becomes a persona. The dramatization of youth grows out of the awareness of its loss.

Youth appears as a persona in the guise of metaphors, such as the mantle and the departed or deceased *ḥabīb*. But these images all display a state of decay (worn-out coat), abandonment (deserted abode), or bereavement (grave). Left behind by the persona of youth, they have lost their prime and life force. The shabbiness of the mantle recalls its former beauty by contrast, as does the abode recall the singing and drinking there with the *ḥabīb*, and the grave the former company of the friend. All these remnants bear witness to happier former states, without themselves being able to help or respond to the addressing poet. Their silence reflects their impotence. In comparison to the persona of *shayb*, which maltreats the poet with its figurative speech and actions, the persona of youth in all its diverse metaphorical guises dwells beyond the poet's reach, remote and unresponsive.

The personae of the strophe, the accuser, white hair, and youth differ greatly in the range of their speech as well as their dramatic development. Personae that speak (or are silent) by figurative attribution, such as white hair and youth, have more latitude than the human persona of the accuser, who is restricted to a single activity. White hair, alias old age, takes on any act or speech the poet sees connected to his physical decay. It is here that one finds the most original interpretations, such as the white hair as a warning like the Koran or a bearer of the good tidings of the reunion with youth. The persona of lost youth – for timeless youth never becomes a persona – dons various metaphorical guises, all of which share a common trait: they are dead, cast-off shells. The persona of youth no longer inhabits them. They convey a non-verbal testimony as youth's metaphorical traces; their message is figurative silence. The poet could not fashion two more different characters: aggressive interfering white hair with a vast range of figurative speech and remote youth, shrouding univocal silence in a variety of metaphors.

Minor fictional personae

In addition to those described above, other personae appear occasionally throughout the encomia and engage the poet in speech. These mostly human figures are briefly listed here, omitting those that only appear in the third person, such as 'the jealous one' and 'evil omens'.[29]

In the strophe, the aging poet encounters the beautiful women (*ayyatuhā l-kawāʿibu*, L1306: 5), from whom he sadly parts or who unjustly severed their bond with him (L191: 27–30; L1611: 2–4).[30] A 'laughing one' (*wa-ḍāḥikin*, L215: 9) is a former beloved, who now mocks the poet. The spy (*yā raqībī*, *murtaqibuh*, L215: 15–16) is placated by the poet's persona at the moment when his role of guarding the poet from committing a misdemeanor is assumed more efficaciously by the white hair. The female neighbor (*jāratī*, 1250: 63), an advocate of moderation, is challenged by the poet's conviction that he had a very fulfilled youth – despite his old age – and which he proceeds to describe in detailed episodes. The poet also crosses paths with a friend (*qultu li-khillin*, L215: 35–59) who wonders at fate and is deluded by appearances and his own strength. In a series of paraphrased statements (*yā man yarā*, 41; *bal yā muhīna l-mahīni*, 43; *bal ayyuhā l-ṭālibu*, 53; *bal ayyuhā l-hāribu*, 52) and responses, the poet lectures him on the treachery of time, appearances that veil the truth, and human weakness.

In the antistrophe, several fictional messengers are charged by the poet's persona with transmitting matters of moment to the *mamdūḥ* or another addressee. The messenger is another figure from pre-Islamic times, more frequently seen in the uni-thematic *qiṭʿa* than the *qaṣīda* and used mainly as a rhetorical device.[31] Ibn al-Rūmī's messenger remains vague and the poet's persona does not enter into debates with him as he does with other pre-Islamic figures. The messenger is only briefly addressed in one verse and not given any quoted or paraphrased statements. Rather, the poet switches his attention immediately to the actual addressee of his missive. The vaguely-treated messenger resembles the witnesses described below except for his active intermediary role, specified in the message phrase.[32] In one case, two messengers are charged to ask the patron (*qūlā li-l-amīri*, L191: 96) why he deprived the poet of his all-encompassing generosity. The long message then addresses the patron. In another case, a messenger is dispatched to ʿAmr the Ṣaffārid (*aliknī ilā ʿAmri bni Laythin risālatan*, L1611: 146), to congratulate him on reinstating ʿUbaydallāh as deputy governor of Baghdad (266/880 or 276/890), proudly proclaiming the appointee's merits.[33] A competitor of the patron (*yā man yujārīhi fī makārimihī*, L215: 122–5) is actively discouraged from challenging him. The poet exposes his fruitless endeavor and declares the patron invincible. Similar to this figure is the challenger (*fa-yā qāʾila l-sūʾā*, F952: 33–4), who tries but fails to equal the patron in glory. A supplicant (*aqūlu li-l-shākī … alā ayyuhā l-shākī*, L1611: 232–3) complaining of hunger and penury is accused by the poet of ingratitude, since the patron had already granted him a safe haven from the claws of fate, which is more than a full stomach. Despite that, he is encouraged to seek the patron's favor. A similar encouragement and warning is directed at the audience (L1307: 23–31). Finally a prospective client for praises (*mustamniḥī madḥan ka-madḥīhi*, L434: 34) approaches the poet's persona, who spurns him out of loyalty to ʿUbaydallāh.

An important agent in both strophes is the concept of time (*zamān*) with its days (*ayyām*) and nights (*layālī*) and its cognate fate (*dahr*) with its blows (*khuṭūb*) and vicissitudes (*ṣurūf*, *ḥawādith*). They are the larger forces in *al-shayb wa-l-shabāb* of the strophe, evoked in the poet's monologues and conversations or confronted by him directly. The vicissitudes chase the poet away from the women and declare them forbidden (*ḥallaʾatnī l-khuṭūbu … wa-abīhā laqad ḥamat …* , L1250': 41–2). They impose the separation of lovers (*sharṭu ṣurūfihā l-tafrīqu*, L1306: 7). A descending blow of fate watches the poet succumb (*khaṭbun mina l-dahri*, L215: 15–16). Both the injustice of the nights (*ẓulmu l-layālī*, L1611: 2–3) and fate (L215: 5) disfigure the poet's hair and body. He denounces and curses fate for unjustly reclaiming his garb of youth (*ʿalima l-dahru anna l-shabāba thawbun ladā l-nāsi …* , L1307: 8–11; *barḥan li-hādhā l-zamāni*, L215: 4), for he had been misled to believe that it was a present (*ghirratī bi-l-zamāni*, L215: 31), and a giver's retrieving of his former gifts violates generosity. Only rarely do the changes of time come to the poet's aid, such as in fulfilling his wish to die (*qul li-banāti dahrī*, L191: 19). Fate is always stronger than him – unless he takes its side – and it is the sole adversary who, when submitted to, does not strip the poet of his dignity.

A different, defeated fate appears in the antistrophe, where the poet, now supported by the patron, summons it sarcastically to wake up: 'I said to the obstinately-assaulting fate, when I held on to your rope, "You shall wake up!"' (*qad qultu li-l-dahri l-mulihhi bi-ṣarfihī lammā ʿtaṣamtu bi-ḥablikum satafīqu*, L1306: 10). Fate's opposite stances never come together in one scene; they appear as irreconcilable roles of the poet's persona in separate strophes of the praise *qaṣīda*.[34]

All fictional personae encounter the poet in short scenes. Human figures, like the *ʿādhila*, play specific, narrowly-defined roles. Their strict conventionality allows them to be sketched with utmost economy. Their standpoints in the conversation do not change, not even if a figure – like the friend – is given multiple turns of conversation. From the human personae, those of white hair, youth, and fate differ, for their actions are projected onto them through interpretation. White hair metamorphoses into a nearly unpredictable interlocutor with multiple roles. The persona of youth has metaphorical 'doubles', documenting its loss, each in a different way. Fate can adopt either the role of the victor or the vanquished, in the first role, unjustly maltreating the poet, in the second, kept in check by the just ruler. There remain two human personae, however, that transcend the above-described narrow scope of action. They mirror the historical individuals – Ibn al-Rūmī and his patron ʿUbaydallāh b. ʿAbdallāh – on whom the praise *qaṣāʾid* bear.

Historical personae

The patron

The patron alternates between three roles, first, as a ruler, responsible for subjects and supplicants, second, as a benefactor of poets, and finally, as a model of praise poetry. In general the patron features more often as a theme in the speech of other personae than as a speaker himself. Occasionally, however, he appears opposite the poet's persona in direct address. There, the poet commends or criticizes him for his acts (and acts of speech).

In the role of the ruler (*amīr*), the patron's acts do not distinguish between the poet and other subjects. Unlike the fictional personae who interact with the poet individually, the ruler acts and speaks in images that indiscriminately affect all of his realm. The subjects, represented by the bystander, the supplicant, and the jealous one, show the effects on them of the patron's acts and attributes. His universality mystifies them (L1611: 223–5), he honors his bond with them, protects them from fate (L1611: 153, 238–42) and spites the jealous ones among them (*al-ḥussād*, L1042: 51; L1611: 297; F952: 35).[35] The ruler fulfills pacts and promises (L1306: 12–14) and defends his honor with generosity (L191:139–40, L1042: 45). As a conscientious ruler he spends the nights alone with his thoughts, solving difficult problems, rather than indulging in sleep or pleasant company (*idhā bitta wa-l-fikra tastakhrijāni miftāḥa amrin*, L1307: 39–42). He is entitled to, and worthy of, his governorship: 'You are the ruler by right' (*anta l-amīru bi-ḥaqqihī*, L1611: 205). 'You deserve this as a realm, as long as you live … as an unalienable governorship' (*bi-ḥasbika hādhī mā ḥuyīta imāratan … wilāyata lā ʿazlin*, L1611: 207–8). Rulership is part and parcel of his nature (*khīm*). If his universality can be analyzed at all, it is split into binary oppositional pairs of good and bad acts (L1611: 223) or promise and threat. They reach cosmic dimensions, as in the example of the latter pair:

إذا وَعَدَ اهتَزّتْ له الأَرْضُ نَضْرَةً   وأَنْبَتَ منها كلُّ ما كان أَسْبَخا
وإنْ أَوْعَدَ ارتَجّتْ وإنْ تمّ سُخْطُهُ   تَهاوَتْ جِبالُ الأرضِ فِى الأَرْضِ سُوَّخا

When he promises, the earth is thrilled by him into moisture,
and every saline [region] of it brings forth plants.

When he threatens, it trembles, and, if his anger is complete,
the mountains of the earth sink, collapsing into the earth.[36]

(L434: 24–5)

The earth oozes moisture when the patron makes a promise, and its mountains collapse when he utters a threat. The entire physical world is governed by his speech. His universality is also split into speech and act, as in the following felicitation:

حَلَفْتُ لأَنتَ القائلُ الفاعِلُ الّذِى   غدا المجدُ محْبوسًا عليه حبائِسُهْ ...
أَلا رُبَّ قولٍ قُلْتَه يا ابنَ طاهرٍ   أَصاخَتْ له بعد الهَدِيرِ قَناعِسُهْ
وفِعْلٍ رآك الفاعِلونَ فَعَلْتَهُ   فأَغْضَوْا وكلٌّ ذُلُّه لكَ عاكِسُهْ
لك القولُ يَستحيِى ذوو القولِ بعدَهُ   مِنَ القولِ حتّى يَتْرُكُ النَّبْسَ نابِسُه
إلى الفعْلِ يَستخْذِى له كلُّ فاعِلٍ   مِنَ النّاسِ حتّى الأَصْيَدُ الرَّأْسِ ناكِسُهْ

I swear you are the one who says and does, the one
to whom the unalienable goods of glory have become restricted …

Many a speech you said, O son of Ṭāhir, to which those
[usually] adept in it (sc. speech)[37] listened silently after chatter.

Many a deed you did which those who do saw
and cast down [their glances],
and of the shame of each you have the opposite (sc. honor).[38]

You have speech, after which speakers are ashamed to speak,
until everyone stops uttering a sound,

In addition to deed, to which every doer among people bows,
until the proud one bends his head.[39]

(F952: 36, 39–42)

ʿUbaydallāh's speech and act mark out his whole range of action. They are not only matchless but stifle any competition, thus becoming unique both in quality and instance. Another passage highlights among his acts generosity, resolve, the gathering of praise, and the defense of his honor (L191: 136–46).[40] Beyond humankind, the whole cosmos acknowledges ʿUbaydallāh as ruler. His acts figure in hyperbolic comparisons; his generosity shames even the rain (L191: 141–9), and his resplendent honor makes the sun turn pale (L1042: 48–51).[41] In hyperbolic inversion personified qualities and acts become his dependents: he is a father to honor, a husband to noble deeds, and a Christ-like resurrector to dead poetry (L1611: 269–72).[42] All of the ruler's acts constantly affect other human beings or personified abstract notions; they never exist for their own sake.

ʿUbaydallāh's two other roles of benefactor and model of praise outline more precisely his patronage relationship with Ibn al-Rūmī. As a benefactor, ʿUbaydallāh has a personal bond with his protégé, resembling, on a larger scale, the ruler's bond with his subjects. This personal bond shields the protégé from the vicissitudes of life (*lammā ʿtaṣamtu bi-ḥablikum ... / amsā mujāwirukum yaḥillu bi-najwatin*, L1306: 10–11; *wa-immā ajarta mina l-ḥādithāti jāran ... ʿaliqat qabḍatāhu ʿuran*, L1307: 43–5; *wa-qad ʿaliqat yadī bi-ʿurwatika l-wuthqā*, L1611: 273). He also composes his own poetry, but in contradistinction to Abū Tammām and al-Buḥturī, who described their patrons' literary skills, Ibn al-Rūmī does not dwell on ʿUbaydallāh's poetry, though it was well respected.[43] He devotes to it a meager three verses in L1611: 189–202 and prefers to highlight instead the complications a versifying patron creates for his poets. The quote continues where the preceding one left off:

عَجِبتُ لِمَن أَهْدَى لكَ الشِّعْرَ تُحْفَةً ... ومَن قال شِعْرًا وهْوَ دونكَ خانِسُهْ
أَيُهدِى إليكَ الشِّعْرَ بعدَ سَماعِه ... بشِعْرِكَ إلّا غافلُ القلبِ ناعِسُهْ؟
وأَنتَ الَّذِى يَدعو الكلامَ بقُدْرةٍ ... فيأْتيه وَحْشِىُّ الْكلامِ وآنِسُهْ
أَذلك أَمْ يَزْويه عنكَ وقَدْ رأَى ... عطاياكَ إلّا عاثِرُ الجَدِّ تاعِسُهْ؟
وأَنتَ الَّذِى سَحَّ النَوالَ بَنانُه ... كما سحَّ غيثٌ ضاحكُ المُزْنِ راجِسُهْ
تَكادُ تَعوقُ الشِّعْرَ عنكَ عوائِقٌ ... إذا قاسَه يومًا بشِعرِكَ قائسُهْ
فَيَحدو به أَنْ لَيْسَ للحَمْدِ بائعٌ ... يَراكَ وإنْ أَغلَى عليكَ تُماكِسُهْ
تقولُ الَّذِى يَنهَى عنِ الشِّعرِ أَهلَه ... بكُلِّ طِرازٍ لمْ يَرَوْا ما يُجانِسُهْ
وتفعلُ ما يَدْعو إليْه فكلُّهُمْ ... يكُرُّ عليْه عائدًا فيُلابِسُهْ
فتَرْكُهُمُ إيّاه إقرارُ أَنفُسٍ ... بأَنَّكَ دونَ الإنْسِ والجِنِّ فارِسُهْ
وقَوْلُهُمُ إيّاه شُكْرٌ تَقودُهُمْ ... إليه بفِعْلٍ لمْ تَشِنْهُ خَسائِسُهْ
عوائدُ عُرْفٍ يوقِظُ الشُّكْرَ نَخْسُه ... وكيف يَنامُ الشُّكْرُ والعُرفُ ناخِسُهْ؟

على أنّهمْ مَن أَحْسَنَ القولَ مِنْهمُ فمِنْكَ ومِن آثارِكَ امْتارَ هاجِسُهْ
تَعَلَّمَ ما قدْ قُلْتَه وفعلتَهُ فأهدَى جَنَى الغَرْسِ الّذى أنتَ غارِسُهْ

I was amazed at anyone, who dedicates poetry to you as a present, and composes[44] poetry, lagging in it behind you.

Would anyone dedicate poetry to you, who has heard your poetry, except one of foolish, careless mind?

For you are the one who summons speech mightily
and to whom speech comes, wild and tame.

On the other hand, would anyone divert it (sc. poetry) from you, who has seen your gifts, except one of tumbling falling luck?[45]

For you are the one whose fingertips pour gifts,
like a shower pouring out of laughing, thundering clouds.

Obstacles nearly keep poetry [by others] away from you,
when someone compares it one day with your poetry.

What incites it (sc. poetry) is that no seller of praise
sees you bargain him down, even if he asks an excessive price.

You say what prevents its people (sc. poets) from poetry,
by every embroidery [of verse] whose like they have not seen.

You do what calls for poetry, so each of them
wheels around to return and practice it.

So their leaving poetry is the confirmation of souls
that you are its hero above man and jinn.

Their saying poetry is gratitude to which you lead them
with an act unblemished by meanness.

The prodding of [your] habits of kindness awakens gratitude
– how can gratitude sleep, with kindness prodding it?[46]

Although, whoever among them excels in speech,
it is from you, and with your deeds his thought supplies itself.

He learnt what you said and did, and dedicated [to you]
the harvest of a seedling you have planted.

(F952: 43–56)

This and the preceding quote unite the three roles of ruler, protector, and model of praise. As a ruler, ʿUbaydallāh's acts are unique; his speech silences other speakers (39, 41), and his poetry other poets. Poets could not venture to dedicate inferior poetry to him (43–4). But as a protector, his unique generosity incites poets to take advantage of it (46–7). His dual role places his poets into a dilemma between dedicating and withholding poetry, which is reiterated in three syntactical pairs alternating between reasons for withholding praise (48, 50, 52) and reasons for uttering it notwithstanding (49, 51, 53). The alternating sets of reasons suggest the poets' long wavering. The position last described, in favor of saying poetry, wins the day, for gratitude cancels shame, and the role of the encouraging benefactor overrides the role of the composing sovereign. The last two verses credit the patron, in his third role as a model of praise, with the poem's contents. This solves logically the problem of the poets' compositions being inferior to those of the patron, by making the latter doubly responsible for the poems dedicated to him. First, his generosity motivated the poets to compose; second, his merits supplied the contents for their poems. These are not deliberate acts of the poets, who cannot be held accountable for them. The quoted passage also establishes a hierarchy among the patron's roles: the generous benefactor affects the poets more than the versifying sovereign, but most influential is the model patron, the poem's idealized subject matter.

As a model of poetry, the patron's relationship with the poet is lifted onto a higher level. This role usually appears in the praise *qaṣīda* around the dedication, and in it panegyrics mean no longer an exchange of separate services (praise for acts) but a fusion between the patron's act and the poet's word. This fusion brings the poem into existence, for example, through acts of the patron that cause, facilitate, or attract the poetry about them, or sometimes endow pre-existing poetry with a more suitable counterpart (L1611: 219, 226–31, 303). At times, the patron's acts even dispense with human language, by conveying messages themselves through physical traces.[47] The acts themselves are flawless and in no need of optimization or aggrandizement – so the poet claims. He merely contributes their arrangement into the *qaṣīda* form. In this fashion, the patron and the poet build the poem together in close interdependence. With the completion of the composition, their co-operation does not cease, since the poem needs to remain true thereafter. If the acts, the true counterparts of the verses, were to subside, the verses would at that moment turn into lies (L191: 155–6). The poet's persona insists that his praise poetry is a true depiction of praiseworthy acts. Such a strict congruity of act and speech is surprising in Abbasid praise poetry, where the poetic lie enjoyed broad acceptance. But much of the medieval Arabic discussion on the poetic lie concerned the acceptability of hyperbole (*ghulūw*) and *takhyīl*. Ibn al-Rūmī's truth was not of the kind to avoid hyperbole or *takhyīl*, he rather claimed it on the ethical level of his own conviction and the commensurateness of the depicted patron with his praise.[48] As such it forms part of Ibn al-Rūmī's ethics of panegyrics.

Can one find fault with a model patron? Indeed, one can, for when the patronage is not satisfactory, the patron may be fragmented into his inexplicable blameworthy acts and his familiar good qualities, both of which are treated as independent parts.[49] The poet's challenge then lies in reconciling dubious acts and reliable qualities, so as to reconstruct the patron's split persona. Troubling acts include depriving the poet of reward (L191: 96, 103–4, 116, 123; L1042: 58–62), breaking a promise of reward (*al-waʿdu mā lam taʿtabiṭhū yadu l-injāzi*: L191: 126–8), and delaying reward (*miṭāl*, *maṭl*, L191: 129–30 and 133), all of which the poet deplores and criticizes. Reliable qualities include the patron's nature (*aʿūdhu bi-ṭībi khīmika*, L191: 129), his origin (*ufakkiru fī niṣābin anta minhū*, L191: 134), his generosity (*li-taʿudh bi-saybikumū l-maṭāmiʿu wa-l-munā*, L1306: 14), and his soul, compared to one of his docile wives (*wa-laysa ʿahdī bi-nafsika min qarāʾinika l-ṣiʿābi … wa-anta qarīnu nafsin tuṭīʿuka*, L191: 130–2). The poet questions the patron's dubious acts based on the previous experience of his good qualities:

وكان الوعدُ ما لمْ تَعْتَبِطْهُ　　يدُ الإنجازِ شَرَّ حِباءِ حابِى
أَعوذُ بطيبِ خيمِك مِنْ مِطالٍ　　حَمانِى وِردَ بَحْرِكَ ذِى العُبابِ
وما هذا المِطالُ وليسَ عَهْدِى　　بنفْسِكَ مِن قرائِنكَ الصِّعابِ
يَروضُ النَّفسَ مَن صَعُبَتْ عليه　　ولمْ تكُ فِى النَّدَى طَوْعَ الجِنابِ
وأنتَ كما عَلِمتَ قَرِينُ نَفْسٍ　　تُطيعُكَ فِى السَّماحِ بلا جِذابِ
فمِن أىِّ الثّنايا ليْتَ شِعرِى　　أَتانِى المَطْلُ أَمْ أىِّ النِّقابِ؟
أُفكِّرُ فِى نِصابٍ أَنْتَ مِنْهُ　　فيُغْلَقُ دونَ عُذْرِكَ كلُّ بابِ
وكمْ فِى النّاسِ مِنْ رجُلٍ مُليمٍ　　يَقومُ بعُذرِه لُؤْمُ النِّصابِ

The [beast of] promise, as long as the hand of fulfillment
does not slaughter it in its fat state, is the worst gift to give.[50]

I take refuge in your nature from a procrastination
that deprives me of drinking from your rolling sea.

What is this delay? I do not know your soul
as one of your difficult wives.[51]

He, whose soul is stubborn and not manageable
in [matters of] generosity, tames it.

You are – as you know – the husband of a soul
that obeys you without haggling about magnanimity.

Through which mountain roads or passes,
if I only knew, did this procrastination come to me?[52]

I think of the origin whence you derive,
and every door is closed to your excuse.

How many a blameworthy man among people
is excused by his low origin!

(L191: 128–35)

The promise and its fulfillment are compared to a gift of a sound fat beast and its quick slaughtering. The delay in the fulfillment, i.e. the figurative slaughtering, makes the beast of promise grow old and worthless (128). Neither the patron's nature (129), nor his generous soul (132), nor his noble origin (134) could be guilty of such procrastination. The poet knows them well (130, 134) and takes his refuge with them (129), but the contradiction poses a challenge to his understanding of the patron's persona. Confused, he seeks reassurance in an anaphoric rhetorical question, 'Are you not that man?' (136, 138).

In sum, the patron plays three roles, in each of which he is perfect by definition. As a ruler, he holds a bond with all his subjects and wields cosmic powers. As a benefactor, he has ties with his poet; they exchange services and interact as personae. This role provides insight into Ibn al-Rūmī's view of praise poetry's social status. As a model of praise, the patron's acts and the poet's words about them are fused, and their congruity is the premise on which the poem's existence and veracity rest. The role of the patron as a model includes the circumstances of the poem's genesis, notably the patron's behavior, as an integral part of the poem's meaning. The patron must assume responsibility for what his poet says about him. The patron's lack of conformity with his role as a praiseworthy model either separates the poetry from him (i.e. makes it untrue) or causes his persona to disintegrate into blameworthy and praiseworthy parts in his poet's eyes. In the second case, shown in L191, the patron's persona fragments into so many contradictory facets, that the reasoning poet struggles to recognize his patron's identity.

Different from the fictional human personae, that of the patron assumes various roles, thus resembling *shayb*. The patron's three roles however, are not bound to separate contexts, as those of white hair or fate, but may concur and overlap within one argument. As a result the patron's persona evolves in the course of long passages with shifting constellations of speakers.[53]

The poet

Among the dramatis personae of Ibn al-Rūmī's praise *qaṣā'id*, that of the poet is the most prominent. He appears in each encounter, whereas his interlocutors change. In this way, his conversation partners contribute the *qaṣīda*'s subthemes, while the poet's persona safeguards its overall continuity. Next to the prosodical structure, the poet's voice gives the poem unity and coherence. The omnipresence of the poet's persona, often as a protagonist, characterizes classical Arabic poetry in general.[54] But the poet is not merely an actor, he simultaneously relates his own and other personae's actions and utterances in present and past encounters. In some passages, however, the poet's persona merges with the background as an unidentified marginal speaker or is entirely eclipsed. This leads Hellmut Ritter to label an example of this type by Ibn al-Rūmī 'objective' poetry.[55] In the encomia of Ibn al-Rūmī, both cases complement each other; the absence of the poet's persona in some passages becomes palpable because of his vivid dramatization in others, and in their conjunction, the author makes his point, which is all but objective. Any persona's position in a given scene is marked by its grammatical person with the important distinction that first or second persons are present and actively engaged in a dialogue, while third persons are absent and spoken about. This basic difference has been elucidated for many languages by Émile Benveniste, who also pointed out its unique reflection in Arabic grammatical terminology: *al-mutakallim* denotes the first person or 'speaker', *al-mukhāṭab* the second person or 'the one spoken to', and *al-ghā'ib* the third person or 'the absent one'.[56] While this division of personal pronouns applies in principle to all dramatis personae, the poet alone explores its full range. Switches in his grammatical person in sequences of scenes fulfill a function similar to the stage directions 'enter' and 'exit' in drama. The poet's persona speaks predominantly in the first person when he is dramatized as hero of *al-shayb wa-l-shabāb*, protégé, or panegyrist. But as hero of *nasīb* and *fakhr* or one of the ruler's subjects in *madīḥ*, where the poet remains a marginal participant or witness, his grammatical person is less fixed.[57] Either the poet's 'I' alternates with 'you' and 'we', or he entirely conceals himself as an implicit or impersonal speaker (see chapter 9). The appeal of such passages lies in their illustrative descriptions or imagery rather than any dramatic action.

As a hero of *al-shayb wa-l-shabāb*, the poet confronts several personae, each of which sets a theme and assumes an attitude to which he responds. The poet's actions, feelings and perceptions are all conveyed through the vehicle of speech. The following discussion of this and other roles focuses on the poet's own utterances and the way in which they characterize him without reiterating the above given descriptions of his interlocutors. How does he approach another persona? Which standpoint does he defend and with which acts of speech?

In his interviews with the accuser (L191: 1–8, L1250': 39–43), the poet asserts that he heeds her admonishment, subjugated as he is by white hair (L191:1, 4, 7) and fate (L1250': 41–2). He faces death (L1250': 39, 44) and vows to abstain from further flirtation: 'The eyes will not see me approach them (sc. the women)' (L1250': 43), and 'I have cast down my eyes neither throwing nor catching a dubious glance' (L191: 5, 8). His rhetorical question confirms his inability to commit sin, even if he so desired: 'How could I possibly attempt to hunt, when my arrows are unevenly feathered (sc. my hair is spotted with white)?' (L191: 6). Glances are commonly compared to arrows shot. Hence the poet's futile suggestive glances, peering from underneath his grizzled hair miss their goal like ill-balanced arrows, whereas the women's glances pierce his own fatal spots.[58] He orders the admonisher to stop, 'Admonish him who listens to you or wake up! The time has come for your shame and mine' (L191: 2), 'Stop the blaming! . . . Leave the blame, that I may not be accused!' (L1250': 39, 43). The poet strives to affect the accuser's mind with his assertions (or assertives, in Searle's taxonomy), and her acts with his orders (or directives), while he assures his obedience with declarations (or declaratives) and promises (or commissives).[59] The acts of speech characterize the poet as a perspicacious adversary, who redefines his physical inability as self-selected moral abstention and then turns around to admonish his accuser. He eliminates her reason to blame him, but denies her the credit for his reform, attributing it instead to fate and white hair. With equal savvy, the poet welcomes and prevails over white hair (L191: 9–19). Again he inverts the expected distribution of roles: instead of white hair threatening him and defeating him, he pronounces it guilty of murder – of former youth — and obliged to redeem the crime to him. In contrast to his adversary, the poet portrays himself as gracefully accepting the offer of redemption. Rejected by the women, he takes a dignified farewell (L1306: 6–7). Whenever the poet stands face to face with a persona, he triumphs over it with his words, turning physical decrepitude into moral integrity or a precondition to heavenly reward.

Not always can the poet achieve a verbal hold over another persona. Youth, for instance, eludes his eloquence, and he must engage with it through an intermediary. He encounters and addresses for example related metaphors, such as the deserted abode (L215: 22–7), the icon of ephemerality *par excellence*, and the worn-out mantle (L191: 65–70). Both are past their prime (inhabitation or newness) at the time of the encounter. In speaking to the metaphorical remnants, the poet does not face youth – as they do not represent it – but the fact of its loss. For instance, he addresses the beloved's deserted abode with the greeting: 'May a shower greet you' (L215: 22, L191: 65). To the worn-out mantle he declares his deep grief about its state: 'It hurts me that you wear out and I remain' (L191: 67). But his words do not draw forth an answer from the abode, as the poet admits himself, 'You have turned dumb after your talking lute urged on the cups' (L215: 25). Nor can his words preserve the newness of the mantle (L191: 69). The hero's speech affects neither of them, and his futile rhetoric, wasted on a mute interlocutor, signals his defeat by youth. Once youth's time has elapsed, it falls outside the range of the poet's direct speech.

Wherever youth is evoked or personified in a dramatic scene, the poet speaks in soliloquy treating it as an absent third person: 'O friend, whom hoariness took from me, his separation made me despair' (L215: 17). He asserts his affliction and shouts it out: 'Alas for the prime of youth' (L215: 21). His greeting of the prime (or time) of youth imitates a salutation to the dead, transmitted by the intermediary of raindrops penetrating into his metaphorical tomb: 'May rain refresh a time joy has made short' (L215: 28).[60] The poet's temporal distance from lost youth is translated into the physical distance between his own first person, sending the greeting, and the absent third person of youth, reached only by the rain clouds. The greeting, moreover, has little power as a speech act, as it counts merely as a courteous recognition without any commitment or interaction between speaker and addressee.[61] Regarding youth, the poet does not possess the fighting spirit of other face-to-face encounters. The weak act of greeting, dispatched to an absent persona, characterizes his helplessness and despair. In reverse, the invigorating presence of youth makes the poet dispense with such greetings. The quote shows both situations juxtaposed:

سقى عهْدَ الشَّبيبةِ كلُّ غيْثٍ أغرَّ مُجلْجِلٍ دانِى الرَّبابِ
ليالِىَ لمْ أَقُلْ سَقْيًا لِعَهدٍ ولمْ أَرْغَبْ إلى سُقْيا سَحابِ

May the time when I knew youth be watered
by every shower with white, thundering, low hanging clouds!

A time, when I did not say, 'May rain fall on a [former] time!' nor wished for water from the clouds.

(L191: 20–1)

Other unreachable personae, such as the women of the past and cursed fate, are similarly cast in the third person, unavailable for dialogue.

But the poet has one weapon at his disposal to fight the course of time: his memory. Encountering the female neighbor, he first concedes his inglorious old age: 'Even if I have aged, and fear of the outcome of sin has killed my vivaciousness.' (L1250': 63–4). Then, in the same breath, he counters present defeat with the boast of past adventure: 'I did often go out early, with youthful vanity shading my branch, as vehemence itself' (L1250': 63).[62] The address of the neighbor shows the poet's present stage, and the following boast depicts his past. Between the two time frames, the women's behavior towards the poet changes. In the present, they mock the poet: 'The women have called me uncle'. In the past, they were attracted to him: 'The long-necked beautiful [gazelles] show themselves to me' (L1250': 66). This perspective of the past lets the poet regain his self-esteem, while he forgets his present.

Forgetting the present makes the past come to life, but unless the poet transcends the present time frame, remembrance of the past brings pain. In one such scene (L191: 24–30), the hero quotes the women's disdain: 'Hoariness is enough humiliation for you and quick separation enough punishment' (L191: 28). Here he fails to step into the obverse of the present and remains prey to what he calls the women's injustice. Memory does not always work to the advantage of the aging hero. Remembering the past without simultaneously forgetting the present only accentuates the loss, as in a lament (L1250': 46–56) that begins as follows (47–8):

قائلٌ قولَ ذاكرٍ خيرَ عَصْرَيْـ ـهِ طويلُ الحَنينِ والتَّهيْامِ
لهْفَ نفسِى على الشَّباب الَّذِى أَصـ ـبَحَ خَلْفِى وذِكرُه قُدَّامِى

[I] am speaking as one, who remembers the better of his two ages,
one who has been yearning and longing without hope
for a long time:

'Oh, grief of my soul for a youth
that is behind me and its memory before me.'[63]

In another passage, the very instances of the present that contrast his former youth overshadow the depiction of youth itself. The memory of the past only underscores the unbearable present: 'What reminds me of youth is long thirst ... shameful chagrin ... deadly arrows' (L191: 31–60). The anaphora leads to the poet's lament:

فَيا أَسَفًا ويا جَزَعًا عَلَيْهِ   ويا حَزَنًا إلى يَوْمِ الحِسابِ

Oh, my pity, oh, my regret for it,
oh, my grief until the Day of Reckoning!

(L191: 61)

In a less emotional rendering of the *shayb wa-l-shabāb* theme, the poet portrays the patronage relationship as a consolation for lost youth (L1306: 9), analogous to the Umayyad transition motif of the *madīḥ* as a distraction from a former love.[64]

The hero of *al-shayb wa-l-shabāb* moves not only between timeframes, but also changes positions within one period of time. When he renounces licentious love because of his white hair, he proposes two interpretations of this act. First, he attributes repenting to white hair as a false idol: 'I am ashamed that I obey my white hair.... Did I, lost like a straying sheep, vow my repentance to something more wicked than myself?' (L1250': 12–28). Then he retraces his steps and reinterprets white hair as heeding a divine warning: 'But I repented to God .... What a warning it (sc. white hair) is for its readers of decaying youth and sudden death' (L1250': 29–38).

As far as the poet as hero remains in the present, his attitude in speaking to other personae is surprisingly close to the reality: He directs his words to interlocutors that are physically present, e.g. the accuser and the white hair, but never demands a response from lost youth. If he addresses the remains of youth, they do not react. His speech thus accurately maps his relative distance from other personae in time. His mode of address tells us about his ability to influence his counterpart: in face-to-face encounters, he wins the argument. He may begin by siding with the personae only to shift his standpoint and defeat the other. A mute or absent interlocutor, however, eludes the power of his word. In confronting a personae, the poet reflects upon his own conduct and adjusts it. But he also changes attitudes between encounters. He can even regain the time of his youth by stepping into the past – though it remains an abstract concept and not a persona he may summon.

Vis-à-vis ʿUbaydallāh, Ibn al-Rūmī depicts himself in two roles, as a protégé and friend, and as a professional poet. As a protégé he entertains with his benefactor a relationship of mutual duties.[65] The protégé has high demands. His own nobility does not tolerate a patron inferior to him (L191: 157–63). He seeks favor, support for his dependents (L1611: 294–5), and protection from unforeseen hardship (L1611: 278–88; L1306: 9–13; L1307: 44–5). He must be able to place full trust in his patron's generosity, the granting of his requests (L1611: 280–92, 296; L1250': 180–7), and his protection:

وَيَصونُ الْوَلِىَّ بالجاهِ والما ـلِ كصَوْنِ الكَمِىِّ نَصْلُ الحُسامِ
ما هُما لِلْوَلِىِّ إلّا كغِمدَيْـ ـنِ لديْهِ كصارِمٍ صَمصامِ

He (sc. the patron) protects a protégé by his rank and wealth, like an iron-clad [fighter], protected by the drawing of the sword.[66]

The two (sc. rank and wealth) are for the protégé
nothing but like two scabbards of him
[who is] like a sharp, tempered [sword].[67]

(L1250': 163–4)

He cannot fathom the patron's not fulfilling these standards:

ومُحالٌ أَلّا يَقومَ بما قَدْ لَدَه الأَوْلياءُ كلَّ القِيامِ

It is unthinkable that he not carry out to its fullest what [other] protectors have observed.

(L1250': 187)

The protégé feels safe with the patron's firm bond and sees him as his last resort:

ولو أَنِّى قَطعْتُ الأَرْضَ طولاً لكانَ إليكَ مِن بَعْدُ انقِلابِى
إذا كُنتَ المَآبَ ولا مَآبَ سِواكَ فأَيْنَ عنكَ بذِى الإيابِ؟

If I were to cross the length of the earth,
I would thereupon turn back to you.
When you are the haven of return, and there is no haven but you, to whom might one return if not to you?

(L191: 172–3)

The protégé considers his protector also as a sincere friend (*ṣadīqin mukhāliṣī*, L1042: 63). As for himself, he feels bound by his loyalty and the favors received (*nuʿmā*, L1250': 180).[68] Thus he spends his life, serving his protector (L1611: 273–7), and foregoes other opportunities:

فذلك عاقَنِى عنْ شَدِّ رَحْلِى وعَنْ عَسْفِى المهامِهَ واجْتِيابِى
ولَوْلاه لما حَنَّتْ قِلاصِى إلى وَطَنٍ لَهُنَّ ولا سِقابِى
ولا أَرْعَتْ على عَطَنٍ قَديمٍ ولا حَفِلَتْ بنَأْىٍ واغْتِرابِ

> That (sc. the patron's rare nobility) hinders me
> from tying my saddlebags
> and crossing and roaming the wayless deserts.
>
> If it were not for him, my sturdy camels and my fillies
> would not be yearning for their homeland.[69]
>
> Nor would they spare (sc. not graze at) an old resting place,
> nor [would they] be burdened by distance and exile.[70]
>
> (L191: 164–6)

The protégé further describes his friendship for the patron (*mawaddatī*, L1042: 52) and his pure love of his character (*fī wazni ʿāshiqin mustahāmī*, L1250': 178). Most of the protégé's speech consists of assertions. When he contemplates alternative scenarios to his relationship with ʿUbaydallāh, as in the above quoted verses, he qualifies them with the negated conditional as unreal (*wa-lawlāhū la-mā ḥannat* ... , L191: 165–7 and *wa-law annī qaṭaʿtu* ... , 171). Inversely, he highlights the constituting elements of protection by posing rhetorical questions that refer to the patron as a last resort (*fa-ayna ʿanka bi-dhī l-iyābī*? L191: 173, quoted above), the protecting bond (L1611: 273), and his own nobility (L191: 150). The poet's verbal acts reflect the support and protection received with assertions, emphasize doubts with rhetorical questions, and obviate his disloyalty with the conditional mood.

The role of the panegyrist has already been observed in invocations and the dedication, in which the poet formally declares what he did and continues to do for his patron.[71] But the panegyrist has less conspicuous facets that make him the poet's most intriguing role. This mostly concurs with requests and complaints about unpaid praises.[72] The panegyrist has invested labor in a piece of work he deems excellent (L1611: 279–99, L191: 105, 107, 120) and of which he expects a return. The panegyrist cherishes the truth of his praise (L1611: 303) and stands by his word, even though doubts assail him. To disavow former praise and turn it into lies by leaving his patron is an unbearable thought; he wishes never to abandon him (L191: 151–6). In reverse, he expects his patron to exemplify his ideal, to give or promise him reward (L191: 126), or at least provide an excuse (L215: 64–7).

Often, the return on his labor is delayed. Then the panegyrist complains to the patron about denying him his due return (*ḥirmān* L191: 109, L1042: 59, *ḥimāya* L191: 110, 129), delaying it (*maṭl*, *miṭāl*, L191: 129–30, 133), and his own mistreatment (*ẓulm*, L1042: 67–8) and grief (L1042: 52–8). Yet he bases his expectation on hope (*rajāʾ*), and doubts raised by delay can always be diffused by renewed favors. The poet, for instance, trusts that the patron can reconcile the poet's deceived grace (*niʿma*) with his hope, with 'grace' personified as a vengeful deceived wife, and 'hope' as her deceiving husband:

وإنَّ رجائِى فيك خَيَّبَ نِعْمتِى　　　فأَضْحَتْ كإحدَى الفارِكاتِ النَّواشِصِ
وكمْ نَشَصَتْ مِن نِعْمَةٍ فعَطَفْتَها　　　على بَعْلِها حتَّى غَدَتْ غَيْرَ ناشِصِ

My hope in you has disappointed my grace,
so that it became like one of the vengeful, obstinate wives.

How often was a grace obstinate, and you softened her
towards her husband, so she was no longer obstinate.

(L1042: 61–2)

But he also expresses hope, based on his own achievements:

لقدْ رجَيّتُ فِى عَمَلِى رَجاءً　　　فلا أُصْدُرْ بلا عَمَلٍ مُثابِ

I truly held hope in my work,
and must not return with [my] work unrewarded.

(L191: 120)

He plainly insists on the right of his poetry:

ولا تَبْخَسَنِّى حقَّ مَدْحِى فإنَّه　　　أَرَى باخِسِى سِيّانِ عندِى وباخصِى

Do not undercut the right of my praise,
for I see as equal him who undercuts me
and him who gouges out my eye.

(L1042: 67)

The term *bakhasa* 'to undercut' alludes to a Koranic verse about the recording of financial debt, 'Let the debtor dictate, and let him fear God his Lord and not diminish aught of it' (Sūrat al-Baqara 2/282).[73] By formulating his expectation of reward like a legal debt, the poet achieves a different result. Where only hope failed, the panegyrist was himself misled (L191: 121–3; L1042: 61, 66); if however his right is slighted, the patron's injustice is to be blamed (L1042: 68). The mention of the poet's right presents a stronger case and presupposes a certain authority of the poetic profession.[74] The panegyrist formulates his complaints about the lack of reward as questions, as if refusing to admit their truth (L191: 97, 101, 105a, 108, 109, 130, 133). Other interspersed rhetorical questions highlight items that would justify a reward, such as the poet's fulfillment of his task (L191: 105b, 107), his sincerity (L191: 156), and the patron's character (L191: 136–8; L1042: 55–6, 68) as the poet has previously known it. He directly advises the patron to reward him in the imperative:

فلا تَضَعَنَّ رِفدَكَ دونَ قَدْرِى　　　فَلَيسَ يَفوتُ بَسْطَتَكَ انْتِصابِى

Do not stay with your gift below my rank,
since my height does not exceed your reach.[75]

(L191: 117)

The panegyrist's fears of deception and disappointment take on the negated jussive:

ولا يَكُنِ الَّذِى أَمَّلْتُ منهُ　　　كَرَقْراقِ السَّرابِ على الحِدابِ

That which I hoped for in him must not be
like a glistening mirage on elevated grounds.[76]

(L191: 121)

فلا أَكُنِ المُهريقَ فَضْلَةَ مائِه　　　غُرورًا بِرَقْراقٍ مِنَ الآلِ وابِصِ

Heaven forfend that I be one who pours away the rest of his water,
being deceived by the glittering pool of a mirage!

(L1042: 66)

The panegyrist reacts to the (non-)action of the patron with a staggered series of speech acts: direct demands for fulfillment in the imperative and questions about the reasons of delay. Disappointment is framed in the negated jussive, as something not fathomed and to be averted.

In trying to prevent the patron from betraying their mutual bond, the poet does not overtly advise him against it, but expresses indirectly his own disbelief. The grammatical mood conveys the panegyrist's subjectivity of doubt mixed with lingering hope.[77] His subjectivity also surfaces in verbs of perception: 'I deem him, know him, think about him' that preface the patron's good qualities (L191: 119, 130, 134). According to Benveniste, such verbs of mental activity denote less the activity itself than the presence of the person executing them. They describe not an operation but an attitude taken towards the utterance made.[78] Here, the poet expresses his own opinion, that the patron will not disappoint him. Disillusionment is envisaged, but phrased in a negated jussive, expressive of his fears. Within this verbal mood, the battle wages between the poet's trust and fear. As above, the poet uses it as a shield against threats he hopes will not come true; the undesirable option is never allowed to become a plain assertion. He denies its positive existence in his speech, as if he could thereby influence reality. His whole linguistic behavior signifies his refusal to accept failure. In giving a clear contour to what he rejects, the poet institutes his personal ethics of praise. This subjectivity of conflicting trust and hope, fear and disappointment reveals a demanding side of the panegyrist, who appeared as dutiful and complying in the speech acts of praise. Both sides evidence a poet whom professional perils have taught to respect his own work and worth.

In one severe grievance, L1042: 52–68, the poet vacillates between the roles of protégé and panegyrist.[79] As a panegyrist, he complains of being starved, unpaid, deceived, and mistreated by the patron. As a protégé and friend, he worries about his reputation and trusts in the patron as a last resort. Where the panegyrist finds no further ground for hope, the protégé upholds his loyalty as a rationale to stay with the patron, without having to lose self-respect. The two conflicting roles are fused into a paradox in the final verse of the *qaṣīda*, where the poet appeals for justice to the same person who may have treated him unjustly.

أَيَظلِمُنِى مَن لَيْسَ فِى الأَرضِ غيْرَه   إذا نيصَ منْ ظُلمٍ مَناصٌ لنائِصٍ؟

> Does he mistreat me, other than whom there is no refuge on this earth
> for a refugee, when seeking refuge from injustice?
>
> (L1042: 68)

The protégé can still expect the justice of which the panegyrist has despaired. This switching of roles allows the self-respecting panegyrist a way out from having to accept the consequences of his ambitious ethics and seek his luck elsewhere.[80] Meanwhile, the role of the panegyrist allows the poet to confess his deepest fears, hopes, and expectations.

Dramatization

As a persona whose speech and acts (alone or in a group) supply the theme.	As a speaker, marginally involved in the action or passively witnessing it.

Role

Hero of *al-shayb wa-l-shabāb*	Protégé	Panegyrist	Hero of *fakhr* and *nasīb*	One of the ruler's subjects/supplicants

Grammatical person of participants

Speaking self: 'I'	Speaking self including the audience: 'We'	Address of self and audience: 'You'	Impersonal speaker: 'He, one'	Implicit speaker: no pronoun

Figure 4 Synopsis of the poet's persona in dramatized roles versus non-dramatized appearances with respective grammatical person

Summarizing the poet's various roles (shown in fig. 4), the poet as a hero of *al-shayb wa-l-shabāb* changes within and between encounters with fictional personae in a linear development. At the same time he passes through a series of varying yet mostly conventional themes. As protégé and panegyrist, the poet becomes a complex persona with different simultaneous and potentially conflicting roles. He tries to solve these conflicts through debates with the patron or in soliloquy. Whatever the role, his speech is the major vehicle of the action, representing his own emotions and his interaction with other personae. What is more, it throws in relief his underlying professional ethics, which he endeavors to impose upon the patron. The full dramatization of the poet as a protégé and panegyrist in conjunction with his appearance in the dedication contributes the main elements for Ibn al-Rūmī's ethics of patronage. With the dedication phrase the poet *performs* an act that constitutes part of his relationship with the patron, while the dramatization *depicts* this relationship in its entirety.

Part III

THE DRAMATURGY

8

THE SCENE

The foregoing discussion of the dramatis personae has shown that their verbal behavior towards each other characterizes their roles. The scenes of their encounters are, logically, the next largest unit in analyzing Ibn al-Rūmī's dramaturgy. The many forms these take are best demonstrated by example; however, a sufficient commonality among them warrants a classification along the major constants. A first subdivision follows the grammatical person of the protagonist(s), distinguishing scenes that include both the first and second persons, from scenes involving only one (first or second) person. The grammatical third person does not appear in scenes; rather, it marks absent personae[1] and characterizes another type of passage, discussed in the following chapter. Secondarily, I distinguish between scenes according to their participants, modalities and limits of space and time.

The dialogue scene

Among the scenes involving the first and second person, the dialogue scene (fig. 5) provides the most explicit dramatic features and will therefore be dealt with first. It shares with other scenes an asymmetrical representation of the personae. The poet's persona (hereafter 'A') directly addresses the interlocutor (hereafter 'B'), whereas the speech of 'B' is conveyed only by the intermediary of 'A'.[2] The two personae converse in what is a poetic rendition of dialogue, reduced to a single round of statement and response, or one turn of conversation.[3] This brevity is achieved by the poet's epitomizing his partner's speech in a characteristic quote, or epithet, and then delivering his own retort in full length.

In the unfolding scene, statement and response occur consecutively unless the other persona's statement is merged into the poet's response. The merged version allows the sketching of a longer dialogue with several rounds of speech, with 'A' referring repeatedly, and from different standpoints, to statements by 'B', which he quotes or paraphrases. By representing the partner's (or adversary's) standpoint indirectly, the response by 'A' sustains the form of dialogue even if the audience only hears his side. Quoted statements from previous encounters add a temporal dimension. Each scene is relatively short as 'A' moves quickly

A↔B
'A responds to statements of B'

A = Poet's persona
B = Interlocutor

Structure
– Introduction of B in the third person
– Address of B in the second person
– Quote or paraphrase of B's statements and their refutation with potential further addresses
– Conclusion by switch of person and/or rhetorical device

Figure 5 Schematization of the dialogue with an argumentative scheme of action and a dramatized poet's persona

between interlocutors; he is addressed by and responds to persona 'B$_1$', to be thereupon addressed by persona 'B$_2$' and so forth, revealing at each stage of the journey a different facet of his evolving persona.

Dialogue scenes are constituted both by real or figuratively-attributed speech. Figurative speaking occurs with personified metonymies, such as white hair (*shayb*) or attributes of the patron. He never addresses the poet within the encomia,[4] for his praiseworthy acts and attributes speak figuratively on his behalf, or his character traits summon speech as a hyperbole. Both figurative and real speech create obligations alike. For instance, the poet's persona holds the patron responsible for 'promises' that the patron's acts figuratively granted. The real counterpart for 'promise' of an act is the poet's expectation of it.[5] This image gives a glimpse of Ibn al-Rūmī's panegyric sophistication.

The portrayal of the poet's persona depends on a scene's scheme of action. An argumentative scheme rests on a strongly dramatized persona, whereas a phatic–rhetorical (univocal) scheme only requires a confirming witness. In the first case, the poet disagrees with his dialogue partner (fig. 5). A scene of this type, quoted in full hereafter, follows the poet's message to ʿAmr b. Layth in which he thanks him for restoring ʿUbaydallāh to the governorship of Baghdad (146–8), vouches for his qualities (178, 203–4) and legitimacy (205–9) and declares himself to be a reliable source about the appointee (223). The poet's subsequent encounter with a supplicant gives him the occasion to act upon his words. (Acts and words of 'A' are italicized, direct addresses and reported acts and words of 'B' are underlined).

أَقول لشاكٍ بَثَّه لَمْ تَزَلْ بِهِ   مِنَ الحالِ أَسمالٌ رِثاثٌ تُرَمَّمُ
أَلا أَيُّها الشّاكِي إلىَّ خَصاصَةً   تُضارِعُهُ فى السِّنِّ بَلْ هِىَ أَقدَمُ
ويُشفِقُ منها فِى بَقِيَّةِ عُمرِه   أَمِنتَ وأَنفُ الدَّهرِ أَجدعُ أَكْثَمُ
أَمِنْ ضيقِ مَثْوَى المرءِ فِى بَطْنِ أُمِّه   إلى ضيقِ مثواه مِنَ القَبْرِ يُسْلَمُ؟
ولَمْ يَلقَ بين الضيقِ والضيقِ فُسْحَةً؟   أَبَى ذاك أَنَّ اللَّهَ بالعَبدِ أَرحَمُ
وأَنَّ عُبيدَ اللهِ للنَّاسِ عِصْمَةٌ   بأَيديهِمُ منها عُرًا لا تُفَصَّمُ

سيزجُرُ عنكَ الدَّهرَ إنْ شِئت زَجرَةً يُصيخُ لها خَوْفًا ولا يَتَرَمرمُ
هو المرءُ أمّا مالُه فمُحلَّلٌ لعافٍ وأمّا جارُه فمُحَرَّمُ
لِجيرانِه منه مَحَلٌّ مُمَنَّعٌ يَضيمُ به الدَّهرَ الذَّليلُ المضيَّمُ
وكفٌّ صَناعٌ تَجبُرُ الكَسرَ منهُمُ وتدمُلُ مِن ذِى كَلْمِهِمْ حينَ يُكْلَمُ
وتَحتاطُ مِن كرِّ الزمانِ عليْهِمُ فتنهاه عَنْهُمْ بالَّتى هِىَ أَحسَمُ
تَتَبَّعُ أَظفارَ الزّمان تتبُّعًا بآثارها فِى أَهلِه أَو تُقَلَّمُ
فسِرْ راشدًا لا تَثْنِيَنَّكَ طِيرةٌ كَذوبٌ ولا رأْىٌ عَنِ القَصْدِ أَضْجَمُ
إلى مَلِكٍ لا تَبْرَحُ الطَّيْرُ دونَه وإن بَرِحتْ لِلرَّكْبِ لَمْ يَتَشاءَموا
إذا ما غدا الغادِى إليه فإنَّه على ثِقَةٍ أَنْ لَيْسَ فِى الطَّيْرِ أَشأَمُ

I say to someone, lamenting his sorrow,
whose situation has not ceased to be worn-out and mended rags:

'O you, who lament *to me* a poverty that is as old as you or older,
And [who] fears it for the [short] remainder of his life,
you are saved, and the nose of fate is cut and maimed!'

Out of his tight dwelling in his mother's womb, is man abandoned [directly] to the tight dwelling of the grave

Without finding between this tight space and that an opening?
No, the fact that God is compassionate for his servant excludes that

And [the fact] that ʿUbaydallāh is for his people a protection
by which their hands hold ties, not [to be] torn.

He will chide fate away from you, if you want,
by a call it obeys fearfully without muttering a word.[6]

He is the man whose wealth is licit for him who asks
and whose protégé is sacrosanct.

His protégés have in him an inaccessible place
in which a humble, oppressed [protégé]
himself oppresses fate.

[They have in him] a skillful hand that sets their broken bones and treats the injured one of them, when [an injury] has been inflicted.

It (sc. his hand) protects them from the assaults of time
and wards it off them by very sharp [claws].

It tracks the claws of time in their marks on his people
[undoing their harm], unless they (sc. the claws of time)
are clipped [by his hand].

Go well-guided, may neither a false omen
nor a distorted opinion divert you from the goal!

To a king before whom the birds never leave,
and if they left a troop, they would not read [in that] ill fortune.[7]

When someone reaches him in the forenoon,
he is assured that there is no ominous one among the birds.
(L1611: 232–46)

The argument is arranged as statement and response. The poet's persona introduces a supplicant who bemoans his poverty (232) and responds to him. First, he ridicules the supplicant's quoted lament by asking whether he has not grown used to poverty after a whole life of it. Then he demonstrates the supplicant's plea to be redundant, for the patron already accorded it as part of the protection from fate he granted to all subjects. The remainder of the scene is taken up by the poet's refutation of the supplicant. He reduces his lament *ad absurdum* with the rhetorical question whether God would ever forsake his subjects (235–7), a question meant as a negation. No more than God would the patron forsake a supplicant, whom he had already shielded from fate, empowered him against it, and healed his wounds (238–43). The poet's response to the supplicant's lament is doubly corroborated by the facts of God's compassion and ʿUbaydallāh's protection. Following his refutation, the poet sends the supplicant to the patron and assures him of a favorable reception. The exhortation carries over to a description of the patron and his fortunate supplicants (245–6).

The dramatized poet addresses the supplicant with a vocative at the beginning (233–4), to recall him again with the idiomatic phrase 'if you want' (*in shiʾta*, 238) and the imperative 'go well-guided' (244). The poet first paraphrases his partner's complaint, rephrases it, and then destroys it with a well-argued retort.[8] At the same time, the poet challenges his interlocutor with interposed phrases and a final exhortation to prove his own words right. To persuade his dialogue partner, the poet pledges his own convictions.

The dialogue is structured as follows: speaking in the first person, the poet introduces the interlocutor in the third, summarizing his statements. Then he responds to him in the second person. He begins by identifying the interlocutor at the beginning with a vocative and a reiteration of his words as well as recurring addresses throughout the retort, which closely adheres to the initial plea. In terms of the grammatical person, the dialogue is characterized by a switch of the conversation partner from the third to second person between the introduction and the poet's response. The closure of the scene is marked formally by a final address and the onset of a new passage in which the former interlocutor is either switched back to the third person or disappears.[9] A dialogue scene can also conclude formally with a sententia, such as in a scene of poet and admonisher.[10] Other than sententiae, exclamations, rhetorical questions and analogies mark closures of scenes (see fig. 5).[11]

In another example several statements are figuratively attributed to the interlocutor, white hair (*shayb*), and merged into the poet's response. By referring to them at different points in the response, the dialogue is expanded. As the scene is quoted above, the following remarks only touch upon its argument.[12] White hair has featured in a preceding scene together with the accuser (*ʿādhila*, L191: 2 and 4) and is introduced in the third person as a dialogue partner (7). Then the poet turns to it in a long response (9–17). In a first turn (9–12), its message is paraphrased as the good tidings of guidance to truth and reunion with youth, and the poet welcomes the bearer of such news. In the short second turn, he mockingly threatens to 'silence' the white hair by dying it black again (13). In the third turn, he represents white hair as the murderer of youth, who repentantly offers redemption in the form of the poet's reunion with youth in his afterlife (14–16). The poet first declares satisfaction (17) and then breaks out in a lament, ordering white hair to hasten his death. White hair is initially portrayed as bringing the poet figurative good tidings. Then, in the second turn, it changes from the bearer of good news to a repenting criminal. In the third turn, it is the poet who grants the wish of white hair. The motif of death only appears at the end as an initiative of the poet: he begs white hair to hasten it.

In both scenes, the poet's persona takes a different standpoint than his interlocutors – the supplicant and white hair – and defeats them with words. The dialogue with *shayb*, containing three sketched turns of conversation, shows a longer development, since the poet imaginatively varies the statements imputed to his abstract opponent.

Argumentative dialogue scenes with the patron's persona tend to be long-winded and show the speaker and addressee in different roles (L191: 96–175): the patron as a benefactor and panegyric model, the poet as a protégé and panegyrist. These dialogues thematize grievances of the poet.[13] In a plaintive tone, he debates his conflicting perceptions and experiences of the patron's acts and attributes, for through these alone the patron 'speaks'. The poet's potential disappointment in the patron challenges his prior knowledge and faith in him, and he tries to resolve the dilemma through debate, though not always with success.[14] Such scenes occur, incorporated into clusters, in the *qaṣāʾid*'s metastrophes and separate poems of admonition. They belong therefore to the composite scenes to be discussed in chapters 10 and 11.

In other scenes, the action unfolds in a phatic–rhetorical scheme (fig. 6), i.e. the poet's words support and confirm the other person's acts. In this type of scene, the interlocutor is always the patron; he initiates it with his actions and the poet responds with a verbal testimony and commentary. The debate shows him as a self-assured panegyrist and a satisfied protégé and friend. In reformulating the patron's acts and qualities with deft use of hyperbole, he infers his own role of conveyance, his literary skill, and his authority to speak for the patron; he vaunts his own sincerity and his direct knowledge of the facts he describes.

A↔B/B_1, B_2 ... 'A responds to previous acts of B'	A = Poet's persona B = Historical persona(e)

Structure
– Account of B's acts
– A's attestation and evaluation of them

Figure 6 Schematization of the dialogue with a phatic-rhetorical scheme of action and a witnessing poet's persona

The poet's recounting of the acts and his attestation either intermix or succeed each other. This essentially univocal scheme with the poet as a dramatized persona occurs in passages of hyperbolic praise around the dedication and demonstrates his full affirmation of the patronage relationship.[15] In some dialogues however, the poet is reduced to sporadic appearances and his voice is diluted by the presence of other supporting speakers, though his role of attestation remains the same.[16]

This marginalized poet tends to appear in dialogues conveying topical praise as the following example illustrates.[17] Here the poet extols the Banū Ṭāhir, soliciting the voices or ears of other witnesses.[18] The poet begins by introducing the Ṭāhirids' achievements as common knowledge, then explains them in more detail, and finally attests to the deeds in his own voice, addressing the Ṭāhirids in the second person plural throughout the *qaṣīda*

بنِى طاهرٍ ما مَن رأى ما بلغْتُمُ   بمستنكرٍ أن يلْمِسَ النَّجمَ لامِسُ
إذا عُدِّدَتْ آلاؤُكمْ آلَ طاهرٍ   أَقَرَّ بها منّا مَسُوسٌ وسائِسُ
بلغْتُمْ مِنَ العَلياءِ والمجدِ رُتبَةً   طوَى كشْحَه مَن رَامَه وَهْوَ يائِسُ
ولِمْ لا وأثمانُ المَعالِى لَدَيْكُمُ   رِغابُ العطايا والنُفوسُ النَفائِسُ
مسامِعُكُمْ نَصْبٌ لِداعِى كريهةٍ   تَساقَى المنايا رَجْلُها والفوارِسُ
وَطورا لملهوفٍ تَعَرَّق لحمَهُ   عَنِ العَظمِ ذؤبانُ الخُطوبِ النَّواهِسُ
تُجيبون كِلتا الدَّعْوَتَينِ كأَنَّكُمْ   غيوثٌ وأحيانًا ليوثٌ عنابِسُ
لأيديكُمُ فِى الموطِنَيْنِ كِلَيْهِما   نَقائِذُ مِن أَيْدِى الرَّدَى وفرائِسُ
مكارِمُ للماضِينَ منكُمْ تقدَّمتْ   وأُخرَى على الباقِينَ منكُمْ حبائِسُ
سأثنِى على الدَّهرِ المذَمَّمِ إذْ أَتَى   بأَمثالِكُمْ أو لا فإنِّى باخِسُ
تضمَّنتُ أَنْ لا يبْخَلَ الدَّهرُ بعدَها   بأَىِّ نفيسٍ بعدكُمْ هُوَ نافِسُ؟
بِكُمْ نَعشَ اللَّهُ الخِلافةَ بعدَ ما   هَوَى جَدُّها عن حالقٍ وهْوَ تاعِسُ

Banū Ṭāhir, he who sees your achievement,
does not deny that the stars have been touched.[19]

When your deeds are enumerated, House of Ṭāhir,
the ruling and the ruled among us confirm them.

You have attained in glory and honor [so lofty] a rank
that he who aspires to it loses countenance in despair.

Why [should he] not? Since the prices of glory for you
are cherished presents and dear souls.

Your ears are open for him who calls to a battle
in which foot soldiers and riders distribute fates of death.[20]

And, at times [your ears are open] for [the call of] a desperate one
whose flesh the snapping wolves of the afflictions devour off the bone.[21]

You answer both calls, as if you were showers
and, at times, ferocious lions.

Your hands in both battlefields have victims,
rescued from the hands of death, and trophies.

Glorious deeds by the deceased of you [Ṭāhirids] have preceded,
and others (sc. glorious deeds) are reserved for the living of you.

I will praise the vituperated fate for bringing the likes of you;
if not, *I hold back [unduly]*.

I pledge that, after them, fate will not be stingy.
Which precious good after you shall it [care to] be stingy with?[22]

With you God revived the Caliphate after its luck,
tripping, tumbled down from high.

(L994: 20–31)

The introductory verses (20–2) relate the Ṭāhirids' achievements as seen and counted not merely by the poet but every human being (20, 21). The historical event referred to is Ṭāhir's killing of al-Amīn, which ended the Civil War and reunited the Abbasid caliphate under his brother al-Ma'mūn (r. 198–218/813–33). By saying 'we', the poet disappears into the crowd of Ṭāhirid subjects.[23] In the scene's middle part (23–7), he asks a rhetorical question and proceeds to answer it himself: The Ṭāhirids' universal excellence is shown in their twofold response to the double attack of war and poverty (24–7). All of the Ṭāhirids' exploits are exchanges: they 'buy' glory with their lives and presents (23). They actively respond to the call of victims of war and the deprived (24–6). Except for the rhetorical question, the speaker does not yet appear explicitly. Only at the end does the poet step out of his mold and pass comment (28–31). He measures the Ṭāhirids' deeds on the scale of time and compares them against the inequities of fate. Pleased with the result, the poet guarantees fate's predilection for the

Ṭāhirids and promises to praise it, inverting the topos of blaming fate. The speech act of the promise given to fate proves the poet's faith in the Ṭāhirids. This is the moment in which the poet steps out as 'I' from the subjects' crowd. He speaks with the authority of someone who gives guarantees, rewards fate, and evaluates history (29–31). But his role remains restricted to that of an affiliate, and his voice to one of assent. He is the Ṭāhirids' 'tongue', and from them derives the authority of his word.

The two extremes of the controversial and univocal schemes of action demarcate the dramatic possibilities of the dialogue scene. These schemes also determine the poet's respective dramatization (excepting scenes of hyperbolic praise, which give the poet's persona a certain leeway he exploits on occasion). A controversial scheme calls for a dramatized poet, taking a moral stance of defiance or refutation toward the interlocutor. In admonitory arguments with the patron, the poet acts out his position as a protégé, friend, and panegyrist who insists on all his rights. The poet's persona does not, however, criticize the patron's acts directly. Instead he stages a debate about his own conflicting perceptions of these acts, so that the apparent object of debate is the (in-) correctness of his own grasp. If mistaken about the patron's nature, the poet has his own judgment to blame and not any malicious deceit by the patron.[24] A univocal dialogue scene that contains topical praise leaves the poet in the background, marginalized as a witness. His only part in the action is that of an authoritative speaker.

However, if a univocal scene contains hyperbolic praise, the poet varies between the marginal role of an anonymous subject and the strong dramatic presence of a panegyrist or protégé. The dramatized persona occurs around the dedication as a way for the poet to take credit for the praise.[25] The dedication lends itself to this, since the poet lays down in it the patron's liabilities and the *qaṣīda*'s benefit for him. Inversely, a weak presence or absence of the poet's persona place him at a distance from the praise.[26] It seems as though he lends a voice to conveying a general opinion, while suspending his own judgment. The veiling of his position toward the praise might imply modesty or doubt. Exploiting this ambivalence, argumentative and hyperbolic dialogues are juxtaposed with sequences, interspersed with monologues.[27] The different roles taken by the poet's persona in the subsequent scenes expose the tensions between his public stand and his inner feelings.

The extended dialogue scene

In the dialogue scene as thus far discussed, two personae meet face to face, but the poet does not only address personae with whom he shares a physical space. He also spans distance and time in extended dialogue scenes. Partners of such dialogues are personified metaphors, such as 'the mantle of youth' (*burdu l-shabāb*), 'the abode of youth' (*dāru l-shabāb*), 'the time of suckling [from the vine]' (*zamānu l-riḍāʿ*), and fate (*dahr*). In the poet's response, they often receive the vocative of distance (*yā*) as opposed to that of closeness (*ʾa-*). The fact that the poet is speaking to them by no means implies their ability to respond: his distant call has the opposite effect. In one scene, the poet describes youth in the third person, then addresses and mourns only its mantle in the second person.[28] He shuns summoning youth itself and only approaches its worn-out garb. Ironically, the choice of this thus derived, somewhat abstract interlocutor makes the distance between the aged poet's persona and his former youth more concrete. In a similar scene, a dialogue with the time of suckling from the vine, he misses the former imbibing and dispatches a greeting to the personification of the elapsed period.

وقضَيْتُ الرِّضاعَ مِن دِرَّة الكَرْ   مِ لِتجريمِ أَربعينَ تَمامِ
ولِتجريمِ أَربعينَ قديمًا   يتناهَى الرِّضاعُ بِابنِ المُدامِ
يا زمانَ الرِّضاعِ أَرضَعَكَ المُزْ   نُ وأَكدَى على زَمانِ الفِطامِ
دعوةً إنْ تُجَبْ بِسُقْيا وإلّا   فسأَسقيكَ بالدُّموعِ السِّجامِ

I have ended the suckling of the milk of the vine,
since forty [years] are fully completed,

From of old, with the completion of forty [years],
the suckling of a son of wine is terminated.[29]

O time of suckling, may the rain cloud nurse you,
and withhold [its rain] from the time of weaning!

[I call it] as an invocation; if it is not answered
with a downpour [by the rain cloud], *I will pour* for you flowing tears.[30]
(L1250': 59–62)

First the suckling is introduced in the third person as of a former period (59–60), then the poet turns to greeting it with the vocative *yā zamāna l-riḍāʿ* (61). The manner of the greeting reveals his double separation from youth by temporal and physical distance, which must be bridged by a travelling rain cloud (62). The obstacles intensify the poet's tenderness for the outgrown suckling, and he sends it a messenger of its own kind, a nursing rain cloud, in a first variation of the familiar rain greeting. But the aging poet doubts his control over the figurative messenger and varies the rain greeting a second time, offering distant youth his own tears. In another scene, a dialogue with the deserted abode of youth, the poet evokes youth as a departed male beloved (*ḥabīb*) in the third person.[31] The opening line 'O friend (sc. youth)' (*yā ṣāḥiban*) is merely a universal vocative and as such a lamentation of unreachable youth. The true addressee of the dialogue is youth's metaphoric campsite trace, playing on the pre-Islamic *aṭlāl* motif.

The unintroduced dialogue

Both regular and extended dialogue scenes begin with an introduction of the poet's partner and his (or her) salient features. This introduction may be substituted by a vocative, rephrasing the information as part of the poet's response, such as 'O you who challenge [the patron]' (*yā man yujārī . . .*). Alternatively it may be condensed into an epithet, such as, 'Sleep my observer' (*nim yā raqībī*).[32] Epithets identify similarly the 'accuser' (*ʿādhil(a)*), the 'calumniator' (*wāshī*), and the 'supplicant' (*ʿāfī, sāʾil, shākī*). Further epithets denote personae with a characteristic behavior, such as the always reasonable but critical 'female neighbor' (*jāra*)[33] and the youth-adoring beautiful women (*kawāʿib*). I refer to this type of scene as unintroduced dialogue. It only occurs with stock figures whose conventional and one-dimensional actions need no elaboration.

In one unintroduced dialogue (L1250': 39–43), following a rueful monologue on youthful impiety, the poet addresses an accuser without any prior introduction:[34]

عاذِلِي قدْ نزعتُ فانْزِعْ عنِ العذْ   لِ وإنْ كُنتَ فِى صَوابِ حَذَامِ
قدْ رأَيتَ الَّذى هويتَ فأَرْضَيـ   ـتُ وأَرغَمتَ فارْضَ لِى إرغامِى
حلَّأَتْنِى الخُطوبُ عنْ شِرَعِ اللَّهْـ   ـوِ فأَصبحتُ حائمًا فِى الحِيامِ
وأَبيها لقد حمَتْ سائغاتٍ   بارداتِ النِّطافِ زُرْقَ الجِمامِ
لَنْ ترانِى العيونُ أَشرَعُ فيها   فدَعِ اللَّومَ ولْيُدَعْ اِتِّهامِى
مِتُّ إلّا حُشاشَةً وادِّكارًا   مِثْلَ أَحلامِ حالِمِ النُّوَّامِ
ومَتَى ما انْقَضَتْ أَجاريُّ طِرْفٍ   ماتَ إلّا صِيامَه فِى المَصامِ

Accuser *of mine, I am dying*, stop the accusing then,
even if you are as right as Ḥadhāmi.[35]

You have seen what you desired, *for I mended my ways*,
and you humbled [*me*], enjoy then *my humiliation!*

The blows of fate *drove me* from the watering places of play,
so I am erring thirstily.[36]

By their father (sc. God)! They kept away those
who taste sweet (sc. the women), whose saliva is cool,
and whose hair, black-blue.

No eyes *will see me* approach them, leave the blaming then
and *may I not be suspected!*

I have expired but for my very breath and a remembrance
like the visions of a dreaming sleeper.[37]

Whenever a stallion's different gaits are past
he has died except for his standing at his place.

(L1250': 39–45)

The vocative opening the response identifies the interlocutor as the female 'accuser of mine' (*ʿādhilī*) in the conventional masculine gender. The vocative comprehends all her action. In vain the poet tries to dissuade her with further imperatives, 'Stop the accusing then' (*fa-nziʿ ʿani l-ʿadhli*), 'Leave the blaming then' (*fa-daʿi l-lawma*). The poet even recounts to the admonisher the humiliation he suffered: fate chased him from the metaphorical watering-places of love and condemned him to endless thirst. The analogy of love with a watering-place (41) is a reprise from an evocation of women earlier in the same strophe (6–11), summarized in verse 42. The response ends with a second address (43), in which the poet equates the loss of love with virtual death, using the analogy of a lame old stallion (45). Other unintroduced dialogues feature the same interlocutor or her companion figure, the spy (*raqīb*).[38] With the personified *shayb* the poet could use his imagination and attribute to it changing statements.[39] This abstract interlocutor was not bound to one role, and it allowed the poet a range of responses. The flat figures of the unintroduced dialogue leave the poet no such room, and his submission or resistance will leave them likewise unaffected.

The address

In the unintroduced dialogue, the dramatic framework is economically reduced. In a further type of scene it is stripped to a minimum. This abbreviated encounter, which I call address, consists of a single apostrophe of a person at the beginning of a speech never to be referred to again, though the poet keeps up the tone and attitude initially assumed toward it.[40] Such an address still distinguishes itself from non-dramatic passages by its inclusion of a dramatized poet, a fictional interlocutor – no mere witness – and the structure of the response, beginning with a paraphrased statement. In one such address, the poet faces the accuser with the vocative *'a-ʿādhilatī* and then defends his right to grieve over the precious garb of youth and condemn fate for stealing it.[41] In an address of the neighbor,[42] beginning with the vocative *jāratī*, he admits to the female neighbor that he is being ridiculed for his old age. Instead of quoting the *jāra*, the poet quotes the women's mocking of him and describes how old age and fear of sins have changed him. Then the interlocutor disappears, and the address is concluded by a conventional *wa-rubba*[43] marking the onset of a new passage, an episode on convivial drinking in a garden (68–71). This is followed by further past adventures, ending in a triumphant exclamation, 'How splendid is love and the abodes of pleasure'.[44] Both examples of address conclude sequences of scenes about the hoariness theme (*al-shayb wa-l-shabāb*), and they help the poet to step out from his nostalgic attitude and redirect his mood. In the former address, he recovers so far as to criticize fate's inequity, while in the latter he switches from mourning to outright boasting of past adventures. Formally, the address is the last scene of a sequence to employ both first and second grammatical person and a bridge to a next group of scenes containing the first person alone.

The evocation

In contrast to the dialogue scene centering on the poet's interaction with other personae, the evocation is defined by the impossibility of encounter. Other personae are still involved but they are marked by the grammatical third person as absent and prevented from speaking with the poet. The personae thus evoked are beyond his reach, such as the 'laughing one' (*ḍāḥik*) and the 'beautiful women' (*al-ghāniyāt*) within the aging theme.[45] Above all youth is evoked as the abstract 'prime', 'time', or 'era of youth' (*sharkhu l-shabāb*, *dahr*, *ʿahdu l-shabība*), as a metaphorical 'verdant branch' (*shabābuka l-ghirnīq*, *ghuṣnun warīq*, *ghuṣnu l-shabāb*), or as a personification of the 'beloved' (*ṣāḥib*).[46] An example of the last illustrates the speaker's intense emotion; it begins yearningly 'O friend, whom hoariness took from me' to end in the disillusioned statement 'Alas for the prime of youth, that laments [of him] have abrogated *nasīb*s of pleasure [in his company]!'[47] Time (*zamān*)[48] is evoked in a curse. Characteristic for the evocation is the poet's attempt to contact or confront the persona beyond his reach. By calling upon the unreachable, the caller isolates himself, and his verbal acts grow all the more intense. Greetings are dispatched across distances, like the invocation of rain, or shouted aloud like the exclamation, the lamentation, or the curse.[49] The poet also tries to summon evoked personae by quoting their words from earlier encounters.[50]

In terms of structure, the evoked one never changes to the second person of the dialogue partner after the introductory phrase but remains outside the scene, in the third person. In this type of scene, the grammatical second person remains void except for intermittent addresses of the general 'you'.[51] In the following example, the aging poet evokes the beautiful women (*kawāʿib*). It follows encounters with the female accuser and white hair. Having argued with both, the poet evokes the women in their changed behavior and quotes their former words:

أجِدَّ الغانياتِ قَلَيْنَ وَصلِى   وتَطْبِينِى إليهنّ الطَّوابِى
صَدَدْنَ بأعْينٍ عنّى نَوابٍ   ولَسْنَ عن المَقاتلِ بالنَّوابِى
ولَمْ يَصدُدنَ مِن خَفَرٍ ودَلٍّ   ولكنْ من بِعادٍ واجْتناب
وقُلْنَ كفاكَ بالشَّيبِ امتِهانًا   وبالصَّرْمِ المُعَجَّلِ مِن عِقابِ
وما أَنصَفنَ إذ يصرِمْنَ حَبْلِى   بذَنْبٍ ليسَ منِّى باكتسابِ
وكُنَّ إذا اعتدَدْنَ الشَّيبَ ذَنْبًا   على رَجُلٍ فليس بمُستَتابِ
وما لكَ عندَ مَن يَعتدُّ ظُلماً   عليْكَ بذنْبِ غيرِكَ مِن مَتابِ

Did the women seriously *dislike meeting me*,
while [motives] *call me* to them?

They (pl. f.) turned away with eyes gliding off me,
and they are not [eyes that] glide off the fatal spots.

They did not turn away for bashfulness or dalliance,
but to distance themselves and avoid [me].

They said 'Hoariness suffices you as a humiliation,
and quick separation as a punishment!'[52]

They were not just in severing *my bond*
because of a sin that *I did not commit.*

When they thus counted white hair as sin of a man
from which he could not be asked to desist.

There is no pardon for you from her
who unjustly counts as yours the sin of another.

(L191: 24–30)

The poet questions himself and the general audience whether the women truly refuse him (24, 30), but he never speaks to the women directly. They are portrayed as unjust in punishing him for his aging, which is not his own doing but an act of time (28–9). Their aloof, scornful treatment of him is rendered in minute detail to the point of quoting their words from an earlier encounter (25–7). When they spoke to him then, he remained silent. Now, in the evocation, he defends his former silence to the general 'you' (28–30): their behavior was such as to leave silence as the only dignified response (30), for an innocent man cannot expect justice from the unjust nor repent a crime he has not committed. But such explanations to the general 'you' do not improve the poet's chances with women; they merely rationalize his failure *post factum*. No longer can the aging poet meet women eye to eye. The evocation is a scene that demonstrates the poet's isolation through his persona's verbal impotence.

The monologue

As opposed to evoking other personae, the poet may dwell upon his own feelings. In long monologues, he dramatizes his situation, lamenting his despair over lost love and youth or inadequate patronage.[53] Formally, the monologue is characterized by a first person pronoun in nearly every verse. The poet frequently uses expressive speech acts, such as the lamentation (*nudba*) in 'Oh, my grief for the branch of youth' (*lahfī li-ghuṣni l-shabābi*) or 'Oh, my sorrow' (*fa-yā asafā*) as well as the invocation and the address of the general 'you'.[54] In two monologues, the pronoun is built into the spine of the anaphorae 'Oh, grief of *my soul* for' (*lahfa nafsī li-…*) and 'What *reminds me* of youth is …'

(*yudhakkirunī l-shabāba* . . .).[55] In the dramatization of the protagonist's situation and his relationship to the audience, there are certain similarities with the 'dramatic monologue' of Robert Browning.[56]

In the monologues of the strophe, the poet impersonates the hero of the hoariness theme. The timeframe of the monologue can open towards past or future. Facing his past, the poet chooses a standpoint close to or distant from it. The changing distance between him and his past is one of the key factors in his persona's development. The monologue echoes the dyadic tension of the dialogue scene – except for placing in oppositional roles not two personae, but the past and present life of the poet. The following monologue, preceded by an unintroduced dialogue, highlights the contrast between both time periods.[57]

غيرَ أنِّى مع انْتِزاعِى وإقلا	عِى ودَفعِى إلى نصيحِى خِطامِى
قائلٌ قَوْلَ ذاكرٍ خيرَ عَصْرَيْـ	ـه طويلِ الحَنين والتَّهيامِ
لَهفَ نفسِى على الشَّبابِ الَّذِى أصـ	ـبَحَ خَلْفِى وذِكْرُه قُدّامِى
لَهفَ نفسِى عليه أنْ صارَ حَظِّى	منه لَهْفًا يُعِضُّنِى إبهامِى
لَهفَ نفسِى على الظِّباءِ اللَّواتِى	عاقَنى عن قَنِيصِهِا إحرامِى
لَهفَ نفسِى على احتكامِى على البيـ	ـضِ وإذْعانِهِنَّ عند احتِكامِى
واقتِحامِى ولِلْهَوَى عَزَماتٌ	يَقتحِمْنَ العِقابَ أَىَّ اقتِحامِ
ودِفاعِى خِلالَ ذلك نفسِى	عَن خِلاطِ الحَرامِ بالإلمامِ
لَهفَ نفسِى على الشَّرابِ السَّرامِىْ	ـىِ وإعمالِه بِطاسٍ وجامِ
وعَزيفٍ عليه مِن مُسمِعاتٍ	وحديثٍ عليه مِن أَحْلامِ
وفُكاهاتِ فِتيَةٍ هُمْ إذا شِئْـ	ـتُ إدامٌ لِلْعَيْشِ خيرُ إدامِ
أَخفَقَتْ رَوْحَتِى مِنَ الرَّبْرَبِ العيـ	ـنِ وطاشَتْ مِنَ الرَّمايا سِهامِى
ولَعهْدِى بهِنَّ قبلَ مَشيبِى	ينْتظِمْنَ القلوبَ أَىَّ انتظامِ

But despite *my abduction*, *my departure*,
and my handing over of my nose-rein to him who counsels me,[58]

[*I*] *am speaking* as one, who remembers the better of his two ages,
one who has been yearning and longing hopelessly for a long time:

Oh, grief of my soul for a youth
that is *behind me* and its memory *before me*.[59]

Oh, grief of my soul that *my share of it*
became a regret that *makes me bite my thumb.*

Oh, grief of my soul for the antelopes
that my pilgrim's state *hinders me* from hunting!

Oh, grief of my soul for my power to persuade the white ones,
and their yielding to *my persuading!*

And *my vehemence*, for love has a resolve
that utterly abandons itself time after time!

And *my guarding of my soul* meanwhile
from confusing the forbidden [adultery] with a short lover's visit![60]

Oh, grief of my soul for the Samarra-wine
and its being put to work with goblets and cups!

And the play of female musicians to it,
and the talk of friends about it,

And the jests of men who, *when I wanted*,
were the best enhancement to life.

My success has failed with a troop of the large-eyed [antelopes, i.e.
women], my arrows have missed the game.

Before *my hoariness*, I had been so used to them (sc. my arrows),
piercing right through the [women's] hearts.

(L1250': 46–58)

Sharing his experiences of life, the poet speaks with knowledge and emotion. Aged and disillusioned, he prefers youth, even though he only possesses its memories. Starting in verse 48, an anaphora enumerates his memories, beginning each line, except 52–3 and 55–6, from the present viewpoint with a lamentation of youth's loss. Finally the poet abandons his nostalgia and confronts his reality, which stands in sharp contrast to youth. Sobered, he admits his exclusion from youthful love (57–8). A subsequent dialogue treats his exclusion from convivial drink (59–62).

In monologues, the poet sets a mood by choosing one of two standpoints: staying in the present and deploring the loss of youth or transcending the present and stepping into the memory of the past. When he remains in the present, as in the previous example, the poet's surrender finds many nuances of tone. He accepts old age either calmly, or with deep remorse for having indulged too long in youthful frivolity.[61] The struggle with remorse is dramatized in L1250', where the poet juxtaposes two agents forbidding sin, white hair and the Koran, and accuses himself of obeying the wrong one, fearing apostasy. Then he clears himself from error by identifying white hair as a God-sent symbol like the Koran.

When the aging poet revisits the past, for instance, in the strophe of L1611, this phase becomes his main angle of vision. He mentions his actual fragile state only in the briefest terms; thereafter glowing memories of youth fill episodes of *fakhr*, a battle scene, and desert journey, involving his persona as a witness.[62]

A remarkable monologue is contained in a debate about the ethics of patronage.[63] The poet contrasts his position as a self-respecting loyal panegyrist, with that of an unprincipled self-serving colleague, probably al-Buḥturī.[64] Trusting his patron's promise of later reward (64, 66), he himself scorns gifts from thieves and misers (65, 68) and refrains from satire (60–3). The other poet in turn satirizes any patron who does not immediately yield riches (70). However, Ibn al-Rūmī's persona does not exclude satire, instead he makes it dependent on the patron being described. He is left to decide, through rewarding a poem or not, whether to affirm or belie a generosity that was attributed to him. If the patron omits the reward, the extolled generosity is left pending and turns into an embarrassing lie in the eyes of the audience (71–2). The normal place for debates on patronage being the metastrophe, the monologue's placement in the strophe disassociates it from ʿUbaydallāh, who is not the one the poet wants to criticize. This notwithstanding, the passage provides an insightful glance into Ibn al-Rūmī's professional code of honor.

In the metastrophes the poet's persona is dramatized as a protégé and panegyrist. In a *qaṣīda* of gratitude (L1250'), the entire metastrophe forms one monologue.[65] The poet speaks in it about his love for the patron's qualities (177–9), his gratitude for material support (180–3), and the protection of his right (*ḥaqq*) (184–7). Both monologue and *qaṣīda* end with a double invocation (189).

Short monologues also interrupt long dialogue scenes.[66] In two *qaṣīda*s that contain demands (L191, L1042), the poet's long debate with the patron is interrupted by short monologues. In them, the angry poet steps aside from the patron to reflect on his past attitudes and future expectations concerning the patronage.[67] He admits doubt and reveals his long suffering due to the patron's acts versus his own loyalty.[68] These monologues contain criticism, though indirectly expressed and softened by renewed pledges of loyalty after the poet has resumed the dialogue.[69] The metastrophe typically addresses needs and affairs of the poet and has logically no addressee other than the patron. If the poet prefers to speak to himself in this part of the *qaṣīda*, his true addressee is still not in doubt. This type of scene is above all an indirect and inoffensive way for the poet to impart his worst fears and complaints.

The monologue concludes the group of scenes containing only one grammatical person.

The implicit and impersonal speaker

In some dialogues, however, a sharp imbalance exists between an omnipresent second person and an elusive speaker who does not take shape as a persona. The poet has already been seen in the marginal role of a witness in a dialogue on hyperbolic praise.[70] In other scenes on this topic, the first person speaker remains entirely implicit, his only palpable imprint being acts of speech, such as wishes and advice, that express a state of sincerity. Utterances indicating such a state are the exclamation, optative, imperative, jussive, and the rhetorical question. They correspond to Searle's expressive and directive speech acts, the former focusing on the speaker, the latter on the addressee. As an implicit speaker, the poet assumes an inscrutable attitude towards a subject.

Inversely he may openly distance himself from his subject and adopt the third grammatical person. Then he becomes an impersonal speaker, since the third person is unidentified by a prevailing dialogue situation and absent from it, according to Benveniste's classification of pronouns. In three scenes of hyperbolic praise, the speaker avoids the first person, and instead identifies himself obliquely, referring to his poetry as 'the speech of someone who does not deem too vast the rule you have assumed' (*maqālatu lā mustaʿẓimin mā walītahū*).[71] The interlocutor is explicitly addressed and named.[72]

In the following example, the poet appears both as an implicit speaker and an impersonal 'protégé'.

إذا بِتَّ والفِكْرَ تَسْتخْرِجا   نِ مفتاحَ أَمرٍ عسيرِ الغَلَقْ
وأَنتَ لأَمرِ الْعُلا مُؤْثِرٌ   علَى كُلِّ ناعِمَةِ المُعْتَنَقْ
وأَبدَى لكَ الصُّبحُ عن واضِحَيْـ   ـنِ رأيِكَ مُنبَلِجًا والفَلَقْ
فلِلَّه صُبحُكَ ماذا جَلا   ولِلَّه ليْلُكَ ماذا وَسَقْ
وإمّا أَجَرْتَ مِنَ الحادِثا   تِ جارًا فلَيْسَ عليْه رَهَقْ
يَرَى الدَّهرُ جارَكَ فِى شاهِقٍ   تَأَزَّرَ مِن لُجَّةٍ وانطَلَقْ
وقدْ عَلِقتْ قَبضَتاه عُرًى   بها عَصَمَ اللَّهُ تِلكَ الوُثَقْ
فهل مِن سبيلٍ إلى مِثْلِه   أَبَى اللَّهُ ذاكَ على مَن خَلَقْ
فدونَكها يابْنَ سَيْفِ المُلو   كِ لهوَ المجالِسِ زادَ الرُّفَقْ

When you and your thoughts spent the night
in extracting the key of a matter intricately locked,

You preferred the noble cause
to every [girl of] sweet embrace,

Morning revealed to you two clear things:
your brilliant insight and the break of dawn,

How splendid was what your morning disclosed!
How splendid, what the night contained!

When you protect *a protégé* from misfortunes,
no evil is against him!

Fate sees *your protégé* on a tall [ship],
surrounding himself with [your] deep sea and escaping [fate].[73]

In it (sc. the sea) *his* two fists cling to ties,
may God protect those bonds!

Is there a way to his like?
God refused that to whom he created.

Take it then, son of the sword of kings,
as an entertainment for [convivial] sessions,
as a provision for people travelling together.

(L1307: 39–47)

The speaker interacts with the patron, commending him and dedicating poetry to him, without identifying himself. Instead he describes himself impersonally as 'a protégé' and 'your protégé' (43–4). Nevertheless, the context of the praise leaves no doubt that it is the poet's persona speaking. The scene privileges the 'you' over the speaker himself. But it makes a strong point without the poet's need to appear. Since the speaker praises and dedicates the poem, his good intentions are evident, and his reticence to take credit reads as modesty. Here the poet's attenuated presence strengthens his message.

However, the impersonal speaker also serves the opposite purpose and protects the poet in undesirable situations. This concerns in particular short switches in monologues from 'I' to 'he'.[74] In these lines, the poet's persona finds himself in a reprehensible position, such as charged with sin, skirting apostasy, or disempowered before a metaphorical wife.[75] He is in a state of embarrassment, despoiled of the garb of youth and exposing his decrepit appearance to his patron.[76] Shielded by the third person, the poet acknowledges these faults and weaknesses. He also complains from behind this protection about the patron and defends himself from allegedly having envied or satirized him.[77] An example of the last case illustrates this:

حسبُ امْرِئٍ من هجاءِ شاعرِه　　　مدْحٌ له فيه خابَ مُنقلَبُهْ

Enough satire of a man by his poet is a praise by him
about [the man] the outcome of which disappointed [the poet].

(L215: 71)

The short switches into the impersonal voice cloak a poet who broaches risky territory – be it self-accusation, self-defense, or complaints against his patron. As with the implicit speaker, the identity of the impersonal 'he' is not in question and sufficiently confirmed by the context. It is, rather, an instance of shunning direct contact with the persona to whom he is speaking.

As a non-dramatized speaker, the poet may bring modesty and self-effacement to bear on his relationship with the patron. But the impersonal voice also shifts the focus to pictorial aspects. In some episodes of *fakhr*, the impersonal voice deflects attention from the protagonist's identity to highlight the particulars of his depiction. The poet, as it were, divides himself between the witness, speaking as 'I', and the impersonal protagonist of a conventional theme.

This abstracted hero is the depiction's aim, be it an elaborate, detailed description or phantasmagoria.[78] For instance, he switches himself to 'he' as a boon companion, fascinated with a female cupbearer.[79] In another episode, shown here, he introduces himself as braving the night, '*I donned* its jet-black darkness, then ripped it apart' (*labistu dujāhu l-jawna thumma hataktuhū*, L1611: 84). Then he proceeds to recount his lone journey in the third person as that of 'a noble man on a noble camel':

يَخوضُ عليها لُجَّةَ الهَوْلِ راكِبٌ   هو السَّيفُ إلّا أنَّه لا يُثَلَّمُ
نجيبٌ مِنَ الفِتيانِ فوقَ نَجيبةٍ   مِنَ العيسِ فِى يَهْماءَ واللَّيْلُ أيْهَمُ
فريدَيْنِ يُمضيها وتُمضيه فِى الدُّجَى   كَسَمْراءَ يمُضيها وتمُضيه لَهْذَمُ
يُريها الهُدَى حَدْسًا وتَنجو بِرَحْلِه   ودونَ الهُدَى سدٌّ مِنَ اللَّيْلِ مُبْهَمُ

On her, *a rider* enters the depth of horror,
he is a sword except he has no notches [like the real sword].

A noble man on a noble camel
in a wayless desert in a starless night.

Both alone, *he* propels her and is propelled by her in the darkness,
like a brown [shaft] a spear head propels and is propelled with.[80]

He shows her the right way, guessing, she races with her burden,
beyond the right way lies the dark high-dam of night.[81]

(L1611: 86–9)

In the conclusion of the episode he resumes the first person to relate the motives of his journey, '*I crossed* it (sc. the night) at random, either to reach tranquility or out of boredom with tranquility' (*taʿassaftuhū immā li-khafḍin anālahū wa-immā saʾāma l-khafḍi*, 95). While the poet claims the journey in the first person as his experience, he turns to the third person to describe it, as if to allow the audience to lose themselves in the depth of the image. The two grammatical persons perform complementary functions, in that the 'I' attests to the experience, and the 'he' impersonates it. Their common identity is again ensured by the narrative. But unlike the impersonal speaker, who dissimulates his voice in the scene, the impersonal speaker of *fakhr* episodes steps aside to emphasize the description over his identity as a participant. The priority lies, for example, in the depiction of ghostly desert sounds as funeral and wedding music, and of the night as an obstructing high-dam. The hero's individuality plays a minor role. Furthermore the theme defers to convention, and the poet's credit lies in recasting it in words, not in re-experiencing it.

The scenes' common denominators are the speakers, or dramatis personae, with their interaction, which constitutes the plot. The action is purely verbal,

Subtype of scene (including its scheme of action)	*Criteria: Grammatical person of participants*	*Medium*	*Definition of time and space*
Dialogue (argumentative scheme)	First person and second person	Face-to-face encounter	Same time and space
Dialogue (univocal scheme)	First person (witness) / implicit speaker / impersonal speaker and second person	Face-to-face encounter	Same time and space
Extended dialogue	First person and second person	Face-to-face encounter	Across time and space
Evocation	First (or second) person about absent third person	No encounter	Across time and space
Monologue	First (or second) person	Interior debate	Same time or across time

Figure 7 Subtypes of scenes and their distinctive criteria

including both real and figuratively-attributed speech (see fig. 7). A dialogue scene consists of two personae with polarized standpoints. They meet face to face within the same space and time and use the first and second grammatical person respectively. The tension played out between them is a function of the poet's dramatization. When the plot is univocal and the poet in harmony with his interlocutor, he does not take a strong stand except in a few dialogues of hyperbolic praise. When the plot is controversial, the poet argues his oppositional stance at length. The extended dialogue scene carries speech across space and time, such as in the poet's dialogue with the metaphors of lost youth. Speaker and personified addressee still converse, but they meet in the realm of the abstract. Two further types of scene focus solely on one actor. In the monologue, the poet's persona, speaking in the first person, is torn between past and present in the theme of hoariness or between hope and fear in the theme of patronage. In the evocation, the poet is likewise alone, but he tries to imagine – in vain – the presence of another. That persona keeps to the absent grammatical third person, never meeting the poet face to face; the evoked one's very elusiveness supplies the scene's tension. Hence the evocation, unable to bridge space and time, is the failed variant of the extended dialogue scene. With the prominence and ubiquitousness of Ibn al-Rūmī's persona, his occasional absence becomes a dramatic factor too. He modulates his presence with great virtuosity between a dominant dramatis persona, a self-effacing voice, and occasionally – for (self-)criticism or visual effects – a cloaked identity.

9

THE EPISODE AND ITS WITNESSES

Scenes with dramatic action alternate with others, of a more contemplative nature, defined as episodes.[1] The attraction of an episode is description with its tropical and rhetorical finish. The detail of depiction and the bravado of trope and *concetto* – not dramatized personae – supply the 'action' of the episode. The referential representation of a theme outweighs the identity of the speaker and the protagonist. An occasional interaction between the speaker and an anonymous hearer, addressed as 'you', does not change this focus, for they are merely defined by their roles of composer and recipient of a work of verbal art. The salient trait of these intermittent voices is their lack of independence; they are not expected to disagree or require persuading, like dramatized personae, and will therefore be referred to as 'witnesses'. They appear in the opening verses and various other places of episodes, notably in the above-quoted night ride episode.[2] This introductory function of direct speech in episodes finds confirmation in Hans Wehr's discovery that the common introductory formula, *wa-rubba*, derives from an old interjection.[3] Within an ongoing episode, witnessing voices also indicate variations in an ongoing theme or announce climax and closure.[4] Moreover, the hearer is often addressed in idiomatic phrases.[5] Though only supporting figures, witnesses fulfill important functions: first, they provide the historical poet and his audience a place within the poem; second, they uphold the contact between them on a phatic level; and third, they presuppose the hearers' acknowledgment, on a rhetorical level.[6] In the *fakhr* episode, they confirm the poet's pure skill of poetic depiction, and in episodes of *madīḥ* they attest to the patron's worthiness.

In comparison with dramatized personae, the witnesses are pale discontinuous figures. They can only appear in a grammatical person by default, if it is not taken by a character in a dialogue, with the exception of the poet, who can shift between a witness and a full-fledged persona. Throughout L1306, which consists mostly of dialogue scenes (of the poet with the women and the Ṭāhirids), hardly a witness appears. The dramatized poet's persona is somewhat of an exception, for he can diminish his voice to that of a witness. In an evocation, where only the first and third person are filled by the speaker and the evoked, the pronouns 'you' and 'we' are free to be used for the voices of witnesses. The episode with a third person protagonist, leaves space for 'you', 'we', and 'I' to attest to the events. In short, the witness is a secondary figure that can only exist in a slot that has not otherwise been taken. Therefore, similar phrases coexist for different grammatical persons, matching the prevailing dramatic context, such as 'by my/your life' (*la-ʿamrī/ʿamruka*), 'when you/I want' (*idhā shiʾta/shiʾtu*) and 'you/I/we see' (*tarā/arā/narā*).

Despite their discontinuity, witnesses may contribute to the structure of larger forms. In L1611 the witnessing 'I' reappears at stable intervals. Throughout the *qaṣīda*, it evolves from the poet as hero to the speaker for the people of Baghdad and supporter of the patron. When the 'I' pledges its veracity at the end, it does so with well-established authority. Similarly it declares itself as an authority about the patron:

عَلِمْتُكَ فيكَ الخيْرُ والشَّرُّ كُلُّه   وكُلُّكَ خيْرٌ عِندَ مَن يَتَفَهَّمُ

I have known you: you hold all the good and bad [to reward and punish],
but you are all good for him who comes to understand you.
(L1611: 223)

In terms of the speech situation, the episode deviates from the dyadic structure of the dialogue scene. On the one hand, the 'I' dwindles at times to an implicit existence in acts of speech, or is replaced by an impersonal 'he'. On the other hand, the witnesses fluctuate between 'I,' 'we', and 'you', and personifications, such as camels, bags, or spears that have temporarily been endowed with speech. Most witnesses appear only once in an episode, except for the 'you', which may recur over a few lines, without, however, constituting a dramatized persona.[7] The witnessing figures add slightly different nuances, the first person occurs more often in *fakhr* episodes, since the theme of *fakhr* encapsulates the poet as hero, while the second person predominates in *madīḥ* episodes to represent the audience's agreement to the contents.[8] The following sections present the different witnesses alone and in combination.

Witnesses speaking or addressed in the episode

As a witnessing 'I', the poet directly observes and guarantees the circumstances described. This role of a conveyor marks the opening and closing formulae but leaves the bulk of an episode to other figures. In episodes of *fakhr*, these are other personae or personified animals and objects, such as veiled urban beauties, a cupbearer of manifold traits, wine, the she-camel, and a group of antelope hunters whom the poet joins.[9] This non-dramatized 'I' spare does not battle with his emotions. Instead the witnessing poet tells of conventional experiences, such as loving, drinking, and crossing the desert, foregrounding his recreation of these situations rather than insisting on his own performance in them, as for example in the dedication. To the composing and pronouncing 'I', the verse, the identity of the protagonist is irrelevant, since the true credit lies in the rendition.

In *madīḥ* episodes, the 'I' attests to conventional acts and attributes of the patron, such as courage and leadership. In this role, the poet as witness assumes responsibility for the suitability of a passage to the historical patron. His acts of speech pledge his commitment and integrity. This moral responsibility is particularly accentuated in L1611, where the poet sends a message to the Ṣaffārid usurper ʿAmr b. Layth, who had been granted the government of Baghdad by the caliph and appointed ʿUbaydallāh as his deputy. In a message to ʿAmr, the poet vouches for ʿUbaydallāh's character and portrays himself as a reliable source about his patron.[10] The witnessing poet first conducts a dialogue scene with the addressee ʿAmr (147–76). Then he reappears in the framing verses of several *madīḥ* episodes (168–204), recalling his role as an authoritative speaker. Depending on the context, the witnessing 'I' claims credit for the poetic rendering in *fakhr*, and authorship and responsibility in *madīḥ*.

In some dialogue scenes, the poet's persona vanishes except for his witnessing voice.[11] Then his focus shifts to his interlocutor whose views he adopts. Conversely, a vocal poet's persona creates a tension with the patron. By portraying himself in a distinct role, the poet implies a distribution of tasks between him and the patron that results in an interdependence, be it on a professional level, between panegyrist and patron, or on an ethical level, between protégé and ruler. Whereas the poet faces fictional conversation partners alone, he rallies himself to other witnesses, such as 'you', 'we,' and quoted third persons, when he addresses historical figures. For instance, in the dialogue scene with the Banū Ṭāhir, their plurality is matched by the plurality of the witnessing subjects' 'we'. Other witnesses also join the 'I' in addressing individuals, such as ʿUbaydallāh or ʿAmr b. Layth.[12] All in all, there is a great variety of ways for the poet to represent himself within the encomia. As a persona, he takes a concrete dramatized role opposite fictional figures or the patron; as a witness, he serves as a conveyor and guarantor; and as an implicit speaker, he hides behind the scene, letting others speak.

The 'we' expands the joys and trials of the dramatized poet to a common experience, e.g. in evocations of the cupbearer's beauty and time's injustice.[13] More often, the 'we' appears where an action is undertaken by a group of people, for instance, the hunters in a *fakhr* episode.[14] In that passage, the protagonists' 'we' is distinguished from the other witnesses, 'I' and 'you'. The boasting 'we' makes the poet a participant in a small group. In *madīḥ*, the witnessing 'we' stands *mutatis mutandis* for the subjects or humankind at large, and it frequently introduces the antistrophe.[15] This praising 'we' aligns the poet with the subjects' voice and standpoint. In both themes, the 'we' encompasses hunters and subjects to denote an actual group, as part of which the poet regards himself for a moment. But the plural harbors ambiguity. Does the poet's voice solicit the subjects' support to strengthen his voice, or does he hide in the crowd, conveying *their* approval of the patron, while reserving his own judgment? A third possible explanation for the poet's preference of 'we' over 'I', is his modesty or dissimulation.[16] Each passage then needs to be scrutinized individually for its configuration of first person witnesses and their implications.

The general 'you' is most frequently called upon as a witness.[17] No arguing is expected, and the anonymous hearer's acquiescence is taken for granted.[18] The force of this 'you' lies in the speaker's confidence that his rendition will stand the test of the audience. He challenges them to see, imagine, and experience, in short, validate his account. This explicit address of the audience does not single out any distinct persona. All thinking and feeling hearers are included in it. This very openness and universality give the 'you' its assertive power, since the facts it is called to perceive become equally universal. The less the witnessing 'you' is limited, the broader its scope of approval becomes, be it for the patron's excellence or the poet's *oeuvre*.

In single occurrences, the 'you' gains a certain deliberateness. It may even represent the poet himself, when he generalizes his experience to share it with the audience (1307: 1–6 and L1306: 1–4). As 'you' he contemplates, together with the audience, his own acts from the outside.[19] The general 'you' is also dramatized occasionally in long passages. Nonetheless it does not build a person with distinct features, for it reunites diametrically opposed behaviors, as in the following example, taken from the end of a *madīḥ* episode:

بلا سَبَبٍ فالْتَمِسْ رِفدَه   فإنَّكَ تَقرَبُ ماءً رَفَقْ

وهلْ يستعدُّ الرِّشاءَ امرُؤٌ   لورِدِ الفُراتِ إذا ما فَهِقْ

ألا فارْجُهُ واخْشَهُ إنَّه   هو البَحرُ فيه الغِنَى والغَرَقْ

ألا فارْجُهُ واخْشَهُ إنَّه   هو الغيثُ فيه الحَيا والصَعَقْ

مُضِرٌّ بمُلتَمِسٍ ضُرَّه   وفيه لمُرتَفِقٍ مُرتَفَقْ

هو السَّيفُ إنْ أنتَ أنحَيْتَه   لِرأْسِكَ أو رَأْسِ قِرنٍ فَلَقْ

هو الماءُ فاشْرَبْه ذا غُلَّةٍ   وذا غُصَّةٍ وتوَقَّ الشَرَقْ

هو النَّارُ فاصْطَلِها واسْتَضِئْ   بها فِي الدُّجَى وتوَقَّ الحَرَقْ

Seek his present without a rope,
for you approach a water easily reachable.[20]

Does a man prepare a well rope
to scoop from the Euphrates when it is flooding?

Oh, ask him and fear him! For he is the sea
in which there is wealth and drowning.

Oh, ask him and fear him! For he is the downpour
in which there is life-giving rain and thunder bolts.

He harms one who seeks his harm,
and he has gentleness for one who is gentle.

He is the sword, if you strike with it your head
or an adversary's it cleaves [it] into halves.

He is water, drink it, O thirsty one
and you with a lump in your throat,
but beware not to choke [from hasty drinking]!

He is fire, warm yourself with it, and take it as light
in the darkness, but beware not to scorch!

(L1307: 24–31)

The 'you' is presumed, by an implicit speaker, to fear the patron and ask his favors, to fight him and be defeated by him, to have recourse to him but to respect him. It has no attributes by itself, but brings out those of the patron. Its scope of experience is coextensive with the patron's diametrically opposed acts. This ubiquity makes the 'you' the ideal witness of the boundless and timeless achievements of poetry's protagonists in their multiform aspects.

Alternatively, the anonymous 'you' can be solicited in specific circumstances or even quoted as speaking. Other occurrences are idiomatic phrases, as old as Arabic itself, such as the demonstrative *tilkumū*, the exclamations *la-ʿamruka*, *ḥasbuka*, *nāhīka*, and *kafāka*, verbs of perception, such as 'you see him, imagine him' (*tarāhu, takhāluhū*), and conditional clauses of the kind 'if you want, require' (*law/idhā shi'ta*) and 'when you require it' (*ḥīna taṭṭalibuh*).[21] These phrases are still stronger than their impersonal cognates,[22] and their currency does not erase their meaning, for their rather pale effect can be revived in judicious combination with less common forms, as in the previous quote. In general they prompt the audience's acknowledgment of recited praise. Given in private, however well rewarded, a praise poem is both invalid and irrelevant, for it purports to enhance a patron's public reputation – that which satire destroys.[23] The general 'you' provides the space for the public to fulfill this requirement: it opens the text for the historical audience to participate in it.[24] In a similar, though more specific way, the historical poet and patron participate in the dedication. The audience's reception provides a basis for the claims of the poet's persona and for his display and offer of the highest poetic skill to a worthy addressee. The formalism of the audience address does not imply its weakness but rather its deep rootedness in the poetic idiom. Benveniste explains the nature of the first and second pronouns as made for such iterative usage:

> It is both an original and fundamental fact that these 'pronominal' forms do not refer to 'reality' or 'objective' positions in space or time but to the utterance, every time unique, that contains them, and [they] thereby reflect their own use.... Language has solved this problem (sc.

> intersubjective communication) by creating a group of 'empty' signs, not referential towards 'reality', always available, and which are 'filled' as soon as a speaker assumes them, in every instance of his speech .... Hence the indicators *I* and *you* cannot exist as virtual signs; they only exist in as far as they are actualized in the instance of speech, in which they mark, by each of their own instances, the process of appropriation by the speaker.[25]

Of course one cannot retrieve from a transmitted text the actual response of the audience during its performance, but one can observe how the author made provision for it by the space he allocated it. In Ibn al-Rūmī's *madīḥ*, the general 'you' offers such an empty space for interaction, whether it was actualized in a given situation or not.

Episodes bring forth different functions of the general 'you'. First, it is called upon to perceive acts and qualities of personae and objects, such as phenomena of the desert or character traits of the patron.[26] Second, the 'you' should ascertain the veracity of acts and qualities. It acknowledges women's slender waists as well as their mercilessness and, likewise, the patron's generosity, popularity, universality, excellence, and the tidings about him.[27] In both, the first and second type, the 'you' emerges as a thinking, rational being called upon to see (*ra'ā*) and encounter (*laqiya*), to indicate (*dalla 'alā*), distinguish (*tabayyana*), and estimate (*iḥtasaba*) facts, as well as to express desire (*shā'a, iṭṭalaba*). The 'you' initiates some of the exchanges by a question (*sa'ala*), a statement (*qāla*), and an intention (*qaṣada*) to which the protagonist reacts. The *tarā/takhālu* phrase occurs only rarely. Sometimes this verificatory task is given to an anonymous messenger, halfway between a witness and a dramatized persona.[28] Third, the 'you' is asked to appreciate the poetic description of objects perceivable by the senses or the imagination. It is called upon to compare the taste and intoxication of wine with a kiss and embrace, to see the color of wine as it moves from the glass into the drinkers' cheeks as yellow turning red, the white-faced antelopes becoming blood-smeared in the hunt as white turning yellow, or the blood-splashed hunting steeds as dyed with henna and redwood.[29] The 'you' is summoned to see the black streak on the back of an oryx as the traced letter *lām* and hear the discordant nocturnal desert sounds as simultaneous funeral and wedding music.[30] Regarding the patron, the 'you' acknowledges common metaphors, such as his war as a fire cooking his enemies, his belligerence and hospitality as two permanent fires, his munificence as gushing springs, and the camels' self-impelled journey towards him.[31] The inner consistency of analogues is also tested by the 'you', e.g. the concomitance of full moons with darkness, as an image for women hidden in camel litters, or the impossibility of touching fire, as a guarantee that consumed wine in a drinker's belly, being fire itself, cannot be touched by the fire of hell.[32] This 'you' accompanies phenomena apparent to one's eye, touch, or imagination. It is frequently contained in phrases, especially where visual (*tarā*) and imaginary (*takhālu*) phenomena are concerned.[33] Tactile phenomena require more variation (*tulāmisu, tamassu*). This third variant of 'you' is limited to passive reception. It loses its interactive quality and becomes a rhetorical device, serving as an anchor for imagery. However, even as a silent, passive observer, the ubiquity of the 'you', still shows the significance of the recipient. In his use of all three aspects of the anonymous hearer, Ibn al-Rūmī does not seek an objective description of events, but a human perception of them. This subjectivity, i.e. the connection of the text to the human standpoint, is a prerequisite for the ethical force with which Ibn al-Rūmī endows his poetry.

Witnesses quoted in the episode

In poem L1611, several episodes of *madīḥ* infer quotations of witnesses other than the three pronouns discussed. An anonymous bystander supposes divine inspiration in the raving panegyrist: 'The themes of poetry obey him (sc. the patron), the rhymes are such that I am told "You receive divine inspiration".'[34] But not only humans are 'quoted'; when the camel mare suffers from thirst and bleeding feet, 'her soul tells her, "Hold on, ʿUbaydallāh has an abundant fountain".'[35] Even a spear calls an oryx to stop and accept death: 'They (sc. the flock of oryx) tried to escape, and our lances spoke to one of them that ran far, "Turn, this is your place of turning (sc. dying)!"'[36] These personifications exemplify the tendency to figurative and fantastic action that distinguishes the episodes from the scenes of this *qaṣīda*.[37]

The encomia greatly vary in the degree of relying on witnesses. Their frequency depends above all on the proportion of scenes and episodes in a *qaṣīda*'s dramaturgy. L191 and L215, with many argumentative dialogue scenes, have few witnesses; L1611, filled with episodes of *fakhr* and *madīḥ*, strongly relies on them. Most *madīḥ* episodes (antistrophe) contain witnesses of several kinds, among which the 'you' predominates. 'I' and 'we' have a tendency to appear together, building up interesting tensions, such as shown in an earlier example of a dialogue between the poet and the Banū Ṭāhir on hyperbolic praise.[38] The subjects begin the speech (L994: 21) and the poet's attestation closes it (29–30), but whereas the subjects merely affirm the Ṭāhirids' paramount place, the poet understands and explains how exactly they attained it, to wit, by their self-sacrificial heroism against fate and their protection of the caliphate. He then interprets their past and projects their future. In the subsequent dialogue scenes, he continues to speak as an implicit speaker (45) without the subjects' support (42, 79).[39] In addition to the 'I' and 'we', other witnesses populate the dialogue scene: 'the one who sees and does not deny' (20), 'he who aspires [to Ṭāhirid ranks]' (22), 'he who calls about a vicissitude' (24), 'a poverty-stricken one' (25), 'victims rescued', and lastly 'blamed fate' who will not care for anyone, after the Ṭāhirids will have gone. Every act of the Tahirids is experienced by some subject, whether sympathetic or hostile. The scene is constructed as a three-way interaction, the Ṭāhirids' dialogue with the witnessing poet and subjects, and their narrated interaction with third persons.

In another episode, L215: 87–104, the poet does not distinguish himself from the subjects (87, 90). Together, they are saved from fate and lavished with presents:

أعتَبَنا الدَّهرُ بالأَميرِ فلا   بُروكُه يُشتكَى ولا خَبَبُه

واسْتَوطأَ الرَّحْلَ مِنه راكِبُه   وطالَ ما قدْ نبا بِه قَتَبُه

راعٍ ومرْعًى فلا رعِيَّتُه   يُلْفَى لها مُشتَكٍ ولا عُشُبُه

تغدو مَتابيعُه مِنَ النَّعَمِ الـ   ـعُوذِ علينْا وتارةً سُلُبُه ...

زينةُ سَقْفِ الأَنامِ لا أَفَلوا   أعلامُه مُمطِراتُه شُهُبُه

مِنهُمْ ذَوو الجَهرِ والأَصالةِ والْـ   ـمَعروفِ والنُّكْرِ حينَ تطَّلِبُهْ

زانوه زَيْنَ الفريدِ واسِطَةَ الـ   ـعِقْدِ زها فى النِّظامِ مُنتخَبُهْ

وزانَهُمْ زَيْنَها صَوَاحِبَها   لا فضَّ ما فِى النِّظام مُنْقَضَبُهْ

كَأَنْ عليْه قِلادةٌ نُظِمَتْ   مِن لؤلؤٍ لا تَشينُها ثُقَبُهْ

Fate *satisfied us* with the prince;
neither his sitting nor his amble is complained of.

His rider finds with him a soft saddle,
after his [own] pack saddle has been uncomfortable
for him for a long time.

A shepherd and his pasture,
with his flock or grass no one [can] find fault.

His ewes with lambs *come to us in the morning*,
and sometimes, those without . . .

The ornament on the roof of humanity,
its guides, its bringers of rain, its seven planets –
may they (sc. the Banū Ṭāhir) *never set!*

Among them are those of fame and sound judgment,
kindness and cunning, if you require it.

They decorate him like pearls decorate the center stone of the necklace,
whose selection radiates in the arrangement.

He decorates them like it (sc. the center stone) decorates the others –
may no breaking scatter the arrangement!

As if he wore a chain,
strung of pearls unblemished by borings.

(L215: 87–90, 99–103)

In the first part (87–90), the subjects as 'we' declare their satisfaction with the patron as ruler. The ruler's qualities are cast in oppositional pairs as a camel's resting and running (87), and his relationship to his subjects and realm compared to that of a shepherd with his flock and pasture (90). The human figures appearing within the images also express their satisfaction with the ruler: 'he who rides' the patron as a metaphoric camel finds his saddle soft (88). In the shepherd analogue, 'no one [can] find fault' with the patron's metaphoric pasture and flock (89). The poet's first person stays aloof, but the episode is still doubly verified by the poet and the subjects, speaking as a group, and by the third person figures at the figurative level. In the second part (99–102), the witnesses disappear except for the 'you', warned not to provoke the Ṭāhirids. Instead, metaphors of stars (99) and a pearl necklace (101–3) illustrate the dynasty's cohesion. The necklace metaphor in particular emphasizes the mutual support of ʿUbaydallāh and his ancestors. Again the 'I' does not appear, but the patron's excellence is twice verified: first, the 'you' is challenged to confirm their qualities on the level of direct dialogue; and second, the implicit speaker voices his support in two invocations in the optative mood: the stars representing the Ṭāhirids shall never set (*lā afalū*, 99), and the pearls in the necklace representing them shall not be scattered (*lā faḍḍa … munqaḍabuh*, 101). Even without the poet's first person, other witnesses and (metaphoric) third person figures sufficiently replace his voice. The episode can now be schematized in contrast with the scene (see fig. 8).

When comparing the preceding example of an episode with the dialogue scene L994: 20–31, one notices a different stance of the first person speaker. *Qaṣīda* L994 shows a self-assured 'I' that steps out of the 'we' of subjects and carries on the dialogue with the Ṭāhirids, praising the absent patron ʿUbaydallāh. In contrast, the speaker in L215 is implicit and replaced by a plethora of other voices. The implicit voice of the poet can be ambiguous. In L215, which is dedicated in a self-effacing fashion, the poet's absence implies modesty. In other poems, however, where a dedication is missing, and the poet is at odds with the patron, his absence from the praise may be construed as hesitation and reserve, as will be shown in the next chapter.

A = Poet's persona or witnessing 'I'
(A) = Implicit speaker
B = Historical persona
C_1 = Witnessing 'we'
C_2 = Witnessing 'you'

A/(A)/C_1 → C_2
'A, (A) and/or C_1 give an account of B's acts to C_2'

Structure
– Account of B's acts
– Attestation or evaluation of the acts by A, (A), C_1 and/or C_2
– Additional attestation or evaluation by third person figures

Figure 8 Schematization of the episode with witnesses

In sum, Ibn al-Rūmī uses the dramaturgy of scene and episode to subtly modulate his persona's voice. Where the poet dramatizes himself in encounters with fictional personae, he does not seek multi-vocal confirmation; rather, his own eloquent self suffices. But the episodes and univocal dialogue scenes show a greater complexity of description and imagery, so as to dispense with dramatic action. However, these passages leave space for a minimal interaction between poet and audience in the guise of witnessing voices. These occur most frequently regarding the patron, sanctioning the poet's words about him, his ancestors, and his overlord.

The salient traits of episodes and scenes may now be reformulated (see figs 9 and 10).[40] The essential difference between both passages is their focus, persuasive and responsible interaction in the scene, versus visualization and focus on intertextuality in the episode. The scene presents as its action a dialogue between two partners, interacting as individuals with their specific standpoints and convictions, or between the conflicting attitudes of one speaker. Vivid exclamations, well-integrated syntactical figures, and a fluid syntax carry the scene. Its argument is distributed judiciously among the dramatized figures. These epitomize at crucial points its gist with rhetorical questions, sententiae and analogies without weighing it down. The beauty of a scene is its whole; it does not survive in partial quotation. The monologue and the evocation

	Scene	*Episode*
Essential	Polarity between two acting personae or within one	Descriptive agenda with sporadic attestation or participation by witnesses
Theme	The relationship between two personae or the acts of one	The protagonist, his acts, attributes, companions, and surroundings

Figure 9 Essential differences of scene and episode

Type of passage	*Speakers*	*Scheme of action*	*Structure*	*Dominant stylistic tools*
Dialogue Monologue Evocation Address	Two acting personae/ attitudes	Argumentative	Dialectic response	Direct speech, figures of closure, and rhetorical figures
Dialogue	One acting persona and one witness/ implicit speaker	Univocal	Affirmation	
Fakhr episode (witnessing 'I' predominates) *Madīḥ* episode (witnessing 'you', 'we' predominate)	Witness(es) and/or implicit speaker	Univocal	Attesting account	Description and various tropes

Figure 10 Subtypes of scenes and episodes

condense the controversy into one persona with his inner tension or yearnings for an unreachable other. The evocation and the *fakhr* episode share both the third person protagonist, e.g. the women evoked or the *mamdūḥ* described, and the second person witness. They differ however in the stance of the speaker, who is a dramatized character in the evocation, but only a marginal figure in the episode.

The *madīḥ* episode presents a state or situation of the patron as conveyed between poet and audience. The focus is on the content, while the act of conveying validates it. Direct speech in the form of quotes and addresses of witnesses performs this attesting role. But the witnesses do not take part in the action. Historical personae take the center stage, described in the third person in habitual or timeless actions, and in literal and metaphorical representation (see Appendix C). In the episode, which is more representational than interactive, the verbal ornament draws on all registers of the archaic lexicon, tropes, rhetorical figures, and phantasmagoria. Therefore, its verses retain their beauty in quotation, isolated from the poem. The *fakhr* episode dramatizes the protagonist represented by 'I' to a certain extent as an agent in a past or present action. This speaker does not describe exploits for the sake of claiming their actual experience; rather, he appropriates both ancient and modern poetic topoi of description: his beloved, a cup of wine, a hunting party, his camel, as well as the physical surroundings of garden or desert. He treats even himself occasionally as an anonymous protagonist and resumes the first person only in instances of witnessing, which changes a passage from the act itself to the description of one. This speaker does not so much lay claim to having performed an act but to having said it anew.

With the controversial dialogue and the episode at both ends of the spectrum, the middle ground is occupied by the scene with a univocal scheme, e.g. the dialogue with the Ṭāhirid ancestors (L994: 21–30). The Ṭāhirids perform the actions that affect the poet as witness and other third person figures, and the poet responds by giving his confirmation. This type of scene resembles the episode in its structure of account and testimony and its ornament of tropes and rhetorical figures, richer than that of the argumentative dialogue. However, the univocal dialogue still differs from the episode by the apostrophe of individuals included in the dialogue, as opposed to the third person account about the episode's protagonist. In other words, the scene contains a direct act of speech, and the episode the description of one. The univocal dialogue scene, though less vivid than the controversial variant, still provides a space for the direct interaction of poet and patron. Poems of felicitation exemplify this; they constitute the act of congratulating and do not merely give an account of it. This gamut of interactive and descriptive units in Ibn al-Rūmī's *madīḥ*, presented here in their subtle gradations, allows for a sophisticated dramaturgy of complete *qaṣā'id*, to be shown in the next two chapters.

10

'THE PASSION OF HIM WHOSE PARTING HAS GRAYED IS AFFECTATION' (L191)

As scene after scene sheds light on the facets of the poet's persona – or as episodes periodically conceal him – he grows into a palpable character animating the *qaṣīda* as a whole. This and the following chapter show how scenes and episodes are built around him into an overarching dramaturgy. *Qaṣīda* L191, whose incipit forms the chapter heading, stands out as composed almost exclusively of scenes. Its strophe, as many others, assembles dialogue scenes, monologues, and evocations, creating with the varying fictional participants a dynamic environment for the poet's persona.[1] Operating in a tight interplay, the fictional personae guide the course of action. According to their character, they confront the poet with word and gesture, prompting his reaction. The personae succeed each other in such a way that a scene dominated by one of them introduces, in the grammatical third person, the persona about to enter in the next scene. White hair, mentioned in the first dialogue scene to the poet's defense, 'O my accuser, the white hair of my head has tamed me for you' (*a-ʿādhila rāḍanī laki shaybu ra'sī*, 2–4), appears as a conversation partner in the second dialogue, 'I said, greeting white hair, "Welcome you guide of the erring towards the truth"' (*wa-qultu musalliman li-l-shaybi ahlan bi-hādī l-mukhṭi'īna ilā l-ṣawābī*, 9–11).

Other scenes are less openly concatenated, and a new persona may ensue by implicit association. At the end of an evocation of lost youth, for example, the poet conjures youth with the metaphorical greeting, 'May the time when I knew youth be watered by every shower!' (*saqā ʿahda l-shabībati kullu ghaythin*, 20–2). Since youth essentially signifies a man's desirability to women (or men), it is logical for the poet to evoke these in the following scene in which he wonders, 'Do the women seriously dislike meeting me?' (*a-jidda l-ghāniyāti qalayna waṣlī*, 24). Whether apparent or implied, the sequence of the personae predicts the course of the argument. Each sets a theme; personified hoariness evokes old age, mocking women lost youth, the female neighbor obstinate love and grief, and so forth. They also take a specific viewpoint of the poet's action, dictating their attitude towards him; the women scorn him, the neighbor criticizes his lack of self-control, while hoariness assumes various positions. The responding poet vaunts, justifies, regrets, or even condemns his past actions.

Despite the fixed themes and viewpoints signalled by the personae, the poet can choose either to submit and pretend to agree, or to rebel, or simply to remain aloof. The poet's attitude also evolves in the spaces between encountering each of these interlocutors, though each is immutable.[2] Having taken a stand *vis-à-vis* one, the poet picks as his next partner a persona whose theme and viewpoint require him to modify that stance. In this fashion, the poet journeys through an itinerary of attitudes with the personae as his stations. The series of scenes, juxtaposing the changing positions of the poet, achieves a dynamic flow, for the encounters' dialectic nature motivates each of his shifts and ensures the cohesion of his evolving persona.

The strophe of L191 begins with such a series of scenes, divided into three parts: dialogue, evocations and monologue, and a return to dialogue (see fig. 11). In the initial dialogue, the poet directs his words at the accuser (2), submitting to her but subordinating her authority to that of white hair (7), the persona of the second dialogue. To white hair (9), the poet responds by turning its warning of imminent death into good tidings and the reward of afterlife, which is a reunion with the poet's slain beloved 'time of youth' (14–17), the persona to appear in the next scene, an evocation. There, the poet greets the time of youth (20) and defines it by negation, as a time without yearning. He then evokes the women as the causes of this yearning (24). Their avoidance of the poet prompts him to

2–8	Dialogue with (female) accuser (*ʿādhila*, 2): She is powerless next to the authority of white hair (*kafā bi-l-shaybi min nāhin muṭāʿin . . . wa-min dāʿin mujābī*, 7).
9–19	Dialogue with white hair (*wa-qultu musalliman li-l-shaybi 'ahlan'*, 9): The poet rejoices at its announcement of his death (*a-lasta mubashshirī . . . bi-washki taraḥḥulī? . . . laqad bashshartanī bi-laḥāqi māḍin*, 10–11), for it signifies the poet's reunion with his former time of youth, or 'twin-brother' of his life (*idhā alḥaqtanī bi-shaqīqi ʿayshī*, 16).
20–23	Evocation of the time of youth (*saqā ʿahda l-shabībati*, 20): Yearning and thirst were absent in it (*layāliya lam aqul 'saqyan li-ʿahdin!' wa-lam arghab ilā suqyā saḥābī*, 21).
24–30	Evocation of the women (*a-jidda l-ghāniyāti qalayna waṣlī*, 24): They condemn the white hair as a sin of the poet (*wa-qulna 'kafāka bi-l-shaybi mtihānan'*, 27; *man yaʿtaddu ẓulman ʿalayka bi-dhanbi ghayrika*, 30).
31–64	Monologue on youth (*yudhakkirunī l-shabāba*, 31–60 passim): Evoked personae and images beginning with women's stinginess (*shuḥḥu l-ghāniyāti*, 32) remind the poet of youth.
65–70	Dialogue across time with Mantle of Youth (*yā burda l-shabābi*, 65): He regrets having worn it out (*balīta ʿalā l-zamāni . . . ʿazza ʿalayya an tablā wa-abqā*, 66–7). He wishes he could have preserved it for the king (*law mulliktu ṣawnaka . . . lam albaska illā . . . yawma ziyārati l-maliki*, 69–70).

Figure 11 Synopsis of scenes in the strophe of L191 (personae underlined)

recite a monologue, containing a series of images that remind him of youth: the women's stinginess in love, their carelessness and their murderous glances. Further images project human emotion into natural scenes: pliant twigs, a languid afternoon sun, a crystal clear pond, the scented breeze from the East, flashes of lightning, cooing doves and the calling of a mother-camel (47–60). The images show that lost youth so occupies the poet's mind that he sees it everywhere around himself – or he perceives only such scenes that echo it. In his banter with white hair, he could still conquer the pain of having lost youth, but to himself he cannot deny it. Youth is ubiquitous for him and its memory inescapable. At the end of the monologue, he finally yields to remembrance. His outbreak of grief strongly contrasts his former pretended welcoming of old age and death. Through contemplating images of youth, the poet accepts its loss and faces his own sadness. Youth's irrevocable loss is then symbolized by the personification of its worn-out 'mantle', the last dialogue partner of the series of scenes.

The poet's pervasive grief has been subdued to acceptance, when he apologizes to the coat for having worn it to shreds. The mantle of youth, in turn, provides a transition to the antistrophe and the patron. Except for the women, every persona in the strophe is introduced explicitly in the scene preceding its appearance. The order of personae proceeds from the present time of accuser and hoariness to the former time of youth and its reminders. The larger movement passes in seemingly circular fashion from dialogue to monologue to dialogue, with the initial and final personae being addressed directly, and those in the middle part only evoked in a greeting or a quote from a previous encounter. But there is more to the dramaturgy. The self-centered middle part culminates in the poet's long monologue, yielding to his grief in many exclamations (61). The return to the dialogue transports him to a higher plain. Looking now beyond the boundaries of time and space, he acknowledges his advanced age, by metaphorically bidding farewell to the personification of lost youth. The order of scenes actually follows an upward spiral, from direct to indirect encounter, to a final direct encounter on the metaphoric level, where the poet transcends the fictional intermediaries that make him aware of his aging, to face and accept obliterated youth itself.

The characterizations of *shayb* (white hair) and *shabāb* (youth) anchor the time frame of the series in the present. Youth remains an elusive concept, and the poet's gaze never leaves the vantage of his actual old age. Every persona and image connected with youth attests above all to its absence. This is the opposite of another strophe (L1250': 63–71), where the poet steps into the past and boastingly claims its memory as timeless. In L191, the characterizations of *shayb* and *shabāb* place memory at an unbridgeable distance. *Shayb* however, directly interacts with the poet, forcing itself – literally – onto him, and keeping essentially to one designation (4, 7, 9, 27, 29). It is humanized in regretting its murder of the beloved youth and desiring to redeem its sin by bringing the two lovers back together in death. *Shabāb* remains an abstract concept like time, the nights, and the past, and becomes only palpable in the marks of its absence, such as hostile women, symbolizing the thirst for love and tears. *Shabāb* is also personified in unreachable figures, such as the poet's departed beloved and deceased twin-brother, or metaphors of loss, such as the worn out mantle. The appearances of youth thus vacillate between an abstract concept and a personification.[3]

The poet's persona is characterized by his verbal acts and his attitude towards remembrance. He does not initiate any dialogue but passively suffers the words and actions of other personae towards him; white hair and the accuser subjugate him (2–3), white hair goads him (9) and brings him news (10), the women shun him (24), and they (31, 34, 40) together with nature (47, 50, 53, 57, 60) force him to recall his youth. His responses only aim at limiting or reinterpreting the other personae's actions. In the initial dialogues, white hair dominates the scene, performing multiple acts, ranging from announcing death or reunion, to taming, promising, bereaving, reconciling, and rewarding:

وأَنتَ وإن فتكْتَ بِحِبٍّ نفسِى　　وصاحبِ لَذَّتِى دونَ الصِّحابِ
فقد أَعْتَبْتَنِى وأَمَتَّ حِقْدِى　　بحَثِّك خَلْفَه عَجِلاً رِكابِى
إذا أَلحَقْتَنِى بشَقيقِ عَيْشِى　　فقدْ وَفَّيْتَنِى فيه ثوابِى
وحَسْبِى مِن ثوابِى فيه أَنِّى　　وإيّاه نَؤوبُ إلى مَآبِ

Even if you have slain the beloved of my soul
and the matchless companion of my pleasure,

You have mended your way and stilled my rancor
by sending my mount quickly after him.

When you reunite me with the twin brother
of my [former] good life (sc. youth),
you grant me thereby my eternal reward.

It is sufficient reward for me regarding him,
that I and he return home.

(L191: 14–17)

The poet obstinately resists white hair as a messenger of death and grief, though he acknowledges his loss of youth, or so it seems. This concept remains vague, wrapped in a double negation (21–3), as if the poet preferred not to face it. But gradually, his fighting spirit weakens. The women, companions of a blissful past, treat the poet in hostile ways that contrast with their once kinder behavior to their erstwhile companion of *shabāb*, which is set off by the conditional mood of its description (35–9, 44). They evoke their former returning of the poet's love by their present cold-hearted rejection (31, 34) and murderous glances (40). All this, the poet does not willingly recall; he is being reminded of it by the women, who torment him to the point that lost love stares at him from every scene of nature. In these dialogues, the poet is still resisting the impulse of memory, and he can counter his dialogue partners with words. But in the monologue, he loses control over the images brought forth by his own mind; women and natural scenes, arranged in an implacable anaphora (*yudhakkirunī l-shabāba*, 47–60), bring his past before his mental eye, and his self-control dissolves into lamentation.

فيا أسَفَا ويا جَزَعَا عليْه   ويا حَزَنَا إلى يومِ الحِسابِ
أأُفجَعُ بالشَّبابِ ولا أُعَزَّى   لقدْ غَفَلَ المُعَزِّى عَن مُصابِى
تَفَرَّقْنا على كُرهٍ جَميعًا   ولَمْ يكُ عَن قِلَى طولِ اصْطِحابِ

Oh, my pity, oh, my regret for it,
oh, my grief until the Day of Reckoning!

Shall I be bereaved of youth and not consoled?
The consoler has neglected my affliction!

We (sc. I and my time of youth) separated entirely against our will,
and not for weariness of long company.[4]

(L191: 61–3)

Thereafter, for the first time, he initiates a dialogue, sending a belated farewell to a metaphor of faded youth.

The personae he encounters affect his attitude toward loss and remembrance. At the beginning, he attempts to limit his loss by reinterpreting it as a gain – reconciliation, reunion, eternal reward – and pretends satisfaction at his approaching end. Above all, Ibn al-Rūmī's persona resists remembrance, but his control gradually slips as he is prompted to remember by the other dramatis personae and his own imagination. At the turning moment in the monologue, the poet's 'I' is almost eclipsed except as the grammatical object of the anaphoric phrases. Ultimately the poet's 'I' resurges in force when he submits to the pangs of his bereavement. In the final dialogue with metaphorical youth, he reiterates this total surrender of control by apologizing for his inability to preserve youth and by bidding it farewell. The earlier denial of grief, and the defensiveness toward the personae reminding him of youth, has given way to a sad acceptance and avowed impotence against fate:

ولو مُلِّكْتُ صَوْنَكَ فاعْلَمَنْهُ   لَصُنْتُكَ فِى الحَريزِ مِنَ العِيابِ

If it had been given me to preserve you,
be assured, I would have kept you in a safe bag.

(L191: 69)

The poet's emerges throughout the scenes as a conflicted character. In speech, he denies the power of memory, defeating the accuser and reversing the figurative statements of white hair. Vainly, though, does he try to block their influence, since his own worst enemy, his memory, emerges from inside and reveals itself in every image of nature. His failing struggle with the personae leads to his larger, doomed struggle with himself and culminates in the recognition and declaration of his defeat. A similar series of scenes constitutes the strophe of *qaṣīda* L215.[5] In both series, the poet's persona undergoes a change through the dialogical process, either from resisting to admitting grief, as in L191, or from being deceived by youth to realizing life's transience and man's weakness, as in L215. Both strophes live in a polarity created through extroverted dialogue scenes, focused on the 'you', and introverted evocations and monologues, centered on the 'I'. They follow an A–B–A pattern in that the scenes either proceed from introverted to extroverted to introverted (L215), or the reverse (L191). The return to the initial orientation brings the poet's development to a conclusion, whether through insight into fate (L215) or acceptance of grief (L191).

There is a tendency of similar adjacent (pairs of) scenes, such as the first two dialogues of L191, or the pairs of evocation and dialogue in L215, to differ in theme and viewpoint, since the introduction of a new persona alters the poet's stance. Inversely, adjacent scenes of different kinds elaborate on the same theme by internalizing or exposing an attitude previously taken. For example, a dialogue following a monologue permits a demonstration before an interlocutor of a conviction previously formed. This is true for the monologue and the final scene of L191 and each pair of scenes in L215. Inversely, a monologue following a dialogue lets the poet further refine an insight gained therein, such as the last monologue of L215, following a dialogue with an anonymous friend. The shifting between introverted and extroverted scenes gives a depth to the poet's persona and a continuity to his consciousness. His development is kept in motion with encounters of interlocutors who motivate its phases. The poet is seen as adjusting to the changing acts of fate – not owing to inconstancy. At the same time, the evolving attitudes of the poet's persona let him recognize the fixed values, among them avoidance of sin, acceptance of fate, and adherence to human modesty. What is more, the poet's persona is characterized by his speech behavior. In L191, he appears mostly as responding to personae and trying to withstand them. In contradistinction to that reactive behavior, the poet's persona of L215 initiates the scenes by confronting his interlocutors, advising them, and soliciting their reactions. His behavior as speaker and his relative control over the dialogue characterize him as sober and self-assured. With all their subtle varieties, both *qaṣīda*s are primarily composed of scenes, dominated by the poet's presence, and they differ from strophes, such as in L1250', that are devoted to mannerist imagery and relegate the poet's persona to the background.

The strophe of L191 stages the poet's tireless yet hopeless struggle against forces larger than himself. His certainty of ultimate failure lends him a touch of tragedy: his character is built only to be broken. Resisting age and fate, he shows a keen sense of justice even toward death itself. With this moral strength he refuses to defend himself before a female character who lacks any sense of justice (30). Once subjected to the vicissitudes of time, the poet reveals a capacity for suffering. As a victim of higher forces, he drops his defense and admits his despair. Yet notwithstanding his defeat, he clings to dignity, epitomized in his futile apology to youth for not having protected it from the ravages of time.

The opening antistrophe relegates the poet momentarily to the background. It is terse, covering less than a fifth of this long *qaṣīda*. The standard catalogue of values is truncated, including only moral praise, and even that is restricted to reliability, protection, charity, and power, the latter clothed in images of unsettling ambivalence, such as the patron as a pliant bamboo stalk and a poisonous viper (78–83). The description is barely witnessed by a general 'you'. Generosity, which usually leads the catalogue of moral virtues, is conspicuously lacking and only appears towards the end, as an occasion for the poet to point out his own exclusion from it (93–5). This leads to the *qaṣīda*'s second cluster of dramatic scenes, constituting the metastrophe.

This third and last part of the *qaṣīda* receives particular emphasis from being framed as a long message dispatched to ʿUbaydallāh, a device further discussed below. The message contains a composite dialogue of the poet with his patron, questioning the latter's honor and justice. In the midst of the dialogue, the poet repeatedly turns aside in soliloquy to meditate his situation. The following presents a survey of the scenes and a characterization of the poet before analyzing the argument in detail (see figs 12 and 13).

In the first dialogue, the poet asserts his exclusion from the patron's generosity. The ensuing monologue (118–22) gives the poet an occasion to evoke his former hope and admit his fear of being disappointed. Resuming the dialogue, he desperately tries to explain the current lack of reward other than as a deliberate exclusion by ʿUbaydallāh. He interrupts his soul-

97–117	Dialogue with ʿUbaydallāh: His exclusion of the poet from reward
118–22	Monologue: The poet's struggle for hope in ʿUbaydallāh
123–63	Dialogue with ʿUbaydallāh in three parts: Delay of reward; hyperbolic praise; the poet's reasons for loyalty
164–71	Monologue: The poet's reaffirmation of allegiance to ʿUbaydallāh despite sacrifices
172–5	Dialogue with ʿUbaydallāh: The poet's renewed declaration of allegiance

Figure 12 Synopsis of scenes in the metastrophe of L191 (see also fig. 13)

searching with hyperbolic praise and affirms a loyalty that is dictated by his own integrity and nobility, not any actions of the patron (157–63). In a second monologue, the poet vaunts his sacrifices for the sake of loyalty, and his tribulations suffered. The two short monologues highlight the damage caused by the patron's actions – whether intentional or not – and the poet's honest attempt to prevail over the injustice and salvage his bruised loyalty. His innocence foregrounds the patron's guilt. The poet's soliloquies abound with accusatory themes, descriptions of indigence, and visions of departure. To thus incorporate criticism of the patron into a monologue circumvents a direct confrontation with him. The surrounding dialogue, however, still identifies ʿUbaydallāh unmistakably as the target. As a result, the monologue places, however softly, the guilt for the poet's sufferings onto the patron's shoulders. Throughout, the poet maintains an ambiguous stance, holding the patron responsible without openly confronting him. Then the poet appeals to the very man who supposedly perpetrated the injustice for the redressing of it, thus heightening duplicity to paradox. Simultaneously the monologue affords the poet a space to discreetly advertise his merit, namely his giving of himself, a fundamental condition for Ibn al-Rūmī's *madīḥ*. This exposing of his inner struggle lets the patron gauge the poet's sacrifices for the sake of faithfulness and loyalty. Accordingly, the patron may deduce the unspoken question of how he will requite his poet's constancy and dispel his doubts. The poet's solemnly offered commitment is not unilateral; it harbors the expectation of a counter gift.

The inserted monologues also transcend the synchronic time frame of the dialogue and open a perspective on the poet's long-term motives.[6] Through them, the poet makes the present situation a mere phase between a former hope and an uncertain future. The temporal progression is marked by his usage of verbal tense, with the poet's hope donning the perfect.[7] But Ibn al-Rūmī deploys other stylistic subtleties as well. In one instance, the poet points to the patron's awareness of his hope with the definite relative pronoun in 'that which I hoped for' (*alladhī ammaltu*, 121). The poetic critic ʿAbdalqāhir al-Jurjānī explains the function of this particle as follows:

> It is used only when a man had been known for a story or affair that occurred to him and distinguished himself for the hearer by that story or affair, and one then wants to point him out. So one says *alladhī*. The explanation is [as follows]: you attach by means of *alladhī* only such a clause of speech as the hearer has previously known, and an affair that is familiar to him . . . . Their (sc. the grammarians') saying, 'It is used only to achieve thereby the description of definite nouns through sentences', signifies, that one applies it in order to distinguish from other cases the mention of a thing with a sentence by which the hearer knew it.[8]

There must be a degree of previous knowledge, whether specific or general (*ʿalā l-jumla*), for the relative pronoun to be meaningful, and it is such prescience that the poet imputes to his patron. The alleged knowledge creates the responsibility to act upon it, by virtue of a single particle. Ibn al-Rūmī shows equal finesse in his use of verbal mood. In speech act theory, the mood of the verb has been identified as 'the way in which the speaker asserts his standpoint toward the statement he makes'.[9] This explanation proves valid here: the poet consistently paints a dreaded future in the negated jussive, and formulates uncomfortable thoughts about departure in the negated conditional.[10] Shielded by modal devices, the soliloquizing poet weighs the possibility of the patron's unworthiness. In dialogue, however, he shows a different face, rejecting a bleak outcome, and affecting an attitude of optimism and obstinate loyalty. The latter is underscored by a long list of motives and an unwillingness to accept disappointment. The combination of dialogue and monologue renders the poet's persona complex: to the patron's face he declares loyalty and trust; in solitude he confesses doubt and intimates the patron's responsibility for his own state. His preference is however clearly indicated by the mood of verbs. The optimistic attitude is readily espoused in affirmative indicative mood, and the alternative averted in negated non-indicative moods. The dramaturgy brings the outer debate with the patron inside the poet's consciousness as a personal dilemma between faith and hope, a dilemma imparted indirectly to him who caused it. In the next discussed *qaṣīda* (chapter 11) this will not be so, but criticism, compounded with a threat of satire, will actually be uttered to the patron's face.

Having established the deep division within the poet's persona, the metastrophe's argument may now be addressed. As mentioned above, the entire final part is highlighted as a message. This is a poetic device bringing a matter – often identical with the poem's motive of composition – to the attention of a specific addressee. It is introduced by an emphatic formula, identifying the recipient, and concluded by a number of figures. The poetic message precedes Islamic times, when it served everything from pleas for peace to tribal satire in war.[11] It either constituted an independent *qiṭʿa* or the final part of a so-called message *qaṣīda* – as distinct from the praise *qaṣīda*.[12] Ibn al-Rūmī uses two messages to mark crucial passages in the *qaṣīda* at hand.[13] The first, one verse long, coincides with the closure of the dialogue between the poet and his personified white hair, discussed above. This message, introduced by the short formula 'Tell!' (*qul li-*), adds nothing new but reiterates the gist of the poet's argument, namely his preference of death over life beyond youth. It is conveyed by the poet's own white hair and addressed to the calamities, personified as the 'daughters of time':

فَقُلْ لبناتِ دَهْرِى فَلْتُصِبْنِى إذا ولّى بأَسهُمِها الصِّيابِ

Tell the calamities of my fate that they must hit me
with their best arrows when he (sc. youth) turns away.

(L191: 19)

The message underscores the poet's rejection of a life falling short of perfect happiness. Placed at the *qaṣīda*'s outset, it foreshadows the poet's high expectations in another context.

The second message comprises the entire metastrophe of 79 verses and is dispatched to ʿUbaydallāh (96–175). After an introductory phrase in which the poet speaks to two fictive messengers, the voices of the sender and the addressee as 'I' and 'you' sustain the format of the message until the *qaṣīda*'s end. Ibn al-Rūmī repeatedly recalls the message format throughout the dramatic scenes, each of which is concluded by a rhetorical figure or a switch of addressee. Through the scenes runs a tight argument, shaped by direct speech, descriptions, syntactical figures, and recurring motifs (see fig. 13).[14] In the first two dialogues, the poet still searches for an explanation for his state through a series of questions. The queries are answered by the poet himself in the manner of *jadal*, eliminating potential answers one by one. In the first dialogue, he invalidates his initial hypothesis, that the patron deliberately withheld his reward, by eliminating plausible reasons for such a consideration. In the second dialogue, he modifies his hypothesis to a delay of reward, which he similarly invalidates. After an interlude of hyperbolic praise, the poet concludes that the only conceivable motive for the missing reward can be a test of his loyalty. He admonishes the patron not to toy with his devotion and demonstrates the futility of such a test, while arguing his loyalty repeatedly.

Along this tight-knit sequence of questions and answers, through three dialogue scenes, the poet undertakes a mental journey from doubt to reassurance. The questions come in anaphoric pairs of interrogative phrases (*a-mā lī*, 1. and 2. Q; *mā li-*, 3. and 4. Q; and *a-lasta l-marʾa lladhī*, 7. and 8. Q) or lesser assonances (*miṭālu and maṭlu*, 5. and 6. Q). The anaphoric pairs also constitute semantic parallelisms. In the initial dialogue, the poet asks the first pair of questions, whether his request is indeed being denied and answers himself in the affirmative (1. and 2. Q and A). To his third question (3. Q) about the reason why he forfeited his reward, he responds by denying the only possible motive for this, a poetic lapse (3. CQ, A, and CQ). The fourth question complements the third, asking inversely why other, inferior poets have triumphed over him (4. Q). He tentatively responds that he did not show any need (4. CQ), but quickly draws an analogy with rain, which refutes the answer: the patron's generosity does not discriminate between needy and wealthy protégés (4. A). At this point in the metastrophe, fathomable reasons for the patron's withholding of the reward, whether due to the poet's uneven verse or the patron's uneven generosity, have been eliminated (116). Hence the reward must be imminent; it has simply been delayed. The poet reformulates his hypothesis accordingly and exhorts the patron not to fail him. In the ensuing first monologue, the poet seeks to reassure himself of his premises, the patron's usually unquestioned liberality (118), and his own fervent hope. The monologue shows the poet's reasoning to rest on deeply-felt convictions.

In the second dialogue, the poet describes himself as ridiculed in public and deceived by the patron. He questions the reasons for the delay:

[*Message formula*] 'Say to the prince' (*fa-qūlā li-l-amīri*, 96):

Dialogue with ʿUbaydallh

1 Q: 'Will *I* not have a request granted from you?' (*a-mā lī min duʿāʾin mustajābin ladayka*)

A: *I* am excluded from your cloud's shadow and rain? It gives to all but me (97–100).

2 Q: 'Will *I* not have a share?' (*a-mā lī ... ḥaẓẓun*)

A: *I* am excluded from your rain? Your water ... quenches the thirst of all except *me* (101–4).

3 Q: 'Why does *my* striking not kindle?' (*haban lī mā li-qadḥī*)

CQ: 'Did *I* not strike the fire with a good fire-stick?' (*a-lam aqdaḥ bi-zandin ghayri kābī*)

A: *My* fire-sticks are well chosen; my horses are winners.

CQ: Did *my* thoroughbreds not come in first? (*a-lam tasbiq jiyādī*, 105–7).

4 Q: Why do second rate steeds triumph? (*fa-mā li-l-tāliyāti* ...)

CQ: Do you deprive *me* because of *my* wealth? (*hal taḥrumunī* ...)

A: The generosity of milch-camels and rain is not dependent on need (108–16).

[*Imp.*] 'Do not stay with your gift below *my* rank!' (*fa-lā taḍaʿanna rifdaka dūna qadrī*, 117).

Monologue

The prince's stream does not miss the hilltops (*wa-mā saybu l-amīri* ... *yuqaṣṣiru an yanāla dhurā l-rawābī*). *I* think him able to teach it to flow uphill (*ẓannī* ... *la-ʿallamahū l-tawaqqula*). *I* held hope in *my* work (*laqad rajjaytu fī ʿamalī rajāʾan*),

[*Juss.*] Let me not return with work unrewarded (*fa-lā aṣdur* ... *bilā ʿamalin muthābī*); let it not be like a mirage (*lā yakun* ... *ka-raqrāqi l-sarābī*, 118–22).

Dialogue with ʿUbaydallāh

Delay of Reward

It is with your generosity 'as if *I* were outwitting shy game' (*kaʾannī addarī* ... *ṣaydan*); people are pointing fingers at *me*. The animal of promise has too long awaited slaughtering. '*I* take refuge with your nature' (*aʿūdhu bi-ṭībi khīmika*, 123–9).

5 Q: 'What is this delay?' (*mā hadhā l-maṭlu* ...)

A: *I* do not know your soul as one of your difficult wives' (*laysa ʿahdī bi-nafsika min qarāʾinika l-ṣiʿābī*, 130–3).

6 Q: 'Through which teeth and veil ... did this procrastination come to *me*?' (*fa-min ayyi l-thanāyā atānī l-maṭlu*)

A: '*I* think about an origin whence you derive: every door is locked to your excuse' (*ufakkiru fī niṣābin anta minhu fa-yughlaqu dūna ʿudhrika kullu bābī*, 133–5).

Hyperbolic Praise

7 RQ: 'Are you not the man to whom no wavering or avarice can be attributed?' (*a-lasta l-marʾa* ...)

A: That man is always generous and prompt (136–7).

8 RQ: 'Are you not the man who levies all the praise?' (*a-lasta marʾa* ...)

A: You flee blame (*tuwāʾilu min lisāni l-dhammi*) and defend your honor (138–40).

We see faults in the generosity of rain but not in your generosity (*naʿuddu maʿāyiban* ... *wajadnā li-l-ghaythi*). Both of you (sc. patron and rain) give without vaunting your gifts (*tajūdāni bilā mtināni*, 141-49)

[*Imp.*] Live joyfully, comfortably and unchallenged! (*fa-ʿish fī ghibṭatin*, 150)

continued ...

Figure 13 Paraphrase of the argument in the metastophe of L191 (see also fig. 12)

The Poet's Reasons for Loyalty

My last speech about you is honest admonition (*wa-ākhiru khuṭbatin lī fīka qawlī*, 151).

[*Imp.*] 'Try *me* with anything you please other than yourself, for you are my goal and patience is *my* habit' (*bi-mahmā shi'ta dūnaka fa-mtaḥinnı fa-ınnaka ghāyatī wa-l-ṣabru dābī*).

I stay with you, because *I* abhor lying (*arā ʿāba l-takadhdhubi sharra ʿābī*, 152–4).

[*Cond.*] If *I* left you, this would not save me from lying in my praises (*wa-in jāwaztu madḥaka lam yazal bī takadhdhubiya l-madāʾiḥa*, 155).

9 RQ: When will *I* ever find anyone whom your praises fit? (*matā ajidu l-madāʾiḥa ... tuʾātī fī siwāka bilā kidhābī*, 156)

10 RQ: How can [another] hand reach my height? (*kayfa tanālunī kaffun bi-naylin*, 159). A: [Another reason for my loyalty is that] no one reaches *my* high rank except a noble patron (*fa-laysa yunīlunī illā munīlun*, 162).

Monologue

That is what hinders *me* from leaving him (*fa-dhālika ʿāqanī*, 164). Only for him do *I* forgo *my* travelling in quest of patrons.

[*Cond.*] If it were not for him, *my* sturdy camels ... would not be yearning (*lawlāhū*, 164–71).

Dialogue with ʿUbaydallāh

[*Cond.*] If *I* were to cross the earth, *I* would return to you (*wa-law annī qaṭaʿtu l-arḍa ... la-kāna ilayka nqilābī*, 172).

11 RQ: 'To whom except to you shall one return? (*fa-ayna ʿanka bi-dhī l-iyābi*).

A: *I* will await with certitude *my* ample share (*sa-aṣburu mūqinan bi-wufūri ḥaẓẓī*); whatever perishes, your praiser's work is not meant for ruin (*mā ʿamalu bni madḥika li-l-tabābī*, 173–5).

(Grammatical persons and names are left unchanged. The speaker is highlighted by italics, the addressee by underlining. Non-indicative verbs are marked 'juss.' for jussive, 'cond.' for conditional, and 'imp.' for imperative. 'Q' stands for question, 'A' for answer, CQ for counter question, and RQ for rhetorical question.)

Figure 13 (*Continued*)

وما هذا المِطالُ ولَيسَ عَهْدِى　　بنَفسِكَ مِن قرائِنِكَ الصِّعابِ

What is this delay? I do not know your soul
as one of your difficult wives.

(L191: 130; 5. Q and A)

فمِن أَىِّ الثّنايا لَيتَ شِعرِى　　أَتانِى المَطلُ أَمْ أَىِّ النِّقابِ

Through which mountain roads or passes,
if I only knew, did this procrastination come to me?

(L191: 133; 6. Q)

The poet answers the question about this delay (5. Q) by segmenting the patron into the different agents: his soul (*nafs*), his nature (*khīm*), and his origin (*niṣāb*).

Based on the poet's best knowledge, none of them could be guilty of procrastination. Delay does not enter into the aspects of the patron's person and must be discounted (135). At this point in the beginning of the second dialogue, the poet's deliberations are heavily marked by his subjectivity. Émile Benveniste identifies linguistic subjectivity by dividing utterances with verbs of mental activity, e.g. 'I suppose that you will be late', into the true utterance 'You will be late' and the marker of subjectivity 'I suppose'. Other verbs marking subjectivity are 'I believe, conclude, presume, and think'. According to Benveniste, these verbs denote less the activity than the presence of the person executing them, as they describe not an operation but an attitude taken towards the utterance made.[15] In this sense one can identify the many verbs of mental activity as the lens through which the poet views the patron, among them 'I deem him' (*ẓannī annahū*, 119), 'I know your soul', (*ʿahdī bi-nafsika*, 130), and 'I think about an origin from which you derive' (*ufakkiru fī niṣābin anta minhū*, 134). They bring into play the poet's prior perception of the patron, which seems to contradict the puzzling yet patent delay. The poet realizes that the true locus of discrepancy lies between the facts and his perception of them (5. and 6. A), which opens up a further pair of questions that represent a point of bifurcation (7. and 8. Q). Depending on their reading, two mutually exclusive interpretations are possible. Paul de Man once traced the ambivalence of the poem 'Among School Children' by William Butler Yeats to two readings of its last verse, summarizing his interpretation as follows.

> Two entirely coherent but entirely incompatible readings can be made to hinge on one line whose grammatical structure is devoid of ambiguity but whose rhetorical [literal or figurative] mode turns the mood as well as the mode of the entire poem upside down.[16]

The ambiguity in de Man's interpretation arises from the reading of the verse 'How can we know the dancer from the dance?' either as a real or a rhetorical question. His interpretation of Yeats's poem helps to recognize a similar 'hinge' of ambiguity in Ibn al-Rūmī's seventh and eighth questions. Their reading offers an alternative of enormous moment for the poem as a whole.

In one reading, the paired questions (7. and 8. Q) are considered as rhetorical devices of emphasis (*li-l-taʾkīd*).[17] The poet confirms that the patron is in fact the man he knows him to be. The anaphoric and semantically parallel questions suggest a match between generosity and promptness, on the one hand, and the 'levying' of praise, on the other. The eighth answer, that the patron flees blame and defends his honor, confirms the rhetorical question. In this reading, the poet has succeeded in convincing himself of the patron's worthiness. Based on this result, he pursues with praises (141–9), an invocation (150) and an inverted comparison placing the patron's generosity above that of rain (141–7).

In an alternate reading, the negative questions are understood as a reproach (*li-l-tawbīkh*), expecting denial (*inkār*). Then, the entire passage acquires a different meaning:

أَلستَ المرءَ لا عزْمٌ كَهامٌ ولا بُخْلٌ إليْه بذِى انتِسابِ
تجودُ بنانُه والغيثُ مُكْدٍ ويَمضِى عَزْمُهُ والسَّيفُ نابِى
أَلستَ المرءَ يَجْبِى كُلَّ حَمْدٍ إذا ما لمْ يكُنْ لِلْحَمدِ جابِ
تُوائِل مِن لِسانِ الذَّمِّ رَكْضاً وتَثْبتُ لِلْمُهَنَّدَةِ العِضابِ
تُظاهِرُ دونَ عِرضِكَ كلَّ دِرْعٍ تُظاهِرُ للطِّعانِ وللضِّرابِ

Are you [really] not the man to whom
no wavering or avarice can be attributed?

His fingers give plenty when rain gives sparsely;
his resolve pierces when a sword bounces off.

Are you [really] not the man who levies all praise,
when there is no collector for praise?[18]

You run for rescue from the tongue of blame,
but you stand firm against sharp Indian swords.

You wear, to defend your honor, every coat of mail
that you don for thrusting [lances] and striking [with swords].
(L191: 136–40)

Now the question pair (7. and 8. Q) is understood literally. From the poet's standpoint, the patron's behavior is inexplicable, and he expects the negative answer that, on the contrary, the patron still is the perfect man of the poet's memory. In this sense, the seventh and eighth answers refer not to ʿUbaydallāh's actual person, but to a perfect image in the poet's mind (129–35). This ideal the poet validates, while distancing himself from the historical addressee. Viewed from this perspective, the assertions of the eighth answer reveal a discrete warning, for only someone who deserves blame and puts his honor at risk needs defend it. By pointing to the patron's endangered honor, the poet subtly advises him to fulfill his promise. A dramaturgic device supports the reading; this middle part of the second dialogue, from the questions through the hyperbolic praise (136–50), is the only place in the metastrophe where the poet's persona vanishes. He withholds his own judgment and leaves it instead to the subjects to attest to the praise (141–4, 146). The hyperbolic praise lavished onto the patron immediately afterwards seems incongruous with the poet's reserve, but a connection between this and other renditions of the rain motif throughout the *qaṣīda* indicates veiled criticism of the patron.[19] The force of the hyperbole contrasts with the tenuousness of its referent; is it the imaginary ideal or the actual person? ʿUbaydallāh still has to prove that it is him the praise describes.

The metastrophe's middle section then allows two mutually exclusive readings. In the first, the poet declares again his unqualified loyalty to a patron he knows well, as if to say, 'This is the man you are'. In the second reading, the praise is advanced tentatively and in good faith, yet to be proven true. This second kind of praise is conditional, conveying merely 'This is the man you could be'. So far, the Janus-headed interpretation has paralleled de Man's reading *mutatis mutandis*, but here the ways part. Unlike Yeats's poem, the *qaṣīda* is part of an ongoing communication and requires a response. This means that the *qaṣīda*'s ambivalence gives the patron the option to eliminate the second reading by an act of generosity. Such an act would re-establish ʿUbaydallāh's identity with the praiseworthy ideal. Through Ibn al-Rūmī's rhetorical ingenuity, the ulterior acts of the *qaṣīda*'s addressee can then restrict it to its positive meaning.[20] That such acts did not always ensue is evidenced in other *qaṣāʾid*.[21]

The end of the second dialogue leaves the issue and returns to the earlier conclusion, that reward can no longer be withheld. The poet has meanwhile identified the only motive for delay: a test of his loyalty (151). He is determined to succeed in this test, like the patient Job, who guiltlessly suffered to prove his faith in God. This Koranic figure is alluded to twice. The wording of the poet's first question for a 'request granted' (*duʿāʾun mustajābun*, 97) echoes God's responding to Job's plea for mercy, 'So We answered him' (*fa-stajabnā lahū*, Sūrat al-Anbiyā' 21/84). Later the poet's alleged constancy in his words 'Because you are my goal and steadfastness my habit' (*fa-innaka ghāyatī wa-l-ṣabru dābī*, 152) recalls God's speech 'Surely We found him (sc. Job) a steadfast man' (*innā wajadnāhu ṣābiran*, Sūrat Ṣād 38/44). The poet carefully motivates his interminable patience and loyalty. First, he abhors lying, and to leave ʿUbaydallāh would mean to lie for the rest of his career.[22] Therefore he admonishes the patron not to test him. Second, the poet's noble rank requires an even nobler patron, which is difficult to find. At this point, any possibility of disloyalty is discounted (159). The second monologue complements the already reached conclusion by rejecting the alternative of departure. A third dialogue, reconfirming his loyalty directly to the patron, concludes the *qaṣīda*.

Now the poet's persona may be assessed as a whole. In the strophe, the poet as hero fights for the ideal world of youth. After long resistance, he admits himself beaten but in the same breath refuses to survive his demise. To that end he charges his victorious adversary, old age (in the metonymy of white hair), to summon the fates of death to him. His defeat by invincible time reveals the poet's staunch adherence to his feelings and beliefs. At the same time, the grand suffering takes the measure of his loss. The antistrophe, given its diminutive size, is a mere interlude. It forecasts an ambivalence in the patron's nature, which causes the poet's undecided stance towards him later in the metastrophe. There, the poet as panegyrist seems to have lost his grip on a second perfect world, that of his venerated patron. The poet's reaction is no longer as simple and direct as it was in the strophe. He couches his doubts in monologues, and expresses optimism in dialogues with ʿUbaydallāh, yet with a contrasting rhetorical undercurrent. Here again, the poet fights for an ideal, but notwithstanding the firmness of his convictions, they might have lost their basis in reality. The outcome of his lengthy argument within himself and with his patron remains open, and in this form the entire metastrophe is dispatched as a message to the historical ʿUbaydallāh. The prolix indirect message delivers the panegyrist's plea to save his perfect world of patronage and not let him end like the hero of the strophe, who chose death over imperfection. Then the poet's voice falls silent and ʿUbaydallāh holds in his hands the *qaṣīda*'s ultimate meaning and its author's fate.

TRANSLATION OF L191

[STROPHE]

The passion of him whose parting has grayed is affectation,
even if he seeks passion, his heart being passionate.

[*Dialogue with the Accuser: her impotence next to the authority of white hair*]
O my accuser, the hoariness of my head has tamed me for you,
were it not for that, taming me would have exhausted you.

Thus accuse him who listens to you or wake up,
for the time of your shame and mine has come.

My hoariness spares you accusing me,
as it spares the eyes [of spies] observing me.

I have cast down my eyes,
neither throwing nor catching a dubious glance.

How could I possibly attempt to hunt,
when my arrows have ill-arranged[23] feathers?

Hoariness is enough as a forbidder,
unwillingly obeyed, and a caller, complied with.

I took my saddlebag down to the tent-peg[24]
for the mount of my vanity was exhausted from racing.

[*Dialogue with White Hair: the poet's joy at its announcement of his death*]
I said greeting hoariness, 'Welcome,
you guide of the erring towards the truth!

Do you not bring me daily the good tidings
of my swift departure in the wake of youth?

You brought me the news of my catching up
with a past dearer to me than the coolness of drink!

I do not call your good tidings an announcement of death,
even if you threaten my soul with departure.

Yours is the good tidings, on my part the good thing is this:
"I'll mend your weakness with dye."

Even if you have slain the beloved of my soul
and the matchless companion of my pleasure,

You have mended your way and stilled my rancor
by sending my mount quickly after him.

When you reunite me with the twin brother
of my [former] good life (sc. youth),
you grant me thereby my eternal reward.

It is sufficient reward for me regarding him,
that I and he, we return home.

By your life, for every living creature,
life, after losing its youth, is mere punishment.

Tell the calamities of my fate, that they must hit me
with their best arrows when he (sc. youth) turns away.'

[*Evocation of the Time of Youth: the absence of yearning in it*]
May the time when I knew youth be watered
by every shower with white, thundering, low-hanging clouds!

A time, when I did not say, 'May rain fall on a [former] time!'
nor wished for water from the clouds.

Nor sighed heavily with regret
for a good life nearly ended.

[But when I] looked with joy at my future, and did not follow
with sadness the departing one (sc. the time of youth).

[*Evocation of the Women: their scorn and condemnation of white hair*]
Did the women seriously dislike meeting me,
while [motives] call me to them?

They (pl. f.) turned away with eyes gliding off me,
and they are not [eyes that] glide off the fatal spots.

They did not turn away out of bashfulness or dalliance,
but [rather] distancing themselves and avoiding [me].

They said, 'Hoariness suffices you as a humiliation,
and quick separation as a punishment!'

They were not just in severing my bond,
because of a sin I did not commit.

When they thus counted white hair as sin of a man
from which he could not be asked to desist.

There is no pardon for you from her
who unjustly counts as yours the sin of another.

[*Monologue on Youth: being reminded of it by images*]
What reminds me of youth is long thirst
for the hail grains of the teeth and sweet saliva,

And the women's stinginess with it
except to a raven-black youth.

When they pour drink for me, they only let me sip;
they do it not for love but for deception.

What reminds me of youth is my shameful chagrin
and the women's turning away when I blame them.

If my blaming were helped by youth blaming [them],
they would return in response and satisfy me.

Those who turn away, would listen
to blame that brings down ibexes from cliffs.

My anger would disturb the rest of the courtesan,
and she would indulge me despite my anger.

I would spend the night with chastity between us:
being the necklace of her embrace above her necklace
[which she did not take off].

If I followed my wild passion there,
I would be her belt beneath her belt.

What reminds me of youth are the deadly arrows,[25]
hitting my fatal spots beneath the skin.

She with winning[26] arrows shot and pierced my heart
from the gap of her face veil.

Then she left lightheartedly,
and I left with a burning wound.

Every one who fights his opponent with hoariness,
will be made prisoner, by your life, not making prisoners.

If youth were martyred, she (sc. the woman) would leave,
by your good life, with twice of what I suffered.

Oh, help me with shackling my revenge,
when revenge has escaped the hand of the claimant!

How often did the hands[27] achieve my revenge,
even if it was between points of spears.

What reminds me of youth are gardens of paradise[28]
on the banks of sweet rivers,

Gusts of wind shake their shadows,
moving the bodies of tender boughs,

When their fringes swing, the weeping birds
call each other, crying mournfully.

What reminds me of youth are high gardens
with blue flies humming between them.

When the late afternoon sun looks at them from the side,
having almost hidden itself behind its veil,[29]

In the darkness of its sunset, it casts a weak ray
like glances of a courtesan.

What reminds me of youth is a road[30] [adjacent to] a pond
with pure water and gentle ripples.[31]

A virgin rain cloud fed it in the morning,
and the East wind made it shimmer like a mirage

On pebbles in a white ground,
as if its soil were exuding pungent perfume.

It has patterns, when they run across it,
you read them as lines of a book.[32]

What reminds me of youth is a moist East wind
with a firm touch, and an exhausted mount.[33]

It came after it had trailed for a while
over the flowers of the hills,

Lavender scent impregnated it,
like the scent of musk that is spread when one takes it away.

What reminds me of youth is the flash of lightning,
the cooing of a dove and the yearning call of an old mother camel.

Oh, my pity, oh, my regret for it,
oh, my grief until the Day of Reckoning!

Shall I be bereaved of youth and not consoled?
The consoler neglected my affliction!

We (sc. I and my time of youth) separated entirely against our will,
and not for weariness of long company.

My thicket belonged to the hand that plucks fruit,
and has fallen afterwards to the hand that gathers firewood.

[*Dialogue with the Mantle of Youth: regret for having worn it out*]
O mantle of youth, for me you were
a good deed and great luck.

You have been worn out with time,
since every mantle is between decay and robbery.

It hurts me that you wear out and I remain,
but [life's] events have no respect.

I wore you for a while not minding to wear [you] out,
though I knew your excellence among garments.

If it had been given me to preserve you,
be assured, I would have kept you in a safe bag

I would only wear you on a day of pride
and the day of visiting the true king.

[ANTISTROPHE]

[*Madīḥ Episode: the patron's ambivalent nature*]
ʿUbaydallāh, Lord of the Banū Zurayq; his name
suffices you as a decision [between true and falsehood].

A man whose traits have of old been pure,
not watery milk or milky water.[34]

They (sc. the traits) are not wholly created from honey,
but mingle honey and bitter juice.

He who combines two different *noble* natures,
does not, however, have a mixed origin.

He owns a composure that chases rashness from him,
like bees chasing [one] away from the honey of the ravines,

The rashness of a composed man in his case is not rashness,
but the sharpness of a claw or a fang.[35]

He treats gently those who show him gentleness,
and harshly the rude rebel.

[*Madīḥ Episode: the patron as pliable bamboo and poisonous viper*]
Beneath his places of bending
lies a forbiddance of rigid inner qualities[36]

Like a bamboo stalk, that shows you pliancy,
but refuses to break to either side.

He who attacks him stirs up in him
a viper whose leaping is feared.

When it glides along it has a scraping sound
that unsettles the hunters of lizards.[37]

Its spittle kills without bite,
and [its] slightest breath [kills] without saliva.

He does so without committing
grave offenses or sins.[38]

[*Madīḥ Episode: the patron as mending rifts and assembling acts of heroism*]
He is pointed out: 'What a means for mending rifts,
when a rift is too serious to mend!'

His flame illuminates every night
so that the darkness parts!

When no [thread] entering holes[39] has yet strung
the boring [of a pearl of glorious deeds], he penetrates it.

No [thread] inserted goes through [the pearl],
except a firmly-twisted [thread of firm resolve].[40]

[*Madīḥ Episode: the patron as mountain and fire*]
He is a mountain under which all mountains
of the earth shrink like[41] hillocks.

One takes him as a safe haven
and around him one pastures a fertile tract.

A benefactor of widows and orphans,
people gather around him as a well-spring.

In his courtyard cauldrons are anchored,
preceded by porringers [sized] like water-troughs.[42]

He has two fires, the fires of hospitality
and of war, either one of them you see burning.

I was astounded and I have never ceased
to be in a state of wonder.

He has the power that protects against[43] fate
and free riches like spoils.

Ever more amazing than that is the fact
that the earth is streaming from the rain of his sky,
except for my ravines!

[METASTROPHE]

[*Dialogue with the Patron: the poet's exclusion from reward*]
Say (dl) to the prince, even if he sees me
in the position of scorned, chased dogs:

'Will I not have a request granted by you,
among the requests granted to others?

The clouds of your kindness grant shade to everything
and give abundant rain to the regions without coercion

Except to me, for I am above them on a plateau,
as if I were beyond [the point] where the sheer rock is exposed.

They (sc. your clouds) lavish forever their downpour
on those other than me and deceive me
with a lightning that does not extinguish.

Will I not have a share from them (sc. your clouds) other than lightning,
which my eyes compare to fire in a reed thicket?

I spend the night watching their course, fighting sleep,
while the furthest place of rainfall is fed with their downpour.

You watered those who came to drink without a well rope,
like the Tigris swollen from the torrents of the hills.

Whereas I let down buckets that did not bring me
a handful or less of your generosity.

What disappointment![44] Why does my striking not kindle?
did I not strike the fire with a good[45] fire stick?

I was sure that I did not go amiss
in my choice and pick of fire sticks.

Did my thoroughbreds not come in first,
[after having] departed with him who leaves from dusty straits?

Why do those of second rank
take the share of the first-come Arab steeds?

Do you deprive[46] me because I have my estates,
and I am not like emaciated starving [camels]?

The milk-giving [camels] do not withhold their milk
when they meet someone with filled milk skins.

They do not favor with their milk the thirsty,
when the milkers come to milk.

They always give freely to every hand
rubbing [the udder] for milk.

Not every shower leaves behind the cultivated land
to go to the abandoned wasteland.

Instead it does not cease to give to each
an abundant shower and a torrential downpour,

Bringing barren land to life and preserving
cultivated land from destruction.

If I am higher than its (sc. the real cloud's) rain,
I am [still] lower than your [figurative cloud's] rain

Do not stay with your gift below my rank,
since my height does not exceed your reach!'[47]

[*Monologue: the poet's struggle for his hope*]
The flood of the prince is not a valley stream
that fails to reach the summits of the hills.

I think, if he were a stream,
he would teach it to ascend mountain passes.

I truly held hope in my work,
and must not return with [my] work unrewarded.

That which I hoped for in him must not be
like a glistening mirage on elevated grounds.

Nor like ashes scattered by strong winds
across the plains,[48] whirled up in the air.

[*Dialogue with the Patron: 1, delay of the poet's reward*]
'As if I am outwitting with your generosity
[wild] game that my proximity and watching alienates.

Therefore, when I pass by
– these things cure the chronic ailments of the jealous –

Hands point me out as deprived, [numerous] like the hands
of people on the day of [casting] pebbles [in Minā].

The waiting for the promise has lasted very long for me,
and the uncertain fate announces separation.

Oh, what a pity for you! If I took it (sc. your promise) to my grave,
what a poor provision!

The [beast of] promise, as long as the hand of fulfillment
does not slaughter it in its fat state, is the worst gift to give.[49]

I take refuge with your nature from a procrastination
that deprives me of drinking from your rolling sea.

What is this delay? I do not know your soul
as one of your difficult wives.

He, whose soul is stubborn and not manageable
in [matters of] magnanimity, tames it.

You are – as you know – the husband of a soul
that obeys you without haggling about magnanimity.

Through which mountain roads or passes,
if I only knew, did this procrastination come to me?

I think about an origin whence you derive:
every door is locked to your excuse.

How many a blameworthy man among people
is excused by his low origin!

[*Dialogue with the Patron: 2, hyperbolic praise*]
Are you [really] not the man to whom
no wavering or avarice can be attributed?

His fingers give plenty, when rain gives sparsely;
his resolve pierces, when a sword bounces off.

Are you [really] not the man who levies all praise,
when there is no collector for praise?

You run for rescue from the tongue of blame,
but you stand firm against sharp Indian swords.

You wear, to defend your honor, every coat of mail
that you don for thrusting [lances] and striking [with swords].

We count several faults in rain –
in the generosity of your hand, nothing is to blame.

We have found that rain destroys what we build,
except exposed tents and domes.

It restricts us from moving
lest we break our necks.

The lights are veiled when it pours on us,
while no light is veiled in your generosity.

Furthermore, the excellence of your gift over its (sc. rain's gift)
is clear and not met with doubt:

Your hands give pure gold,
when the rain distracts us with drizzle.

Your generosity does not stay away on the second day –
the generosity of the rain often comes later.

You two coincide in a noble trait
and share it with each other in lawful partnership.

You two give to mankind without enumerating
or calculating the rain for which you are asked.

Live in joy, ease of mind, and a kingdom
that does not fear the hand of usurpation!

[*Dialogue with the Patron: 3, the poet's reasons for loyalty*]
My last speech about you is my words
– and admonishing you is not trying to vanquish –

Try me with anything you please other than you,
for you are my goal, and patience is my habit.

That (sc. my being loyal to you despite my doubts) is not because
my way is blocked, nor because I am unable to earn a livelihood
and seek my gain.

But I think – not praising myself –
that forged lies are the worst fault.

Even if I relinquish [my] praising you, the forging of false praises
and demanding [favors from other patrons] does not stop for me.[50]

If I only knew when I will ever find [my] praises
fit people other than you without lying?

Furthermore, I am on a tall [mountain],
the turban of its summit are shreds of clouds.

Noble fathers made me dwell there,
who surrounded their heads with the crowns of kings.

How can a hand reach me with gifts,
when the hand of the eagle does not reach me?[51]

The hands of people except you are beneath mine,
and their length[52] falls short of me.

My high plateau towers above every stream,
and my noble wood[53] is beyond the spray of the lower parts of the valleys.

Only such a benefactor can reach me,
who looks down on me like the clouds.

The sources of [hard] Nabʿ-trees are, God forbid,
not fed by water accumulated in cisterns!'

[*Monologue: the poet's sacrifices for the sake of his loyalty*]
That (sc. the patron's rare nobility) hinders me
from tying my saddlebags
and crossing and roaming the wayless deserts.

If it were not for him, my sturdy camels and my fillies
would not be yearning for their homeland.

Nor would they spare (sc. not graze at) an old resting place,
nor [would they] be burdened by distance and exile.[54]

Nor would they find their far-travelled [rider] stingy
with [his] exhausted [camel] to the hungry wolves.

Nor would they cease to cut the night
with necks like trunks of loaded palm trees.

For the stars do not travel at night like me,
nor do the vipers glide along like me.

[Then] my sturdy camels would graze with flocks of antelopes,
where parts of their herds are separated from them.

They would swim across flat sands,
and [also] where piled-up sand dunes obstruct their way.

[*Dialogue with the Patron: the poet's renewed declaration of loyalty*]
'If I were to cross the length of the whole earth,
I would thereupon turn back to you.

When you are the haven of return, and there is no haven
but you, to whom except you might one return?

I will be persistent, sure of my ample share,
since the reward of the persistent is not calculated.

Whatever work and word perish,
the work of the "son" of your praise is not destined for ruin.'

11

'THEY AIMED AT MY HEART FROM THE GAPS OF VEILS' (L1042)

The second *qaṣīda* presented in full constitutes Ibn al-Rūmī's most serious grievance against ʿUbaydallāh in a praise *qaṣīda*. Its unexceptional length is offset by the difficult rhyme letter *ṣād* Ibn al-Rūmī defiantly boasts. His tone in the metastrophe is more strident than in the above-discussed L191. In its layout, L1042 differs from L191 most visibly in the strophe, a single episode. The *qaṣīda*'s strophe and metastrophe have close dramaturgic parallels in other *qaṣā'id*. Careful comparison of L1042 with them discloses variations in corresponding places from which this *qaṣīda*'s message can be deduced.

The strophe of thirteen verses is the briefest in proportion to the *qaṣīda*'s length of sixty-eight verses. It is an episode, describing a group of courtly women, loosely based upon the pre-Islamic morning-of-separation motif.[1] Except for the metaphor of the ostrich egg as a simile for the womens' smooth white faces, the motif is transposed into an urban environment, where secluded ladies preserve their complexions in shady courtyards. These women seem the perfect consorts for an *adīb* like the poet. But they remain cruelly aloof except for throwing him the piercing glances that form the *qaṣīda*'s incipit:

رَمَيْنَ فؤادِى مِن عُيونِ الوَصاوصِ بلَحْظٍ له وقْعٌ كوقعِ المشاقِصِ

They aimed for my heart from the gaps of veils[2]
with glances that stuck like [iron] arrow heads.

(L1042:1)

The poet's obstructed view of the women lasts for a few verses, describing their beautiful faces as shining through their veils and comparing them to sunlight penetrating clouds (4, 6). Then his voice fades away. In L191 the poet struggled long before abandoning his doomed quest for women's love. Here he evades any confrontation and, by not engaging, remains inscrutable. Yet the implied author displays his virtuousity in description. He steps behind the veils and discovers their wearers' hidden beauty.

قرى ماءَه فيهِنَّ عِشرينَ حِجَّةً   نعيمٌ مُقيمٌ ظِلُّه غيرُ قالِصِ ...
ثقيلاتِ أَردافٍ نبيلاتِ أَسْوُقٍ   وما شِئتَ مِن قُبِّ البُطونِ خَمائِصِ
مِنَ اللّائِى عمَّتْها المحاسِنُ لا الأُلَى   مَحاسِنُها مِن خَلقِها فِى الخَصائصِ

For twenty seasons, the water of sweet life gathered
in the [luster of their faces], while [life's] shade stood unfading...

Heavy-bosomed, with noble legs
and as thin-waisted and lank-bellied as you fancy

Of those whom beauty pervades,
not those whose bodily beauty lies in details.

(L1042: 5, 8–9)

But the heroines' beauty is not confined to the physical realm. Noble, morally impeccable, and sophisticated, they distinguish themselves from amoral, swarthy slave girls and uncultured Bedouin women. Their cold-hearted rejection of the poet is counterbalanced by their consummate perfection in lineage, moral values and culture, paralleling the patron's catalogue of virtues in the antistrophe to which the poet presently turns.

The antistrophe follows a dramaturgy that also occurs in L994 (see fig. 14) but differs in the rendition of ʿUbaydallāh's portrait. The reading of L1042's antistrophe is therefore prefaced with a discussion of its counterpart in L994.

Antistrophe of L994:

20–31	Dialogue with Ṭāhirids
32–7	Episode: Ṭāhir b. al-Ḥusayn
38–42	Dialogue with Ṭāhirids
43–61	Episode: ʿUbaydallāh
62	Dialogue with Ṭāhirids
63–84	Episode: ʿUbaydallāh
	(ʿUbaydallāh's praise occupies 34 of 84 total verses.)

Antistrophe of L1042:

14–16	Dialogue with the Banū Muṣʿab (i.e. the Ṭāhirids)
17	Episode: Ṭāhir b. al-Ḥusayn
18–21	Dialogue with the Banū Muṣʿab
22–32	Episode: 'Each bold knight' (*kullu fārisi buhmatin*)
33–40	Dialogue with the Banū Muṣʿab
41–7	Episode: ʿUbaydallāh
	(ʿUbaydallāh's praise occupies 7 of 47 total verses.)

Figure 14 Synopses of the antistrophes of L994 and L1042

Unlike most *qaṣāʾid*, L994 can be dated to (or shortly after) 253/867, when young ʿUbaydallāh first ascended to the governorship of Baghdad, an achievement for which Ibn al-Rūmī congratulates him in verses 84 and 88. L1042, whose date is unknown, most likely followed L994 and played off of it, as the following juxtaposition suggests.

Both antistrophes unfold as long composite scenes, each held together by a dialogue between the historical figures. These consist of the poet and the ancestors of the *mamdūḥ*, the Banū (or Ālu) Ṭāhir, or Banū Muṣʿab and Banū Zurayq, after more distant forebears. They participate as a group, addressed in the second person plural. Intermittently, the framing dialogue is interrupted by episodes that highlight individual members of the dynasty. The alternating focus creates the effect of a spotlight wandering between the characters on a stage. This is realized dramatically by switches between the third person, for the hero of a vignette, and the second person plural, for the interlocutors. So far, both antistrophes structurally coincide. They diverge in the way the vignettes' protagonists relate to the surrounding dialogue. Their acts and attributes may either be identical with those of the ancestors or not.[3] From the perspective of the *mamdūḥ*, resemblance with his ancestors makes him partake in their renown, whereas a lack of resemblance disassociates him from them.

I begin with the antistrophe of L994, which depicts a *mamdūḥ* in harmony with his ancestors. The poet reminds the Ṭāhirids (*Banū Ṭāhir*, 20, *Ālu Ṭāhir*, 22) of their rank, their past and future heroism, historical significance, and the protection and generosity they bestowed on others. Not only the poet but all the subjects acknowledge the Ṭāhirids' standing. What is more, God chose them to be his instruments.[4] This motif of divine agency (31) provides the transition to the first episode, which is devoted to Ṭāhir b. al-Ḥusayn (*iṣlāḥu Ṭāhir*, 32, *Abū l-Ṭayyib*, 35). He appears as a savior of Islam and the caliphate by ending the fratricidal war between al-Maʾmūn and al-Amīn. The episode concludes with a Koranic allusion to divine punishment, administered through human hands, and a further mention of God's direct intervention.[5] Conversely the adversaries, allies of al-Amīn, are associated with pagan figures.[6] The second dialogue with the ancestors elevates the first example to a general rule: whenever the caliphate is in danger, the Ṭāhirids send a savior.[7] To the Ṭāhirid guardian role (39), the second dialogue adds determination as a further family trait. This determination is figuratively interpreted as the true piercing force of the Ṭāhirids' swords and spears (40). This leads to the second episode with ʿUbaydallāh as the protagonist:

أَعُمُّكُمْ مَدْحًا وأَخْتَصُّ مِنكُمْ   فَتاكُمْ عُبيدَ اللّهِ والرَّأْسُ رائِسُ

I praise <u>you</u> all and distinguish among <u>you</u>
<u>your</u> hero ʿUbaydallāh, for the head is heading.

(L994: 42)

A list of ʿUbaydallāh's general leadership qualities, such as glory (43), courage (47), dignity (49–50), and propriety (51), heralds the episode. Then he is shown to exemplify the above-defined 'Ṭāhirid' traits of resolve and guardianship. Regarding the first, the young governor outdoes his forefathers. Their firm resolve endows their swords and spears with sharpness (a mock etiology, recurring in L1042):

بأَحكامِكمْ تمَضِى السُّيوفُ مَضاءَها   وتَقْضِى قضاياها الرِّماحُ المَداعِسُ

By your decisions, the swords cut
and the unbending spears pass sentences.

(L994: 40)

ʿUbaydallāh's firmer resolve entirely replaces the sword, and it gushes forth more indomitably than a torrent.[8]

له عَزَماتٌ ليْسَ للسَّيْفِ مِثلُها   مَضاءً ولا لِلسَّيْلِ والسَّيْلُ مارِسُ

He has a resolve whose like no sword has in cutting,
and no torrent – though a torrent is all-destructive.

(L994: 57)

Praise of ʿUbaydallāh's guardian role concludes the episode. At this point, the two Ṭāhirid traits of guardianship and determination have been attested in the *mamdūḥ*. The poet returns to the ancestors in one short verse, identifying ʿUbaydallāh's reliability with theirs (62, quoted below). The rest of the antistrophe is formed by a third episode about ʿUbaydallāh's individual virtues, which recognizes in him the generosity and protection of the Ṭāhirids, evoked in the initial dialogue (23–7). ʿUbaydallāh's magnanimity (65), gentleness (67), and his enormous gifts (71) single him out. Above all, he acknowledges poetry as a register of virtues, which earns him the hyperbolic praise that follows.[9] The structure of the episodes places ʿUbaydallāh on a par with Ṭāhir b. al-Ḥusayn as an instrument of God (61, 72) and a leader among men (45, 76). What is more, ʿUbaydallāh outdoes his illustrious ancestor by virtue of the caliphs' recognition of his own rank (44).

Usually the ancestry of a praised individual is stated by description, honoring him through his affiliation to them. In this composite scene, the poet testifies before the *mamdūḥ*'s ancestors about their offspring. The dialogue achieves what a description does not; it reverses the direction of affiliation. No longer does the ancestors' lore automatically reflect on a (passive) scion, but the latter is called upon to keep their lore alive.[10] He bears the burden of proof for his descendance, and the implied author sits as judge. Thus Ibn al-Rūmī turns the concept of ancestry from inherited honor into inherited duty. He proceeds by defining a 'prototypical' Ṭāhirid and then comparing with him actual family members:

Ṭāhir and ʿUbaydallāh. In *qaṣīda* L994, the juxtaposition results in an overlap between dialogue and episode in terms of personal lore, divine sanction, allegiance to the caliphate, as well as the weapon imagery. These similarities are proudly presented to the ancestors, for instance, in the mention of ʿUbaydallāh's reliability:

وفىٌّ وتِلكُمْ شيمَةٌ طاهِرِيَّةٌ　　　له سَلَفٌ فيها قَديمٌ قُدامِسُ

[He is] reliable, and this[11] is a Ṭāhirid quality
in which he has ancient predecessors.

(L994: 62)

This verse does not contain an explicit address, but the choice of the demonstrative variant *tilkum* echoing the personal suffix marker of the dialogue (*-kum*), can be interpreted as an implicit address. Here the ancestors are called to acknowledge the affiliation, because their heroism is kept alive through their offspring (41). When, at the closure of the antistrophe, the poet recounts ʿUbaydallāh's genealogy, he really implies that the young governor's performance has 'earned' him the descendence from Zurayq, Muṣʿab, al-Ḥusayn, Ṭāhir, and ʿAbdallāh. Deeds, not birth, have made him the sixth of these 'five fathers' (79–80).

At the end of the first scene, the poet's persona steps out from the collective voice of the subjects (30) and begins to speak as a witness and guarantor for ʿUbaydallāh (43, 79). But it is ʿUbaydallāh who has previously supplied the poet with the facts.[12] His deeds, reinacting those of the Ṭāhirids, are the proof visible to all (Ṭāhirids, 20, ʿUbaydallāh 44, 45, 76). In identifying ʿUbaydallāh's individual traits with those of his ancestors, the poet has cleverly molded individual and ancestral praise into one. Consequently, the attributes and their realization were not the governor's own choice but a given with which he had to conform. In L994, he succeeded, and his poet pledged his own word for it to the ancestors.

The antistrophe of *qaṣīda* L1042 bears a dramaturgic resemblance with that of L994, but its message drastically differs.[13] The dialogue scene with the ancestors, here called Banū Muṣʿab, mentions their outstanding glory and introduces the motif of the kingdom rescued from schism.[14] This is illustrated as before by an episode with Ṭāhir b. al-Ḥusayn (*iṣlāḥu Ṭāhir*, 17). The resuming dialogue, this time, claims victory over a downtrodden foe as a Ṭāhirid habit (18–19). Then the dialogue introduces a further episode as proof.

ولِمْ لا وفيكمْ كلُّ فارسِ بُهمَةٍ　　　يُغادِرُ فُرسانَ الوَغَى بالمَداحِصِ

Why not? since each bold hero among you leaves behind
the [hostile] heroes of the battle convulsed in death.

(L1042: 21)

The indeterminate 'bold hero' is said to fight lion-like (25–8) as a defender and protector (28–9), with his infectious verve pervading even horses and arms (cf. ancestors, 19). The episode concludes with a variation on the sword etiology, in which the cutting is performed by the hero's noble lineage, not by the sword's edge:

عَلى أَنَّه يمُضيهِ لَيْسَ بِحَدِّه   ولكنْ بِعِرْقٍ مُصْعَبىٍّ مُصامِصِ
بأَمثالِهِ تمَضِى السُّيوفُ مَضاءَها   وتَنْفُذُ أَطرافُ الرِّماحِ العَوارِصِ

Although he does not cause it (sc. sword) to cut with its edge,
but with a noble Muṣʿabite origin.

With [origins] of its kind swords cut,
and quivering points of lances pierce.

(L1042: 31–2)

The short third dialogue scene with the Ṭāhirids repeats the sword etiology with a change in pronouns:

وقِدمًا مَضَتْ أَسْيافُكُمْ ورِماحُكُمْ   بأَعراقِكُمْ دونَ الظُّبا والمَخارِصِ

From old <u>your</u> swords and spears have been cutting
with <u>your</u> origins, not with edges and points.

(L1042: 33)

The remainder of the dialogue enumerates virtues of patronage such as generosity (34–6), popularity (37), discernment (38), ambition (39), and universal perfection (40). Then the third episode, devoted to ʿUbaydallāh, is introduced:

ومِنْكُمْ عُبيدُ اللَّهِ فُتُّمْ بسَعْيِه   ذَوِى السَّعْىِ فَوْتًا بائِصًا أَىَّ بائِصِ

From you is ʿUbaydallāh. With what forbidding distance
did <u>you</u> surpass – by his striving – all those who strive!

(L1042: 41)

What follows next, however, fails to corroborate what preceded it. Generosity and protection do not characterize ʿUbaydallāh but rather an ambivalent mix of generosity and ferocity. The image of the unpredictable ruler fits a situation in which a poet needs to point out mistreatment without short-changing his addressee's status. This has been seen above in the antistrophe of L191, which is full of ambivalence.[15] ʿUbaydallāh's moral integrity in the last episode of L1042 is presented in a series of doubly-negated rhetorical figures, called 'praise resembling blame' (*taʾkīdu l-madḥi bi-mā yushbihu l-dhamm*).[16] The patron is said to be cowardly in sacrilege (44), anxious for honor (45), and armored against defamation (46). While the rhetorical ornament emphasizes his care for his reputation, the subtext implies that his behavior is calculated – the opposite of veritable integrity. One of the episode's few non-ambivalent verses states that soiled honor cannot be cleansed. The author hints that ʿUbaydallāh may not be by nature righteous and open-handed – this is, 'Ṭāhirid' – but merely presenting himself as such, and that is exactly the question occupying the poet's persona in the metastrophe.

But before turning to that last part, the three episodes within L1042's antistrophe need to be compared. The first and second echo themes and imagery of the dialogues, particularly the second one, which is longer and replete with praising motifs and imagery. Its protagonist is only alluded to as 'each bold hero' and vaguely designated as Muṣʿabite in the opening and closing verses (22, 31–2), which makes him stand for the entire dynasty. This vignette is the most seamlessly integrated of all three; its parallels with the dialogue include the victory theme (Banū Muṣʿab, 20; 'bold hero', 25–30), the agency of horses and spears (Banū Muṣʿab, 19; 'bold hero', 22–3), and the sword etioloy (Banū Muṣʿab, 33; 'bold hero', 31–2). The 'bold hero' is none other than the prototypical Ṭāhirid, who manifests himself in each worthy male member of the clan. His lack of individuality does not make him anonymous, for the praise of an unknown man would benefit neither poet nor audience.[17] The clue lies in him whom the designation of 'each bold hero' excludes and replaces, for in L994, it was ʿUbaydallāh who featured in the second episode. In L1042, ʿUbaydallāh's acts have obviously not furnished his poet with enough proof to convince the patron's ancestors. So the poet chooses an unnamed representative of the worthy members of the dynasty to illustrate the argument of Ṭāhirid perfection. He says so in his own voice:

كَمُلْتُمْ فمَهْما أَسْأَلِ اللَّهَ فيكُمُ مِنَ الأَمْرِ لا أَسألْه تَكْميلَ ناقِصِ

You [Ṭāhirids] have attained perfection;
for whatever matter *I* beg God regarding you,
I shall not beg Him to complete a deficiency.[18]

(L1042: 40)

The poet ostensibly renounces God's succor with the faultless Muṣʿabite forebears. His oblique supplication nonetheless allows for such a need in the future, notably with ʿUbaydallāh, who has not yet made his appearance in the *qaṣīda*. He enters the *qaṣīda* only in the third episode of L1042, which corresponds to the third episode in L994. Different from its parallel, however, the ambiguous and extremely short description disassociates ʿUbaydallāh from the surrounding dialogue. While the first two episodes overlap with the dialogue and confirm it, as in L994, the third one fails to do so. In the composite scene of L994, the persona of the patron takes a celebrated central place, whereas in

L1042, ʿUbaydallāh is marginalized by an undetermined Muṣʿabite. The final bifurcation of dialogue and episode in the latter *qaṣīda* proves an ingenious way of critiquing the patron with his own hereditary standards, not a poet's willful demands. Ibn al-Rūmī's dialogues propound the view that all praiseworthy attributes are ancestral, and the extent to which an individual perpetuates ancestral lore determines his claim to it. ʿUbaydallāh's disappointing portrayal results from the poor facts he has supplied to his poet, and which the latter merely arranged to the best of his capacity. Nowhere does the poet take responsibility for the patron's acts, or his *qaṣīda*'s contents. In this sophisticated dramaturgy, the patron morally disinherits himself. Meanwhile the poet still remains the patron's advocate – he has not yet disclaimed his own good faith in the patron's ability to revive ancestral virtue.

The antistrophe has set up the patron as a target for criticism, which the metastrophe will dispense. This last part has a dramaturgic parallel too, in L191. Both metastrophes are again composite scenes, i.e. dialogues between poet and patron, alternating with the poet's monologues (see fig. 15). The inserted monologues of L1042 echo the diachronic perspective of those in L191. The poet's past experience takes on the perfect tense, and his dreaded future the conditional and jussive moods,[19] with the poet looking at his past to guide his future. As L191's metastrophe has been treated in the previous chapter (figs 12

48–62 Dialogue with ʿUbaydallāh (*Abā Aḥmad*, 48; *Ibna Ṭāhir*, 58):

Your rank is outstanding and generally conceded (48–51).

[*Cond.*] If it were not for *my* friendship, *I* would desert you (*ʿalā annahū law lā dawāʾī mawaddatī raḥaltu rikābī ʿanka*, 52).

I am emaciated due to *my* fear for your reputation, since what you did to *me* provides the enemy with words of satire (*wa-fīka bi-mā awlaytanī yā bna Ṭāhirin maqālun, la-ʿamrī, li-l-ʿaduwwi l-muqāriṣī*, 53–8).

You decided to deprive *me* so that *my* hope has come to mislead my benefit, personified as husband and wife (*athbattanī l-ḥirmāna .... wa-inna rajāʾī fīka khayyaba niʿmatī*). *My* benefit resents that, but you can reconcile it with hope again (59–62).

63–66 Monologue:

ʿUbaydallāh betrayed *me* by causing *my* impoverishment (*wa-mā khiftu ghishshan min ṣadīqin mukhāliṣī*, 63).

[*Juss.*] May *I* not be deceived into wasting *my* other chances (*fa-lā akuni l-muhrīqa faḍlata māʾihī ghurūran bi-raqrāqin mina l-āli*, 66).

67 Dialogue with ʿUbaydallāh:

[*Imp.*] Do not undercut the due of my praise (*wa-lā tabkhasannī ḥaqqa madḥī*).

68 Monologue:

[Q:] Does ʿUbaydallāh, the ultimate recourse, do me injustice? (*a-yaẓlimunī*).

Figure 15 Paraphrase of the metastrophe of L1042 (for the abbreviations, see fig. 13, p. 167)

and 13), this discussion focuses on the variations introduced in L1042 and the conclusions to be inferred. In terms of the dramaturgy, the poet's disappointment about being neglected and his thoughts of departure are moved from the monologue (L191: 120, 165) to the dialogue (L1042: 52–3, 61). What was a private reflection is now asserted directly to the patron's face. This makes an accusation of what had before been only an indirect plea.[20] In terms of the general tone, the poet's voice has become more strident. In the opening dialogue scene of L1042, he presents his case more strongly than in L191. The patron's exclusion and deprivation of him, which had been in question before (L191: 97, 101 and 109), are now affirmed as a *fait accompli* (L1042: 58–9). Furthermore, the poet's persona threatens obliquely with satire, reflecting aloud that his starved condition provides food for satire by an enemy (58–60). Despite his envisioning a potential satirist, however, the poet conducts himself still as his patron's friend. In the short second dialogue, he demands his reward from the patron face to face as his right.[21] Although the patron's generosity has previously failed to meet the poet's expectations, Ibn al-Rūmī's persona urges him now to correct his record and prove himself just. The tone of the monologues is likewise stronger than in L191; the poet accuses the patron first of betrayal (*ghishsh*, 63), then injustice (*ẓulm*, 68). At that point in L191, a third dialogue had brought a rejoinder in which the poet reaffirmed his loyalty (L191: 171–5). In L1042, the accusatory second monologue remains his unmitigated last word.

In L191, the spectrum of the poet's attitudes extended from hope, uttered in dialogue, to doubt, confined to monologue. In L1042 the range shifts to doubt and despair. The dialogues convey shock and dissatisfaction, but still a faint readiness to reconcile, whereas the monologues have passed this point and condemn the patron as an unjust impostor.[22] They show no more hope, only consternation and loss of faith. In sum, both poems share the tension between dialogue and monologue and the different perspectives of the poet's persona. In dialogue the poet attempts to maintain his understanding with the patron and show his good will; in monologue he shows scepticism and exposes the patron's faults. But the two encomia are set apart by a substantial gradation. In L191, most of the conflict occurs as an internalized dilemma, which the patron is indirectly asked to realize and solve. In L1042, this agony is past, the poet has lost faith, and bitterness renders him careless enough to openly condemn the patron's misdemeanors.

The study of L1042 reveals a dramaturgy with intertextual depth. In the antistrophe, the marginalization of the *mamdūḥ* ʿUbaydallāh must have reminded him of his once celebrated central place in his inaugural *qaṣīda* L994. Now he has to struggle to regain his former dynastic status. In the metastrophe, the poet explicitly condemns ʿUbaydallāh's unreliability and injustice towards himself in a way that seems to leave no space for reconciliation, as had been the case in L191. There, the patronage relationship had deteriorated from the ideal state, but the dramaturgy of the indirect plea had invited a rejoinder. In L1042, the poet's uncompromising tone leaves no opening for that. He no longer protests hurt feelings but argues hurt self-esteem; his awareness of his rights and his powers (of satire) have obviously grown. In this light, the unique strophe comes to bear. The poet as hero, though scorned and mistreated by veiled women, refrained from engaging in a dispute or unveiling his inner feelings. Instead he kept aloof and described the women in isolation as perfect in their beauty and breeding, but imperfect in their cruelty. This attitude of proudly rejecting injustice sets the *qaṣīda*'s theme and is brought to a climax in the last verse, where the panegyrist wonders about his patron with faint hope of being proven wrong:

أَيظلِمُني مَن لَيْسَ فِى الأَرضِ غَيْرُهُ   إذا نيصَ مِن ظُلمٍ مَناصٌ لِنائِصِ

Does he mistreat me, other than whom there is no refuge on this earth
for a refugee, when seeking refuge from injustice?

(L1042: 68)

TRANSLATION OF L1042

[STROPHE]

[*Evocation of women as secluded urban beauties*]
They aimed for my heart from the gaps of veils
with glances that stuck like [iron] arrow heads.

Those veils have not been asked to hide unseemly faces
or complexions of black shameless ones.

Rather they have been entrusted the complexions
of white noble ones with hues[23] of pure true ancientness.

They shield faces, spotless like full moons,
shining behind the face veils.

For twenty seasons, the water of sweet life gathered (5)
in the [luster of their faces], while [life's] shade stood unfading.[24]

[They are] as if the eyes of the beholders
distinguished them as suns behind piled clouds.

The unblemished and smooth-faced ones of the convivial[25] courtyards,
like eggs in a clutch of ostriches, not sand grouse.

Heavy-bosomed, with noble legs
and as thin-waisted and lank-bellied as you fancy.

Of those whom beauty pervades,
not those whose bodily beauty lies in details.

[They are] candid, except for being elusive –
antelopes that the arrows of hunters do not chase.

They play with their similes, female oryx
with eager calves [running] between them.

They collect the white blossoms of camomile,
scorning those who gather truffles between halting [Bedouin] groups.

In Mauliya in whose slopes the sand grouse finds
a sheltering prairie with soft nesting hollows.

[ANTISTROPHE]

[*Dialogue with the Banū Muṣʿab: their rescue of the caliphate*]
Children of Muṣʿab, you have reached every virtue,
and treated those who wish you ill, to imperfections.

If [mankind's] grasp of glory is assessed, your grasp [of it]
is the double of every thing [held] in every grasping pair of hands.

Through you the widening tear in the realm was stitched,
if it had not been for you, no stitcher could have coped with it.

[*Episode: Ṭāhir b. al-Ḥusayn*]
The reform of Ṭāhir called back discord,
as it was riding on the bucking back of evil.

[*Dialogue with the Banū Muṣʿab: their determination*]
When blue spears look at flanks [as targets]
like blue eyes, staring with fixed gaze,

Then your sword edge is not fearful in the tryst,
neither do your horses shrink from the mêlée.

By your tread the rebellious are humbled,
and the cheeks of enemies [placed] under the arches of feet.

Why not? since each bold hero among you leaves behind
the [hostile] heroes of the battle convulsed in death.

[*Episode: the protoptypical Ṭāhirid*]
His horses deem the chewing of the bit-mouth in battle
more plentiful than the grazing of fresh herbage.

He has a sharp-eyed lance point that casts ahead a glance,
fixed on the [opponent's] fatal spots.

The onager does not fear him, except when he – with good [hunter's] luck –
selects it for [his] spear thrust, instead of [his] fat camels.

[He is] stronger in attack than an indomitable torrent,
standing firmer than a lion, who will not budge from his place.

He weaves[26] avenues of assault in every tight spot,
when the one among them weaves routes of escape.

As if the openings of his mail coat were made
for a full moon and a staunch lion.[27]

Lions of intimidating courage, when seeing him,
obediently wag their tails.

His enemy is in fear, his neighbor in safety
like tame doves in a home with dovecotes.

He has a dented sword blade from [his] long striking
the helmet tops of those in shining armor.

Although he does not cause it (sc. sword) to cut with its edge,
but with a noble Muṣʿabite origin.

With [origins] of its kind swords cut,
and quivering points of lances pierce.

[*Dialogue with the Banū Muṣʿab: collective praise*]
From old your swords and spears have been cutting
with your origins, not with edges and points.

From old, generosity mistreats you, and towards you
incline the sternums of dancing camels.

If the doors of kings are passages,
your doors are the place where the saddles
of far-travelling camels are thrown down [to stop].

With you alights each [she-camel] with bleeding sole,
because she was wounded by the stones she eagerly crushed.

You have swarming visitors as guidance, whenever we lose our way
– may you avoid small swarming [worms in drying watering-holes].[28]

Your minds penetrate a difficult view,
when nobody is hoped to penetrate it.

When people, in many affairs, shoot at the legs [of a horse],
you aim at the jugular veins.

You [Ṭāhirids] have attained perfection;
for whatever matter I beg God regarding you,
I shall not beg Him to complete a deficiency.

[*Episode: ʿUbaydallāh*]
From you is ʿUbaydallāh. With what forbidding distance
did you surpass – by his striving – all those who strive!

A man who feeds hungry birds meat with his sword
and feeds [people] in years of hunger.

At times he milks the milch camels of courage,
and at others the milch camels of generosity, never short of milk.[29]

Fearful of unseemly actions, he retreats from them,
whereas he meets the fates of death advancing, not retreating.

Anxious about honor – he knows,
when it is stained, no washing cleanses it.

Bold in terror – he is bareheaded for the spears
and armors himself with kindness against biting words.

His foe and the pursuer of his gift are constantly
on the verge of [receiving] a gift and [meeting] unexpected death.

[METASTROPHE]

[*Dialogue with ʿUbaydallāh: the poet's complaint of mistreatment*]
Abū Aḥmad, no station of honor remains
that you have not, by [many] ranks, outstripped.

If the sun boasted with you, it would pale
at your boast like a blinking star.

I deem everything knowable to be known by examination,
whereas your excellence is known without any one's examining [it].

If the jealous ones do not see that like I do,
they look as one-eyed [seers] with one eye taken out.

Although, if it were not for the reasons of my friendship [for you],
I would mount my camel to depart from you.

Its emaciation and leanness have spread,
however, everyone[30] takes charge himself to gain [his] benefit.

– Even if the gifts of others than you are licit only
when the meat of carcasses is licit.[31]

Do you let your, [once] perfect[32] grace for me become imperfect,
after I have been innocent of imperfect actions?

The hands of those asking you are given [gifts],
whereas I am not given a gift – not the smallest trifle of one.

Nothing of this starved me but my fear
of the evil imputed to you for what you have accorded me.

[There is] in that which you accorded me, Ibn Ṭāhir,
by my life, a speech about you for an insulting foe.

You determined to deprive me, then
– as the most hurtful rejector –
cast me out, the foremost of the assembly[33]

[In recompense] for my stringing for you precious pearls in necklaces
and my having dived for them into the depths.

My hope in you has disappointed my grace,
so that it became like one of the vengeful, obstinate wives.

How often was a grace obstinate, and you softened her
towards her husband, so that she was no longer obstinate.

[*Monologue: the poet's deprivation*]
He indicated me to freely open my hand; I obeyed him
and did not fear fraud from a sincere friend.

Then my shirt of livelihood became tight,
like the cut of a shirt that has not been let out.

By God, I did not retreat stout and big-bellied.
How many stout ones retreat!

Heaven forfend that I be one who pours away the rest of his water,
being deceived by the glittering pool of a mirage!

[*Dialogue with ʿUbaydallāh: exhortation*]
Do not undercut the right of my praise,
for I see as equal him who undercuts me
and him who gouges out my eye.[34]

[*Monologue: ʿUbaydallāh's injustice*]
Does he mistreat me, other than whom there is no refuge on this earth
for a refugee, when seeking refuge from injustice?

Part IV

VERBAL ORNAMENT

12

SUPPORTING FIGURES OF SPEECH

The dramaturgic outline of the *qaṣāʾid*, traced in the preceding chapters, abounds with verbal ornament, performing a variety of functions. As in the rain motif of L191, these can be supportive or subversive, as the figures of speech may themselves be sparse or frequent. This chapter examines both single and complex figures that have more than a local impact, affecting the structure of passages. Accordingly, the first half is devoted to syntactic figures that supply the weft of a passage, such as anaphora and reprise. The second half treats semantic figures, or tropes, that support an argument within a passage, such as sententia and analogy, or that relate separate passages, such as the recurring motif. Tight-knit arrangements of figures, or phantasmagoria, which create an abstract action of their own, form another chapter. The following is a selection, not a survey, of Ibn al-Rūmī's rhetorical figures and imagery with the purpose of illustrating functions they fulfilled in his praise *qaṣāʾid*.

Syntactic figures

Anaphora

The anaphora appears in monologues, enumerating motifs of grief or doubt, and in one dialogue scene, reiterating a challenging question.[1] But the most frequent and effective uses of the anaphora are found in episodes of praise, listing acts and attributes of the *mamdūḥ*. The following example contains descriptive epithets of rulership almost devoid of imagery:

صاحِبُ السَّيْفِ والمكايِدِ والنَّقْـ　　ـضِ لتِلكَ الأُمورِ والإجْرامِ

لا تراهُ يَخِفُّ للمستَخَفّا　　ـتِ ولا يستَكينُ لِلآلامِ

جَبَلُ الأَرْضِ ذو الشَّماريخِ والأَطْـ　　ـوادِ والنّاسُ حوْلَه كالرُّضامِ

صاحِبُ الدَّعْوةِ الَّتِى رَدَّتِ الحَقْـ　　ـقَ على أَهْلِه برَغْمِ الرَّغامِ

والَّذِى أَسْرَعَ الإجابةَ واسْتَعْـ　　ـجَلَ قبْلَ الإسراجِ والإلْجامِ

صاحِبُ النُصرَةِ الَّتِى شَفَعَتْ نُصْـ   ـرَةَ أَهلِ الفَسيلِ والآطامِ

صاحِبُ الشُّرْطَةِ الَّتى انْهزَمَ الطا   غوتُ إذْ كافَحَتْه أَىَّ انْهِزامِ

صاحِبُ الرَّايةِ المُظَفَّرَةِ السَّوْ   داءِ تهفْو على الخَميسِ اللُّهامِ

صاحِبُ الحَرْبةِ الَّتِى تنفُثُ المَوْ   تَ كَنَفْثِ الأَفْعَى ذُعافَ السِّمامِ

The holder of the sword, stratagems, and destruction
for those things (sc. the vicissitudes) and for the perpetration of crime.

You do not see him make light of matters deemed light,[2]
nor succumb to [great] pains.

[He is] the mountain of the earth with fruit-laden [palm trees]
and hills, the people around him are like stones.
The holder of the call that returns the right to its people,
despite [their] humiliation,

He who responds [with aid] and hastens
before saddling and bridling [his steeds].
The holder of the victory, that redoubles the victory
of the people of palm shoots and fortresses.[3]

The holder of the guard by which, when it struck the rebellious,
he suffered such a surrender![4]
The holder of the victorious black flag
that flutters over the five-partite army.

The holder of the lance that spits death,
as a viper spits deadly venom.[5]

(L1250': 120–8)

The anaphora is constituted by the repetition of *ṣāḥib* 'the holder of', a weak noun that merely denotes ownership of, or association with, the following element. The figure begins with general elements of good rulership, the 'sword, stratagems and destruction', with which he combats the vicissitudes of poverty and crime, beleaguering his subjects. Military items are the 'call' answering the request for protection, and his constant God-given 'victory'. The list concludes with his official rank, the 'guard' of Baghdad, and his stewardship of the Abbasid insignia, the 'black banner' and the 'lance' of Solomon.[6] The anaphora is built with epithetic noun phrases, not full sentences; they are qualified by syndetic relative clauses, which resume the praised item with the definite relative pronoun (*alladhī/allatī*, 122–8).[7] Only a few images illustrate these items, such as the metaphor of a protective mountain covered with fruit trees for the patron (122), and his lance's comparison with a spitting viper (128). The beginning of the anaphora is expanded by intervening verses, an insertion technique that reappears below.

Other anaphorae are entirely devoted to comparisons, metaphors, or hyperboles.[8] The next example lists character traits of the patron in inverted comparisons:

مَن كزُرَيْقٍ ومَنْ كمُصْعَبِهِ أَو كَحُسَينٍ وطاهرٍ قُرُبُهْ؟
أَو مِثْلُ عبدِ الإلهِ ذِى الشَّرَفِ الـ ـباذِخِ يُلقَى إلى العُلَى سَبَبُهْ؟
كالسَّيْفِ فِى القدِّ والصَّرامَةِ والـ ـرَّوْعَةِ لكنَّ حَلْيَهُ أَدَبُهْ
كالغَيْثِ فِى الجود والتَّبرُّعِ والـ إطْباقِ لكنَّ صَوبَهُ ذَهَبُهْ
كالبدْرِ فِى الحُسْنِ والفَخامةِ والـ ـرِفعَةِ لكنَّ ضَوْءهُ حَسَبُهْ
كالدَّهرِ فِى النَّفْعِ والمَضَرَّةِ والـ ـحُنْكَةِ لكنَّ غَيْبَهُ غَضَبُهْ

Whose ranks are like Zurayq and his [son] Muṣʿab,
or like Ḥusayn and Ṭāhir?

Or [who is] the like of ʿAbdallāh, the one of high honor,
whose rope is thrown up into the heights [to climb up it].[9]

Like a sword in length, sharpness, and frightfulness,
except that his ornament is his culture.

Like rain in generosity, charity, and wide coverage,
except that his shower is his gold.

Like the full moon in beauty, majesty, and height,
except that his light are his achievements.

Like fate in benefit, harm, and wisdom,
except that his incertitude is his wrath.

(L215: 144–9)

The anaphora concludes an episode about ʿUbaydallāh's uniqueness. It begins by describing him as a foreigner in his hometown (L215: 140–1), standing out by his very self, not by virtue of any affiliation (142). This uniqueness is accentuated in two sets of rhetorical questions. The first, an analogy, asks 'Does one look at the morning on the horizon with the aid of lamps?' (143). The second set, quoted here, asks rhetorically for him who compares with ʿUbaydallāh and his ancestors (144–5), and the ensuing anaphora answers with potential contenders. Its core consists of the particles of similarity ('like' *ka-*) and opposition ('except that' *lākinna*). In each verse, an object of comparison (sword, rain, full moon, and fate) illustrates three matching features of the patron. Then, the comparison is extended into a fourth area of the object in which the patron outdoes it, turning the comparison upside down. For instance, the sword's length, sharpness, and threat compare to the height, resolve, and intimidating presence of the patron.

The comparison is then extended to ornament in which the patron's intellectual decorum outdoes the sword's material decoration. Similarly, rain illustrates the trait of permanent, kind-hearted, and widespread giving, but in extending the comparison to the gift itself, rainwater pales before gold, and so forth. Item by item, the poet searches for an appropriate analogy for the patron, but each one, when fully matched with him, reveals a flaw. The plethora of shortcoming analogies demonstrates the patron's matchlessness. The anaphora as a whole proves the poet's initial assertion, that uniqueness defies comparison, and he openly admits his incapacity:

وكلُّ أَشْباهِهِ الَّتِى ذُكِرَتْ　　　دونَ الَّذِى بلَّغَتْ به رتُبُهْ

All his objects of comparison that have been mentioned
lag behind [the gallop] of his ranks giving [their horses] the reins.[10]
(L215: 150)

As in the first example, intervening verses can interrupt and expand an anaphora. This is accomplished systematically in the antistrophe of L1611.[11] Seven instances of repetition each open a small passage. In the following, the anaphoric verses are quoted, and intervening verses paraphrased:

فتًى مِنهُمْ فِى فضْلِه مُتقَدِّمٌ　　　على أَنَّهُ فى سِنِّهِ مُتقَدَّمُ ...
فتًى لا أُسمِّيه فتًى لحَداثةٍ　　　ولكنْ لأَخلاقٍ لهُ لا تَكَهَّمُ ...
فتًى ليس مِن يَومٍ يمرُّ ولا يُرَى　　　لنُعماه فيه أَوْ لبُؤْساه ميسَمُ ...
فتًى عَزمُهُ سيفٌ حُسامٌ وسيفُهُ　　　قَضاءٌ إذا لاقَى الضَّرِيبةَ مُبْرَمُ ...
فتًى لوْ رَأَى النَّاسُ الأُمورَ بعينهِ　　　لَما جهِلوا أَنَّ المحامِدَ مَغْنَمُ ...
فتًى حَسُنَتْ أَسماؤهُ وصِفاتُهُ　　　فأَضحَتْ بها أَيْدِى الكواعبِ توشَمُ ...
فتًى كمُلَتْ فيه الفَضائِلُ كلُّها　　　هَنيئًا له الحَظُّ الوَفاءُ المُتَمَّمُ ...

A youth of them (sc. the Ṭāhirids), preceding them in his excellence,
although he is preceded in his age.
(L1611: 105)

[His foremost position, 106; his uniqueness, 107; and the permanence of his achievements, 108]

A youth, I do not call him 'youth' because of his age,
but for traits that do not blunt.
(L1611: 109)

[His generosity and courage, 110; his kissed sandal, 111; his foot, ahead in glory, 112]

A youth, no day passes without one seeing in it
an imprint of his grace or harm.

(L1611: 113)

[Presents and death fates carry his acts towards people, 114; generosity and bravery are his motivation, 115; wealth and enemies supply the material for his acts, 116]

A youth, his resolve is a cutting sword,
and his sword, inevitable fate, when it meets a victim.[12]

(L1611: 117)

[His fighting of enemies without armor and of blame with the metaphoric armor of generosity, 118; his hand, kissed on its back and giving with its palm, is compared to al-Ḥaṭīm and Zamzam in the Muslim pilgrimage, 119–20][13]

A youth, if people saw him in person, they would not be unaware
that praiseworthy acts are [easy] spoils [for him].[14]

(L1611: 121)

[His gregariousness and his mark (*sīmā*) of nobility, guiding supplicants to him, 122; his unwillingness to decline a plea, 119; his preference for losing wealth over gaining it, 124]

A youth, his names and attributes are [so] handsome,
that the hands of beautiful [women] are tattooed with them.

(L1611: 125)

[His praise would not hurt if branded into foreheads, 126; his mention, if concealed, would divulge itself by the recipients' sweet breath in analogy with wind-spread musk, 127–8]

A youth in whom all virtues are completed,
may he enjoy his share of a long and fulfilled life!

(L1611: 129)

[Paradox of his subdivision among all good traits versus his perfection in each, 130–1; he is the goal of everyone's striving, 132; his resolve reunites good traits in analogy with a string holding pearls, 133–4]

The anaphora proper consists of *fatā* with the double meaning of 'youth' and 'man in full possession of his strength', which opens every passage. The first two passages play on the meaning of 'youth'. The first contrasts young age with excellence, the second defines youth metaphorically as the freshness of his character traits. Then, *fatā* shifts to the meaning of 'man'. Each passage contains four lines (the last one, six) with a unity of theme and style. The first establishes

ʿUbaydallāh's outstanding achievements in general, the second specifies acts of generosity and courage, the third constitutes the acts' motivation and their effect on people. Until this point, very little imagery is involved. The following passages thematically reiterate the first three, but elaborate them in many figures. The fourth passage reunites antithetical virtues of ferocity and generosity under the common denominator of resolve. Its opening verse contains a *concetto* matching his real sword (*wa-sayfuhū qaḍāʾun … mubramū*, 117) with the metaphoric sword of resolve (*ʿazmuhū sayfun*). The following line opposes, in an antithetical parallelism ʿUbaydallāh's real fighting without armor (*wa-hwa ḥāsirun*) to his metaphorical fighting 'armored' with generosity (*wa-hwa mulaʾʾamū*). The patron's hand, which bestows and which people kiss, is equated with the wall and fountain of the Kaaba. The fifth passage explains through a causal hyperbole (i.e. an imaginary cause) the attraction of the patron's generosity for people: it acts as an emblem guiding them towards him. The passage also motivates the generosity by his nature and piety, not any personal advantage. The sixth passage elaborates on the second, adding further causal hyperboles about the traces and memories of the patron's acts among the people.[15] The beauty of his attributes makes women tattoo them onto their hands, and the pleasant content of his praise turns the pain of branding people's foreheads with it into pleasure. His mention divulges itself by sweetening people's breath, supported with an analogy of musk that imbues the wind with its scent. The seventh passage forms a paradox. With the multiform array of ʿUbaydallāh's virtues, how can he reach perfection in each one without any shortcoming? The paradox is solved through the double meaning of *marīra*, 'resolve' and 'well-twisted thread', which forms the basis of an analogy between a thin, strong thread holding finely bored pearls and a firm resolve uniting perfect character traits.[16] The rhythm of the anaphora guides the development from concrete to abstract themes, and stylistically from literal description to a climax of speech figures, including *concetto*, antithesis, causal hyperbole, and paradox.

Short anaphorae can be enhanced with morphological and syntactical parallelisms.[17] The following example contains an anaphora of two lines, namely the personified presents, travelling to the patron's supplicants (*wa/fa-ʿaṭāyā*, 153–4) combined with syntactically parallel participles in feminine plural.[18] (The anaphora is italicized and parallelisms underlined).

لَيْسَ يَنفَكُّ مِن عطايا تُبارِى   سائِراتٍ خواطِرَ الأَفهامِ
حاصِلاتٍ وهنَّ مِن عِظَمِ القَدْ   رِ كبعضِ المُنَى أَوِ الأَحلامِ
وعَطايا كَوامِنٍ فى المواعيـ   ـدِ كُمونَ الثِّمار فِى الأَكمامِ
فعَطاياهُ دانِياتٌ يدَ الدهْـ   ـرِ توالَى كأَنَّها فِى نِظامِ
ساعياتٌ إلى رجالٍ قُعودٍ   سارِياتٌ إلى أُناسٍ نِيامِ
مُعْفَياتٌ مِنَ السُّؤالِ مُصفًّا   ةٌ أَلا هكذا عَطاءُ الكِرامِ
مُعْفِياتٌ مِنَ الهَوانِ وُجوهًا   عبَّدَتْها مُطالَباتُ اللِّئامِ

He does not cease with presents that race
in travelling with the ideas of minds.

Real, although, in their enormous size,
they seem like a wish or a dream.

And *presents*, hidden in the promises,
like the hiding of fruit in calyxes,

For *presents* of his are close, following each other,
as if they were [strung] on a thread,

Running towards sitting men,
journeying by night towards sleeping people,

Spared request, cleared [or it] –
oh, such is the gift of the noble ones!

Sparing humiliation to men of rank,[19]
whom the seeking of their due from lowly [patron's]
has turned into slaves.

(1250': 151–7)

The first description of 'presents' (*'aṭāyā*) covers two verses; they are 'travelling' (*sā'irātin*) faster than ideas, and they are 'real' (*ḥāṣilātin*) in spite of their fantastic proportions. Then, the anaphora returns with presents (*'aṭāyā*) as fulfilled promises (153–4). Further descriptions of the presents replace the noun with its epithets, describing the presents as running fast and journeying by night, while their recipients sit back and sleep (155). This inverts the ancient *raḥīl* motif in which the travelling poet must exert himself to earn his patron's grace.[20] The presents also save the recipients' pride and rank by pre-empting their requests and demands (*su'āl, muṭālabāt*, 156–7). This extended anaphora avoids becoming static; it begins with personifying the presents and moves gradually to their behavior towards their recipients. This changes the material act of giving into an attitude of concern and respect for the addressees, with the presents as messengers.

Reprise

Poem L215 contains, in addition to the above-described anaphora the repetition of a full verse.[21] Its first instance follows the conclusion of ancestral praise:

زانوه زيْنَ الفَريدِ واسِطَةَ الـ   ـعِقْدِ زَها فِى النِّظامِ مُنتَخَبُهْ
وزانهُمْ زيْنَها صَواحِبَها   لا فضَّ ما فِى النِّظامِ منقَضَبُهْ
كأَنْ عليْهِ قلادةٌ نُظِمَتْ   من لُؤلُؤٍ لا تَشينُهُ ثُقَبُهْ
وأَحْسَنُ الحَلْى مَنِطقٌ حَسَنٌ   يَكْثُرُ مَحْفوظُهُ ومُكتَتَبُهْ

They [his ancestors] decorate him like pearls decorate the center stone
of the necklace, whose selection radiates in the arrangement.

He decorates them, like [a center stone] decorates its neighbors –
may no breaking scatter the arrangement!

As if he wore *a necklace, strung of pearls*
unblemished by borings.

The best jewelry is beautiful speech,
much memorized and asked to be dictated.

(L215: 101–4)

Ancestors and patron are compared to a string of pearls with a central gem. The mutual enhancement of pearls and gem is compared to the ancestors and ʿUbaydallāh bestowing glory on each other (101–2). It is noteworthy that the descendant not only gains luster from the ancestors, but his achievements reflect back on them. This concludes the ancestral praise. The next thematic block presents individual praise, including the poet's pledge to praise (103–7) and its fulfillment with several subthemes of *madīḥ* (108–49).[22] Slightly transformed, the necklace image introduces this section; now the patron *alone* is adorned by it. The ensuing verse reinterprets the necklace as widespread beautiful speech. In the context of individual praise, these verbal jewels symbolize the patron's individual achievements. The image has thus been transferred from collective to individual personal praise. Meanwhile, the superlative in 'the best jewelry' (104) seems to imply that poetry about one's own deeds provides a *better* decoration than that about ancestral ones. At the same time, the audience anticipates the shift of the necklace image from ancestral glory to poetry as its more familiar topic. Later – and after the above-quoted anaphora – the introductory verses return as a reprise and closure of the individual *madīḥ*:

وكلُّ أَشْباهِهِ الَّتِى ذُكِرَتْ   دونَ الَّذِى بَلَّغَتْ به رُتَبُهْ
خُذْها أَميرِى قِلادةً نُظِمَتْ   مِن لُؤلُؤٍ لا يَشينُها ثُقَبُهْ
وأَحْسَنُ الحَلْىِ مَنِطقٌ حَسَنٌ   يَكْثُرُ محفوظُهُ ومُكتَتَبُهْ

All the comparisons with him that have been mentioned
are beneath [the speed of] his ranks letting loose [their reins].

Take them, my prince, *as a necklace, strung of pearls*
unblemished by borings.

The best jewelry is beautiful speech,
much memorized and asked to be dictated.

(L215: 150–2)

The verses dedicating and describing the poem claim that personal deeds, when versified, count more than those of ancestors. Though repeated verbatim, the reprise conveys a different meaning in its second instance, as the necklace image has been identified and dedicated as a recognition of individual acts. The supremacy of newly-earned *madīḥ* is now stated simply as *quod erat demonstrandum*:[23] poetry composed of individual achievements overrides the glory of one's forebears.[24] Such an attitude of course benefits a praise poet, who gains nothing from the generosity of those long gone.

Both repetition and anaphora exemplify Ibn al-Rūmī's tendency to develop a theme throughout a passage or a series of passages. Particularly versatile, the anaphora can be simple or expanded. It assembles either plain, descriptive phrases or ornate ones, charged with rhetorical figures (parallelism, antithesis, paradox) and tropes (comparison, metaphor, analogy, hyperbole), or mixes the two on occasion. The unobtrusive regularity of the anaphora is well-suited to pace a development; it guides movements from general to specific, concrete to fantastic, or material to ethical. Occasionally, its rhythm adds a meaning of its own, such as the patron's matchlessness.

Semantic figures

Sentencia and analogy

While supporting syntactic figures structure whole passages, semantic figures, or tropes, accentuate or shade crucial moments within them. Among these tropes, those that mark the closure of a scene are of particular importance. They include the sententia, exclamation, rhetorical question, and apostrophe.[25] The sententia predominates in frequency and is often combined with other figures.[26] A sententia summarizes and affirms the argument that precedes it as a general truth.

In a scene where the hoary poet bids the women farewell, he rounds off his greeting with the sententia:

لَمْ تَجْمَعِ الأَيَّامُ شَمْلَ أَحِبَّةٍ إلّا وشَرْطُ صُروفِها التَّفريقُ

The days have not reunited lovers, without separation
being the condition of their vicissitudes.

(L1306: 7)

Among the tropes, the analogy (*tamthīl*) serves as a closure. It supports the argument as a whole, by adducing a plausible analogous image, in other words, a figurative summary. Ibn al-Rūmī's images derive from the known physical world: human activities, familiar objects, plants, animals, and natural phenomena.[27] Like the sententia, the analogy may be combined with the other figures.[28] In one monologue (L1611: 1–9), the poet concludes his reflections on youth and old age with the analogy of dreaming and awaking:

رأيتُ سَوادَ الرأسِ واللَّهوَ تحتَهُ   كلَيْلٍ وحُلْمٍ باتَ رائيهِ يَنْعَمُ
فلمّا اضمَحَلَّ اللَّيلُ زالَ نعيمُهُ   فلَمْ يبقَ إلّا عهدُهُ المتوهَّمُ

I see the black-haired head and the pleasure under it
as a night and a dream whose dreamer spends the night in ease.

And when the night dwindles, his easy life ends,
and nothing remains but its fantasized time.

(L1611: 8–9)

This use of analogy has been classified by the poetic critic al-ʿAskarī as a rhetorical figure, called 'adducing evidence and argumentation' (*al-istishhād wa-l-iḥtijāj*), and explained as follows.[29]

> It operates like the paraphrase (*tadhyīl*) in engendering a motif (*tawlīd al-maʿnā*). It consists of one's presenting a motif and then confirming it by means of another motif, adduced as evidence for the former [motif] and as the argument in favor of its soundness.

Al-ʿAskarī mentions that most instances of this figure qualify as comparisons (*tashbīh*), a general term that in his usage includes analogy. As an example, al-ʿAskarī quotes Abū Tammām:

فاضْمُمْ قواصِيَهُمْ إليكَ فإنَّهُ   لا يَزخَرُ الوادِى بِغَيْرِ شِعابِ
والسَّهْمُ بالرِّيشِ اللُّؤامِ ولَنْ ترى   بيْتًا بلا عَمَدٍ ولا أَطْنابِ

Bring close to you their straying ones,
for a wadi does not fill up without remote watercourses.[30]

An arrow [flies straight only] with tightly set feathers,
and you will not see a tent [raised] without poles or ropes.

The poet intercedes with the tribal chief Mālik b. Ṭawq al-Taghlibī on behalf of the related clan of Usāma, who ask for his forgiveness. The poet argues that only such a tribe is strong whose clans are united with it, and he adduces three images demonstrating the importance of peripheral parts to a whole. Al-Jurjānī however treats analogy (*tamthīl*) among the tropes and amply discusses its psychological impact (*taʾthīr*).[31] He describes in particular such analogies that follow unusual images, giving a verse by al-Buḥturī as an example:

دانٍ على أيدِى العُفاةِ وشاسِعٌ   عنْ كلِّ نِدٍّ فى النَّدَى وضَرِيبِ
كالبَدْرِ أَفرَطَ فِى العُلُوِّ وضَوْءُهُ   للعُصبَةِ السّارِينَ جِدَّ قرِيبِ

[He is] close to the hands of supplicants
and distant from any equal and companion in generosity.[32]

Like the moon: it is of extreme height, while its light
is very close to the group of nocturnal travellers.[33]

Al-Buḥturī explains the paradox of a simultaneously reachable and unreachable patron by analogy with the moon; nobody can reach its height, but its light reaches down to every traveller. Ibn al-Rūmī uses this type of explanatory analogy as a device for closure. In the following episode on ʿUbaydallāh's generosity, he condemns hoarded wealth and compares it to rotting meat. Then he supports this image with the analogy of water turning foul from stagnation. (The analogy is italicized.)

يَتَّقِى جودُهُ صُلولَ القَناطيـ ـرِ كَما يُتَّقَى صلولُ اللِّحامِ
والقناطيرُ لا تَصِلُّ ولكنْ مَنْعُها الحَقَّ أَيُّما اسْتِذْمامِ
وصُلولُ اللِّحامِ يُسْقِمُ لكِنْ سَقَمُ البُخلِ أَبرَحُ الأَسْقامِ
وكذا الماءُ طَيِّبٌ ما اسْتَقَوْهُ آجِنٌ آسِنٌ على الإجْمامِ
يَعْذُبُ المَوْرِدُ الَّذى يُسْتَقَى مِنـ ـهُ ولا تَعْذُبُ المِياهُ الطَّوامِى

His generosity fears the stench of *qinṭārs*,
as one fears the stench of [rotting] meat.[34]

Qinṭārs do not [really] stink, but their denying
of the right [of generosity] – what a thing asking for blame!

The stench of meat is sickening, but the sickness
of avarice is the most serious sickness.[35]

Thus is water: palatable, as long as [people] draw from it, but altered
for the worse and undrinkable from being left to gather.

A watering place from which one draws [water] is sweet,
whereas swollen watering-holes are not.[36]

(L1250': 144–8)

By rendering money analogous to meat, the stench of meat corresponds to the blameworthiness of hoarding money, while the sickness, a consequence of the stench, parallels the blame and humiliation[37] of hoarding. In addition, the objects of comparison, 'stench' and 'sickness' invade the level of the topic as the metaphors 'stench of *qinṭārs*' and 'sickness of avarice'.[38] But they are immediately distinguished from their topical counterpart: '*Qinṭārs* do not [really] stink', rather they are blameworthy, and a physical ailment is minor compared to 'the sickness of humiliation'. The whole comparison pretends that 'hoarding' causes 'stench,' without explaining how the one leads to the other. This might well be left to the imagination, but Ibn al-Rūmī supports his image with a second analogy of water in a cistern. If constantly scooped, the water remains palatable, whereas if left untouched, it stagnates and begins to smell. The transparent analogy of smelling stagnant water replaces the moral assumption of shameful hoarded riches. The physical analogy provides effective support precisely because it replaces the weaker causality of the moral assumption. Its vividness distracts from the fact that its relationship with the argument is not one of logically-binding identity, but merely similarity. Medieval poetic critics and philosophers differed as to the truth value of such analogies and the poetic syllogisms on which they were based. Al-Jurjānī considered analogies (*tamthīl*) involving fantastic interpretation (*takhyīl*) at least as having a semblance of truth.[39] But philosophers generally considered poetic premises and the syllogisms built with them as false, with the exception of al-Qarṭājannī, who accepted their truth under certain conditions.[40] Both al-Jurjānī and al-Qarṭājannī agree however in placing more importance on an analogy's evocative impact than its truth value.

More often than episodes, Ibn al-Rūmī concludes scenes with a supporting sententia or analogy. In many cases, a sole image provides an effective closure. In the following rather atypical dialogue scene – the poet's persona opposes a friend, probably al-Buḥturī, in numerous turns of address and response – many of the responses are thus ended. The high frequency of turns and interior closures may be unique in the corpus, but it is useful for the sake of the example:

قُلْتُ لخِلٍّ خلا تَعَجُّبُهُ　　　إلّا مِنَ الدَّهْرِ إنْ خلا عَجَبُهْ
يَعْجَبُ مِنه ومِن تَلَوُّنِهِ　　　وكيْفَ يقْفو نوالَه حَرَبُهْ
لا تَعْجَبَنْ للزَّمانِ إنْ كَثُرَتْ　　　مِنهُ أَعاجيبُهُ ولا ذَرَبُهْ
فالدَّهْرُ لا تَنْقضِي عجائبُهُ　　　أَوْ يَتقضَّى مِنَ اهلِه أَرَبُهْ
كم جَوْرةٍ للزَّمانِ فاحِشَةٍ　　　قادَ بِها الرَّأْسَ مُذْعِنًا ذَنَبُهْ
وافتَرَسَ اللَّيْثَ مِنه ثَعْلَبُهُ　　　وصارَ يَصْطادُ صَقْرَهُ خَرَبُهْ
يا مَن يرَى الأَجربَ الصَّحيحَ فلا　　　يلقاه إلّا مُبَيَّنًا نَكَبُهْ
ما جَرَبُ المَرْءِ داءَ جِلْدَتِهِ　　　بلْ إنّما داءُ عِرضِهِ جَرَبُهْ
بلْ يا مُهينَ المَهينِ يَصحَبُهُ　　　رُبَّ مَهينٍ كفاكَ مُنْتَدَبُهْ
لا تَحْقِرِ المُنصُلَ الخَشيبَ فقدْ　　　يُرْضيك عِندَ المِصاعِ مُخْتَشَبُهْ
كم مِن قوِيٍّ إذا أَخلَّ بهِ　　　فَقْدُ مَهينَيْه فاتَه غَلَبُهْ
كالسَّهْمِ ذِى النَّصْلِ لا نُهوضَ بهِ　　　ما لمْ يَكُنْ ريشُهُ ولا عَقَبُهْ
الشَّىْءُ بالشَّىْءِ يُسْتَخَفُّ بهِ　　　والجِذْعُ ما لا يَصونُهُ شَذَبُهْ

لا تيأَسَنْ أَنْ يَتوبَ ذو سَرَفٍ — يُضْحِي ويُمسِي كثيرةً حُوَبُهْ
وايْأَسْ مِنَ المَرْءِ أَنْ يُنيبَ إذا — ما المَرْءُ كانتْ كثيرةً تُوَبُهْ
بلْ أَيُّها الطّالبُ المُجِدُّ بهِ — فِي كلِّ يومٍ وليْلَةٍ قَرَبُهْ
قدْ شَفَّهُ حِرْصُهُ وحالَفَهُ — طولَ عَناءٍ وحَسْرَةٍ وَصَبُهْ
بلْ أَيُّها الهارِبُ المُخامِرُهُ — خوْفٌ وكَرْبٌ مُخَنَّقٌ لَبَبُهْ
أَلْقِ المقاليدَ إنَّهُ قَدَرٌ — ما لامْرِئٍ صَرْفُهُ ولا جَلَبُهْ
قدْ يَسْبِقُ الخيْرَ طالِبٌ عَجِلٌ — ويَرْهَقُ الشَّرُّ مُمْعِنًا هَرَبُهْ
والرِّزْقُ آتٍ بلا مُطالَبَةٍ — سِيّانِ مَدْفوعُهُ ومُجْتَذَبُهْ
لا يُحْزِنُ المرْءَ أَنْ يُنَبَّزَ بالـ — ـأَلْقابِ بلْ أَنْ تَشينَهُ خُرَبُهْ
وما معيبٌ بعادِمٍ لَقَبًا — كلُّ مَعيبٍ فعيْبُهُ لَقَبُهْ
فاسْلَمْ مِنَ العَيْبِ أَوْ فَكُنْ رجُلاً — مِمَّن تَهادَى عُيوبَهُ غِيَبُهْ
فقَلَّما عُدَّ مُخْطِئًا رجُلٌ — قدْ كَثَرَتْ خاطئاتِهِ صُيُبُهْ

I said to a friend who wonders only about fate,
[even] if his wondering [in general] has ceased.[41]

He wonders about it and its changing, and how upon its bestowing
its plundering ensues.

'Do not be amazed at time, when its miracles abound,
nor [when] its violence [abounds].

The miracles of time do not cease
unless its aiming for people ceases.[42]

How often in a shameless tyranny of time,
a tail led an obedient head!

The fox broke the neck of the lion,
and the bustard preyed upon the falcon.

O you who see the scabby, [morally] sound [man],
and do not meet him without his mange being exposed.[43]

The scab of a man is not the illness of his skin,
rather, his scab is the illness of his honor.[44]

No, you who despise the despised companion; often the response
of a despised one [you called upon in need] sufficed you.

Do not despise the unpolished sword! [Your] having picked it
in its rough state may please you in a fight.

How often victory escaped a strong one,
when the loss of his two despised [companions] left him in need.

Like an arrow [furnished] with a head, which does not
fly straight as long as it lacks feathers and a tail.[45]

One thing [exists] with [the help of] another thing one despises,
a [dead] trunk is that which no bark and leaves protect.

Do not give up on a corrupted man, who enters
[every] morning and evening with many sins.

Give up on the return of a man
whose repentances are many.

No, you who strive, whose craving plagues him
each day and night,

His greed has worn him thin, and illness cleaves to him
from long struggle and pain.

No, you who flee, whom fear and sorrow beleaguer,
whose throat is constricted,

Surrender! it is destiny,
which man can neither avert nor attract.[46]

Sometimes the hasty striver outruns the good,
and evil catches up with him who escapes far.

[God's] bestowal comes without demand,
similarly [that which is] given and taken.

A man is not saddened by being called names,
but by [real] faults disgracing him.[47]

No blameworthy one is without a name;
for each blameworthy one, his fault becomes his name

Therefore, be free of fault, or be a man regarding whom
evil speeches behind his back trade his faults between them.[48]

For rarely is a man called 'missing [a goal]' whose
winning shots outnumber his misses.'[49]

(L215: 35–59)

The poet's interlocutor, reported in the poet's words throughout the dialogue, holds certain beliefs about fate and the standards of a man's worth, which the poet challenges. Nearly all of the seven turns of paraphrase and response are supported by sententia or analogy or both.

To the friend's wondering about the changes of fate in the first turn (35–40), the poet declares change and deceit to be fate's intrinsic qualities. He underscores it with a sententia and three analogies of weaker and inferior animals (fox, bustard) and body parts (tail) as triumphing over their stronger and superior counterparts (lion, falcon, head). The images narrow the unpredictability of fate to a reversal of the hierarchy between strong and weak. In the second turn (41–2), the friend's criticism of mange, a skin disease, is dismissed by the poet as merely physical in contrast to more serious moral deficiency.[50]

The strongest accumulation of analogies occurs in the third turn (43–7), where the friend despises a lowly man. The poet adduces analogies with inferior objects that are vital in certain contexts, such as the rough sword in a fight, or minor parts essential to whole entities, such as the feather and tail that ensure an arrow's straight flight or the bark and leaves that keep a tree alive. The images replace the message of the first turn – the seemingly weak as dominating the strong – with a complementary relationship of weak and strong part of a whole as equally essential.[51] In the fourth and fifth turn (48–9), two imperatives remind the friend of the reversibility of human acts. The friend should not judge human sinfulness nor penitence at face value, since it can change at any moment. No sententiae or arguments are adduced. In the last two exchanges (50–1 and 52–9), the poet remains in the human realm and proceeds to the theme of ambition. The friend's striving, both in gaining and avoiding certain things, is called erring and failed. The poet repeats and confirms his criticism of both kinds of striving in two sententiae. Knowing God's grace, striving is unnecessary (55) and virtually counterproductive (54). The poet adds further sententiae: one should distinguish false insults from real faults, as the latter provide the really harmful insults, while false insults have no power over a blameless man. The poet concludes that faultless acts protect from false blame and supports that with the analogy of a good archer, judged by the majority of his good shots, not hearsay. In this turn, the poet brands as futile every human endeavor if not directed at avoiding faults.

The sententiae and analogies follow and reinforce the literal assertions. Those are nearly devoid of imagery. It is the occurrence of the figures after literal passages that increases their impact. The poet's general argument bears on the deceptiveness of appearances. In the third and the seventh turn of conversation, he develops it further. On the one hand, hierarchies are reversible and human self-reliance is self-deception, for humans cannot direct their own fates. On the other, humans are held responsible for their sins and must avoid them. The poet's persona directs human endeavor to moral integrity and away from short-sighted ambition. The whole argument prepares the ground for the following scene, in which the poet expounds his own professional ethics and refuses to satirize an unnamed individual (L215: 60–72). The argumentation on its own is coherent and lucid, but the sententiae and analogies lend it charm and persuasion.

The function of sententia and analogy in the examples can be characterized as auxiliary. They do not direct attention to themselves, but support and reiterate a preceding statement either literally or figuratively. Both epitomize the content of a preceding scene or episode. As a trope, the analogy is psychologically effective in a predominantly literal context. Due to its double-layered structure, it also has a wider field of application than the sententia, for it resonates in other occurrences of the same motif within a *qaṣīda*.

The recurring motif

The long dialogue on missing reward, discussed in chapter 10 (L191: 96–150), contains several recurring motifs, for example the milch camels and the stream or ocean.[52] The most interesting one is the rain motif because it both underscores and undercuts the argument. Rain recurs in different tropes in connection with the generosity of the patron, namely as metaphor, analogy, and inverted comparison. Adjacent motifs of lightning, mirage, and dust storm symbolize the poet's fears, while the mountain motif serves his boast and his demands.[53] The following quotes show how Ibn al-Rūmī gradually transforms the metaphorical relationship between the patron and rain.

In the poet's first dialogue with the patron (L191: 97–117), asking for the reason why he has not received a reward, the genitive metaphor 'clouds of your kindness' identifies his patron's generosity with clouds. These metaphorical clouds exclude and disappoint the poet, although they rain on others and even reach distant regions:

أَظلَّ سَحابُ عُرفِك كلَّ شَىْءٍ   ودرَّ على البِلاد بلا عِصابِ
سِوایَ فإنَّنِى عنه بظَهرٍ   كأَنِّى خَلفَ مُنقَطِعِ التُّرابِ
يجودُ بِسَيْبِهِ أَبدًا لِغَيْرِى   ويخلُبُنِى ببرْقٍ غيرِ خابِى
أَما لِى مِنْه حَظٌّ غيْرُ برْقٍ   تُشبِّهُهُ العُيونُ حريقَ غابِ؟
أَبيتُ أَشيمُهُ وأَذودُ نَومِى   ويُرزَقُ صوبَه أَقصَى مَصابِ

The clouds of your kindness grant shade to everything
and give abundant rain to the regions without coercion.[54]

Except to me, for I am above them on a plateau,
as if I were beyond [the point] where the sheer rock is exposed.

They lavish forever their downpour
on others than me and deceive me
with a lightning that does not extinguish.

Will I not have a share from them (sc. your clouds) other than lightning,
which my eyes compare to fire in a reed thicket?

I spend the night watching their course, fighting sleep,
while the furthest place of rainfall is fed with their downpour.
(L191: 98–102)

The patron's generosity in the guise of clouds is not principally in question, but called far-reaching and constant. The poet only criticizes the patron's ignoring of himself. The poet then pursues a line of questioning to find the reason for missing his patron's generosity, using the rain image to couch criticism of him in praise. After dismissing several answers, he arrives at a potential explanation:

أَتَحْرُمُنِى لِإنِّى مُسْتَغِلٌّ   وأَنِّى لسْتُ كالرَّزْحَى السِّغابِ؟

Do you deprive me because I have my estates,
and I am not like emaciated starving [camels]?[55]

(L191: 109)

Could the poet's wealth have caused the patron's withholding? The poet shirks a literal answer, responding instead in two analogies. He deduces the patron's behavior from that of milch camels (110–12) and rain:

وما يَطوِى العِمارةَ كلُّ غَيْثٍ   إلى الأَرضِ المُعطَّلةِ اليَبابِ
ولكنْ لا يَزالُ يجودُ كُلًّا   بجَوْدٍ أَو بِوَبْلٍ ذِى انْسِكابِ
لإحياءِ الَّتِى كانتْ مَواتًا   وحِفظِ العامِراتِ مِنَ الخَرابِ

Not every shower leaves behind the cultivated land
for the abandoned wasteland,

But it does not cease to give to each
an abundant shower and a torrential downpour,[56]

Bringing barren land to life and preserving
cultivated land from destruction.

(L191: 113–15)

The nature of real rain to shed water everywhere indiscriminately seems to criticize the patron's bestowing as selective, but immediately negates the poet's hypothesis that the patron's rain cloud could have intentionally deprived him. According to the poetic analogy, the patron's generosity cannot be selective, but should treat wealthy and poor with equal measure. This ends the first dialogue, excluding the possibility of the patron's denial of reward. After a monologue of doubt, the poet reformulates the denial of reward as a temporary delay.

In both instances of the rain motif, the role of the poet is active. In the rain cloud metaphor, his deprivation is motivated by his high position, which also connotes nobility;[57] the patron's rain clouds cannot reach him because he is 'above them on a plateau' (99). In the subsequent analogy, the poet modifies his earlier statement:

وإن أكُ مِن نَداهُ على صُعُودٍ   فإنِّي مِن نداكَ على انصِبابِ

If I am higher than its (sc. the real cloud's) rain,
I am [still] lower than your [figurative cloud's] rain.[58]

(L191: 116)

This verse reiterates the poet's deprivation, but declares the patron able and worthy of remedying it. Now the poet distinguishes between real rain clouds and the patron's sublime metaphorical ones, which alone are able to climb to the poet's height. More important, the verse establishes the superiority of figurative rain above literal rain – a tendency already noted. This inequality is heightened when the rain motif returns two scenes later in a hyperbolic dialogue with the patron to compete with its metaphorical counterpart. This is not true dispute poetry (*munāẓara*), as the competitors do not debate with each other. Instead, rain is only adduced in the third person,[59] and it forms an expanded comparison in which the relationship between topic and image is inverted.

نعدُّ مَعايِبًا للغَيْث شتَّى   وما فِي جودِ كفِّكَ مِن مَعابِ
وَجَدْنا الغيْثَ يَهدِمُ ما بَنَيْنا   سِوَى الخَيْمِ المُبدَّى والقِبابِ
ويمنَعُنا الحَراكَ أَشَدَّ مَنْعٍ   وإلّا سامنَا حَطْمَ الرِّقابِ
ويحتجِبُ الضِّياءُ إذا سَقانا   وما ضَوْءٌ بِجودِك ذو احْتِجابِ
وفَضْلُ جَداكَ بَعْدُ على جَداهُ   مُبِينٌ لا يُقابَلُ بارْتِيابِ
تَجودُ يداكَ بالذَّهَبِ المُصَفَّى   إذا ما الغَيْثُ عَلَّلَ بالذِّهابِ
وجودُك لا يُغِبُّ الناسَ يومًا   وجودُ الغَيْثِ تاراتُ اعْتِقابِ

We count several faults in rain –
in the generosity of your hand, nothing is to blame.

We have found that rain destroys what we build,
except exposed tents and domes.[60]

It restricts us from moving
lest we break our necks.

The lights are veiled when it pours on us,
while no light is veiled by your generosity.[61]

After that, the excellence of your gift over [rain's]
is clear and not met with doubt:

Your hands give pure gold,
when the rain distracts us with drizzle.[62]

Your generosity does not stay away on the second day –
the generosity of the rain often comes later.

(L191: 141–7)

The moral notion of generosity puts its object of comparison (e.g. real rain) to shame, as it reveals many shortcomings: it destroys habitations, limits people's movement, spreads darkness and is unreliable. Finally, its gift is mere water, not gold like that of the patron. However, the initial advantage of real rain's indiscriminate giving – contrasting the selective giving of the patron – is not modified. The competition closes on a common trait: both types of rain never vaunt favors given:

وتَتَّفِقانِ فِى خُلُقٍ كريمٍ فَتَشْتَرِكانِهِ شِرْكَ الطِّيابِ
تجودانِ الأَنامَ بلا امتِنانٍ بما تُسْتَمْطَرانِ ولا احْتِسابِ

Both of you coincide in a noble trait
and share it with each other in lawful partnership.[63]

Both of you give to mankind without enumerating
or calculating the rain solicited from you.

(L191: 148–9)

The inverted comparison concludes the argument on delayed reward. Throughout it, the positions of rain and generosity have been reversed. The rain motif, usually a hackneyed metaphor for generosity, is revealed in changing facets, which include even avarice. In the beginning, metaphorical rain, identified with the patron's generosity, was criticized as selective. Then, the analogy with real rain disproved that criticism. Here real rain was posited first as superior to the patron's gifts and then as vindicating them. At the end, however, actual rain is outdone by the patron's metaphorical rain. This last relationship is developed as a point-by-point comparison, in which real rain proves to be inferior in almost all of its traits, except those it shares with the patron. By its constant recurrence, the rain motif cumulates its meanings, which continue to resonate in each new instance, notably the initial criticism. Even the ostentatious final praise does not erase the negative aspect of the patron's limited versus rain's unlimited giving. This aspect is no more touched upon in the rest of the *qaṣīda*, only counterbalanced by other positive aspects of the patron's generosity. The rain motif accentuates the direct argument of this composite scene: the poet struggles to believe in the patron's justice and ends on an ambivalent note. The recurring motif mirrors this ambivalence. Overtly, it gives preference to metaphorical over real rain, but it also suggests a counterposition. The bipolar figurative layer of the recurring motif aptly parallels the bifurcating argument of this composite dialogue.

In general, the figures' dramatic functions depend upon the context in which they are adduced. The semantic figures of sententia, analogy, and recurring motif highlight an argument at crucial points and closures. They do not perform but support the actions of the plot. This occurs predominantly, but not exclusively, in dramatized monologues and dialogues between the poet and a conversation partner. Such scenes exhibit what Gregor Schoeler has called Ibn al-Rūmī's 'style with sparse imagery' (bildarmer Stil).[64] He describes it as the reduction of a topic to a few essential motifs, characterized in a sensuous, concrete fashion, and expressed in predominantly non-figurative speech.[65] To this, the closing analogy adds a final spice. Conversely, select syntactic figures prevail in episodes of *madīḥ*, which center on the patron. Anaphora and reprise provide a structure for non-figurative descriptions or straight-forward imagery. The anaphora lends itself in particular to the exhaustive enumeration of familiar praising epithets, illustrating the universal uniqueness of the *mamdūḥ* as the underlying meaning of an antistrophe. The figure's repetitive rhythm drives home the patron's matchlessness in ever new guises. But not all verbal ornament is relegated to supporting roles, as will be seen in the next chapter.

13

PHANTASMAGORIA

The previous chapter has explored figures that enhance the dramaturgy of passages without playing a predominant role themselves. The opposite is true for some episodes in which a theme serves as a mere prop for an arrangement of figures and tropes. These create an abstract fantastic action that is initially removed from and eventually inverts the depicted reality. The shift of focus from depicting an (often highly conventionalized) reality to developing existing motifs of poetry, characterizes *muḥdath* poetry in general and rightly deserves the name of mannerism, which Wolfhart Heinrichs and later Stefan Sperl applied to it.[1]

In Ibn al-Rūmī's nature poetry, Gregor Schoeler identified two variants of mannerism and one more concrete style.[2] In the episodes of *madīḥ* analyzed below, Ibn al-Rūmī achieves an astonishing fusion of figurative elements, which justifies the label of *phantasmagoria*. Benedikt Reinert offers a definition of the term, based on European baroque concettism.

> Phantasmagoria are essentially always based on a terminological duplicity (begriffliche Doppelbödigkeit). Two levels of terms are placed into a relationship with each other by means of a poetic trick (Kunstgriff). From the tension between the two levels, i.e. the identity, similarity, or difference of their corresponding elements, games of meaning (Sinnspiele) arise.[3]

With this poetic 'trick', Reinert means a trope, such as a comparison or metaphor, that associates a verse's topical level with a metaphorical level. Inversely, an element of the metaphorical level may be naturalized and play a part in the topical level. Irrespective of which level invades the other, the result is always an amalgamation of the two. Instances of it are the paradox, the oxymoron, and the incoherent harmony of terms.[4] Reinert's concept of phantasmagoria has the benefit of including the elements of Heinrichs's typology of paired metaphors for *muḥdath* poetry, which is adopted below for a close analysis of examples. The typology is based on samples of *muḥdath* poetry, mainly drawn from the *Kitāb al-Badīʿ* by the prince and poet-critic Ibn al-Muʿtazz (d. 296/908), a contemporary of Ibn al-Rūmī. The typology should facilitate an understanding of the internal logic of Abbasid mannerist poetry. According to Heinrichs, the technique of pairing metaphors 'affords us something of a magnifying glass by which certain generating mechanisms in the poetical language of the Abbasid poets will become apparent'.[5] He distinguishes four categories of increasing complexity. The first contains one topic and one analogue, both consisting of several elements; the second unites one topic to two or more analogues, describing perhaps different aspects of the topic. In the third category, two topics are combined with two analogues, with the resulting image being tied together by some additional figure of speech, notably the harmonious choice of images (*murāʿāt al-naẓīr*). In the fourth category, two topics, one plain, the other expressed through an image, are tied together by an additional figure of speech.[6] Heinrichs identifies the trend towards a 'formal unity' as one of the generating mechanisms. This term signifies 'that two or more traditional motifs which are contiguous in the ancient poetry are unified and made coherent on a purely literary level by the use of rhetorical figures and imagery'.[7] By applying the typology to Ibn al-Rūmī, the nuclei of his metaphors can be extracted, and other elements isolated. This way of proceeding tests Ibn al-Rūmī's mannerism against a *muḥdath* common ground.[8] The following admittedly technical analyses are vital because much of what requires explanation for modern readers was well-known to educated Baghdadians. Without some direction as to what Ibn al-Rūmī presupposed from his audience, the fine points that render his poetry ingenuous artistry cannot be distinguished.

The long strophe of L1611: 1–101 unites a plethora of themes, beginning with *al-shayb wa-shabāb*, followed by a kaleidoscope of *fakhr* episodes.[9] The following quotes derive from its middle part, a *khamriyya* (19–55), which contains descriptions of wine (10–18) and of a female figure in varying guises. First she appears as a cupbearer, then an alluring beauty, and finally a singer and musician (19–45). The woman's real action is limited to a terse narrative frame (19, 44–5), while the bulk of twenty-three verses reduces her to a backdrop for phantasmagoria. An abstract dispute springs up between her smooth cheek and the beholder's intruding eye (22–31), a *metaphora continuata* dresses the woman in the vocabulary of flower and garden poetry (32–6), and her simultaneously uniform and diversified charms form a paradox (37–43).[10] This is followed by a description of the garden in which this takes place (46–8), and a coda (49–55).[11] Two episodes describing her appearance and the coda are selected for scrutiny, beginning with the last.

The *khamriyya*'s coda summarizes and condenses all preceding topics. The woman's actions as a cupbearer and a singing lute-player are captured in the metaphor of a 'gazelle' (*ghazāl, ẓaby*), which is juxtaposed with the actual animal. The first verse recalls the garden as the *khamriyya*'s physical backdrop (44):

يُغازِلُنى فيها غَزالانِ مِنهُما   رَبيبُ الفيافِى والرَّبيبُ المُتَوَّمُ
إذا نَصَبا جيدَيْهِما فكِلاهُما   سَواءٌ وإبريقٌ لَدَىَّ مُفَدَّمُ
ثلاثةُ أظْبٍ نَجْرُها غَيْرُ واحِدٍ   لِذى اللَّهْوِ فيها كُلِّها مُتَنَعَّمُ
غَزالٌ وإبريقٌ رَذومٌ وغادَةٌ   تُحَرِّكُ مِنْ أَوْتارِها وتُنَغِّمُ
فظَبْىٌ يُغَنِّيهِ وظَبْىٌ يَعُلُّه   وظَبْىٌ يرودُ التَّلْعَ أَوْ يَتَجَرْثَمُ
لِعَيْنَىْ مُراعِى شَخْصِه فيهِ مَأْنَسٌ   ومَلْهًى ولِلْمُسْتَطْعِمِ الصَّيْدِ مَطْعَمُ
فَقَدْ عَكَفَتْ منها عليْه بما اشْتَهَى   هُنالِك أظآرٌ مِنَ العَيْشِ رُوَّمُ

In it (sc. the garden)[12] two gazelles dally with me;
one reared in the deserts, one wearing a necklace.

When both of them stretch their necks
they are equal to my strainer-covered ewer.

Three young gazelles, not of a single origin;
for a man of pleasure, there is in all of them delight:

A gazelle, a brimming jug, and a girl,
who plucks her strings and sings.

Then one gazelle is singing to him,
one gazelle pouring him a second drink,
and one gazelle roaming the hillsides or hovering in one place.

For the eyes of him who beholds [the gazelle's] shape,
there is in her companionship and pleasure;
for him who desires to feed himself by hunting, there is tasting.[13]

In her, for whatever he wants from life,
wet-nurses stand eagerly at his beck and call.[14]

(L1611: 49–55)

A composite metaphor of over two lines opens the passage as a summary (49–50). Its first verse, belonging to Heinrichs's fourth category, consists of two topics, one plain, the other expressed in an image. The plain topic is the actual 'gazelle reared in the deserts'. Matched with it is a metaphorical 'ear-ringed gazelle' based on the simile of the long-necked gazelle for the bejewelled singing lute-player.[15] The two topics oppose the true animal to its metaphorical counterpart. In the following verse, a ewer is added as a further topic, based again on the simile of the long neck. As a result, three topics of gazelle, singer, and ewer share a single term, merging reality and fantasy. In this case, Ibn al-Rūmī's inventiveness expands the fourth category as defined above. No further metaphors are introduced, but the existing ones are reiterated, detailed, reshuffled, and naturalized. Verse 51 adds an antithesis between the gazelles' diversity and their shared quality of giving pleasure. The following verse pair adds the figure of 'proper explanation' (*ṣiḥḥat al-tafsīr*, 52–3).[16] It lists the three topics of gazelle, ewer, and singing lute-player, and then, in reverse order, their naturalized metaphors of a singing gazelle, a pouring gazelle, and an actual gazelle. The final pair of verses recalls the speaker as a 'man of pleasure' who enjoys the concept of gazelle in its real and imagined manifestations (54–5). The episode's attraction rests on the initial triple meaning of gazelle and its subsequent detailed explanation. As a whole, it sums up the previous episodes' topics of wine, cupbearer, and musician. For cupbearer and women, the gazelle simile is common; for the wine cup, Abū Nuwās already used the gazelle image to establish a formal unity with gazelle-like women.[17] But Ibn al-Rūmī achieved a greater inclusiveness by naturalizing the gazelle metaphor, i.e. adding the real animal as a third party.

Another phantasmagoric passage presents the cupbearer as a paradox of unity and diversity:

تفاوَتَ منها الخَلْقُ فِى حُسْنِ صورةٍ   تَفاوُتَ إبْداعٍ فَرابٍ وأَهْضَمُ
وجَدْلٌ وممشوقٌ وأَبيضُ ناصِعٌ   وأَسْوَدُ غِرْبيبٌ وأَقْنى وأَخْثَمُ
إذا استَعْرَضَتْها العينُ دَقَّ مُوَشَّحٌ   لها ورَبا رِدْفٌ وجَلَّ مُخَدَّمُ
مراكبُ لِلَّذّاتِ منها مُضَمَّرٌ   وما مسَّها ضُمْرٌ ومِنها مُطَهَّمُ
لها فِرَقٌ شَتَّى مِنَ الحُسْنِ أَجْمَعَتْ   على أَنْ يُلَقَّى البَرْحَ منها مُتَيَّمُ
أَما عَجَبٌ إجْماعُ مُخْتَلِفاتِها   على قَتْلِ مَنْ لاقَتْه لا تَتَأَثَّمُ
كذا السَّهْمُ يُصمِى وَهْوَ شَتَّى نِجارُه   حَديدٌ وريشٌ وابْنُ غيلٍ مُقَوَّمُ

Her body is diverse, in a beautiful shape, like the diversity of creation,
for [it is] well-rounded and thin,

Plump and bony, radiant white and jet black,
a high-ridged [nose] and flat [nostrils].[18]

When the eye approaches her from the side, her waist is slight,
her buttocks, well-rounded, her ankles, strong.

They are mounts for pleasures [to ride on], some of them, lean –
though untouched by hunger – others, plump.[19]

She has diverse parts of beauty that rally
to distress an enslaved [lover].

Is it not strange, the consensus of her different [parts]
to kill whom they meet without repentance?

Thus is the arrow; it hits fatally though of diverse origins:
iron, feathers, and a straightened piece of shrub.

(L1611: 37–43)

The passage contains two images; one of them (39–40) belongs to the first category with one topic, the woman's limbs, and one analogue, the riding beast. The second rather peculiar metaphor is non-imaginary, since it has a real counterpart in the limbs.[20] The image is generated by an analogy between the eye travelling across the body and a man riding different animals. The 'pleasures' belong to the level of the topic, 'fullness', and 'leanness', to both levels of limbs and metaphorical riding beasts. The second paired metaphor (41–2) also spans two lines and belongs to the first category. In it, the limbs' figurative 'throwing' of the lover 'into distress' and 'killing' him 'without holding back', are non-imaginary action-metaphors that correspond to the reality of the admirer's fascination. The 'consent' of the limbs, however, is an imaginary metaphor that has no basis in reality, since it results merely from the personification of the limbs as wilful murderers. Underlying the metaphors is an analogy between diverse limbs that charm an observer, and a motley band of rogues plotting the murder of an innocent victim. In this connection, the common motif of the beloved's murderous glances comes to mind, but our image differs from it in not attributing the infamous deed to a conscious action of the beloved, but a fantasized conspiracy of her limbs. The two paired metaphors of the passage are cumulative. The second metaphor overlays the motif of diversity from the first metaphor with the motif of the limbs' 'consensus', creating a paradox, which prompts the poet's feigned wondering, 'Is it not strange'? The metaphors are connected by means of the limbs' personification. Furthermore, we find in the opening lines a Koranic allusion to the effect that diversity is a proof of God's creation.[21] The conclusion is provided by an explanatory analogy, as discussed in the previous chapter.[22] It is the familiar arrow image that demonstrates how different agents (wood, feathers, and iron, or here, diverse body parts) can share the same goal (hitting the mark or, here, murder). The remarkable unity of this episode also manifests itself in its gradual ascent to the metaphoric sphere. The literal description combined with the Koranic allusion is first matched with one paired metaphor, then another, creating a paradox that sparks the witnessing poet's feigned wondering, and countered in turn by the concluding analogy. Conversely, reality is progressively estranged to baffling phantasmagoria before the viewer's very eye. Though paired metaphors and personifications provide the core, the adventurous mental trajectory is Ibn al-Rūmī's.

Another episode revolves around the cupbearer's cheek and the viewer's eye, personified as two adversaries:

كهمِّ الخَلِيِّ اسْوَدَّ فَرْعٌ ومَكْحَلٌ   لها خِلْقَةً وابْيَضَّ ثَغْرٌ ومَلْغَمُ
وأَشْرَقَ منها صَحْنُ خَدٍّ مُضَرَّجٍ   يَظَلُّ بما فيه مِنَ الماءِ يُضْرَمُ
مُفَدًّى يُسَمَّى بِاسمِ فيها مُقَبَّلاً   إذا قيلَ للخَدِّ الشَّتيمِ مُلَطَّمُ
وأَنَّى يُسَمَّى مَلْطَمًا وَهْوَ مَلْثَمٌ   فَدَى حُسْنَهُ مِن ذاكَ خَدٌّ مُلَطَّمُ

على أَنَّه مُغْرًى به العَضُّ مولَعٌ — وليسَ له ذَنْبٌ سِوى الحُسْنِ يُنْقَمُ
يُعَضُّ وما أَسْدَى إلى العَينِ سَيِّئًا — وليس بمظلومٍ وإنْ كانَ يُظْلَمُ
يَظَلُّ إذا أَبدَى لنا مِنه صَفَحَةً — تَلُذُّ بها أَبصارُنا وتَنَعَّمُ
نُوَلِّيه أَطرافَ الثَّنايا وإنَّهُ — لَيَدْمَى مِنَ الأَلحاظِ بلْ حينَ يُوهَمُ
بذاك قضَى قاضِي الهَوَى وَهْوَ ظالِمٌ — على الخَدِّ للْعَينِ الَّتِى هِىَ أَظْلَمُ
وما زالَ فِى القاضِى الغَشومِ تحامُلٌ — على الخصْمِ للخَصْمِ الَّذِى هُوَ أَغْشَمُ

Like the sorrow of a solitary man,
her hair and eye rims are black by nature,
and white are the opening and corners [of her mouth].

In her shines the surface of a blood-smeared cheek,
constantly set afire by its [own] water.

A cherished [cheek] which should be called 'place of kissing'
by the name of her mouth,
whereas to a blamed cheek one says 'place of slapping'.[23]

How should it be called 'place of slapping'
when it is a 'place to be kissed'? May a blamed cheek
ransom the beauty of [this blameless cheek] from that![24]

However, 'biting' is charmed and spellbound by [the cheek],
although it [committed] no sin to be avenged except [its] beauty.

[The cheek] is bitten without having hurt the eye,
although it is not one to be mistreated, even if [here] treated thus.

When it (sc. the cheek) exposes its side to us,
our eyesight delights and revels in it,[25]

We show it the edges of our front teeth, but it bleeds already
from the glances, no, [already] from being imagined.

Thus ruled the judge of desire, unjust to the cheek
and favoring the more unjust eye.

A corrupt judge will always be prepossessed against one adversary,
favoring the more corrupt adversary.

(L1611: 22–31)

The passage contains three paired metaphors. The first (23) belongs to the second category of one topic, the redness of the cheek, and the two analogues of bleeding and burning. The second analogue is joined with the frequent metaphor of 'water' for skin based on their similar sheen. Together, the water-for-skin simile and the fire-for-blushing analogue create the paradox of water kindling a fire. Another paired metaphor belongs to the third category of two topics and two analogues. The first topic, the gaze of an eye fixed on a beautiful cheek, is rendered by the analogue of 'biting' it, which personifies the eye. Having a real counterpart in staring, biting is a non-imaginary metaphor, although its attributes 'charmed' and 'spellbound', developing the personification, are imaginary. The second topic is the perfection of the cheek, placed in analogy with innocence from sin. The personified cheek's 'sinning' and 'hurting' are then imaginary verb metaphors.[26] The two analogues of the eye's 'biting' and the cheek's 'innocence' are then connected by the motif of the eye's injustice. The third and last paired metaphor (30) derives from the first category. It naturalizes the injustice motif and transfers the phantasmagoric action onto a human level. The love-maddened eye biting the cheek becomes the new topic, placed in turn in analogy with a corrupt litigant. The evildoer is favored by an equally corrupt judge, identified with desire by a genitive metaphor. The judge's 'unjust ruling' and 'favoring' are imaginary verb metaphors that derive from the personification of desire. The three paired metaphors are again cumulative; the first centers on the cheek, the second adds the eye and the connective motif of injustice, and the third supplies desire as the motivation for injustice.

In addition to the paired metaphors and the resulting personifications, the attribute 'blood-smeared' (23), gives rise to a fantastic etiology of the delicate cheek's 'bleeding' from glances (29). The author further toys with the etymologies of mouth and cheek (24–5) and fleshes out the action with a descriptive line (28). A closing sententia (31), syntactically parallel with the last paired metaphor, claims such injustice to be universally true.

The paired metaphors supply the vignettes for a sequence of illusions, which can be paraphrased as follows. The first part introduces the two protagonists cheek and mouth (22–4). The blameless (white) mouth is kissed, whereas the blood-smeared (flushed) cheek is blamed and slapped. In a second step, the poet wonders at this, given the beauty of the cupbearer's cheek, and asks why no ugly cheek has ransomed hers from such abuse (25). In answer to his question, the perpetrator appears. It is the eye that bit the cheek, unjustly to be sure, but hopelessly enslaved by desire (26–7). The following verse adds the cheek's bleeding to the misdeeds of the eye. The action ends in an imaginary tribunal in which a partial judge (desire) favors the guilty defendant (eye) over the innocent plaintiff (cheek), as an analogy between injustice and desire. A sententia takes the imaginary plot back to reality and proclaims it as true. The action of the passage rests on single and paired *muḥdath* metaphors and the play on etymology. Together with personifications and fantastic etiologies, they produce a coherent plot, complete with description and closure. A pertinent trait are the curious moral dilemmas of the personified facial organs: the cheek is ransomed and avoids sin, whereas the eye commits it. The original topic of a woman's face has become a fantastic theater of desire.

The examples have shown the combination of tropes to be the mainstay of Ibn al-Rūmī's *fakhr* episodes. But they are deftly expanded, layered, and joined with other figures, notably personifications, which are the 'dramatis personae' of fantastic scenarios: intense activity rages in what is in reality a quiet scene, such as a man gazing at a woman's face. Intermittent descriptions, explanations, and marked conclusions smooth the progression of the imaginary plots in which even moral questions find a place.

This highly complex yet consistent mannerism manifests Ibn al-Rūmī's larger compositional vision. His unit of thought is the entire passage to which each verse and image contributes, not the single verse or image itself, as was the case for most of his contemporaries. The poetic critic al-Marzubānī mentioned Ibn al-Rūmī's habit of giving summaries and then proceeding to the details.[27] Ibn Rashīq for his part took the poet to task for stretching too far the treatment of single motifs, though he did acknowledge the poet's inventiveness in motifs (*ikhtirāʿ*).[28] The style resembles that which Schoeler has termed one of Ibn al-Rūmī's mannerist styles, describing it as the poet's attaching himself to one phenomenon and representing it in numerous different images, with a predilection for far-fetched comparisons and phantasmagoria.[29]

Episodes in this style are reserved for the strophe, where the poet figures at best as a witness. There is no immediately recognizable link between them and the panegyric *qaṣīda*'s general purpose to praise. Rather the poet shows his virtuosity, removed from those sections of the *qaṣīda* that serve its purpose. These obligatory episodes of *madīḥ* in the antistrophe are shaped by straightforward figures of speech that retrace a catalogue of *madīḥ*. The more daring verbal artistry – whether dramatic or phantasmagoric – is placed in the *qaṣīda*'s peripheral parts of strophe and metastrophe,[30] extended by Ibn al-Rūmī to intimidating length. The strophes of L1611 and L1250' abound with phantasmagoria, while the strophes and metastrophes of L191 and L215 shine with their dramaturgy. These surrounding parts establish the poet's skill and the value of his *qaṣīda* as a work of art without jeopardizing its official purpose to praise. This functional understanding of the *qaṣīda*'s parts coincides with the views of Jamal Eddine Bencheikh and Thomas Bauer on the relationship of *nasīb* and *madīḥ*.[31]

Though Ibn al-Rūmī would hone his mannerist style with later patrons, such as al-Qāsim b. ʿUbaydallāh b. Wahb, its elements are already present in ʿUbaydallāh's panegyric corpus. With this early patron he focused however on the human aspects and moral dimensions of their relationship to which the last part of this book is devoted.

Part V

IBN AL-RŪMĪ'S ETHICS OF PATRONAGE

14

IN THE MIRROR OF *MADĪḤ*

Arabic literature can boast of no more enduring element than *madīḥ* (panegyrics), which antedates Islam and survives, in some form, until this day. And one cannot find a more visible example of the socio-political role of literature in medieval Arabic-Islamic culture. *Madīḥ* fulfilled a twofold role as a ruler's commemorative portrayal and as an occasion for him to practice patronage. In addition, *madīḥ* commanded the lion's share in the works of most professional poets of that era. All of this combined makes *madīḥ* and its paragon genre, the *qaṣīda*, an ideal nexus for examining the relationship between patrons and poets. The *madīḥ* of Ibn al-Rūmī offers a unique opportunity to look at this relationship from *within*, for Ibn al-Rūmī constructs in his praise poems an ethics of praise poetry. Ethics is understood here in the sense of the principles of conduct of the parties in a patronage relationship, on a human level as well as on a professional one. While Ibn al-Rūmī's ideas, of course, may not have been widely held, they represent the standpoint of an expert practitioner of *madīḥ*.

It is intriguing that poems serving to glorify those to whom they were addressed, whether caliphs, generals, viziers, or other dignitaries, gave the poet Ibn al-Rumī an occasion to eloquently argue his own professional standards and claims. The ethics of *madīḥ* not only occupied a fair share of his *qaṣā'id* and shorter pieces dedicated to ʿUbaydallāh b. ʿAbdallāh, but, of all themes, it also received the most dramatic treatment. If one believes Wayne Booth's contention that authors tend to deploy their most intense rhetoric on such topics that are likely to meet resistance from the audience,[1] then fervent rhetoric allows one to identify controversial issues in the author's mind. Can it then be inferred that Ibn al-Rūmī was waging a battle against an audience with low esteem for the panegyric profession?

There are indeed certain external arguments supporting such a position. The famous essayist al-Jāḥiẓ himself placed the orator above the poet, deploring the latter's decline of power in his own lifetime.[2] Second, in early Abbasid days, praises alone were no longer enough for a poet to earn his keep; most poets had to entertain their patrons as familiars (*julasā'*) or boon companions (*nudamā'*) in their circles, observing the rules of elegant conduct (*ẓarf*), or even to provide them with diversions on their travels – in addition to composing poetry. Third, the class of government scribes (*kuttāb*) developed *adab*, a canon of mainly literary, anthological knowledge, which required familiarity with the 'classical' Jāhilī and early Islamic poetry as well as the ability to compose light poetry as *divertissement*. This 'disinterestedness' of the scribes' verses as opposed to the panegyrists' material interest in theirs was a source of pride for the scribes.[3] However, not only the amateur, but even a true professional like ʿAlī b. al-Jahm would claim disinterestedness in poetry in order to boost his trustworthiness and loyalty.[4] In sum, although praise had a firm place in the Abbasid court ceremonial, its status as a profession seems to have been unresolved, at the least.

Still, there are arguments for a different position. The historian al-Ṭabarī, for instance, accompanied his reporting of salient events with quotations of poetry composed on the occasion side by side with transcripts of official decrees or epistles. His account of the second half of the third/ninth century contains *madīḥ* by al-Buḥturī, Marwān b. Abī l-Janūb, his son Muḥammad and others.[5] If praise poets had lacked any official status and power of attestation, quoting them would have been a futile exercise. Moreover, with the caliphal court in Samarra, the competing Persian and Aramean families of viziers and the gubernatorial residence in Baghdad, literary patrons abounded, as is evident in the amount and diversity of addressees in the *dīwāns* of al-Buḥturī or Ibn al-Rūmī.[6] From this point of view, praise poetry did not so much lose ground as evolve from a caliphal prerogative to a showy accoutrement many members of the elite could afford and of which they considered themselves to be qualified critics. The poets' success, therefore, depended on their readiness to cope with multiple, poetically 'interfering' patrons.

And finally, could the case for the ethics of praise have been simply a stylistic choice of Ibn al-Rūmī? He was, after all, known for his creativity, especially his ability to infuse a human dimension into many of his themes.

These observations do not amount to an overall assessment of the state of praise poetry at the time of Ibn al-Rūmī, and they cannot replace a larger survey of individual cases of patronage. However, they certainly signal that Ibn al-Rūmī's ethics of praise may be read as internal evidence of his reaction to the contemporary circumstances of panegyrics. The intense effort and ingenuity the poet deployed in this topic suggest he may have found himself in a situation where old concepts of the panegyric genre had to accommodate new socio-economic requirements, and he chose to carve for himself an identity with the poetic resources he commanded.

The scenes between poet and patron

The *madīḥ* Ibn al-Rūmī dedicated to ʿUbaydallāh b. ʿAbdallāh contains passages in which he and his patron meet as dramatis personae. Within their encounters, the poet performs several speech acts that presuppose specific conditions pertaining to the patronage. Ibn al-Rūmī uses the encounters to tie the historical addressee ʿUbaydallāh to an ideal depiction of him and a firm relationship with his poet. Such passages hence reflect Ibn al-Rūmī's ethics of patronage, but they simultaneously criticize the current state of the historical relationship. A word about the structure of the encounters is in order.

The encounters occur at the end of the long praise *qaṣā'id* and *tahānī* after the poet's persona has met and spoken with a series of other personae. The scenes also constitute independent poems of *ʿitāb* and general epigrams on praise poetry. The last two groups of poems define rights or claims more directly and succinctly than is found in the more ceremonial *qaṣā'id* and *tahānī*.

As for the content of the encounters, the poet and the patron face each other as dramatized historical personae. They may adopt more than one role, e.g. the patron, the role of benefactor and model patron, and the poet as protégé and panegyrist. In the course of the passage, the poet brings to the fore his own merit, i.e. his impeccable service in the form of loyalty, friendship, and masterful compositions. His service culminates in the dedication, a speech act by which he hands over to his addressee the entire *qaṣīda* with all its verbal power, glory, and durability. In return, he demands his due of protection, generosity, and reward. He makes it integral to his strategy to match his rights, which he spells out in much detail, with those of the patron. In presenting his claims, he performs further direct acts of speech, invokes blessings, provides advice, and enumerates the mutual obligations of poet and patron. He plays an ambivalent role in requesting reward or recognition; for, immediately thereafter, he wonders about the outcome – whether his supplications will be fulfilled – and how non-fulfillment will affect the meaning of the poem as a whole. This makes it possible to extract the ethics of patronage between Ibn al-Rūmī and ʿUbaydallāh b. ʿAbdallāh.

In terms of dramaturgy, the encounters between poet and patron take on the same form as other encounters between the poet and fictional or historical personae in Ibn al-Rūmī's *qaṣā'id*; they include dialogues, monologues, and combinations of both (hereafter referred to as patronage scenes).[7] In a dialogue scene that follows an argumentative scheme of action, the poet's persona typically finds himself in a state of tension with the patron's recent actions. At times, an intercalated monologue complements the dialogue, giving the poet two different voices. With these elements of dramaturgy, Ibn al-Rūmī constructs a highly complex set of relationships.[8]

The historical relationship

The dialogue on patronage distinguishes itself from other dialogues in that it identifies its historical participants – author and recipient – and addresses actual declarations, demands, or pleas to this recipient.[9] But it also comments on the everyday patronage relationship by posing and defending an ideal image of it, and exposing the contrast between the ideal and the reality. Hence, the dialogues propagate ethical norms. Ibn al-Rūmī's frequent self-representation as poor and needy has been recognized by Said Boustany as a role in which the poet liked, strangely enough, to portray himself.[10] More precisely, his self-portrayal in these scenes alternates between the two roles of protégé and panegyrist, while ʿUbaydallāh adopts the roles of benefactor and model patron.[11] Both portrayals serve the construction of a patronage ideal, which is staged in scenes and formulated in a simple direct style. The code of behavior invoked by the poet must have conformed with ʿUbaydallāh's views; the ideal captured an image of him he condoned. The direct, crystal-clear style of argumentation must have responded to the patron's tastes,[12] as Ibn al-Rūmī carefully heeded his patron's poetic suggestions in other respects.[13] Given Ibn al-Rūmī's long relationship with ʿUbaydallāh – twenty-three years at minimum – and the wealth of poetry it inspired, it is implausible to assume that the poet was ethically at odds with this patron. Considering ʿUbaydallāh's authority as governor of the Abbasid metropolis, the poet's professional ethics could not but fall within generally held conceptions of patronage, and it therefore is a partial reflection of educated Baghdadian society in the third/ninth century.

The function of the poem

The scenes investigated do not yield a single monolithic model of patronage. Rather, they dramatize two concurrent relationships in varying states of satisfaction or disappointment: a broad relationship between the protégé and his benefactor and a more specific relationship between the panegyrist and his model. Both require mutual commitments, but they differ in the order of performance (who initiates and who reciprocates), as well as in the way the poem is presented. In the first relationship, the poem serves as a token of the poet's moral commitment, without a literary function of its own. In the second relationship, however, poetic speech has an intrinsic value, variously articulated. It can be vaunted or offered modestly. It may be true, partially true, or it may be a lie. It anticipates, acts, or reacts. Finally, it may be personified and endowed with a will of its own. The two relationships are not given equal weight. The first dominates most poems, while the second is occasionally woven into the first, particularly in poems of admonition. The second relationship provides the poet with a counter-position from which he can argue his case with more credit. The next two chapters discuss the mutual duties either relationship entailed as well as poems that dramatize these at various levels of satisfaction.

15

MUTUAL DUTIES AND RIGHTS OF BENEFACTOR AND PROTÉGÉ

In this relationship, both parties have a long-term commitment to each other. The patron affords the poet protection from penury and slander.[1] His generosity comes easily, and he does not remind people of it. His motivation for generosity is not gain; rather, this virtue is inherent in his noble nature. Generosity counts toward his honor and grants him credit toward his afterlife.[2] Generosity is also bound to other virtues, such as respect of the recipient's honor, reliability in the fulfillment of promises, and anticipation of wishes and hopes.[3] Finally, generosity is a power exerted over free people, and therefore it needs to be exercised justly toward both the needy and those who merit it by virtue of their excellent work.[4] The tax expert and poetic critic Qudāma b. Jaʿfar (d. 327/938) agreed with connecting justice to generosity. In his discussion of *madīḥ*, he offers a broad subdivision of praiseworthy virtues for males, which include *ʿaql* (reason), *shajāʿa* (courage), *ʿadl* (justice), and *ʿiffa* (decency). *Samāḥa* (generosity) falls under the heading of *ʿadl* and is substituted by it later in the text. Most virtues listed under *ʿadl* (justice) are associated with giving: *samāḥa* (generosity) as opposed to *taghābun* (cheating in buying and selling), *inẓilām* (taking upon oneself injustice and difficulty), *al-tabarruʿ bi-l-nāʾil* (charity), *ijābat al-sāʾil* (granting the plea of a supplicant), and *qirā l-aḍyāf* (hospitality).[5] These good deeds (*niʿam*) place a burden on the protégé.[6] He acknowledges his gratitude and obligation to his benefactor by reciprocating with gratitude, loyalty, and trust.[7] This, in turn, entitle the poet to renewed generosity, protection, and so forth.[8] If the patron does not perform as expected, the poet chastises him for delaying or breaking his promise, for administering his generosity unjustly, or neglecting his devoted protégé and sincere friend. The poet's commitments are fulfilled by poetry, but that is poetry's only function here, and its specific character as a literary form is not of great importance. The poem is a token of the poet's ongoing allegiance, just as the patron's gifts and benefits were tokens of his ongoing protection and benevolence. To this end, the poem performs a service and thereby repays the patron's gifts and relieves the poet of some of his liability.[9] The relationship emerges as a mutual exchange. However, it is not one of discrete transactions of giving and thanking; rather, it represents an ongoing process. This exchange in essence mirrors the relationships in commercial trade. In his study on the Būyids in the century following Ibn al-Rūmī's lifetime (334–440/945–1050), Roy Mottahedeh compares the loyalty arising from benefit to a long-term trade relationship:

> The commercial analogy fitted the continuing barter of *niʿmah* and gratitude. . . . But it was an analogy appropriate to a commerce of long-standing patterns of trade, in which, for all the calculus of benefit, neither seller nor customer wanted a final 'reckoning' of accounts between them, since such a reckoning would sever the bonds of loyalty that the exchange had created.[10]

Here, the trade analogy includes the exchange of tangible goods as well as the intangible quality of trust and protection of each other's interests. From the Koran, we know the purchase as an image for a (usually disadvantageous) exchange of immaterial things. Unbelievers sell guidance for error; the hereafter for the here; belief for unbelief; etc.[11] When Ibn al-Rūmī uses the trade image, he emphasizes the calculated benefit, be it material or immaterial. In praise, such calculation is the opposite of honorable disinterested giving:

مَتى يُطاوِلْ شريفًا يَعْلُهُ شَرَفًا   وإنْ يُوازِنْهُ يَسْفُلْ عنهُ رُجْحانا

إذا اشْتَرَى الحمدَ أَفْناءُ الملوكِ رأى   بينَ التِجارةِ والإفْضالِ فُرقانا

When vying with an honorable man, he is higher than him in honor,
and when weighing himself with him, he is lower, outweighing him [in importance].

When all and sundry kings [just] buy praise,
he sees a distinction between trade and giving favors.[12]
(S1312': 3–4 to an anonymous patron)[13]

The payment of money for praise stands in negative contrast to the noble disinterested favor that earns praise by its very self. Where Ibn al-Rūmī does use the trade analogue in the second relationship, it represents moral worthiness, for example when renown or praise result from selfless personal endeavor.[14] But more important are the mutual personal commitments upon which all giving and receiving rest – so much so, that the poet justifies his claim with his sincere devotion, not with hopes or claims of reward.

أَحَقُّ برِفْدِك مِن آمليـ   ـه مَن لمْ يُؤمِّلْهُ فِى الآملينَ

ومَن كان وُدُّكَ لا للجَدا   ولكنْ لنَفْسِك حَقًّا يَقينا

وإنِّى لَمَنْ أَخْلصَتْ نَفْسُهُ   لك الوُدَّ قِدمًا مع المُخلِصينَ

ولكنَّنِى اضْطَرَّنى حادِثٌ   إليْك فكُنْ لِى عليه مُعينا

More worthy of your present than those who hope for it,
is someone who does not hope for it, among those who hope.

He, [whose] affection for you – not for your generosity
but for yourself – is certain truth.

For, among the sincerely devoted, I am one
whose soul has devoted sincere affection to you from of old.

But an event forced me to you;
be then my helper against it!

(E1448' to an anonymous patron)[15]

The following examples show how, in Ibn al-Rūmī's eyes, gifts and praise poetry act as material tokens of mutual commitments, and how commitment is the necessary basis for all exchanges.

Examples of scenes: A1160, F1243, and A1510

Several dialogues between poet and patron in the roles of protégé and benefactor dramatize the relationship in various degrees of fulfillment. The first two (A1160, F1243) depict the situation intact; in the third (A1510), it has failed. Each scene is dominated by certain acts of speech. In the following discussion, I rely on John Searle's concept of the speech act. Searle divides the speech act into its propositional content and certain constitutive conditions on whose fulfillment the act's validity depends. These are the preparatory condition, the sincerity condition, and the essential condition.

First example

The poem of admonition A1160 consists of a long dialogue scene between poet and patron in which the poet acknowledges the esteem received, recalls a need, complains about delay, and finally protests his devotion, all in direct acts of speech. A detailed examination of the speech acts shows that the conditions that constitute them, in Searle's terms, are identical with the intact relationship described above. The poet begins with the speech act of thanking, acknowledging the patron's (unspoken) esteem of him:

وإنّي وصِدْقُ المَرْءِ مِن خَيرِ قَولِهِ   لَراضٍ بحِظْيِ مِن ضَميرِكَ قانِعُ

I am pleased and satisfied with your favoring me in your mind –
and a man's sincerity is among his best speech.[16]

(A1160: 2)

For a valid act of thanking, Searle's preparatory condition requires that 'the act benefits the speaker and the speaker believes that it benefits him', while the sincerity condition stipulates that 'the speaker feels grateful or appreciative of the act'. Both conditions are literally covered in the formulation of the second verse. The poet is 'pleased and satisfied' and says so, as a man whose 'sincerity is among his best [kinds of] speech'. In the following verse, the poet requests a public show of esteem:

ولكنَّ بِى مِن بَعْدِ ذلك حاجَةً   إلى أنْ يَرى راءٍ ويسْمَعَ سامِعُ
لِيُكبَتَ أعْدائِى ويرغَمَ حُسَّدِى   ويَقمَعَهُمْ عَن شِرَّةِ البَغْىِ قامِعُ

But after that (sc. your unspoken esteem),
I have a need that a seer sees and a hearer hears [too].

So that my enemies be felled, those begrudging me, humiliated,
and that someone suppress the evil of their tyranny!

(A1160: 4–5)

As an indirect request, he expresses to the patron his wish not to be deprived:

فلا أَكُنِ المحرومَ منكَ نَصيبَهُ   بلا أُسْوَةٍ إنِّى لذلك جازِعُ

May I not be the one, without precedent,
to be deprived of his share in you[17] – I do fear that.

(A1160: 17)

According to Searle, a valid request must suffice the preparatory condition: 'The hearer is able to do the act. The speaker believes the hearer is able to do the act.' It must also suffice the sincerity condition: 'The speaker wants the hearer to do the act.'[18] In the poem, the preparatory condition follows immediately after the request: the patron is not known for putting off supplicants or bartering with praise poets.

مَتَى استَبْطَأَ العافونَ رِفدَكَ أمْ مَتَى   تقاضاك أَثمانَ المدائحِ بائعُ؟

When did supplicants ever find your presents slow?
When did a seller ever extort from you prices for praises?

(A1160: 18)

The poet's persona challenges the patron to acquiesce. The second condition, the poet's real desire for fulfillment, is explained at length. First, his enemies must be silenced by visible proof (5–7); but, more fundamentally, his need for the patron never ceases (9–11). He deplores the delay in the fulfillment, first through a question (8), then with an assertion, when he fearfully grasps that he might not see his wishes realized (16, 19–20).[19] But he calms himself by interpreting the delay as temporary (8, 21) and by dismissing the possibility of indefinite deprivation (17–18, both quoted above). The poet overcomes his innermost fears and repeats his requests and wishes in the hope that the patron will grant them (26–7), believing that the patron will eventually do so (6), although he concedes that doubt is justified in a situation like his:

فكُنْ عندَما أَمَّلْتُ منكَ فلَمْ تكُنْ   لِتُخْلِفَنِى مِنك البُروقُ اللَّوامِعُ

Be as I hoped you to be, so that your shining beams of lightning
have not been there to deceive me about you.[20]

(A1160: 26)

Up to this point, the poet has acknowledged the patron's presumed commitment to him and is requesting more substantial proof. Then he proceeds to demonstrate his own commitment to the patron. The speech act predominating in the poem is the assertion. The poet asserts his material dependence as perpetual and not one that can be resolved by a single act of bestowing gifts and expressing thanks. This bolsters his request (quoted above), but also guarantees his permanent loyalty:

أَأَنْ قلْتُ إنِّى ما انتَجَعْتُك مُجْدِبًا   أَبا أَحْمدٍ تُحمَى علىَّ المَراتِعُ
فلسْتُ غنِيًّا عَنْك ما ذرَّ شارِقٌ   ولوْ سالَ بالرِّزقِ التِّلاعُ الدَّوافِعُ
شَهَدْتُ متَى استَغْنَيْتُ عنك بأَنَّنِى   غَنِىٌّ عَنِ الماءِ الَّذِى أَنا جارِعُ

Is it [because of] my saying 'I did not seek pasture with you, finding
a barren soil', Abū Aḥmad, that places of pasture are denied to me?

I do not dispense with you as long as a rising [sun] shines,
even if the gushing mountain streams were flowing with sustenance.

If ever I find you dispensable, I am testifying
that I would dispense with the water I swallow.

(A1160: 8–10)

He also asserts his humility to ʿUbaydallāh:

مديحِى وإنْ نَزَّهتُهُ لكَ مِبذَلٌ   وخَدِّى وإنْ صعَّرتُهُ لكَ ضارِعُ

My praise is – even if I ensured its beauty –
a shabby daily garb for you;[21]
my cheek is humble to you, even if I proudly turn it [to you].

(A1160: 12)

The poet, then, presents his verse not as a proud achievement, but as a token of humility. This is reinforced by the image of the humble cheek, a Koranic allusion to proud behavior.[22] Further assertions, introduced by a rhetorical question, qualify this loyalty as exclusive:

أَتعلَمُنِى مِن مَدْحِ غيرِكَ صائِمًا   صِيامًا له قِدمًا على فِىَّ طابِعُ
وحلَّأْتُ نفسِى عَنْ شرائعَ جَمَّةٍ   لتَروِيَنِى ممّا لديْكَ الشَّرائعُ

Do you know that I am fasting[23] from the praise of others,
in a fast that has left from of old an imprint on my mouth?

I chased my soul from brimful watering places,
so that the watering-places of yours give me drink.

(A1160: 14–15)

The poem is the token of exclusive loyalty – since the poet extols no one else – phrased again in a religious metaphor (fasting). According to Searle, the requirements of a valid assertion are, first, that 'the speaker has evidence for the truth of the proposition' (preparatory condition) and, second, that 'the speaker believes the proposition' (sincerity condition). Both conditions are fulfilled here, because the poet speaks about his own acts, and, since the assertions describe an ongoing situation, they also act as commitments. The poet strengthens his assertions by analogical images. In his need for him, he compares the patron with water (10). He places the primacy of loyalty before material ambitions as analogous to a sword's sharpness before its gleam, or a religious duty before additional good deeds:

قَبولُك مَيْلِى وانْقِطاعِى وخِدمتِى   قُصارِى ولكنْ للْقَضاءِ تَوابعُ
ومَقصودُ ما يُبغَى مِنَ السَّيفِ مَضرَبٌ   حُسامٌ إذا لاقَى الضَّريبةَ قاطِعُ
على أَنَّه مِن بعْدِ ذلك يُبْتَغَى   له رَونَقٌ يستأْنِقُ العَينَ رائعُ
كذلك مَحْضُ الوُدِّ مِنكَ فَريضتِى   ونافِلَتِى فيكَ الجَدا والمنافِعُ

Your accepting of my inclination, my exclusive devotion,
and my service is my utmost striving,
but there are additions to the fulfillment [of striving].

The object required in a sword, when it slays a victim,
is a sharp cutting edge.

Although after this one requires in it
a brilliant shine that delights the eye.

Similarly, pure love is my religious duty to you;
[striving for] gift and favors my supererogatory deed in you.[24]

(A1160: 22–5)

The poet's primary duty is the devotion to his patron; only secondarily does he regard his patron as a provider of sustenance. That hicrarchy already appeared in the opening line:

رَفَعتُ إلى وُدِّيك أَبْصارَ هِمَّتِى　　　لِتَرْفَعَ مِن قَدْرِى فهَلْ أَنْتَ رافِعُ؟

> I elevated the glances of my endeavor to my love for you,
> so that you elevate my rank – are you elevating it?
>
> (A1160: 1)

The acts of speech strengthen each other as a chain of mutual acts, each of which is a reaction to a previous act and a cause of a further one. The sequence of the speech acts reflects this concatenation.[25] Furthermore, the conditions for making the thanking, requesting, and asserting successful acts have been explicitly fulfilled, often in more than one way. The speech acts confirm the poet's sincere commitment to the relationship, and they acknowledge the patron's past commitment and future compliance, despite the expression of residual fears about the future. In these conditions, one can recognize the patronage relationship described above: on the poet's part, devotion, loyalty, and service; and on the patron's, inexhaustible munificence and protection. The poet's direct claims then assume the long-term mutual commitment as intact. Or, the give and take of praise and reward can be seen as a vehicle for inculcating these mutual moral obligations. Among all speech acts, the assertions of loyalty stand out through their repetitiveness and their solemn religious imagery. The poet emphasizes what he gives over what he requires. By giving the greatest weight and figurative corroboration to assertions of his own fulfillment, the poet tilts the patronage balance in his favor, placing the moral onus on the patron to reciprocate. The poem contains, then, not only the direct request for outstanding reward, but also an indirect moral pressure on the recipient to match his poet's commitment.

Second example

In the felicitation F1243, the poet welcomes the patron back from his pilgrimage, describing him as a Kaaba for supplicants (1–9). In the metastrophe, he exhorts him to live up to his reputation for generosity (10–15) and to bestow this generosity justly (10–24). All this occurs in a dialogue with the patron. Intermittently, the poet steps aside and speaks to himself (16–17). Finally, he accuses the patron of injustice toward him, warning him about becoming a bad patron (25–33). He concludes by excusing his brash speech as a sincere and necessary reprimand (34–8). At first, he urges the patron to confirm the hearsay about his generosity and fulfill his promise and the poet's hope:

فأَعِذْنِي مِن أَنْ أَرَى بَيْن ظَنِّي ويَقينِي فيما رَجَوْتُ اخْتِلافا
أَوْ أَرَى المجدَ قاعِدًا لِي عَن كفْـ ـفِكَ وعْدًا مُثمِرًا إخلافا
وأَنِلْنِي يا مَن رَأَيْتُ سُؤالِيـ ـهِ سَواءً فِي نَيْلِهِ والعَفافَ

Concerning what I asked [from you], save me
from seeing a difference between my presumption and my certainty!

Or – by breaking an [already] fruit-bearing promise –
from seeing glory absent itself from your palm with me.[26]

And grant me gifts, O you with whom
my asking for gifts is the same as modesty.[27]

(F1243: 12–14)

As to the first request of confirmation (12), the sincerity condition has been fulfilled previously, when the poet expressed the belief that the patron's favors (*faḍl*) are signs of his excellence (*faḍluka*, 11). The poet now pleads with the patron to make his presumption (*ẓann*) a certainty (*yaqīn*) instead of destroying it. The second request (13), combines with the first the fulfillment of a promise, although the emphasis remains on the patron's preservation of his glory. The preparatory condition to fulfill both requests is met, because the patron customarily protects his honor by destroying material wealth (10), and his promise has borne fruit already (13). The third request names the gift directly (14). In all three, the patron's generosity is triply needed: for the patron's own honor, for the poet's belief in him, and for the offering of the gift. A longer series of requests (19–24) adds yet a fourth motive for generosity: as generosity governs free people, it must treat them with justice:

إنّما إمرَةَ الجَوادِ على الأَحْـ ـرارِ فاعدِلْ وأَعمِلِ الإنصافَ
لا تَدَعْ مَعشرًا سِمانًا يُكَظّو نَ سُمانَى وآخَرِينَ عِجافا
أَعقِبِ المُجْدِبينَ مِن أَهلِ خِصْبٍ قدْ رَعَوْا رَوضَكَ الرَتِعَ ائْتِنافا
وأَدِلْ مُعْطِشيك مِنْ أَهلِ رَيٍّ شرِبوا العُرفَ مِن يَدَيْكَ سُلافا

The rule of the generous governs the free,
thus be just and act equitably!

Do not let a group of fat people be stuffed with quails
and others stay meager![28]

Let the drought-stricken take the place of the prosperous
who have grazed in your plentiful garden for the second time.[29]

Let those with thirsty camels triumph over the satiated
who drank pure the good deeds from your palms.

(F1243: 19–22)

This series of requests urges ʿUbaydallāh to give to the hungry, the drought-stricken, and the thirsty before the people of plenty. The object of generosity should either be the needy alone (21–2) or all people (23–4). These requests are based on a strong and binding rationale: since generosity empowers the generous over other free people, it is a form of rule, subject to justice and equity (18–19). Thus the poet expects a generous man to be just (the sincerity condition). In the context of justice, a previous poem is cited as a case of the patron's tyranny and injustice: he did not give to the laboring exhausted poet, but to another lazy person. Finally, the poet reformulates the previous requests, by informing the patron of the consequences his inaction would entail, and warning him not to let matters come to that. The patron might drive him into the arms of other, inferior patrons:

صُنْ مَديحِي ومَطلَبِي عَنْ أُناسٍ　　　لمْ أَزَلْ عَنْ لِقائهِمْ صَدّافا

Protect my praise and my pursuit from people
from whose encounter I constantly distance myself.

(F1243: 29)

He invokes again ʿUbaydallāh's honor, but this time only for that patron's sake:

صافِ دونَ الأَموالِ عِرضَك واعْلَمْ　　　أَنَّه دونَ بَذلِها لَنْ يُصافَى

Love truly your honor, not your possessions,
and be aware that it (sc. honor) will not be truly loved
without their (sc. the possessions') being squandered.

(F1243: 33)

These requests ostensibly concern the patron's honor, the keeping of his promise, and his justice. Their fulfillment lies in his interest. To all these virtues generosity is bound. By asking, the poet gives the patron the opportunity to redeem and distinguish himself. For himself, the poet wants only to serve a perfect patron and to receive his gift. His material gain from generosity is outweighed by the patron's moral gain in three aspects – honor, reliability, and justice.

The requests alternate with warnings. The poet warns his patron not to force his protégé to give up on him. The poet does so not with harmful intent, but because he could not bear to see a deficiency in his patron:

لا يكُنْ حَسْرةً نَداكَ على النَّفْـ　　　ـسِ فأَقنَى الغِنى وأَرضَى الكَفافَ

May your generosity not be a grief on [my] soul
lest I keep to [my] self-sufficiency
and be satisfied with what I have [refraining from asking you].

(F1243: 15)

A warning requires the preparatory condition that 'the hearer has reason to believe an event will occur and it is not in the hearer's interest' while the sincerity condition demands that 'the speaker believes that the event is not in the hearer's best interest'.[30] The possibility of the threat is intimated in the verse itself. That the hearer fears it, is clearly stated in the monologue: the patron fears the anger of his supplicants and their dislike of 'the trough of his good deeds' (16–17). It is the duty of a loyal poet to warn his patron of the danger. The monologue also reveals the poet's belief, that his mere voicing of concern will suffice to prompt such a caring patron as ʿUbaydallāh to mend his ways. He repeats his warning more precisely (28), in a third instance in the negative form, confronting the patron with what he might become:

فلْيَعِظْكَ امرؤٌ غدا فِى يَدَيْهِ　　　حَسَبٌ مُبتلىً ومالٌ مُعافَى

May a man be your lesson in whose hands
a reputation is troubled and possessions are spared.

(F1243: 32)

The deficient patron is described and modelled exactly as the opposite of ʿUbaydallāh and yet portrayed with the same motifs. His Qibla of hope has been deserted (30); ʿUbaydallāh's Qibla is circled by supplicants (4). The bad patron's wealth is safe, his reputation, however, suffers (31). The impending moral is stated by the poet: ʿUbaydallāh's wealth has to suffer so his honor can be safeguarded (10). The poet has reason to fear that in his case the usually fair and good patronage of ʿUbaydallāh might take the opposite direction. By warning him, he means well and believes in a successful outcome, as is evident from the monologue.

Unlike the previous poem, here the focus of the patronage relationship is on the patron. Generosity is not so much owed to the poet; rather it is what the patron owes to himself in order to safeguard his honor and justice. The poet holds up a mirror to the patron so that he might erase any shameful attributes. The poet wishes his impression of the patron to be proven true for his own sake, both ideally and materially. The ultimate decision, however, lies with the patron. All the poet can do is be sincere and courageous, even at the risk of inculpating his patron:

لا وعيدًا أَقولُ ذاكَ ولكنْ　　　قلتُ حاءً من المَقالِ وقافا
إنَّ أَهلَ القَرِيضِ طَورًا يرقُّو　　　نَ وطَورًا تَراهمُ أَجْلافا
وإذا أُسخِطُوا رَأَوْا ذَمَّ سابو　　　رَ ولوْ كانَ يَنزِعُ الأَكتافَ
همْ إذا شِئتَ نَحْلُ شَهْدٍ وإن شِئـ　　　ـتَ أَفاعٍ رُقْشٌ تَمُجُّ الزُّعافَ
لا يكونَنَّ ما سمِعْناه مِن جو　　　دِكَ فى كُلِّ مَحْفِلٍ إرْجافا

I do not say this as a threat but I [simply] say
the *ḥā'* and *qāf* of speech (sc. حق 'truth').

Poets are delicate at times
and at others you deem them rude.

When angered, they would consider blaming Shāpūr,
even if he used to tear off [men's] shoulder blades.[31]

When you so desire, they are honey bees;
and when you want, speckled vipers spitting quick-killing poison.

May that which we hear about your generosity
in every meeting-place not be a spreading of false news!

(F1243: 34–8)

The poet qualifies his previous warning as the speech of a concerned truthful observer. In this poem, the roles of benefactor and protégé are articulated as those of the just ruler and his well-meaning adviser. Compared to the patron's attaining of perfection, the price of a gift to the poet is small. In the previous example, A1160, the poet solicited the patron's renewed commitment to the relationship by his own perfect fulfillment of his role. In the present example, he stands aside in order to achieve the patron's perfect fulfillment of his part. Although the patron has behaved unjustly, the poet feels confident enough to appeal to him and show him the danger of his error. Above his own material needs, he cherishes and upholds his image of ʿUbaydallāh as a perfect patron.

Third example

In the admonition A1510, the relationship of the protégé to the benefactor has been disturbed. The poet makes a request without fulfilling the conditions for this act of speech. The poem contains three scenes: a monologue with the poet's doubts about the patronage (1–9); a dialogue reprimanding the patron (10–19); and a second monologue declaring his departure from him (20–5). In the middle dialogue scene, the poet requests from the patron the fulfillment of his promises and protection:

أبا أحمدٍ طالَ هذا المِطا ... لُ وحَسْبُكَ بالدَّهرِ مِن غائلِ
فأنجِزْ عِداتِكَ أوْ أعْطِنِي ... أماناً مِنَ الحَدَثِ النّازِلِ

Abū Aḥmad, this delaying has dragged on!
Fate is already enough for you as a bringer of evil
(sc. no need for you add to it)!

Fulfill your promises then, or give me safety
from a deepening misfortune!

(A1510: 11–12)

However, the following verses indicate that the poet does not believe his own words: the patron's promise is decried as deceitful, sterile, and worthless (15–17). The preparatory condition of the speech act – 'The hearer is able to do the act' – has lapsed. In the second request, the poet does not ask for anything but the recognition that he has fulfilled his own part of the relationship properly: the composing of countless poems of praise.

تَذَكَّرْ فكَمْ لِىَ مِن مِدْحَةٍ　　　تركَّضْتُ فى ذَيلِها الذَّائلِ
وكائِنْ كَسَوْتكَ مِن حُلَّةٍ　　　مَشَيْتَ بها مِشيَةَ الرَّافِلِ

Remember! How many praises did I have [for you],
urging myself in [weaving] their trailing train!

How often did I dress you in a garment in which you strutted,
proudly dragging its skirts![32]

(A1510: 13–14)

Here, the poem stresses the poet's eagerly-accomplished service and the patron's benefit from it. The dialogue closes with a summary of the failed exchange of duties:

منحتُكَ مدحِى فلم تَجْزِهِ　　　ألا ضَلَّ سَعْيِى مِن عامِلِ
كأنّى فِى كُلّ ما قُلْتُهُ　　　زَرَعْتُ حَصًى فى صفًا صاملِ

I had dedicated to you my praise, and you did not requite it.
Oh, my effort as a worker is lost.

As if, in everything I said,
I sowed pebbles on smooth hard stones.[33]

(A1510: 18–19)

The poet begins the dialogue with an abortive attempt to perform a request and ends it by proclaiming the failure of the relationship. This request is a pointless act of speech.

The surrounding monologues provide direct insight into the poet's disillusionment. In the first monologue, the poet measures his striving and suffering for the patron against his good deeds that count towards his afterlife. Having placed his hope for so long on the former, he fears he would be a fool to forsake the latter. He faces a dilemma of allegiance between patron and God. A refrain (5, 10) divides the monologue into two sections, the first containing his vacillation between the here and the hereafter, and the second scathing self-accusations. The argument breaks off with the onset of the first dialogue. At this point the poet could still succeed in convincing himself of his patron's worthiness – as is evident in a parallel case.[34] His deprivation by his patron is formulated as questions and conditional clauses, and not yet stated explicitly. But with his half-hearted request in the dialogue, he positively asserts the barrenness of the patron's promise. In the second monologue, he confronts again his initial dilemma, and now *acts* upon it by abandoning the patron and finding his last refuge with God (20–1). He gives the patron a jab in the closing lines, in the absent third person, by describing how much grief an imperfect patron causes his panegyrist. The poet's fears and warnings to the patron about the danger of divergence between the ideal and the reality have now been realized, and he, as praising poet, has to suffer for it.[35] The following verses describe the patron in general terms:

إذا مَدَحَ المادِحُ النّاقصيـ — ـنَ ذَكَّرَهُم فَوْزَةَ الفاضِلِ
فأَهدَى لهمْ مِدْحَةً حَسْرَةً — لِتَقصيرِهِمْ عَنْ مَدَى الكامِلِ

When a panegyrist praises deficient [men],
he reminds them of the triumph of an excellent [man].[36]

And he dedicates praise to them,
grieving for their falling short of a perfect [man's] measure.
(A1510: 24–5)

The framing monologue places the middle dialogue within a larger movement, from doubt and guilt before God (first monologue), to aborted request and reprimand (dialogue), and then departure (second monologue). The poem focuses on the poet's inner struggle, his foolish clinging to the patron, his reluctant realization of the patron's unworthiness, and his own final self-salvaging breakaway. He holds on to the patron almost to the point of jeopardizing his own salvation. At this point, he does not pit ʿUbaydallāh against any other human; God alone is more deserving of the poet's loyalty. His hard struggle displays his self-respect and integrity. He deplores not so much the material loss – although he regrets it – but the damage to his word and to his integrity as a consequence of having claimed perfection for a deficient patron. With his blemished tongue and soiled honor (21), the poet still knows his own worth (22). In contrast to the exemplary poet, the patron's unreliability is amply delineated. His promise is a dry lightning (15), a barren female (16); he himself, a stone on which the poet sowed pebbles (19); and his generosity a careless lover who deserves to be abandoned:

فلوْ كُنتُ أَعشَقُ جَدوَى يَدَيْكَ — لَحانَ ذُهولى مَعَ الذّاهِلِ

If I felt passion for generosity of your palms,
it would be time for me to neglect the neglectful [beloved].
(A1510: 23)

The poem shows how the severing of the mutual relationship and the shattering of the ideal image of the patron and benefactor makes the poet's dialogue with him unsuccessful. Having lost his belief in the patron, the poet can no longer address him with requests. Against the patron's unfavorable depiction, the poet stands out as a man of integrity and one who fulfills his duty. Still, the poem does not mean the end of their relationship – there are several of this kind in the corpus. But it raises the threshold of sacrifices the patron needs to make in order to regain the poet's loyalty. In this way, the overt inability to request itself becomes an even more challenging request.

The two first examples (A1160 and F1243), mostly consisting of dialogues, are based on the intact relationship between benefactor and protégé. The poet utters requests as a continuation of a long-standing mutual commitment. In A1160, he needs protection from slander in return for his exclusive devotion and loyalty. In F1243, he leads the patron with requests and warnings back to his usual perfection after a short lapse in performance. In both cases, be it directly or indirectly, he appeals to their mutual duties, soliciting the patron's reciprocation by stressing his own performance, according to the principle of *do ut des*. In the third example, dominated by monologues, the relationship has floundered, and the poet has lost his faith. No longer can he request anything since he does not believe he will attain it. Taking the consequences, he cuts his losses and seeks refuge with God. His fears, along with his departure, are no longer of concern to the patron, so the poet withdraws from his confidence and speaks to himself.

All examples share two traits. First, they esteem ethical values over material benefits. Whatever material aspects come into play serve only to confirm ethical values. A gift affirms the justice and honor of its giver (which have been in doubt), and a poem expresses the humbleness and devotion of its author. The second trait concerns the figure of the poet. If one adds up the material and immaterial benefits, the patron always gains more, and the poet subtly maneuvers himself into the position of the benefactor: he bestows his loyalty, his friendship, and his advice; and when things go wrong, he grieves for the patron's lost perfection. He requests and receives in order to give the patron opportunities to shine. Most important, he portrays himself as faithful to his duties, as a man who prizes his sincerity and integrity above all. Even in abandoning the relationship (A1510), he argues his case as a matter of remaining true to himself – saving his soul from futile worldly endeavors in the nick of time.

16

ACTS AND WORDS BETWEEN PANEGYRIST AND MODEL

In the relationship described thus far we have seen the poet giving his patron immaterial presents, such as devotion, loyalty, gratitude, honor, and justice and accepting, in return, material tokens of generosity. But even if the poet's persona gives more then he receives, the exchange of generosity for gratitude is still centered on the patron's gift and leaves the poet in a reactive position. The type of exchange does not allow him to advertise his specific merits as a poet, nor the specific beauties and powers of his poem. The poem is fixed in the transaction as a token of the poet's moral response to the patron. The situation is different in the second relationship, that between the poet's persona as a panegyrist and the patron as his model. Here the poet portrays his specific role with more authority and gives his poem its full weight as a piece of literature and a depiction of the reality of patronage. This second relationship presupposes a co-operation of poet and patron of which the poem is the result. There is variety in the order of the contributions, i.e. whether acts precede words or the reverse, and in their commensurability, i.e. whether acts and words truly fit each other. Ibn al-Rūmī will be found to insist on the truthfulness of his poetic speech.

What is the truth of a praise poem? As the following discussion demonstrates, the 'truth' the poet's persona so often invokes is the truth of personal conviction and that of historical fact, i.e. his patron's actions.[1] These levels of truth are to be distinguished, on the one hand, from the philosophical truth, which deals with the truth value of poetry in general and the soundness of its syllogisms, and, on the other, from the aesthetic truth, which is concerned with such matters as fantastic etiology and hyperbole, including their effects and permissibility. As to aesthetic truth, critics like ʿAbd al-Qāhir al-Jurjānī (d. 471/1078) and Ḥāzim al-Qarṭājannī (d. 864/1285) distinguished different degrees of lie and truth, ranging from the truthful, to the potential (or fictive), impossible, and absurd. Both critics privileged, at least overtly, the first category – labelled variously 'rational' (*ʿaqlī ṣaḥīḥ*) or 'empirical' (*ḥāsil*) – which al-Jurjānī exemplifies with a line by Ibn al-Rūmī on glory as something to be earned individually. Though critics were generally reserved about the extreme hyperbole, or *ghuluww*, they found ways to accept the regular hyperbole (*mubālagha*) and other fantastic imagery. This, however, concerned only poetry's way of representation.

Al-Jurjānī did not condone inappropriate praise or unjustified satire. Al-Qarṭājannī evaluated the permissibility of the (partial) lie according to the poetic genres. Whereas truth was to be mostly respected in paraenetic poetry, it could be bent to the purposes of panegyric and satire.[2] Ibn al-Rūmī's persona *claimed* sincerity precisely on the levels of personal and historical truth, imposing on himself stricter standards than those of poetic criticism. (This, of course, did not apply to the historical Ibn al-Rūmī). His persona required an ideal relationship with his patron, a man deserving his praise *and* his faith. Such a relationship made it impossible or, at least, extremely difficult, for the poet to praise a patron who showed an inadequacy and lost his poet's faith. Nor could the poet extol a virtue at a moderate level. Only its perfect measure deserved praise and the poet ultimately depended on a model patron in order to be able to praise at all.

Acts and words, their order and congruity

The exact manifestation of the panegyric relationship varies in every poem according to the sequence of words and acts and their degree of congruity. Different configurations compel either the poet or the patron to take a position of commitment. The following cases excerpted from the poems exemplify five different sequences.

When the praiseworthy acts appear first, the poet has to match them with poetry. Since the acts are excellent – otherwise he would not deign to praise them – he has nothing to add beyond rendering them into verse. Still, there are differing degrees of fidelity in his poetic rendering.

The praise matches the acts

When the poet's persona formulates the acts in matching verses, he refrains from additions or embellishments. He emphasizes his 'mere' arranging of the scattered pearls provided by the patron.[3] As he asserts in the praise of ʿAlī b. Yaḥyā b. al-Munajjim, 'An enemy cannot but say the same about you as a friend'.[4] Praise becomes a mere attestation. The poet is free to praise to his full ability, without risking insincerity.[5]

The praise cannot live up to the acts

If the acts are so excellent that they fall outside poetic speech, they may either stretch the boundaries of speech and enrich it with motifs so as to include the acts, or the acts may leave the speech behind altogether. In the former case, poetry gains vicariously through the patron, because he extends its realm. In the latter case, the poet still tries to approach the acts with his words, but he can only declare his inability to do them justice. This is insufficient truth, not a lie, since the poet cannot match the facts despite his sincere endeavor. The very incommensurability of the praise proves the matchlessness of the acts –

a sophisticated hyperbole.[6] The poet excuses himself all the same for not doing the patron justice and is convinced of the latter's understanding.[7]

The acts themselves compose praise through causal hyperbole

Through causal hyperbole and personification, the praise can be directly connected with the patron or his acts.[8] Poetry is owed to the patron as a possession; it can be tamed by him like a wild animal; or it can offer allegiance to him like a human being.[9]

The acts claim ancient praise and re-attribute it to the patron

Ancient praise may be taken from its original addressee and re-attributed to ʿUbaydallāh, since he outdid the former addressee and deserves to appropriate the praise from him.[10] Here, the truth of the acts in relation to the words becomes a right of ownership.[11]

This and the previous variant represent the highest degree of fidelity between act and word. The poetry is immediately connected to the patron's acts, bypassing the poet. Ibn al-Rūmī can afford to efface himself modestly, because he is unmistakably present in his work. Within the literary context, his authorship is not in question.[12]

Praise precedes the acts

When the verses come first, the patron has to match them with acts. The poet has advanced him praises for future acts (mainly generosity) and trusts his patron to carry them out. The patron is expected to redeem the 'advance' praise by ratifying his noble portrayal with a noble gift or a recompense.[13] Thereby he grants truth to the praise and safeguards the sincerity his poet pledged for him. The risk of advancing praise is high, for the patron may default partially or totally in carrying out what the praise contains.[14] Then the 'advance' praise remains suspended without a factual counterpart, threatening to stand as a lie and consequently branding the poet a liar. In one case, the poet's tongue is silenced by the absence of a performance of praiseworthy acts. He compares his tongue to a dull, dented sword and advises the patron to repair it.[15] In another case, unredeemed advance praise already 'reeks of admonition'.[16] In most cases, the poet's persona speaks only of lies and satire in terms of his fears and warnings. He is wont to blame another poet whose praises have not been redeemed for engaging in satire.[17]

Sincerity is one of the poet's two most cherished qualities; trust in his patron is the other.[18] For without trust, he cannot pledge his sincerity for the patron. Both are necessary conditions for praises that precede acts. As shown above, Ibn al-Rūmī treats sincerity as co-operation: when the poet anticipates acts that the addressee has to redeem, the poet's sincerity passes out of his sole control and is shared with the addressee. But can a hearer be made responsible for the truth of what is said about him? Searle's rules of speech acts, which have proved illuminating in the analysis so far, cannot accommodate this concept. Searle's sincerity condition concerns only the speaker; an ulterior reaction on the part of the hearer cannot be included in it and would count as a separate act (of speech). Richard Ohmann includes the reaction of the participants to a speech act in its success or failure, a position that draws sharp criticism from Stanley Fish.[19] According to Searle (whom Fish follows), the rules of a speech act only determine whether the speaker has correctly performed it, not whether the hearer has reacted in the desired way. If Ibn al-Rūmī does things with words inconceivable in speech act theory, what effect does he aim for and what are its implications?

When the sincerity of speech about the hearer can be influenced by him, he takes responsibility for it. By executing an announced praised act he confirms the praise. In failing to do so, he actively transforms it to satire. Hence, the recipient makes and unmakes his own praise, by sharing in its sincerity, and the praising poet can put him on the spot.

Shared sincerity also poses a hazard for the poet. When the advanced praise is not substantiated, he suffers shame as a liar in the public eye, which sees only his authorship. Before the patron, however, the poet remains innocent and deplores his compromised word. He may accept all that for the sake of his loyalty, or he may punish the patron indirectly by continuing to utter words of praise that, given the lack of corresponding acts, are indirect words of satire.

The poet's persona can also become a prisoner of his own sincerity. Though he doubts ʿUbaydallāh, he still holds on to him, for he knows the difficulty of finding other worthy patrons:[20]

وَلَيسَ لأَنَّنِى سُدَّتْ سَبيلِى   ولا عَجَزَ اصْطِرافِى واضْطِرابِى
ولكنّى وما بِى مَدْحُ نَفْسِى   أَرَى عابَ التَّكذُّبِ شَرَّ عابِ
وإنْ جاوَزْتُ مَدْحَكَ لمْ يَزَلْ بِى   تَكَذُّبِىَ المَدائِحَ واجْتلابِى
مَتَى أَجِدُ المَدائِحَ لَيْتَ شِعرِى   تُؤاتِى فِى سِواكَ بلا كِذابِ؟

That (sc. my loyalty to you despite my doubts) is not
because my way is blocked, nor because I am unable
to earn a livelihood and seek my gain.

But I think – not praising myself –
that forged lies are the worst fault.[21]

Even if I relinquish [my] praising you, the forging of false praises
and demanding [favors from other patrons] does not stop for me.[22]

If I only knew when I will ever find [my] praises
fitting people other than you without lying?

(L191: 153–6)

The poet adheres to the letter of his praise in order to maintain his integrity.[23] If he were to desert his patron, he would belie his former praise, compromise his sincerity, and lose self-respect. The poet can risk surrendering his sincerity only if he trusts the patron to respect the indemnity of his own word and honor. For the patron can, by not redeeming praised acts, hurt the poet's veracity in the eye of the public. Therefore it is crucial for the poet to find and hold on to someone with whom he can share his sincerity.

Trust is the other precondition of any praise. When trust in the patron justifies the risk, it counts in the poet's favor, for he pledges his most valuable good, his professional integrity. Such trust honors and obliges the recipient. Again, the poem functions as a token of underlying commitments. The risk taken by the poet's trust also proves the poet's conviction of the patron's worthiness. Any praise spoken without that, for the mere extortion of gifts, is manipulation and abuse. Praise without trust can be construed as indirect satire:

مَديحُكَ مَن تُطالِبُهُ برِفدٍ　　هِجاءٌ مِنكَ فيه بلا كَلامِ
لأَنَّك لمْ تَثِقْ مِنه بمَجْدٍ　　فتَقْنَعَ باللِّقاءِ وبالسَّلامِ

Your praise of someone, asking him for gifts,
is satire by you of him without words.

For you have no faith in his glory,
and wanted to convince yourself [of it]
by face-to-face encounter and [proof of his] integrity.

(E1252')[24]

With trust being an unavoidable risk, the poet must choose his patron carefully. If he is so unwise as to praise an undeserving patron, he wastes his effort and makes the *mamdūḥ* aware of his faults, thereby forfeiting any right to reward:

ما تستحِقُّ ثوابَ مَن كابَرْتَهُ　　ورَمَيْتَهُ بالإفْكِ والعُدْوانِ
قومٌ تُذَكِّرُهُمْ فَضائِلَ غَيْرِهِمْ　　فيَرَوْنَ ما فيهمْ مِنَ النُّقْصانِ
فإذا مَدَحْتَهُمُ فَتَحْتَ عليْهِمُ　　بابًا مِنَ الحَسَراتِ والأَحْزانِ
ظَلَمَ امْرُؤٌ أَهدَى المَديحَ إليهِمُ　　ثُمَّ استَثابَ مَثُوبَةَ الإحْسانِ

You do not deserve the reward of someone
you [falsely] magnify and insult with lies and enmity –

People whom you remind of the virtues of others,
so that they see the deficiency in themselves.

For when you praise them,
you open for them a door to sorrow and sadness.

Unjust is a man who dedicates [injurious] praise to them,
and then asks for the reward of kindness.[25]

(E1307': 2–5)[26]

The demonstrated conditions of trust and shared sincerity place the poet in the position of the giver. He entrusts his word and his integrity to his patron. The loss of these values, which are specific to his poetic trade, would affect his honor and livelihood. They in turn place the patron under equal moral obligation to prove himself worthy. The relationship between panegyrist and model, with words preceding acts, poses a counterweight to the relationship between benefactor and protégé in which the poet is the recipient. Ibn al-Rūmī knew well the psychology of values of his time and gave the panegyrist a firm honorable place within them. The diagram (fig. 16) summarizes the relationships demonstrated so far.

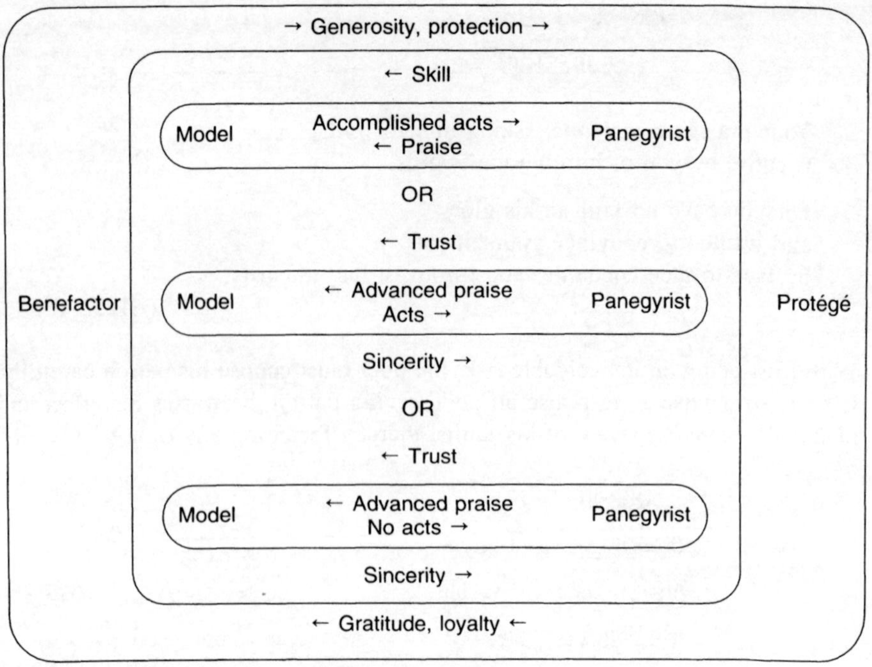

Figure 16 Diagram of the two relationships between poet and patron

Examples of scenes: A694, F1373', A464/F1373', and A1171/A212/L215

In praising acts after they have occurred, the poet does not need trust; nor does he put his sincerity at risk. Therefore, he faces the patron self-confidently in univocal dialogue scenes.

The acts precede the praise, and the praise matches them

In the admonition A694, dedicated either to ʿUbaydallāh or his brother Muḥammad, the poet reprimands the addressee for competing with him in poetry (1–7). He then lectures him on his actual princely tasks, such as care for the supplicant, the poor, the prisoner, fighting calamities, and waging war (8–11). From all these tasks, the poet distinguishes his own task of praising them:

عليكَ بأَفعالِ المُلوكِ وخَلِّنِى   وتَقْرِيظَ ما تَأْتِى مِنَ العُرفِ والنُّكرِ

Busy yourself with the acts of the kings and leave to me
the praising of your kindness [to your subjects]
and your cunning [against your enemies]!

(A694: 12)

Both tasks, acts and praise, are different but they are matched exactly to each other. The poet asserts this twice, once to the patron (12), and a second time when he quotes himself as addressing the audience (14):

فحَسْبُ المَساعِى كلِّها بكَ ساعِيًا   وحَسْبُكَ وَصْفِى ما تَرِيشُ وما تَبْرِى
أَقولُ وتُعطِى نائلاً بعدَ نائلٍ   فتَغْرِفُ مِن بَحْرٍ وأَقْلَعُ مِن صَخْرِ
إذا الشّاعِرُ الرّومِىُّ أَطرَى أَميرَهُ   فناهيكَ مِن مُطرًى وناهيكَ مِن مُطرِى

Your striving is enough for all the glorious pursuits, and
my describing of what you give and take is enough for you.[27]

I say [to the bystander], while you give present upon present,
so that you are scooping from a sea,
and I am wrenching away rocks:

'When the Byzantine poet praises his prince,
how excellent is the praised one and
how excellent the praising one!'[28]

(A694: 13–15)

The different tasks, in the metaphors of a sea for acts and of rock for poetry are perfectly commensurate in their excellence, and together they suffice for every audience (14). The repetition of 'is enough' (*ḥasbu*) and 'how excellent' (*nāhīka*) highlights the congruity of acts and poetry. The closing verse reiterates the perfect match between word and act by negating the contrary: the poet has added nothing and only strung the pearls (of acts) into a necklace (of a monorhyme *qaṣīda*):

وما لمديحي في ثَناك زِيادةٌ سِوَى أَنَّني نظّامُ لؤلؤِك النَّثْرِ

My praise, extolling you, contains no addition,
except that I am stringing your scattered pearls.

(A694: 16)

The praise cannot live up to the acts

At the end of a long felicitation, full of fantastic motifs, for the Mihrajān festival, the poet excuses himself for choosing an easy rhyme letter (*n*). He justifies his choice by noting the many diverse meanings he had to accommodate:

إنْ تكُنْ سَهلةَ القَوافِي فليستْ فِي المعانِي بِسَهلَةِ الوِجدانِ

If it (sc. the poem) has easy rhymes,
it does not have meanings easy to find.

(F1373': 261)

The felicitation in 272 verses, with the same number of rhyme words, ending in one letter, would have been indeed difficult in a rare rhyme letter, i.e. one not belonging to the frequent six *b, d, r, l, m, n*.[29] The poet excuses himself in the same way for the easy meter, the lyrical *khafīf*, which is less suitable to *madīḥ* than the majestic *ṭawīl*, *basīṭ*, *kāmil*, and *wāfir* meters.[30] Again, the poet justifies his choice of rhyme with the patron, who offers so many motifs, by insisting that only an easy meter can hold them all. He further explains that only a simple lengthy *tahni'a* can accommodate them. And indeed the felicitation is brimming with astounding causal hyperboles. The poet sacrifices fanciful prosody for excellent motifs; in other words, form for content:

وابْسُطِ العُذرَ فِي ارْتخاصِ القَوافِي واتِّباعِي سُهولةَ الأَوْزانِ
أنتَ أَلجأْتَنِي إلى ما تَراهُ بالّذِي فيكَ مِن فُنونِ المَعانِي
أيُّ وَزْنٍ وأيُّ حرفِ رويٍّ لهُما بالمديحِ فيك يَدانِ؟
ضاقَ عَن مأْثُراتِكَ الشِّعرُ إلّا فاعِلاتُنْ مُستَفْعِلُنْ فاعِلانِ

Excuse my taking cheap rhymes
and pursuing a simple meter.
You forced me to resort to what you see (sc. easy rhyme
and meter) by the [many] kinds of meanings you contain.
Which meter and which rhyme letter
are capable to convey your praise?
Poetry is too narrow for your causes of glorification,
except for *fāʿilātun mustafʿilun fāʿilāni* (sc. the *khafīf* meter).

(F1373': 263–6)

Then the poet goes so far as to deny poetry the ability to fully express the patron's praise:

لیسَ مدْحٌ یفِی بِمدْحِكَ إلّا   صَلَواتُ المَلیكِ فِی القُرآنِ

There is no praise that fulfills your [true] praise,
except the prayers to the King in the Koran.[31]

(F1373': 267)

Rhyme, prosody, no, the whole of praise poetry lags behind the excellence of its subject ʿUbaydallāh.

The acts themselves compose praise through causal hyperbole

The admonition A464 contains a dialogue scene in the form of a message in which Ibn al-Rūmī lectures ʿUbaydallāh on the production of praise. He criticizes the concept of buying poetry as merchandise and contrasts it with the inherent moral value of a generous act that moves the recipient to praise:

لیسَ الجَوادَ مُشْتَرِی القَصائدِ
بَلِ الجَوادُ مُشْتَرِی المحامدِ
مِن جائرٍ فِی مدحِهِ وقاصدِ

Generous is not he who
purchases *qaṣāʾid* [of praise].

Generous is he who
purchases praiseworthy acts

From him who deviates from his praise
and from him who intends it.

(A464: 3–5)

Verse 3 explicitly denies the commercial analogy as a material exchange. Generosity does not consist in buying *qaṣāʾid*. Verse 4 contrasts the buyer of *qaṣāʾid* with him 'who purchases praiseworthy acts' and recasts purchasing as a metaphor for earning through sacrifice. The repetition of buying in the literal and metaphorical senses underscores the fundamental difference between purchasing praise and deserving praise for personal effort and sacrifice. Verse 5 qualifies the praiseworthy act further: it must be devoid of ulterior motives, and it must include all people, not just those whose gratitude is guaranteed by virtue of their social or political dependence or personal indebtedness. This aspect is elaborated further:

بَلِ الجَوادُ باذِلُ المَرافِدِ
لشاكِرٍ نِعمَتَهُ وجاحِدِ
يُعطِي العَطايا لَيْسَ لِلْعَوائِدِ
لا كالمُفِيدِ طَلَبَ الفَوائِدِ

No, rather the generous one
is he who bestows gifts,

Upon him who gives thanks for his favor
and upon him who denies it,

He gives gifts not for [returning] favors,
Not like a benefactor pursuing benefits.

(A464: 6–9)

Only the unpremeditated act of generosity is worthy of praise. Poetry is clearly distinguished from merchandise and defined as a poet's immediate reaction to pure generosity. The poet's persona returns with a variation of the commercial analogy:

يُرِيغُ بالمَعروفِ حَمْدَ الحامِدِ
إراغَةَ البائعِ نَقْدَ النّاقِدِ

He seeks by doing good the praise of a praiser,
As a seller seeks an assayer's [positive] verdict

(A464: 10–11)

The verses reiterate an earlier line, elevating the trade image to a metaphorical level: 'Generous is he who purchases praiseworthy acts (4).' But this transaction is limited to the patron. He exerts effort to acquire praiseworthy acts for his own credit. The poetry stands outside the transaction. It enters the scene as an objective assayer of the patron's 'coin of good deeds' only after the transaction has been completed. Hence the poet is the critical examiner of the deeds' worth, and he passes his verdict on them in his praise. Praise depends on the true quality of the deed, its sincerity and disinterestedness.

The acts claim ancient praise and re-attribute it to ʿUbaydallāh

In the already quoted felicitation F1373', ancient poetry is made to refer to ʿUbaydallāh by causal hyperbole. First, poetry appears and is personified as a supplicant, receiving from the patron benefits in the form of motifs. Since he enriches poetry, it feels obligated to him, and it bequeaths him two-thirds of its total amount, or the share of an only son:

أَصبحَ الشِّعرُ شاكرًا لكَ دونَ النـ　　　ـناسِ نَعْماءَ مُنْعِمٍ مِحْسانِ
أَنْتَ تَرْعاهُ وَهْوَ يَرعَى بكَ المجْـ　　　ـدَ فيا بِئْسَ ما رَعَى الرّاعِيانِ
كلُّ مَدْحٍ قدْ قيلَ فِى النَّاسِ قِدمًا　　　لكَ فيه بحَقِّكَ الثُّلُثانِ
وبهذا قضَى لكَ الشِّعرُ شُكْرًا　　　لكَ يا خَيْرَ قَيِّمٍ ومُعانِى

Poetry gives you thanks, excluding [all] other people,
for the benefits (*naʿmāʾ*) of an excellent benefactor.

You herd it (sc. poetry) and it herds glory along with you.
How miserable, what the two shepherds herd [in comparison]![32]

Of all the praise said about people from of old,
you by right own two-thirds.[33]

Poetry thus passes judgment in your favor
out of gratitude to you, O you best manager and tender [of it]!
(F1373': 178–81)

The following verses enumerate the total amount of poetry from which these two-thirds are deducted. It includes all the praise for the pre-Islamic dynasties of Kinda (Āl Naṣr), Ghassān, and the early Islamic Umayyads (Āl Ḥarb, Banū Marwān). Their praises are bequeathed to ʿUbaydallāh and the real descendants disinherited (185). The re-attribution of all the ancient Arab praises to a Khurāsānian governor may have Iranian nationalist (*Shuʿūbī*) undertones, especially in a poem celebrating the Iranian *Mihrajān* festival. But the passing of judgments through poetry is not a far-fetched idea. Classical Arabic poetry is the literary canon from which medieval Arab linguists, genealogists, and other scholars take evidentiary verses (*shawāhid*) to support their arguments. In this way ancient poetry 'judges' many a scholarly case. A further causal hyperbole reverses time and history even more drastically. The ancient poets themselves appear and declare ʿUbaydallāh as the object of all their verses. They do so without ever having seen or met him. His excellence reaches them across time and outdoes the original addressees of their praises:

فيكَ قالتْ أَئِمَّةُ الشِّعرِ ما قا　　　لتْ بلا رُؤيَةٍ ولا لُقيانِ
كامْرِئِ القيسِ قَرمِهِمْ وزُهَيْرٍ　　　وزيادٍ أَخِى بنِى ذُبيانِ
وكأَوْسٍ فَصيحِهِمْ ولَبيدٍ　　　وعَبيدٍ أخِى بنِى دودانِ
كلُّهُمْ بالمَديحِ إيّاك يَعنِى　　　كانيًا عنْك كانَ أَوْ غيرَ كانِى
فكَأَنْ قَدْ شَهَدْتَ كُلَّ قديمٍ　　　وبِكَمْ قَدْ تَفاوَتَ الحَرَسانِ
كمْ قَريضٍ فِى مَدْحِ غَيْرِكَ أَضحَى　　　لك مَعناهُ واسْمُهُ لِفُلانِ

The *imāms* of poetry said about you what I have said, without
[having to convince themselves by] sight or encounter [of you],[34]

As their chief Imru'ulqays and Zuhayr [b. Abī Sulmā]
and Ziyād [b. Muʿāwiya], the brother of the Banū Dhubyān.[35]

As Aws [b. Ḥajar] the eloquent one among them,
and Labīd [Rabīʿa], and ʿAbīd [b. al-Abraṣ],
the brother of the Banū Dūdān.[36]

Each of them means you in [his] praise,
whether he was alluding to you or not.

It is as if you had been present before each ancient [poet];
how day and night do differ![37]

How much well-wrought praise of someone else becomes yours in meaning, while the name it bears is So-and-so.

(F1373': 186–91)

As the perfect model for the motifs of ancient poetry, ʿUbaydallāh gains ownership of it and deprives its nominal owners. The fidelity of word and act reaches its limit by breaking the laws of chronology, history, and ownership.

Praise preceding acts and not yet redeemed

In the admonition A1171, in the form of a monologue, the poet deplores the fact that his sincerity is compromised and that he is deprived of the possibility of giving voice to any further praise. He compares his tongue, now avoiding lies by silence, to a dented and damaged sword:

أيَرضَى الأَميرُ أَطالَ الإلهُ   بقاءَ الأميرِ عزيزًا مُطاعا
بأَنْ فلَّ حِرمانُهُ مِقْوَلِي   فأَحْذاه بَعْدَ المَضاءِ انْقِطاعا
وكانتْ قَوافِيَّ فِي مَدْحِهِ   مِئينَ فقدْ صِرنَ فيه رُباعا
وما كانَ إلّا حُسامًا أُضيعَ   ومهما أُضيعَ مِنَ الأَمرِ ضاعا
فَلَوْ شاءَ صَيْقَلُهُ ردَّهُ   جديدًا وولّاهُ كفًّا صَناعا
تُعيدُ شَباهُ إلى حالِهِ   وتُلْقِي على صَفَحَتَيْهِ شُعاعا
لِيَومٍ تَقَنَّعُ فيه الرِّجالُ   وتَحسِرُ فيه النِّساءُ القِناعَ

Is the prince satisfied – may God give him long life
as a powerful, obeyed [ruler]! –

That his depriving [me] dents my tongue
and renders it silent after it had been cutting.[38]

For my rhyme words in his praise were hundreds
and have been reduced to quatrains.

It is only a sword's edge that has been destroyed –
whatever is destroyed is lost.

And if its polisher wanted, he could make it new again
and entrust it to a skillful hand,[39]

Which would return the tip to its [former] state,
and throw a shine on its broad blades.

For a day on which men gird themselves [with their swords],
and women expose their faces.[40]

(A1171)

The poet's tongue, unable to enunciate more praises – until they are confirmed by palpable acts – is compared to a sharp sword that has been dented. Only the patron can repair the broken sword and thereby give the advance praise substance. His polishing hand may sharpen and shine it, that is, grant the poet favors that lead him to praise again. The poet's shame will be erased in public and his audience amazed by him again. Here, the dented sword is the poet's tongue, the repaired sword is the speaking tongue, and the skillful hand sharpening and shining it is the patron's generosity. In a related motif, the sword's primary purpose of cutting and secondary purpose of shining are analogous to the poet's primary devotion to his patron and his secondary quest for benefits.[41] The choice of the monologue shows that the poet can no longer face the patron, having lost trust in him. But, by indirect lament, the poet makes him aware of his responsibility.

The poem of admonition A212 also consists of a monologue. It concerns an earlier unrewarded praise poem, the acts of which have not yet come true. The poem has now reached the threshold of becoming a lie. That is also obvious to any hearer, since the praise contains 'no single rhyme' about a demonstration of generosity to the poet. Therefore the poem 'reeks' of admonition and will lapse before long into satire, unless the patron makes it come true:

أَيَسيرُ مدْحِى فِى الأَميرِ وكُلُّهُ   يا لَلرِّجالُ مؤرَّجٌ بعِتابِ؟
ما قلتُ قافِيَةً تُخَبِّرُ أَنَّهُ   فيما يُثيبُ أَثابَنِى بِثَوابِ

Does my praise of the prince circulate – O men, help me! –
and the whole of it is reeking with admonition?

I did not mention a single rhyme
stating that he considered me for one of his rewards.

(A212: 1–2)

The poet fears the shame of having pledged his word for something that will not materialize. For the public will perceive only *his* lie and not the patron's misleading of him. The poet protests this double disappointment by his patron, along with the wasted work and public dishonor, and he laments these ill rewards after having demonstrated his consistent good faith.

ظَنّى لَئِنْ أَنا دامَ لِى حِرمانُهُ لأُلَقَّبَنَّ بشاعِرٍ كَذّابِ
يا بؤسَ لِلشُّعَراءِ يَسْهَرُ لَيْلُهمْ ويُلَقَّبونَ بأَسْوَإِ الأَلقابِ

I think – if his depriving of me continues –
I am bound to be labelled a lying poet.[42]

Oh, affliction of the poets whose nights are spent sleepless
while they are given the worst labels (sc. liars)![43]

(A212: 3–4)

The praise is on the verge of turning into admonition and then to satire. The third verse contemplates the risk of shared sincerity: 'If *his* (sc. the patron's) depriving of me continues, *I* will be labelled a lying poet.' The poet's plea is for his own sincerity, not for a material benefit; yet the power to achieve sincerity lies with the patron alone since the poet trusted him. As in the previous example of admonition (A1171), the poem as a whole takes the form of a monologue, with the patron assumed absent. No direct plea to him is voiced, and it ends in a lamentation (4). But the poet's fears have not yet materialized; hence, they are formulated as a question and projected as a potential future state. Only the lack of reward is positively asserted. The poet speaks in monologue, for he lacks the trust to directly address the patron any longer. But in lamenting – albeit ostensibly to himself – how his patron disappointed and dishonored him, he is indirectly accusing him.

In both monologues, A1171 and A212, the poet has compromised his sincerity and lost his trust. The basis of their relationship is shaken; the poet no longer addresses the patron, and he is unable to compose further praises. But it is hoped that the indirect utterance of his fears and grievance will nudge the patron into taking responsibility and restoring his poet's faith in him. ʿUbaydallāh can be assumed to have realized this in time, since Ibn al-Rūmī hardly ever stooped to satirizing him.[44] He mostly kept satire confined to the context. According to him, praise not redeemed can be recognized as such by the audience and signifies (indirect) satire. In the strophe of one encomium, L215: 62–70, the poet's persona criticizes another poet for turning from praise to satire. It was, in fact, a rival poet, al-Buḥturī, who satirized ʿUbaydallāh anonymously after he had praised him earlier.[45] Ibn al-Rūmī contrasts his own honorable abstinence from satirizing (this patron) with al-Buḥturī's greed and fickleness, and in so doing, defends his patron:

بلْ لا أُريغُ النَّوالَ مِن لَحِزٍ — سِيّانِ مُمتاحُهُ ومغتصَبُهْ
ولا أَلومُ الهَجينَ إنْ سَبَقَتْ — خَيْلٌ عِتاقٌ وخانَهُ عَصَبُهْ
كالمُتْبِعِ المدْحَ بالهِجاءِ إذا — ما المرءُ لمْ يَفدِ عِرضَهُ سَلَبُهْ

I do not desire the presents of a stingy man; what he is asked for
and what is extorted from him [are] the same.

I do not blame the low-bred [horse]
if the thoroughbreds win and its [own] sinews betray it.

Like him who follows his encomium by satire,
if a man's spoils (sc. readily given riches)
have not redeemed his honor.[46]

(L215: 68–70)

The poet's persona condemns al-Buḥturī's inconsistency. To begin with, one should not expect excellence from a deficient patron; second, a stingy man's present is no token of true generosity; and third, satire is unnecessary since it can be construed through inference from the context:

حَسْبُ امرئٍ من هجاءِ شاعرِهِ — مدْحٌ لهُ فيه خابَ مُنقَلَبُهْ
فى المدحِ ذَمٌّ لكلِّ مُمْتَدَحٍ — حارِدَ عِندَ احْتِلابِهِ حَلَبُهْ

Enough satire by a poet for a patron lies in his praise
for him whose yield was disappointing.

For a reprimand lies in the praise of every one
whose milk dries up at the [moment of] milking.

(L215: 71–2)[47]

The poet compares a patron whom the poet entrusted with praise and who failed to substantiate the trust with a milch camel whose udder seems full yet yields little when milked. The poet's trust has been deceived, but he values his own integrity too much to further contradict himself (by satirizing whom he had praised). He lets the contradiction between his word and the surrounding situation speak for itself. That discrepancy – or contextual satire, as one might call it – is sufficient to embarrass the patron.

Recapitulation

The scene of patronage (in metastrophes and separate admonitions) is the crucial passage on which the meaning of the whole *qaṣīda* hinges. It comments on the state of the patronage by depicting it as fulfilled or unsatisfactory. Thereby, it constructs a context for the poem. As a consequence, the patronage scene presents the rest of the poem in a certain light, e.g. as a token of gratitude, a testimony, or a lie. The encomium offers here literally an interpretation of itself.

Within the scenes, Ibn al-Rūmī constructs the patron's persona in two well-defined relationships, as depicted in the diagram (fig. 16). In one relationship – benefactor-protégé – the patron's honor and justice and the poet's belief in him are tied to a material gift for the poet. In the other – panegyrist-model – the poet's words pre-empt the patron's future acts and place certain contingencies on him. Direct speech acts addressed to the patron constantly recall and solicit either relationship. In terms of distribution, the dialogue scene portrays the intact state of the relationship, whereas monologue occurs whenever the relationship is disturbed.

The poet and patron perform mutual duties, both giving and taking from each other. But the poet's role in giving is emphasized over his role in receiving gifts. His presents are of the immaterial kind and consist primarily of loyalty, gratitude, sincerity, and trust. Hence he portrays himself as a man of professional pride, self-respect, and integrity. As a praise poet, he claims moral values that, according to him, other poets like al-Buḥturī did not care for; and he took less leeway with the truth than Arabic critics allowed.

In the scenes of patronage, the poet's persona comments on the historical situation and places contingencies on each act of the addressee, including his inaction. Ibn al-Rūmī fits the historical patronage with an ideal mirror image, which enables him, in the guise of the poet's persona, to draw the addressee into an argument and commit him to acts he has not (yet) performed.

CONCLUSION

Dramaturgy as a rhetoric of ethics

Viewing Ibn al-Rūmī's *madīḥ* for ʿUbaydallāh b. ʿAbdallāh as a literary speech situation allows one to isolate the components of its dramaturgy, namely (a) the dramatis personae and their characterizations, especially the persona of the panegyrist, (b) the typology of the scenes, and (c) the articulation of an ethics of patronage.

Once defined, Ibn al-Rūmī's elements of dramaturgy can be identified in other poets as well. The two earlier contemporaries and caliphal praise poets, ʿAlī b. al-Jahm (d. 249/863) and Diʿbil al-Khuzāʿī (d. 244/859 or 246/860), used a similar yet less complex style. In terms of characterization, both poets also portrayed themselves in dialogues with fictive and historical personae.[1] Yet the form of their dialogue scene includes both dialogue partners equally as speakers, whereas in Ibn al-Rūmī's dialogue scene, the poet's persona usually paraphrases his interlocutor. The number of their participants at times exceeds Ibn al-Rūmī's customary two speakers. ʿAlī b. al-Jahm, in particular, also used dialogue as a gradual transition from the *nasīb* to the *madīḥ* and as a structure for entire poems.[2] All three poets, however, applied the dramatic style to ethical issues. Dramatic scenes abound in Ibn al-Rūmī's encomia containing demands (L191, L1042), whereas descriptive and mannerist episodes predominate in encomia without claims (L1611, L1250'). Diʿbil adopted the dramatic style in defense of his honesty as a poet and to exhort a patron to true generosity.[3] ʿAlī, on the other hand, used it in defense of himself as a non-professional poet, and as a loyal follower of the caliph al-Mutawakkil and his return to orthodoxy, i.e. his abolishing of the doctrine of the created Koran.[4] Hence, dramatic scenes seem to have been solicited for the sake of their persuasive powers. But not everywhere did ethical issues receive this treatment; al-Buḥturī, for example, used descriptive imagery in an exhortation for reward.[5]

As for the substance of Ibn al-Rūmī's dramatized ethics of patronage, it allows comparison with the ruler image in the wisdom and advice literature.[6] For instance, the epistle of his patron's grandfather, Ṭāhir b. al-Ḥusayn, the general of al-Maʾmūn and governor of Khurāsān, to his son ʿAbdallāh[7] stipulates duties that closely resemble the duties Ibn al-Rūmī prescribed for the patron towards the protégé. The epistle was distributed by al-Maʾmūn to all his governors and

Ibn Khaldūn considered it exemplary. In it, Ṭāhir requires from his son, as a ruler, protection and kindness for his subjects and respect for their rights and duties (305/140).[8] Comparing his role to that of a shepherd (309/150–1), he specifically enjoins his son to observe pacts and promises (306/144), not to turn away poor petitioners (307/147), to acknowledge the rights of the grateful and to reward them (306/146). His particular care should be with the needy, the victims of accidents, and those unaware of their rights or unable to claim them (309/153). His paramount duties are justice and generosity. Establishing justice among the subjects is the ruler's first task before God (308/149), and generosity his best investment (306/146).[9]

> You should know that property, once it is gathered and stored in treasuries, does not bear fruit, but if it is invested in the welfare of the subjects and used for giving them what is due to them and to prevent them from need, then it grows and thrives.... Therefore, let it be your way of gathering up treasures to spend money on building up Islam and the Muslims.

Avarice, in turn, constitutes a serious disobedience to God (307/148). Ṭāhir also offers recommendations for how the ruler should treat governors and nobles. Nobles deserve the ruler's good faith (305/143); those who have fallen into poverty particularly merit his generosity (309/153). The ruler should reserve the highest honor for a noble man who dares to point out the ruler's mistakes to him (310/155).[10]

> Consider those the most honorable of your protégés and intimates who, when they notice a fault (in you), are not deterred by their respect for you from informing you about it in secret or from calling your attention to the shortcoming that lies in that fault. People of that sort are your most sincere friends and helpers.

The duties of the ruler towards the noble in Ṭāhir's treatise clearly resemble Ibn al-Rūmī's claimed duties of the benefactor to his protégé. On the surface, the duties the poet sets forth appear fair and reasonable, and he does not lower himself by insisting upon them. But on closer inspection, his more demanding poems L191 or L1042 relate favors and reward specifically to *poetry.* Ibn al-Rūmī thus adapts the general ruler image into the narrower context of literary patronage, grafting onto patronage an accepted system of mutual duties. (The second relationship Ibn al-Rūmī postulated between the panegyrist and his model is operative only within his *madīḥ* and presupposes a direct correspondence of word and act.)

With these literary parallels for Ibn al-Rūmī's dramatic style and ethical substance, there remains the question of his motive. An answer can be attempted from two perspectives, artistic and historical. According to the first, Ibn al-Rūmī manifests a predilection, across the genres, for dramatizing personae and human relationships. From here, his self-portrait as a panegyrist and a matching portrayal of his patron seem a logical next step, and one that must have appealed to ʿUbaydallāh. From a historic viewpoint, given the inconclusive evidence for the state of patronage, Ibn al-Rūmī's system of ethics may provide a working hypothesis for an absence of firm norms and customs in patronage. However, a broader examination of several historical patronage relationships is needed to assess the degree to which literary patronage was an institution with rights and claims, and to gauge the weight and currency of such terms as a poet's right (*ḥaqq*) and a patron's justice (*ʿadl*). That Ibn al-Rūmī was motivated simultaneously by inspiration and necessity should not be ruled out.

But the discussion of Ibn al-Rūmī's dramaturgy draws even wider circles. He used dramaturgy also in other genres, for example in the personal and the official lament (*rithāʾ*). In his personal lament for the singer Bustān, the poet's persona enacts a respectful lover and deep admirer, speaking to the deceased singer and beloved companion in a long dialogue scene that brings out the central theme of loss and despair.[11] The poet's struggle over 165 verses – from his realization of Bustān's death to his categorical refusal to be consoled – takes the measure of his bereavement.

In an official lament of the people of Basra, massacred by the revolting African slaves (Zanj), Ibn al-Rūmī arouses in a daring way the guilt of all Muslims for failing to save their co-religionists.[12] He even dramatizes God and the prophet speaking in two soliloquies set on Judgment Day, each on blaming the Muslims for forsaking their Basran brothers and sisters. Thereupon the poet's persona turns to the Muslims and urges them to act so as to prevent a scene like the one depicted from being witnessed again. In both laments, the dramaturgy highlights the respective central theme, personal grief and the duty to rescue and avenge fellow Muslims. During the Spanish Reconquista, official lamentations combined with calls for revenge become common for Andalusian cities, such as Valencia, Seville, and Granada.

Further uses of the dramatic style appear in the genres of devotional and mystical poetry. In sum, the elements of dramaturgy gleaned from Ibn al-Rūmī's *madīḥ* can provide, with the necessary adaptations, an analytical tool for any poetry that dramatizes issues of secular or religious ethics.[13] It thereby fosters a better understanding of the fundamental role of poetry in Arabic-Islamic society.

APPENDICES

A. Themes of the *Qaṣā'id*
B. Speech acts in the *Qaṣā'id*
C. Witnesses in the episodes
D. Poetry dedicated to ʿUbaydallāh b. ʿAbdallāh
E. Concordance with Boustany

Appendix A

THEMES OF THE *QAṢĀ'ID*

Qaṣīda	*Strophe*	*Verses*	*Antistrophe*	*Verses*	*Metastrophe*	*Verses*	*Total*
L191	*al-shayb wa-l-shabāb* (melancholic)	70	Individual praise (ambivalence, power, protection)	22	Neglectedness, loyalty (to patron's soul), hyperbolic praise, *fakhr* (poet's truthfulness, rank, loyalty, departure), praise of poem	83	175
L215	*al-shayb wa-l-shabāb* (resigned)	72	Individual praise (protection), rulership, ancestors, individual praise (ideal *mamduḥ*, generosity), rulership (milit., adm. praise, stability)	76	Dedication, praise of poem, hyperbolic praise	5	154
L434	*al-shayb wa-l-shabāb* (resigned)	11	Ancestors, individual praise (generosity), rulership	22	Loyalty	2	35
L994	*nasīb* (morning of separation, *waṣf al-ḥabīb*)	19	Ancestors, individual praise (reliability, generosity, courtliness), rulership	75	Praise of poem, dedication, hyperbolic praise (name, acts of patron), invocation	16	110
L1042	*nasīb* (morning of separation)	13	Ancestors (patron described in only seven verses)	38	Neglectedness, *fakhr* (service, departure, shame for patron), admonition, fear of deception	17	68
L1306	*al-shayb wa-l-shabāb* (reconciled)	7	Rulership, individual praise (reliability)	8	Hyperbolic praise (patron is owed all *madīḥ*)	3	18
L1307	*al-shayb wa-l-shabāb* (vindictive)	11	Individual praise (generosity, ideal *mamdūḥ*, sincerity), rulership (felicitation)	31	Protection, loyalty, invocation, hyperbolic praise, dedication	5	47

Qaṣīda	*Strophe*	*Verses*	*Antistrophe*	*Verses*	*Metastrophe*	*Verses*	*Total*
L1611	*al-shayb wa-l-shabāb* (ending in *fakhr: khamriyya, ṭardiyya, raḥīl*)	101	Individual praise (incl. generosity), ancestors, rulership (protection, courtliness, legitimacy), invocation, patronage (easy as *mamdūḥ*, popularity, indulgence with poets, connoisseur of poetry)	171	Hope and need, neglectedness, trust in patron, financial needs, dedication, praise of poem, invocation (to ruler and patron)	31	303
L1250'	*al-shayb wa-l-shabāb* (ending in *fakhr: ṭardiyya, khamriyya, raḥīl)*	105	Rulership, individual praise (generosity, reliability, protection), apotheosis (Islamic)	66	Gratitude loyalty (love) invocation (for life and afterlife)	19	190

In L1611, the last section of the antistrophe, following the invocation, praises ʿUbaydallāh's patronage in preparation for the poet's claim to be raised in the metastrophe.

Appendix B

SPEECH ACTS IN THE *QAṢĀ'ID*

Function	*Section of the qaṣīda*	*Speech act*
Establishment of poetic authority	Strophe	No direct speech act
Praise	Antistrophe	Intention to praise (expressive performative)
Mutual obligations of patronage	Metastrophe	Dedication of the *qaṣīda* (declarative performative)

Figure 17 Functional correlation between the sections of the *qaṣīda* and the speech acts occurring within them

	Antistrophe		*Antistrophe/Metastrophe*		*Metastrophe*
Qaṣīda	(1) *Naming of patron*	(2) *Intention to praise*	(3) *Invocations/ advice*	(4) *Message*	(5) *Dedication*
L191	71	–	117/121–2 150	/96, 151	[129, 152–6, 172–5]
L215	73	(73–4), 105–6	/(152–3)	–	150–1
L434	13, 19	(18)	(32–3)/	–	(34–5)
L994	(20), 42	(29)	84–5/107, 110	–	102
L1042	(14), 41	–	/66–7	–	[58–60, 66–8]
L1306	8	8–9	14/	–	(16–18)
L1307	12	(23–34)	/(46)	–	47
L1611	104	104, 147–50	207, 269–70 /301–3	146/	297, 300
L1250'	106	–	/189–90	–	[176–83]

(The forward slash separates invocations occurring within the antistrophe from those within the metastrophe. Parentheses indicate indirect or figurative synonyms of the speech acts, e.g. the naming of the *mamdūḥ*'s ancestors instead of the *mamdūḥ* himself; brackets mark thematically unrelated substitutes. In L1611, the intention to praise is also declared to the *mamdūḥ*'s Ṣaffārid overlord.)

Figure 18 Synopsis of the occurrence of speech acts within the encomia

Appendix C

WITNESSES IN THE EPISODES

Type of Witness	*Evocation*	*Dialogue with: fictional persona*	*historical persona*	*Episode of: fakhr*	*madīḥ*	*Total*
'You'	1	–	–	9[1]	21[2]	31
'I'	–	–	6	14	8	28
'We'	1	–	7[3]	8[4]	3	19

Figure 19 The distribution of witnesses according to passages, counting every verse containing a witness as one instance

Strophe: one witness	*several witnesses*	*Antistrophe: one witness*	*several witnesses*
L191 30 Ev (*ḥabīb*) L215 4 Ev (time)	L994 *3* Ep 1 imp. Ep 2 Ep L1042 1 Ep (*ghāniyāt*) 8 Ep L1611 *19, 44–5, 49–50, 56, 82–3, 95* Ep 12, 16, 61, 72, 94, 101 Ep 28–9, 60, 62–3, 71–2, 75 Ep L1250' *68, 73, 103* Ep 80 Ep	L191 71 Ep (opening) 92 Ep (closure) L215 141 Ep (closure) 142–3 imp. Ep L434 15, 22, 26–7 Ep L1250' 113–15, 121, 179 Ep	L215 99, 101 imp. Ep 100 Ep 87, 90 Ep L994 45 imp. Ep *29–30, 42, 79* Ep 21 Dia (Banū Ṭāhir) L1041 *40* Ep 24, 26–27, 29–31 Ep 37 Dia (Banū Ṭāhir) L1307 23–5, 29–31 Ep 12 Ep L1611 *104, 109,*[5] *145–6, 171, 189, 203, 223, 254* Ep 127, 132, 247 Ep 147–50, 211 Ep

(In this corpus, no witnesses appear in the metastrophe. The passages are abbreviated 'Ev' for evocation, 'Ep' for episode, and 'Dia' for dialogue; the verse numbers for witnessing 'I' are marked *cursive*, for 'you', underlined, for 'we', left roman, and the implicit speaker is abbreviated 'imp.'.)

Figure 20 The combination of witnesses in passages of strophe and antistrophe

Appendix D

POETRY DEDICATED TO ʿUBAYDALLĀH B. ʿABDALLĀH

Sixty-four pieces in 2373 verses, distributed as follows:

No.	*Verses*	*Date*	*Dīwān eds Naṣṣār/Salīm*	*Rhyme*	*Meter*
9 long encomia (S–AS–MS) in 1100 verses					
L191	175		i: 255–64 /ii: 366–94	*-ābī*	*wāfir*
L215	154		i: 300–15 /ii: 488–511	*-buh*	*munsariḥ*
L434	35		ii: 573–5	*-akhā*	*ṭawīl*
L994	110	*c.* 253/867	iii: 1220–6	*-āCisū*	*ṭawīl*
L1042	68		iv: 1366–70	*-āCiṣī*	*ṭawīl*
L1306	18		iv: 1684–5	*-ī/ūqū*	*kāmil*
L1307	47	(incomplete)	iv: 1685–8	*-aq*	*mutaqārib*
L1611	303	276/890	v: 2091–109	*-amū*	*ṭawīl*
L1250'	190	261/875	vi: 2366–77	*-āmī*	*khafīf*
20 felicitations (AS-MS) in 883 verses					
F21	16		i: 76–7	*-āʾī*	*basīṭ*
F458	74	255–6/869–70	ii: 627–31	*-ī/ūdī*	*basīṭ*
F462	17	263/877	ii: 636–7	*-ad*	*majzūʾ al-kāmil*
F463	40		ii: 637–40	*-ādī*	*basīṭ*
F484	14		ii: 667–8	*-īdī*	*sarīʿ*
F538	12		ii: 704	*-īdū*	*mukhallaʿ al-basīṭ*
F690	15		iii: 926–7	*-Crā*	*khafīf*
F952	82		iii: 1170–4	*-āCisuh*	*ṭawīl*
F986	34		iii: 1207–9	*-aCsī*	*kāmil*
F1122	46	266/880 or 276/890	iv: 1465–7	*-ūʿī*	*kāmil*
F1124	7	266/880 or 276/890	iv: 1468–9	*-aʿā*	*ṭawīl*
F1174	83	266/880 or 276/890	iv: 1533–7	*-Cʿah*	*kāmil*
F1243	38		iv: 1620–2	*-āfā*	*khafīf*
F1365	26		v: 1816–18	*-ākā*	*basīṭ*
F1557	8	268/882	v: 2011	*-alī*	*basīṭ*
F1634	41		v: 2131–3	*-āCimā*	*kāmil*
F1320'	21	260/874	vi: 2445–6	*-ānī*	*wāfir*
F1342'	12		vi: 2462	*-ānī*	*khafīf*
F1373'	272		vi: 2492–508	*-ānī*	*khafīf*
F1495'	25		vi: 2609–11	*-īhī*	*khafīf*

No.	Verses	Date	Dīwān eds Naṣṣār/Salīm	Rhyme	Meter
10 short encomia (AS, MS) in 46 verses					
S30	5		i: 95	*-Cā*	*ṭawīl*
S532	14		ii: 697–8	*-aydī*	*majzūʾ al-ramal*
S543	8		ii: 715–16	*-adih*	*majzūʾ al-wāfir*
S561	2		ii: 729	*-ūdī*	*kāmil*
S810	1		iii: 1062	*-arā*	*ṭawīl*
S976	5		iii: 1199	*-āCisū*	*ṭawīl*
S1569	3		v: 2021	*-al*	*kāmil*
S1216'	6		vi: 2314–15	*-īmū*	*sarīʿ*
S1349'	2		vi: 2472	*-Cnūnī*	*basīṭ*
12 admonitions and requests ((AS-)MS) in 153 verses					
A212	4		i: 298	*-ābī*	*kāmil*
A464	15		ii: 640	*-āCidī*	*rajaz*
A674	4		ii: 816	*-ādhū*	*munsariḥ*
A694	16		iii: 932–3	*-Crī*	*ṭawīl*
A1160	28		iv: 1503–5	*-āCiʿū*	*ṭawīl*
A1171	7		iv: 1527	*-āʿā*	*mutaqārib*
A1204	15		iv: 1561–2	*-Cfī*	*khafīf*
A1241	4		iv:1619	*-a/ifū*	*ṭawīl*
A1368	4		v: 1819	*-aykā*	*ṭawīl*
A1510	25		v: 1947–8	*-āCilī*	*mutaqārib*
A1518	10		v: 1951–2	*-alī*	*munsariḥ*
A1369'	21		vi: 2489–90	*-ānahū*	*kāmil*
1 satire (MS)					
H1512	6		v: 1949	*-ālihī*	*sarīʿ*
4 epigrams and occasional poems in 27 verses					
[E492	1 by ʿUbaydallāh		ii: 671	*-adī*	*majzūʾ al-rajaz*]
E492	6		ii: 671	*-adī*	*majzūʾ al-rajaz*
[E1216	4 by ʿUbaydallāh		iv: 1578–9	*-awfā*	*wāfir*]
E1217	6		iv: 1579	*-awfā*	*wāfir*
E1398	7		v: 1845–6	*-ākā*	*khafīf*
E1552'	8		vi: 2645–6	*-iyyī*	*basīṭ*
9 answers to ʿUbaydallāh's *Risālat al-Shukr* in 158 verses					
37	14		i: 99–100	*-āʾī*	*ṭawīl*
201	14		i: 278–9	*-ābū*	*madīd*
287	10		i: 370	*-atī*	*basīṭ*
341	10		i: 407–8	*-āthū*	*wāfir*
365	19		ii: 491–2	*-ajū*	*kāmil*
409	36		ii: 550–2	*-Cḥī*	*hazaj*
438	19		ii: 577–8	*-akhū*	*rajaz*
559	26		ii: 727–8	*-ādī*	*ramal*
670	10		ii: 814	*-dhādh*	*sarīʿ*
Poems related to or mentioning ʿUbaydallāh					
206	34		i: 289–90	*-ūbū*	*basīṭ*
291	61		i: 374–7	*-ātī*	*ṭawīl*
693	66		iii: 928–32	*-ārī*	*kāmil*
1032	92		iii: 1251–7	*-āshī*	*munsariḥ*
1546	81		v: 1994–9	*-ālū*	*ṭawīl*
1234'	9	247–8/861–2	vi: 2340	*-amū*	*basīṭ*

POETRY DEDICATED TO ʿUBAYDALLĀH B. ʿABDALLĀH

No.	*Verses*	*Date*	*Dīwān eds Naṣṣār/Salīm*	*Rhyme*	*Meter*
Poems dedicated to the Banū Ṭāhir collectively					
Encomia					
65	2		i: 122	*-ā'ihā*	*mutaqārib*
620	11		ii: 792	*-Cdī*	*ṭawīl*
1306	see poetry dedicated to ʿUbaydallāh and chapter 5, note 52				
1561	3		v: 2013	*-ū/īlū*	*khafīf*
1242	2		vi: 2345	*-ujūmū*	*kāmil*
Admonitions					
577	6		ii: 746	*-id*	*ramal*
1599	8		v: 2052–3	*-īlī*	*ṭawīl*
1322'	12		vi: 2448–9	*-in*	*mutaqārib*
Satire					
106	7		i: 148–9	*-ibah*	*mutaqārib*
1066	3		iv: 1406	*-aḍī*	*kāmil*
1392	2		v: 1841	*-ākā*	*mukhallaʿ al-basīṭ*
1199	3		vi: 2278	*-āCimā*	*ṭawīl*

Appendix E

CONCORDANCE WITH BOUSTANY

Boustany's dated poems (1967, 147, note 5):

Naṣṣār	*Boustany*	*Rhyme*	*Meter*	*Verses*	*Date AH*	*Occasion*
F458	B32=Is^{1}29b	*-di*	*basīṭ*	74	255–6	Reconciliation with brother
F462	B153=Is^{1}83a	*-ad*	*majzū᾽ al-kāmil*	17	263	Fortieth birthday
F1122	Is^{2}31a	*-ʿi*	*kāmil*		266	Congratulation to *ʿĪd al-Aḍḥā*
F1557	Is^{2}231a	*-li*	*basīṭ*		268	Four festivals
L1250'	Es71a	*-mi*	*khafīf*	188	261	Pure *madīḥ*
F1320'	Es185b	*-ni*	*wāfir*	21	260	*ʿĪd al-Aḍḥā* and *Mihrajān*

Boustany's pure panegyrics (1967, 147, note 6):

Naṣṣār	*Boustany*	*Rhyme*	*Meter*	*Verses*
S30	S^{1}72	*-a*	*ṭawīl*	
L215	S^{1}488	*-buh*	*munsariḥ*	153
L434	S^{2}116	*-kha*	*ṭawīl*	
F463	B29=Is^{1}27b	*-di*	*basīṭ*	
F484	B157=Is^{1}85a	*-di*	*sarīʿ*	
S532	B28=Is^{1}27a	*-di*	*majzū᾽ al-ramal*	
F538	B53=Is^{1}46b	*-du*	*mukhallaʿ al-basīṭ*	
S543	B31=Is^{1}29a	*-dih*	*majzū᾽ al-wāfir*	
F690	B318=C101b	*-ra*	*khafīf*	
S810	B280=Is^{1}148a	*-ra*	*ṭawīl*	
F952	C135b	*-suh*	*ṭawīl*	
F1122	Is^{1}31a	*-ʿi*	*kāmil*	
L1307	Is^{2}127b	*-aq*	*mutaqārib*	
F1557	Is^{1}231a	*-li*	*basīṭ*	
L1611	Es47a	*-mu*	*ṭawīl*	322
L1250'	Es71a	*-mi*	*khafīf*	188
F1342'	Es187a	*-ni*	*khafīf*	
F1373'	Es176a	*-ni*	*khafīf*	272

Boustany's panegyrics with request (1967, 148, note 1):

Naṣṣār	*Boustany*	*Rhyme*	*Meter*	*Verses*
L191	$S^1$366	*-bi*	*wāfir*	175
A212	$S^1$485	*-bi*	*kāmil*	
A464	B27=$Is^1$26b	*-di*	*rajaz*	
A674	B215=$Is^1$94b	*-du* (sic)	*munsariḥ*	
L1042	$Is^2$244a	*-ṣi*	*ṭawīl*	
A1160	$Is^2$36b	*-ʿu*	*ṭawīl*	
A1171	$Is^2$37b	*-ʿa*	*mutaqārib*	
A1368	$Es^2$271b	*-ka*	*ṭawīl*	
S1569	C233a	*-al*	*kāmil*	
S1216'	Es123b	*-mu*	*sarīʿ*	
S1349'	Es229b	*-ni*	*basīṭ*	

NOTES

1 THE BACKGROUND: POETRY AND POETS IN EARLY ABBASID SOCIETY

1 Cf. *Dīwān*, iii: 932 note 5. ʿUbaydallāh was indeed an ambitious poet. All translations are the author's unless otherwise noted.

2 Or: 'Do not make me go beyond my limit [if you infringe on my territory, I could do the same]', although *AEL* does not give *ʿadā* in this causative meaning. Another possibility is to emend *bī* to *fī* 'do not run in my [length of] step', i.e. 'do not imitate my trade'. Cf. the poet's 'rank' *qadr* L191: 117 and 'right' *ḥaqq* L1042: 367 and E110.

3 *Najr* also means type. Both meanings, however, render the same sense that the sovereign has no equal to compete with; he is above all others.

4 The *qiṭʿa* also served other genres.

5 Sourdel 1960, Mez 1937, 132–46 give no indication of poetry in the official Abbasid court ceremonial. Mez mentions praise poetry, however, in a caliphal session with his familiars; ibid., 143. Cf. also Grabar 1977, 58–9 on the Umayyads; and Canard 1951, Sanders 1984, on the Fāṭimids.

6 Bencheikh 1975a, 1975b, 1975c, and 1977.

7 Bencheikh 1975a, 21.

8 Ibid., 24–7, Boustany 1967, 33–4.

9 Bencheikh 1977, 36.

10 *Ẓarf* adds itself to the social ideals of *muruwwa* 'virtue' and *adab* 'accomplishment', or 'cultivation'; Boustany 1967, 47 and Ghazi 1959, 63–5.

11 Boustany 1967, 52 and 55.

12 Ibid., 37–8.

13 This *Kitāb al-Shukr*, or *Risālat al-Shukr*, is not preserved; Boustany 1967, 168.

14 In respect to the *ʿarabiyya*, the poets fell into two classes, established by grammarians and poetic critics: the ancients (*mutaqaddimūn*), who furnished the rules for the classical *ʿarabiyya*, and the moderns (*muḥdathūn*), who had to abide by them. The break-off point lay approximately at the end of the Umayyad period.

15 Cf. Lyons 1999, 126–7 for blame of ignorant audiences.

16 Heinrichs 1987–8, 360.

17 Heinrichs 1974, 27–8 sees the focus of artistic endeavor (*Kunstwille*) in the poetic idiom rather than reality, or 'the ignition from within', as justifying the application of the term. Sperl 1989, 158–64 adds as a further ingredient a tension between the classical model and its ulterior variations. His concept of mannerism resides in this tension between reality and representation, i.e. the discord between signifier and signified.

18 *Dīwān* i: 75–6 translated also by Boustany 1967, 142 note 7 and Bencheikh 1977, 50. See also the preceding poem to the same addressee. For a more subtle criticism, see note 35.
19 Bencheikh 1975b, 313.
20 Bencheikh (1975b, 275, 282, 291, 300, 311) mentions panegyrics by M. b. ʿAbdalmalik al-Zayyāt (176–233/792–847), minister of al-Muʿtaṣim; Ibrahīm b. al-ʿAbbās al-Ṣūlī (176–243/783-857), secretary under al-Mutawakkil; Ibrāhīm b. al-Mudabbir (d. 279/893), governor of Basra and later minister of al-Muʿtamid; the polymath ʿAlī b. Yaḥyā al-Munajjim (d. 275/888); and the army secretary Khālid b. Yazīd (d. 262/876 or 269/883). Bencheikh 1975c, 143–4 [30–1] also mentions the female poets Faḍl (d. 257/871 or 260/874) and Sakan (d. bef. 230/845) who composed *madīḥ*, which is preserved. See also Ibn al-Muʿtazz, *Ṭabaqāt*, 425 for al-Khansāʾ, the slave-girl of Hishām al-Makfūf, who praised caliphs.
21 Bencheikh 1975b, 311.
22 Ibn Rashīq *ʿUmda*, ii: 109–10, translated also in Bencheikh 1975b, 267–8. For the quote, see Kushājim *Dīwān*, no. 93, verses 32–3.
23 Bencheikh 1975c, 128 [15] and 131–2 [18–19].
24 Ibid., 134 [21].
25 But cf. songs on ceremonial themes, such as congratulation of a sovereign on the birth or circumcision of a male heir, investiture to an office, military victory, and praise of caliphate and vizierate; see Sawa 1998, 128–9, 132, and 134.
26 L1600 (*Dīwān*, v: 2055–70).
27 L585 (*Dīwān*, ii: 751–7).
28 D. Sourdel 1959–60, i: 328. For patronage of the translation movement, see Gutas 1998, 121–36.
29 Diʿbil's unconcealed Shiism represents an exception.
30 Bencheikh (1975a, 32) mentions for example Ibn al-Zayyāt, Ibrāhīm b. al-ʿAbbās al-Ṣūlī, and the brothers Wahb. For an analysis of their poetry, see Bencheikh 1975b.
31 Bencheikh 1975b, 313.
32 Ibn al-Zayyāt is praised for his poetry by Abū Tammām (*Dīwān*, i: 252–4, no. 18: 39–42) and al-Buḥturī (*Dīwān*, i: 636–8, no. 259: 31–41).
33 Cf. Lyons 1999, 143–5.
34 See chapter 2.
35 See F952: 43–56.
36 Bencheikh 1975a, 30.
37 e.g. Ṣafwān al-Anṣārī and later ʿAlī b. al-Jahm; see Rubinacci 1990, 193–5.
38 Bencheikh 1975a, 20–1.
39 Boustany 1967, 311.
40 Bencheikh 1975a, 29.
41 Cf. Walzer and Gibb 1960, 326b, Ayalon 1991, 261a, Gutas 1990, 356, and al-Qāḍī 1978, 88. For an example, see Pellat 1976. On the early history of this genre, see Richter 1932.
42 Bencheikh 1975a, 30 and Meisami 1987, 5–9.
43 Cf. Lyons 1999, 142–2 and Ouyang 1997, 67–70.
44 Bencheikh 1977, 38.
45 *GAS* ii: 455–7.
46 *GAS* ii: 528–9. For his use of *badīʿ*, see Heinrichs 1994.
47 See note 17.
48 *GAS* ii: 551–8.
49 Abū ʿUbāda al-Walīd b. ʿUbayd al-Buḥturī, panegyrist to all caliphs from al-Mutawakkil to al-Muʿtaḍid; *GAS* ii, 560–4.
50 *GAS* ii: 529–32.

51 Abū l-Ḥasan ʿAlī b. al-Jahm b. Badr, preferred panegyrist of al-Mutawakkil; *GAS* ii: 580–1.
52 Bencheikh 1975a, 162–3, esp. p. 163, note 61 on Diʿbil and ʿAlī b. al-Jahm. For the latter, see also chapter 2.
53 For the rise of ceremonial poetry, see Bencheikh 1975a, 14–15 and 35–8; for that of lay poetry, see Bencheikh 1975b, 265, introductory footnote.
54 Bencheikh 1975a, 114.
55 For length, see Bencheikh 1975a, 109 and Boustany 1967, 320–1; for rhyme letters, ibid., 322.
56 e.g. E1398.
57 See note 31.
58 Cf. Lyons 1999, 141–6.

2 THE FORM: THE ABBASID PRAISE *QAṢĪDA*

1 Jacobi 1982, 2 and 18.
2 Heinrichs 1973, 37–43.
3 Ibid., 44–6 and notes 116–19.
4 For beginnings, see van Gelder 1982, 29–32; for transitions, see ibid., 32–7.
5 Hamori, 1984 and 1991.
6 Cf. Montgomery 1997, 6 and 38–40.
7 For the *qaṣīda* as a multilingial genre of world literature, see Sperl and Shackle 1996; for the Arabic *qaṣīda* in al-Andalus, see Gruendler 2000b.
8 On molecularity according to Kowalski and von Grunebaum, see Heinrichs 1969, 20–7; on stereotype and lack of emotion according to von Grunebaum and others, see Sells 1987, 320–1. For a thorough overview of modern research on the unity and coherence of the *qaṣīda*, see van Gelder 1982, 14–22.
9 Bloch 1948, 123–31. He explains the term as ‘*al-maqālatu l-maqṣūdatu (sic) bihā li-fulānin* "that composition (*Gesätze*) which is addressed [to someone], dispatched [to someone]".’ Cf. also Jacobi 1971, 1–3.
10 Bloch 1948, 109–16. Cf. also Jacobi 1971, 27, 71, and 101, Wagner 1987–8, i: 88.
11 Jacobi 1996.
12 Jacobi 1971, which is based on Ahlwardt 1870.
13 Jacobi 1971, 100–5.
14 Ibid., 49–53, 61–5, and 86–91.
15 Cf. e.g. J. Stetkevych 1994 and Sells 1993, 1994a, and 1994b.
16 Jacobi 1982, 14–19.
17 Ibid., 19–21.
18 Scheindlin 1974, 60–80 and 93–109. Al-Muʿtamid's elegiac poetry belongs to the ceremonial genres.
19 Meisami 1985 and 1987, 24–8.
20 In poems by Abū Nuwās (Hamori 1974, 101–6) and in poems by Abū Nuwās, Abū Tammām, and Ibn al-Rūmī (Hamori 1977).
21 Badawi 1978.
22 Sperl 1989, 19–27. For a more comprehensive list of themes, see Sperl 1977, 25–31 and chart, ibid., 22.
23 For the vocative, see Scheindlin 1974, 88, 162, 171 and Hamori 1981, 200–1, and idem 1992, 19 (also including other syntactic breaks, such as the interrogative and the imperative). For parallel syntax, see Scheindlin (1974, 87, 157, 163. For perfect verbs, see Hamori 1981, 197, 201–2 and idem 1992, 7 and 19. For switches from third to second person and the appearance of the poet in the first, see ibid., 19; for another function of this switch, see van Gelder 1983, discussed in chapter 3.

24 For *ḥikam*, see Hamori 1981, 203 and 1992, 20; for *ḥikam* ending poems, see ibid., 1. For aphorisms, rhetorical questions, and apostrophes, see Scheindlin 1974, 113; for invocations and optatives ending whole poems, see Hamori 1992, 1. For balanced hemistiches, see Scheindlin 1974, 129, 132, 138. For slowing patterns, see Scheindlin 1974, 125, 127–9, 131; for the function of *taqsīm* 'tripartite report' as a slowing pattern, see Hamori 1992, 25; however his first example (ibid., 25) exhibits four equal parts similar to Scheindlin's balanced hemistiches.

25 For *mujmal–mufaṣṣal*, see Hamori 1980, 203–4, 1984, 43, and 1992, 46–50. For narrative, see Hamori 1991, 15–18 and 1992, 6.

26 For word repetition, see Hamori 1991, 19–20; for verse repetition in the Koran, see Hamori 1984, 40–1. For explanation (*bayān*), see Hamori 1991, 18–19.

27 For pre-Islamic and Umayyad poetry, see Bauer 1992, i: 250–62, 1993a, and 1993b and Montgomery 1995 and 1997; for Abbasid Poetry, see Bencheikh 1975a, 136–46.

28 *Concetto* in the narrower sense as 'the creative idea generated by the shaping of the motive', the third meaning of Latin *conceptus*; see Reinert 1990.

29 See chapter 1, note 17.

30 e.g. Bauer 1992, i: 215.

31 For collective functions, see Montgomery 1986, 2–6, Jacobi 1971, 196; for tribal *mufākhara* and messages, see ibid., 74–84; tribal virtues also apply to the personal *mufākhara*. For an application of C. Lévi-Strauss's technique of myth analysis, see Abu Deeb 1975 and 1976; for an application of the lack – mediation – lack-liquidation scheme from V. Propp's analysis of Russian folk tales, see Haydar 1977 and 1978. For various applications of the separation – liminality – aggregation model of van Gennep and V. Turner, see S. Stetkevych 1983, 98–107, 1993 and 1994a. J. Stetkevych (1993, 1–49) proposes a triple rationale: a rhetorical explanation following Ibn Qutayba, a musical analogy with the Romantic sonata form, and an archetypal rationale, which subsumes the two preceding ones. The concept of the *qaṣīda* underlying his argument, however, differs from that of Bauer (1992) and Montgomery (1997), who deny the existence of a 'regular *qaṣīda*'; cf. note 33. J. Stetkevych (1993, 2) conversely maintains that 'the sections of the *qaṣīdah* are obvious. In its sequential thematic structure there are three main thematic nuclei', i.e. first, the *nasīb*, second, the *raḥīl*, and third, the *fakhr*, *madīḥ*, or *hijā'*.

32 Montgomery 1986.

33 Montgomery 1997, 6 and 76–7. He cautions that 'no two pre-Islamic poems are identical' (ibid., p. 258), concurring with Bauer's statement, 'Da es in der arabischen Dichtung kaum etwas gibt, was es nicht gibt, muß man bei jeder Klassifikation immer eine Rubrik "Sonstiges" bereithalten' (1992, i: 74).

34 For legitimation, see S. Stetkevych 1979. For ruler iconology, see Sperl 1989; for a subdivision of caliphal rulership into the three components of virtue, divine sanction, and mythical power, see Sperl 1977, 20–5.

35 Bencheikh 1975a, 46–50.

36 Meisami 1987, 18–20.

37 But cf. Meisami's studies on Bashshār and Heinrichs's comments on Ibn al-Rūmī, mentioned above in notes 3 and 19.

38 Bencheikh 1975a, 136.

39 Ibid., 137.

40 For buildings as dominant topics, see ʿAlī b. al-Jahm's descriptions of al-Wāthiq's Hārūnī palace (*Dīwān*, no. 9), al-Buḥturī's descriptions of al-Mutawakkil's Jaʿfarī palace (*Dīwān*, ii: 1039–42, no. 411) and lake (ibid., iv: 2414–21, no. 915) and of Chosroe's Īwān (ibid., ii: 1152–62, no. 470); cf. also Sperl 1989, 38–47, 196–9 and Meisami 1998. For dialogue as a structural device, see the poem of ʿAlī b. al-Jahm, discussed pp. 21–4. For new themes, see Abū Tammām's praise of his own poetry and

benevolent patronage, al-Buḥturī's praise of a patron's literary skill (Bencheikh 1975a, 145 and 1975b, 277), and Ibn al-Rūmī's praise of intercession (chapter 1, notes 25 and 26) and his complaint of homesickness (Boustany 1967, 277).

41 Cf. the parallel concepts in linguistic anthropology of text and context as processes of entextualization and contextualization and the performer's role in orienting these processes; see Bauman and Briggs 1990, 66–78.

42 Al-Buḥturī *Dīwān*, iii: 1770–4, no. 679. On him, see chapter 1, note 49.

43 Verses 17–23 and 34, which al-Buḥturī added when rededicating the poem to al-Ḥusayn b. Muḥammad al-Ṭaʾī, are omitted.

44 *Tajnīs* of *mawāzin* 'measures' and *muwāzan* 'balanced'.

45 Cf. Lyons 1978, 59 [2. 349 and 2. 385].

46 *Kunya* of ʿUbaydallāh.

47 Verse 34 is omitted, cf. note 43.

48 i.e. one of the rhymes, not he who recites them.

49 The antithesis alludes to the sequence of praise and generous deeds. Verses 32 and 39 suggest that praise comes first, but verse 33 assumes the deeds as preceding.

50 In the second attribution of this poem, the vagueness in *madīḥ* and dedication is eliminated by the insertion of additional verses. Both additions begin with a statement by the poet about his attitude to the patron: 'I have sworn' (*ḥalaftu*), 'I have hoped' (*rajawtu*), and the second patron's name. The first insertion (17–23) acknowledges a benefit received; the second (34) asserts that the poet had asked the patron previously for a favor.

51 Holt, Lambton, and Lewis 1970, 126. The doctrine of the created Koran itself was shared by Jahmite Ḥanafites and Muʿtazilites, cf. M. Hinds 1993, van Ess 1967–8, and Melchert 1996. Verses 14 and 15 of the *qaṣīda*, however, describe specifically Muʿtazilī tenets, namely, their negation of divine attributes (*taʿṭīl*), their rejection of all anthropomorphic representations, as well as the principle of the necessary justice of God; cf. Gimaret 1993.

52 On him, see chapter 1, note 51.

53 *Dīwān*, 71–6, no. 23, and, for the chronology, page 71, note 1.

54 Verse 23 of the *qaṣīda* alludes to Muslim soldiers captured by the Byzantines. Al-Wāthiq gave the order only to redeem those prisoners who acknowledged that the Koran had been created and denied the sight of God on Judgment Day. From the standpoint of the orthodox *ahl al-sunna*, this was similar to forcing them to become unbelievers; cf. *Dīwān*, 73, note 4.

55 Verses 1–5, 6–9, 10–15, 16–17, and 18–45.

56 *Majūsī* (pl. *majūs*) originally designated an Iranian priestly caste and is used in Arabic primarily for Zoroastrians.

57 A play on the caliph's name al-Mutawakkil bi-llāh 'He who relies on God'.

58 The anecdote, transmitted by the judge's son, is classified under poetic mistakes. 'It [verses 36–7] shocked Abū ʿAbdallāh b. Abī Duʾād and he looked down. [ʿAlī] b. al-Jahm said to him, "Abū ʿAbdallāh, you have not heard a praise like this!" [The judge] answered, "Neither me nor anyone else, nor did I fathom anybody daring such a thing",' al-Marzubānī *Muwashshaḥ*, 384. Ibn Abī Duʾād suffered a paralytic stroke in 233/848 giving the poem an *ante quem*.

59 Note the word play on *khalīfa* 'caliph, successor'.

60 Cf. also the Banū Hāshim as 'noble ones' (*ghurr*, 37).

61 Cf. verses 5, 6, and 9 in Abū Bakr al-Ẓāhirī al-Iṣfahānī *K. al-Zahra* and verses 38–9 in ʿAbdalqāhir al-Jurjānī *al-Ṭarāʾif al-adabiyya*; see al-Buḥturī *Dīwān*, iii: 1771 and 1774.

62 See chapter 4, notes 23 and 24.

3 THE APPROACH: *MADĪḤ* AND PRAGMATICS

1 For intertextuality in poetry, see chapter 2, note 27, in poetic criticism under the heading of literary borrowing (*sariqa*), see Heinrichs 1987–8.

2 This is the position of Austin, Searle, and Grice who see the meaning of language in its use, and pragmatics as equal to semantics. Rudolf Carnap and Jerrold J. Katz distinguish between the domain of an abstracted, context-free, and literal meaning (semantics and syntax) and the domain of a contextualized meaning of the language user (pragmatics); see Searle, Kiefer, and Bierwisch 1980, viii–xi.

3 Briggs and Bauman 1992, 160, 165 voice a similar concern in linguistic anthropology for an integration of the minutiae of linguistic structure and broader social, cultural, and political units.

4 For anticipation–resolution, see Scheindlin 1974, 84 and 174–6; for indirection, see Meisami 1987, 18–20.

5 Heinrichs 1973, 40, note 100, points to a correlation between *gharaḍ* in the narrow sense of a poet's 'intention', and the fact that poetry was usually addressed to a person and pursued a tangible motive. For some medieval authors, however, *gharaḍ* stood for the broader meaning of the poet's '"aim" in writing a line of poetry'. *Gharaḍ* is an important term for the medieval categorization of poetry. Among the *aghrāḍ*, the medieval critics mainly distinguished between *madīḥ* (praise) and *hijā'* (satire), subsuming other genres under these two headings, with the exception of one author allowing a middle position for *ʿitāb* (admonition) and *ighrā'* (incentive); see ibid., 38–43.

6 This self-reflectiveness distinguishes the Abbasid *qaṣīda* from the pre-Islamic and early Islamic *qaṣīda*, which fulfills but does not reflect on its function, e.g. threat of satire, message, and dedication; see van Gelder 1982, 28.

7 Cf. Betten 1994, 521.

8 Ibn al-Jawzī *Muntaẓam*, v: 165, no. 310 without verses 3 and 5–8. For the admonition A111, see *Dīwān*, i: 150–1. Cf. also al-Jurjānī (*Asrār*, 242, no. 293), who quotes only the first verse as an example of rational (*ʿaqlī*) poetry as opposed to fantastic (*takhyīlī*) poetry.

9 Searle, Kiefer, and Bierwisch 1980, x. Searle uses direct versus indirect speech act to render the discrepancy between language meaning (literal meaning) and speaker's meaning (contextualized meaning). For the interpretation of one type of speech act (statement) as another (request), see Searle 1979, 31–2, 49–50. He modifies his previous explanation of indirect speech acts (as questions for conditions of appropriateness) and admits that indirect speech acts rely on the hearer's general powers of rationality and inference, including (a) a theory of speech acts, (b) general principles of co-operative conversation, (c) standard idiomatic forms, and (d) mutually-shared background information.

10 For an approach widening Searle's semantic bipolarity to a succession of possible meanings, by allowing for one utterance an unlimited number of communicative (i.e. contextualized) senses, resulting from an equally unlimited number of possible definitions of interactional settings (i.e. context of a linguistic utterance larger than its language context), see Bierwisch 1980. For a critical view of the *ad hoc* use of certain elements of context in the interpretation of discourse, see Hymes 1974, 154–8. Conceding, however, the absence of a system of social meanings, he accepts a consistent *ad hoc* approach.

11 Pratt 1977, 88–99. For genre as a framework of orientation and not only a precondition for illocutionary force, see Briggs and Bauman 1992, 142–3 and 146–7.

12 For criticism of Searle and Ohmann, treating literature as 'suspended illocutions' and 'pretended speech acts' respectively, see Pratt 1977, 89–99 and Hess-Lüttich 1985,

203. On the existence of the co-operative principle of conversation in literature as well as its exploitation, see notes 20 and 21.

13 Pratt 1977, 86 and 99. Compare, in linguistic anthropology, the much larger role given to genre including the ascription to it of illocutionary force; see Bauman and Briggs 1990, 63–4.

14 Hess-Lüttich 1981, 109.

15 Pratt 1977, 100–115.

16 Hess-Lüttich 1981, 109–10.

17 Pratt 1977, 170.

18 Ibid., 132–51.

19 Pratt 1977, 154 and Grice 1975, 49–58.

20 Grice 1975, 45 and Pratt 1977, 153.

21 The four maxims cover quantity, quality, relevance, and manner (clarity, perspicuity, brevity, order) of an utterance. For a complete list, see Grice 1975, 45–6 and Pratt 1977, 129–30.

22 Pratt 1977, 163 and 171.

23 For the theory of speech acts, see the section following after the next.

24 Pratt 1977, 173.

25 Similarly A694: 16 وما لمديحِى فى ثَناكَ زِيادةٌ سِوَى أَنَّنِى نظّامُ لؤلؤكَ النَّثْرِ 'My praise, extolling you, contains no addition, except that I am arranging your scattered pearls'.

26 No *madīḥ* of al-Buḥturī or Abū Tammām exceeds ninety verses, while 96 per cent of Abū Tammām's *madīḥ* is under sixty verses, and 97 per cent of al-Buḥturī's *madīḥ* under fifty; cf. Bencheikh 1975a, 106–7.

27 The patron's support before this public is requested in A1160, L1250: 180–2. For an *adīb* asked to assess a poem's value, see al-Marzubānī *Muwashshaḥ*, 517–18 and Ibn al-Rūmī *Dīwān*, i: 99.

28 Al-Marzubānī *Muwashshaḥ*, 398–9 and al-Ḥuṣrī *Zahr al-Ādāb*, i: 272–3.

29 On him, see chapter 4, note 28.

30 *Wa-hādhā ẓulmun min Abī l-Ṣaqri li-bni l-Rūmī wa-qillatu ʿilmin minhu bi-l-farqi bayna l-hijāʾi wa-l-madīḥ*, al-Marzubānī *Muwashshaḥ*, 399. This patron later learnt the difference, as Ibn al-Rūmī satirized him; see Boustany 1967, 161–6.

31 Hence genre acts as a field of intertextuality and as an orientating framework that puts into place interpretative procedures and sets of expectations between actors and audiences; cf. Briggs and Bauman 1992.

32 See Pratt 1977, 132–51 and note 18.

33 For an in-depth discussion of the dedication, see chapter 5.

34 Dramatic scenes also appear in laments (*rithāʾ*), such as those for the Alid rebel Yaḥyā b. ʿUmar (*Dīwān*, ii: 492–500, no. 366), the singing slave-girl Bustān, and the people of Basra (*Dīwān*, vi: 2377–82, no. 1251', translated in Arberry 1965, 62–72). Each genre, however, requires a separate study for the function dialogue fulfills in it.

35 The poet switches from the first to the second and third person; the patron from the second to the third.

36 Van Gelder 1983.

37 This feature is also discussed under the heading of *ibtidāʾ*, 'beginnings [of poems]'.

38 Van Gelder (1983, 29) uses Ibn al-Athīr's purely grammatical term *tawassuʿ* 'expansion' (of the first to the second person) to describe this concept of collective experience.

39 Ibid., 27.

40 See, e.g. L191 and L1306 in which the patron switches from third to second person.

41 For parallelism with *istidlāl* by Bashshār, see Meisami 1985; for antithesis by Abū Tammām, see Badawi 1978, and by al-Buḥturī, see Sperl 1989, 19–27, 47. Cf. also chapter 2, notes 18–22.

42 For other integral parts, such as analogy and sententia, see chapter 12.

43 Hess-Lüttich 1981, 112–15 and 1985, 201–2.
44 Hess-Lüttich 1981, 110.
45 e.g. in the composite dialogues for which see chapters 10 and 11.
46 Hess-Lüttich 1981, 110 and 1985, 200.
47 Note the difference of the implied author, or the manifestation of the author in the text, on the one hand, from the historical character in all his aspects of life and changes over time, and on the other, from the first person of the poet's persona. The implied author can distance himself in space and time, morals, and intellect from the poet-speaker. Cf. Booth 1961, 155.
48 See example A1510, chapter 15.
49 For examples, see ibid.
50 Hess-Lüttich (1981, 103–4 and 1985, 208) reviews current classificatory models for dialogue types and criticizes them as theoretically and methodologically imprecise as well as lacking an integrative perspective. He advises against establishing types at all and suggests instead selecting categories that suit a specific corpus and arriving heuristically at a typological system which – if defined in a dynamic way – can be adapted to other text groups. His set of criteria includes the number, constellation, relationship, and social position of participants, medium, senses, degree of formality, scheme of action, function of discourse, orientation towards addressee, definition of time and space, and modality of the dialogue.
51 ʿAlī b. al-Jahm *Dīwān*, 41–7 (no. 14), 50–1 (no. 16), 71–6 (no. 23), and 220–3 (al-Ruṣāfiyya).
52 Diʿbil *Dīwān*, 13 (no. 8), 13–14 (no. 9), 31 (no. 37), 53 (no. 54), 65 (no. 73), 72 (no. 80), 77 (no. 87), 87 (no. 108) all *madīḥ*; ibid., 134 (no. 178), 145 (no. 199) all *ʿitāb*; and ibid., 171 (no. 5) *hijāʾ*.
53 With the limited set of praise poems studied and in anticipation of later and broader application, the present typology should be regarded as provisional and expandable.
54 The terms 'argumentative' and 'phatic–rhetorical' are taken from Hess-Lüttich after Jakobson.
55 In pre-Islamic poetry, Jacobi (1971, 47–9) calls both types episodes, though she distinguishes between 'verbal exchanges that appear fictional' (*fiktiv wirkende Wechselreden*) and 'reminiscences' (*Remineszenzen*), introduced by *wa-rubba*, where the more original and individual examples are to be found. Ibn al-Rūmī's *wa-rubba* passages typically contain conventional topoi of boast and praise, while his original dialogues deserve their own term.
56 The application of speech art theory to literature has been treated in-depth by Pratt 1977, 100–32 for narrative, by Fish 1976 and Felman 1980 for drama, and by Ohmann 1972, 1973 for several genres. Whereas Ohmann extends the notion of speech act to the behavior of the participants afterwards (e.g. whether a promise is executed, an order followed), Fish adheres strictly to Searle's rules, which limit the speech act to its utterance only. Searle and Ohmann treat the literary speech act as pretended and 'unserious'. Fish 1976, 1011–23 and Pratt 1977, 89–99 criticize Ohmann for making such a generic distinction between 'serious' and literary discourse and for claiming a suspension of the truth conditions in the latter. Instead Pratt includes the special conditions of literary communication as part of the literary speech context and equates the conditions of appropriateness of speech act theory with the genre in literature; see also note 11. Cf. also Bauman and Briggs 1990, 62–6 for a critical survey of applications of speech act theory in linguistic anthropology.
57 Smith 1978, 79–106.
58 Fish 1976, 1002 and 1024.
59 Austin and Searle belong to the philosophical branch, Ohmann and Pratt to the literary. For linguistic anthropology, see Bauman and Briggs 1990, 62–6.

60 Benveniste 1966, i: 267–76, summarized by Felman 1980, 19–22.
61 'Illocutionary' designates that quality of language that is present in an assertion, request, command, and other acts of speech; see Searle 1969, 22–3. For the illocutionary force as inherent in larger forms, such as the genre, see Bauman and Briggs 1990, 62–4.
62 Searle 1969, 66–7.
63 Searle 1979, 12–20. Pratt and Traugott (1979, 229–30) reduce Searle's five categories to three, based on the part of the speech act they affect: (a) affecting the mind of the addressee (expressive, assertive); (b) denoting the act of the speaker, being of contractual character (commissive, declaration); and (c) affecting the act of the addressee (directive).
64 Searle 1969, 67.
65 Fish 1976, 990–1.
66 Ibid. and Felman 1980.
67 Fish 1976, 994 and 1001–2 with a concept of speech act based on Searle.
68 Felman 1980, 24–31 with a concept of performative based on Benveniste.
69 Ohmann 1973, 89.
70 They are excluded in Searle's model of the speech act, but included in Ohmann's.
71 See L191: 155 (and chapter 5, note 89), L215: 71–2, and the felicitations and admonitions discussed in chapter 16.
72 Ohmann 1972, 50; see also Ohmann 1973, 87 and 90.
73 Fish 1976, 1004–8.

4 THE PROTAGONISTS: IBN AL-RŪMĪ AND HIS PATRON ʿUBAYDALLĀH B. ʿABDALLĀH

1 *Ūliʿa bi-l-ṭīra, maʿrūfun bi-l-taṭayyur*; see al-Maʿarrī *Risāla*, 468–75, esp. 470 and 498.
2 *GAS* ii: 585–8, Boustany 1967, 187–91, and *EAL* i: 364–5.
3 Boustany 1967, 99–119.
4 Ibid., 119–25.
5 *Dīwān*, ii: 497, no. 366: 51–8.
6 According to older editions and manuscripts, 80 per cent (Boustany 1967, 34), but see note 20.
7 Al-Buḥturī *Dīwān*, v: 2921–2.
8 Cf. also McKinney 1998, 96, note 7.
9 S. Stetkevych 1979, 1991, Sperl 1977, 1989, and al-Sāmarrāʾī 1970–1. But compare von Grunebaum 1948–53, Meisami 1985, and al-Qaysī and al-Nājī 1994. For the poetic breadth of Ibn al-Rūmī, see Schoeler 1974, 167–234 (on nature poetry), idem 1994 and 1996 (on poetry and thought), van Gelder 1996, McKinney 1998 (on variations of the *raḥīl*), and Smoor 1996 (on elegies).
10 *GAS* i: 375, *GAS* ii: 612, Boustany 1967, 145–9, al-Khaṭīb al-Baghdādī *Taʾrīkh*, x: 340–4, no. 5479, al-Iṣfahānī *Aghānī*, ix: 39–47, Ibn Khallikān *Wafayāt*, ii: 304–6, further references in al-Ṣafadī *Wāfī*, xix: 379, no. 357, notes.
11 On the extensive literary patronage of the Ṭāhirids, see Bosworth 1969, esp. 71–6.
12 For the criticism, see E1478; for the reconciliation, F458.
13 Boustany 1967, 145–6.
14 For his prose, see al-Ḥuṣrī *Zahr*, ii: 615–16; for his poetry, al-ʿAskarī *Ṣināʿatayn*, al-Ḥuṣrī *Zahr*, Ibn Abī ʿAwn *Tashbīhāt*, passim, and al-Marzubānī *Muwashshaḥ*, 396–7.
15 Al-ʿAskarī *Ṣināʿatayn* 147.
16 For correspondence with Muḥammad, see Ibn ʿAbdrabbih *ʿIqd*, ii: 254, with Ibn al-Muʿtazz, see al-Iṣfahānī *Aghānī*, x: 296 [*Akhbār ʿAbdallāh Ibn al-Muʿtazz*], and with al-ʿAlāʾ, see Ibn al-Rūmī *Dīwān*, i: 99–100, no. 37.

17 On Dimashqī, see Boustany 1967, 295; on Ibrāhīm, probably the author of the *Kitāb al-Maḥāsin wa-l-masāwī*, see EI^2 i: 1132; on Muḥammad b. ʿAlī, see Boustany 1967, 283; on al-Buḥturī, ibid., 266; on Aḥmad, ibid., 279; and on Muḥammad b. ʿArūs, ibid., 286 and Ibn al-Muʿtazz *Ṭabaqāt*, 418–20.
18 Boustany 1967, 147, note 5.
19 Northedge 1991, 84, fig. 11.
20 See Appendix D, which supersedes the numbers given in Boustany 1967, 148, note 7.
21 Ibid., 147–9.
22 Ibid., 148 and Bencheikh 1975a, 109.
23 Heinrichs 1969, 38; see also Boustany 1967, 149 and chapter 16, note 45.
24 *Dīwān*, i: 272, no. 196: 43–50.
25 Discussed on pp. 210–13 and 260–1.
26 Bosworth 1969, 74–5.
27 It is attested in al-Ḥuṣrī *Zahr*, i: 273, 301–2, al-Marzubānī *Muwashshaḥ*, 398. The poetry of both is quoted side by side in Ibn al-Rūmī's *Dīwān* (E492, E1216 and E1217), by Ibn Abī ʿAwn (*Tashbīhāt*, 114, 191–2), and al-Ḥuṣrī (*Zahr*, i: 236 and ii: 1032–3).
28 Boustany 1967, 157–66, Sourdel 1959–60, i: 315–26 and 315, note 2 for further reference.
29 Boustany 1967, 158.
30 Al-Ḥuṣrī *Zahr*, i: 272. See also pp. 31–2 above.
31 Boustany 1967, 157–66.
32 A *zindīq* was an adherent of *zandaqa*, referring to the dualist sect of the Manichaeans or heresy in general. Manichaeism was indeed spread among Islamized Iranian intellectuals for reasons expounded by van Ess 1991–7, i: 423–7.
33 Sourdel 1959–60, i: 319 and 316, note 7.
34 Sourdel 1959–60, i: 321 and al-Marzubānī *Muwashshaḥ*, 377.
35 Boustany 1967, 166–170.
36 Sourdel 1959–60, i: 316.
37 Boustany 1967, 174–91, Sourdel 1959–60, i: 326–57 and 346, note 4.
38 Al-Qāsim became vizier still under the reign of al-Muʿtaḍid (288–9/901–2) and continued in this position during the first years of the reign of al-Muktafī 289–91/902–4. For the number of poems to his name and the pension allotted, see Boustany 1967, 176–7.
39 *Dīwān*, iii: 1030–2, no. 779 and Boustany 1967, 180.
40 Sourdel 1959–60, i: 352, note 7, Ibn Khallikān *Wafayāt*, 44, no. 436 and al-Masʿūdī *Murūj*, iv: 318–20. For other death versions, see Boustany 1967, 70–91.
41 Boustany 1967, 136.
42 Ibid., 137–40.
43 al-Marzubānī *Muʿjam*, 145. On Ibn al-Rūmī's satire, see Yārid *Kull mā qālahū Ibn al-Rūmī fī l-hijāʾ*.
44 al-Khaṭīb al-Baghdādī *Taʾrīkh*, xii: 23–6, no. 6387.
45 Ibn Rashīq *ʿUmda*, i: 286.
46 Al-Marzubānī *Muwashshaḥ*, 375–6.
47 Cf. also E10.

5 THE *MADĪḤ* EXCHANGED BETWEEN IBN AL-RŪMĪ AND ʿUBAYDALLĀH

1 Mez 1937, chapters 7, 9, 10, and 23, Ahsan 1979, 275–96. Bencheikh (1975a, 114), however, discounts praise in familiar sessions. D. Sourdel (1960) lacks accounts of poetic recitation. The formal-informal distinction differs from that of Sawa (1998, 111–18) for musical sessions, as he calls 'formal' any large or small session convened by a patron, as

opposed to *ad hoc* meetings without invitation, hosted by a poet, a commoner, or the musician himself. For a detailed classification of sessions, see Najar 1987, 156–60.

2 For enthronement, see Ahsan 979, 294–5; for designation of an heir, ibid., 295; for birth, ibid., 292; for victory, ibid., 296; and for *Nawrūz*, ibid., 287. The caliph's receiving of presents from his subjects on *Mihrajān* seems another likely occasion; ibid.

3 Only chapter headings survive of al-Masʿūdī's *Akhbār al-zamān* on the etiquette of *majālis*; cf. al-Masʿūdī *Murūj*, iv: 255–6.

4 Al-Ṣūlī *Akhbār Abī Tammām*, 144 and Mez 1937, 254–5 and 255, note 1.

5 Mez 1937, 143–4 after al-Ṣūlī and al-Masʿūdī. On literature as a subject of sessions, see also Ouyang 1997, 81–2.

6 Mez 1937, 96 and 104.

7 Ibid., 285 after al-Khaṭīb *Taʾrīkh*, viii: 249–50 and xii: 95–6, no. 4352. Cf. ʿAlī b. al-Jahm *Dīwān*, 6–7.

8 Al-Ṣūlī *Akhbār Abī Tammām*, 117 and Ibn al-Jarrāḥ *Waraqa*, 47

9 For *dirham* sums, see al-Ṣūlī, *Akhbār Abī Tammām*, 124, Yarshater 1985–, xxxiv: 185–8, and al-Masʿūdī 1986, iv: 105–6; for *dīnār* sums, see al-Ṣūlī, *Akhbār Abī Tammām*, 145, Ahsan 1979, 288, note 99, and Yarshater 1985–, xxxiv: 187; cf. also Ouyang, 1997, 74. The *dīnār* had been fixed at 4.25 grams of gold in 696–7 AH, and the *dirham* at 2.97 grams of silver in 698–9 AH. One *dīnār* equalled 20–2 *dirhams* at the beginning of the third/ninth century and rose to 25 *dirhams* by the middle of this century; see Ehrenkreutz 1977, 92–3 and 96.

10 Ibn al-Jarrāḥ *Waraqa*, 99 and al-Marzubānī *Muʿjam*, 322.

11 Al-Marzubānī *Muwashshaḥ*, 377 and al-Ṣūlī *Akhbār al-Buḥturī*, 128.

12 For salaries, see Ashtor 1961, 52 [34].

13 Ibn al-Jarrāḥ *Waraqa*, 100.

14 Canard 1946, 33 and Mez 1937, 96 and 104.

15 Bencheikh 1975a, 87.

16 Var. Naṣṣār: *Aʿqabta*, 'you caused [shame] as a consequence [of your action]'.

17 Cited by al-Marzubānī *Muʿjam*, 147. See also E1261.

18 See al-Marzubānī *Muwashshaḥ*, 376.

19 See *Dīwān*, i: 99 and chapter 4, note 16.

20 For al-ʿAlāʾ, see p. 45; for the epistle, *Dīwān*, i: 5–25 and *GAS* ii: 587.

21 Cf. also a similar arrangement in al-Ṣūlī's *Akhbār Abī Tammām* and *Akhbār al-Buḥturī*.

22 See note 19.

23 See chapter 2, note 22.

24 L1306.

25 For a similar intercalation of eulogy and plea in a pre-Islamic *qaṣīda*, see Montgomery 1997, 160.

26 Boustany (1967, 147, note 6) mentions the version of Escurial MS 277, 47a with 322 verses. For an excerpt of L1600, see chapter 3.

27 To L1306, addressed to the Banū Ṭāhir, see note 52.

28 A *tahniʾa* names its occasion in the first line and mirrors it in the choice of themes; F952 on the autumn festival of *Mihrajān* contains a *khamriyya*, and F1243 on the return from pilgrimage compares the patron to the Kaaba.

29 The male oryx antelope occurs in the pre-Islamic *qaṣīda* in independent comparisons with the poet's camel, which develop into complex narrative episodes; cf. Jacobi 1971, 56–7 and Montgomery 1997, 110–65. The female oryx, with its large eyes and long neck, is a common simile for a woman.

30 For the *khamriyya*, see chapter 13.

31 For the persona of *shayb*, see chapter 7.

32 L994, though containing a felicitation, is a *qaṣīda* by form and includes a strophe.

33 See note 23.
34 On the motif of *hieros gamos*, see Gruendler 1999.
35 This theme of renewed royalty is followed by a lacuna in the text.
36 Cf. A1171: 2, A212: 3–4, imparting stronger messages, namely the poet's threat of silence and his regret at having announced a generosity that, having failed to materialize, turns him into a liar.
37 Jacobi 1971, 78–85 and 103–4 and Bauer 1992, i: 72–3.
38 For the message formula as an act of speech see, pp. 59, 65, and 73.
39 This poem is noteworthy for containing a section on poetic ethics in the strophe: the poet rates an honorable promise higher than a stolen or grudgingly-given gift.
40 About the two-faced nature of this hyperbolic praise, see pp. 168–70.
41 Cf. pp. 55 and 270.
42 For a partial antithesis, see note 24 above.
43 Bencheikh 1975a, 145–6.
44 Bauer 1992, i: 267.
45 For Abū Tammām, see Bencheikh 1975b, 277 and chapter 1, note 32.
46 Bencheikh 1975a, 145.
47 For *ism*, see L191: 70, L215: 73; for *nasab*, see L434: 13 (Ibn Ṭāhir), L434: 13 (Ṭāhir, son of the Banū Ṭāhir); for *kunya*, see L434: 19, L1307: 12 (Abū Aḥmad).
48 In L994: 109 the bags themselves figuratively pronounce the praise; see chapter 6.
49 *Faṣl al-khiṭāb* 'what decides between true and false, what decides the judgment, the obligatory proof or oath' or 'sufficing as plain speech'; *AEL* ii: 2406.
50 Similarly L1611: 104.
51 Similarly L994: 20 (Banū Ṭāhir) and 42 ('Ubaydallāh).
52 The encomium L1306 addresses the Banū Ṭāhir (8). Its parallels with L1307, however, suggest a similar date of composition. It may have been addressed to 'Ubaydallāh as the last representative of the Banū Ṭāhir, without specifying him. Then the second person plural would count as a rhetorical device. The poem's hammering second person addresses stand out in deed (*-ka* for the poet, *-kunna* for the women, and *-kum* for the Ṭāhirids).
53 Similarly L434: 11.
54 Cf. the felicitation in the *madīḥ* of al-Nābigha; see Jacobi 1971, 99.
55 Compare God's agency, unmediated by the poet in 'That by which God has singled you out attests that you are his chosen and selected one' (L215: 152), 'With him God aided the caliphate, after its foundation had weakened and disintegrated' (L434: 32–3) and 'Is there a way to his like? God has refused that to the creation' (L1306: 46).
56 Naṣṣār's يمم, which violates the meter, is emended to يَنعِم.
57 Similarly L191: 121, L1042: 66. For the verbal trope in L1306: 14, see page 92.
58 Similarly L1611: 301–3. L1611: 301 and 303, both addressed to the patron, combine wishes from him and statements in his favor.
59 This ancient Iranian festival, dedicated to the God Mithra, survived, like *Nawrūz*, deprived of its original religious function in the Islamic context. It was celebrated by the Abbasid caliphs and their semi-independent Turko-Iranian vassals around the autumnal equinox with wine and music, the reception of presents from subjects, or the distribution of autumn and winter clothes; see Calmard 1993, 18.
60 *rawāmis* (s. *rāmisa*) 'winds that transport the dust from one district to another which is some days distant from the former'; see *AEL* i: 1155a.
61 Naṣṣār's حبيت emended to حُبيتَ.
62 <**al'ik*, a defective imperative derived from *mal'ak* 'angel'; see *WKAS* ii: 51–5.
63 Mainly as introductory lines of shorter poems (*qiṭa'*) conveying hostile and defying messages, threats, warnings, or supplications and pleas for reconciliation; see Bloch 1948, 117–22, Jacobi 1971, 81–2, and *WKAS* ii: 51.

64 Cf. also A464: 1–2. For the entire message of L191, see chapter 10.
65 For *dawiya* as 'being consumed with sickness or rancor', see *Lis* xiv: 278. The message contains ʿUbaydallāh's appointment as a deputy governor, which guarantees a safe future for the people of Baghdad, notwithstanding the vicissitudes of time.
66 Cf. Fischer 1972, 91 and Wright 1896–8, ii: 1.
67 Cf. Bloch 1948, 121–2. For the dedication in the *madīḥ* of al-Nābigha and Zuhayr, see Jacobi 1971, 94, 97, and 99.
68 For a repetition of verses 151–2 in L215 and an intervening anaphora, see chapter 12.
69 Cf. also L1611: 231, L191: 104.
70 For the nocturnal traveller, see L994: 102.
71 Cf. also F952: 74.
72 Abū Tammām used *ʿiqāb* 'mountain-passes' in a similar double meaning and added a matching metaphor for the patron's response (Heinrichs 1986, 15, Abū Tammām *Dīwān*, ii: 6, no. 42: 7):

فَرَعْتُ عِقابَ الأَرضِ والشّعرِ مادِحًا   له فارْتَقَى بِى فِى عِقابِ المحامِدِ

I ascended the mountain-passes of earth and of poetry praising him, so he took me up the mountain-passes of glorious deeds.

(trans. Heinrichs)

73 See also the surrounding verses L191: 157–63.
74 On friendship, see L1042: 52, 57.
75 See Sūrat al-Baqara 2/256 and Sūrat Luqmān 31/22.
76 Emendation of Naṣṣār's *maʾābun* to *maʾāba*.
77 For the patron's spell over rhymes, see L994: 96, 101, and over rare words, see L994: 95, 100. Cf. also L1611: 253 for motifs and rhymes as springs that flow only for him. For speech as a trope, see chapter 6.
78 Cf. the innovation to this theme in L1611: 303.
79 For the hyperbole in this verse, see pp. 87–8.
80 For the hyperbole, see pp. 86–7. For the relationship of words and acts, see chapter 16.
81 I follow Salīm (*jāwaztu*) not Naṣṣār (*jāwazta*) since the poet debates his own allegiance in the whole passage; cf. chapter 10. To leave ʿUbaydallāh would force him into a life of permanent lying, for no one could match the poet's praises with acts except him. Cf. also L1600: 249–50.
82 Emending Naṣṣār's *yaẓlumunī* to *yaẓlimunī*.
83 On speech act theory in literature, see chapter 3.
84 For sincerity in its uttered form, taking the responsibility for having an intention, and not an elusive inner sincerity, see Searle 1979, 62.
85 Benveniste 1966, 265–6.
86 Ibid., 227–8.
87 Fish 1976, 991.
88 For a poem as a first initiative, see al-Buḥturī *Dīwān*, iii: 1770–4, no. 679, as a response to a previous favor, see L1250: 180–90. For the concept of *do ut des*, see Mauss 1950, 8–18.
89 For a patron's failure to do so, see L215: 70–2 and E110.
90 Cf. also Lyons 1999, 141–6.

6 SPEECH AS ACTION

1 For women quoted, see L191: 27 and L1250': 64, a bystander, L191: 84, L1611: 254. For a paraphrased spy, see L215: 15–16, a complaining supplicant, L1611: 233–46, a potential client for *madīḥ*, L434: 34–5, and a competitor of the patron, L215: 121–4.

For personae, i.e. figures who speak or listen during an entire passage, see the following chapter.

2 For Zuhayr's use of the motif, see Jacobi 1971, 42.

3 For this motif, see also L1306: 4.

4 For sayings of the admonisher, *ḥabīb*, or enemy, motivating the poet's response in pre-Islamic poetry, see Wagner 1987–8, i: 171. For the reverse sequence, see L1611: 84 and 263.

5 L215: 35–59.

6 For averted eyes, see L191: 25–6.

7 Throughout the strophe, the persona of youth takes the place of the customary beloved (cf. *bāna shabābī*, L215: 1, *yā ṣāḥiban fātanī l-mashību bihī*, 17, *lahfī li-sharkhi l-shabābi*, 21). The scholion to verse 9 explains the masculine gender of the *ḥabīb* as the conventional periphrasis for the feminine. In this case, however, the gender coincides with masculine *shabāb* cast in the role of the departed *ḥabīb* (17–20).

8 Literally *maltham* means 'place of kissing'; see *WKAS* ii: 199–200.

9 L1611: 63 and L1611: 250.

10 For causal hyperbole, see Reinert 1990, 376.

11 Var. in Naṣṣār: *anfāsuhum*. For the same motif, see L434: 21, L1250': 179, L1611: 196 (as not concealable), and L1307: 33–5 (as not lying).

12 Abu Deeb 1979, 178–89.

13 For the patron's call as halting fate, see L1611: 238. Cf. also Sperl (1989, 5–19) on the cosmic powers of the ruler in the Abbasid *madīḥ*, particularly that of fertilizing a wasteland.

14 For *takhyīl*, see Heinrichs 2000 and Abu Deeb 1979, 159–63. Elements of *takhyīl* are, e.g. the reified metaphor, personification, and etiology, see Heinrichs 1991, 181–2. Reinert (1990, 376–80) lists as further paralogical figures (i.e. that map a causal relationship from the level of the image to the level of the topic) the causal hyperbole, the fantastic etiology, the translation, and the imaginary action in a quiet scene.

15 For the patron's mention as sweet-smelling and sounding, see L1250': 179, as tattooed or branded, see L1611: 125–6, as marking foreheads, see L1611: 122.

16 L1611: 113.

17 Cf. A464, discussed in chapter 16.

18 Von Grunebaum 1960, 1115 and al-Jāḥiẓ *Ḥayawān*, i: 33–5.

19 Al-Rummānī *Nukat*, 98.

20 Isḥāq b. Ibrāhīm al-Kātib *Burhān*, 9–17.

21 فهِى وإن كانت صامتةً فى أَنفسِها فهِى ناطقةٌ بظاهرِ أَحوالها؛ وعلى هذا النّحوِ استنطقتِ العربُ الرَّبْعَ وخاطبتِ الطللَ؛ ونطَقتْ عنه بالجوابِ، على سبيلِ الاستعاراتِ فِى الخِطاب ... فاستنطقَ ما لاينطق بلسانه، لأَنّ أَحوالَه مُظهِرةٌ لبيانه ... وأَجاب عن صامتٍ غير مُجيبٍ، لِما ظهر من حاله للقلوب ... وإنّما تُعبِّرُ هذه الأَشياءُ لِمَن اعتبرَ بها، وتُبيِّنُ لِمَن طلبَ البيانَ منها ... قد قُلنا إنّ الأَشياءَ تُبيِّنُ بذواتها لِمَن تَبَيَّنَ، وتُعبِّرُ بمعانيها لِمَن اعتبر.

(Isḥāq b. Ibrāhīm *Burhān*, 10–11 and 18)

22 See previous note. Here *istiʿāra* is synonymous with *majāz* (cf. Heinrichs 1991–2, 271) and not to be confused with its other meaning of a *tamthīl*-based metaphor.

23 On him see p. 43.

24 Cf. Mottahedeh 1980, 63–4

25 For his name passing decisions, see L994: 99, L191: 71; for his generosity causing speech, see L994: 76, for its causing poetry, see F952, 51, 53, 55; and for his acts weaving praise, see L994: 105, L1611: 226–31.

26 Cf. Heinrichs 1987–8, 359–60.

27 For racing oryx and thirsty camels, see L994: 99–100, L215: 105.
28 L994: 96.
29 For *shayb*'s forbidding, see L1250': 12–14, 17 and L191: 7; for its warning and guiding, see L191: 9, L434: 1, L1250': 31–8; for its announcing death, see L191: 12, L215: 3 and 9, L1250': 5–7; and for its promising to return youth, see L191: 10–19.
30 I follow *khalīlatī* after Salīm, instead of the misprinted *khalīlayyatī* in Naṣṣār.
31 Metonymy is not included by al-Jurjānī (*Dalā'il*, 70–2, 262, 306–14, 431) under *kināya*, which is limited to the allusion or attribution of praiseworthy qualities. However, in one of his examples, the personifications of generosity and liberality evoke and lament the deceased Barmakid Muḥammad b. Yaḥyā (314).
32 Quoted pp. 82–3. Similarly, in L1250': 5–8, the poet first claims that the death warning of white hair has scared him and cooled his passion. Then he admits the real cause to be that the women eschew him, imposing his abstention, while some color still remains in his hair.
33 The metaphorical 'book' of white hair, lacking any reading signs, is understood more clearly and unmistakably than any real book with diacritics and vowel markers.
34 *Ghuflun* of a Koran codex means 'without *'awāshir*', i.e. the signs marking groups of ten verses, or, of a book, 'anonymous', *AEL* ii: 2276a. The surrounding imagery suggests the first meaning.
35 For the warning, see verse 5 of this poem. For the determinate transitive active participle in construct with a direct object in *li-l-qāri'īhi* and *akuffu l-sā'ilīka* (L1042: 56), see Ullmann 1998, nos. 274–82.
36 *Tamthīl* is taken in the sense of al-Jurjānī, as a similarity of the relationship between several objects at the level of the image with a relationship between elements at the level of the topic; see Abu Deeb 1979, 145–8.
37 For youth as a dramatized persona, see the following chapter.
38 For fate forbidding the poet women, see L1250': 42; for its abrogating youth, see L434: 7 (cf. also the lament for youth as abrogating love poems (*manāsib*) in L215: 21); for fate's inscribing of hoariness onto the poet's head, see L1250': 35–6 in the preceding quote.
39 L994: 93, L1306: 13.
40 L191: 126–8.
41 L215: 66–7.
42 Literally, 'The wish that promised his favor is not being complained of as lying or faking', i.e. any wish addressed to the patron is granted.
43 Cf. the metaphor of the patron's governorship vowing its permanence, L1611: 153.
44 Reinert (1990, 366–71) also offers two broader definitions.
45 For the motif of the patron as last resort in hyperbolic praise, see L191: 172–3 and L1042: 68.
46 For this style, see Schoeler 1974, 174–5, 181 and chapter 12.

7 THE DRAMATIS PERSONAE

1 As a convention the female accuser, like the *ḥabīb*, appears in the masculine gender.
2 For pre-Islamic *fakhr*, see Jacobi 1971, 70 and Wagner 1987–8, i: 109–111; for pre-Islamic *rithā'*, see Wagner 1987–8, i: 125, S. Stetkevych 1993, 161–205, and Borg 1997. For Umayyad love poetry, see Wagner 1987–8, i: 62-3, Jacobi 1985, and Bauer 1998, 38–55; for Umayyad wine poetry (also as *wāshī*), Wagner 1987–8, ii: 36, 38 and Kennedy 1997, 94–7, 104–10 and 154–70. For Abbasid love poetry, see Wagner 1965, 251, 324 and Bauer 1998; for Abbasid wine poetry, Wagner 1965, 291–6; 1987–8, ii: 41–2, and Kennedy 1997.

3 For the full passages, see L191: 2–7, L1250': 1–3, 39–45, and L1307: 7–11.
4 But cf. Jacobi (1971, 70) for the disregarded blamer in the pre-Islamic individual *fakhr*.
5 Paraphrased in L191 and L1250' or implied in L1307.
6 For the pre-Islamic period, see Jacobi 1971, 41–2, Wagner 1987–8, i: 91, and Bauer 1998, 382.
7 See chapter 6.
8 For women mocking the poet, see Jacobi 1971, 42.
9 For white hair as forbidding, as warning and guiding, see pp. 88–90.
10 Another meaning of *thaghām* is 'a tree with a white blossom and fruit'; see *AEL* i: 339.
11 Cf. L215: 2–3, 10–11 and L1250': 5–8.
12 For the motif of blindness, see also L434: 1.
13 The straight-feathered arrows of the fates of death, hunting him (similar to the glances of women, 25), contrast his own unevenly feathered arrows in his 'hunting' for love (6). Naṣṣār's *ṣuyyāb* (s. *ṣā'ib*) is emended to *ṣiyāb*.
14 L1611: 5–103.
15 Cf. same motif in the nostalgic mood, *mithla aḥlāmi ḥālimi l-nuwwāmi*, L1250': 44.
16 For anaphoric lamentations, see L191: 47–60; L1250': 48–56. For their occurrence in pre-Islamic laments, see Wagner 1987–8, i: 119–20 and Borg 1997, 83 and 152–61; for internal rhyme, S. Stetkevych 1993, 182.
17 For old age as a failed hunt, due to broken and unevenly feathered arrows, see L1307: 1–6, L1611: 5 and L1250': 57–9. In the metaphor of the still successful hunt of women as oryx (L1611: 5–9 and L1250': 63–7), youth acts as a persona. For old age as firewood, see L191: 64 and L215: 33–4. In L1306: 4 youth is still a fresh bough (*ghuṣn*) whose shade attracts the oryx.
18 L191: 65–70 (quoted hereafter), L215: 4, and L1307: 1 and 8–11.
19 From the sample of encomia it is not possible to say which of both was at the origin, the personification of youth as a deceased person or the analogy of its memory with a tomb – or whether they developed in conjunction.
20 For an appeal to youth to remain close, see L1306: 1 (*lā yabʿadanna shabābuka l-ghirnīqu*); for the poet's call for consolation, see L191: 62–3 (*a-ufjaʿu bi-l-shabābi wa-lā uʿazzā?*). For the rain-greeting, see L191: 20–1 (*saqā ʿahda l-shabībati kullu ghaythin … layāliya lam aqul saqyan li-ʿahdin*); L215: 28 and 30 (*saqyan li-dahrin … wa-lam aqul ʿinda dhāka min asafin saqyan li-dahrin*); and L1306: 2 (*saqyan li-azmānin*). In a *fakhr* episode, the resurrected time of youth becomes metonymically the 'time of suckling from the vine', and the rain cloud is called to breast-feed it, in a formal unity of the image; see L1250': 59–62 (*yā zamāna l-riḍāʿi arḍaʿaka l-muznu*).
21 Cf. Wagner 1987–8, i: 117 and 120–1.
22 Cf. Jacobi 1971, 22–7.
23 The alternate meaning for *ajzaʿa*, 'to leave a remainder of less than half', would fit better but is only attested as intransitive; see *AEL* i: 419a.
24 i.e. rarely does a friend mourn such an excellent friend.
25 There are no clearings (*juwab* s. *jawba*) between the single rain clouds, so that the rain is continuous. The pores (*furūgh* s. *fargh*) of the clouds, however, and the drops they produce are so big as to be compared, in their enormous size, to clearings between clouds.
26 This refers back to verse 22. Instead of *munsakabu l-damʿi … munsakabuh*, Naṣṣār, I follow Salīm's vocalization, *munsakiba l-damʿi … munsakibuh*, conforming with the scholion: the shower (as subject) imitates the tears (as object).
27 Female oryx, gazelles, and ostriches giving birth to their offspring belong to the pre-Islamic *aṭlāl* motif. They show the abode's state of desertion in contrast with its former human habitation; cf. Jacobi 1971, 25–6, Wagner 1987–8, i: 96, and Lichtenstädter 1932, 33–4. In Ibn al-Rūmī's verse both animals are male.

28 Wagner 1987–8, i: 117 and Borg 1997, 150–2.
29 For those jealous of the patron, see L1042: 51, L1611: 297, and F952: 35, and for the one envying the poet, see L191: 124–5, L1042: 51, and L1611: 293. For evil omens deterring the poet, see L215: 106–7 and the supplicant, see L1250: 244–6.
30 *Kawāʿib* literally means 'full-breasted'.
31 Jacobi 1971, 81–2 and note 86.
32 For the witnessing 'you', see chapter 9, for the message phrase, pp. 59, 65, and 73.
33 Cf. also F1364, which is entirely cast as a message, beginning, *qul li-l-amīri*.
34 For a structural opposition between fate and Islamic ruler, and the *qaṣīda* as the place of the ruler's struggle and temporary defeat of fate, see Sperl 1989, 22–4.
35 For the patron as a protector in the third person, see L434: 13, L1306: 10–11, L1611: 237.
36 This allusion to Koranic descriptions of Judgment Day (e.g. Sūrat al-Muzammal 73/14) confers cosmis powers upon the patron.
37 *Qunāʿisun* pl. *qanāʿisu* normally referring to one strong in body (*Lis* vi: 184b) applies here to *qawl* 'speech'; cf. the parallel *fārisuh* 'hero in it (sc. speech)', in verse 52.
38 Literally, 'and each one, his shame, you have its reverse'.
39 *Ilā* may alternately be translated as 'towards (a deed)'.
40 Cf. L1042: 45–6, L1307: 38.
41 Cf. the patron in the third person in L1306: 15.
42 For inverted hyperbole, see chapter 6.
43 For these poets' praises of literary talent, chapter 1, note 32. For ʿUbaydallāh's poetry, see chapter 4, note 14.
44 Literally, 'who says poetry'.
45 *Tāʿisuh* 'tumbling, falling' is emended from Naṣṣār's misprinted *nāʿisuh*, which occurs as a rhyme word two verses earlier.
46 *ʿAwā'idu* is taken as plural of *ʿādatun* 'custom, habit'. It is also the plural of *ʿā'idatun* 'a female visitor' and 'favor, benefit, advantage', see *AEL* ii: 2191b.
47 For acts attracting poetry or conveying meaning themselves, see chapter 6.
48 Heinrichs 1969, 59–65, nos. 3–4, Jacobi 1970, 93–8, and Bürgel 1974, 24–5 (nos. 3 and 5) and 54–87. For hyperbole, see also Reinert 1990 and pp. 84, 86–8, and 90–2. For *takhyīl*, see chapter 6, note 14.
49 Ancestral praise offers a similar way of criticizing by splitting the patron into his praiseworthy reliable Ṭāhirid heritage and his individual acts, which are either insufficient or questionable. See L994: 20–84 and L1042: 14–47.
50 The reading follows Salīm, whose image of promptly slaughtering the beast of promise in its young healthy state is more apt than Naṣṣār's ما لم تعطنيه 'as long as you have not granted it to me'. For the gift, see verse 123.
51 The obstinate wife recurs as the poet's deceived benefit in L1042: 61–2. The figurative use of the bride or wife is not unusual, especially as the wife's obedience is asserted; cf. the noble deeds as the patron's wives (L1611: 270), Tihāma and Najd as his brides (L994: 91), the world as a divorced wife after his death (L1250': 190), as well as the dedicated poem as an orthodox wife (L1611: 300), and the daughters of poetry given to the patron as brides (F952: 81). For the different roles of wives in *madīḥ*, see Gruendler 1999. Alternate meanings of *qarīna* are 'side camel' and 'soul', the latter in the phrase *asmaḥat (sāmaḥat) qarīnatuhū* 'his companion allowed [it]', i.e. his soul agreed to it; see *Lis* xiii: 339a.
52 Cf. verse 119 in which the patron's stream of generosity is said to ascend mountain passes, with the mountain water course as a source of the valley stream. The poet, expecting streams of generosity from the patron's metaphorical mountain passes, receives procrastination instead.
53 To be shown with the example of L191 in chapter 10.
54 Ritter 1927, 15. Ibn al-Rūmī is presented as untypical in this respect.

55 Ibid., 16. The poem contains a quoted prayer of monks and God's response, qualifying as a dialogue scene as defined in chapter 8.
56 Though Benveniste (1966, i: 228) argues for a universal difference between the first and second person, as present in a dialogue, and the third, as absent from it, only the Arabic linguistic tradition so distinguishes the speech situation in its pronouns.
57 Note, however, that the hero of *fakhr* is dramatized in L1611: 56–76 (group hunt), 77–81 (battle), and 97–101 (noonday journey).
58 Cf. L191: 25 and 40–1.
59 For the terminology of speech acts, see chapter 3.
60 For the rain greeting, see note 20.
61 Searle 1969, 66 and Fish 1976, 995.
62 For a similar motif without the neighbor, see L1611: 5–9.
63 To Naṣṣār's metrically corrupt *aḍḥā*, I prefer the variant *aṣbaḥa*, also found in Salīm.
64 Jacobi 1982, 14, 16.
65 For this role, see L191: 157–74, L434: 34–5, L1042: 52–68 (combined with panegyrist), L1306: 9–13, L1307: 44–5, L1611: 273–96, and L1250': 172–87.
66 *Walī* pl. *awliyā'* means both 'guardian, protector' and 'friend, protégé' but the objective genitive in 'like the protecting of an iron-clad figher', *ka-ṣawni l-kamiyyi*, parallel to *yaṣūnu l-waliyya*, equals the protected figher with the protégé. *Naṣlu* is emended for Naṣṣār's *naṣla*.
67 See also the sword metaphor in L1250': 186.
68 Regarding these mutual duties, see chapter 15.
69 *Siqābi* is emended to *siqābī* as a parallel subject to *qilāṣī*.
70 Cf. also L191: 164–71 and L434: 34–5.
71 See pp. 65–70.
72 L191: 96–140, 151–6; 215: 64–72; L994: 95–101, 105–6; L1042: 52–68 (combined with protégé); L1611: 297–9, 303.
73 *Fa-l-yaktub wa-l-yumlili lladhī ʿalayhi l-ḥaqqu wa-l-yattaqi llāha rabbahū wa-lā yabkhas minhu shay'an*. See also Koran 7/85, 11/85, 26/173 (involving humans) and 11/15, 72/13 (involving God).
74 Cf. also A1638 on the right of the man of letters (*ḥaqq al-adīb*) addressed to al-Qāsim b. ʿUbaydallāh b. Sulaymān b. Wahb and E110. Cf. also al-Ṣūlī (*Akhbār Abī Tammām*, 3–4), *tarā aktharahum . . . yūfīhi ḥaqqahū fī l-madḥ*, 'You see most people . . . observe [Abū Tammām's] due in panegyrics'.
75 Cf. also previous quote and L191: 152.
76 Var. Naṣṣār: *ka-raqrāqi l-saḥābi ʿalā l-jidābi*, 'like the coming and going of clouds over drought'.
77 The moods of the verb are part of what constitutes the 'world-constitutive' component of the direct explicit speech act as defined by Petöfi and Kayser (1978, 19), i.e. the way in which the speaker asserts his standpoint toward the statement he makes.
78 Benveniste (1966, i: 263–5) see verbs of mental activity as markers of subjectivity. Petöfi and Kayser (1978, 19) divide subjectivity into the 'performative-modal' and 'world-constitutive' components of their speech act model. Cf. chapter 10, note 15.
79 Discussed in chapter 11.
80 But cf. A1510, where he takes the consequences and departs.

8 THE SCENE

1 For semantic aspects of the grammatical person, see pp. 36–9, 73–4, and 111–12.
2 'Address' stands for speaking to someone in the second person (*mukhāṭaba*) and not for the vocative (*nidā'*), though many addresses begin with a vocative, exclamation, lamentation (*nudba*), or a call for help (*istighātha*).

3 For a dialogue scene with several rounds, see L215: 35–59. For a definition of the conversational turn, see Sacks, Schegloff, and Jefferson 1974.
4 But ʿUbaydallāh addresses an epigram to Ibn al-Rūmī, who responds (E1217), and once asks him to perform a *taṣḥīf* (E492). Ibn al-Rūmī is also commissioned to compose a poem in his patron's voice about the number forty (E462).
5 Cf. pp. 90–2.
6 Emending Naṣṣār's *zajratun* to *zajratan* as cognate accusative with ʿUbaydallāh as subject.
7 Emending Naṣṣār's *yatasha''amū* to the sixth form because of the plural subject.
8 The structure of the refutation resembles a *muʿāraḍa* (cf. van Ess, 1970, 41), and poetry belongs indeed to the subjects using disputation (*jadal*); see Isḥāq b. Ibrāhīm al-Kātib *Burhān*, 117. The use of logical argumentation (*jadal* or *kalām*) in literature has to my knowledge only been treated by Heinrichs (1975, 464) in connection with prose dialogues in the work of Najm al-Dīn al-Ṭūfī. These are not *munāẓarāt* in the strict legal sense, and only a few use *jadal* techniques.
9 For the first case, see the dialogue between poet and patron (L191: 97–117), terminated by a monologue, switching the patron to the third person as 'the prince' (*saybu l-amīri*, 118-22). For the second case, see the evoking scene L1250': 61–2 with the 'time of suckling [from the vine]' (*zamānu l-riḍāʿ*), which is terminated by the disappearance of youth and the arrival of the persona of the neighbor, addressed in the second person (*jāratī*) within a dialogue scene (63–71).
10 L1250': 39–45. In addition, the closure is marked by the onset of a monologue (46–60), including as a third person '[him] who recommends to me my nose-rein' (*naṣīḥī khiṭāmī*), identical with the accuser (40, 43). For the latter's gender, see chapter 7, note 1.
11 For the dramatic function of these figures, see chapter 12.
12 L191: 7–19.
13 For argumentative dialogues, see L191: 97–117, 123–35, 151–63, 172–5; L1042: 52–62, 67; L1611: 273–96.
14 e.g. A1510, A1171 and A212.
15 For dialogues of hyperbolic praise, including the dedication, with the poet as a dramatized persona, see L994: 95–110, L1306: 16–18, and L1611: 297–303.
16 For the poet as witness, see chapter 9.
17 For topical (e.g. general, individual, ancestral, and courtly) praise with the poet as a witness, see L434: 13 (unique address of patron), L994: 20–31 (with 'we' in 21, and 'I' in 29–30), 38–42 (with 'I' in 42), 84–93 (impersonal poet in 85), L1042: 14–21 (without 'I'), 33–41 (with 'I' in 40, 'we' in 37), L1306: 8–15 ('I' in inserted dialogue, 10), and L1611: 205–31 (with 'we' in 211, and 'I' in 223).

For hyperbolic praise with the poet as a witness, see L191: 136–150 (with 'we'), L215: 149–53 (with 'I' in the dedication, 150), and L1042: 48–51 (with 'I' in 51). For hyperbolic praise without the poet's persona, see L994: 84–94, L1307: 39–47 (with dedication), and L1611: 269–72.
18 This scene opens the antistrophe and is followed by an episode with the patron's ancestor Ṭāhir b. al-Ḥusayn as an historical example
19 Cf. *WKAS* ii: 1362b.
20 For *karīha* as battle, see *WKAS* i: 155a and 165a. Naṣṣār's *raḥluhā* is emended to *rajluhā*, forming an oppositional pair with *al-fawāris*.
21 Cf. *WKAS* ii: 1539a.
22 *Baʿdahā* logically refers to the human antecedents *amthālikum*; the non-human *makārim* fit grammatically but not logically, since fate is stingy with the Ṭāhirids' lives, not only their deeds.
23 For more detail on the witnessing 'I', 'we', and 'you', see chapter 9.

24 On choosing a bad patron, see E1307 and A1510: 24.
25 Cf. note 15 above.
26 For the poet's weak presence, see note 17. For the two dedication formulae, which either include the poet (*manaḥtukahā*) or exclude him (*khudhhā! dūnakahā! hākahā*), see pp. 65–6 and 73. For the poet's absence, see the two possible readings of L191: 136–49 in chapter 10.
27 See for example a sequence of argumentative and hyperbolic dialogues (L191: 123–35 and 36–50 with ambivalent verses 136–40) or hyperbolic and argumentative dialogues (L1024: 48–51 and 52–62). The poet assumes everywhere the role of the protégé. For interspersed monologues, see L994: 118–22, 164–71 and L1042: 63–6 and 68.
28 This is an address of the mantle of youth (L191: 60–70). First youth is introduced (60–3), then the poet speaks to its metaphoric mantle (65–70).
29 For the span of forty years, cf. Diʿbil, 'Wake up from your blaming me, O departing one, the passing of forty years saves you the blame' (*afīqī min malāmiki yā ẓaʿīnā / kafāki l-lawma marru l-arbaʿīnā, Dīwān*, 148, no. 204: 1)
30 Literally, '[I call the rain] by a call as to which, if it is answered [it is good], if not, I will pour for your flowing tears [answering in the rain's stead]'.
31 L215: 21–6 consisting of an introduction (17–21) and a response (22–6), concluded with a greeting in the optative (28). The same figure is mentioned in the poet's dialogue with white hair (L191: 7–19).
32 For a rephrasing vocative, see L215: 122–5 (or *mubārī, musābiq*); for the epithet, L215: 15–16.
33 Cf. Lichtenstädter 1932, 83–5.
34 This accuser appears already at the *qaṣīda*'s beginning (1250': 1–3 in an argument with the poet, where she counts on his white hair to help her tame him.
35 A keen-sighted woman.
36 The contents reiterate an earlier motif in the poem (L1250': 9–11).
37 Breathing and remembering are equated here as virtual death, though memory is used as a productive source in the camel ride (*raḥīl*) later in the *qaṣīda*.
38 L191: 2–6 (with accuser and concluded by hyperbole) and L215: 15–16 (with spy).
39 L191: 9–19; for a rare reinterpretation of a fictional persona, see the dialogue with a friend L215: 37–59.
40 One might add here two short addresses of the poet's self, which are similar in form and purpose and lead to the *raḥīl* (L1250': 72) or *madīḥ* (L434: 11).
41 L1307: 7–11.
42 L1250': 63–7.
43 On this pre-Islamic introductory formula of *fakhr* themes, see Jacobi 1971, 47–8 and 54, note 57 and Wagner 1987–8, i: 98.
44 L1250': 71 (*darra darru l-ṣibā wa-darru maghānī l-lahwi*).
45 For the first example, see L215: 9–14, beginning 'A laughing one hurt me with his laughter' (*wa-ḍāḥikin sā'anī bi-ḍaḥkatihī*). It describes the male beloved's laughter (9–10), the poet's reaction (11–12), and his remembrance of him (13–14). For the male gender of this beloved, see chapter 6, note 7. For the second example, see L191: 24–30, beginning 'Do the women seriously dislike meeting me?' (*a-jidda l-ghāniyāti qalayna waṣlī?*)
46 Abstract youth occurs in L215: 21, L1307: 6, L215: 28–34, and L191: 20–3. L215: 28–34 opens with an invocation of rain (28), 'May rain refresh a time joy has made short, its years are like the hours of another [time]' (*saqyan li-dahrin ṭawathu ghibṭatuhū kānat ka-sāʿāti ghayrihī ḥiqabuh*), following with a quote of the poet's past speech (30), a lamentation (32), and two sententiae. L191: 20–3 begins 'May every

shower with lightening, thunder, and low clouds refresh the time of youth' (*saqā ʿahda l-shabībati kullu ghaythin agharra mujaljilin dānī l-rabābī*), containing an invocation of rain (20).

Metaphorical youth occurs in L1306: 1–4, L215: 32–4. L1306: 1–4 begins 'Your tender youth shall not be far, in the days when it looked handsome on you / May the rain refresh times ...' (*lā yabʿadanna shabābuka l-ghirnīqu ayyāma manẓarihī ʿalayka anīqū / saqyan li-azmānin* ...), and it ends in the historical present, 'In you a verdant branch, whose shade the antelopes seek, is trembling with the joys of youthful love' (*yahtazzu fīka li-aryaḥiyyāti l-ṣibā ghuṣnun tafayyāhu l-ẓibāʾu warīqū*). L215: 32–4 begins 'Oh, my regret for the bough of youth is that its twigs return as firewood after [their former] freshness' (*lahfī li-ghuṣni l-shabābi an rajaʿat muḥtaṭaban baʿda naḍratin shuʿabuh*).

47 L215: 17–21 (*yā ṣāḥiban fātanī l-mashību bihī* ... *lahfī li-sharkhi l-shabābi an nasakhat manāsiba l-lahwi baʿdahū nudabuh*). Elements of the syntax recur in another evocation in this *qaṣīda* (32–4) as well as in L191: 61–4, beginning 'Oh, my sorrow ... Am I bereaved of youth and not consoled?' (*fa-yā asafā* ... *a-ufjaʿu bi-l-shabābi wa-lā uʿazzā?*)

48 L215: 4–8, beginning 'Shame upon time: it dresses us with the garb of good life, then robs it' (*barḥan li-hādhā l-zamāni yulbisunā sirbāla naʿmāʾa thumma yastalibuh*).

49 For invocations of shade, clouds, rain, or dew for a dwelling or, figuratively, for a time period, see L191: 20, L215: 28, L1306: 2, and L191: 21 (negated). For an exclamation, see L215: 17 (*yā ṣāhiban*) in an evocation of the personified youth, describing his departure (17–18) with the poet's weeping and mourning of him (19, 17, 21). For lamentations, see L215: 21, 32 (*lahfī li-*), L191: 61 (*fa-yā asafā wa-yā jazaʿā ʿalayhī wa-yā ḥazanā*). When a lamentation is unvocalized and combined with the particle *yā*, e.g. *yā ṣāḥibā* 'Alas for my friend', it is indistinguishable from an impersonal vocative, *yā ṣāḥiban* 'O friend': see Wright 1896–8, ii: 93–4. The ambiguity might be intended and could be interpreted as a hopeless or failed apostrophe. For the curse, see previous note.

50 For a quote of evoked personae, see L191: 27 below. For a quote of the poet, see L191: 21 'Nights when I did not say "May rain refresh a [former] time"' (*layāliya lam aqul saqyan li-ʿahdin*).

51 L191: 30. For the general 'you', see chapter 9.

52 Naṣṣār and Salīm offer the variant *kafāka bi-l-tashbībi dhanban* 'Composing love poetry is enough sin for you', anticipating the sin (*dhanb*) referred to in verses 28 and 30. But the poet's real sin is his age, not his composing of love poetry, lest he could not claim innocence in verse 28. The separation is one from women and life, as already mentioned in verse 15.

53 See, e.g. L191: 31–64, L215: 60–72, L1042: 63–6, 68, L1611: 1–9, 78–81, 97–103, and L1250': 1–38, 175–7, 180–5, 189.

54 For lamentations, see L215: 32, L191: 61; for invocations, L191: 20, L215: 28, 30; for address of the general 'you', L191: 30.

55 L191: 31–59 and the next quote.

56 Booth 1983, 162. See for example Browning's 'Rabbi Ben Ezra' (1874, 94, stanzas 15–17):

> Youth ended, I shall try
> My gain or loss thereby;
> Be the fire ashes, what survives is gold:
> And I shall weigh the same,
> Give life its praise or blame:
> Young, all lay in dispute; I shall know, being old.

For note, when evening shuts,
A certain moment cuts
The deed off, calls the glory from the gray:
A whisper from the west
Shoots – 'Add this to the rest,
Take it and try its worth: here dies another day.'

So, still within this life,
Though lifted o'er its strife,
Let me discern, compare, pronounce at last,
'This rage was right i' the main,
That acquiescence vain:
The Future I may face now I have proved the Past.'

57 L1250': 39–45.
58 Naṣṣār's *annā* has been emended to *annī*.
59 Naṣṣār's var. أصبح, not أضحى, fits the meter.
60 For *ilmām* as 'a short call, visit of lovers', see *WKAS* ii: 1321a.
61 For a calm monologue, see L434: 1–11 (closing with an admonition to patience, 11); for a grieving one, see L191: 31–64 (in eight episodes connected by anaphora) and 1250': 44–56 (also with anaphora, connecting images and episodes); and for a remorseful one, see L1250': 15–38.
62 For present old age, see L1611: 1–9; For *fakhr* of the past, see L1611: 77–81, 96–103.
63 L215: 60–72.
64 See chapter 4, notes 24 and 25.
65 L191: 172–89.
66 L191: 118–22, 164–71 and L1042: 63–6 and 68.
67 L191: 118–22.
68 L1042: 46–66, 68 (suffering due to the patron) and L191: 164–70 (due to loyalty).
69 In L1042: 68. See also the dialogue scene L191: 171–5.
70 Cf. L994: 20–31, cited earlier in this chapter.
71 L994: 85. See also verses 43–4 of the next quote. The hyperbolic dialogues are L994: 84–94, L1307: 39–47, L191: 136–50.
72 For the interlocutor's address, see the double exclamation 'How splendid' (*lillāhi*, L1307: 42) and the dedication 'Take it (sc. the *qaṣīda*)' (*dūnakahā*, 47). For his naming 'O son of the noblest' (*yā bna l-akramīna*), see the congratulation L994: 84.
73 For *shāhiq* as 'high mountain, building, or other object', see *Lis* x: 192a.
74 On the switch from the first to the second person, see van Gelder 1983 and chapter 3, notes 38 and 39.
75 For the poet as sinner, see L191: 29 ('They counted white hair as a man's sin' *iʿtadadna l-shayba dhanban ʿalā rajulin*). For the poet as an apostate, see L1250': 25–7 ('The argument of him who returns to white hair is null and void .... What is the excuse for him who does not return to God?' *dahaḍat ḥujjatu l-munībi ilā l-shaybi ... ayyu ʿudhrin li-tāʾibin lā ilā llāhi*). For the poet as a disempowered husband, see L1042: 62 ('How many a favor was obstinate [like an obstinate wife], and you (sc. ʿUbaydallāh) softened her towards her husband' *wa-kam nashaṣat min niʿmatin fa-ʿaṭaftahā ʿalā baʿlihā*).
76 For the poet's lost youth, see L1307: 8–9 ('Fate knows youth in people as a garb... So it robs it from them' *laqad ʿalima l-dahru anna l-shabāba thawbun ladā l-nāsi ... fa-yaslubuhū salaban*). The verse's *mutaqārib* meter is corrupt and Naṣṣār's ending *lā ka-l-saraq* could be emended to *fa-yaslubuhū salaban ka-l-saraq*. For the poet's decrepitude, see L1611: 275 ('What is the excuse of him who meets you (sc. ʿUbaydallāh) with a decrepit appearance?' *wa-mā ʿudhru man yalqāka wa-l-ʿarḍu adsamū*).

77 The complaining poet is designated as 'your neighbor' *jāruka* in L1307: 43–5. For the poet rejecting the charge of envy, see L1250': 178 ('When an envious one is free of ill-will, he takes the form of a love-maddened lover' *wa-idhā ḥāsidun ṣafā min ghalīlin fa-hwa fī wazni ʿāshiqin mustahāmī*).

78 See chapter 13.

79 L1611: 51–5, as 'he who enjoys' (*dhū l-lahwi*), in an episode introduced in the first person (49), partially quoted and discussed in pp. 220–5.

80 The hero and his camel, he guiding her and she trotting with him, move in unison, like the point and shaft of a driven spear.

81 Literally, her saddle, including the utensils carried in it; cf. L994: 24. Cf. *WKAS* ii: 1512b.

9 THE EPISODE AND ITS WITNESSES

1 See fig. 2, p. 34.

2 Cf. L1611: 82–96.

3 Wehr 1951, 122.

4 Cf. chapter 2, notes 23 and 24, referring to vocative and rhetorical question. Van Gelder (1983, 24–5) mentions the hearer's refreshment among the goals of *iltifāt*. For the exact distribution of the witnesses, especially in L191 and L215, see Appendix C.

5 Verbs of perception or mental activity in the imperative, indicative, or conditional.

6 Hess-Lüttich's criteria of 'scheme of action' and 'orientation' (chapter 3, note 50) replace Jakobson's 'functions' of speech.

7 L215: 142–3, L434: 26–7, L1250': 113–14, and L1307: 23–31.

8 For examples of *fakhr*, see the strophe of L1611; for *madīh*, the antistrophes of L434, L1250' (with 'you'), L1307 (with 'you' and 'we'), and L1611 (with all three and further witnesses).

9 For the women, see L1041: 1–13 ('I' in verse 1); for the cupbearer, L1611: 19–55 ('I' in verses 19, 28–9, 44–5, 49–50, beginning each episode); for wine, see L1611: 10–18 (implicit speaker and *wa-rubba* in verse 10). For the *nāqa* in an independent comparison with an oryx bull, see L1250': 72–105 ('I' at the beginning, 73, and end, 103–5); for the *nāqa* in a nocturnal desert ride, see L1611: 82–96 ('I' at the beginning, 82, 84, and end, 94–5). For the hunt, see 1611: 56–76 ('we' in verses 56, 60–3, 71–3, 75–6).

10 *Fa-innī ḍāminun* (1611: 171), *ʿajibtu* (189), *ḥalaftu* (203–4), *ʿalimtuka* (223).

11 e.g. the message of L1611 and the antistrophes of L994, L1042.

12 For 'we' in dialogue with the Ṭāhirids, see L994: 21, L1042: 37; in dialogue with ʿUbaydallāh, see L1611: 211, in an episode with him, L215: 87, 90. For 'we' in dialogue with ʿAmr b. Layth, see L1611: 147–50.

13 L1611: 28–9 and L215: 4.

14 L1611: 60–72 with both 'I' in verse 56, and 'you' (var. 'I'), in verse 61.

15 L1611: 147–50, L215: 87, 90, and L1307: 12.

16 L1307: 12–31, L215: 87–102, and L191: 136–50.

17 Dramatized bystanders, supplicants, competitors, or enemies fulfill this function in scenes.

18 But see the responding and commenting 'you' in L1611: 114.

19 Cf. also van Gelder 1983.

20 *Sabab* also means 'motive'. Note Naṣṣār's var. *dafaq* 'that overflows'.

21 L994: 62 (*tilkumū*), A694: 15 (*nāhīka*), L215: 100 (*ḥīna taṭṭalibuh*).

22 L215: 100 (*yurā*), L1611: 94 (*yukhālu*), L994: 1, L1611: 94 (*tus'alu*). See also L1611: 110 for the less formulaic *mina l-aryaḥiyyāti llatī tumtarā l-nadā*.

23 See p. 51.

24 Cf. Benveniste (1966, i: 252–3), 'The definition [of the personal pronoun] can then be refined as follows: *I* is "the individual, uttering the present instance of speech that contains the linguistic instance *I*". Hence by introducing the situation of "addressing" one obtains a symmetrical definition for *you* as "the individual addressed by the present instance of speech that contains the linguistic instance *you*".'

25 Benveniste 1966, i: 254–5.

26 For perception of mirages and sandstorm, see L1611: 101 (*tarā l-āla fīhā*). For perception of the patron's handsomeness, sound judgment, good and evil, see L215: 100 (*ḥīna taṭṭalibuh*); for his individual fame as needing no tribal affiliation, see L215: 142 ('Indicate him by [virtue of] himself' *udlul ʿalayhi bihī*); for his scholarship, see L434: 26 (*wa-lasta tulāqī ʿāliman*); for his deeds for people as evident without speech, see L1611: 127 (*tabayyantahū fīhim wa-lam yatakallamū*); for his closing of any irreparable breach, see L1250': 114 (*idhā qulta lāta ḥīna lti'āmī*); for his giving everything its due weight, see L1250': 121 (*lā tarāhū yakhiffu*).

27 For women's slender waists, see L1042: 8 (*wa-mā shi'ta min qubbi l-buṭūni khamā'iṣī*); for their injustice and lack of mercy, see L191: 30 (*mā laka ʿinda ... min matābī*, a section closure). For the patron's stunning generosity, see L215: 114 (*yuʿṭīka ... fawqa mā kunta minhu taḥtasibuh*); for his popularity, even among the jealous, see L434: 15 (*matā sā'alta nāfisa ḥaẓẓihim ... bakhbakhā*); for the patron as everyone's goal, see L1611: 132 (*ilā ayyi mā fīhī qaṣadta ḥasabtahū huwa l-gharaḍu*); for him as an excellent model of praise, see A694: 15 (*nāhīka min muṭran*); for his tidings (var. *thanāhu* 'his praise') as tasting and sounding sweet, see L1250': 179 (*lasta tadrī nathāhu aḥlā madhāqan*).

28 See pp. 103–4.

29 For wine's effect and color, see L1611: 16 (*bāta minhū taḥta khaddika miʿṣamū*) and L1611: 12 (*wa-in badat li ʿaynayka*). For the oryx, see L1611: 60–1 (*ra'aytahā tuʿaṣfiruhā muthʿanjirātun*). For the horse, see L1611: 73 (*takhāluhū ṭilā'an*).

30 For the oryx, see L1250': 80 (*fa-tarāhā ka'annahā khaṭṭu lāmī*); for the desert sounds, see L1611: 94 (*tukhālu bihā ...* [*var. yukhālu*]).

31 For the fire of war, see L434: 27 (*lam tara nāran*, a section closure); for his two fires, see L191: 92 (*lahū nārāni ... tarā kiltayhimā dhāta ltihābī* 'He has two fires ... either of them you see burning', a section closure); for his munificence, see L215: 23 (*taẓallu matā ṣāfaḥta asrāra kaffihī tamassu ʿuyūnan*), a rather dead metaphor; for the camels, see L1611: 247 (*lā tarā qalūṣan ... tugharramū*).

32 For the women, see L994: 2 (*wa-lan tarā budūran badat laysa lahunna ḥanādisū*); for the wine, see F952: 15 (*wa-mā kāna jismu l-nāri jismun tulāmisuh*).

33 Cf. further uses of *tarā* for comparison (L1250': 80), metaphor (L434: 27, L994: 2) and personification, e.g. of mirage (L1611: 101) and camels (L1611: 247).

34 L1611: 254 (*ḥattā qīla lī anta mulhamū*).

35 L1611: 250 (*wa-in ẓami'at qālat lahā l-nafsu shammirī fa-ʿinda bni ʿAbdillāhi ʿiddun qalaydhamū*).

36 L1611: 63 (*ʿarrij fa-hādhā l-mukhayyamū*).

37 For the scenes, see L1611: 146–204; for fantastic action, see chapter 13.

38 L994: 21–30.

39 For a similar combination, see L1042: 37–40 and, in expanded form, L1611: 145–204.

40 Cf. fig. 3, p. 35. For the criteria, see chapter 3, note 50.

10 'THE PASSION OF HIM WHOSE PARTING HAS GRAYED IS AFFECTATION' (L191)

1 Cf., however, the strophes of L215, L1306, L1307, and L1250', which also contain episodes.

2 For one interlocutor with a changing viewpoint, see the dialogue with 'a friend' (*khill*) in L215: 35–59.

3 *Māḍin aḥabba ilayya min bardi l-sharābī*, 11; *ḥubbu nafsī, ṣāḥibu ladhdhatī*, 14; *shaqīqu ʿayshī*, 16; *al-shabāb*, 10, 18, 62; *al-shabība* 20, 32).

4 'We' stands for 'I and my time of youth'.

5 The strophe of L215 is structured as follows:

I: Monologue an old age (1–8);
II: Evocation of the cruel beloved (9–14), dialogue with the spy (15–16); evocation of the departed beloved (17–21); dialogue across time with the abode of youth (22–7); evocation of the time of youth (28–34); dialogue with a friend (35–59);
III: Monologue on the ethics of *madīḥ* (60–72).

6 On the timeframe of the monologue, see pp. 139–40 and 144, fig. 7.

7 *Laqad rajjaytu* (120), *alladhī ammaltu* (121).

8 Al-Jurjānī *Dalāʾil*, 200 and Weisweiler 1958, 81 and 101–2.

9 Petöfi and Kayser (1978, 3) include the verbal mood within 'the world-constitutive component' of a direct speech act.

10 For negated jussive, see *fa-lā aṣdur* (120), *wa-lā yakun* (121); for negated conditional, see *wa-lawlāhū lammā ḥannat qilāṣī* (165), *wa-lā arʿat* (166), *wa-lā alifat* (167), *wa-lā bariḥat* (168).

11 Cf. Jacobi 1971, 78–85, Wagner 1987–8, i: 108–15, Bauer 1992, i: 72.

12 The pre-Islamic message *qaṣīda* is discussed by Jacobi 1971, 103–4. For parallels between the introductory formulae of messages and *madīḥ*, see ibid., 81; and for the formulae's style, ibid., 82.

13 On his message phrase, see p. 65, and on the persona of the messenger, pp. 103–4. Ibn al-Rūmī's third message (L1611: 146–204) is addressed to ʿAmr b. Layth. For felicitations as messages, see F986 and A464.

14 For syntactical figures and recurring motifs, see chapter 12.

15 Benveniste 1966, i: 263–5, Petöfi and Kayser 1978, 19. Benveniste's subjectivity marker combines Petöfi and Kayser's performative-modal and world-constitutive components of the direct explicit speech act, Benveniste's true utterance corresponds with their descriptive component.

16 De Man 1979, 131.

17 See also 'Are you not the one who attacks fate?' *a-lasta lladhī yuʿdī ʿalā l-dahri* (L1611: 206), which precedes a statement of ʿUbaydallāh's legitimacy as governor. For the rhetorical question, see al-Jurjānī *Dalāʾil*, 111–21 and Weisweiler 1958, 80 and 84–6. According to him, interrogative *ʾa-* followed by a perfect or imperfect verb is a rhetorical question expecting confirmation (*taqrīr*) and when followed by a noun, a reproach (*tawbīkh*) expecting denial (*inkār*). The imperfect verb with future meaning negates either the following verb or noun. Regarding the psychological intention, Weisweiler paraphrases al-Jurjānī, 'Der tiefere Sinn dieses Bestreitens besteht darin, den Befragten zum Nachdenken zu bewegen, ihn zu beschämen und mundtot zu machen, weil er etwas tun zu können behauptet hat, was er nicht tun kann'; ibid., 85. Cf. also al-ʿAskarī *Ṣināʿatayn*, 450 [*'faṣl al-khabar wa-l-waṣf fī ṣūrat al-istifhām'*] and Kanazi 1989, 188–9, with *istifhām* as a new figure of *badīʿ*. Kanazi further mentions Ibn Qutayba's division of *ʾa-* into *taqrīr* (rhetorical question) and *tawbīkh* (reproach) in his *Mushkil* (ibid.).

18 *Jābī* refers normally to a tax collector, i.e. the patron is the only one rightfully deserving praise. The result of this collection is *madīḥ*.

19 For this interpretation of the recurring rain motif, see chapter 12.

20 On the patron's share in the praise, see also chapter 16.

21 Unredeemed praise becomes satire in L215: 71–2 and motivates it in L1042: 57–8.

22 The context (156) supports the reading of future lies for other patrons; alternatively the leaving (*takadhdhubiya l-madā'iḥa*, 155) could be seen as the poet's recanting his earlier praises of ʿUbaydallāh.
23 Cf. *WKAS* ii: 878.
24 *Nuhā* means both 'tent-peg' and 'reason'. Throwing down the saddlebags at the tent hook and dismounting from the mount of vanity is an image for the poet's relinquishing youthful love. The analogy bifurcates at the homonym *nuhā*. The image is an exhausted rider throwing down his bag and dismounting in order to pitch a tent. The topic is the poet, abandoning youthful vanity for reason. The matching elements in topic and image, mount and vanity, are brought together in a genitive metaphor. The homonym *nuhā* operates on both levels.
25 The heart-piercing glances of the beloved.
26 The beloved's fatal arrows (glances) evoke the Koranic parallel of God's inescapable fire (punishment) attaining the sinners' hearts in Sūrat al-Humaza 104/6–7 'The Fire of God kindled / roaring over the hearts' (*nāru llāhi l-mūqada / allatī taṭṭaliʿu ʿalā l-afʾida*).
27 Of the revenge.
28 From *ʿadana* 'to dwell'; thence the phrase *jannātu ʿadnin* 'gardens of perpetual abode' for paradise; see *AEL* ii: 1876b.
29 The sun's 'hiding behind the veil' is a Koranic allusion to the moment when Solomon realizes his erroneous preference of worldly goods over the remembrance of God and repents. His return can be seen as a parallel to the poet's realization of his age and repenting for former youthful folly. Cf. Sūrat Ṣād 38/31–2 'When in the evening were presented to him the standing steeds, / he said, "Lo, I have loved the love of good things better than the remembrance of my Lord, until the sun was hidden behind the veil"' (*idh ʿuriḍa ʿalayhi bi-l-ʿashiyyi l-ṣāfinātu l-jiyād / fa-qāla innī aḥbabtu ḥubba l-khayri ʿan dhikri rabbī ḥattā tawārat bi-l-ḥijāb*).
30 Other meanings of *sarāh* (pl. *sarawāt*): (a) back, highest part, mountain; (b) the middle of the day; and (c) a wide tract of land; see *AEL* i: 1355–6.
31 Other meanings of *ḥabāb*: (a) utmost (*ḥabābuka*); (b) mass of water, bubbles, dewdrops; see *AEL* i: 497.
32 Cf. al-Buḥturī's poem on al-Mutawakkil's lake, *Dīwān*, iv: 2418, no. 915: 19.
33 The wind, carrying heavy rain clouds, is compared to a mount carrying a rider.
34 *Shahāb* equals exactly two-thirds of water and one-third of milk.
35 After literal rashness as synonym of foolishness has been denied in the preceding verse, rashness is reinterpreted as a mature man's boldness. Cf. also a reinterpretation of jealousy, L1250': 175–8.
36 *Maksir* (pl. *makāsir*) 'inner quality'; see *WKAS* i: 186.
37 'Lizard eater' is a (usually pejorative) attribute of Arab Bedouins as opposed to Iranian city dwellers. The reading *yumīru* (root *m-w-r*) 'to stir up' is preferred to *yamīru* (root *m-y-r*) 'to feed'. Salīm explains the meaning as a viper shedding pieces of skin (*saḥīf*) that provide bait for the hunters of lizards.
38 Literally, 'without climbing the backs of grave sins or riding them'. *Irtakaba* 'to ride (a mount), to commit (a sin)', is used in the second meaning, but the first establishes a (rather flat) verbal metaphor in formal unity with 'climbing the backs'.
39 Salīm's *niqāb* (s. *naqb*): (a) mountain pass; (b) breach, hole; Naṣṣār's *thiqāb* 'tinder, fuel' does not fit.
40 Ibn al-Rūmī uses this image also in L1611: 133–4 and, in more detail, in the encomium for ʿAlī b. Yaḥyā b. al-Munajjim (*Dīwān* v: 2055–70, no. 1600: 57–81). The fairly abstract image combines the patron, collecting glorious deeds with his firm resolve, as a topic, and a firmly-twisted wire, stringing precious pearls, as an image. Cf. also the ancestors as a necklace, L215: 101–2.

41 Read *mithla*.
42 The cooking utensils allude to those of fantastic size made by the *jinn* for Solomon, 'fashioning for him whatsoever he would – places of worship, statues, porringers like water-troughs, and anchored cooking-pots' (*yaʿmalūna lahū mā yashāʾu min maḥārība wa-tamāthīla wa-jifānin ka-l-jawābi wa-qudūrin rāsiyātin*; Sūrat Saba' 34/13).
43 To *ʿalā* with *ajāra*, cf. *yujīru wa-lā yujāru ʿalayhi* 'He protects but none is protected against him'; *AEL* i: 483.
44 Perhaps derived from the literal meaning 'Dust on me!' *haban* < *habāʾ*.
45 *Ghayri kābī* literally 'not failing to produce fire'.
46 Salīm; Naṣṣār: *taḥrumunī*.
47 Cf. L191: 152 and L1042: 67.
48 The Koranic allusion of 'ashes on which the wind blows' compares the poet's unrewarded work with the work of unbelievers annihilated by God, 'The likeness of those who disbelieve in their Lord: their works are as ashes, whereon the wind blows strong upon a tempestuous day; they have no power over that they have earned' (*mathalu lladhīna kafarū bi-rabbihim aʿmāluhum ka-ramādini shtaddat bihī l-rīḥu fī yawmin ʿāṣifin lā yaqdirūna mimmā kasabū ʿalā shayʾin*; Sūrat Ibrāhīm 14/18)
49 Cf. L191: 123.
50 Var. Salīm; Naṣṣār: *jāwazta*.
51 This recalls the image from verses 116–19.
52 A Koranic allusion of the distance between Muḥammad and a divine vision, described as 'two bows'-length away, or nearer' (*qāba qawsayni aw adnā*; Sūrat al-Najm 53/9).
53 *Nabʿa*: (a) a tree with very hard wood; (b) noble origin.
54 Cf. also L191: 164–71 and L434: 34–5.

11 'THEY AIMED AT MY HEART FROM THE GAPS OF VEILS' (L1042)

1 Cf. Jacobi 1971, 27–35.
2 *Waṣwāṣ* (pl. *waṣāwiṣ*, *waṣāwīṣ*) here means face veil, not curtain hole; cf. the parallel L191: 41 (*ramat qalbī ... min khalali l-niqābī*).
3 For the first case, see F1122: 30-46.
4 For the subjects, see verse 20 (*mā man raʾā ... bi-mustankirin*); for God, verse 31 (*bi-kum naʿasha llāhu l-khilāfata*).
5 For direct agency, see verse 38 (*bihī allafa llāhu l-qulūba*); for indirect agency, see verse 36 (*fa-jāsa ... ʿuqra diyārihā*), alluding to Sūrat al-Isrā' 17/5, 'So, when the promise of the first of these [corruptions of the Children of Israel] came to pass, We sent against you servants of Ours, men of great might, and they went through the habitations, and it was a promise performed' (*fa-idhā jāʾa waʿdu ūlāhumā baʿathnā ʿalaykum ʿibādan lanā ulī baʾsin shadīdin fa-jāsū khilāla l-diyāri wa-kāna waʿdan mafʿūlā*).
6 Verses 32 (*ghabrāʾu ... wa-dāḥisu*) and 34 (*jinnatu l-nafri*).
7 Verse 38 (*wa-mā zāla minkum li-l-khilāfati midrahun*).
8 *Maḍā* means both 'to cut' and 'to flow'.
9 Verse 74 (*raʾā l-shiʿra dīwāna l-makārimi*).
10 Cf. the *madīḥ* for Ismāʿīl b. Bulbul, *Dīwān*, vi: 235–7, no. 1302: 87–8.
11 The second person ending of the demonstrative, here in the masculine plural variant (Fischer § 275, note 2, Ullmann 1984, 811), is only a pale and implicit designation of an addressee, but it gains force in the context of the poem's consistent address of groups.
12 For the patron enabling his poet to speak, cf. also L1611: 252.
13 This includes a rendition of the sword metaphor (L994: 40 and 57, L1042: 31–3) and a parallel hemistich on Ṭāhir's rescue of the caliphate (L994: 32, L1042: 17).

14 Verse 16 (*bi-kum ḥīṣa fatqu l-mulki*).
15 See above p. 162.
16 Ibn al-Muʿtazz *Badīʿ*, 62.
17 One may also understand *wa-fīkum kullu fārisi buhmatin* (21) more precisely as all Ṭāhirids except ʿUbaydallāh, who has not yet been mentioned, and, when he appears is described differently. This reading would exclude him altogether from the ancestral praise.
18 Emendation of Naṣṣār's *as'alu* to *as'al(i)*.
19 For the perfect, see verses 63 (*fa-aṭaʿtuhū, mā khiftu*), 64 (*aṣbaḥa sirbālī ... ḍayyiqan*), and 65 (*mā tamākhaṣtu bādinan*); for the conditional, see verse 52 (*lawlā dawāʾī mawaddatī raḥaltu*); for the jussive, see verse 66 (*fa-lā akuni l-muhrīqa faḍlata mā'ihī*).
20 In L191, it appears as negated jussive in the monologue, outside of the patron's presence (120).
21 Verse 67 (*wa-lā tabkhasannī ḥaqqa madḥī*) infers the poet's right, whereas 191: 117 (*fa-lā tadaʿanna rifdaka dūna qadrī*) only infers his rank.
22 Note the indicative mood of the question *a-yaẓlimunī*? In L1042: 68.
23 The translation does not reflect the *double entrendre* of *najr*, 'hue' and 'origin'.
24 Emendation of Naṣṣār's *muqīmu* to *muqīmun*, fitting the meter.
25 Naṣṣār's var. *majālis* is chosen over *maḥāsin*, 'ornate [courtyards]', which occurs two verses later.
26 The mock escape and attack are compared with the zigzagging motion of weaving.
27 Cf. al-Nābigha al-Dhubyānī, *wa-fī l-waghā ḍayramun fī ṣūrati l-qamari*, and Muslim b. al-Walīd, *ka'anna fī sarjihī badran wa-ḍirghāmā*; al-ʿAskarī *Dīwān*, 20.
28 The visibility of these worms in a pond indicates its low water-level. The image implies a diminishing of the patron's generosity.
29 Cf. *WKAS* ii: 1071a.
30 Var. *mulāwiṣun*, 'a planning, scheming [man]'.
31 Cf. Sūrat al-Mā'ida 6/3 'Forbidden to you are carrion ...' (*ḥurrimat ʿalaykumū l-maytatu ...*).
32 *Ṣaṭmun, ṣaṭamun*, 'firm, perfect, completely paid [sum]'; *Lis* xii: 332.
33 Emendation of Naṣṣār's *ʿawāliṣ*, which is unattested in the active first form, to *ʿawākiṣ* from *ʿakaṣa* 'to reject a man, deprive him of his need'; *Lis* vii: 57.
34 Cf. Sūrat al-Baqara 2/282 '... So let him (sc. the scribe) write, and let the debtor dictate, and let him fear God his Lord and not diminish aught of it ...' (*fa-l-yaktub wa-l-yumlili lladhī ʿalayhi l-ḥaqqu wa-l-yattaqi llāha rabbahū wa-lā yabkhas minhu shay'an*) and 7/85, 11/85, 26/183 among humans, and 11/15, 72/13 by God.

12 SUPPORTING FIGURES OF SPEECH

1 For anaphorae comprising motifs of grief and doubt in *al-shayb wa-l-shabāb*, see L1250': 48–56, L191: 31–49, and Schoeler 1974, 171–4; for *fakhr*, see L191: 165–8, describing the poet's metaphorical camels ('If it were not for him, my sturdy camels would not be yearning ... Nor would they spare ... Nor would they be accustomed ... Nor would they cease ...' *wa-lawlāhū la-mā ḥannat qilāṣī ... wa-lā arʿat ... wa-lā alifat ... wa-lā bariḥat ...*); for questions, see L191: 136 and 138 ('Are you not the man ...?' *a-lasta l-mar'a*).
2 Emendation of Naṣṣār's *mustakhiffāt* to the passive.
3 *Uṭm* (pl. *āṭām*) 'fortress, high house in a city esp. in Yemen'; *Lis* xii: 19–20. *Fasīla* (pl. *fasīl, fasā'il*) 'small palm tree, palm shoot'; al-Fīrūzābādī *Qāmūs* iv: 30. The whole expression seems to imply farmers and city dwellers, perhaps of the Sawād.
4 Var. *allatī* for *alladhī*, both Naṣṣār.

5 Similarly L1250': 133–4 ('The one with the clear eloquence ... The one with the moist (sc. generous) palm' *dhū l-bayāni l-mubīni ... dhū l-yadi l-tharrati*) and L1250': 160–1 ('Delegations of request ... delegations of greeting and gratitude' *fa-wufūdu l-su'āli ... wa-wufūdu l-salāmi wa-l-shukri*).

6 This lance was carried for instance by ʿUbaydallāh in the caliphal procession on the occasion of the sacrificial feast (ʿĪd al-Aḍḥā) in 251/866; cf. al-Ṭabarī *Ta'rīkh*, x: 1638–9 and Yarshater 1985–, xxxv: 104.

7 Except for verse 121. In verse 127, *allatī* is omitted by poetic license.

8 For metaphors, combined with the general 'you', see L1307: 25–31; for hyperbolae, see L1250': 110–13 ('he is ...' *wa-hwa ... fa-hwa ...*).

9 *Sabab* 'a strong rope by means of which one ascends and descends', *AEL* ii: 1285.

10 Figuratively speaking, his personified ranks let their horses go at full gallop.

11 Similarly in L191: 31–49, see note 1.

12 Literally, 'ratified destiny', *AEL* i: 196a.

13 Al-Ḥaṭīm is the semi-circular wall north-west of the Kaaba, Zamzam the fountain next to it.

14 Nassār's *umūra bi-ʿaynihī* is emended to *amīra*.

15 Cf. the speech of objects in chapter 6.

16 Cf. also L1611: 56–7.

17 For morphological parallelism, see L1250': 130–1 ('Wearing refinement and weapon ... Cutting in heart and tongue (sc. determined and eloquent) ...' *ḥāmilu l-ẓarfi wa-l-silāḥi ... ṣārimu l-qalbi wa-l-lisāni*). For syntactic parallelisms, see L994: 96–100 ('To you I called ... To you [rhymes] called me ... I came to you ... crossing ... I called ... and I composed' *ilayka dhaʿartu ... ilayka tadāʿatnī ... ataytuka ... ujāwizu ... daʿawtu ... fa-allaftu*). Other parallelisms gather attributes of the patron into the image of a horse race ('A thoroughbred ... Coming first ... Reaching,' *Jawādun ... sabūqun ... laḥūqun*, L1611: 200–3) or stations of pilgrimage ('Hope of the hopeful ... Qibla of the hopeful ... Haven of the fearful,' *amalu l'āmilīna ... qiblatu l-āmilīna ... maʿqilu l-khā'ifīna*, L1250': 139–43).

18 Except for one feminine plural adjective (*kawāmin*).

19 Alternate meaning: 'faces [of petitioners]'.

20 See especially the Umayyad praise *qaṣīda*, Jacobi 1982, 16.

21 L215: 144–9.

22 Praise of individual achievements (e.g. good rulership and moral virtues) and hyperbolic praise.

23 This mathematical way of proof is similar to the above effect of the reprise, since it starts by stating the equation to be proven, undertakes the proof in reverse direction and ends with 'what had to be proven' as the result.

24 Cf. also the admonition A111 (*Dīwān*, i: 150) of the patron's brother and predecessor Muḥammad b. ʿAbdallāh b. Ṭāhir (d. 253/867).

25 For exclamation, see L1611: 71 and 105; for rhetorical question, L191: 6 and L1250': 28; for apostrophe, L191: 19 and L1250': 43 (imperatives).

26 L215: 16, 38, 42, 54–5, 56–7, and 69, L434: 9, L994: 70 and 106, L1306: 7, L1250': 45 and 147. All of these close scenes, except L994: 70 and L1611: 31, which conclude episodes. For combinations of sententia with exclamation, see L191: 7, 18 and 135, L215: 45, and L1611: 38; with rhetorical question, L1611: 235–6 (including the answer); and with apostrophe, L191: 30, 43.

27 For human activities, see L215: 59 (archer); L1611: 31 (judge); for objects, see L215: 46, and L1611: 43 (arrow); L215: 44, L994: 52, L1611: 96 (sword); L1611: 133–4 and L1600: 56–7 (threaded pearls); L1611: 128 (musk); for plants, see L215: 3 (tree); L191: 64 and L215: 33 (branch); L215: 47 (trunk); L191: 67 (palm tree); for animals, see L191: 110–12 (camels); L215: 39–40 (fox, lion, bustard, falcon); L215: 69 and

122–4 (horse); and for natural phenomena, see L191: 113–15 (shower); L1611: 8–9 (nocturnal dream); and 1250': 144–8 (meat, water).

28 For a combination of analogy with rhetorical question, see L215: 42, 67, and L1611: 128; with direct address, L215: 214; and with apostrophe, L215: 44 (imperative).

29 Al-ʿAskarī *Ṣināʿatayn* 434–7 (for the quotes, see ibid., 434–5) and Kanazi 1989, 178–80. For the quote, see Abū Tammām *Dīwān*, i: 88–9, no. 4: 32–3.

30 Var. *Dīwān: aqāṣiyahum*, 'their furthest ones'.

31 Al-Jurjānī *Asrār*, 101–3 on the psychological impact of the analogy (*tamthīl*, translated by Ritter as Gleichnis). Cf. also, in philosophical poetics, the 'rhetorical analogy' (*al-tamthīl al-khiṭābī*) used by al-Qarṭājannī (Heinrichs 1969, 1980 [translation] and Schoeler 1983, 58–60). For the quote, see al-Buḥturī *Dīwān*, i: 248–9, no. 81: 27–8.

32 Var. *Dīwān: fī l-ʿulā.*

33 Var. *Dīwān: jiddu qarībī.*

34 As a unit for gold, a *qinṭār* equalled 42,3 kilograms or 10,000 *dīnārs*. As a weight measure, it equalled 100 *raṭls*, amounting to 130 weight *dirhams* of 406.25 grams, or sometimes the double of that (100 *manns*), in early medieval Baghdad. However, many different kinds of *qinṭārs* existed, varying between 45 and 228 kilograms, depending on the region and the merchandise; see Hinz 1955, 24–7 and 31. Regarding meat that stinks from not being cooked and shared as a metonymy for shame, see *WKAS* ii: 351.

35 Naṣṣār's var. *bukhl* 'avarice' fits better than his *dhull* 'humiliation', which would have to be interpreted as the consequence of showing avarice. *Bukhl* can also be understood as the '[label of] avarice', earned by such behavior.

36 Cf. also L215: 42 and L1611: 8–9, 31, 43, 128, and 133–4.

37 Or, '[the label of] avarice'.

38 According to the variant, 'the sickness of [the label of] avarice'.

39 Schoeler 1983, 60 and al-Jurjānī *Asrār* 245–6.

40 Heinrichs 1969, 187–91 and Schoeler 1983, 76–7.

41 Salīm explains *in* as a negation, 'Though about fate, his wondering has not ceased'. Cf. also Fischer 1972, §322.

42 Emending Naṣṣār, the *hamza* in *ahl* is elided *metri causa*.

43 Salīm; Naṣṣār, *mubayyinan* 'exposing'.

44 The accusative in *dā'a* is due to *mā al-ḥijāziyya*, Wright 1896–8, ii: 104–5 and Fischer 1972, §367, note 1.

45 Salīm; Naṣṣār: *ʿaqabuh* 'sinew'.

46 Literally, 'throw down the keys!' cf. *WKAS* ii: 1187b–88b.

47 Cf. *WKAS* ii: 1052b.

48 Literally, 'his absences offer each other his faults as presents', i.e. his absences encourage people to gossip about his faults.

49 Salīm; Naṣṣār's *khāṭī'ātihī* is a misprint.

50 The elevation of the figurative over the real disease echoes that of moral stench, or shame, over real stench; see p. 209 above.

51 Cf. also p. 208 for Abū Tammām's arrow image.

52 For the former, see L191: 98 and 110–13; for the latter, L191: 103–4, 118–19, 129, 133, and 161.

53 Respectively L191: 100–2 and 121–2.

54 *ʿIṣāb* literally means the tying of the camels thighs during milking.

55 Salīm; Naṣṣār: *taḥrumunī* and *mustaqillun* 'independent'.

56 Syntactic parallelism with verse 112a.

57 This is developed in a later episode of *fakhr* (157–63).

58 Salīm; Naṣṣār *ʿalā ṣaʿūdin* 'on an elevation'.

59 Cf. Wagner 1963, 440–1.

60 Alternatively, *mubaddā* signifies 'in the desert' as a denominative of *bādiya*. *Khaym* follows Salīm; Naṣṣār's *khiyam* (pl.) does not fit the gender of *mubaddā*. The verse may intend that masonry domes and flexible tents resist rain unharmed but mud-brick architecture suffers.
61 Salīm's vocalization. Naṣṣār's unvocalized text allows the reading *bi-jawdika* 'in your downpour'.
62 Note the paronomasia of cognate roots *dhahab* 'gold' and *dhihāb* (s. *dhihba*) 'drizzle'.
63 Salīm reads *ṭiyāb* as *ṭīb* meaning 'lawfulness' or 'a Basran species of date palms'; cf. al-Fīrūzābādī *Qāmūs*, i: 105.
64 Schoeler 1974, 174–5 and 181.
65 Ibid. 170–6 on L191: 47–60.

13 PHANTASMAGORIA

1 For a practical definition of *muḥdath* poetry, see Heinrichs 1986, 1. On mannerism, see Heinrichs 1974 and Sperl 1989, 155–80. Their concepts of it differ however, cf. p. 6, note 17 and p. 16.
2 For the manneristic styles, see Schoeler 1974, 180–203 and 232–4 with a discussion of Ritter and von Grunebaum; for the concrete style, see ibid., 174–5 (on L191).
3 Reinert 1990, 372–80 esp. 373.
4 This is the treatment of one semantic field, e.g. the female physique, with terms from another semantic field, e.g. fruit, leaving some of the original verbs in place, such as in L1611: 34–5. The result is an incoherence between the metaphors and their actions:

> Grapes of paradise (sc. hair) and apples of Eden (sc. cheeks)
> for which each soul pines longingly.
> Towards the two rise the bosom's pomegranates,
> which hyacinth and pearl strings conceal from the eye.

5 Heinrichs 1986, 3.
6 Paraphrase of Heinrichs 1986, 10–16.
7 Heinrichs 1986, 14. For the coinage of the term, see Heinrichs 1973, 63, 65, and 67.
8 I do not propose to explain the historical genesis of his metaphors, which only a motif-historical study can reveal; e.g. in a metaphor that is based on a simile and analogy simultaneously, it is often difficult to assess which type of comparison originally generated the metaphor.
9 See thematic overview in Appendix A.
10 For the *metaphora continuata*, see Schoeler 1974, 201–3; for a paradox in the patron, see L1611: 120–33.
11 For an overview of *khamriyya* themes, cf. Wagner 1987–8, ii: 34–46, esp. 42 and idem 1965, 289–308.
12 *Fīhā* could also refer to the *ḥabīb* as combining different natures; cf. verses 37–45.
13 Reading Naṣṣār's *murāʿā* as active part. *murāʿī*, parallel to *al-mustaṭʿim* in the second hemistich. For the participle construction, see Ullmann 1989, nos. 274–82.
14 Cf. L1250': 56, a description of young men as 'the best enhancement to life' *idāmun li-l-ʿayshi khayru idāmī*.
15 *mutawwam* is a denominative of *tūm* (s. *tūma*), a silver ear-ring in the shape of a bead. Al-Aʿshā uses it as an epithet for a male cupbearer:

يَطوفُ بها ساقٍ عَلَيْنا مُتَوَّمٌ   خَفيفٌ ذَفيفٌ ما يَزالُ مُفَدَّما

> An ear-ringed cupbearer makes it circle among us,
> svelte, nimble, [his mouth] covered with a cloth all the time.
> (*Dīwān*, 200, no. 55: 6)

In Ibn al-Rūmī's passage, the epithet marks the women as a musician. Her role as cupbearer is introduced only afterwards by the motif of the ewer.

16 Here, two or more terms occurring in one verse are repeated and briefly explained in the following verse in the same or a different order; see Qudāma *Naqd*, 142–4 and al-ʿAskarī *Ṣināʿatayn*, 355–7.

17 Cf. the comparison between a wine cup and a girl with pearl necklace or a gazelle-like boy (Wagner 1965, 303) and the combination of wine cup and gazelle-like women, (ibid., 308).

18 *Ghirbīb* alludes to the Sūra cited in note 21. The literal meaning is 'a species of excellent black grapes of Ṭāʾif'. Bunches of grapes (*ʿanāqīd*) commonly represent hair, as in this poem, verse 33.

19 *Muṭahham*: (a) 'fat'; (b) 'lean'; (c) 'perfect in plumpness and leanness'; cf. al-Fīrūzābādī *Qāmūs*, iv: 147.

20 The non-imaginary metaphor has a counterpart on the level of the topic, as opposed to the imaginary metaphor, which does not; cf. Heinrichs 1986, 3–7 and 9.

21 'Hast thou not seen that God sends down out of heaven water, and therewith We bring forth fruits of diverse hues? And in the mountains are streaks white and red, of diverse hues, and pithy black' (*a-lam tara anna llāha anzala mina l-samāʾi māʾan fa-akhrajnā bihī thamarātin mukhtalifan alwānuhā wa-mina l-jibāli judadun bīḍun wa-ḥumrun mukhtalifun alwānuhā wa-gharābību sūd*; Sūrat al-Malāʾika 35/27).

22 Cf. the arrow analogues above, pp. 208, 212, and 306, note 27.

23 For *mulaṭṭam* 'hit, struck (part of the body)' or 'place of slapping', see *WKAS* ii: 761a.

24 For *malṭam* normally 'cheek', see *WKAS* ii: 758a. Ullmann reads the verses as referring to the mouth. The larger context however, equates *malṭam* with *mufaddā, muḍarraj*, and *ṣaḥn*. It is also the cheek that fails to ransom its beauty and is later bitten by the eye (30). For the inverse interpretation of the *etyma*, see the satire H1243: 81–3 (*Dīwān* vi: 2350):

وَمَلثَمٍ يُظْلَمُ باسْمِ مَلْثَمِ
وَمَلْطَمٍ حَقَّ لهُ اسْمُ مَلْطَمِ
نِعْمَ العَتادُ لِحُضورِ المأْتَمِ

A mouth, unjustly named 'place to be kissed',
A cheek, deserving the name 'place of slapping',
What excellent utensils for attending a funeral!

For *maltham*, 'place to be kissed; lips, mouth', see *WKAS* ii: 199–20. The improper repetition of the rhyme word (*mulaṭṭam*) indicates a corrupt text.

25 Emendation of Naṣṣār's *yaẓalla* to *yaẓallu*.

26 They could also be non-imaginary metaphors, if they are thought of as actual blemishes in the cheek, which 'insult' the eye.

27 'He mixed into his speech logical terms and summed up their ideas and then detailed them in the best description and the smoothest wording' (*wa-yakhliṭu kalāmahū bi-alfāẓin manṭiqiyyatin yujmilu lahā l-maʿānī thumma yafṣiluhā bi-aḥsani waṣfin wa-aʿdhabi lafẓ*; al-Marzubānī *Muʿjam*, 145). Unfortunately, al-Marzubānī gives no examples for these logical terms.

28 For his criticism, see Ibn Rashīq *ʿUmda*, ii: 238, 'Ibn al-Rūmī hung on to ideas, being stingy with them. He used to take a single idea and paraphrase it, so that he did not stop turning it over and taking it through every aspect and level, until he killed it and knew that no flavor was left in it for anyone [else].' For praise of his originality, see ibid., i: 265 and 286, ii: 244–5, and Ibn Sharaf *Masāʾil*, 34.

29 Schoeler (1974, 187–200) on L1223: 1–45. Schoeler sees in the second style the ambition of outdoing other poets. Schoeler also describes another mannerist variant,

not represented in this corpus. In it, the poet jumps from one phenomenon to the next in the pursuit of exciting images, without relationship to the real world; see ibid., 180–7 on L956: 1–31 and ibid., 201–3 on L1302: 1–8. For the first style 'with little imagery', see note 2.

30 See pp. 53–4, 56–8.

31 Discussed on pp. 58–9.

14 IN THE MIRROR OF *MADĪḤ*

1 Booth 1961, 177–82.

2 Bencheikh 1975a, 29.

3 Bencheikh 1975b, 267–8 and Ibn Rashīq *ʿUmda*, ii: 109.

4 See his *Dīwān* 146, no. 51: 30–1 commented upon by Ibn Rashīq *ʿUmda*, i: 42.

5 For Marwān's *qaṣīda* on the deposition of al-Mustaʿīn and that of his son praising al-Muʿtazz, see Yarshater 1985–, xxxv: 117–21 and 134–6. On the attribution of the latter poem to Muḥammad, not his father, see *GAS* ii: 582. See also the *qaṣīda* by Muḥammad b. ʿAlī b. Qayd (or Fayd) al-Ṭāʾī (fl. third/ninth century) on the battle of 262/876 between Yaʿqūb b. Layth al-Ṣaffār and the caliphal army in ibid., xxxvi: 172–4 (cf. Sukkar 1419/1999, 367 no. 502); and the *qaṣāʾid* of Yaḥyā b. Muḥammad al-Aslamī and Yaḥyā b. Khālid b. Marwān on the victory of 270/883 by al-Muʿtamid's brother al-Muwaffaq over the Zanj in ibid., xxxvii: 140–3 (cf. Sukkar 1419/1999, 420–1, nos. 577 and 579).

6 Sourdel 1959–60, i: 328.

7 See chapter 8.

8 These elements include the reduction of a theme to a tension between two personae or attitudes (e.g. between former youth and old age); the delineation of a character through forms of address (e.g. the third versus second grammatical person; the construction of an argument throughout single or composite scenes; a simple, direct style; and supporting figures of speech).

9 For the speech acts of praise, see the latter part of chapter 5.

10 Boustany 1967, 350–4.

11 For their individual roles, see the latter part of chapter 7.

12 Ubaydallāh's preference for clear rational poetry is evident in his dispute with al-Buḥturī, see pp. 44 and 210.

13 On the poetry produced, see pp. 43–4, 52–9 and Boustany 1967, 147–8 whose numbers are superseded with Naṣṣār's complete *Dīwān* edition. Regarding ʿUbaydallāh's influence, e.g. his predilection for difficult rhyme, rare words, and excessive length, see above p. 44. See also F1373': 260–7, where the poet makes ʿUbaydallāh responsible for letting the *maʿānī* (motifs) of his excellence dominate his own rhyme and meter.

15 MUTUAL DUTIES AND RIGHTS OF BENEFACTOR AND PROTÉGÉ

1 The motifs of the firm bond (*ḥabl, al-ʿurwa al-wuthqā*, passim; *awākhī ṣidq*, L1611: 253) and the last refuge (*najwa*, L1306: 11; *manāṣ*, L1042: 68; *maʾāb*, L191: 173; *maḥall mumannaʿ*, L1611: 240; *shāhiq*, L1307: 44) are discussed pp. 105, 116–7, and 120. Cf. also the motif of sacrificing sleep in solving the supplicant's difficulties in L1307: 39–42 and L1250': 162. Particular duties and rights are not cross-referenced, as most of them recur in each poem containing this relationship.

2 For the motif of honor tied to the destruction of material wealth, see L994: 78, F1122: 10–13, F1243: 10 and 33–4 (admonition); for generosity as an armor in the defense of honor and the warding off of blame, see L191: 139–40, L1042: 45–6, L1307: 38,

L1611: 118, L1250': 144–8, and F1373': 250–3. For the motif of readily given riches as licit spoils, see L1611: 284 and passim.

3 e.g. L1250': 155–7.

4 F1243: 18–24 and E765.

5 Further virtues, such as *ḥimāya* (protection) and *difāʿ* (defense), fall under *shajāʿa*, while *injāz al-waʿd* (fulfillment of a promise) is a combination of *ʿaql* and *sakhāʾ* (generosity). See Qudāma *Naqd* 96–8.

6 On the motif of free men burdened or enslaved by good deeds, see F458: 63–4, F1369: 4–9, and S880; on the image of presents summoning men to gratitude, see S30: 2–3.

7 Cf. Mottahedeh's (1980, 72–8) description of the loyalty between individuals based on gratitude for benefits in the Būyid era. For a general treatment of the gift as a binding obligation, along with systems of liberality, honor, and money based on the exchange of gifts, see Mauss 1990, 8–46.

8 For the poet's entitlement, see also L1042: 68 and E1341. Poems containing this relationship alone are the metastrophes of L434: 34–5, L1307: 46–7, and L1250': 172–190. Poems that mix the relationship with that of the panegyrist and his model include L191: 96–150 and 157–75, L1042: 48–68, and L1611: 273–303. See in addition the felicitations F458: 39–70, F690: 9–15, F952: 43–56, F1122: 41–6, F1243: 9–38, and F1557: 6–8; the admonitions A674, A1160, A1241, A1368, and A1510; and the satire H1512.

9 For a poem devoted to squaring the accounts, see A464: 12–15; as a new (*mubdiʿ*) gift, E1137 and E1342; and as a reciprocation, F1243: 9.

10 Mottahedeh 1980, 78.

11 e.g. Sūrat al-Baqara 2/16 and 86, Sūrat Āl ʿImrān 3/177.

12 Emendation of Naṣṣār's *afḍāl* to *ifḍāl*.

13 This is negated in the patron's case in A1160: 18.

14 See A464 discussed in the next chapter.

15 See also A1160: 22-5, where devotion outweighs benefit.

16 Emendation of Naṣṣār's *bi-ḥaẓẓī* 'with my share [of your mind]'.

17 Alternate translation: 'deprived by you of his share'.

18 Searle 1969, 66–7. The second preparatory condition, stipulating that the event warned against is not obvious, is assumed as given, since a superfluous poem of admonition would not exist at all. In all quotes, Searle's abbreviated clauses are written out.

19 For wishes as promises, see pp. 90–2.

20 Literally, 'be in accordance with what I hoped for in you'. For the motif, see L191: 98–102.

21 The division of the verse differs from that in Naṣṣār's edition.

22 Cf. Sūrat Luqmān 31/18.

23 i.e. abstaining from praising others.

24 If one takes the alternate meaning of *nāfila* (pl. *nawāfil*) 'additional benefit', the end of the verse should be translated as 'gifts and favors are my additional benefit in you'.

25 Thanks (2), request (4), thanks (8), assertions of loyalty (12–13, 22–5), request (26), invocation (27), assertion of loyalty (28).

26 Second meaning of *muthammir*: 'churned [milk], about to become butter'.

27 Literally, 'my asking him for gifts and [keeping my] modesty are equal'.

28 Emendation of Naṣṣār's second *simānan* to *sumānā* 'quails' as lectio difficilior. The parallel plurals *simānan* and *ʿijāfan* are used in their passive sense of 'fattened' and 'emaciated'; cf. *WKAS* i: 223a.

29 Emendation of Naṣṣār's *martaʿ* 'place of pasturing' to *ratiʿ* 'abundant, plentiful [herbage]', fitting the meter.

30 Searle 1967, 66–7.

31 Shāpūr II b. Hormuzd, also called Dhū l-Aktāf, the Sasanian king (310–79 CE). He led an expedition against Arab tribes who encroached on his territory and tore out the shoulder blades of the defeated, hence his name Dhū l-Aktāf; see Ibn Qutayba *Maʿārif*, 657 and al-Masʿūdī *Murūj*, i: 263–4. The blaming of Shāpūr is derived from an anecdote related by al-Masʿūdī (ibid., 264–6). When Shāpūr, fearing the prophesied Arab rule, attacks the Banū Tamīm in Baḥrayn, they all flee before him, except their old chief ʿAmr b. Tamīm b. Murr, who convinces Shāpūr to stop the killing in order to make the Arabs indebted to him.

32 *Kāʾin* is a variant of *kaʾayyin* 'how often'.

33 Note the strong image and the sound repetition of the gutturals (*kaʾanniya / kulli / qultuhū*) and the emphatic sibilant (*ḥasan / ṣafan / ṣāmilī*), which underscore the harsh frustration of constantly wasted labor.

34 The dilemma of choosing between two allegiances – the patron or God – recalls a scene (L1250': 1–38) in which the aging persona of the poet is caught in the dilemma of offering repentance to a personification of white hair instead of to God. At first, the poet dwells on the dangerously misguided nature of such repentance, but then he resolves the dilemma by interpreting the apparently heathenish idol of white hair as a divine warning.

35 For fears come true, see F1243: 12 and 38; for suffering, F1243: 15.

36 Var. *al-bākhilīna* 'the stingy'. The motif appears in E1307'.

16 ACTS AND WORDS BETWEEN PANEGYRIST AND MODEL

1 This corresponds to the second and fourth levels of truth in Bürgel's classification (1974, 23–4).

2 Ibid., 63–87, esp. 70 and 84–5.

3 For praise without exaggeration, see L1611: 252–4 and E387; as arranged facts, A694: 16.

4 L1600: 251.

5 Metastrophes L1611: 219–31, 251–65 and 303, F694: 13–16, F952: 74–80, and F986: 29–34.

6 Metastrophes L215: 149–53, F458: 71–4, F1243: 1, F1373': 257–67, F1342': 5–6 and 11–12.

7 e.g. L1611: 257–60.

8 See pp. 83–8.

9 e.g. in the motif of a buyer from the merchants of praise in F463: 14–18; as a tax-collector in L191: 138 and F458: 10; and as the resurrector of poetry in 1611: 272 and F1342': 2.

10 F1373': 178–95 and L1306: 16–18.

11 This relationship takes up metastrophes L994: 95–110 and L1306: 16–18 in their entirety. It also appears in part in L1611: 252–4, 289; F952: 43–56, 81–2; F1373': 178–92; and A464: 12–15.

12 For the context in literature, see pp. 27–32.

13 L1042: 68, general E1341. On the concept of redemption in Jāhilī poetry, see S. Stetkevych 1994. Stetkevych's concept of redemption differs from the one proposed here in so far as the pre-Islamic poet redeems a life *in exchange for* a poem, whereas Ibn al-Rūmī urges the patron to redeem himself as *worthy of* a poem.

14 The praise is partially redeemed in A1204 and A1369': 13–21; it is not yet redeemed in A212, A1171; and it has lapsed in L215: 68–72 and epigrams E110 and E681.

15 For the sword image, see A1171: 2, discussed below; for the plea, A1171: 4–6. The same plea is addressed to God in A1510: 21. The fourth relationship is mixed with the first relationship in metastrophes L191: 151–6 and L1042: 55–60, 67.

16 A212: 1, discussed below.
17 L215: 68–72, discussed below.
18 For sincerity see, e.g. L191: 154–6, L994: 104, L1611: 303, F986: 21, and A1160: 2.
19 See Ohmann 1972, 50, idem 1973, 87 and 90, Fish 1976, 1004–8 and 1011–21.
20 Cf. L191: 155–6.
21 Naṣṣār; Salīm gives the variant *ghāb* 'reed thicket', alluding to the danger hidden in lies.
22 Salīm; Naṣṣār gives the variant *jāwazta* 'you have transgressed your praise (sc. by not doing what I say you do)'. See also L1600: 249–50.
23 The same motif appears in E371.
24 Cf. also the anonymous epigram E876:

مَديحُكَ مَن تُطالِبُ منهُ رِفدًا   هِجاءٌ مِنكَ فيه بالضَّميرِ
لأَنَّك لمْ تَثِقْ منه بمَجْدٍ   يَنوبُ عنِ المديحِ ولا بِخيرِ

> Your praising of someone, by asking him for a gift
> is satire by you of him in [your] mind.
>
> For you do not trust glory or generosity in him
> to stand up for the praise.

Other epigrams in this vein include E414, E858, and E940
25 Emendation of Naṣṣār's *istatāba* to *istathāba*.
26 Cf. A1510: 24–5. A stingy man's present is declared illicit in L215: 68–9. Note also the case of a praising epigram (E68) for which Ibn al-Rūmī found no worthy recipient, so that it remained undedicated:

طوَيْتَ بَسيطَ آمالِي برِفْدٍ   كفانِي أَنْ أُؤَمِّلَ ما سِواهُ
أَقولُ وقدْ طوَيْتُ بهِ رَجائِي   لِيَطْوِ كذا رَجائِي مَن طَواهُ

> You fulfilled my simple hopes with a favor that is enough for me
> to dispense with hoping for another [favor].
>
> I speak and have already achieved my request;
> may someone fulfilling my request fulfill it thus!

27 Literally, 'what you feather and pare', i.e. the antithetical description of the patron's acts in the previous verse.
28 The poet refers to himself by the *nisba* derived from his Greek grandfather.
29 For the distribution of rhyme letters, see Bencheikh 1975a, 169–73.
30 Only one of nine encomia for ʿUbaydallāh has the *khafīf*, but the *khafīf* appears in five out of nineteen felicitations. The encroaching of the lyrical *khafīf* on ceremonial genres is a trend of the third/ninth century, especially in ʿAlī b. al-Jahm and al-Buḥturī, before Ibn al-Rūmī. See Bencheikh 1975a, 216–20 and 224 (graph).
31 Cf. the reference to God as *malīk muqtadir* 'Mighty King' in Sūrat al-Qamar 54/55.
32 Sun and moon as guardians of night and day. See also note 37 below.
33 This amount presupposes a single male heir, i.e. the patron, with a sixth for each of the parents (Sūrat al-Nisāʾ 4/11), so that nothing remains for the real descendants of those praised rulers. See also verses 185 and 192.
34 Cf. *WKAS* ii: 2118a. See also E1252'.
35 Ziyād b. Muʿāwiya is al-Nābigha al-Dhubyānī. All those mentioned are famous pre-Islamic poets and, with the exception of Aws b. Ḥajar, authors of a *muʿallaqa*.
36 Dūdān b. Asad b. Khuzayma is an ancestor of ʿAbīd b. al-Abraṣ. See al-Tibrīzī *Sharḥ* 364.

37 Literally, 'the two stars [of day and night]', a comparison of the nominal addressee of the poetry in the pagan dark ages with ʿUbaydallāh in his luminous era.
38 The translation does not capture the double meaning of *maḍā'*, which works both at the topical level of the tongue as 'moving', and at the figurative level of the sword as 'cutting'.
39 Note the play with the root of *ṣanīʿa* 'benefit'.
40 The translation does not convey the paranomasia tying together the antithetical elements of sword and veil, with *qināʿ*, 'face veil' being a metonymy for sword and *taqannaʿa* meaning 'to gird oneself with [a sword]'. A literal rendering would be: 'For a day on which men "veil their faces", and women wear no face veil.'
41 Cf. A1160: 22–5, A1510: 21.
42 Var. *khayyāb* 'dry (lightning), not producing rain' in Salīm.
43 The full risk of trusting a patron with one's sincerity is spelled out in an epigram (E18) alluding to Sūrat al-Shuʿarā' 26/226. After God has already chastised the poets for lying, the patrons pile more lies on them. The poets are the victims of patrons who cannot match with deeds the praises offered to them:

يقولونَ ما لا يَفعَلونَ مَسَبَّةٌ مِنَ اللّهِ مسبوبٌ بها الشُّعراءُ
وما ذاكَ فيهمْ وَحْدَهُ بل زيادةٌ يقولونَ ما لا يَفعَلُ الأُمراءُ

'They say what they do not do' is an insult by God
with which the poets are insulted.

Not only this [is an insult] to them,
but, furthermore, that they say what princes do not do!

Emendation of Naṣṣār's *masabbatan* to the nominative as *khabar* of the Koranic quote, which is the *mubtada'*.
44 There is one case of mild satire, H1512.
45 Al-Buḥturī's praise is quoted and discussed on pp. 18–21. In a later encomium, dedicated to Ibn Bisṭām (*Dīwān*, i: 277–81, no. 96), al-Buḥturī satirizes ʿUbaydallāh, without naming him. He reprimands him for being a neglectful friend (7–16) and calls him obscure (20), lacking virtues (*khiṣāl*, 22), fine culture (*adab*, 22), and personal achievements (*ḥasab*, 23). Al-Ṣayrafī notes that Ibn al-Rūmī's indirect response to al-Buḥturī (L215) shares the same rhyme and meter as ʿUbaydallāh's direct response (ibid., iv: 2481–90, no. 1) and al-Buḥturī's original attack. Ibn al-Rūmī also satirizes al-Buḥturī directly (Ibn al-Rūmī *Dīwān*, i: 269–74, no. 167). For the ascription, see al-Buḥturī *Dīwān*, iv: 2476–7 and 2481, note 1. Al-Ṣayrafī hence disproves Boustany's claim (1976, 149) of Ibn al-Rūmī's impartiality in the dispute between ʿUbaydallāh and al-Buḥturī.
46 Cf. the motif of licit spoils for readily given riches L191: 94, L215: 110, and L1611: 284.
47 Cf. also E10 and E110.

CONCLUSION: DRAMATURGY AS A RHETORIC OF ETHICS

1 In one dialogue, Diʿbil's persona defends his generosity; see Diʿbil *Dīwān*, 13, no. 9. In another, ʿAlī b. al-Jahm's persona proclaims his loyalty as a subject; see ʿAlī b. al-Jahm *Dīwān*, 50–1, no. 16. For a discussion of their dramaturgic styles, see Gruendler 2000a.
2 For dialogue as a transition, see ʿAlī b. al-Jahm *Dīwān*, 50–1, no. 16 and 220–3 (al-Ruṣāfiyya); as a poem's structure, ibid., 71–4, no. 23 and 41–7, no. 14 (al-Dāliyya).
3 On honesty, see Diʿbil *Dīwān*, 134, no. 178; on generosity, ibid., 65 no. 73.

4 On non-professionalism, see ʿAlī b. al-Jahm *Dīwān*, 220–3 (al-Ruṣāfiyya); on loyalty, ibid., 71–4, no. 23.
5 See pp. 20–1 and al-Buḥturī *Dīwān*, iii: 1770–4, no. 679: 35–9.
6 Gutas 1990, 346–65.
7 Ibn Khaldūn *Muqaddima*, 302–11 (chapter 3, faṣl 51) translated by Rosenthal 1958, ii: 139–56. For the earliest version of the epistle, see Ibn Abī Ṭāhir Ṭayfūr *Kitāb Baghdād*, 26–34. Cf. also Gutas 1990, 357–8.
8 The page numbers in parentheses refer to Ibn Khaldūn *Muqaddima* and Rosenthal 1958, ii.
9 واعلَمْ أنَّ الأَموالَ إذا اكْتُنِزَتْ وادُّخِرَتْ فى الخَزائِنِ لا تَنمو وإذا كانتْ فى صَلاحِ الرَّعِيَّةِ وإعطاءِ حُقوقِهمْ وكَفِّ الأَذيَّةِ عنْهمْ نمَتْ وزكَتْ ... فلْيكُنْ كَنزُ خَزائِنِك تفريقَ الأَموالِ فى عِمارة الإسلامِ وأَهلِهِ.

For Ibn al-Rūmī, see chapter 15, note 2.

10 ولْيكُنْ أَكرمُ دُخلاءِك وخاصَّتِك عليْك مَن إذا رأَى عَيْبًا فيك لمْ تَمنَعْه هيْبَتُك عنْ إنهاءِ ذلكَ إليك فى سِرِّك وإعلانِك بما فيه مِن النَّقْصِ فإنَّ أولَئِك أَنصَحُ أَوْلِيائِك ومُظاهِرون لك.

For Ibn al-Rūmī depicting himself as a devoted and concerned friend, see pp. 117, 189–90 and fig. 15, and 233–5 as well as L1042: 52–62, F1243: 34–7, and E1448’.
11 Ibn al-Rūmī *Dīwān*, iii: 914–34, no. 687.
12 Ibn al-Rūmī *Dīwān*, vi: 2377–82, no. 1251’.
13 For an adaptation of this dramaturgy to other Abbasid poets, see Gruendler 2000a; and to the Andalusian *qaṣīda*, Gruendler 2000b.

APPENDICES

1 Two instances have variants with the first and the third person passive.
2 Six instances derive from only one passage (L1307: 12–31), an episode of *madīḥ* in a very reserved *qaṣīda*.
3 Four instances derive from the beginning of a dialogue between ‘we’ and a historical addressee (L1611: 147–50) belonging to a message.
4 Six instances derive from only one passage (L1611: 60–75), a hunting episode with participants speaking as ‘we’ and witnessed by ‘I’.
5 Here with witnessing ‘I’ replaces the more frequent ‘we’.

BIBLIOGRAPHY

DĪWĀN EDITIONS IN CHRONOLOGICAL ORDER

(Ibn and Abū are disregarded in the alphabetical order.)

Salīm, M. Sh. (ed.) (1335/1917), *Dīwān Ibn al-Rūmī*, 2 pts, Cairo: Maṭbaʿat al-Hilāl (edition and commentary until rhyme letter *b*).

Kīlānī, K. (ed.) (1924), *Dīwān Ibn al-Rūmī*, Cairo: Maṭbaʿat al-Tawfīq al-Adabiyya.

Boustany, S. (ed.) (1961), 'Ibn ar-Rūmī: Dīwān', thesis, Paris.

Naṣṣār, Ḥ. *et al.* (eds) (1973–81), *Dīwān Ibn al-Rūmī*, 6 vols, Cairo: Maṭbaʿat Dār al-Kutub (complete critical edition).

Yārid, N. S. (ed.) (1988), *Kull mā qālahu Ibn al-Rūmī fī l-hijāʾ*, London: Dār al-Sāqī.

Muhannā, ʿA.ʿA. (ed.) (1411/1991), *Dīwān Ibn al-Rūmī*, 6 vols, Beirut: Dār wa-Maktabat al-Hilāl (based on Naṣṣār).

Basaj, A. Ḥ., (ed.) (1415/1994), *Dīwān Ibn al-Rūmī*, 3 vols, Beirut: Dār al-Kutub al-ʿIlmiyya (based on Naṣṣār).

Ṭarrād, M., Ḥaydar, U., Aslim, F., Nuʿayyim, A., and Māyū, Q. (eds) (1418/1998), *Dīwān Ibn al-Rūmī*, 7 vols, Beirut: Dār al-Jīl (based on Naṣṣār).

SOURCES

Ibn ʿAbdrabbih (n.d.), *al-ʿIqd al-farīd*, ed. M. S. al-ʿAryān, 8 pts in 4 vols, Beirut: Dār al-Fikr.

Ahlwardt, W. (1870), *The Divans of the Six Ancient Arabic Poets Ennābiga, ʿAntara, Tharafa, Zuhair, ʿAlqama and Imruulqais*, repr. Osnabrück: Biblio, 1972.

ʿAlī b. al-Jahm (1949), *Dīwān*, ed. Kh. M. Bek, Damascus: Lajnat al-Turāth al-ʿArabī, 2nd annotated edition, 1959.

al-ʿAqqād, ʿA. M. (1404/1984), *Ibn al-Rūmī: Ḥayātuhū min shiʿrihī*, repr., Beirut: Manshūrāt al-Maktaba al-ʿAṣriyya.

al-Aʿshā, Maymūn b. Qays (1928), *Dīwān* [Die Gedichte von Abū Baṣīr Meimūn ibn Qais al-ʾAʿšā nebst Sammlungen von Stücken anderer Dichter des gleichen Namens], ed. R. Geyer, E. J. W. Gibb Memorial Series, N. S., vol. 6, London: Luzac.

al-ʿAskarī, Abū Hilāl (1971), *K. aṣ-Ṣināʿatayn*, ed. ʿA. M. al-Bijāwī and Abū l-Faḍl Ibrāhīm, Cairo: Dār al-Fikr al-ʿArabī.

Ibn Abī ʿAwn (1369/1950), *Kitāb al-Tashbīhāt*, ed. M. ʿA. Khān, E. J. W. Gibb Memorial Series, N. S., vol. 17, London: Luzac.

al-Buḥturī (1977–8), *Dīwān*, ed. Ḥasan Kāmil al-Ṣayrafī, 5 vols, Cairo: Dār al-Maʿārif.

Diʿbil b. ʿAlī al-Khuzāʿī (1962), *Dīwān*, ed. M. Y. Najm, Beirut: Dār al-Thaqāfa.

—— (1961), *Diʿbil b. ʿAlī: The Life and Writings of an Early ʿAbbāsid Poet*, ed. L. Zolondek, Lexington: University of Kentucky Press.

Divans: see Ahlwardt.

al-Fīrūzābādī, Majd al-Dīn ([1301]/1884), *al-Qāmūs al-muḥīṭ*, 4 vols, Būlāq, repr. Beirut, n.d.

al-Ḥuṣrī al-Qayrawānī, Abū Isḥāq Ibrāhīm b. ʿAlī (1969–70), *Zahr al-ādāb wa-thamr al-albāb*, ed. ʿA. M. al-Bijāwī, Cairo: ʿĪsā al-Bābī al-Ḥalabī.

al-Iṣfahānī, Abū l-Faraj ʿAlī b. al-Ḥusayn (1401/1981[5]), *K. al-Aghānī*, 25 vols, various editors vols 1–14, ed. ʿA. A. Farrāj vols 15–25, Beirut: Dār al-Thaqāfa.

Isḥāq b. Ibrahīm b. Sulaymān b. Wahb al-Kātib, Abū al-Ḥusayn (1402/1982), *al-Burhān fī wujūh al-bayān* [publ. as Pseudo-Qudāma, *Naqd al-nathr*], ed. ʿA. al-ʿIbādī, repr. Beirut: Dār al-Kutub al-ʿIlmiyya.

al-Jāḥiẓ, Abū ʿUthmān ʿAmr b. Baḥr (1385/1965[2]), *K. al-Ḥayawān*, 7 vols, ed. ʿA. M. Hārūn, Cairo: Maktabat Muṣṭafā al-Bābī al-Ḥalabī.

Ibn al-Jarrāḥ, Abū ʿAbdallāh Muḥammad b. Dawūd (1372/1953), *al-Waraqa*, ed. ʿA. ʿAzzām and ʿA. A. Farrāj, Cairo: Dār al-Maʿārif.

Ibn al-Jawzī (1355–9), *al-Muntaẓam fī ta'rīkh al-mulūk wa-l-umam*, 10 pts in 3 vols, Haydarābād: Maṭbaʿat Dār al-Maʿārif al-ʿUthmāniyya.

al-Jurjānī, ʿAbdalqāhir (1404/1984), *Dalā'il al-iʿjāz*, ed. M. M. Shākir, Cairo: Maktabat al-Khānjī.

—— (1954), *Asrār al-balāgha*, ed. H. Ritter, Istanbul, repr. Cairo: Maktabat al-Mutanabbī, 1399/1979.

Ibn Khaldūn (1981[4]), *al-Muqaddima*, first publ. 1879, Beirut: Dār al-Qalam.

Ibn Khallikān, Abū l-ʿAbbās Aḥmad b. Muḥammad (1367–9/1948–50), *Wafayāt al-aʿyān wa-anbā' abnā' al-zamān*, ed. M. M. ʿAbdalḥamīd, 6 vols, Cairo: Maktabat al-Nahḍa al-Miṣriyya.

al-Khaṭīb al-Baghdādī, Abū Bakr Aḥmad b. ʿAlī (1931/1349), *Ta'rīkh Baghdād*, 14 vols, Cairo: Maktabat al-Khānjī.

Kushājim, Maḥmūd (b. Muḥmammad) b. al-Ḥusayn (1390/1970), *Dīwān*, ed. Kh. M. Maḥfūẓ, Baghdād: Mudīriyyat al-Thaqāfa al-ʿĀmma.

Ibn al-Muʿtazz, ʿAbdallāh (1935), *Kitāb al-Badīʿ*, ed. I. Kratchkovsky, E. J. W. Gibb Memorial Series, N. S., vol. 10, London: Luzac, repr. Baghdad: Qāsim Muḥammad al-Rajab, 1399/1979.

—— (1981), *Ṭabaqāt al-shuʿarā'*, ed. ʿA. A. Farrāj, Cairo: Dār al-Maʿārif.

al-Maʿarri, Abū l-ʿAlā' (1950[2]), *Risālat al-Ghufrān*, ed. Bint al-Shaṭi' [ʿĀ'isha ʿAbdarraḥmān], Cairo: Dār al-Maʿārif.

al-Marzubānī, Abū ʿUbaydallāh Muḥammad b. ʿImrān (1415/1995), *Kitāb al-Muwashshah fī ma'ākhidh al-ʿulamā' ʿalā l-shuʿarā'*, ed. M. Ḥ. Shamsaddīn, Beirut: Dār al-Kutub al-ʿIlmiyya.

—— (1379/1960), *Muʿjam al-shuʿarāʿ*, ed. ʿA. A. Farrāj, Cairo: ʿĪsā al-Bābī al-Ḥalabī.

al-Masʿūdī, Abū l-Ḥasan ʿAlī b. al-Ḥusayn (1406/1986), *Murūj al-dhahab wa-maʿādin al-jawhar*, 4 vols, ed. M. M. Qamīḥa Beirut: Dār al-Kutub al-ʿIlmiyya.

Ibn Qutayba, Abū Muḥammad ʿAbdallāh b. Muslim (1981), *Kitāb al-Maʿārif*, ed. Th. ʿUkkāsha, Cairo: Dār al-Maʿārif.

Qudāma b. Jaʿfar, Abū l-Faraj (1399/1979), *Naqd al-shiʿr*, ed. M. ʿA. al-Khafājī, Cairo: Maktabat al-Kulliyya al-Azhariyya.

Ibn Rashīq al-Qayrawānī, Abū ʿAlī al-Ḥasan (1401/1981[5]), *al-ʿUmda fī maḥāsin al-shiʿr wa-ādābihi wa-naqdihi*, ed. M. M. ʿAbdalḥamīd, Beirut: Dār al-Jīl.

al-Rummanī, Abū al-Ḥasan ʿAlī b. ʿĪsā (n.d.), '*al-Nukat fī iʿjāz al-Qurʾān*', in: M. Khalafallāh and M. Zaghlūl Salām (eds), *Thalāth rasāʾil fī iʿjāz al-Qurʾān li-l-Rummānī wa-l-Khaṭṭābī wa-ʿAbd al-Qāhir al-Jurjānī*, Cairo: Dār al-Maʿārif, 67–104.

Ibn Sharaf al-Qayrawānī (1953), *Questions de critique littéraire* (Masāʾil al-intiqād): *Texte arabe établi d'après deux éditions et traduction française avec une introduction et des notes*, ed. and trans. Charles Pellat, Algiers: Jules Carbonel.

al-Ṣafadī, Khalīl b. Aybak (1931–98), *al-Wāfī bi-l-wafayāt*, 29 vols, ed. Ritter *et al*., Leipzig: F. A. Brockhaus, Wiesbaden: Steiner, Berlin: Das arabische Buch, and other publishers.

al-Ṣulī, Abū Bakr Muḥammad b. Yaḥyā (n.d.), *Akhbār Abī Tammām*, ed. Kh. M. ʿAsākir, M. ʿA. ʿAzzām, and Naẓīr al-Islām al-Hindī, Beirut: al-Maktab al-Tijārī li-l-Ṭibāʿa wa-l-Tawzīʿ wa-l-Nashr.

—— (1378/1958), *Akhbār al-Buḥturī*, ed. Ṣ. al-Ashtar, Damascus: al-Majmaʿ al-ʿIlmī al-ʿArabī.

al-Ṭabarī, Abū Jaʿfar Muḥammad b. Jarīr (1879–90), *Tarīkh al-rusul wa-l-mulūk*. ed. M. J. de Goeje *et al*., 14 vols in 3 pts, Leiden: Brill.

Ibn [Abī] Ṭāhir Ṭayfūr (1368/1949), *Kitāb Baghdād*, ed. M. Z. al-Kawtharī, Cairo: ʿIzzat al-ʿAṭṭār al-Ḥusaynī.

al-Tibrīzī, Abū Zakariyyāʾ Yaḥyā b. ʿAlī (1407/1987^2), *Sharḥ al-qaṣāʾid al-ʿashr*, ed. ʿA. al-Ḥufī, Beirut: Dār al-Kutub al-ʿIlmiyya.

SECONDARY LITERATURE

Arberry, A. J. (1955), *The Koran Interpreted*, repr. New York: Macmillan, 1986.

—— (1965), *Arabic Poetry: A Primer for Students*, Cambridge: Cambridge University Press.

Abu Deeb, K. (1975), 'Towards a Structural Analysis of Pre-Islamic Poetry (I)', *International Journal of Middle East Studies* 6: 148–84.

—— (1976), 'Toward a Structural Analysis of Pre-Islamic Poetry (II): The Eros Vision', *Edebiyat* 1:3–69.

—— (1979), *Al-Jurjānī's Theory of Poetic Imagery*, Warminster, Wiltshire: Aris and Phillips.

AEL: see Lane

Ahsan, M. M. (1979), *Social Life under the Abbasids, 170–289 AH/786–902 AD*, London and New York: Longman.

Ashtor, E. (1961), 'Essai sur les prix et les salaires dans l'empire califien', *Rivista degli studi orientali* 36: 16–69.

Ayalon, A. (1991), 'Malik', *EI*^{2} vi: 261–2.

Badawī, M. M. (1980), 'From Primary to Secondary *Qaṣīda*s,' *JAL* 11: 1–31.

—— (1978), 'The Function of Rhetoric in Medieval Arabic Poetry: Abū Tammām's Ode on Amorium', *JAL* 9: 43–56.

Bauer, T. (1992), *Altarabische Dichtkunst: Eine Untersuchung ihrer Struktur und Entwicklung am Beispiel der Onagerepisode*, 2 vols, Wiesbaden: Harrassowitz.

—— (1993a), 'Formel und Zitat: Zwei Spielarten von Intertextualität in der altarabischen Dichtung', *JAL* 24: 117–38.

—— (1993b), 'Wie fängt man eine Qaṣīde an? Formelhafte und nichtformelhafte Nasīb-Einleitungsverse', *Zeitschrift für arabische Linguistik* 25: 50–75.

—— (1998), *Liebe und Liebesdichtung in der arabischen Welt des 9. und 10. Jahrhunderts: Eine literatur- und mentalitätsgeschichtliche Studie des arabischen Gazal,* Diskurse der Arabistik, vol. 2, Wiesbaden: Otto Harrassowitz.

Bauman, R. and Briggs, C. L. (1990), 'Poetics and Performance as Critical Perspectives on Language and Social Life', *Annual Review of Anthropology* 19: 59–88.

Bencheikh, J. E. (1975a), *Poétique Arabe. Précédée de: Essai sur un discours critique*, 2nd edition with prefatory essay, Paris: Gallimard, 1989.

—— (1975b), 'Les secrétaires poètes et animateurs de cénacles aux IIe et IIIe siècles de l'Hégire. Contribution à l'analyse d'une production poétique', *Journal Asiatique* 263: 265–315.

—— (1975c), 'Les musiciens et la poésie. Les écoles d'Isḥāq al-Mawsilī (m. 225 H.) et d'Ibrāhīm Ibn al-Mahdī (m. 224 H.)', *Arabica* 22: 114–52.

—— (1977), 'Le cénacle poétique du calife al-Mutawakkil (m. 247): Contribution à l'analyse des instances de légitimation socio-littéraires', *Bulletin d'Études Orientales* 29: 33–52.

Benveniste, É. (1966), *Problèmes de linguistique générale*, vol. 1, Paris: Gallimard.

Betten, A. (1994), 'Analyse literarischer Dialoge', in: G. Fritz and F. Hundsnurscher (eds), *Handbuch der Dialoganalyse*, Tübingen: Max Niemeyer, 519–44.

Bierwisch, M. (1980), 'Semantic Structure and Illocutionary Force' in: J. Searle, F. Kiefer, and M. Bierwisch (eds) (q.v.), 1–35.

Bloch, A. (1948), 'Qaṣīda', *Asiatische Studien* 2: 106–32.

Booth, W. (1961), *The Rhetoric of Fiction*, 2nd edition, Chicago: University of Chicago Press, 1983.

Borg, G. (1997), Ufarriju hamma ṣadrī bi-l-qarīḍī: *Mit Poesie vertreibe ich den Kummer meines Herzens: Eine Studie zur altarabischen Trauerklage der Frau*, Istanbul: Nederlands Historisch-Archeologisch Instituut.

Bosworth, C. E. (1969), 'The Tahirids and Arabic Culture', *Journal of Semitic Studies* 14: 45–79.

Boustany, S. (1967), *Ibn ar-Rūmī. Sa vie et son oeuvre, vol. 1: Ibn ar-Rūmī dans son milieu*, Beirut: Imprimerie Catholique.

Bürgel, J. C. (1974), '"Die beste Dichtung ist die lügenreichste:" Wesen und Bedeutung eines literarischen Streites des arabischen Mittelalters im Lichte komparatistischer Betrachtung', *Oriens* 23–4: 7–102.

Briggs, C. L. and Bauman, R. (1992), 'Genre, Intertextuality, and Social Power', *Journal of Linguistic Anthropology* 2: 131–72.

Browning, R. (1874), *Dramatis Personae*, Boston: James R. Osgood & Co.

Calmard, J. (1993), 'Mihragān', *EI²* vii: 15–20.

Canard, M. (trans.) (1946), *Akhbār Al-Rāḍī billāh wa'l-Muttaqī billāh (Histoire de la dynastie Abbaside de 322 à 333/934 à 944) par Mohammed ben Yahyā as-Sūlī*, Algiers: 'La Typo-Litho' and Jules Carbonel.

—— (1951), 'Le cérémonial fatimide et le cérémonial byzantin: Essai de comparaison', *Byzantion* 21: 355–420.

EAL: see Meisami and Starkey

Ehrenkreutz, A. S. (1977), 'Money', in: Spuler (ed.) (1997) (q.v.), 84–97.

EI²: see individual authors

Ess, J. van (1967–68), 'Ḍirār b. ʿAmr und die 'Cahmiyya': Biographie einer vergessenen Schule', *Der Islam* 43: 241–79, 44: 1–70 and 318–20.

—— (1970), 'The Logical Structure of Islamic Theology', in: G. E. von Grunebaum (ed.), *Logic in Classical Islamic Culture*, 21–50, Wiesbaden: Otto Harrassowitz.

—— (1991–7), *Theologie und Gesellschaft im 2. und 3. Jahrhundert Hidschra. Eine Geschichte des religiösen Denkens im frühen Islam*, 6 vols, Berlin: Walter de Gruyter.

Felman, S. (1983), *The Literary Speech Act: Don Juan with J. L. Austin, or Seduction in Two Languages* [first publ. as *Le scandale du corps parlant*, 1980, trans. C. Porter, Ithaca: Cornell University Press.

Fischer, W. (1972), *Grammatik des klassischen Arabisch*, 2nd edition, 1987, Wiesbaden: Otto Harrassowitz.

Fish, S. (1976), 'How to Do Things with Austin and Searle: Speech Act Theory and Literary Criticism', *Modern Language Notes* 91: 983–1025.

GAP ii: see Gätje

GAS ii: see Sezgin

Gätje, H. (1987), *Grundriß der Arabischen Philologie, vol. 2: Literaturwissenschaft*, Wiesbaden: Dr. Ludwig Reichert.

Germanus, A. K. J. (1956), 'Ibn-Rūmī's Dichtkunst', *Acta Orientalia Academiae Scientiarum Hungaricae* 6: 215–86.

Gelder, G. J. H. van (1982), *Beyond the Line: Classical Arabic Literary Critics on the Coherence and Unity of the Poem*, Studies in Arabic Literature, vol. 8, Leiden: E. J. Brill.

—— (1983), 'The Abstracted Self in Arabic Poetry', *JAL* 14: 22–30.

—— (1996), 'The Terrified Traveller: Ibn al-Rūmī's Anti-*Raḥīl*', *JAL* 27: 37–48.

Ghazi, M. F. (1959), 'Un groupe social: "Les raffinés" (Ẓurafā')', *Studia Islamica* 11: 39–71.

Gimaret, D. (1993), 'Muʿtazila', EI^2 vii: 783–93.

Grabar, O. (1977), 'Notes sur les cérémonies Umayyades', in: M. Rosen-Ayalon (ed.), *Studies in Memory of Gaston Wiet*, Jerusalem: Institute of Asian and African Studies, Hebrew University, 51–60.

Grice, H. P. (1975), 'Logic and Conversation', in: P. Cole and J. L. Morgan (eds), *Syntax and Semantics, vol. 3: Speech Acts*, New York and London: Harcourt Brace Jovanovich, 41–58.

Gruendler, B. (1996), 'Ibn al-Rūmī's Ethics of Patronage', *Harvard Middle Eastern and Islamic Review* 3: 104–60.

—— (1999), 'The Motif of Marriage in Select Abbasid Panegyrics', in: A. Neuwirth, B. Embaló, S. Günther, and M. Jarrār (eds), *Myths, Historical Archetypes and Symbolic Figures in Arabic Literature*, Beiruter Texte und Studien, vol. 64, Beirut/Stuttgart: Franz Steiner, 109–22.

—— (2000a), 'ʿAbbāsid Praise Poetry in Light of Dramatic Discourse and Speech Act Theory', in: B. Gruendler and V. Klemm (eds), *Understanding Near Eastern Literatures: A Spectrum of Interdisciplinary Approaches*, Wiesbaden: Dr. Ludwig Reichert, 157–70.

—— (2000b), 'The Qasida', in: M. Menocal, R. Scheindlin, and M. Sells (eds), *The Cambridge History of Arabic Literature: The Literature of Al-Andalus*, Cambridge: Cambridge University Press.

Grunebaum, G. E. von (1948–53), 'Three Arabic Poets of the Early Abbasid Age (The Collected Fragments of Muṭīʿ b. Iyās, Salm al-Ḫāsir and Abū š-Šamaqmaq)', *Orientalia* 17 (148): 160–204, 19 (1950): 53–80, and 22 (1953): 262–83.

—— (1955), *Kritik und Dichtkunst: Studien zur arabischen Literaturgeschichte*, Wiesbaden: Otto Harrassowitz.

—— (1960), 'Bayān', *EI*[2] i: 1114–16.

Guest, R. (1944), *Life and Works of Ibn er Rūmī, 'Alī ibn el 'Abbās, Abū el Ḥasan: A Baghdad Poet of the 9th Century of the Christian Era: His Life and Poetry*, London: Luzac.

Gutas, D (1990), 'Ethische Schriften im Islam', in: W. Heinrichs (ed.) (1990) (q.v.), 346–65.

—— (1998), *Greek Thought Arabic Culture: The Graeco-Arabic Translation Movement in Baghdad and Early 'Abbāsid Society* (2nd–4th/8th–10th centuries), London and New York: Routledge.

Hamori, A. (1974), *On the Art of Medieval Arabic Literature*, Princeton: Princeton University Press.

—— (1977), 'Form and Logic in Some Medieval Arabic Poems', *Edebiyat* 2: 163–72.

—— (1981), 'Reading al-Mutanabbī's Ode on the Siege of al-Ḥadaṯ', in: Wadad al-Qadi (ed.), *Studia Arabica et Islamica: Festschrift for Iḥsān 'Abbās on His Sixtieth Birthday*, Beirut: American University in Beirut, 195–208.

—— (1984), 'Did Medieval Readers Make Sense of Form?: Notes on a Passage of Al-Iskāfī', in: A. H. Green (ed.), *In Quest of an Islamic Humanism: Arabic and Islamic Studies in Memory of Mohamed al-Nowaihi*, Cairo: American University in Cairo Press, 39–47.

—— (1991), 'Some Schemes of Reading in al-Marzūqī, al-Iskāfī and Fakhr al-Dīn al-Rāzī', in: S. Somekh (ed.), *Israel Oriental Studies, vol. 11: Studies in Medieval Arab and Hebrew Poetics*, 13–20.

—— (1992), *The Composition of Mutanabbī's Panegyrics to Sayf al-Dawla*, Studies in Arabic Literature, vol. 14, Leiden: E. J. Brill.

al-Ḥāwī, Ī. S. (1980), *Ibn al-Rūmī, fannuhū wa-nafsiyyatuhū min khilāli shi'rihī*, Beirut/Cairo: Dār al-Kutub al-Lubnānī/Dār al-Kutub l-Miṣrī.

Haydar, A. (1977–8), 'The *Mu'allaqa* of Imru' al-Qays: Its Structure and Meaning', *Edebiyat* 2: 227–61 and 3: 51–82.

Heinrichs, W. (1969), *Arabische Dichtung und griechische Poetik: Ḥāzim al-Qarṭāǧannīs Grundlegung der Poetik mit Hilfe aristotelischer Begriffe*, Beiruter Texte und Studien, vol. 8, Beirut/Wiesbaden: Franz Steiner.

—— (1973), 'Literary Theory: The Problem of its Efficiency', in: G. E. von Grunebaum (ed.), *Arabic Poetry: Theory and Development*, 19–69.

—— (1974), '"Manierismus" in der arabischen Literatur', in: R. Gramlich (ed.), *Islamwissenschaftliche Abhandlungen Fritz Meier zum sechzigsten Geburtstag*, 118–28. Wiesbaden: Franz Steiner.

—— (1975), 'Ǧadal bei aṭ-Ṭūfī': Eine Interpretation seiner Beispielsammlung', *ZDMG Supplement iii, 1* (XIX. Deutscher Orientalistentag, Freiburg, 1975, ed. W. Voigt), 463–73.

—— (1986), 'Paired Metaphors in *Muḥdath* Poetry', *Occasional Papers of the School of Abbāsid Studies* 1: 1–22.

—— (1987–8), 'An Evaluation of *Sariqa*', *Quaderni di studi arabi* 5–6: 357–68.

—— (1991), 'Rose versus Narcissus: Observations on an Arabic Literary Debate', in: G. J. Reinink and H. L. J. Vanstiphout (eds), *Dispute Poems and Dialogues in the Ancient and Mediaeval Near East: Forms and Types of Literary Debates in Semitic and Related Literatures*, Leuven: Peeters Press, 179–98.

—— (1991–2), 'Contacts Between Scriptural Hermeneutics and Literary Theory in Islam: The Case of *Majāz*', *Zeitschrift für Geschichte der Arabisch-Islamischen Wissenschaften* 7: 253–84.

—— (1994), 'Muslim b. al-Walīd and *Badīʿ*', in W. Heinrichs and G. Schoeler (eds), (1994) (q.v.), 211–45.

—— (2000), 'Takhyīl', *EI*² x: 129–32.

Heinrichs, W. (ed.) (1990), *Orientalisches Mittelalter*, Neues Handbuch der Literaturwissenschaft, vol. 5, Wiesbaden: Aula.

Heinrichs, W. and Schoeler, G. (eds) (1994), *Festschrift Ewald Wagner zum 65. Geburtstag. Bd. 2: Studien zur arabischen Dichtung*, Beiruter Texte und Studien, vol. 54, Beirut/Stuttgart: Franz Steiner.

Hess-Lüttich, E. W. B. (1981), *Grundlagen der Dialoglinguistik, vol. 1: Soziale Interaktion und literarischer Dialog*, Berlin: Erich Schmidt.

—— (1985), 'Dramatic Discourse', in: T. van Dijk (ed.), *Discourse and Literature: New Approaches to the Analysis of Literary Genres*, Amsterdam and Philadelphia: John Benjamins, 199–214.

Hinds, M. (1993), 'Miḥna', *EI*² vii: 2–6.

Hinz, W. (1955), *Islamische Masse und Gewichte umgerechnet ins metrische System*, Handbuch der Orientalistik, Abt. 1, Suppl. vol. i, Leiden: E. J. Brill.

Holt, P. M., Lambton, A. K. S., and Lewis, B. (eds) (1970), *The Cambridge History of Islam, vol. 1A: The Central Islamic Lands from Pre-Islamic Times to the First World War*, repr. 1985, Cambridge: Cambridge University Press.

Hymes, D. (1974), *Foundations in Sociolinguistics: An Ethnographic Approach*, Philadelphia: University of Pennsylvania Press.

Iser, W. (1972), *Der implizite Leser*, München: Wilhem Fink.

Jacobi, R. (1970), 'Dichtung und Lüge in der arabischen Literaturtheorie', *Der Islam* 49: 85–99.

—— (1971), *Studien zur Poetik der altarabischen Qaṣide*, Wiesbaden: Franz Steiner.

—— (1982), 'The Camel-Section of the Panegyrical Ode', *JAL* 13: 1–22.

—— (1985), 'Time and Reality in *Nasīb* and *Ghazal*', *JAL* 16: 1–17.

—— (1996), 'The Origins of the Qasida Form', in: Sperl and Shackle (eds) (1996) (q.v.), i: 21–34.

James, H. (1958), *The Figure in the Carpet* in: *Eight Tales From the Major Phase*: In the Cage *and Others*, repr. London and New York: W. W. Norton, 1969, 134–73.

Kanazi, G. J. (1989), *Studies in the Kitāb aṣ-Ṣināʿatayn of Abū Hilāl al-ʿAskarī*, Leiden: E. J. Brill.

Kennedy, P. F. (1997), *The Wine Song in Classical Arabic Poetry: Abū Nuwās and the Literary Tradition*, Oxford: Clarendon Press.

Lane, E. W. (1863–77), *Arabic-English Lexicon, London*, 2 vols, repr. 1984. Cambridge: Islamic Texts Society.

Lassner, J. (1970), *The Topography of Baghdad in the Early Middle Ages: Text and Studies*, Detroit: Wayne State University Press.

Lichtenstädter, I. (1932), 'Das *Nasīb* der altarabischen *Qaṣīde*', *Islamica* 5: 18–96.

Lyons, M. C. (1978), 'Notes on Abū Tammām's Concept of Poetry', *JAL* 9: 57–64.

—— (1999) *Identification and Identity in Classical Arabic Poetry*, Gibb Literary Studies, vol. 2, Warminster, Wiltshire: Aris and Phillips.

de Man, P. (1979), 'Semiology and Rhetoric', in: J. V. Harari (ed.) *Textual Strategies: Perspectives in Post-Structural Criticism*, 121–40, Ithaca: Cornell University Press.

Mauss, M. (1990), *The Gift: The Form and Reason for Exchange in Archaic Societies* (first publ. as *Essai sur le don*, 1950), trans. by W. D. Halls, London and New York: W. W. Norton.

McKinney, R. (1998), 'Ibn al-Rūmī's Contribution to the "Nautical *Raḥīl*" Tradition: The Expression of Meaning through Form and Structure', *JAL* 29: 95–135.

Meisami, J. S. (1985), 'The Uses of the *Qaṣīda*: Thematic and Structural Patterns in a Poem of Bashshār', *JAL* 16: 40–60.

—— (1987), *Medieval Persian Court Poetry*, Princeton: Princeton University Press.

—— (1998), 'Places in the Past: The Poetics/Politics of Nostalgia', *Edebiyat* 8: 63–106.

Meisami, J. S. and Starkey, P. (eds) (1998), *Encyclopedia of Arabic Literature*, 2 vols, London and New York: Routledge.

Melchert, C. (1996), 'Religious Policies of the Caliphs from al-Mutawakkil to al-Muqtadir, A.H. 232–295/A.D. 847–908', *Islamic Law and Society* 3: 316–42.

Meyer-Hermann, R. (ed.) (1978), *Sprechen – Handeln – Interaktion: Ergebnisse aus Bielefelder Forschungsprojekten zu Texttheorie, Sprechakttheorie und Konversationsanalyse*, Tübingen: Max Niemeyer.

Mez, A. (1937), *The Renaissance of Islam* (first. publ. as *Die Renaissance des Islams*, 1922), trans. by S. Khuda Bukhsh and D. S. Margoliouth, Patna: Jubilee Printing and Publishing House.

Mir, M. and Fossum, J. E. (eds) (1993), *Literary Heritage of Classical Islam: Arabic and Islamic Studies in Honor of James Bellamy*, Princeton: Darwin Press.

Montgomery, J. E. (1986), 'Dichotomy in *Jāhilī* Poetry', *JAL* 17: 1–20.

—— (1995), 'The Deserted Encampment in Ancient Arabic Poetry: A Nexus of Topical Comparisons', *Journal of Semitic Studies* 40/2: 283–316.

—— (1997), *The Vagaries of the* Qaṣīdah: *The Tradition and Practice of Early Arabic Poetry*, Gibb Literary Studies, no. 1, Warminster, Wiltshire: Aris and Phillips.

Mottahedeh, R. P. (1980), *Loyality and Leadership in an Early Islamic Society*, Princeton: Princeton University Press.

Najar, Brahim (1987), *La mémoire rassemblée: Poètes arabes 'mineurs' des IIe/VIIIe et IIIe/IXe siècles*, Paris: La Française d'Édition et d'Imprimerie.

Northedge, A. (1991), 'Creswell, Herzfeld, and Samarra', *Muqarnas* 8: 74–93.

Ohmann, R. (1972), 'Speech, Literature and the Space Between', *New Literary History* 4: 47–63.

—— (1973), 'Literature as Act', in: S. Chatman (ed.), *Approaches to Poetics: Selected Papers from the English Institute*, New York and London: Columbia University Press, 81–107.

Ouyang, W. (1997), *Literary Criticism in Medieval Arabic-Islamic Culture: The Making of a Tradition*, Edinburgh: Edinburgh University Press.

Pellat, C. (ed. and trans.) (1976), *Ibn al-Muqaffaʿ, mort vers 140/757: 'Conseilleur' du Calife [al-Risāla fī l-Ṣaḥāba]*, Paris: G.-P. Maisonneuve et Larose.

Petöfi, J. S. and Kayser, H. (1987), 'Sprechhandlungen und Semantische Interpretation', in: Meyer-Hermann (ed.) (1978), (q.v.), 1–48.

Pratt, M. L. (1977), *Toward a Speech Act Theory of Literary Discourse*, Bloomington: Indiana University Press.

Pratt, M. L. and Traugott, E. C. (1980), *Linguistics for Students of Literature*, New York: Harcourt Brace Jovanovich.

al-Qāḍī, W. (1978), 'An Early Faṭimid Political Document', *Studia Islamica* 48: 71–108.

al-Qaysī, N. and al-Nājī, H. (1994), *Arbaʿat shuʿarāʾ ʿabbāsiyyūn*, Beirut: Dār al-Gharb al-Islāmī.

Reinert, B. (1990), 'Der Concetto-Stil in den islamischen Literaturen', in: Heinrichs (ed.) (1990) (q.v.), 366–408.

Richter, G. (1932), *Studien zur Geschichte der älteren arabischen Fürstenspiegel*, Leipzig: J. C. Hinrichs'sche Buchhandlung.

Ritter, H. (1927), *Die Bildersprache Nīẓāmīs*, Berlin and Leipzig: Walter de Gruyter.

Rosenthal, F. (trans.) (1958), *Ibn Khaldūn: The Muqaddimah: An Introduction to History*, 3 vols, New York: Pantheon.

Rubinacci, R. (1990), 'Political Poetry', in: J. Ashtiany *et al.* (eds), *The Cambridge History of Arabic Literature: ʿAbbasid Belles-Lettres*, Cambridge: Cambridge University Press, 185–201.

Sacks, H., Schegloff, E. A. and Jefferson, G. (1974), 'A Simplest Systematics for the Organization of Turn-Taking for Conversation', *Language* 50: 696–735.

Sāmarrāʾī, Y. A. (1970–1), *Al-Buḥturī fī Sāmarrā'*, 2 vols, Baghdad: Maṭbaʿat al-Irshād.

Sanders, P. (1984), *Ritual, Politics and the City in Fatimid Cairo*, Albany: SUNY Press.

Sawa, G. D. (1989), *Music Performance Practice in the Early ʿAbbāsid Era 132–320 AH/ 750–932 AD*, Toronto: Pontifical Institute of Mediaeval Studies.

Scheindlin, R. P. (1974), *Form and Structure in the Poetry of al-Muʿtamid ibn ʿAbbād*, Leiden: E. J. Brill.

Schoeler, G. (1974), *Arabische Naturdichtung: Die Zahrīyāt, Rabīʿīyāt und Rauḍīyāt von ihren Anfängen bis aṣ-Ṣanaubarī: Eine gattungs-, motiv- und stilgeschichtliche Untersuchung*, Beiruter Texte und Studien, vol. 15, Beirut/Stuttgart: Franz Steiner.

—— (1983), 'Der poetische Syllogismus: Ein Beitrag zum Verständnis der "logischen" Poetik der Araber', *ZDMG* 133: 43–92.

—— (1994), 'Ibn ar-Rūmī's Gedicht über die Dichtung und seine Gedankenlyrik', in: Heinrichs and Schoeler (eds) (1994) (q.v.), 318–36.

—— (1996), 'On Ibn al-Rūmī's Reflective Poetry: His Poem about Poetry', *JAL* 27: 22–36.

Searle, J. R. (1969), *Speech Acts: An Essay in the Philosophy of Language*. Cambridge: Cambridge University Press.

—— (1979), *Expression and Meaning: Studies in the Theory of Speech Acts*, Cambridge: Cambridge University Press.

Searle, J., Kiefer, F. and Bierwisch, M. (eds) (1980), *Speech Act Theory and Pragmatics*, Dordrecht, Boston, and London: D. Reidel.

Sells, M. A. (1987), 'The Qaṣīda and the West: Self-reflective Stereotype and Critical Encounter', *Al-ʿArabiyya* 20: 305–57.

—— (1993), '"Along the Edge of Mirage": The *Mufaḍḍalīyah* of al-Mukhabbal as-Saʿdī, an Interpretation', in: Mir and Fossum (eds) (1993), 119–36.

—— (1994a), 'Guises of the *Ghūl*: Dissembling Simile and Semantic Overflow in the Classical Arabic *Nasīb*', in: S. Stetkevych (ed.) (1994b) (q.v.), 130–64.

—— (1994b), 'Like the Arms of a Drowning Man: Simile and Symbol Worlds in the Nāqa Section of Bashāma's *Hajarta Umāma*', in: Heinrichs and Schoeler (eds) (1994) (q.v.), 18–41.

Sezgin, F. (1975), *Geschichte des arabischen Schrifttums, vol. 2: Poesie bis ca. 430H.*, Leiden: E. J. Brill.

Smith, B. H. (1978), *On the Margins of Discourse: The Relation of Literature to Language*, Chicago and London: University of Chicago Press.

Smoor, P. (1996), 'Elegies and Other Poems on Death by Ibn al-Rūmī', *JAL* 27: 49–85.

Sourdel, D. (1959–60), *Le vizirat ʿAbbāside de 749 à 936 (132 à 324 de l'Hégire)*, Damascus/Beirut: Imprimerie Catholique.

—— (1960), 'Questions de cérémonial ʿAbbaside', *Revue des Études Islamiques* 28: 121–48.

Sperl, S. (1977), 'Islamic Kingship and Arabic Panegyric Poetry in the Early 9th Century', *JAL* 8: 20–35.

—— (1989), *Mannerism in Arabic Poetry: A Structural Analysis of Selected Texts (3rd Century AH/9th Century AD – 5th Century AH/11th Century AD)*, Cambridge: Cambridge University Press.

Sperl, S. and Shackle, C. (eds) (1996), *Qasida Poetry in Islamic Asia and Africa, vol. 1: Classical Traditions and Modern Meanings; vol. 2: Eulogy's Bounty, Meaning's Abundance: An Anthology*, Leiden: E. J. Brill.

Spuler, B. (ed.) (1997), *Wirtschaftsgeschichte des Vorderen Orients in islamischer Zeit*, Handbuch der Orientalistik, 1. Abt., vol. 6, pt. 6, Leiden/Köln: E. J. Brill.

Stetkevych, J. (1975), 'The Arabic Lyrical Phenomenon in Context', *JAL* 6: 57–77.

—— (1993), *The Zephyrs of Najd: The Poetics of Nostalgia in the Classical Arabic* Nasīb, Chicago and London: University of Chicago Press.

—— (1994), 'Toward an Arabic Elegiac Lexicon: The Seven Words of the *Nasīb*', in: S. Stetkevych (ed.), 1994b (q.v.), 58–129.

Stetkevych, S. P. (1979), 'The 'Abbāsid Poet Interprets History: Three Qaṣīdahs by Abū Tammām', *JAL* 10: 49–64.

—— (1983), 'Structuralist Analyses of Pre-Islamic Poetry: Critique and New Directions', *Journal of Near Eastern Sudies* 42: 85–107.

—— (1991), *Abū Tammām and the Poetics of the 'Abbāsid Age*, Studies in Arabic Literature, vol. 13, Leiden: E. J. Brill.

—— (1993), *The Mute Immortals Speak: Pre-Islamic Poetry and the Poetics of Ritual*, Ithaca: Cornell University Press.

—— (1994a), 'Pre-Islamic Panegyric and the Poetics of Redemption: *Mufaḍḍalīyah 119* of 'Alqamah ibn 'Abdah and *Bānat Su'ād* of Ka'b ibn Zuhayr', in: S. Stetkevych (ed.), (1994b) (q.v.), 1–57.

Stetkevych, S. P. (ed.) (1994b), *Reorientations/Arabic and Persian Poetry*, Bloomington: Indiana University Press.

Traugott: see Pratt

Ullmann, M. (1970–), *Wörterbuch der klassischen arabischen Sprache*, 2 vols, Wiesbaden: Otto Harrassowitz.

—— (1989), *Adminiculum zur Grammatik des klassischen Arabisch*, Wiesbaden: Otto Harrassowitz.

—— (1984), 'Vorklassisches Arabisch', in: R. Traini (ed.) *Studi in onore di Francesco Gabrieli nel suo ottantesimo compleanno*, 2 vols, Rome: Università di Roma 'La Sapienza': Dipartimento di Studi Orientali, ii: 807–18.

Ullmann, M. and Peltz, C. (1993), *Adminiculum zur Grammatik des klassischen Arabisch: Wörterverzeichnis*, Wiesbaden: Otto Harrassowitz.

Wagner, E. (1965), *Abū Nuwās: Eine Studie zur arabischen Literatur der frühen 'Abbāsidenzeit*, Wiesbaden: Franz Steiner.

—— (1963), *Die arabische Rangstreitdichtung und ihre Einordnung in die allgemeine Literaturgeschichte*, Akademie der Wissenschaften und der Literatur, Abhandlungen der geistes- und sozialwissenschaftlichen Klasse, Jahrgang 1962, no. 8, Wiesbaden: Franz Steiner.

—— (1987–8), *Grundzüge der klassischen arabischen Dichtung, vol. 1: Die altarabische Dichtung; vol. 2: Die arabische Dichtung in islamischer Zeit*, Darmstadt: Wissenschaftliche Buchgesellschaft.

Walzer, R. and Gibb, H. A. R. (1960), 'Akhlāḳ', *EI*[2] i: 325–6.

Wehr, H. (1951), 'Starre syntaktische Schemata als affektische Ausdrucksformen im Arabischen', *ZDMG* 101: 107–24.

Weisweiler, M. (1958), ''Abdalqāhir al-Jurjānī's Werk über die Unnachahmlichkeit des Korans und seine syntaktisch-stilistischen Lehren', *Oriens* 11: 77–121.

Wright, W. (1896–8), *A Grammar of the Arabic Language*, 2 vols, 3rd edition, repr. 1985, Cambridge: Cambridge University Press.

WKAS: see Ullmann

Yarshater, E. (gen. ed.) (1985–), *The History of al-Ṭabarī*, various translators, Albany: SUNY Press.

INDEX OF VERSES

Synopses (*italicized*) and paraphrases (underlined) of passages are listed under the beginning verse.

Abū Tammām
Dīwān, no. 4
32–3 208

Dīwān, no. 42
7 290 n77

ʿAlī b. al-Jahm
Dīwān, no. 23
1–9 21–2
27–30 22
36–8 23
49–51 23–4

al-Aʿshā
Dīwān, no. 55
6 308 n15

Dīwān, no. 42
7 290 n77

al-Buḥturī
Dīwān, no. 81
27–8 208–9

Dīwān, no. 679
16 19
24–5 19
32–3 19–20
35–9 19–20

Diʿbil
Dīwān, no. 204
1 297 n29

Ibn al-Rūmī
Long encomia
L191
Full translation 171–81
2–70 157 fig. 11
9 97
10–11 80, 97
12–13 97
14–17 97–8, 159
18 97–8
19 97–8, 164
20 114, 297–8 n46
21 114
24–30 136–7
61 115, 160
62–3 160
65–70 99–100
69 160
71 60
96–175 166–7 fig. 13
96 65
97–175 162 fig. 12
98–102 214
109 215
113–15 215
116 216
117 64, 119
120 118
121 64, 119
122 64
128–35 110
130 167
133 167
136–140 169

141–7 217–18
148–9 217
150 62
151 65
152 69
153 250
154 69, 250
155–6 72, 250
162 68
164–6 116–17
172–3 69–70, 116
174 69
175 67

L215
1–72 302 n5
2–3 89
4 298 n48
9–12 82
17–20 101
21 101, 298 n47
22–27 101–2
28 297 n46
32 298 n46
35–59 210–12
68–70 261
71 142, 261
72 261
73–4 60
87–90 152
99–103 152
101–4 265–6
106–7 61
115 91
144–9 201
150 66, 202
151–2 66, 206

L434
18 61
24–5 106
32–3 289 n55
34–5 71

L994
20–84 183, fig. 14
20–31 130–1
40 185
42 184
57 185
62 186
84–5 64

95–102 67–8
103–4 66
105–6 70
109 83
110 62

L1042
Full translation 191–5
1 182
5 183
8–9 183
14–47 183 fig. 14
14 60
21 186
31–2 187
33 187
40 188
41 60, 187
48–68 189 fig. 15
61–2 118
66 63, 119
67 63, 118
68 72, 120, 191

L1306
1 298 n46
4 298 n46
5–6 79–80
7 79–80, 207
8–9 60–1
14 63, 92
15 63
16–18 71–2, 87
46 289 n55

L1307
24–31 148–9
39–46 141–2
47 66, 141–2

L1600
248–51 30

L1611
8–9 208
22–31 223–4
34–5 308 n4
37–43 222
49–55 221
86–9 143
104 61
105 202

109 202
113 202–3
117 202–3
121 202–3
125 202–3
127–8 84
129 202–3
146 65
153 86
197 83
207 65
223 146
226 71
231 70
232–46 126–8
250 301 n35
252 70, 87
253–4 87–8
269–70 63
273 69
292 91
297 67
300 67
301 62
303 62

L1250'
30–2 96
33–8 89–90
39–45 134–5
46 138
47–8 114, 138
49–58 138–9
59–62 133
63–5 81
120–8 199–200
144–8 209
151–2 204–5
153 91, 204–5
154–7 204–5
163–4 116
178 300 n72
187 116
189–90 62

L1302'
86 31
87 31

Felicitations
F458
66 69

F952
1 64
36 106
39–42 106
43–56 107–8
74 67

F1243
12–14 240
15 241
19–22 240
29 241
32 242
33 241
34–8 242–3

F1373'
178–81 257
186–91 257–8
261 254
263–6 254
267 255

Short encomia
S1312'
3–4 234

Admonitions
A212
1–2 259
3–4 260

A446 50

A464
3–5 255
6–9 256
10–11 256

A694
2–8 3–4
12 3–4, 253
13–15 253
16 254

A1160
1 239
2 235
4–5 236
8–10 237
12 237
14–15 238

17 236
18 236
22–5 238
26 237

A1171 258–9

A1510
11–12 243
13–14 244
18–19 244
23 245
24–5 245

Satire
H1243
81–3 309 n24

Epigrams
E18 314 n43

E19 7

E68 313 n26

E110 47

E876 313 n24

E1448’ 234–5

E1252’ 251

E1307’
2–5 251–2

Kushājim
Dīwān, no. 93
32–3 8

al-Makhzūmī, al-Ḥārith b. Khālid
Burhān, 10 (var. of *Aghānī*, iii: 331) 85

GENERAL INDEX

ʾa- (vocative) 133; *see also* vocative
ʾa- (interrogative) 302 n17
ʿAbbās 43
Abbasid(s) ix, 10–11, 23, 43, 45, 289 n59; administration 9; ideology ix; insignia 200; *see also* caliphs
ʿAbdallāh b. Ṭāhir b. al-Ḥusayn 186, 201, 263
ʿAbīd b. al-Abraṣ 258, 313 n36
abstraction *see tajrīd*
Abū Aḥmad *see* ʿUbaydallāh b. ʿAbdallāh
Abū l-ʿAtāhiya 5
Abū Nuwās 5, 222, 280 n20
Abū Tammām 5, 45, 48; as innovator 12, 52, 59; as panegyrist 10, 17, 107, 295 n74; poetry of 15, 208, 279 n32, 280 n20, 281 n40, 284 nn26, 41, 290 n72
accounts *see akhbār*
accuser (female): persona of 32–3, 39, 81, 94–8, 103, 105, 112–13, 115, 161; pre-Islamic 94, 292 n2; in scenes 129, 134–6, 156–7, 159
act of speech *see* speech act
acts and words *see* patron; praise; words
adab, ādāb 5–6, 8, 12, 230, 278 n10, 314 n15
adab literature ix, 43
adab story 50
address 125, 295 n2; as scene 135–6, 144 fig., 154 fig.; of two companions 19; *see also* vocative
addressee: of dedication 66, 74; of message 104; of poem 14, 27, 36, 49; of speech act 75; *see also* dedicatee; dedication; *mamdūḥ*; patron
ʿādhil(a) see persona of the accuser
adīb, udabāʾ 31, 43, 51, 182; *ḥaqq al-* 295 n74
ʿadl 233, 265
admonisher *see* accuser
admonition *see ʿitāb*
ʿAdnān 31
advice *see* speech acts of praise
advice literature 11, 263
affiliation: ethnic 9; religious 9
ʿāfī 134; *see also* persona of the supplicant
Aḥmad Ibn Abī Ṭāhir *see* Ibn Abī Ṭāhir Ṭayfūr
Aḥmad b. Muhammad b. Ṭāhir *see* al-ʿUqaylī
akhbār ix, 50
akhdh 6; *see also* borrowing; *sariqa*
al-ʿAlāʾ b. Ṣāʿid 6, 9, 43, 45, 51–2
ʿalāma (sign) 85; *see also bayān*
ʿAlī b. Abī Ṭālib 42
ʿAlī b. al-Furāt 49
ʿAlī b. al-Jahm 5, 12, 21–4, 33, 279 n37, 280 nn51–2; as panegyrist 21–4, 230, 263, 281 n40, 282 n58, 314 n1; poetry of 13, 35, 313 n30
ʿAlī b. Yaḥyā b. al-Munajjim 9, 30, 44, 53, 248, 279 n20
Alid rebel 42, 284 n34
aliknī 65, 104; *see also* speech act
alladhī 163, 200; *see also* relative pronoun; relative clause
allusion *see talmīḥ*
ʿamal see poet: work of
amateur *see* dilettante
ambiguity 33; *see also madīḥ*
ambivalence *see* ambiguity; *madīḥ*
al-Amīn 131, 184
amīr 105; *see also* patron; patron's persona; patronage relationship; ruler
'Among School Children' 168
ʿAmr b. Bāna 8

ʿAmr b. Layth 43–4, 65, 86, 94, 104, 126
ʿAmr b. Tamīm b. Murr (chieftain) 312 n31
analogy, analogical (trope) 90, 135, 150, 154, 306–7 n27; definition of 292 n36; in dramaturgy 20, 129, 199, 207–15, 218, 238; as part of phantasmagoria 225; rhetorical 307 n31; *see also* dialogue scene; figures of speech; image; metaphor; motif; sententia
anaphora, anaphoric 54–5, 57, 115, 137–9, 160, 165, 199–205, 207, 218
ancients, the *see mutaqaddimūn*
al-Andalus 280 n7
Andalusian cities 265
anecdote(s) 32
anthropology 17; linguistic 37, 283 n3; *see also* theory: anthropological
antistrophe 53, 72–4; definition of 15; function of 59, 271 fig.; imagery in 88, 202, 226; themes of 54–6, 206
antithesis 15, 204, 207; *see also* parallelism
aphorism 16
apostrophe (punctuation) xiii; *see also* vocative
apotheosis 55
approach: contextual 14, 16–18; intertextual 14, 16, 18, 26; pragmatic x, 26–7; synchronic x; textual 14–16
ʿaqd (counting on fingers) 85
ʿaql, ʿaqlī 233, 247, 283 n8, 311 n5
Arab(s) 85; genealogy 31; Northern 31
Arabic: background 6; literature 229; script 31, 85; *see also* audience; civilization; genealogists; grammatical terminology; linguistic tradition; linguists; philosophers; poetic critics; scholars; society
Arabic-Islamic civilization ix, 229; *see also* society
Arabic-Islamic culture *see* Arabic-Islamic civilization
ʿarabiyya 6, 17, 30–1, 278 n14
Aramean background 6, 230
architect 45
argumentation (speech figure) *see istishhād*
al-Aʿshā, Maynūn b. Qays 308 n15
al-ʿAskarī 43, 208
assertion *see* speech act
assertive see speech act
aṭlāl: motif 15, 18–19, 53, 85, 100–2, 293 n27; as metaphor 102, 113, 133
attitude (behavioral) *see* poet; speaker
attitude (posture) *see niṣba*
audience(s) (hearers or readers) 10; medieval Arabic 5–10, 18, 24, 26–7, 33, 47, 260; courtly 17; double, simultaneous 34–5; educated, critical 32, 58; *see also* court; society
audience(s) (event): official, public *see majlis ʿāmm*; semi-private *see majlis al-uns*
Austen, Jane 28
Austin, John L. 37, 40, 283 n2
avarice 209; *see also* generosity
Aws b. Ḥajar 258, 313 n35
āya 53; *see also* Koran; Sūra
ayyām 104; *see also* fate

background: ethnic 6; non-Arab 31; *see also* Arabic; Aramean; Byzantine; Greek; Persian; Sasanian
badīʿ 11–12, 43
badīʿ-style 12, 17; *see also muḥdath*
Baghdad, Baghdadian ix, 5, 18, 42–3, 45, 49, 65, 68, 104, 184, 200, 220, 230, 232, 290 n65, 307 n34
Bakr b. al-Naṭṭāḥ 5
Barmakids 49, 292 n31
Basaj, Aḥmad Ḥasan 51
Bashshār b. Burd 11, 15, 48, 284 n41
Basra 5, 265, 279 n20, 284 n34
battle scene 53, 139
Bauer, Thomas 58, 226, 281 nn31, 33
bayān (speech figure) 16
bayān (way of signifying) 85; *ʿilm al-* 85
bayt 68
bear xi
Bedouin 5
begriffliche Doppelbödigkeit 219
beloved *see ḥabīb*; persona of ‘laughing one’; youth
Bencheikh, Jamal Eddine 7, 58, 226
benefactor 18
Benveniste, Émile 37–8, 40, 73–4, 119, 141, 149, 168
bildarmer Stil 218
Bloch, Alfred 14
boast *see fakhr*
boon companion *see nadīm*
Booth, Wayne 229
borrowing *see akhdh*; *istiḥqāq*; *sariqa*
Boustany, Said 231; concordance with 276–7 fig.

Browning, Robert 138, 298 n56
al-Buḥturī 5, 12, 33, 43–6, 48; as panegyrist 10, 17–18, 24, 50, 107, 263; poetry of 13, 19–20, 52, 209, 230, 279 nn32, 49, 281 n40, 282 n43, 284 nn26, 41, 313 n30; relations with Ibn al-Rūmī 45, 140, 210, 260–2, 314 n45; relations with ʿUbaydallāh b. ʿAbdallāh 18, 20, 44, 261, 314 n45
Bureau of Poety *see dīwān al-shiʿr*
Bustān 265, 284 n34
Būyid(s) 49, 86, 234, 311 n7
bystander *see* persona
Byzantium, Byzantine ix; background 6, 94, 282 n54

calamities *see* fate
caliph(s), caliphate 8, 12–13, 22–3, 42, 44, 229, 289 n55
caliphal circle *see* circle
caliphal family 5
caliphal praise *qaṣīda see* praise *qaṣīda*
call for help *see istighātha*
camel description *see raḥīl*
camel section *see raḥīl*
campsite traces *see aṭlāl* 15
canon *see* corpus
Carnap, Rudolf 283 n2
ceremonies, public 8; *see also* audience (event); *majālis*
chamberlain *see ḥājib*
characterization 39–41, 76, 79, 263
characters *see* dramatis personae; persona
charity *see al-tabarruʿ bi-l-nāʾil*
cheating in trade *see taghābun*
Chosroe 281 n40
Christ 107
circle(s) 5–8; caliphal 6, 278 n5; courtly ix; literary *see majlis al-uns*; lower 6; middle, upper 9; of al-Mutawakkil 11; of ʿUbaydallāh b. ʿAbdallāh 30
Civil War 5, 131
civilization *see* Arabic-Islamic
clients 5
closure: device(s) of 16; of poem 20
collected works *see dīwān*
commerce *see* motif of trade
commissive see speech act
commitment(s): mutual, reciprocal 72, 81, 92, 115, 231–2, 239, 244, 246, 262, 264; unilateral 74, 81; *see also* patron; patronage relationship; relationship; speech; words
communication: conditions of 52; historical 33; levels of 34; mode of 7; (non-)verbal 85; reciprocal 33; *see also madīḥ*; patronage; patronage relationship; patronage scene; praise *qaṣīda*
comparison(s) 201, 207–8; inverted 214, 216–17; received 16; textual 17
compensation 9, 62; *see also* reward
composers 8
composition: larger forms of 13; of sections 13
conceit *see concetto*
concettism, baroque 219
concetto, 16, 91, 93, 145, 204, 281 n28
condition(s): of appropriateness 28–9, 285 n56; essential, 74, 235; preparatory 38, 74, 235–6, 238, 240, 242; sincerity 38, 74–5, 235–6, 238, 240–2, 244
conditional mood 117, 245; negated 117, 164, 166–7 fig.
congratulation *see* speech acts of praise: felicitation; *see also tahniʾa*
connoisseur 6, 10
contemplation *see iʿtibār*
context 27–32, 283 n10; historical 72; *see also* literary speech situation
conversation: in *majālis* 48; maxims of 29, 284 n21; rules, expectations of 28–9; turn(s) of 125, 210, 212–3
co-operation *see* patronage relationship
co-operative principle 29
Coriolanus 37–9
corpus, pre-Islamic 14, 257
counting on fingers *see ʿaqd*
courage 19, 22, 55, 233, 311 n5
court: Abbasid 3, 49, 230; ceremonial 11, 278 n5; literature 17
courtier 11
courtier-poet 11
courtly culture 6, 55
craft *see ṣanʿa*; *ṣināʿa*
criticism 3; *see also* poetic criticism; ʿUbaydallāh
cupbearer 53, 143, 220, 222–3, 308–9 n15

ḍāḥik see person a of 'laughing one'
dalāla 85
dahr 96, 104; *see also* fate
decency *see ʿiffa*

declarative see speech act
decrees 230
dedicatee: non-paying 47; *see also* addressee
dedication 11, 18–20, 40–1, 50, 56–7, 269–70 fig.; double function of 75, 121; as entire passage 67, 296 n15; first 27; omitted 34, 69, 72; pre-Islamic 290 n67; in scenes 130, 231; second 282 n50; speech act of 59, 65–72, 73–4, 149, 271 fig.; *see also manaḥtukahā*
denial *see inkār*
descriptive passage *see waṣf* episode
descriptive poetry *see waṣf*
desert journey 53, 139, 146
deserted abode *see aṭlāl*
device: dramatic 33; structural, structuring 15–16, 18
Dhū l-Aktāf *see* Shāpūr
Dhū l-Wizāratayn *see* Ṣā'id b. Makhlad
dialogue 23–4, 33, 35, 79, 263; between dramatis personae 33, 35; dramatic, literary 34; everyday 35; fictional 35; forms, levels of 12, 34, 36; hyperbolic (i.e. with hyperbolic praise) 130, 140, 216, 296 nn15, 17, 299 n71; poetic, criteria and types of 32–6, 285 n50; with *shayb* 98; typology of 35, 285 n50; *see also* dramaturgy; dialogue scene; episode; persona; *qaṣīda*; speech
dialogue scene 125–32, 126 fig., 130 fig., 140, 144 fig., 154 fig., 263, 295 n55; argumentative 126–9, 126 fig., 132, 154–5, 231, 296 n13, 310 n8; in dramaturgy 156–8, 160–5, 166–7 fig., 170, 183 fig., 184, 186–90, 189 fig.; extended 132–3; imagery in 214; unintroduced 134–5, 138; univocal 126, 129–32, 130 fig., 154–5; *see also* address; evocation; impersonal speaker; implicit speaker; monologue; patronage scene
Di'bil al-Khuzā'ī 5, 7, 12, 33, 263, 280 n52, 314 n1
dignitaries, religious 5
dilapidated abode *see aṭlāl*
dilettante(s) 7, 12; poet 8, 230; poetry 9, 12
Dimashqī, friend of Ibn al-Rūmī 43
dīnār (currency) 45, 49, 288 n9
direct speech acts *see* speech acts of praise
directive see speech act
dirham (currency) 49, 288 n9
display text(s) 28
disputation *see jadal*
dispute poetry *see munāẓara*
divertissement 7–8, 230
dīwān, dawāwīn ix
dīwān al-shi'r 11
doctrine: of created Koran 21, 263, 282 n51; Ḥanafī 21; Mu'tazilī 21; *see also* Koran; policy; Sūra
do ut des 74, 246; *see also* patron; patronage relationship; poet; relationship
Dome of the Poets *see qubbat al-shu'arā'*
Don Juan 39
double entendre 305 n23
drama 58; German 33
dramatic discourse x, 27, 35, 39; model 33; *see also* dialogue; speech act
dramatis personae 33, 36, 39, 76, 79, 125, 143, 226, 230, 263; as opposed to personifications 88, 90, 94; as opposed to witnesses 146, 150; *see also* persona; speech
dramaturgy 33, 39, 41, 75, 79, 154–5 figs., 231, 263, 265, 310 n8; of antistrophe 162, 183–4, 183 fig., 186–9; of metastrophe 162–5, 162 fig., 182, 189–90, 189 fig.; of strophe 156–8, 157 fig., 182–3; timeframe of 138, 144, 163; *see also* accuser; analogy; dialogue scene; dramatis personae; episode; evocation scene; figures of speech; *'itāb*; monologue scene; patronage scene; persona; praise *qaṣīda*; scene; speech; *tahni'a*; witnesses
Dūdān, Banū 258
dūnakahā see dedication
duty *see* commitment; patron; poet
dynasties, pre-Islamic 257; *see also* Abbasid(s); Būyid(s); Umayyad(s)

education, level of 6
effort *see jahd*
emphasis, rhetorical *see ta'kīd*; *see also* question
encomium *see* praise *qaṣīda*
encounter *see* scene
enemy *see* persona
English literature 37
enthronement *see* occasions of felicitation
epigram(s) 4–5

episode 34–5, 145–6, 150–4, 153–4 figs, 155; containing speech 92; in dramaturgy 183 fig.; imagery in 226; introduced by *wa-rubba* 53, 285 n55; narrative 35; *see also fakhr* episode; *madīḥ* episode; phantasmagoria; *wa-rubba*; *waṣf* episode
epistle(s) 230, 263; doctrinal 11
ethics 37, 39; *see also* patronage
etiology 80, 187–8; fantastic 225, 247, 291 n14; mock 84, 93, 185; *see also* motif
etymon 15
eulogy 7, 26; *see also madīḥ*; praise poetry; praise *qaṣīda*
evocation scene 136–7, 144 fig., 145, 154 fig.; in dramaturgy 156, 161; *see also* address; dialogue scene; monologue scene
exclamation 129, 140, 207
excuse *see iʿtidhār*
exhortation 3
expansion (grammatical term) *see tawassuʿ*
explanation *see bayān*
expressive see speech act

Faḍl 279 n20
fakhr, mufākhara 4–5, 40, 53–4, 58, 220, 281 n31
fakhr episode 99, 143, 147, 151, 154 fig., 155; dearth of personae in 94; speaker in 139, 142, 147, 151; themes of 146, 269–70 fig.; *see also* episode; impersonal speaker; *madīḥ* episode; witnesses
familiar *see jalīs*
fantastic action *see* phantasmagoria
al-faraj baʿda l-shidda 50
farewell *see* speech act of greeting
faṣl al-khiṭāb 60, 289 n49
fate: in antistrophe 105, 107, 203, 253; blame, curse of 132, 136; personification of 39; in strophe 95–6, 104, 112–13, 134–6, 161–2, 170, 211, 213; injustice (*ẓulm*) of 53
felicitation *see tahniʾa*
Felman, Shoshana 39
festivals: Easter 44; *Ḥajj* 203, 239; *ʿĪd al-Aḍḥā* 46, 48, 306 n6; *ʿĪd al-Fiṭr* (Breaking of the Fast) 44, 46, 48; *Mihrajān* 46, 48, 64, 257, 288 nn2, 28, 289 n59; *Nawrūz* 44, 46, 48, 289 n59; Passover 44
field, semantic 11, 15
figure(s) of speech 199; binary 15; combination of 219; in dramaturgy 219; paralogical 291 n14; placement of 58; rhetorical 11, 16, 33, 126, 154 fig., 155, 165, 199; semantic 199, 218, 207, 213; syntactic 16, 59, 154, 165, 199, 218; *see also* formal unity; image; imagery; metaphor; phantasmagoria; *takhyīl*
Fihrist 51
Fish, Stanley 37–8, 74, 250, 285 n56
flattery 3
formal unity 220, 222, 290 n72; 303 n38
forms: large 14; literary 17; non-contiguous 14
French literature 37
fulfillment *see* performance
functionary *see* official
Fürstenspiegel see mirrors for princes

gain *see takassub*
Gelder, Jan Geert van 33
genealogist(s), medieval Arabic 42, 257
general(s) 13, 229
general 'you' *see* witnessing 'you'
generosity 19, 32, 34, 55, 107, 110, 214–17, 247, 249, 255–6, 264; functions of 241–2; as justice 233, 240–2, 246; lacking 56, 88, 140, 162, 165, 187, 245; unlimited 55; *see also* image; motif; personification
Gennep, Arnold van 281 n31
genre(s) 27–32, 248, 283 n5; ceremonial 5, 13, 280 n18; functions of 283 n11, 284 nn31, 34, 285 n56; ignorance of 31; light, informal 8, 13; multilingual 280 n7; panegyric i, x; poetic 31; *see also fakhr*; *ghazal*; *hijāʾ*; *ʿitāb*; *khamriyya*; *madīḥ*; *ṭardiyya*
gesture *see ishāra*
al-ghāʾib (grammatical term) 112, 295 n2
ghāniyāt 103; *see also* personae of the women
gharaḍ, aghrāḍ 13, 59, 68, 283 n5
gharīb 11
Ghassān 257
ghazal ix, 5, 13, 51, 94, 102, 146
ghuluww see hyperbole: extreme
gift(s) 20; *see also* compensation; reward
glosses 12
God 21–3
good deeds *see niʿma*

governor(s) 5–6, 13, 263–4; *see also* ʿUbaydallāh
grammarian(s) *see* linguists
grammatical mood 119
grammatical person(s) 32, 120 fig., 125, 128, 144 fig., 295 n56; first 137; first and second (present) 36, 73, 112, 125 128, 144, 149; first and third (evocation) 145; lacking first 141; lacking second 136; second plural 130, 289 n52; shift from first to third 142–3; shift from second to first 33, 284 n40; shift from third to second 33, 128; switch of 16, 33, 112, 126 fig.; third (absent) 73, 112, 114, 125, 133, 136, 141, 143–4, 151, 156, 245; of witnesses 145–6; *see also* address; dialogue scene; dramaturgy; evocation; impersonal speaker; implicit speaker; persona; scene; speaker; speech
grammatical terminology, Arabic 112
grammatical tradition 74
Granada 265
granting a plea *see ijābat al-sāʾil*
gratitude 108, 234, 311 n7; *see also* poem of gratitude
gray hair *see shayb*
Greek: background 42, 313 n28; sciences 46
Grice, Paul 29, 283 n2
guard *see shurṭa*

ḥabīb 15, 291 n7, 292 n1, 297 n45; *see also* youth
Ḥadhāmi (seer) 134
ḥājib 45
Ḥajj 203; *see also* festivals
ḥāl: accusative, clause 66; as signifier 85
Hamori, Andras 15
Ḥanafite(s) 282 n51
han(n)aʾa 64
ḥaqq 140, 265; *see also adīb*; poet
Ḥarb, Āl *see* Umayyads
harmonious choice of images *see murāʿāt al-naẓīr*
Hāshim, Banū 23
al-Ḥaṭīm 203, 303 n13
ḥawādith 96, 104; *see also* fate
Heinrichs, Wolfhart 6, 44, 219–21, 278 n17, 296 n8
hemistich(es), balanced 16
Hess-Lüttich, Ernest W. B. 28, 33, 35
Hibatallāh, son of Ibn al-Rūmī 42
hieros gamos see motif of bride, wife
hijāʾ, ahājī ix, 4–5, 10, 31, 46–7, 51, 149, 190–1, 283 n5; criticism of 213, 260–1; lie in 248; indirect, contextual, praise turned into 142, 250–1, 259–61, 302 n21; of ʿUbaydallāh 44, 249
ḥikma, ḥikam 16
historian(s) 42
historiography 11
history 17; Islamic 17
ḥiwār 85; *see also* dialogue
hoariness *see shayb*
Holy Book *see* Koran
homonym 68, 303 n24, 314 n38; *see also double entendre*
honor 55; as wealth destroyed 105, 241–2, 310–11 n2
honor code *see muruwwa*
hospitality *see qirā l-aḍyāf*
hunt *see* onager; oryx
al-Ḥusayn b. al-Ḍaḥḥāk 5
al-Ḥusayn b. Muḥammad al-Ṭāʾī 282 n43
al-Ḥusayn b. Muṣʿab 186, 201
al-Ḥuṣrī 44
hyperbole 19, 109, 207, 249; causal 30, 80, 84–7, 90–1, 93, 204, 249, 254–7, 291 n14; extreme 247; inverted 87–8, 107
hyperbolic comparison 107
hyperbolic dialogue *see* dialogue
hyperbolic expression 90
hyperbolic praise *see* praise
hyperbolic reinterpration 82

ʿibāra 85
Ibn Abī Duʾād 23, 282 n58
Ibn Abī Ṭāhir Ṭayfūr 43
Ibn al-Athīr, Ḍiyāʾ al-Dīn 33, 284 n38
Ibn Bisṭām 314 n45
Ibn Firās 45
Ibn al-Ḥājib (*Dīwān* redactor) 51
Ibn al-Jawzī 27
Ibn Khaldūn 264
Ibn al-Mudabbir *see* Ibrāhīm
Ibn al-Muqaffaʿ 11
Ibn al-Musayyab al-Kātib 51
Ibn al-Muʿtazz 43, 220
Ibn Nubāta 51
Ibn Qutayba 13, 281 n31
Ibn Rashīq 7, 46, 226
Ibn al-Rūmī x, 3–5, 7, 25; as author 140, 185, 190, 199, 207, 209–10, 214,

218–19, 222, 231, 246, 249, 309 n28, 309–10 n 29; as dramatist 160–5, 168, 189; as innovator 12, 56, 59, 75, 93, 126, 170, 223, 225–6, 230, 264; pessimism, superstition of 42; as poetic critic 51; relationship with ʿUbaydallāh 30, 43–4, 48, 50, 184, 230–2, 262, 265; relevance of dramatic discourse, speech act theory for 27, 32–3, 35, 37–40, 73; vita and patrons 10, 17, 30–1, 42–7, 49; *see also* al-Buḥturī; poet; poet's persona; ʿUbaydallāh b. ʿAbdallāh
Ibn Ṭayfūr *see* Ibn Abī Ṭāhir Ṭayfūr
Ibn Wahb al-Kātib *see* Isḥāq b. Ibrāhīm
Ibn al-Zayyāt 279 nn20, 30, 32
Ibrāhīm al-Bayhaqī 43
Ibrāhīm b. al-Mahdī 8
Ibrāhīm b. al-Mudabbir 50, 279 n20
ibtidāʾ 13, 284 n37
ʿĪd see festivals
ideology *see* Abbasids
ʿiffa 233
ighrāʾ 283 n5
ijābat al-sāʾil 233
ikhtirāʿ 226
illocutionary acts 38
illocutionary force 37, 75, 283 n11
iltifāt 33
image(s): for acts and poets 253; for fear 214; for generosity 201, 214, 217; for *qaṣīda* 24; for verse 20; *see also* motif; iconology
imagery: fantastic 11; Islamic 54–5; mythical 54; pre-Islamic 54; stereotyped 14, 16; *see also* antistrophe; metastrophe; monologue; praise *qaṣīda*; semantic figures; strophe
imaginary action *see* phantasmagoria
imperative 118–9, 128, 140, 167 fig.
implicature 28
implied audience 34; *see also* audience
implied author 34, 182, 285 n47
improvisation 9, 44
Imru'ulqays 258
incentive (poetry) *see ighrāʾ*
incoherent harmony of terms 219, 308 n4; *see also* formal unity
inferential thinking *see istidlāl*
inkār 168, 302 n17; *see also* question
intention(s) 28, 37; authorial *see gharaḍ*; to praise *see* speech acts of praise
interaction: via poetry 32; within poetry 32, 145, 150, 155; *see also madīḥ*; praise *qaṣīda*
intercession 9, 20, 45, 50
intersubjectivity 73–4, 150
intertextuality 6, 158, 161, 183 fig., 186–90
invocation *see* speech acts of praise
inzilām 233
Iranian *see* festivals, Persian, *shuʿūbiyya*
Iraq 19
irony 29
Isḥāq b. Ibrāhīm b. Sulaymān b. Wahb al-Kātib 85–6
Isḥāq al-Mawṣilī 8
ishāra 85
al-Iskāfī 14
Islam ix, 184, 289 n59
ism, asmāʾ 60
Ismāʿīl b. Bulbul 9–10, 44–6, 284 n30
istiʿāra see metaphor; speech: figurative attribution of
istidlāl 85, 284 n41
istifhām (speech figure) 302 n17
istighātha 295 n2
istinṭāq 291 n21
al-istishhād wa-l-iḥtijāj 208
ʿitāb: classification of 283 n5; direct 57–8; dramaturgy of 40, 75, 261; *in lieu* of dedication 69; in message 65; poems of 3–4, 51, 129, 231–2, 235–9, 243–6, 253–6, 258–61; of ʿUbaydallāh x, 44, 52
iʿtibār 85
iʿtidhār 4, 56; poem of 45
istiḥqāq 87
iʿtiqād 85

jābī 169, 302 n18
Jacobi, Renate 13–15
jadal 165, 296 n8
jahd see poet: work of
Jāhiliyya ix, 17
al-Jāḥiẓ 11, 42, 45, 85, 229
Jahmite(s) 282 n51
Jakobson, Roman 33
jalīs, julasāʾ 11, 48, 229
jāra see persona of the neighbor
jinn, jinnī
Job 170
judge(s) 5
al-Jurjānī, ʿAbdalqāhir 84, 163, 208, 210, 247–8, 292 n36, 302 n17

jussive mood 140; negated 119, 164–5, 166–7 fig., 295 n77
justice *see ʿadl*

Kaaba 19, 204, 239, 288 n28, 306 n13
kalām (logical argumentation) 296 n8; *see also jadal*
kātib, kuttāb 8, 230; *see also* scribe
Katz, Jerrold 283 n2
kawāʾib see personae of the women
khabar see akhbār
Khālid b. Yazīd (scribe) 7, 279 n20
khamriyya ix, 4–5, 13, 94, 139, 146, 220, 288 n28; themes of 53, 269–70 fig.
al-Khansāʾ (slave-girl of Hishām al-Makfūf) 279 n20
al-Khaṭīb al-Baghdādī 46
khaṭṭ see Arabic script
khill see persona of friend
khudhhā see dedication
Khurāsān, Khurāsānian x, 43, 263
khuṭūb 104; *see also* fate
kināya see metonymy
Kinda 257
kitāb (writing) *see* Arabic script
Kitāb Akhbār al-zamān 288 n3
Kitāb al-Badīʿ 219
Kitāb al-Maḥāṣin wa-masāwī 287 n17
Kitāb al-Shukr see Risālat al-Shukr
Koran 89–90, 96–7, 103, 139, 170, 234; codex 292 n34; *see also āya*; doctrine; Sūra
Koranic allusion 69, 223, 238, 255, 290 n75, 294 n36, 303 nn26, 29, 304 nn42, 48, 52, 5, 305 nn31, 34, 309 n21, 311 n22, 313 n31, 314 n43; *see also* Sūra
Koranic exegetes 14
Koranic figure(s) 303 n29
Kufa, Kufan 5, 42
kunya, kunā 60
Kushājim 8

Labīd Rabīʿa 258
lafẓ, alfāẓ 85, 87
lamentation 102, 136–7; *see also marthiya*; *nudba*
lampoon *see hijāʾ*
landowner(s) 5
layālī 96, 104; *see also* fate
leaders, leadership ix; military 5; *see also* governor; ruler
Lévi-Strauss, Claude 281 n31
lexicographer(s) ix
licentious poetry *see mujūn*
lie, poetic 210, 247–9, 260; *see also madīḥ*; praise *qaṣīda*; premise; speakers; syllogism
linguistic(s) 6, 37, 74
linguistic tradition, Arabic 295 n56
linguists, medieval Arabic 157, 163, 278 n14
lisān al-ḥāl see istinṭāq; *see also bayān*
literary aesthetic ix
literary form 3
literary genre *see* genre
literary patronage *see* patronage
literary prestige ix
literary production 28
literary services 9, 57
literary speech situation 27–32, 249, 263, 285 n56; of Abbasid poetry 29; medium, preparation, unidirectionality of 28
literati 7
logic 44
love, unfulfilled 19; *see also ḥabīb*; *nasīb*; youth
love lyric, love poetry *see ghazal*
loyalty *see* poet
lute-player(s) ix, 220–2

al-Maʿarrī 42
madīḥ, madāʾiḥ; Abbasid ix-x, 4–5, 7–8, 10, 13, 18–19, 21–4, 33–4, 37; ambivalence of x, 163, 168–71, 187, 217; claimed 87; classification of 283 n5; as communication 59, 170; conventions, themes of 19, 23, 30; criticism within 182, 189; functions of 25, 229, 232, 235, 251; as income 43; length of 52; longevity of 229; of long-term patrons 46, 244; as mirror 229, 242, 262; performance of 48; practice of 48–51; and pragmatics 26–7, 30–33, 37; pre-existing 18; price of 45, 49, 108, 243; significance of ix-x; speech in 79; standard catalogue of 34, 40, 54–6, 58, 162; transfer of 231, 247; truth of 109, 247–9, 255; of ʿUbaydallāh b. ʿAbdallāh 43–4, 52–3, 273–4 fig.; Umayyad 10, 15; *see also* antistrophe; patronage; praise; praise *qaṣīda*; reward

madīḥ episode 145–8, 151, 154 fig., 155, 183 fig., 183–9, 219; *see also* witnesses
majāz 291 n22
majlis, majālis: access to 50; *ʿāmm* ix, 13; etiquette, protocol of 48; *al-uns* 5–6, 8, 13, 287–8 n1; *see also* circle
majūs(ī) see Zoroastrian
make-believe *see takhyīl*
Makhlad, Banū 45
Mālik b. Ṭawq al-Taghlibī 208
mamdūḥ 15, 33, 47; *see also* addressee; dedicatee; patron
al-Maʾmūn 5, 11, 21, 184, 263
Man, Paul de 168, 170
maʿnā, maʿānī 11; as content 87; *see also* figure of speech; image; motif
manaḥa 65
manaḥtukahā 38, 73–4; *see also* dedication; patronage relationship; speech acts of praise
Manichaeism *see zandaqa*
mannerist, mannerism 6–7, 12, 16, 161, 219–20, 226, 263, 278 n 17, 308 nn1–2, 309 n29; *see also concetto*; figures of speech; *hyperbole*; *muḥdath* poetry; *takhyīl*
manners 5; *see also adab*
al-Manṣūr Mosque 49
manuscript sources 51
marthiya ix, 5, 13, 51, 265, 284 n34; motifs of 100; *see also nudba*
Marwān, Banū *see* Umayyads
Marwān b. Abī l-Janūb 49, 230, 310 n5
al-Marzubānī 31, 46, 226, 309 n27
al-Marzūqī 14
al-Masʿūdī 288 n3
al-Mathal al-sāʾir 33
meaning, indication of *see dalāla*
merchand(s) 5
merchandise ix, 8
message 14, 38, 104; ideological 17; long 162, 164–5, 166 fig., 171; *see also* speech acts of praise
metaphor(s) 80, 85, 93, 203, 207, 214, 216–17; analogue in 220, 224–5; imaginary 223, 225; naturalized 221–2; non-imaginary 223, 225, 309 n20; paired 219, 223–5; received 16; terminology 291 n22; topic in 220–5; typology of 219–20; *see also* figure; image; imagery; motif; phantasmagoria
metaphora continuata 11, 220
metaphorical expression 90
metaphorical level 19
metastrophe 53, 65, 72–4; definition of 15, 52; dramatization of 58; function of 59, 271 fig.; imagery in 226; scenes in 129, 140; themes of 56–9
meter 58, 254, 273–7; *basīṭ* 254; *kāmil* 254; *khafīf* 30, 254, 313 n30; *ṭawīl* 254
metonymy, metonymical 80, 89, 95–6, 126, 170, 314 n40; *see also* figure of speech; metaphor; personification
Miftāḥ al-ʿulūm 33
miḥna 21
Mihrajān see festivals
minister(s) 5–6
mirrors for princes 11, 279 n41
missionaries (*duʿāh*) 11
mock etiology *see* etiology
modern poetry see *badīʿ*; *muḥdath* poetry
moderns, the *see muḥdathūn*
molecularity 14
Molière (Jean-Baptiste Poquelin) 39
monologue scene 35, 39, 56, 79, 137–40, 144 fig., 154 fig.; in dramaturgy 156, 158, 160–5, 166–7 fig., 170, 189–90, 189 fig.; imagery in 207, 215; intercalated 132; *see also* address; dialogue scene; evocation; patronage scene
monorhyme 253
Montgomery, James 17, 281 n31
motif(s) 16, 208, 256; ancient 18–19; arrow 112, 182, 208, 212–13, 223, 293 n13, 303 n26, 306 n27; of bride, wife, *hieros gamos* 55, 62, 67, 110, 116, 142, 294 n51; gazelle 220–2; morning of separation 14, 18, 182, 269 fig.; panegyric x; pearl string v, 203, 206–7, 253, 308 n4; pre-Islamic, Umayyad 11, 98, 101, 182; rain 199, 201–2, 210, 214–17; recurring 165, 199, 214–18; sword 116, 143, 149, 185, 187–8, 201–2, 204, 210, 238, 258–9, 304 n13, 306 n27; trade x, 234–5, 255–6; *see also* etiology; image
motif derivation *see tawlīd l-maʿnā*; *see also* image; metaphor
Mottahedeh, Roy 234
muʿallaqa 313 n35
muʿāraḍa 296 n8
mubālagha see hyperbole
mubārāh (poetic competition) 54
al-Mubarrad 42, 45
mufākhara see fakhr

mughāzalāt see ghazal
Muḥammad (the prophet) 31, 304 n52; family of 23
Muḥammad, son of Ibn al-Rūmī 42
Muḥammad b. ʿAbdallāh b. Ṭāhir 3–4, 27, 43, 253
Muḥammad b. ʿAbdalmalik b. al-Zayyāt *see* Ibn al-Zayyāt
Muḥammad b. ʿAlī al-Bayn (singer) 43
Muḥammad b. ʿArūs al-Shīrāzī (poet) 43
Muḥammad b. Ḥabīb 42
Muḥammad b. Marwān b. Abī l-Janūb 49, 230, 310 n5
Muḥammad b. Qayd (or Fayd) al-Ṭāʾī 310 n5
Muḥammad b. Yaḥyā (Barmakid) 292 n31
Muhannā, ʿAbd al-Amīr 51
muḥdath metaphors *see* metaphors: paired
muḥdath poetry 12, 219–20, 308 n1; *see also badīʿ*; mannerism
muḥdath poets *see muḥdathūn*
muḥdath style 11–12, 21, 93
muḥdathūn 56, 278 n14
al-Muhtadī 6
mujmal-mufaṣṣal 16
mujūn 5, 51
al-mukhāṭab, mukhāṭaba 112, 295 n2
al-Mukhayyim al-Rāsibī 49
al-Muktafī 287 n38
munāẓara 216, 296 n8
al-Muntaṣir 46
murāʿāt al-naẓīr 220
muruwwa 10–11, 17, 278 n10
Muṣʿab, Banū Muṣʿab 60, 184, 186–7, 189, 192, 201; *see also* Ṭāhirids
al-Musayyabī *see* Ibn al-Musayyab
music, musician(s) 5, 8, 43, 53, 309 n15; female 5
Muslim b. al-Walīd 11, 305 n27
Muslim pilgrimage *see* festivals: *Ḥajj*
al-Mustaʿīn 46, 310 n5
muṭābaqa see ṭibāq
al-Muʿtaḍid 44, 46, 279 n49, 287 n38
al-mutakallim (grammatical term) 112, 295 n2
al-Muʿtamid 5, 44–5, 48, 279 n20
al-Muʿtamid b. ʿAbbād 15, 33, 280 n18
al-Mutanabbī 17, 33
mutaqaddimūn 56, 87, 258, 278 n14
al-Muʿtaṣim 5, 7, 279 n20
al-Mutawakkil 5, 11, 21–2, 24, 42, 263, 279 nn20, 49, 280 n51, 281 n40
Muʿtazilite 42, 282 n51; *see also* doctrine
al-Muʿtazz 310 n5
al-Muwaffaq 45, 310 n5
al-Nābigha al-Dhubyānī 258, 290 n67, 305 n27, 313 n35
nadīm, nudamāʾ 11, 48, 143, 229
nasab 60
nasīb, manāsib 4, 13–14, 18, 21, 48, 103; function of 58–9; as theme of strophe 52, 269 fig.; dearth of personae in 94; pre-Islamic 102
Naṣr, Āl *see* Kinda
Naṣṣār, Ḥusayn 51
nationalism, Iranian *see shuʿūbiyya*
nature poetry *see waṣf*
Nawrūz see festivals
Nestorian background 45
new style *see badīʿ*-style; *muḥdath* style
nidāʾ see vocative
niʿma, niʿam, naʿmāʾ, nuʿmā 116–17, 233–4, 256
nisāʾ see personae of the women
niṣba 85
nostalgia 4, 139
nudba 102, 137, 295 n2; *see also marthiya*
nuhā 303 n24

obligation *see* commitment
occasion 15, 18; *see also* situation
occasions of felicitation 44, 288 n28; birth of child 48; celebration of victory ix, 48; designation of an heir 48; enthronement ix, 48
ode *see* praise *qaṣīda*; *qaṣīda*; *tahniʾa*
office, governmental 9
official(s) 5, 9
Ohmann, Richard 40, 250, 285 n56
onager hunt 53
optative mood 140, 295 n77
orator 229
orthodoxy *see Sunna*
oryx 70, 288 n29, 293 n17, 300 n9; hunt 53, 150–1

Pahlavi 11
panegyric profession 11; *see also* poet; poet's persona
panegyric *qaṣīda see* praise *qaṣīda*
panegyrics *see madīḥ*
panegyrist *see* praise poet
paper 49

paradox: in phantasmagoria 220, 222–4; as speech figure 120, 203–4, 207, 219; *see also* virtues
parallelism 15, 19, 207; antithetic 19
parallelism, syntactic 15, 204
paraphrase (speech figure) *see tadhyīl*
paronomasia *see tajnīs*
patron(s) 9–10, 20, 24, 27, 32–3; Abbasid 9; achievements of 20; acts of 52, 70, 83, 108, 130, 248–9; acts and attributes of 54, 126, 199; acts and words of 85–6, 106–7; duties and benefits of 10, 20, 64, 68, 240, 244, 246; expert 10; finding a 50, 250, 313 n26; iconology of 13, 40, 55; ignorance of 10; as last refuge 117, 120, 310 n1; literary skills of 9–10, 107–9; oppositional, universal qualities of 104, 106, 131; rank of 115–16; sincerity of 55–6; *see also* addressee; *mamdūḥ*; patron's persona; ʿUbaydallāh; virtues; words
patron-*adīb* 10
patron's persona 39, 105; as benefactor 92, 105, 107–9, 111, 231, 233, 237, 240–3, 246–7; as model 70, 105, 107–11, 170, 231, 241, 245–9, 254, 258; as ruler 105–8, 111, 183–6, 199–200; in scenes 129; in syntactic figures 199, 201–2, 204, 206, 218
patronage x; ethics of 34, 51, 76, 119, 121, 140, 213, 229–31, 263, 265, 289 n39, 302 n5; literary i, x, 4, 39, 59; medium of 26; practice of 229; *see also* commitments; *madīḥ*; patron; patron's persona; patronage relationship; patronage scene; poet; poet's persona; relationship
patronage relationship 4, 27, 40, 71, 107 247; between benefactor and protégé 139, 232–5, 242–3, 246–7, 252 fig., 262, 311 n8; commitments of 52, 92; co-operation in 71, 75, 109, 247, 249; damaged 190, 259–60; failed 235, 243–6; as firm bond 69, 105, 107, 116, 141, 310 n1; ideal 171, 231–2, 248; intact 235–9, 243, 246, 253, 255–6; long-term 17, 75; between panegyrist and model 232, 245, 247–8, 252 fig., 262, 264–5, 311 n8; reciprocal 71, 75, 92, 149
patronage scene(s) 130, 230–1, 261; dialogue(s) 235, 243–6, 252, 262; in metastrophes 261; monologue(s) 244–6, 258–60; in *qaṣīda*, *tahni'a*, and *ʿitāb* 231, 261
pattern: of anticipation and resolution 26; slowing 16
pension, monthly 45; *see also* compension; *dīnar; dirham*; reward
performance(s) ix, 27; initial 33; musical 8; of praise poem 26
performative *see* speech act
performative phrase(s) 33
Persia, Persian ix; background 6, 9, 11, 31, 42, 230, 287 n32
persona(e): of bystander 39, 52, 105; of calumniator 134; of competitor, challenger 39, 104; of enemy 52; of fate 90; fictional 32, 36, 39, 111, 121, 135, 156–7, 263; fictional, major 94–103; fictional, minor 103–5; of friend 103, 115–16, 210–13; historical 32, 36, 39, 130 fig., 184, 263; human 92, 96, 98, 105, 111; of jealous one 39, 105; of 'laughing one' 82, 103, 136; of messenger 103–4, 150; of neighbor (female) 39, 81, 103, 114, 134–5, 156; of observer, spy 39, 96–8, 103, 134–5; order of appearance of 158; of rejected *mamdūḥ* 104; pre-Islamic 92, 94, 104–5, 291 n4; of supplicant(s) 83, 104–5, 126, 128–9, 134, 203–4, 206, 236, 253; of women 81, 95–8, 103, 112, 114, 134, 136–7, 145, 157–60, 182–3, 191, 203; *see also* accuser; characterization; dramaturgy; patron's persona; poet's persona; *shayb;* speech; youth
personal pronoun *see* grammatical person; pronoun
personification(s) 39, 93, 151, 249; of desire as corrupt judge 225; of favor 142 n75; of glory and noble deeds 63; of generosity 245, 292 n31; of grace and hope 117–8; of poet's eye 225; of poetry 88, 256; of presents 204–5; of qualities and acts 107; of soul 110; of speech 87–8; of woman's limbs 223; of woman's cheek and mouth 223–5; of world 62; *see also* dramatis personae; fate; generosity; *shayb*; youth
persuasion *see iʿtiqād*
phantasmagoria 40, 143, 151, 155, 199, 219, 222, 225–6, 247, 291 n14
philologists 6, 42

philosopher(s), medieval Arabic 210
philosophy 37 *see also* truth
phrases of praise *see* speech acts of praise
pilgrimage *see* festivals
pleasure *see taṭarrub*
poem(s): beginnings of *see ibtidāʾ*; of gratitude 50, 140, 247, 262; of intercession 9; ordering in *Dīwān* 51; recycling of 50; short *see qiṭʿa*; uni-thematic *see qiṭʿa*
poet(s) 7–8, 10–12, 23, 27; attitude of 52, 55, 115; as audience 6; competing with scribe 8; female 6, 279 n20; as friend 116, 129, 132; loyalty of 9, 69, 71–2, 75, 116, 140, 163–4, 169–70, 231, 237–9, 242, 245–7, 262, 269–70 fig.; pre-Islamic 11, 17, 75, 313 n35; professional, vocational 5–8, 17, 229–30; rank of 64; rights, benefits, and duties of 12, 64, 71, 118, 140, 191, 229–31, 239, 242, 246, 265, 305 n21; self-portrayal of 24, 231, 265; shared sincerity of 58, 250, 252; sincerity of 40, 62, 68, 118, 129, 235, 239, 242–3, 246, 248–9, 251, 260, 262; trust of 57, 120, 240, 249, 251–2; Umayyad 11; virtues of 69; as witness 147, 186, 189; work of 30, 67, 120, 181, 241, 244, 304 n48, 312 n33; *see also* dilettante; *muḥdath*; poet's persona; praise poet; speaker
poet-scribe(s) 7
poet's persona 12, 34–6, 39, 111–21, 120 fig.; conflicting roles of 120, 129, 132, 161, 164, 190; development of 126, 156–7, 159–63, 165–8, 166–7 fig., 170–1, 182–4, 186, 189–91, 244–5; as hero of *al-shayb wa-l-shabāb* 39, 75, 112–15, 121, 171, 191; as panegyrist 75, 112, 115, 117–21, 129, 132, 140–2, 191, 231–2, 245, 247–9, 263, 295 n72; as protégé 92, 112, 115–17, 129, 132, 140–2, 231–3, 241, 243, 246–7, 295 n65; in scenes 125, 126 fig., 130 fig., 138; silence of 136–7, 169
poetic critic(s) and criticism, medieval Arabic 7, 13, 26, 33, 208, 210, 233, 248, 262, 278 n14, 283 n5
poetic genre *see* genre
poetic speech 232
poetry: Abbasid 6, 220; ceremonial 5; classification of 13; early Islamic 230, 257; knowledge of 55; light 5; pre-existing 6; pre-Islamic 33, 230, 257; professional 9; rational, empirical 247, 283 n8; research on 43; sociocultural role of 229, 265; *see also badīʿ*; dilettante; mannerism; *muḥdath*; *takhyīl*; *waṣf*
police governorship *see shurṭa*
policy, anti-Shiite 45
position(s), administrative 6
posture *see* attitude
pragmatics 26–41, 283 n3
praise(s): act of 38, 51; ancestral 55, 184–6, 205–6, 269–70 fig., 294 n49 anticipatory, advanced 20, 249–50, 258–61, 312 n15; composed by acts 248, 255–6, 312 n9; falling short of acts 248–9, 254–5, 312 n6; false 72; fidelity to acts 248–9, 253; of governorship 56, 64–5; hyperbolic 54–7, 130, 132, 140, 144, 165, 166 fig., 169, 185, 269 fig.; individual 55, 185, 206–7, 269–70 fig.; matching acts 248, 253–4, 312 n5; of patronage 59; re-attributed 50, 86, 249, 256–8, 282 n50, 312 n11; of rulership 55, 269–70 fig.; topical 130, 296 n17; unredeemed 170, 258, 302 n21; *see also* antistrophe; *hijāʾ*; lie; *madīḥ*; occasions; patron; patronage; poet; praise *qaṣīda*; speaker; *taʾkīdu l-madḥ*; words
praise poem *see ʿitāb*; *madīḥ*; praise *qaṣīda*; *qiṭʿa*
praise poet(s) 4, 9, 11, 32
praise poetry *see* panegyrics; *madīḥ*
praise *qaṣīda* x, 3–4, 9, 15, 30–1, 36; Abbasid 13–25, 109; caliphal 26, 45; dramaturgy of 156, 161, 165, 182, 186, 188, 190–1; imagery in 214, 217–8, 226; interactive potential of 17; power of 67, 231; pre-Islamic 26, 52, 288 n56; relevance of 229; themes of 52–9, 269–70 fig., 281–2 n40; to ʿUbaydallāh b. ʿAbdallāh 48, 52–9; Umayyad 15, 52; *see also madīḥ*; patronage relationship
Pratt, Mary Louise 28, 286 n63
pre-Islamic *see* corpus; dedication; dynasties; imagery; motif; *nasīb*; persona; poet; poetry; praise *qaṣīda*; *qaṣīda*; theme
premise, poetic 210; *see also* lie; syllogism
Pride and Prejudice 28
promise *see* speech act

pronoun(s) 36, 39, 73, 141, 150; *see also* grammatical person
propaganda: doctrinal 11; political 10
proper explanation *see ṣiḥḥat al-tafsīr*
prophet, the *see* Muḥammad
Propp, Vladimir 281 n31
prose 9–10
prose-stylist 43
prosody 44, 254–5; *see also* meter; monorhyme; rhyme; rhyme letter
protection 9–10, 55
protégé(s) 5; *see also* poet's persona
psychological impact *see ta'thīr*
pure art 4, 8

al-Qarṭājannī 210, 247–8, 307 n31
qaṣīda, qaṣā'id: Abbasid 15, 18, 21, 281 n40, 283 n6; bipartite 15, 17, 52, 54; as convention 18; as dialogue 23, 140; etymology of 280 n9; final part of 14; Hebrew 14; history of research 13–17, 280 n8, 281 n31; as interaction 26; memorial 14; message 14, 302 n12; objectivity of 14, 16; orthodox 24; Persian 14; pre-Islamic 14, 17, 58, 102, 283 n6; themes of 14, 18; tripartite 14, 17; Umayyad 13–15, 58; unity of 14; *see also* antistrophe; metastrophe; molecularity; praise *qaṣīda*; stereotype; strophe
al-Qāsim b. ʿUbaydallāh b. Sulaymān b. Wahb 45–6, 226, 287 n38, 295 n74
Qibla 242, 306 n17
qinṭār (unit of weight) 209, 307 n34
qirā l-aḍyāf 233
qiṭʿa, qiṭaʿ 4, 14, 104, 164, 278 n4, 289 n63
quatrain 259
qubbat al-shuʿarā' 49
Qudāma b. Jaʿfar 233
question(s) 119, 165–9, 166 fig., 245; rhetorical 117–8, 128–9, 140, 154, 166–7 fig., 168, 201, 207, 238, 302 n17
qul(ā) li- 65, 104, 164; *see also* speech acts of praise: message
quod erat demonstrandum 207
quotation *see taḍmīn*; *speech*

'Rabbi Ben Ezra' 298 n56
al-Rāḍī 48
raḥīl 13–15, 68, 297 nn37, 40
raḥīl motif 205
raqīb 134; *see also* persona of the spy, observer
rāwī, ruwāh 14, 31, 73
al-Rāzī 14
reason *see ʿaql*; *nuhā*
reception 13, 26, 59
recipients *see* persona of the supplicant
reciprocal obligation *see* patronage relationship
Reconquista, Spanish 265
recurring motif *see* motif
redemption 312 n13; *see also hijā'*; praise
reduction *ad absurdum* 128
Reinert, Benedikt 219
relationship: dialogical 36; fantastic 93; with individual addressee 26; between personae 36; between poet and patron; between speakers 28, 35; *see also* patronage relationship
relative clause 200
relative pronoun 163–4
repetition *see* reprise
reprimand, poem of *see ʿitāb*
reprise 199, 205–7, 253, 306 n23
reproach *see tawbīkh*
reward: act(s) of 50; affirming praise 140; call for 63, 118–9; by currency 45, 49, 234; delay of 119, 166 fig., 168, 215, 235; denial of 3–4, 50, 110, 215; by fief 49; future 34; by material objects, positions, slaves 49; request for 57, 239; *see also* compensation; *dīnār*; *dirham*
rhyme 58, 255, 259, 290 n77, 314 n45; *see also* monorhyme
rhyme letter(s), difficult 44, 182, 254
ribald poetry *see mujūn*
Risālat al-Shukr 51–2, 274 fig., 278 n13
rithā' see marthiya
Ritter, Hellmut 111
ruler(s), ideal 17, 55; *see also* image; patron; patron's persona; patronage relationship; ʿUbaydallāh
al-Rummānī 85

sacrificial feast *see* festivals
Ṣaffārid(s) *see* ʿAmr b. Layth; Yaʿqūb b. Layth
Ṣafwān al-Anṣārī 279 n37
al-Ṣāḥib Ibn ʿAbbād 49
Ṣāʿid b. Makhlad 9, 45
sā'il 134; *see also* persona of the supplicant
Sakan 279 n20
al-Sakkākī 33

Salīm, Sharīf 51
samāḥa see generosity
Samarra, Samarran ix, 5, 43–4, 48
Samarra-wine 139
ṣanʿa 7, 12
ṣanīʿa 314 n39
sariqa, sariqāt 6
Sasanian(s) 11; background 6
Satan 22–3
satire *see hijāʾ*
scene(s) 39, 79, 156, 161–3; composite 35, 132, 162 fig., 166–7 fig., 183 fig., 184–5, 189, 217; dramatic 32, 34–5, 59, 76, 113, 145, 263; in dramaturgy 156, 157 fig., 183 fig.; series of 157–8, 161, 207; speech in 92; typology 125, 143–4, 144 fig., 154 fig., 263; *see also* address; dialogue scene; evocation; monologue; patronage scene
Scheindlin, Raymond 15
Schoeler, Gregor 218–19, 226
scholar(s), medieval Arabic 5, 31, 85, 257
scribe(s) 5–9, 13, 31; chancellery 6; handbooks for 6
Searle, John 37–8, 40, 74–5, 112, 235–6, 238, 250, 283 n2, 285 n56
secretary *see* scribe; *kātib*
section opening(s) 15; *see also* composition: of sections
Sells, Michael 15
sententia(e) 129, 154, 199, 207, 210–14, 218, 225; *see also* analogy
session *see majlis*
service through poetry, verses 20
Seville 265
shabāb 33, 53–4, 80; silence of 90; *see also al-shayb wa-l-shabāb*
shāʿir, shuʿarāʾ see poet(s)
shajāʿa see courage
Shakespeare, William 37–9
shākī see persona of the supplicant
Shāpūr II 242–3, 312 n31
shawāhid 257
shayb 53–4; development of 156–9, 164; as persona 32–3, 39, 82, 94–9, 101, 103, 105, 111–13, 115, 159; in scenes 98, 126, 129, 136–7, 139, 156; speech of 88–90
al-shayb wa-l-shabāb 4, 15, 39, 48, 220; poet in 112–5, 121; as theme of strophe 52–4, 269–70 fig.; timeframe of 99, 102, 138–9, 144 fig.
Shaybān, Banū 31, 45
Shiism, Shiite(s) 42, 45, 279 n29
shiʿr see shāʿir
shiʿr ʿaqlī ṣaḥīḥ see poetry, rational; *see also takhyīl*
shiʿr ḥāṣil see poetry, empirical
shurṭa 43
shuʿūbiyya 257
sign *see ʿalāma*
ṣiḥḥat al-tafsīr 222
ṣināʿa 7
singers 5, 8, 220–2
situation: historical 17; *see also ḥāl*
skills: administrative 7–8; social 12
slaves, educated 5
slowing pattern 16, 281 n24
social class(es): educated 17; middle, higher 5–6
society: Abbasid x, 3–10, 26, 75; Abbasid urban ix; Arabic-Islamic 265; Baghdadian 232; Near Eastern i; tribal 16; urban elite 16; *see also* Arabic-Islamic civilization
sociocultural expression 7
sociology 17
Solomon 200, 303 n29, 304 n42
song: ban on 6; on ceremonial themes 279 n25
sovereign(s) 4, 7; *see also* addressee; *mamdūḥ*; patron; ruler
speaker 70, 75; attitude of 28, 168, 242; authority of 73, 129, 132; explicit 65; female 14; impersonal (in third person) 112, 140–3, 146; implicit 66, 112, 140–2, 146, 151; marginal 111, 132; of truth 70
speech: of abstract concepts 39, 79–80, 83–90, 92–4; of bags 83–4, 86; of breath 84, 86; direct 39, 76, 83, 145, 155; of fictional personae 82; figurative attribution of 85–6, 88, 90, 92, 94, 103, 126, 129, 169, 291 nn21–2; figurative reinterpretation of 80, 90–2; function of 79; of humans 81–3, 92–4; of inanimate objects 79–80, 83–90, 92–4; paraphrased 125, 126 fig., 134, 212, 263; of personifications 39, 79, 92, 94; quoted 125–6, 126 fig., 128, 135; of tears 83–4, 86; types, levels of 76, 79; as vehicle of action 79, 82, 112, 143; *see also shayb*
speech act(s) 29, 36–41, 74–5, 92, 239, 311 n25; *assertive*, of assertion 38, 112, 117, 233, 237–9; *commissive* 38, 112;

declarative 38, 73, 112; *directive* 38, 73, 112, 140; *expressive* 38, 140; felicity of 40; of greeting 79–80, 114, 133, 136, 156, 160; indirect 236, 283 n9; performative 37–40, 73–5; of promise 80, 90–2, 106, 110–11, 126, 132, 233, 240–1, 243–5, 264, 289 n39; of request 236–7, 239–41, 243, 246; of thanking 235–6, 239; types of 37, 286 n63
speech act(s) of praise 230–1, 235, 239, 271 fig.; advice 3, 59, 63; intention to praise 59–61, 73–4; invocation, felicitation 38, 57, 59, 61–5, 71, 73, 136, 140, 155, 184, 231, 298 n49; message 59, 65, 104, 164; naming 59, 60, 73; *see also* dedication
speech act theory x, 27–8; application to literature 285 n56; excursus into 36–9
Sperl, Stefan 15, 219, 278 n17
spring *see* description of nature
stereotype 14, 16
Stetkevych, Jaroslav 15, 281 n31
Stetkevych, Suzanne 281 n31, 312 n13
strophe(s) 105; definition 15; function of 58–9, 226, 271 fig.; imagery in 220, 226; lack of speech acts in 73; themes of 53–4, 121
structuralism *see* theory
style(s): epistolary 8; panegyric x; *see also* *badīʿ*-style; *muḥdath* style
sub-genre 9
subjectivity 26, 119, 168, 295 n78
Sulaymān b. ʿAbdallāh b. Ṭāhir 43
Sulaymān b. Wahb 45
al-Ṣūlī, Muḥammad b. Yaḥyā 48, 279 nn20, 30
Sunna 21–3; *ahl al-* 282 n54
supplicant(s) *see* persona
Sūra: Sūrat Āl ʿImrān 3/177 311 n11; al-Anbiyāʾ 21/84 170; al-Baqara 2/16 311 n11; al-Baqara 2/86 311 n11; al-Baqara 2/204 95; al-Baqara 2/256 290 n75; al-Baqara 2/282 118, 305 n34; al-Humaza 104/6–7 303 n26; Ibrāhīm 14/18 304 n48; al-Isrāʾ 17/5 304 n5; Luqmān 31/18 311 n22; Luqmān 31/22 290 n75; al-Māʾida 6/3 305 n31; al-Malāʾika 35/27 309 n21; al-Muzammal 73/14 294 n36; al-Najm 53/9 304 n52; al-Nisāʾ 4/11 313 n33; al-Qamar 54/55 313 n32; al-Rūm 30/9 85; Sabaʾ 34/13 304 n42; Ṣād 38/31–2 303 n29; Ṣād 38/44 170; al-Shuʿarāʾ 26/226 314 n43; al-Zumar 39/10 69
ṣurūf 104; *see also* fate
syllogism, poetic 210, 247
symbol 15; divine *see āya*
syntax 37; *see also* parallelism, syntactic
Syria 5

al-Ṭabarī 230
al-tabarruʿ bi-l-nāʾil 233
tadhyīl 208
taḍmīn 6
taghābun 233
Ṭāhir b. al-Ḥusayn 60–1, 106, 184–6, 192, 201, 263–4, 296 n18
Ṭāhirid(s), Banū Ṭāhir 43–4, 56, 60, 94, 106; excluding ʿUbaydallāh 153, 305 n17; glory of 86–7, 131; *madīḥ* of 275 fig.; as personae 130–2, 145, 151–3, 155, 183–8, 202; reliability of 186
tahniʾa, tahānī: dramaturgy of 10, 40; in *qaṣīdas* 55; formulae of 64; poems of x, 4, 30, 40, 52, 239–43, 254–8; *see also* *han(n)aʾa*; occasions; speech acts of praise
tajnīs 314 n40
tajrīd 33
takassub 8
takhalluṣ 13, 54, 263; motifs of 14; Umayyad 115
takhyīl 84, 86, 93, 109, 210, 291 n14
takhyīlī (poetry) 283 n8
taʾkīd 168; *see also* question
taʾkīdu l-madḥi bi-mā yushbihu l-dhamm 187
taking injustice upon oneself *see inẓilām*
talmīḥ 6, 31; *see also* Koranic allusion
Tamīm, Banū 312 n31
tamthīl see analogy
taqrīr (stylistic term) 302 n17
taqsīm (speech figure) 281 n24
ṭardiyya 53, 99, 147, 295 n57
Ṭarrād, Majīd 51
tashbīh see comparison
taṣḥīf 52, 296 n4
taṭarrub 8
taʾthīr 208, 307 n31
tawassuʿ 284 n38
tawbīkh 168, 302 n17
tawlīd al-maʿnā 208
tax collector *see jābī*
tax expert 233
tellability 28, 32

Tha'lab 42
theft *see* borrowing; *sariqa*
thematic goal *see gharaḍ*
theme(s): new 12; panegyric x; pre-Islamic, Umayyad 11; received 16; stereotyped 16
theologians 6
theology, dogmatic 11
theory: anthropological 17; philosophical-linguistic 36; structuralist 17; *see also* dramatic discourse; speech act theory
ṭibāq, muṭābaqa
time *see* fate
timeframe *see* dramaturgy; *al-shayb wa-l-shabāb*
trade *see* motif; *ṣināʿa*
tradition: classical 6; play on 26; textual 18
transition *see takhalluṣ*
translation (speech figure) 291 n14
transmitter(s) *see rāwī*
tribe(s) 10
trope *see* figure of speech; phantasmagoria
truth: aesthetic 247; personal and historical 248; philosophical 247; suspended 285 n56; *see also* lie; *madīḥ*; premise; speaker; syllogism
al-Ṭūfī, Najm al-Dīn 296 n8
Turner, Victor 281 n31

ʿUbaydallāh b. ʿAbdallāh b. Ṭāhir x, 3–4, 6, 17–18, 24, 27, 31, 94, 171; as addressee of al-Buḥturī 20, 314 n45; as addressee of message 162–3, 165, 170–1; as author 43, 51, 278 n1, 286 nn14, 16, 287 n27; criticism of 57, 140, 142, 168, 182, 184–5, 187–90, 239, 251, 255; criticism of, indirect 209–10, 214–17, 294 n49; as (deputy) governor 24, 55, 65, 86, 104–5, 126, 184, 232, 290 n65, 302 n17; historical relationship with Ibn al-Rūmī 30, 43–4, 48, 50, 184, 226, 230–2, 262, 265, 273–4 fig.; as *mamdūḥ* 52, 55, 60, 71, 118, 127, 184–5, 187, 237, 273–4 fig.; naming of 60–1, 289 n47; *see also* addressee; *madīḥ*; patron; patron's persona; speech acts of praise; Ṭāhirid(s)
ʿUbaydallāh b. Sulaymān b. Wahb 45
Umayyad(s) 10, 257, 278 nn5, 14
al-ʿUqaylī, Aḥmad b. Muhammad b. Ṭāhir 51
urban environment 182
Usāma, clan of 208

utterance(s) 28; context-dependent meaning of 27; direct 37; linguistic 27; *see also ʿibāra*; *lafẓ*; speech

Valencia 265
values: doctrinal ix; ethical ix; ideological ix; *see also* antistrophe; ideology; *madīḥ*: standard catalogue; patronage: ethics of
verbal act *see* speech act
verbal action *see* speech
verbal ornament *see* figures of speech; phantasmagoria; *see also* dramaturgy; mannerism
verbs, past tense 15
verse, evidentiary *see shawāhid*
verse repetition *see* reprise
vicissitudes *see* fate
victory *see* praise: occasions of
vignette(s) 184, 188, 225
virtues: common 19; contrasting, paradox of 54; enumeration of 59; *see also* antistrophe; *madīḥ*: standard catalogue; patron; poet; praise
viziers, vizierate 9, 48, 229–30
vocabulary, rare *see gharīb*
vocative 15, 81, 128, 133–5, 207, 295 n2; *see also* address; pronouns

Wahb, Banū 43, 45, 279 n30; *see also* al-Qāsim, Sulaymān, and ʿUbaydallāh
wa-rubba 135, 145, 285 n55, 297 n43; *see also* episode; *fakhr* episode
wasf, awṣāf 5, 13, 51, 150; of spring, of nature 4, 54, 158, 160, 220; of women 54, 220; *see also* personae of women
wasf episode 182, 219, 222
wāshī see persona of the calumniator
al-Wāthiq 281 n40, 282 n54
Wehr, Hans 145
white hair *see shayb*
wine, ban on 6; *see also* Samarra
wine-drinking 8
wine song *see khamriyya*
witnesses 52, 104, 145–6, 150, 153–4, 154 fig., 272 fig.; combination of 152–3, 272 fig.; in *fakhr* episode 146–7, 151; frequency of 151; in *madīḥ* episode 146–8, 151–3; in scenes 300 n17; quoted 151; speaking and addressed 146–51
witnessing 'I' 145–8, 151, 153, 300 nn8–10

witnessing 'we' 145–8, 151–3, 300 nn13–16
witnessing 'you' 135–7, 145–51, 162; functions 150–1, 300 nn26–33
women *see* personae of women; *waṣf* episode
word(s): correspondence to act(s) 75, 109, 247–9, 253, 258, 264; *see also* commitments; dialogue; patron; patronage; patronage relationship; praise; speech
world-view, Islamic ix
writing *see* Arabic script

Yaḥyā b. Khālid b. Marwān 310 n5
Yaḥyā b. Muḥammad al-Aslamī 310 n5
Yaḥyā b. ʿUmar (Alid rebel) 42, 284 n34
Yaʿqūb b. Layth 310 n5
Yeats, William Butler 168, 170
youth: as absent 133; as abstract notion 90, 100, 102, 114–15, 136, 297 n46; as departed *ḥabīb* 96, 98, 100–3, 133, 136, 158–9; development 157; as persona 94, 98, 100, 103, 105, 113–5, 293 n17; as personified metaphor or metonymy 39, 81, 99–100, 103, 105, 113, 132–3, 135, 158–60, 157 fig., 293 nn19–20, 298 n46; *see also ḥabīb*; *al-shayb wa-l-shabāb*

zamān 96, 104; *see also* fate
Zamzam 203, 306 n13
zandaqa, zindīq 45, 287 n32
Zanj 265, 310 n5
ẓarf 6, 12, 229, 278 n10
ẓarīf, ẓurafāʾ 5–6
zindīq see zandaqa
Ziyād b. Muʿāwiya *see* al-Nābigha al-Dhubyānī
Zoroastrian, Zoroastrianism 21–2, 282 n56
Zuhayr b. Abī Sulmā 258, 290 n67
ẓulm see time
Zurayq, Banū Zurayq 60, 94, 175, 184, 186, 201

Lightning Source UK Ltd.
Milton Keynes UK
12 October 2010

161091UK00001B/71/P

9 780415 595797